Contents

Introduction 4
Pricing Information.................................4
Abbreviations 5
The Barbie® Doll Family 6
Barbie® Dolls
    Listed Alphabetically 32
    Listed by Stock Number.....................74
    Listed by Year 114
    Listed by Store/Collection 156
Ken® Dolls
    Listed Alphabetically 184
    Listed by Stock Number.....................188
    Listed by Year 192
Skipper® Dolls
    Listed Alphabetically 196
    Listed by Stock Number.....................198
    Listed by Year 200
Family & Friends Dolls
    Listed Alphabetically 202
    Listed by Doll 213
    Listed by Stock Number.....................224
    Listed by Year 235
Barbie® Doll Outfits
    Listed Alphabetically 246
    Listed by Stock Number.....................273
Ken® Doll Outfits
    Listed Alphabetically 300
    Listed by Stock Number.....................307
Francie® Doll Outfits
    Listed Alphabetically 313
    Listed by Stock Number.....................317
Skipper® Doll Outfits
    Listed Alphabetically 321
    Listed by Stock Number.....................327
Miscellaneous Doll Outfits
    Listed Alphabetically 332
    Listed by Doll 334
Accessories 336
Adult Accessories 338

Adult Clothing 338
Barbie® Bazaar Magazine 339
Barbie® Doll Reading Books 341
Cases...342
Catalogs 344
Children's Accessories..........................345
Children's Clothing 346
Children's Riding Toys 346
Coloring & Activity Books 347
Tea Sets & Dishes 348
Electronics 348
Enesco
    Listed Alphabetically 350
Furniture 353
Games 356
Gift Sets
    Listed Alphabetically 357
    Listed by Year 362
Greeting Cards 367
Jewelry & Jewelry Boxes 368
Keychains 369
Kitchen 369
Lunchboxes & Thermoses 370
Barbie® Doll's Make-up 370
McDonald's® Barbie® Dolls 373
Miscellaneous.....................................375
Ornaments...377
Paper Dolls 380
Pets...384
Plates...........................386
Puzzles 387
Real Estate 388
Records &
    Cassettes 390
Paper Products 391
Vehicles.............393
Watches &
    Clocks 394
Bibliography....396

Introduction

We would like to thank all of those who have purchased our prior editions. Every effort has been made to make this the most complete edition. However, due to the number of items being released by Mattel and their licensees, it is becoming nearly impossible to track down everything. We will continue to do our best to locate everything and will keep updating our next edition.

My wife and I have spent many hours going over all the entries in this book to make sure they are accurate to the best of our ability. If we missed some, we are sorry and will try to correct them in our next edition.

There are over 3,600 different entries for Barbie® doll and her family & friends dolls including gift sets, and there are over 2,500 different entries for cases, pets, vehicles, miscellaneous, books, clothing, Enesco, furniture, and structures. There is a combined total of over 14,000 entries when you count the multiple entries for dolls, outfits, gift sets, and Enesco. We have also included photographs of every type of vintage Barbie® doll.

This book does not include all the dolls issued by Mattel.
We hope this book is of great value and an asset to all Barbie® collectors.

– Patrick & Joyce Olds

Pricing Information

The current values in this book should be used as a guide only. These prices were gathered from shows, mailing lists, dealers, Barbie® doll clubs, auctions, and various other sources. These are the average selling prices from across the country. As I gathered the information for this sixth edition, I put all the prices into my computer and averaged all of them. Prices vary from state to state, and from different parts of the country. The conditions of the items and of the boxes play important parts in determining the values of the items. All prices listed here are based on NRFB (never removed from box) unless otherwise noted.

Although every attempt has been made to do so, it is impossible to determine values for every item listed in this book. Further revisions of this book will list values of items not given at this time. Every effort is being made to have prices for all items marked with N/A or Retail for the next edition. If you find an item not listed or an incomplete listing in this book, please drop the author a note including the name of the item, stock number, date of issue, whether or not it was a special edition, current value if known, and any other information about the product. Also, send a picture if possible. Please send to The Barbie Doll Years, 3235 W. Bennington, Owosso, MI 48867. All assistance will be appreciated.

Abbreviations

Here is a list of abbreviations that you will often see used in listings or advertisements.

ACC . . . . .Accessories	MNB . . . . .Mint no box
A/O . . . . .All original	MOC . . . . .Mint on card
B.L. . . . . .Bendable leg	MU . . . . .Make-up
B.C. . . . . .Bubble cut	NM . . . . .Near mint
BK . . . . .Book	NRFB . . . . .Never removed from box
C . . . . .Complete	OF . . . . .Outfit
CLO . . . . .Clothes	OO . . . . .Original outfit
C/M . . . . .Complete & mint	OSS . . . . .Original swimsuit
C.T. . . . . .Close toe	OT . . . . .Open toe
D.S.S. . . . . .Department store special	OW . . . . .Otherwise
EC . . . . .Excellent condition	PC . . . . .Poor condition
FC . . . . .Fair condition	PD . . . . .Paper doll
FUR . . . . .Furniture	RE . . . . .Real estate
GC . . . . .Good condition	REC . . . . .Record
GS . . . . .Gift set	RTL . . . . .Retail
HTF . . . . .Hard to find	SD . . . . .Store display
I . . . . .Incomplete	S.L. . . . . .Straight leg
JE . . . . .Jewelry	SS . . . . .Swimsuit
M . . . . .Mint	TNT . . . . .Twist & turn
MIB . . . . .Mint in box	VEH . . . . .Vehicles
MIP . . . . .Mint in package	VGC . . . . .Very good condition
MISC . . . . .Miscellaneous	

The Barbie Doll Family

The Barbie doll family is broken down into three sections: Barbie doll's family, friends, and pets.

BARBIE® b. 1959

Family

SKIPPER b. 1964
(Barbie doll's sister)

TODD b. 1966
(Barbie doll's brother, twin to Tutti)

TUTTI b. 1966
(Barbie doll's sister, twin to Todd)

FRANCIE b. 1966
(Barbie doll's cousin)

JAZZIE b. 1989
(Barbie doll's cousin)

STACIE b. 1992
(Barbie doll's sister)

KELLY b. 1994
(Barbie doll's baby sister)

KRISSY b. 1999
(Barbie doll's littlest sister)

Friends (Skipper)

Ricky b. 1965
Skooter b. 1965
Fluff b. 1971
Tiff b. 1972
Ginger b. 1976
Scott b. 1980
Courtney b. 1989
Kevin b. 1990
Nikki b. 1997
Sidney b. 1999

Friend (Tutti)

Chris b. 1967

Friend (Francie)

Casey b. 1967

Friends (Jazzie)

Dude b. 1989
Chelsie b. 1989
Stacie b. 1989

Friends (Stacie)

Whitney b. 1994
Janet b. 1993

Friends (Kelly)

Becky b. 1996
Chelsea b. 1996
Nia b. 1999
Maria b. 1999
Melody b. 1996
Deidra b. 1996
Marissa b. 1998
Tamika b. 1999
Belinda b. 1999
Deidre b. 1999
Desiree b. 1999
Jenny b. 1999
Kayla b. 1999
Keeya b. 1999
Maria b. 1999
Lorena b. 1999
Lianna b. 1999

Pets (Skipper)

Honey (Pony)
b. 1983

Friends

Ken b. 1961

Family

Tommy b. 1997
(Ken doll's little brother)

Friends

Allan b. 1964
Brad b. 1970
Curtis b. 1975
Todd b. 1983
Derek b. 1986
Steven b. 1988
Alan b. 1991

Midge b. 1963
Twiggy b. 1967
Christie b. 1968
Buffy b. 1968
Stacey b. 1968
P. J. b. 1969
Truly Scrumptious b. 1969
Jamie b. 1970
Steffie b. 1972
Kelley b. 1973
Cara b. 1975
Carla b. 1976
Tracy b. 1983
Dana b. 1986 (Rocker)
Dee Dee b. 1986 (Rocker)

Diva b. 1986 (Rocker)
Miko b. 1987
Whitney b. 1987
Becky b. 1988 (Sensations)
Belinda b. 1988 (Sensations)
Bopsy b. 1988 (Sensations)
Midge b. 1988
Shani b. 1988
Teresa b. 1988
Devon b. 1989 (Dance Club)
Kayla b. 1989 (Dance Club)
Nikki b. 1989
Kira b. 1990
Nia b. 1990
M.C. Hammer b. 1991

Marina b. 1992
Tara Lynn b. 1993
Shani b. 1994
Becky b. 1997 (Wheelchair)
Ana b. 1999 (Generation Girl)
Chelsie b. 1999
Nichelle b. 1999 (Generation Girl)
Tori b. 1999 (Generation Girl)
Brandy b. 1999
Rosie O'Donnell b. 1999
Lara b. 1999 (Generation Girl)
Mari b. 1999 (Generation Girl)
Nichelle b. 1999 (Generation Girl)
Becky b. 1997
Chelsie b. 1999

Pets

Tahiti b. 1965 (bird)
Dancer b. 1971 (horse)
Beauty b. 1980 (Afghan dog)
Beauty's Pups b. 1982 (puppy)
Dallas b. 1981 (horse)
Midnight b. 1982 (horse)
Dixie b. 1984 (pony)
Prancer b. 1984 (horse)
Fluff b. 1983 (kitten)
Prince b. 1985 (poodle)
Blinking Beauty b. 1988 (horse)
Ginger b. 1988 (giraffe)
Sun Runner b. 1990 (horse)
Snowball b. 1990 (dog)
All American b. 1991 (horse)
Sachi b. 1992 (dog)

Honey b. 1992 (kitten)
Rosebud b. 1992 (horse)
Tiffy b. 1992 (cat)
Wags b. 1992 (dog)
Butterfly b. 1993 (pony)
Chelsie b. 1993 (pony)
Stomper b. 1993 (horse)
Western Star b. 1993 (horse)
High Stepper b. 1994 (horse)
Mitzi Meow b. 1994 (cat)
Ruff b. 1994 (puppy)
Tropical Splash b. 1994 (seahorse)
Calico b. 1996 (cat)
Collie b. 1996 (dog)
Keiko b. 1996 (whale)
Nibbles b. 1996 (horse)

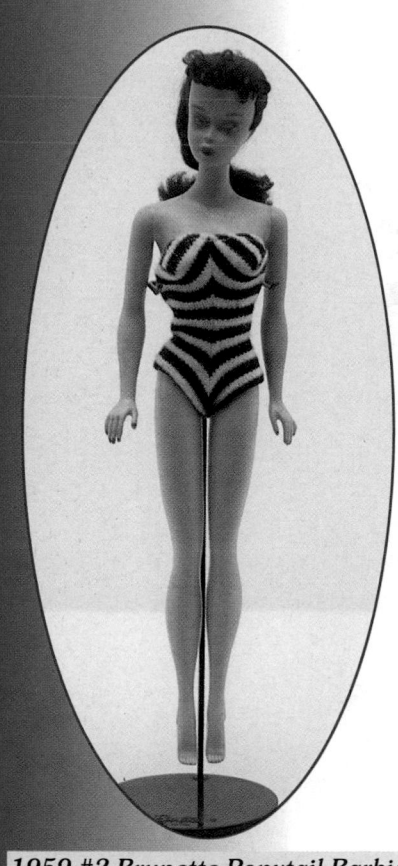

1959 #2 Brunette Ponytail Barbie

1960 #3 Ponytail Barbie

1961 #5 Ponytail Barbie

1961 Blonde Bubble Cut Barbie

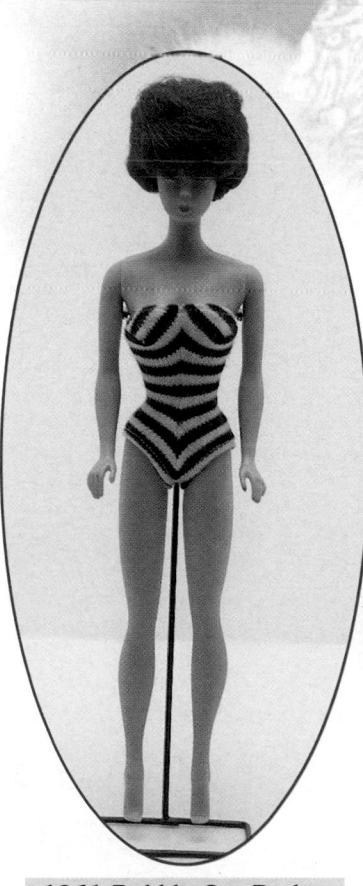

1961 Bubble Cut Barbie

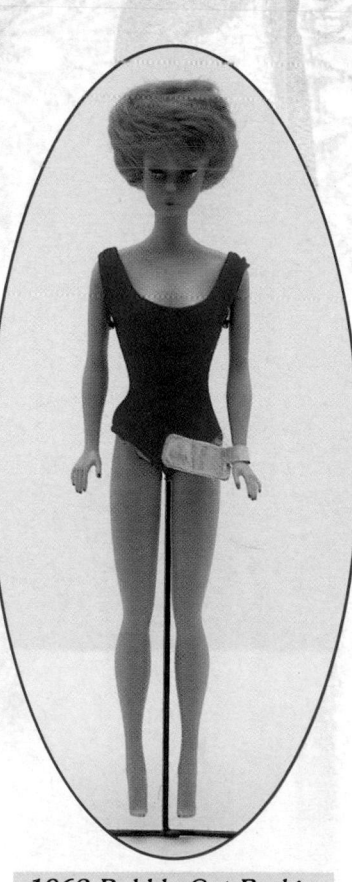

1962 Bubble Cut Barbie

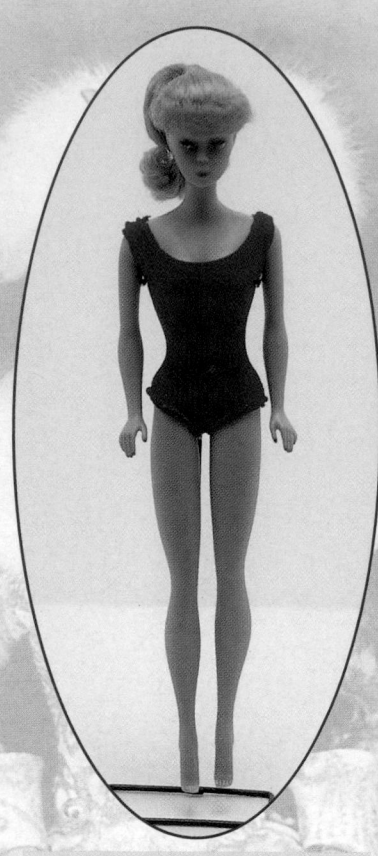

#6 Blonde Ponytail Barbie

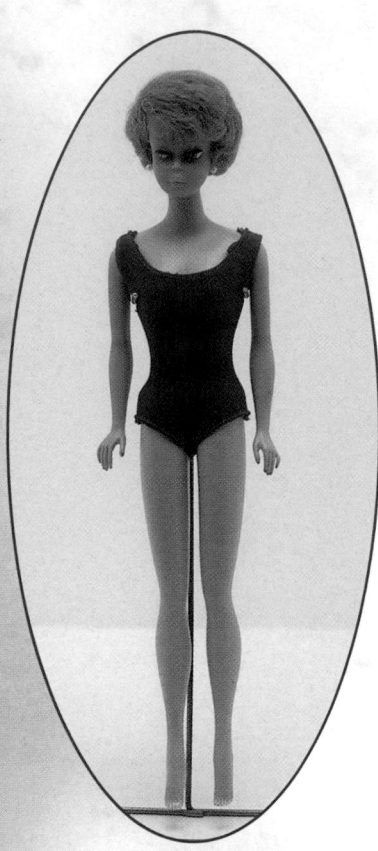

1963 Bubble Cut Barbie

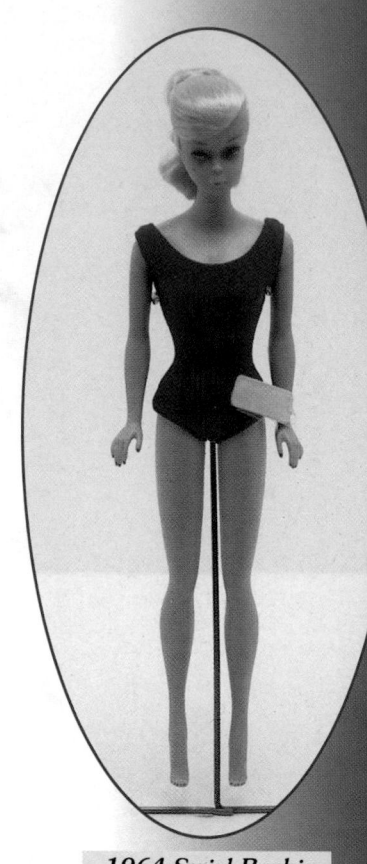

1964 Swirl Barbie

1964 Miss Barbie

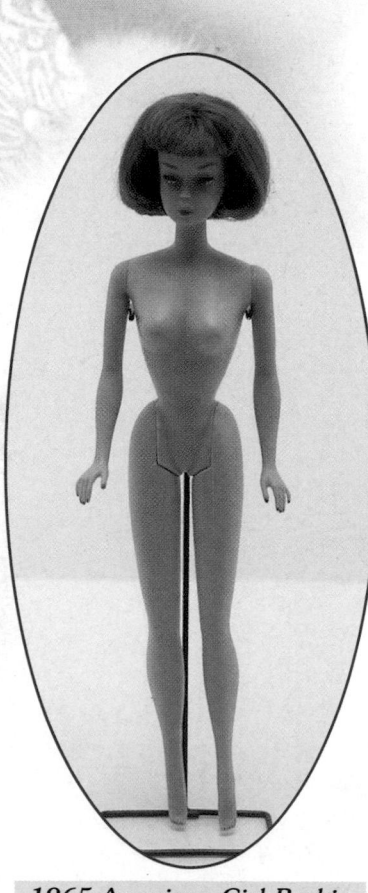

1965 American Girl Barbie

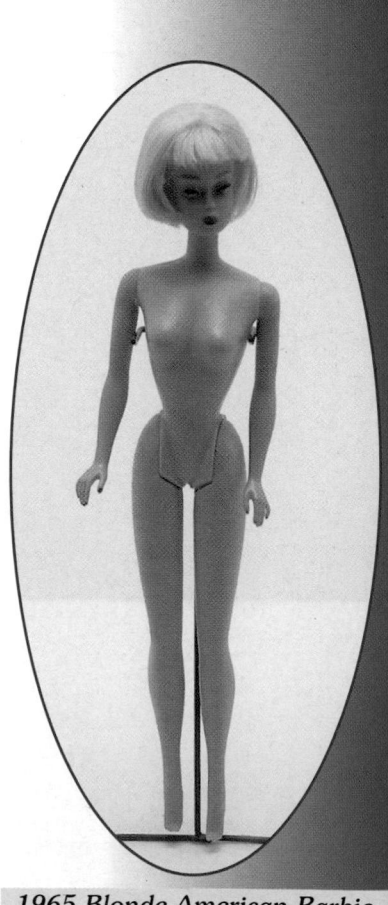

1965 Blonde American Barbie

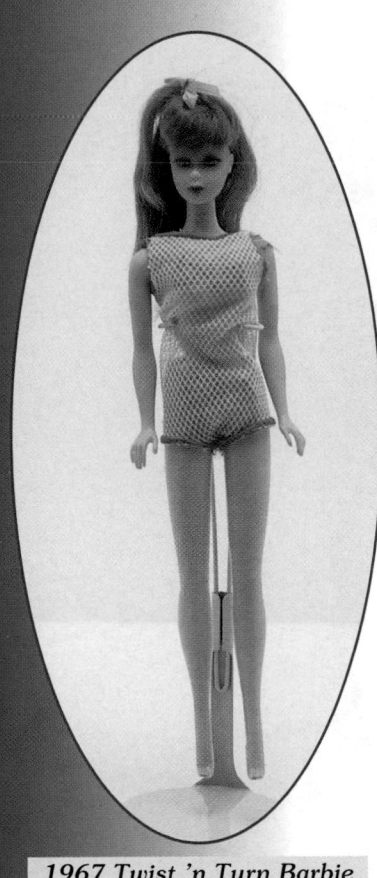

1967 Twist 'n Turn Barbie

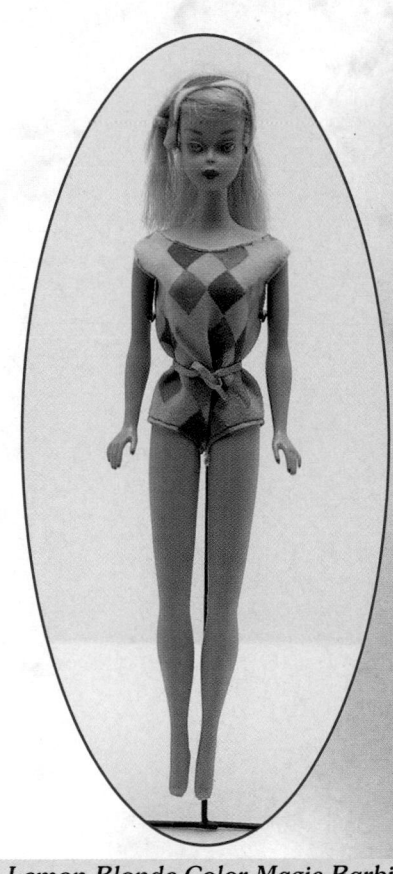

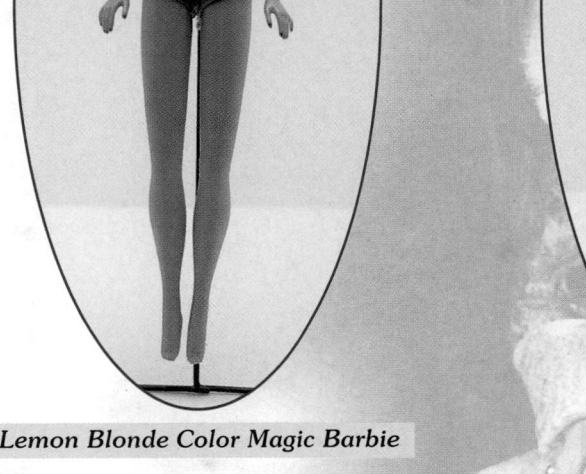

Lemon Blonde Color Magic Barbie

1967 Standard Barbie

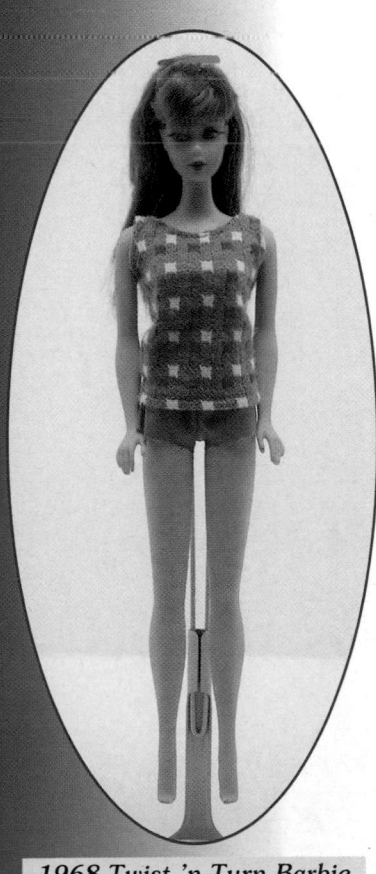

1968 Twist 'n Turn Barbie

First Talking Barbie

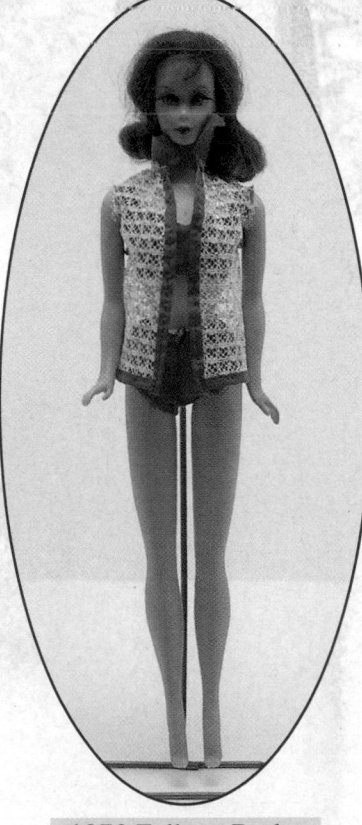

1970 Talking Barbie

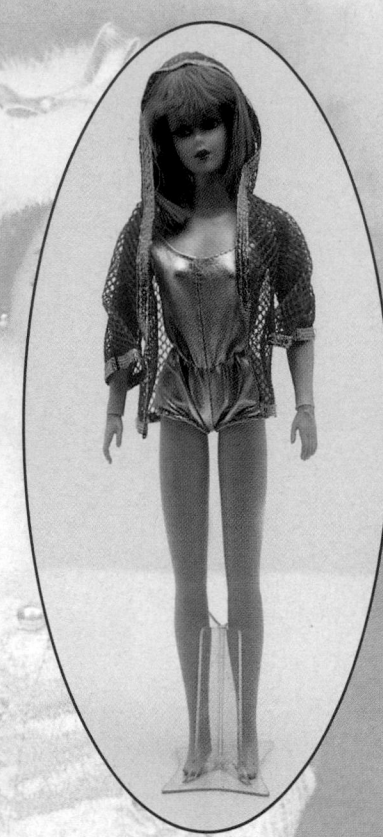

1970 Living Barbie

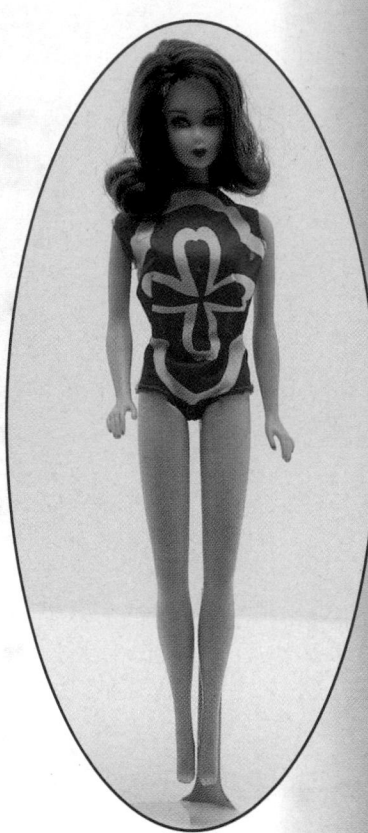

1970 Twist 'n Turn Barbie

1971 Twist 'n Turn Barbie

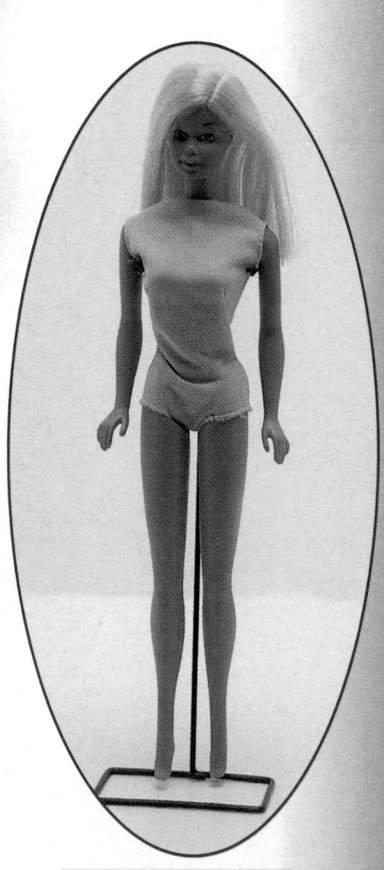

1971 Malibu Barbie

Bob Mackie Queen of Hearts musical and plate by Enesco

1993 Winter Royale Barbie, Wholesale Clubs Special

1994 Evergreen Princess Barbie, blonde

1996 Midnight Waltz Barbie, blonde

Braniff Airlines outfits with 1964 Sports Plane

1996 Special Occasion Barbie, The Mercantile Company store special

1994 Extravaganza Barbie

Barbie doll in Easter Parade, Sweater Girl, and Commuter Set

Russell Stover candy tins

1994 Southern Belle, part of the Great Eras Collection

Barbie doll Mix-n-Match Set, 1962 – 1963

1967 New Talking Barbie doll in Dinner Dazzle Set

1964 Skipper doll in School Days, 1965 American Girl Barbie doll in Student Teacher, and 1967 Twist 'n Turn in Sorbonne (Austrian market only)

1965 American Girl Barbie doll in Pan American Airways Stewardess

#1 Barbie wearing Roman Holiday outfit

Barbie Goes Traveling Carrying Case

1972 Put-Ons and pets, outfits: Kitty Kaper, Hot Togs, & Poodle Doodles

1964 Swirl Ponytail Barbie doll and Ken wearing 1964 Yachtsman

1995 Musical Barbie by Enesco

1970 gift set, Sears Exclusive

1967 Braniff Air Hostess gift set

16

One of four Twiggy doll outfits released in 1966

Barbie doll as Scarlett O'Hara in red velvet dress, barbecue dress, and green drapery dress (1994 – 1995)

Ken doll as Rhett Butler and Barbie doll as Scarlett O'Hara in Honeymoon in New Orleans (1995)

1996 Barbie Millicent Roberts' Goin' to the Game

1996 Barbie Millicent Roberts' Picnic Perfect

1961 blonde bubblecut Barbie doll in Solo in the Spotlight

1998 Ponytails Barbie doll

1994 Theater Elegance released by Spiegel

1996 Fourth Edition Native American Barbie doll

1996 Elizabethan Queen, part of the Great Eras Collection

1997 Summer Splendor, part of the Enchanted Seasons Collection

1996 plate, ornament, and musical depicting Barbie as My Fair Lady

1992 Plantation Belle Barbie doll, porcelain figurine

Swirl Ponytail Barbie doll coffee cup by Enesco

1992 Benefit Ball Barbie doll, part of the Classique Collection

1992 Crystal Rhapsody Barbie, part of the Presidential Porcelain Barbie Collection

1991 Gay Parisienne Barbie doll

Bob Mackie Goddess of the Moon and Goddess of the Sun musicals

Enesco's Barbie as Dorothy musical

*1995 Spring Bouquet Barbie doll, part
of the Enchanted Seasons Collection*

*1994 Dutch Barbie doll, from the
Dolls of the World Collection*

*1996 Autumn Glory Barbie, part of
the Enchanted Seasons Collection*

1993 Romantic Bride Barbie doll

Left, Black Francie, 1967; right, Black Francie, 1968

1964 Sports Plane with Ken wearing 1964 Braniff Pilot uniform made by Marx Company

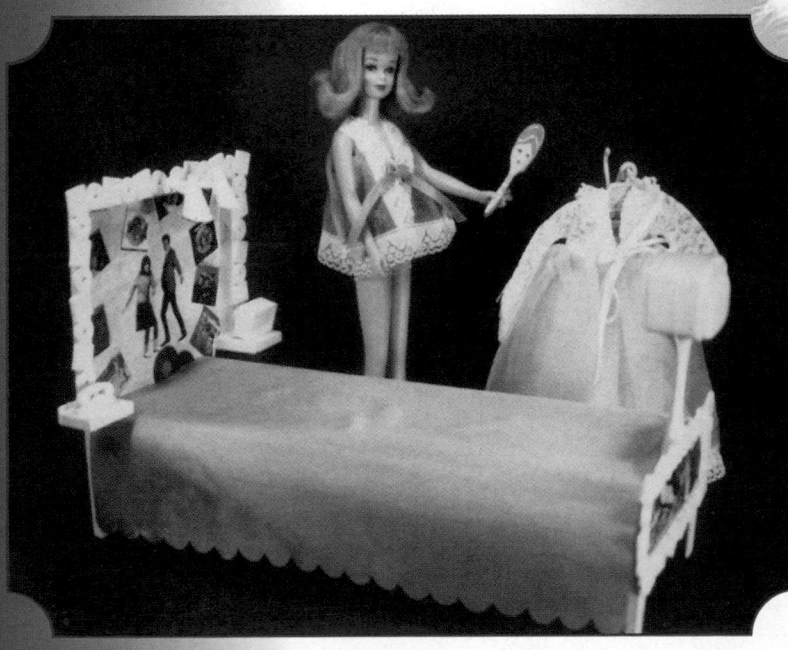

Twist 'n Turn Francie wearing Snooze News in her Francie modern bedroom set. Rise 'n Shine is pictured on the right.

1971 Jamie doll's Strollin' in Style gift set

1993 Desert Storm gift set

1969 Sleek Sportster with Skooter doll wearing Rainy Day Checkers and Skipper doll wearing Can You Play

1964 Elgin Co. clocks

Enesco miniature figurines

1996 Barbie doll Family House

1966 bendable leg Francie doll

King Seeley Thermos Company Barbie doll Lunch Kit from the early 1960s

One of many vintage outfits from Japan

1995 Christian Dior Barbie doll

26

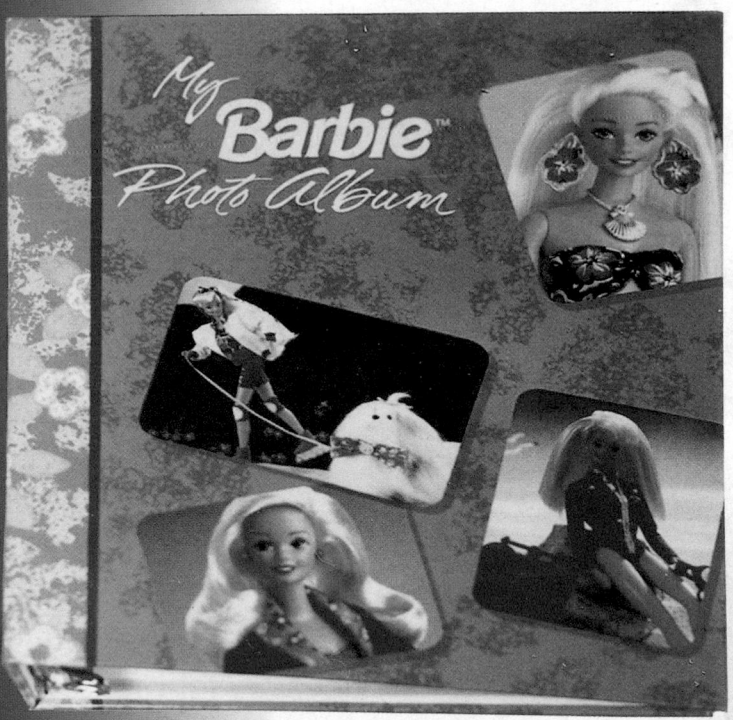

Hallmark Barbie doll photo album

Hallmark Barbie doll sticker packet

1963 Barbie doll
Mix 'N Match Set

Barbie Goes Traveling
Carrying Case, Sears
Exclusive

1995 Hot Skatin' Barbie doll

1994 brunette Snow Princess for the Orlando Convention at Walt Disney World

1994 Bicyclin' Barbie doll

1994 Cut and Style Barbie doll

1995 Teacher Barbie doll with two students and classroom accessories

1965 American Girl Barbie Gold

1995 Medieval Lady Barbie doll

1993 Gibson Girl Barbie doll

Mattel's 50th Anniversary Barbie doll

Enesco box from Gone With the Wind

Graduation Barbie

Barbie wearing 1959 Wedding Day
outfit and Ken wearing 1961 Tuxedo

1959 #1 Barbie, blonde

1959 #1 Barbie, redhead

Barbie Dolls

Listed Alphabetically

Item	Number	Year	Value	Specials
#1 Ponytail (blonde)	850	1959	$6,900.00	
#1 Ponytail (brunette)	850	1959	$7,000.00	
#2 Ponytail (blonde)	850	1959	$6,400.00	
#2 Ponytail (brunette)	850	1959	$6,400.00	
#3 Ponytail (blonde)	850	1960	$1,000.00	
#3 Ponytail (brunette)	850	1960	$1,100.00	
#4 Ponytail (blonde)	850	1960	$700.00	
#4 Ponytail (brunette)	850	1960	$700.00	
#5 Ponytail (blonde)	850	1961	$550.00	
#5 Ponytail (brunette)	850	1961	$550.00	
#5 Ponytail (titian)	850	1961	$675.00	
#6 Ponytail (ash blonde)	850	1962	$500.00	
#6 Ponytail (blonde)	850	1962	$500.00	
#6 Ponytail (brunette)	850	1962	$500.00	
#6 Ponytail (titian)	850	1962	$500.00	
#6 Ponytail (wheat blonde)	850	1962	$500.00	
#6 Ponytail (yellow blonde)	850	1962	$500.00	
1 Modern Circle Barbie	B2523	2003	$30.00	1 Modern Circle
1 Modern Circle Barbie	B2527	2004	$33.00	1 Modern Circle
101 Dalmatians	17248	1997	$25.00	Toys "R" Us
101 Dalmatians (black)	17601	1997	$25.00	Toys "R" Us
101 Dalmatians Barbie (brunette)	21377	1999	$20.00	Toys "R" Us
101 Dalmatians Barbie (strawberry blonde)	21375	1999	$20.00	Toys "R" Us
1850s Southern Belle	11478	1994	$42.00	Great Eras Collection
1920s Flapper Barbie	4063	1993	$55.00	Great Eras Collection
1950s Barbie	15820	1996	$30.00	Sam's Club/Wholesale Club
25th Anniversary	3939	1972	$650.00	Montgomery Ward
35th Anniversary (redhead)	11591	1994	$425.00	Mattel Festival Doll
35th Anniversary Barbie (blonde with arched eyebrows)	11590	1994	$23.00	Nostalgic
35th Anniversary Barbie (blonde with curved eyebrows)	11590	1994	$28.00	Nostalgic
35th Anniversary Barbie (brunette with arched eyebrows)	11782	1994	$24.00	Nostalgic
35th Anniversary Barbie (brunette with curved eyebrows)	11782	1994	$36.00	Nostalgic
35th Anniversary Barbie Keepsake Collection	11591	1994	$77.00	Nostalgic
35th Anniversary Festival Barbie	12670	1994	$200.00	Barbie Festival
35th Anniversary Target	16485	1997	$25.00	Target
35th Anniversary Target (black)	17608	1997	$25.00	Target
35th Anniversary Wal-Mart	17245	1997	$25.00	Wal-Mart
35th Anniversary Wal-Mart (black)	17616	1997	$25.00	Wal-Mart
40th Anniversary Barbie (black)	22336	1999	$45.00	40th Anniversary Collection
40th Anniversary Barbie (blonde)	21384	1999	$45.00	40th Anniversary Collection
40th Anniversary Barbie (brunette)	24842	1999	$150.00	Collectors Convention 1999
40th Anniversary Bumblebee Gala Barbie	23041	1999	$80.00	40th Anniversary Collection
45th Anniversary Barbie and Ken Gift Set	C4656	2004	$97.00	Barbie Fashion Model/FAO Schwarz
45th Anniversary Barbie (black hair)	B3454	2004	$150.00	Bob Mackie

Item	Number	Year	Value	Specials
45th Anniversary Barbie by Bob Mackie (black)	B3453	2004	$60.00	
45th Anniversary Barbie by Bob Mackie (blonde)	B3452	2004	$50.00	
45th Anniversary Barbie by Robert Best	B8955	2004	$49.00	Barbie Fashion Model
45th Anniversary Barbie by Robert Best (black)	B0445	2004	$50.00	Barbie Fashion Model
70s Disco Barbie (blonde)	19928	1998	$25.00	Wholesale Clubs
70s Disco Barbie (brunette)	19929	1998	$25.00	Wholesale Clubs
A Model Life Barbie Gift Set	B0147	2003	$80.00	
A Nod for Mod Barbie	C6261	2004	$80.00	Barbie Fan Club Exclusive
Action Accents Set (auburn)	1585	1969	$800.00	Sears
After Five	934	1963	$600.00	Dressed Boxed Dolls
After the Walk	17341	1997	$48.00	Coca-Cola Fashion Classic Series
Air Force	3360	1991	$30.00	Stars 'n Stripes
Air Force Academy	21166	1999	$14.00	University Barbie
Air Force Thunderbirds	11552	1994	$20.00	Stars 'n Stripes
Air Force Thunderbirds (black)	11553	1994	$20.00	Stars 'n Stripes
Alabama	19170	1998	$10.00	University Barbie
Alabama (black)	19422	1998	$10.00	University Barbie
Alice in Wonderland	21933	1998	$16.00	Disney Classics
All American	9423	1991	$28.00	Reebok
All That Glitters Barbie	55426	2002	$27.00	Diva Collection
American Airlines Stewardess	984	1963	$700.00	Dressed Boxed Dolls
American Beauty Queen	3137	1991	$35.00	
American Beauty Queen (black)	3245	1991	$35.00	
American Girl (ash blonde)	1070	1965	$1,500.00	
American Girl (blonde)	1070	1965	$1,500.00	
American Girl (brown)	1070	1965	$1,500.00	
American Girl (brunette)	1070	1965	$1,500.00	
American Girl (brunette)	1070	1966	$2,500.00	
American Girl (color magic face)	1070	1966	$3,000.00	
American Girl (redhead)	1070	1965	$2,500.00	
American Girl (side part/blonde)	1070	1966	$3,000.00	
American Indian	14715	1996	$25.00	American Stories Collection
American Indian II	17313	1997	$28.00	American Stories Collection
Amethyst Aura	15522	1997	$90.00	Bob Mackie Jewel Essence
Andalucia	15758	1996	$40.00	
Angel Face	5640	1983	$35.00	
Angel Lights	10610	1993	$50.00	
Angel of Joy Barbie	19633	1998	$45.00	Timeless Sentiments
Angel of Joy Barbie (black)	20929	1998	$45.00	Timeless Sentiments
Angel of Peace	24240	1999	$40.00	Timeless Sentiments
Angel of Peace (black)	24241	1999	$40.00	Timeless Sentiments
Angel Princess	15911	1997	$24.00	
Angel Princess (black)	15912	1997	$24.00	
Animal Lovin'	1350	1988	$30.00	
Animal Lovin' (black)	4824	1988	$30.00	
Anne from Anne of Green Gables	50726	2002	$14.00	When I Read, I Dream
Anne Klein Barbie	17603	1997	$40.00	Macy's
Anniversary Edition Golden Qi-Pao Barbie	20649	1998	$75.00	Hong Kong Commemorative Edition
Anniversary Star	2282	1992	$30.00	Wal-Mart
Antique Rose	15814	1996	$190.00	FAO Schwarz
Applause Barbie	3406	1991	$35.00	Applause
April Diamond Barbie	B3412	2003	$40.00	Birthstone Collection/Wal-Mart
April Diamond Barbie (black)	C0586	2003	$40.00	Birthstone Collection/Wal-Mart
Aquarius Barbie		2005	$20.00	Zodiac
Aquarius Barbie (black)		2005	$20.00	Zodiac

Item	Number	Year	Value	Specials
Arabian Nights	874	1964	$1,270.00	Dressed Boxed Dolls
Arcadian Court Barbie	62889	1996	$85.00	Hudson's Bay Company Canada
Archie Comics Betty Barbie	H7614	2005	$20.00	
Archie Comics Veronica Barbie	H7615	2005	$20.00	
Arctic	16495	1996	$25.00	Dolls of the World
Aries Barbie		2005	$20.00	Zodiac
Aries Barbie (black)		2005	$20.00	Zodiac
Arizona Jean Company I	15441	1996	$25.00	JCPenney
Arizona Jean Company II	18020	1997	$25.00	JCPenney
Arizona State University	19162	1998	$10.00	University Barbie
Army	3966	1989	$25.00	American Beauty Collection
Army	21159	1999	$14.00	University Barbie
Army Desert Storm	1234	1993	$24.00	Stars 'n Stripes
Army Desert Storm (black)	5816	1993	$24.00	Stars 'n Stripes
Astronaut	2449	1986	$65.00	
Astronaut	12149	1994	$45.00	Toys "R" Us
Astronaut (black)	1207	1986	$60.00	
Astronaut (black)	12150	1994	$45.00	Toys "R" Us
Atlanta Hawks	20734	1998	$20.00	NBA
Atlanta Hawks (black)	20735	1998	$20.00	NBA
Auburn University	17699	1997	$10.00	University Barbie
Auburn University (black)	18346	1997	$9.00	University Barbie
August Peridot Barbie	B3416	2003	$40.00	Birthstone Collection/Wal-Mart
August Peridot Barbie (black)	C0578	2003	$40.00	Birthstone Collection/Wal-Mart
Australian Barbie #1	3626	1993	$32.00	Dolls of the World
Australian Barbie #2	3626	1993	$34.00	Dolls of the World
Austrian Barbie	21553	1999	$18.00	Dolls of the World
Autumn Glory	15204	1996	$48.00	Enchanted Seasons
Autumn in London	22257	1999	$30.00	City Seasons Collection
Autumn in Paris	19367	1998	$35.00	City Seasons Collection
Avon Representative Barbie	22202	1999	$50.00	Avon
Avon Representative Barbie (black)	22203	1999	$40.00	Avon
Avon Representative Barbie (Hispanic)	22204	1999	$50.00	Avon
B Mine Barbie	11182	1994	$22.00	Supermarket
Back to School	10217	1993	$25.00	Supermarket
Back to School	17099	1997	$10.00	Supermarket
Back to School (black)	17100	1997	$10.00	Supermarket
Badgley Mischka Bride Barbie	B8946	2004	$139.00	Designer Dolls
Baking Fun Barbie	52639	2004	$12.00	
Ballerina	4983	1983	$40.00	Mervyn's
Ballerina (1st version)	9093	1976	$70.00	
Ballerina (2nd issue)	9093	1979	$45.00	
Ballerina (black)	4984	1983	$60.00	Mervyn's
Ballerina Barbie on Tour	9613	1976	$125.00	Department Store
Ballerina Barbie on Tour (no wrist tag)	9613	1979	$110.00	Department Store
Ballerina Barbie on Tour (with wrist tag)	9613	1979	$120.00	Department Store
Ballerina Dreams Barbie	20676	1999	$14.00	Supermarket
Ballerina Barbie on Tour (1st hair version)	9613	1976	$140.00	
Ballerina Barbie on Tour (2nd hair version)	9613	1979	$90.00	
Ballet Lessons	26774	1999	$11.00	
Ballet Lessons (black)	26775	2000	$50.00	
Ballet Star	29195	2000	$11.00	
Ballet Star (black)	29196	2000	$12.00	
Ballroom Beauty	3678	1991	$30.00	Wal-Mart
Banquet Set Barbie Doll (blonde)	850	1994	$299.00	Barbie Festival

Item	Number	Year	Value	Specials
Banquet Set Barbie Doll (redhead)	850	1994	$299.00	Barbie Festival
Barbie	G8469	2004	$6.00	
Barbie & Champion	13181	1995	$45.00	Hill's
Barbie & Ginger	17116	1997	$35.00	
Barbie & Ginger (black)	17369	1997	$35.00	
Barbie 2000	27409	2000	$48.00	
Barbie 2000 (black)	27410	2000	$48.00	
Barbie 2001	50841	2001	$102.00	
Barbie 2001 (black)	50842	2001	$70.00	
Barbie 2002	53975	2002	$44.00	
Barbie 2002 (black)	53976	2002	$38.00	
Barbie 2003	B0144	2003	$65.00	
Barbie 2003 (black)	B0145	2003	$65.00	
Barbie 2003 (redhead)		2003	$125.00	
Barbie and *Curious George*	28798	2001	$28.00	Keepsake Treasures
Barbie and Her Super Fashion Fireworks #1	9805	1997	$90.00	K-Mart/Kresge
Barbie and Her Super Fashion Fireworks #2	9805	1997	$90.00	K-Mart/Kresge
Barbie and Her Super Fashion Fireworks #3	9805	1997	$90.00	K-Mart/Kresge
Barbie and Ken as Arwen and Aragorn from *The Lord of the Rings*	B3449	2004	$180.00	Hollywood
Barbie and Snoopy	55558	2002	$60.00	
Barbie and Snowball Her Pet Dog	7272	1990	$15.00	
Barbie and the All Stars	9099	1990	$25.00	
Barbie and the Beat	2751	1990	$25.00	
Barbie and *The Tale of Peter Rabbit*	19360	1998	$28.00	Keepsake Treasures
Barbie as Beauty	24673	2000	$30.00	Children's Collector Series
Barbie as Catwoman	B5838	2004	$20.00	Barbie Loves Pop Culture
Barbie as Cinderella	16900	1996	$24.00	Children's Collector Series
Barbie as Dorothy	25812	2000	$25.00	Wizard of Oz
Barbie as Dorothy	25812	1999	$18.00	Wizard of Oz
Barbie as Dorothy 2nd Edition	12701	1996	$75.00	Wizard of Oz
Barbie as Elle Woods from *Legally Blonde 2*	B9284	2003	$35.00	Barbie Loves Pop Culture
Barbie as Empress Sissy	15846	1996	$55.00	Royal House of Europe
Barbie as Flower Ballerina from *The Nutcracker*	28375	2001	$25.00	Classic Ballet Series
Barbie as Galadriel from *The Lord of the Rings*	H1179	2004	$40.00	Hollywood
Barbie as Glinda	25813	2000	$25.00	Wizard of Oz
Barbie as Glinda	25813	1999	$18.00	Wizard of Oz
Barbie as Jeannie from *I Dream of Jeannie*	29913	2001	$40.00	Barbie Loves Pop Culture
Barbie as Juliet	B5655	2004	$30.00	Classic Ballet Series
Barbie as Little Bo Peep	14960	1996	$55.00	Children's Collector Series
Barbie as Marzipan from *The Nutcracker*	20851	1999	$26.00	Classic Ballet Series
Barbie as Peppermint Candy Cane from *The Nutcracker*	57578	2003	$33.00	Classic Ballet Series
Barbie as Princess Annika	G8399	2005	$20.00	
Barbie as Rapunzel	13016	1995	$24.00	Children's Collector Series
Barbie as Samantha from *Bewitched*	53510	2002	$30.00	Barbie Loves Pop Culture
Barbie as Sleeping Beauty	18586	1998	$25.00	Children's Collector Series
Barbie as Snow White	21130	1999	$28.00	Children's Collector Series
Barbie as Snowflake from *The Nutcracker*	25642	2000	$27.00	Classic Ballet Series
Barbie as Swan Ballerina	53867	2002	$24.00	Classic Ballet Series
Barbie as That Girl	56705	2003	$40.00	Barbie Loves Pop Culture
Barbie as the Sugar Plum Fairy from *The Nutcracker*	17056	1997	$29.00	Classic Ballet Series
Barbie as the Swan Queen from *Swan Lake*	18509	1997	$22.00	Classic Ballet Series
Barbie as the Swan Queen from *Swan Lake* (black)	18510	1997	$22.00	Classic Ballet Series
Barbie as Titania	C3819	2004	$27.00	Classic Ballet Series

Item	Number	Year	Value	Specials
Barbie as Wonder Woman	24638	2000	$18.00	Barbie Loves Pop Culture
Barbie at Bloomingdale's	16290	1996	$35.00	Bloomingdale's
Barbie at FAO	17298	1997	$30.00	FAO Schwarz
Barbie Babysits (yellow)	7882	1974	$70.00	
Barbie Celebration	9146	1987	$30.00	
Barbie Doll	1511	1991	$80.00	McGlynn's Bakery
Barbie Doll (black)	1534	1991	$80.00	McGlynn's Bakery
Barbie for President	26288	2000	Retail	Career
Barbie for President (black)	26284	2000	Retail	Career
Barbie for President (black, Presidential seal)	3940	1991	$45.00	Toys "R" Us
Barbie for President (Hispanic)		2000	Retail	Career/Online Exclusive
Barbie for President (Presidential seal)	3722	1991	$65.00	Toys "R" Us
Barbie for President (white star)	3722	1992	$40.00	Toys "R" Us
Barbie Had a Little Lamb	21740	1999	$25.00	Nursery Rhyme
Barbie in Holland	823	1964	$820.00	Dressed Boxed Dolls
Barbie in India	9910	1993	$50.00	
Barbie in Mexico	820	1964	$820.00	Dressed Boxed Dolls
Barbie in Switzerland	822	1964	$820.00	Dressed Boxed Dolls
Barbie Loves Patrick	C3699	2005	$15.00	
Barbie Loves Shrek	H1703	2005	$17.00	
Barbie Loves Tweety	21632	1999	$35.00	Warner Bros. Studio Store
Barbie Millicent Roberts Matinee Today	16079	1996	$40.00	Barbie Millicent Roberts
Barbie Millicent Roberts Perfectly Suited	17567	1997	$35.00	Barbie Millicent Roberts
Barbie Millicent Roberts Pinstripe Power	19791	1998	$30.00	Barbie Millicent Roberts
Barbie on Bay	63987	1997	$35.00	Hudson's Bay Company Canada
Barbie Pet Doctor	G8815	2004	$16.00	
Barbie Sign Language	25837	1999	$20.00	
Barbie Sign Language (black)	26394	1999	$20.00	
Barbie Style	14476	1997	$20.00	
Bard Barbie Doll, The	B2511	2004	$60.00	Legends of Ireland
Baseball	4583	1993	$30.00	Target
Bath Blast	4159	1993	$15.00	
Bath Blast (black)	3830	1993	$15.00	
Bath Boutique Barbie (brunette)	22359	1999	$15.00	
Bath Boutique Barbie (black)	22358	1999	$15.00	
Bath Boutique Barbie (blonde)	22357	1999	$15.00	
Bath Magic	5274	1992	$15.00	
Bath Magic (black)	7951	1992	$15.00	
Bathtime Fun	9601	1991	$15.00	Wal-Mart Wholesale Clubs
Bathtime Fun (black)	9603	1991	$15.00	Wal-Mart Wholesale Clubs
Batik Princess Barbie	C4558	2004	$25.00	Online Exclusive
Baywatch	13199	1995	$20.00	
Baywatch (black)	13258	1995	$20.00	
Beach Blast	3237	1989	$15.00	
Beach Blast (black)	3253	1989	$20.00	
Beach Time	9102	1985	$25.00	
Bead Blast (black)	18889	1997	$15.00	
Bead Blast (blonde)	18888	1997	$15.00	
Bead Blast (brunette)	18891	1997	$15.00	
Bead Blast (redhead)	18890	1997	$15.00	
Beautiful Bride	9599	1976	$200.00	Department Store
Beautiful Bride	9907	1978	$175.00	Department Store
Beautiful Bride Barbie		2004	$15.00	
Beauty Secrets Barbie Pretty Reflections	1290	1980	$75.00	Department Store
Bedtime	11079	1993	$15.00	

Item	Number	Year	Value	Specials
Bedtime (black)	11184	1993	$15.00	
Bedtime Barbie with Bed	12184	1994	$30.00	Wholesale Clubs
Bedtime Stories w/book	29426	2000	$25.00	Toys "R" Us
Bedtime Stories w/book (black)	29427	2000	$25.00	Toys "R" Us
Benefit Ball	1521	1992	$45.00	Classique
Benefit Performance	5475	1988	$235.00	Nostalgic Porcelain
Benetton	9404	1991	$30.00	
Benetton Shopping	4873	1991	$30.00	
Between Takes Barbie	27684	2000	$50.00	Hollywood Movie Star Collection
Beyond Pink	20017	1998	$15.00	
Bicyclin'	11689	1994	$25.00	Toys "R" Us
Bicyclin' (black)	11817	1994	$25.00	Toys "R" Us
Bill Blass	17040	1997	$80.00	Designer Collection
Billions of Dreams	17641	1997	$199.00	Ultra Limited Edition
Birthday	11333	1994	$30.00	
Birthday	12954	1995	$25.00	
Birthday	15998	1997	$20.00	
Birthday (black)	11334	1994	$30.00	
Birthday (black)	12955	1995	$25.00	
Birthday (black)	15999	1997	$20.00	
Birthday (blonde)	20017	1998	$20.00	
Birthday (brunette)	18292	1998	$20.00	
Birthday (Hispanic)	13253	1995	$25.00	
Birthday (Hispanic)	16000	1997	$20.00	
Birthday Party	3388	1993	$30.00	
Birthday Party (black)	7948	1993	$30.00	
Birthday Party Barbie	18351	1998	$12.00	Supermarket
Birthday Party Barbie	22907	1999	$20.00	
Birthday Party Barbie (black)	18352	1998	$12.00	Supermarket
Birthday Party Barbie (black)	22906	1999	$20.00	
Birthday Surprise	3679	1992	$40.00	
Birthday Surprise	16491	1997	$15.00	Supermarket
Birthday Surprise (black)	4051	1992	$40.00	
Birthday Surprise Barbie (black)	17320	1997	$15.00	Supermarket
Birthday Wishes Barbie	21128	1999	$26.00	Birthday Wishes Series
Birthday Wishes Barbie #2	24667	2000	$24.00	Birthday Wishes Series
Birthday Wishes Barbie #2 (black)	24668	2000	$24.00	Birthday Wishes Series
Birthday Wishes Barbie #3	28434	2000	$27.00	Birthday Wishes Series
Birthday Wishes Barbie #3 (black)	28435	2000	$27.00	Birthday Wishes Series
Birthday Wishes Barbie (black)	21509	1999	$26.00	Birthday Wishes Series
Birthday Wishes Barbie (black)	24668	2000	$25.00	Birthday Wishes Series
Birthday Wishes Barbie (black)	28435	2001	$27.00	Birthday Wishes Series
Birthday Wishes Barbie (black)		2004	$24.00	Birthday Wishes Series
Birthday Wishes Barbie (black)	G8061	2005	$30.00	Birthday Wishes Series
Birthday Wishes Barbie, Aqua		2004	$19.00	Birthday Wishes Series
Birthday Wishes Barbie, Green		2004	$24.00	Birthday Wishes Series
Birthday Wishes Barbie, Lavender		2004	$19.00	Birthday Wishes Series
Birthday Wishes Barbie, Peach		2005	$30.00	Birthday Wishes Series
Birthday Wishes Barbie, Pink		2004	$19.00	Birthday Wishes Series
Birthday Wishes Barbie, Red	C6229	2004	$24.00	Birthday Wishes Series
Birthday Wishes Barbie, Violet	C6228	2004	$37.00	Birthday Wishes Series
Birthday Wishes Barbie, Yellow		2004	$19.00	Birthday Wishes Series
Black Barbie Doll	1293	1980	$75.00	Birthday Wishes Series
Black Magic Ensemble	1609	1964	$860.00	Dressed Boxed Dolls
Blossom Beautiful	3817	1992	$225.00	Sears

Item	Number	Year	Value	Specials
Blossom Beauty	3142	1991	$40.00	Shopko/Venture
Blossom Beauty	17032	1997	$20.00	
Blossom Beauty (black)	17033	1997	$20.00	
Blue Elegance	1879	1992	$50.00	Hill's
Blue Rhapsody	1364	1991	$140.00	Service Merchandise
Blue Rhapsody	1708	1986	$299.00	Porcelain
Blue Starlight	17125	1997	$35.00	Sears
Blush Becomes Her Fashion	29652	2001	$75.00	Barbie Fashion Model
Blushing Bride		2000	$30.00	Avon
Blushing Bride (black)		2000	$30.00	Avon
Blushing Orchid Bride (porcelain)	16962	1997	$125.00	Wedding Flower Collection
Bohemian Glamour Barbie	B2512	2003	$39.00	Style Set
Boston Celtics	20716	1998	$20.00	NBA
Boston Celtics (black)	20717	1998	$20.00	NBA
Boston College	21189	1999	$16.00	University Barbie
Boston University	21226	1999	$16.00	University Barbie
Boulevard Fashion	29653	2001	$60.00	Barbie Fashion Model
Bowling Champ Barbie	25871	2000	$30.00	Sports
Brazilian	9094	1990	$27.00	Dolls of the World
Bride Barbie (brunette)		2000	$60.00	My Design Friend of Barbie
Bride Barbie (redhead)		2000	$60.00	My Design Friend of Barbie
Bride's Dream	947	1964	$910.00	Dressed Boxed Dolls
Bridesmaid	9608	1991	$30.00	
Brigham Young University	19152	1998	$10.00	University Barbie
Bronze Sensation Barbie	20022	1998	$55.00	Wholesale Clubs
Brunette Brilliance Barbie	B0585	2003	$100.00	Bob Mackie
Bubble Angel	12443	1995	$20.00	
Bubble Angel (black)	12444	1995	$15.00	
Bubble Cut (blonde)	850	1961	$400.00	
Bubble Cut (blonde)	850	1962	$400.00	
Bubble Cut (brunette)	850	1961	$975.00	
Bubble Cut (brunette)	850	1961	$400.00	
Bubble Cut (brunette)	850	1962	$400.00	
Bubble Cut (Japanese, side part)	850	1965	$2,995.00	
Bubble Cut (side part)	850	1965	$445.00	
Bubble Cut (titian)	850	1961	$400.00	
Bubble Cut (titian)	850	1962	$400.00	
Bubble Cut (white ginger)	850	1961	$925.00	
Bubble Fairy	22087	1998	$20.00	
Bubbling Mermaid	16131	1997	$15.00	
Bubbling Mermaid (black)	16132	1997	$15.00	
Burberry Barbie	29421	2001	$70.00	Designer Burberry
Busy (Talking)	1195	1972	$350.00	
Busy Barbie	3311	1972	$200.00	
Busy Gal	13675	1995	$42.00	Nostalgic Vinyl Series
Butterfly Art	20359	1998	$10.00	
Butterfly Princess	13051	1995	$25.00	
Butterfly Princess (black)	13052	1995	$25.00	
Butterfly Princess (Hispanic)	13238	1995	$25.00	
Caboodles	3157	1993	$20.00	
Caboodles Barbie with child-sized Caboodles Case	11285	1993	$35.00	JCPenney
Café Society Barbie	18892	1998	$68.00	Barbie Collector's Club
Cali Girl Teresa	C6463	2004	$8.00	
California Barbie	4439	1987	$20.00	
California Barbie (with Beach Boys record)	4442	1987	$30.00	

Item	Number	Year	Value	Specials
California Dream	4439	1988	$30.00	
Calla Lily Barbie, The	29912	2002	$57.00	Flowers in Fashion
Calvin Klein Jeans Barbie	16211	1996	$55.00	Bloomingdale's
Calvin Klein Jeans Barbie	16211	1996	$70.00	Hudson's Bay Company Canada
Camp	11074	1994	$25.00	
Canadian	4928	1988	$35.00	Dolls of the World
Cancer Barbie		2005	$20.00	Zodiac
Cancer Barbie		2005	$20.00	Zodiac
Capricorn Barbie		2005	$20.00	Zodiac/FAO Schwarz
Capricorn Barbie (black)		2005	$20.00	Zodiac
Capucine Barbie	B0146	2003	$100.00	Barbie Fashion Model
Career Girl	954	1964	$858.00	Dressed Boxed Dolls
Carnival Barbie	J0927	2005	$20.00	Festivals of the World
Carnival Cruise Lines	15186	1997	$30.00	Wessco
Carolina Herrera Bride Barbie	B9797	2005	$140.00	Designer Dolls
Caroling Fun	13966	1995	$20.00	Supermarket
Case with Doll (swirl ponytail)	2000	1966	$800.00	
Celebration Barbie	1998	1986	$65.00	Sears
Celebration Barbie	28269	2000	$34.00	Holiday Dolls
Celebration Barbie (black)	28270	2001	$45.00	
Celebration Cake Barbie (black)	22903	1999	$20.00	
Celebration Cake Barbie (blonde)	22902	1999	$20.00	
Celebration Cake Barbie (brunette)	22904	1999	$20.00	
Charity Ball Barbie	18979	1998	$30.00	Toys "R" Us
Charity Ball Barbie (black)	19132	1998	$30.00	Toys "R" Us
Charleston Barbie, The	24252	2001	$250.00	Bob Mackie
Charlotte Hornets	20698	1998	$20.00	NBA
Charlotte Hornets (black)	20699	1998	$20.00	NBA
Chataine Barbie	B4425	2003	$425.00	Barbie Fashion Model
Chic	18218	1999	$5.00	K•B Toys
Chicago Bulls	20692	1998	$20.00	NBA
Chicago Bulls (black)	20693	1998	$20.00	NBA
Chicago Cubs Barbie	23883	1999	$29.00	Major League Baseball
Chicago Cubs Barbie (black)	24473	1999	$35.00	Major League Baseball
Chicago Cubs Fan Barbie	22857	1999	$85.00	Chicago Cubs
Children's Day Barbie	18350	1998	$15.00	K•B Toys
Children's Day Barbie	18350	1998	$15.00	Children's Day
Children's Doctor	29461	2000	$20.00	
Chilean	18559	1997	$25.00	Dolls of the World
Chinese	11180	1994	$23.00	Dolls of the World
Chinese Empress Barbie	16708	1997	$32.00	Great Eras Collection
Chinese Empress Barbie	16708	1997	$88.00	Hong Kong Commemorative Edition
Chinese New Year Barbie	J0928	2005	$20.00	Festivals of the World
Chinoiserie Red Midnight Barbie		2004	$175.00	Barbie Fashion Model
Chinoiserie Red Moon Barbie	B3431	2004	$50.00	Barbie Fashion Model
Chinoiserie Red Sunset Barbie		2004	$115.00	Barbie Fashion Model/Online Exclusive
Chocolate Obsession Barbie	G8878	2005	$35.00	Flavor Obsession
Christian Dior I	13168	1995	$60.00	Designer Collection
Christian Dior II	16013	1997	$68.00	Designer Collection
Chuck E Cheese	14615	1996	$30.00	Chuck E Cheese Pizza
Cincinnati	21231	1999	$16.00	University Barbie
Cinderella	872	1964	$858.00	Dressed Boxed Dolls
Cinnabar Sensation	23420	1998	$76.00	Byron Lars Runway Collection
Cinnabar Sensation (black)	19848	1998	$76.00	Byron Lars Runway Collection
Circus Star	13257	1995	$70.00	FAO Schwarz

Item	Number	Year	Value	Specials
Citrus Obsession Barbie	J0933	2005	$35.00	Flavor Obsession
City Shopper	16289	1996	$40.00	Macy's
City Smart Barbie		2003	$510.00	Barbie Fashion Model
City Sophisticate	12005	1994	$50.00	Service Merchandise
City Style Barbie	10149	1993	$35.00	Classique
City Style Barbie	15612	1996	$20.00	Target
City Style Barbie	17237	1997	$15.00	Target
City Style Barbie	10149	1995	$105.00	Hudson's Bay Company Canada
City Style Barbie	18952	1998	$16.00	Target
City Style Barbie	18952	1999	$14.00	Target
Civil War Nurse	14612	1996	$25.00	American Stories Collection
Classic Grace Barbie		2002	Retail	Prima Ballerina
Clemson University	17753	1997	$10.00	University Barbie
Clemson University (black)	18349	1997	$9.00	University Barbie
Cleveland Cavaliers	20736	1998	$20.00	NBA
Cleveland Cavaliers (black)	20737	1998	$20.00	NBA
Club Couture	26068	2000	$70.00	Barbie Collector's Club
Club Wedd Barbie (black)	20423	1998	$20.00	Target
Club Wedd Barbie (black)	22361	1999	$20.00	Target
Club Wedd Barbie (blonde)	19717	1998	$20.00	Target
Club Wedd Barbie (blonde)	22360	1999	$20.00	Target
Club Wedd Barbie (brunette)	19718	1998	$20.00	Target
Club Wedd Barbie (brunette)	22362	1999	$20.00	Target
Coca-Cola Barbie #2 (brunette)	24637	2000	$60.00	American Classics
Coca-Cola Barbie (blonde)	22831	1999	$60.00	Coca-Cola Series
Coca-Cola Barbie (brunette) Walt Disney World	23934	1999	$198.00	Coca-Cola Series
Coca-Cola Barbie (Cheerleader)	53974	2001	$46.00	Coca-Cola Series
Coca-Cola Barbie (Majorette)		2002	$35.00	Coca-Cola Series
Coca-Cola Barbie (Sweetheart)	24637	2000	$40.00	Coca-Cola Series
Coca-Cola Brand Party Barbie	22964	1999	$12.00	Supermarket
Coca-Cola Drive-In Waitress	22831	1999	$60.00	American Classics
Coca-Cola Picnic Barbie	19626	1998	$15.00	Supermarket
Coca-Cola Picnic Barbie (black)	19627	1998	$15.00	Supermarket
Coca-Cola Soda Fountain	26980	2000	$140.00	Coca-Cola Series
Colonial	12578	1995	$25.00	American Stories Collection
Color 'N Curl Set (molded Barbie head only)	40389	1965	$585.00	
Color 'n Curl Set (head only)	4839	1965	$500.00	
Color 'n Wash My Hair Barbie	15139	1997	$50.00	Avon
Color Magic (cardboard box, blonde)	1150	1967	$3,000.00	
Color Magic (cardboard box, midnight black)	1150	1967	$4,200.00	
Color Magic (plastic box, blonde)	1150	1966	$1,800.00	
Color Magic (plastic box, midnight black)	1150	1966	$3,000.00	
Color Magic Barbie (brunette)	B3437	2004	$40.00	Collectors' Request
Color Magic Barbie (blonde)	B3437	2004	$175.00	Collectors' Request
Color Magic Barbie (redhead)	B3437	2004	$210.00	Collectors' Request
Color with Me Barbie	19047	1998	$15.00	Supermarket
Commuter Set Barbie	21510	1999	$50.00	Collectors' Request
Continental Holiday Barbie Gift Set	55497	2002	$100.00	Barbie Fashion Model
Convention 2000 Barbie Democrat (black)		2000	$120.00	
Convention 2000 Barbie Democrat (blonde)		2000	$95.00	
Convention 2000 Barbie Democrat (brunette)		2000	$110.00	
Convention 2000 Barbie Republican (black)		2000	$130.00	
Convention 2000 Barbie Republican (blonde)		2000	$97.00	
Convention 2000 Barbie Republican (brunette)		2000	$115.00	
Cool 'n Sassy	1490	1992	$25.00	Toys "R" Us

Item	Number	Year	Value	Specials
Cool 'n Sassy (black)	4110	1992	$25.00	Toys "R" Us
Cool Blue Barbie	20122	1998	$15.00	
Cool Clips Barbie	26425	2000	$14.00	
Cool Collecting	25525	2000	$36.00	
Cool Looks	5947	1990	$25.00	Toys "R" Us
Cool Looks Fashion Designer CD-ROM	24746	1999	$28.00	Meijer
Cool Shoppin'	17487	1997	$20.00	
Cool Shoppin' (black)	17488	1997	$20.00	
Cool Skating Barbie	25887	2000	$20.00	
Cool Skating Barbie		1999	$20.00	
Cool Times	3022	1989	$25.00	
Corduroy Cool (black)	26107	1999	$15.00	
Corduroy Cool (blonde)	24658	1999	$15.00	
Corduroy Cool Barbie (brunette)	24659	1999	$9.00	
Costume Ball	7123	1991	$30.00	
Costume Ball (black)	7134	1991	$30.00	
Countess of Rubies Barbie	26972	2001	$80.00	Jewel Collection
Country & Western Star	11646	1994	$30.00	Wal-Mart
Country & Western Star (black)	12096	1994	$30.00	Wal-Mart
Country & Western Star (Hispanic)	12097	1994	$30.00	Wal-Mart
Country Bride	13614	1995	$20.00	Wal-Mart
Country Bride (black)	13615	1995	$20.00	Wal-Mart
Country Bride (Hispanic)	13616	1995	$20.00	Wal-Mart
Country Charm	26464	2000	$25.00	Cracker Barrel Restaurant
Country Charm (black)	29332	2000	$25.00	Cracker Barrel Restaurant
Country Fair	1603	1964	$595.00	Dressed Boxed Dolls
Country Looks	5854	1993	$25.00	Ames
Country Rose	17782	1997	$42.00	Grand Ole Opry
Country Rose	17864	1997	$50.00	Sam's Club/Wholesale Club
Country Star Western Horse	12271	1994	$25.00	Wal-Mart
Cruisin' the Boardwalk Barbie and River	C4212	2004	$33.00	My Scene
Crystal	4598	1984	$30.00	
Crystal (black)	4859	1984	$30.00	
Crystal Fairytopia Barbie	G6261	2005	$17.00	
Crystal Glitter (black)	22070	1999	$15.00	
Crystal Glitter (blonde)	22069	1999	$15.00	
Crystal Glitter (brunette)	22071	1999	$15.00	
Crystal Glitter (redhead)	22071	1999	$15.00	
Crystal Jubilee Barbie	21923	1999	$155.00	Jubilee Series
Crystal Rhapsody (blonde)	1553	1992	$220.00	Presidential Porcelain
Crystal Rhapsody (brunette, Disney)	10201	1992	$350.00	Presidential Porcelain
Crystal Splendor	15136	1996	$25.00	Toys "R" Us
Crystal Splendor (black)	15137	1996	$25.00	Toys "R" Us
Cut and Style (black)	12642	1995	$20.00	
Cut and Style (blonde)	12639	1995	$20.00	
Cut and Style (brunette)	12643	1995	$20.00	
Cut and Style (redhead)	12644	1995	$20.00	
Cute 'n Cool	2954	1991	$30.00	Target
Cynthia Rowley Barbie	G8064	2005	$80.00	Cynthia Rowley
Czechoslovakian	7330	1991	$55.00	Dolls of the World
Dallas Mavericks	20728	1998	$20.00	NBA
Dallas Mavericks (black)	20729	1998	$20.00	NBA
Dance 'n Twirl	11902	1994	$50.00	
Dance 'n Twirl (black)	12143	1994	$45.00	
Dance 'Till Dawn Barbie	19631	1998	$40.00	Great Fashions of the 20th Century

Item	Number	Year	Value	Specials
Dance Club with Tape Player	3509	1989	$55.00	Child's World
Dance Magic	4836	1990	$25.00	
Dance Magic (black)	7080	1990	$25.00	
Dance Moves	13083	1995	$15.00	
Dance Moves (black)	13086	1995	$15.00	
Dance Sensation	9058	1984	$60.00	Toys "R" Us
Dancing Fire Barbie	26327	2000	$60.00	Essence of Nature
Daria Celebutante		2004	Retail	Model of the Moment
Daria Shopping Queen		2005	Retail	Model of the Moment
David's Bridal Eternal Barbie		2005	Retail	David's Bridal
David's Bridal Eternal Barbie (black)		2005	Retail	David's Bridal
David's Bridal Eternal Barbie (Hispanic)		2005	Retail	David's Bridal
David's Bridal Unforgettable Barbie		2004	Retail	David's Bridal
David's Bridal Unforgettable Barbie (black)		2004	Retail	David's Bridal
David's Bridal Unforgettable Barbie (Hispanic)		2004	Retail	David's Bridal
Day in the Sun (blonde)	26425	2001	$35.00	Hollywood Movie Star Collection
Day in the Sun (brunette)	26426	2001	$70.00	Hollywood Movie Star Collection
Dayton Hudson Cute 'n Cool	2954	1991	$25.00	
Day-to-Night	7929	1985	$40.00	
Day-to-Night (black)	7945	1985	$30.00	
Day-to-Night (Hispanic)	7944	1985	$40.00	
Dazzlin' Date	3203	1992	$30.00	Target
December Turquoise Barbie	B2397	2003	$40.00	Birthstone Collection/Wal-Mart
December Turquoise Barbie	C5330	2004	$40.00	Birthstone Collection
December Turquoise Barbie (black)	C0582	2003	$40.00	Birthstone Collection/Wal-Mart
Definitely Diamonds Barbie	20204	1998	$55.00	Jewelry Collection Series
Definitely Diamonds Barbie	20204	1998	$110.00	Service Merchandise
Delphine Barbie	26929	2000	$95.00	Fashion Model
Deluxe Quick Curl	9217	1976	$100.00	Jergens
Deluxe Tropical Barbie	2996	1985	$30.00	
Deluxe Tropical Barbie	2996	1986	$40.00	Department Store
Denim 'n Lace	2452	1992	$28.00	Ames
Dentist (black)	17478	1997	$20.00	
Dentist (blonde)	17255	1997	$20.00	
Dentist (brunette)	17707	1997	$20.00	
Denver Nuggets	20730	1998	$20.00	NBA
Denver Nuggets (black)	20731	1998	$20.00	NBA
Designer Spotlight by Heather Fonseca		2004	Retail	Designer Spotlight
Designer Spotlight by Katiana Jimenez	B0836	2003	$450.00	Designer Spotlight
Detroit Pistons	20706	1998	$20.00	NBA
Detroit Pistons (black)	20707	1998	$20.00	NBA
Diamond Dazzle	15519	1997	$100.00	Bob Mackie Jewel Essence
Diana Ross by Bob Mackie	B2017	2004	$32.00	Celebrities
Dinner at Eight	946	1964	$595.00	Dressed Boxed Dolls
Dinner Date (blonde)	19016	1998	$15.00	Wholesale Clubs
Dinner Date (redhead)	19037	1998	$20.00	Wholesale Clubs
Disney Fun Barbie	10247	1992	$50.00	Disney
Disney Fun Barbie	12957	1995	$55.00	Disney Europe
Disney Fun Barbie	18970	1998	$27.00	Disney
Disney Fun II	11650	1994	$45.00	Disney
Disney Fun III	13533	1995	$35.00	Disney
Disney Fun IV	17058	1997	$35.00	Disney
Disney Special (black)	9385	1990	$45.00	Child's World
Disney Special (with mouse hat)	4385	1991	$45.00	Child's World
Disney Weekend	10723	1993	$50.00	Disney

Item	Number	Year	Value	Specials
Disney Weekend Barbie	12957	1992	$60.00	Disney Europe
Disney Weekend Barbie & Ken Deluxe	10724	1993	$75.00	Disney Europe
Disney's Animal Kingdom Barbie	20363	1998	$28.00	Disney
Disney's Animal Kingdom Barbie (black)	20989	1998	$28.00	Disney
Doctor Barbie	3850	1988	$55.00	
Doctor Barbie	3850	1990	$45.00	Toys "R" Us
Doctor Barbie	15803	1996	$30.00	Toys "R" Us
Doctor Barbie (black)	14315	1995	$25.00	Toys "R" Us
Doctor Barbie (black)	15804	1996	$30.00	Toys "R" Us
Doctor Barbie (black, with white baby)	11814	1994	$38.00	
Doctor Barbie (brunette)	12903	1994	$100.00	Mattel Festival Doll
Doctor Barbie (white with 3 babies)	14309	1995	$25.00	Toys "R" Us
Doctor Barbie (with black baby)	11160	1994	$30.00	
Dolls of the World Limited Edition Set	12043	1994	$49.00	Dolls of the World
Dolls of the World Limited Edition Set	13939	1995	$45.00	Dolls of the World
Dolls of the World Limited Edition Set	15283	1996	$40.00	Dolls of the World
Donna Karan NY (blonde)	14545	1995	$85.00	Bloomingdale's
Donna Karan NY (brunette)	14452	1995	$85.00	Bloomingdale's
Dorothy (Wizard of Oz)	12701	1995	$72.00	Hollywood Legends
Dorothy with Toto Porcelain #1		2000	Retail	Wizard of Oz
Dramatic New Living (blonde)	1116	1971	$195.00	
Dramatic New Living (brunette)	1116	1971	$250.00	
Dramatic New Living (redhead)	1116	1971	$150.00	
Dream Bride Barbie	1623	1992	$60.00	
Dream Bride Barbie	17153	1997	$35.00	Service Merchandise
Dream Bride Barbie (black)	17933	1997	$25.00	Service Merchandise
Dream Dancing	11902	1994	$16.00	
Dream Dancing (black)	12143	1994	$16.00	
Dream Date	5868	1983	$40.00	
Dream Fantasy	7335	1990	$35.00	Wal-Mart
Dream Glow	2248	1986	$25.00	
Dream Glow (black)	2242	1986	$25.00	
Dream Glow (Hispanic)	1647	1986	$30.00	
Dream Princess	2306	1992	$40.00	Sears
Dream Time	9180	1985	$25.00	Toys "R" Us
Dream Wardrobe Barbie	3331	1992	$35.00	Wholesale Clubs
Dream Wedding	27374	2000	$16.00	
Dreamtime Barbie	5868	1982	$20.00	
Dreamtime Barbie	9180	1988	$35.00	Toys "R" Us
Dress 'n Fun	10776	1994	$15.00	
Dress 'n Fun (black)	12143	1994	$15.00	
Dress 'n Fun (Hispanic)	11102	1994	$15.00	
Duchess Emma Barbie	B3422	2004	$80.00	Portrait Collection
Duchess of Diamonds Barbie		2001	Retail	Jewel Collection
Duke University	17750	1997	$10.00	University Barbie
Duke University (black)	19665	1997	$9.00	University Barbie
Dusk to Dawn Barbie Gift Set	29654	2001	$145.00	Barbie Fashion Model
Dutch	11104	1994	$29.00	Dolls of the World
Earring Magic	7014	1993	$20.00	
Earring Magic (black)	2374	1993	$20.00	
Earring Magic (brunette)	10255	1993	$30.00	
Earring Magic Barbie Doll Software Pak	25-1992	1993	$30.00	Radio Shack
East Carolina University	19155	1998	$10.00	University Barbie
East Carolina University (black)	19426	1998	$10.00	University Barbie
Easter Barbie	16315	1997	$15.00	Supermarket

Item	Number	Year	Value	Specials
Easter Barbie (black)	16317	1997	$15.00	Supermarket
Easter Basket	14613	1996	$18.00	Supermarket
Easter Fun	11276	1994	$25.00	Supermarket
Easter Party	12793	1995	$20.00	Supermarket
Easter Style Barbie	17651	1998	$12.00	Supermarket
Easter Style Barbie (black)	17652	1998	$12.00	Supermarket
Easter Surprise Barbie	20542	1999	$10.00	Supermarket
Easter Surprise Barbie (black)	20543	1999	$10.00	Supermarket
Easy Chic Barbie	17590	1996	$750.00	Harrods England
Egyptian Queen	11397	1994	$48.00	Great Eras Collection
Elektra Barbie	H1699	2005	$15.00	
Elizabethan Queen	12792	1995	$40.00	Great Eras Collection
Embassy Waltz Barbie	22836	1999	$60.00	Barbie Collector's Club
Emerald Elegance	12322	1994	$35.00	Toys "R" Us
Emerald Elegance (black)	12323	1994	$35.00	Toys "R" Us
Emerald Elegance	12322	1994	$33.00	Society Style
Emerald Elegance (black)	12323	1994	$33.00	Society Style
Emerald Embers	15521	1997	$88.00	Bob Mackie Jewel Essence
Emerald Enchantment	17443	1997	$55.00	Toys "R" Us
Empress Bride	4247	1992	$460.00	Bob Mackie
Empress Josephine Barbie	G8051	2005	$250.00	Women of Royalty/Avon
Empress of Emeralds	25680	2000	$100.00	QVC/Royal Jewel
Enchanted Evening	2702	1991	$75.00	JCPenney
Enchanted Evening	3415	1987	$228.00	Porcelain
Enchanted Evening (blonde)	14992	1996	$25.00	Nostalgic Vinyl Series
Enchanted Evening (brunette)	15407	1996	$25.00	Nostalgic Vinyl Series
Enchanted Mermaid Barbie	53978	2002	$200.00	
Enchanted Princess	10292	1993	$50.00	Sears
English	4973	1992	$37.00	Dolls of the World
Escada	15948	1996	$48.00	Designer Collection
Eskimo	3898	1982	$65.00	Dolls of the World
Eskimo (reissue)	9844	1991	$32.00	Dolls of the World
Evening Elegance	7057	1990	$75.00	JCPenney
Evening Enchantment	3596	1989	$38.00	Sears
Evening Enchantment Barbie	19783	1998	$35.00	JCPenney
Evening Enchantment Barbie	19783	1998	$45.00	Evening Elegance
Evening Extravaganza	11622	1994	$40.00	Classique
Evening Extravaganza (black)	11638	1994	$44.00	Classique
Evening Flame	1865	1991	$150.00	Home Shopping Club
Evening Flame	15533	1996	$30.00	Sears
Evening Glamour	14070	1995	$75.00	Glamour Collection
Evening Illusion Barbie	23495	1999	$72.00	Nolan Miller Designer Collection
Evening Majesty	17235	1997	$40.00	JCPenney
Evening Pearl	12825	1996	$140.00	Presidential Porcelain
Evening Sensation	1278	1992	$50.00	JCPenney
Evening Sophisticate Barbie	19361	1998	$30.00	Classique
Evening Sparkle	3274	1990	$35.00	Hill's
Evening Splendor Barbie	G8890	2005	$50.00	Collectors' Request
Evening Splendour	961	1964	$635.00	Dressed Boxed Dolls
Evening Star Princess	27690	2000	$45.00	Celestial Collection
Evening Symphony Barbie	19777	1998	$25.00	Service Merchandise
Evergreen Princess (blonde)	12123	1994	$42.00	Winter Princess Collection
Evergreen Princess (redhead)	13173	1994	$295.00	Mattel Festival Doll
Evergreen Princess (redhead)	12123	1994	$151.00	Disney/Winter Princess (Theme)
Exotic Beauty Barbie	B0149	2003	$26.00	Style Set

Item	Number	Year	Value	Specials
Exotic Beauty Barbie (black)	B0150	2003	$54.00	Style Set
Exotic Intrigue Barbie		2004	Retail	Avon
Exotic Intrigue Barbie (black)		2004	Retail	Avon
Exotic Intrigue Barbie (Hispanic)		2004	Retail	Avon
Fabulous Forties Barbie	22162	2000	$55.00	Great Fashions of the 20th Century
Fabulous Fur	7093	1986	$65.00	Mervyn's
Faerie Queen Barbie (brunette)	B3456	2004	$185.00	Legends of Ireland
Faerie Queen Barbie	B3456	2004	$50.00	Legends of Ireland
Fair Valentine Barbie	18091	1998	$30.00	Hallmark
Fairy of the Forest	25639	2000	$42.00	Enchanted World of Fairies
Fairy of the Garden	28799	2001	$45.00	Enchanted World of Fairies
Fairytopia Enchantress Barbie	G8065	2004	$35.00	
Fancy Frills	3474	1992	$40.00	
Fantastica	3196	1992	$60.00	Wholesale Clubs
Fantasy Ball Barbie	18594	1997	$20.00	K•B Toys
Fantasy Ball Barbie (black)	18595	1997	$20.00	K•B Toys
Fantasy Goddess of Africa	22044	1999	$280.00	Bob Mackie International Beauty
Fantasy Goddess of Asia	20648	1998	$100.00	Bob Mackie International Beauty
Fantasy Goddess of the Americas	25859	2000	$135.00	Bob Mackie International Beauty
Fantasy Goddess of the Arctic	50840	2001	$140.00	Bob Mackie
Far Out Barbie	21911	1999	$40.00	Twist 'n Turn Collection
Fashion Avenue Barbie	20782	1998	$15.00	K•B Toys
Fashion Brights	1882	1992	$20.00	Toys "R" Us
Fashion Brights (black)	4112	1992	$20.00	Toys "R" Us
Fashion Designer	29399	2000	$22.00	
Fashion Designer Barbie		2002	$95.00	Barbie Fashion Model
Fashion Editor Barbie		2001	$110.00	Barbie Fashion Model
Fashion Fun Barbie	H6482	2005	$8.00	
Fashion Jeans	5315	1982	$30.00	
Fashion Jeans (black)	5313	1982	$30.00	
Fashion Luncheon	17382	1997	$49.00	Nostalgic Vinyl Series
Fashion Photo	2210	1978	$60.00	
Fashion Play	2730	1992	$15.00	
Fashion Play	5766	1990	$20.00	Woolworth
Fashion Play	9429	1987	$30.00	
Fashion Play	9629	1991	$15.00	
Fashion Play (black)	3842	1992	$15.00	
Fashion Play (black)	5953	1991	$15.00	
Fashion Play (Hispanic)	3860	1992	$15.00	
Fashion Play (Hispanic)	5954	1991	$15.00	
Fashion Play (pink & white jumpsuit)	7193	1983	$25.00	
Fashion Play (turquoise dress)	2713	1991	$25.00	
Fashion Queen	870	1963	$450.00	
Fashion Show Barbie	G3673	2004	$23.00	
Fashion Show Teresa	G3675	2004	$23.00	
Fashion Wardrobe	27788	2000	Retail	
Fashion Wardrobe (black)	27789	2000	Retail	
February Amethyst Barbie	B3410	2003	$40.00	Birthstone Collection/Wal-Mart
February Amethyst Barbie	C5332	2004	$40.00	Birthstone Collection
February Amethyst Barbie (black)	C0584	2003	$40.00	Birthstone Collection/Wal-Mart
Feelin' Fun (2nd version)	4808	1988	$20.00	
Feelin' Fun (1st version)	1189	1988	$30.00	
Feelin' Fun (black)	4809	1989	$20.00	
Feelin' Fun (Hispanic)	7373	1989	$20.00	
Feelin' Groovy	3421	1987	$175.00	Department Store

Item	Number	Year	Value	Specials
Fern from *Charlotte's Web*	50724	2001	$15.00	When I Read, I Dream
Ferrari Barbie	25636	2000	$47.00	Sports
Ferrari Barbie	25636	2001	$35.00	Sports
Ferrari Barbie	H6466	2005	$105.00	
Ferrari Barbie #2	28534	2001	$50.00	Barbie Loves Sports
Festiva	10339	1993	$50.00	Wholesale Clubs
Festive Season Barbie	18909	1998	$14.00	Supermarket
Festive Season Barbie (black)	18910	1998	$14.00	Supermarket
Fifties Fun	13613	1996	$35.00	Wholesale Clubs
Fire and Ice Barbie	53511	2002	$45.00	Barbie Loves Pop Culture
Fire and Ice Barbie (black)	53863	2002	$45.00	Barbie Loves Pop Culture
Fire Fighter	13553	1995	$50.00	Toys "R" Us
Fire Fighter (black)	13472	1995	$40.00	Toys "R" Us
Flamingo Barbie	22957	1999	$55.00	Birds of Beauty Series
Flight Time Barbie	9584	1990	$35.00	
Flight Time Barbie (black)	9916	1990	$30.00	
Flight Time Barbie (Hispanic)	2066	1990	$57.00	
Flip 'n Dive Barbie	18980	1998	$20.00	
Florida State University	19161	1998	$10.00	University Barbie
Florida Vacation	20535	1998	$10.00	
Florida Vacation Beach Time Fun Barbie	23740	1999	$22.00	Wholesale Clubs
Flower Fun	16063	1997	$6.00	
Flower Fun (black)	16064	1997	$6.00	
Flower Fun (Hispanic)	16065	1997	$6.00	
Flower Power	29002	2000	$9.00	
Flower Power (black)	29003	2000	$9.00	
Flying Butterfly Barbie	29345	2000	$13.00	
Flying Hero	14030	1996	$15.00	
Flying Hero (black)	14278	1996	$20.00	
Foam 'n Color (blue)	15099	1996	$15.00	
Foam 'n Color (pink)	14457	1996	$15.00	
Foam 'n Color (yellow)	15098	1996	$15.00	
Forest Fairy	25639	2000	$40.00	Fairy Series
Forget-Me-Nots (baggie)	3269	1972	$195.00	Kellogg Company
Fountain Mermaid	10393	1993	$20.00	
Fountain Mermaid (black)	10522	1993	$20.00	
Free Moving	7270	1974	$160.00	
French	16499	1997	$25.00	Dolls of the World
French Lady	16707	1997	$28.00	Great Eras Collection
French Quarter Barbie Fashion	B2518	2003	$29.00	Barbie Collector's Club
Friendship Barbie Berlin Wall I	5506	1990	$24.00	Friendship
Friendship Barbie Berlin Wall II	2080	1991	$29.00	Friendship
Friendship Barbie Berlin Wall III	3677	1992	$25.00	Friendship
Frills & Fantasy	1374	1988	$45.00	Wal-Mart
Fruit Fantasy Barbie (blonde)	21386	1999	$25.00	Avon
Fruit Fantasy Barbie (brunette)	20319	1999	$30.00	Avon
Fun to Dress	4558	1988	$15.00	
Fun to Dress	1372	1989	$15.00	
Fun to Dress	4808	1990	$15.00	
Fun to Dress	3240	1993	$15.00	
Fun to Dress (black)	7668	1988	$15.00	
Fun to Dress (black)	1373	1989	$15.00	
Fun to Dress (black)	4939	1990	$15.00	
Fun to Dress (black)	2570	1993	$15.00	
Fun to Dress (Hispanic)	7373	1990	$15.00	

Item	Number	Year	Value	Specials
Fun to Dress (Hispanic)	2763	1993	$15.00	
Fun to Dress (Hispanic)	4809	1992	$15.00	
Funtime (black)	1739	1986	$30.00	Toys "R" Us
Funtime (blue watch)	3717	1987	$30.00	Toys "R" Us
Funtime (pink watch)	3718	1987	$30.00	Toys "R" Us
Funtime (purple watch)	1738	1987	$30.00	Toys "R" Us
Gap Barbie	16449	1996	$60.00	Gap Stores
Gap Barbie (black)	16450	1996	$60.00	Gap Stores
Garden Party	1953	1989	$20.00	Wal-Mart
Garden Party	931	1963	$600.00	Dressed Boxed Dolls
Garden Party Fashion	26933	2000	$90.00	Barbie Fashion Model
Garden Tea Party	1606	1964	$595.00	Dressed Boxed Dolls
Gay Parisienne (blonde)	9973	1991	$350.00	Nostalgic Porcelain
Gay Parisienne (brunette)	9973	1991	$135.00	Nostalgic Porcelain
Gay Parisienne (redhead/porcelain)	9973-9999	1991	$350.00	Disney
Gay Parisienne Barbie (blonde)	57610	2003	$200.00	Collectors' Request
Gay Parisienne Barbie (brunette)		2003	$37.00	Collectors' Request
Gay Parisienne Barbie (redhead)		2003	$185.00	Collectors' Request
Gemini Barbie		2005	$20.00	Zodiac
Gemini Barbie (black)		2005	$20.00	Zodiac
Generation Girl Barbie	19428	1999	$20.00	
Generation Girl Barbie Dance Party	25766	2000	$20.00	
George Washington Barbie	17757	1997	$50.00	FAO Schwarz
Georgetown University	17749	1997	$10.00	University Barbie
Georgetown University (black)	18341	1997	$10.00	University Barbie
Georgia Tech	19159	1998	$10.00	University Barbie
Georgia Tech (black)	19427	1998	$10.00	University Barbie
German	3188	1987	$50.00	Dolls of the World
German (reissue)	12698	1995	$22.00	Dolls of the World
German Talking	4767	1991	$55.00	
Ghanian	15303	1996	$24.00	Dolls of the World
Gibson Girl	3702	1993	$45.00	Great Eras Collection
Gift Giving	1205	1989	$35.00	
Gift Giving	1922	1986	$35.00	
Giggles 'n Swing Barbie & Kelly	20333	2000	$15.00	
Giggles 'n Swing Barbie & Kelly (black)	20534	2000	$15.00	
Giorgio Armani Barbie	B2521	2003	$135.00	Giorgio Armani
Givenchy Barbie	24635	2000	$60.00	
Glam 'n Groom Barbie	27271	1999	$9.00	
Glam 'n Groom Barbie	26251	2000	$15.00	Dressed Boxed Dolls
Glamour Barbie	18594	1997	$15.00	K•B Toys
Glamour Barbie (black)	18595	1997	$15.00	K•B Toys
Glamour Gal Betty Boop		2001	Retail	Barbie Loves Pop Culture
Glinda the Good Witch	14901	1996	$68.00	Hollywood Legends
Glitter Beach	3602	1993	$15.00	
Glitter Hair (black)	11332	1994	$15.00	
Glitter Hair (blonde)	10965	1994	$20.00	
Glitter Hair (brunette)	10966	1994	$20.00	
Glitter Hair (redhead)	10968	1994	$20.00	
Goddess of Beauty and Love	27286	2000	Retail	Inspirational Series
Goddess of Beauty Barbie		2000	$82.00	Goddess Collection
Goddess of Spring	28112	2000	Retail	Inspirational Series
Goddess of Spring Barbie		2000	$79.00	Goddess Collection
Goddess of the Americas	25859	2000	$189.00	
Goddess of the Sun	14056	1995	$95.00	Bob Mackie

Item	Number	Year	Value	Specials
Goddess of Wisdom Barbie		2001	$119.00	Goddess Collection
Gold	5405	1990	$500.00	Bob Mackie
Gold 'n Glamour Barbie	54185	2002	$42.00	Collectors' Request
Gold and Lace	7476	1989	$35.00	Target
Gold Jubilee	12009	1994	$345.00	Jubilee Series
Gold Medal Barbie and Her U.S. Olympic Wardrobe	9044	1975	$90.00	Sears
Gold Medal Skater	7262	1975	$75.00	
Gold Medal Skier	7264	1975	$75.00	
Gold Medal Swimmer	7233	1975	$75.00	
Gold Medal Winter Sports	9042	1975	$85.00	Sears
Gold Sensation	10246	1993	$180.00	Porcelain
Golden Allure Barbie	22961	1999	$32.00	Home Shopping Club
Golden Anniversary Barbie	20038	1998	$90.00	Toys "R" Us
Golden Dream	1874	1981	$50.00	
Golden Dreams	3533	1981	$70.00	Department Store
Golden Dreams (2nd issue, big hair)	3533	1981	$70.00	Department Store
Golden Evening	2587	1990	$45.00	Target
Golden Greetings	7734	1989	$100.00	FAO Schwarz
Golden Hollywood Barbie	22832	1999	$95.00	FAO Schwarz
Golden Hollywood Barbie (black)	23877	1999	$95.00	FAO Schwarz
Golden Qi-Pao Barbie	20866	1998	$65.00	Spiegel
Golden State Warriors (black)	20743	1998	$20.00	NBA
Golden State Warriors	20742	1998	$20.00	NBA
Golden Waltz Barbie (blonde)	22976	1999	$25.00	Wholesale Clubs
Golden Waltz Barbie (redhead)	23220	1999	$30.00	Wholesale Clubs
Golden Winter	10684	1993	$50.00	JCPenney
Goldilocks and The Three Bears	29605	2001	$30.00	Storybook Favorites/Kelly
Golf Date	10202	1993	$30.00	Target
Gone Platinum Barbie (black)	53868	2002	$40.00	Diva Collection
Gone Platinum Barbie	52739	2002	$40.00	Diva Collection
Got Milk	15121	1996	$20.00	Toys "R" Us
Got Milk (black)	15122	1996	$20.00	Toys "R" Us
Governor's Ball Barbie	14010	1996	$90.00	Hudson's Bay Company Canada
Graduation Barbie		2000	$55.00	My Design Friend of Barbie
Graduation Barbie (black)		2000	$55.00	My Design Friend of Barbie
Graduation Barbie Class of '97 (black)	16489	1997	$15.00	Supermarket
Graduation Barbie Class of '98 (black)	17831	1998	$10.00	Supermarket
Graduation Class of '96	15003	1996	$20.00	Supermarket
Graduation Class of '97	16487	1997	$15.00	Supermarket
Graduation Class of '98	17830	1998	$10.00	Supermarket
Grand Entrance Barbie	28533	2001	$45.00	Grand Entrance
Grand Entrance Barbie #2	53841	2002	$30.00	Grand Entrance
Grand Entrance Barbie #2 (black)	53842	2002	$30.00	Grand Entrance
Grand Entrance Barbie (black)	29662	2001	$45.00	Grand Entrance
Grand Hotel	50576	2001	$20.00	Toys "R" Us
Grand Premier	16498	1997	$79.00	Barbie Collector's Club
Grease Barbie	B2510	2003	$100.00	Barbie Loves Pop Culture
Grease Barbie #2	B4773	2004	$30.00	Barbie Loves Pop Culture
Great Shape	7025	1984	$30.00	
Great Shape (black)	7834	1984	$25.00	
Grecian Goddess	15005	1996	$34.00	Great Eras Collection
Greek	2997	1986	$38.00	Dolls of the World
Groovy '60s Barbie	27676	2000	$38.00	Great Fashions of the 20th Century
Growin' Pretty Hair	1144	1971	$375.00	
Guinevere	873	1964	$645.00	Dressed Boxed Dolls

Item	Number	Year	Value	Specials
Gymnast (black)	12153	1994	$14.00	
Gymnast (blonde)	12126	1994	$14.00	
Gymnast (brunette)	11921	1994	$35.00	Mattel Festival Doll
Hair Fair	4043	1967	$210.00	
Hair Fair	4044	1971	$250.00	
Hair Fair Set (re-issue)	4043	1974	$125.00	
Hair Happenin's	1174	1971	$1,075.00	
Hanae Mori Barbie	24494	2000	$75.00	
Happenin' Hair Barbie	22882	1999	$12.00	
Happy Birthday	1922	1981	$45.00	
Happy Birthday	12954	1994	$15.00	
Happy Birthday	14649	1996	$20.00	
Happy Birthday	7914	1991	$36.00	
Happy Birthday	22902	1999	$20.00	
Happy Birthday (2nd issue)	1922	1984	$25.00	
Happy Birthday (3rd issue)	1922	1984	$30.00	
Happy Birthday (black)	7913	1991	$35.00	
Happy Birthday (black)	9561	1990	$35.00	
Happy Birthday (black)	14662	1996	$20.00	
Happy Birthday (black)	22903	1999	$20.00	
Happy Birthday (brunette)	22904	1999	$20.00	
Happy Birthday (Hispanic)	14663	1996	$20.00	
Happy Birthday Barbie	G8490	2004	$16.00	
Happy Go Lightly Barbie	G8889	2005	$70.00	Barbie Fashion Model
Happy Holidays 1988	1703	1988	$390.00	Happy Holidays Collection
Happy Holidays 1989	3523	1989	$125.00	Happy Holidays Collection
Happy Holidays 1990	4098	1990	$65.00	Happy Holidays Collection
Happy Holidays 1990 (black)	4543	1990	$40.00	Happy Holidays Collection
Happy Holidays 1991	1871	1991	$65.00	Happy Holidays Collection
Happy Holidays 1991 (black)	2696	1991	$40.00	Happy Holidays Collection
Happy Holidays 1992	1429	1992	$50.00	Happy Holidays Collection
Happy Holidays 1992 (black)	2396	1992	$38.00	Happy Holidays Collection
Happy Holidays 1993	10824	1993	$48.00	Happy Holidays Collection
Happy Holidays 1993 (black)	10911	1993	$32.00	Happy Holidays Collection
Happy Holidays 1994	12155	1994	$50.00	Happy Holidays Collection
Happy Holidays 1994 (black)	12156	1994	$36.00	Happy Holidays Collection
Happy Holidays 1994 (brunette)	12155	1994	$550.00	Mattel Festival Doll
Happy Holidays 1995	14123	1995	$28.00	Happy Holidays Collection
Happy Holidays 1995 (black)	14124	1995	$24.00	Happy Holidays Collection
Happy Holidays 1996	15646	1996	$28.00	Happy Holidays Collection
Happy Holidays 1996 (black)	15647	1996	$28.00	Happy Holidays Collection
Happy Holidays 1997 (all variations) (brunette)	20416	1997	$20.00	Happy Holidays Collection
Happy Holidays 1997 (black)	17833	1997	$20.00	Happy Holidays Collection
Happy Holidays 1997 (blonde)	17832	1997	$64.00	Happy Holidays Collection
Happy Holidays 1998	20200	1998	$25.00	Happy Holidays Collection
Happy Holidays 1998 (black)	20201	1998	$25.00	Happy Holidays Collection
Happy Holidays Barbie	13545	1995	$40.00	Happy Holidays International
Happy Holidays Barbie	15816	1996	$32.00	Happy Holidays International
Happy Holidays Barbie	12432	1994	$65.00	Happy Holidays European
Happy Holidays with Ornament	14124	1995	$80.00	JCPenney
Happy New Year	14024	1995	$45.00	
Happy New Year	16093	1997	$44.00	
Hard Rock Café Barbie	G7915	2004	$105.00	Barbie Loves Pop Culture
Hard Rock Café Barbie	J0963	2005	$70.00	Barbie Loves Pop Culture
Harley Quinn Barbie	H7616	2005	$24.00	

Item	Number	Year	Value	Specials
Harley-Davidson Barbie	29207	2000	$70.00	
Harley-Davidson Barbie	29208	2001	$100.00	
Harley-Davidson Barbie #1	17692	1997	$450.00	Toys "R" Us
Harley-Davidson Barbie #2	20441	1998	$150.00	Toys "R" Us
Harley-Davidson Barbie #3	22256	1999	$95.00	Toys "R" Us
Harpist Angel Barbie	18894	1998	$45.00	Angels of Music
Harpist Angel Barbie (black)	20551	1998	$45.00	Angels of Music
Hawaii Barbie	24614	1999	$5.00	
Hawaiian	7470	1975	$50.00	Department Store
Hawaiian (one-piece swimsuit)	7470	1982	$50.00	Department Store
Hawaiian (two-piece swimsuit)	7470	1983	$40.00	Department Store
Hawaiian Fun	5940	1991	$20.00	
Hawaiian SuperStar	2289	1978	$175.00	
Heartstring Angel Barbie	21414	1999	$60.00	Angels of Music
Heartstring Angel Barbie (black)	21915	1999	$60.00	Angels of Music
Heidi	52900	2002	$10.00	When I Read, I Dream
Hip 2 Be Square (black)	28314	2000	$6.00	
Hip 2 Be Square (blonde)	29410	2000	$8.00	Value Pack
Hip 2 Be Square (brunette)	29663	2000	$8.00	Value Pack
Hip 2 Be Square (redhead)	28316	2000	$6.00	
Hispanic Barbie	1292	1980	$60.00	
Holiday Angel	28080	2000	$32.00	
Holiday Angel (black)	28081	2000	$30.00	
Holiday Angel Barbie #2	28081	2001	$36.00	Holiday Angel
Holiday Angel Barbie #2 (black)	28080	2001	$34.00	Holiday Angel
Holiday Ball	18326	1997	$65.00	Holiday Porcelain Series
Holiday Barbie		2004	$39.00	
Holiday Barbie (black)		2004	$39.00	
Holiday Barbie by Bob Mackie (blonde)	G8058	2005	$40.00	
Holiday Barbie by Bob Mackie (ethnic)	H0178	2005	$40.00	
Holiday Caroler	15760	1996	$70.00	Holiday Porcelain Series
Holiday Celebration Barbie		2002	$65.00	
Holiday Celebration Barbie (black)		2002	$65.00	
Holiday Dreams	12192	1994	$30.00	Supermarket
Holiday Gift Barbie	20128	1998	$90.00	Holiday Porcelain Series
Holiday Hostess	10280	1993	$40.00	Supermarket
Holiday Jewel	14311	1995	$100.00	Holiday Porcelain Series
Holiday Memories	14106	1995	$30.00	Hallmark
Holiday Season	15581	1996	$16.00	Supermarket
Holiday Season (black)	15583	1996	$16.00	Supermarket
Holiday Sensation	19792	1999	$35.00	Holiday Homecoming Series
Holiday Traditions	17094	1997	$45.00	Hallmark
Holiday Treasures Barbie		1999	$120.00	
Holiday Treasures Barbie	27673	2000	$78.00	Club Exclusive
Holiday Treasures Barbie		2001	$110.00	
Holiday Treats Barbie	17236	1997	$15.00	Supermarket
Holiday Treats Barbie (black)	17618	1997	$15.00	Supermarket
Holiday Treats Fiesta Barbie (Hispanic)	18012	1997	$15.00	Supermarket
Holiday Voyage Barbie	18651	1998	$40.00	Hallmark
Hollywood Cast Party Barbie	50825	2001	$65.00	Hollywood Movie Star Collection/ FAO Schwarz
Hollywood Divine Barbie (blonde)		2004	$65.00	Barbie Fan Club Exclusive
Hollywood Divine Barbie (brunette)	B3426	2004	$70.00	Barbie Fan Club Exclusive
Hollywood Hair	2308	1993	$25.00	
Hollywood Hair Barbie Deluxe Play Set	10928	1993	$25.00	Wholesale Clubs

Item	Number	Year	Value	Specials
Hollywood Nails (black)	24557	1999	$15.00	
Hollywood Nails Barbie	17857	1999	$12.00	
Hollywood Premiere Barbie	26914	2000	$36.00	Hollywood Movie Star Collection
Home for the Holidays Barbie	52834	2001	$34.00	
Home Pretty	2249	1990	$20.00	
Horse Lovin'	1757	1983	$40.00	
Horse Lovin'	14879	1996	$20.00	
Horse Lovin' SE	15648	1997	$10.00	
Horse Ridin'	19268	1998	$10.00	
Horse Ridin' Barbie (black)	19269	1997	$13.00	
Horse Riding Barbie with Riding Club CD-ROM	24788	1999	$28.00	Meijer
Hot Dancin' Set	4841	1990	$40.00	
Hot Looks	5756	1992	$25.00	Ames
Hot Skatin'	13511	1995	$20.00	
Hot Skatin' (black)	13512	1995	$18.00	
Hula Hair	17047	1997	$18.00	
Hula Hair (black)	17048	1997	$18.00	
Hula-Hoop	18167	1997	$16.00	Hill's
I Love Barbie	20668	1999	$5.00	
I'm a Toys "R" Us Kid (50th Anniversary)	18895	1998	$30.00	Toys "R" Us
I'm a Toys "R" Us Kid Barbie (black)	21040	1998	$25.00	Toys "R" Us
Ice Breaker	942	1964	$695.00	Dressed Boxed Dolls
Ice Capades	9847	1991	$30.00	
Ice Capades 50th Anniversary	7365	1990	$50.00	
Ice Capades 50th Anniversary (black)	7348	1990	$25.00	
Ice Cream Barbie	19280	1998	$16.00	Ames
Icelandic	3189	1987	$45.00	Dolls of the World
Illusion Barbie	18667	1997	$80.00	Masquerade Gala
Imperial Elegance	19816	1998	$290.00	Faberge Porcelain
Imperial Splendor	27028	2000	$310.00	Faberge Porcelain
In The Limelight (black)	17031	1997	$140.00	Byron Lars Runway Collection
In the Pink Barbie	27683	2001	$140.00	Barbie Fashion Model
India	3897	1982	$75.00	Dolls of the World
Indian	14451	1996	$25.00	Dolls of the World
Indiana	20044	1998	$15.00	University Barbie
Indigo Obsession Barbie	26935	2000	$165.00	Byron Lars Runway Collection
In-Line Skating	15473	1996	$25.00	
International Haute Couture Rainbow Barbie	None	1994	$199.00	Barbie Festival
International Pen Friend Barbie	13558	1995	$18.00	Toys "R" Us
International Travel Barbie #1	15184	1996	$45.00	Wessco
International Travel Barbie #2	13912	1995	$50.00	Wessco
International Travel I	13912	1995	$40.00	Wessco
International Travel II	16158	1996	$50.00	Wessco
Inuit Legend Barbie		2005	Retail	World Culture Collection
Iowa	20367	1998	$15.00	University Barbie
Iris Barbie, The	53935	2002	$70.00	Flowers in Fashion
Irish	7517	1984	$75.00	Dolls of the World
Irish (reissue)	12998	1995	$34.00	Dolls of the World
Island Fun	4061	1988	$20.00	
Italian	1602	1980	$150.00	Dolls of the World
Italian (reissue)	2256	1993	$36.00	Dolls of the World
JAL Barbie	64347	1997	$150.00	Japan Air Lines
Jamaican	4647	1992	$28.00	Dolls of the World
James Bond 007 Ken and Barbie Gift Set	B0150	2003	$55.00	Barbie Loves Pop Culture
January Garnet Barbie	B3409	2003	$40.00	Birthstone Collection/Wal-Mart

Item	Number	Year	Value	Specials
January Garnet Barbie	C5331	2004	$40.00	Birthstone Collection
January Garnet Barbie (black)	C0583	2003	$40.00	Birthstone Collection/Wal-Mart
Japanese	9481	1985	$70.00	Dolls of the World
Japanese (reissue)	14163	1996	$23.00	Dolls of the World
Jewel Girl	28066	2000	Retail	
Jewel Hair Mermaid	14586	1996	$15.00	
Jewel Hair Mermaid (black)	14587	1996	$15.00	
Jewel Jubilee	2366	1991	$65.00	Wholesale Clubs
Jewel Princess (blonde)	15826	1996	$25.00	Winter Princess Collection
Jewel Princess (brunette)		1999	$95.00	Disney/Winter Princess
Jewel Secrets	1737	1987	$30.00	
Jewel Secrets (black)	1756	1987	$20.00	
Jewel Skating Barbie	23239	1999	$12.00	Wal-Mart
Jewel Skating Barbie (black)	23240	1999	$12.00	Wal-Mart
Jewel Splendor	14061	1995	$90.00	FAO Schwarz
Jewelia Fairytopia Barbie	G6262	2005	$17.00	
Jewelry Fun My First Barbie	16005	1997	$10.00	
Jewelry Fun My First Barbie (Asian)	16008	1997	$10.00	
Jewelry Fun My First Barbie (black)	16006	1997	$10.00	
Jewelry Fun My First Barbie (Hispanic)	16007	1997	$10.00	
Jo from *Little Women*	50723	2001	$15.00	When I Read, I Dream
Joyeux Barbie	B3430	2003	$115.00	Barbie Fashion Model
Joyeux Barbie (redhead)	B3431	2003	$320.00	Barbie Fashion Model
Jude Deveraux The Raider Barbie and Ken Gift Set		2003	$50.00	Romance Novels
Judith Leiber Barbie		2005	Retail	Designer Dolls
Juicy Couture Barbie Doll	G8079	2005	$100.00	Juicy Couture
July Ruby Barbie	B3415	2003	$40.00	Birthstone Collection/Wal-Mart
July Ruby Barbie	C5325	2004	$40.00	Birthstone Collection
July Ruby Barbie (black)	C0577	2003	$40.00	Birthstone Collection/Wal-Mart
June Pearl Barbie	B3414	2003	$40.00	Birthstone Collection/Wal-Mart
June Pearl Barbie	C5324	2004	$40.00	Birthstone Collection
June Pearl Barbie (black)	C0576	2003	$40.00	Birthstone Collection/Wal-Mart
Kansas State	19156	1998	$10.00	University Barbie
Kate Spade Barbie	B2513	2004	$79.00	Kate Spade
Kellogg Quick Curl	3197	1974	$60.00	Kellogg Company
Kenyan	11181	1994	$23.00	Dolls of the World
Kissing (bangs style)	2597	1979	$45.00	Department Store
Kissing (extra dress)	2597	1979	$45.00	Department Store
Kitty Fun (black)	28624	2000	$15.00	
Kitty Fun (blonde)	28612	2000	$16.00	
Kitty Fun (brunette)	28866	2000	$16.00	
Knitting Pretty (pink version)	957	1964	$1,265.00	Dressed Boxed Dolls
Knitting Pretty (royal version)	957	1964	$635.00	Dressed Boxed Dolls
Korean	4929	1988	$35.00	Dolls of the World
Kraft Treasures	11546	1994	$50.00	Kraft
L. A. Clippers	20744	1998	$20.00	NBA
L. A. Clippers (black)	20745	1998	$20.00	NBA
L. A. Lakers	20704	1998	$25.00	NBA
L. A. Lakers (black)	20705	1998	$20.00	NBA
Lady Camille Barbie		2003	Retail	Portrait Collection
Lady Liberty		2000	$225.00	Bob Mackie Custom Limited Edition
Lady Liberty		2000	$225.00	
Ladybug Fun	17695	1997	$18.00	Ames
Lavender Looks	3963	1989	$35.00	Wal-Mart
Lavender Surprise	9049	1990	$32.00	Sears

Item	Number	Year	Value	Specials
Lavender Surprise (black)	5588	1990	$35.00	Sears
Le Nouveau Theater de la Mode (Billy Boy) France	6279	1985	$220.00	
Le Papillon Barbie	23276	1999	$214.00	Bob Mackie Custom Limited Edition
Le Papillon Barbie	23273	1999	$175.00	FAO Schwarz
Lemon-Lime Sorbet Barbie	20318	1999	$25.00	Avon
Leo Barbie		2005	$20.00	Zodiac
Leo Barbie (black)		2005	$20.00	Zodiac
Libra Barbie		2005	$20.00	Zodiac
Libra Barbie (black)		2005	$20.00	Zodiac
Lighter Than Air Barbie	29905	2001	$120.00	Prima Ballerina
Lights 'n Lace	9725	1991	$30.00	
Lilac and Lovely	7669	1988	$45.00	Sears
Lilly Pulitzer Barbie and Stacie Doll Gift Set	H0187	2005	$50.00	
Lily	17556	1997	$125.00	FAO Schwarz
Lingerie (blonde)	26930	2000	$255.00	Fashion Model
Lingerie (brunette)	26931	2000	$265.00	Fashion Model
Lingerie Barbie #3	29651	2001	$100.00	Barbie Fashion Model
Lingerie Barbie #4 (blonde)	55498	2002	$54.00	Barbie Fashion Model
Lingerie Barbie #5 (black)	56120	2002	$50.00	Barbie Fashion Model
Lingerie Barbie #6	56948	2003	$42.00	Barbie Fashion Model
Lisette Barbie	7438	2001	$104.00	Barbie Fashion Model
Little Debbie Barbie Series I	10123	1993	$60.00	Little Debbie Snacks
Little Debbie Barbie Series II (bent arms)	14616	1996	$30.00	Little Debbie Snacks
Little Debbie Barbie Series II (straight arms)	14616	1996	$25.00	Little Debbie Snacks
Little Debbie Barbie Series III	16352	1998	$22.00	Little Debbie Snacks
Little Red Riding Hood and The Wolf	52899	2002	$22.00	Storybook Favorites/Kelly
Live Action (baggie)	1155	1973	$165.00	
Live Action (blonde)	1155	1971	$160.00	
Live Action (ranch)	10412	1971	$100.00	Montgomery Ward
Live Action on Stage	1152	1971	$233.00	
Living	1116	1970	$250.00	
Locket Surprise	10963	1994	$20.00	
Locket Surprise (black)	11224	1994	$20.00	
Lone Star Great Barbie		2005	Retail	Barbie Fan Club Exclusive
Los Angeles Dodgers Barbie	23882	1999	$27.00	Major League Baseball
Los Angeles Dodgers Barbie (black)	24472	1999	$32.00	Major League Baseball
Lounge Kitties Leopard	B3417	2004	$70.00	Lounge Kitties
Lounge Kitties Panther	C3553	2004	$36.00	Lounge Kitties
Lounge Kitties Tiger	C2478	2004	$36.00	Lounge Kitties
Loving You	7072	1983	$55.00	
Loving You	7583	1983	$50.00	
LSU	21219	1999	$16.00	University Barbie
LSU (black)	21220	1999	$16.00	University Barbie
Lunch at the Club Fashion	26932	2000	$77.00	Barbie Fashion Model
Madame Du Barbie	17934	1997	$225.00	Bob Mackie
Mademoiselle Isabelle Barbie	55387	2002	$79.00	Portrait Collection
Madison Avenue	1539	1992	$100.00	FAO Schwarz
Magic Curl	3856	1982	$55.00	
Magic Curl (black)	3989	1982	$40.00	
Magic Hair Styler CD-ROM	24748	1999	$28.00	Meijer
Magic Moves	2126	1986	$60.00	
Magic Moves (black)	2127	1986	$40.00	
Magical Mermaids Barbie & Krissy	26837	2000	$25.00	
Magical Mermaids Barbie & Krissy (black)	26838	2000	$25.00	
Magna Doodle Barbie	23275	1999	$15.00	Ames

Item	Number	Year	Value	Specials
Make-A-Valentine Barbie	20339	1999	$10.00	Supermarket
Make-A-Valentine Barbie (black)	20340	1999	$10.00	Supermarket
Making Friends	19592	1998	$18.00	Military
Making Friends (black)	19593	1998	$18.00	Military
Malaysian	7329	1991	$25.00	Dolls of the World
Malibu	1067	1975	$45.00	
Malibu (baggie)	1067	1972	$150.00	
Malibu (Sunset)	1067	1971	$65.00	
Malibu Barbie	56061	2002	$24.00	Barbie Loves Pop Culture
Malibu Barbie – The Beach Party with Case	1703	1980	$60.00	
Malibu Barbie & Her Ten-Speeder Set	10456	1974	$95.00	Montgomery Ward
Malibu Barbie Beach Party, The	1703	1980	$55.00	Department Store
Malibu Fashion Combo	2753	1978	$65.00	Catalog Showroom
Malt Shop	4581	1993	$35.00	Toys "R" Us
Mann's Chinese Theatre	24636	2000	$48.00	FAO Schwarz
Mann's Chinese Theatre (black)	24998	2000	$60.00	FAO Schwarz
March Aquamarine Barbie	B3411	2003	$40.00	Birthstone Collection/Wal-Mart
March Aquamarine Barbie	C5333	2004	$40.00	Birthstone Collection
March Aquamarine Barbie (black)	C0585	2003	$40.00	Birthstone Collection/Wal-Mart
March of Dimes Walk America Barbie	18506	1998	$20.00	K-Mart
March of Dimes Walk America Barbie (black)	18507	1998	$20.00	K-Mart
Mardi Gras	4930	1988	$45.00	American Beauty Collection
Maria (Sound of Music)	13676	1995	$36.00	Hollywood Legends
Marie Antoinette Barbie	53991	2003	$250.00	Women of Royalty
Marie Therese Barbie	55496	2002	$64.00	Barbie Fashion Model
Marilyn Monroe (pink dress)	17451	1997	$55.00	Hollywood Legends
Marilyn Monroe (red dress)	17452	1997	$60.00	Hollywood Legends
Marilyn Monroe (white dress)	17155	1997	$50.00	Hollywood Legends
Marine Biologist		1999	$15.00	Career
Marine Biologist (black)		1991	$15.00	Career
Marine Corps	7549	1992	$25.00	Stars 'n Stripes
Marine Corps (black)	7594	1992	$25.00	Stars 'n Stripes
Marshall	21245	1999	$16.00	University Barbie
Martina McBride Barbie	G8887	2005	$23.00	
Masquerade	944	1964	$635.00	Dressed Boxed Dolls
Masquerade Ball	18667	1997	$235.00	Bob Mackie
Masquerade Ball (scented)	10803	1993	$275.00	Bob Mackie
Massachusetts	21192	1999	$16.00	University Barbie
Mattel Golden Anniversary	14479	1995	$170.00	Porcelain
May Emerald Barbie	B3413	2003	$40.00	Birthstone Collection/Wal-Mart
May Emerald Barbie	C5323	2004	$40.00	Birthstone Collection
May Emerald Barbie (black)	C0575	2003	$40.00	Birthstone Collection/Wal-Mart
Mbili Barbie		2002	$135.00	Byron Lars
Medieval Lady	12791	1995	$36.00	Great Eras Collection
Mermaid	1434	1992	$20.00	
Mexican	1917	1989	$25.00	Dolls of the World
Mexican (reissue)	14449	1996	$23.00	Dolls of the World
MGM 75th Anniversary Barbie	22832	1999	$70.00	
Miami Heat	20694	1998	$20.00	NBA
Miami Heat (black)	20695	1998	$20.00	NBA
Mickey Mouse Barbie	H6468	2005	$15.00	
Midnight Gala	12999	1995	$34.00	Classique
Midnight Moon Princess	27687	2000	$50.00	Celestial Collection
Midnight Princess Barbie (blonde)	17780	1997	$25.00	Winter Princess Collection
Midnight Princess Barbie (brunette)	18486	1997	$86.00	W.D.W. Teddy Bear & Doll Con.

Item	Number	Year	Value	Specials
Midnight Tuxedo Barbie	28796	2001	$77.00	Club Exclusive
Midnight Tuxedo Barbie (black)	29307	2001	$400.00	Club Exclusive
Midnight Waltz (blonde)	15685	1996	$35.00	Ballroom Beauties
Midnight Waltz (brunette)	16705	1996	$52.00	Ballroom Beauties
Millennium Bride	24505	2000	$285.00	Millennium Collection
Millennium Grad w/black gown (black)	25750	2000	$5.00	Supermarket
Millennium Grad w/blue gown (black)	25740	2000	$5.00	Supermarket
Millennium Princess Barbie	24154	1999	$45.00	Millennium Collection
Millennium Princess Barbie (black)	23995	1999	$45.00	Millennium Collection
Millennium Wedding (black)	27674	2000	$36.00	The Bridal Collection
Millennium Wedding (Hispanic)	27765	2000	$45.00	The Bridal Collection
Millennium Wedding (white)	27674	2000	$36.00	The Bridal Collection
Milwaukee Bucks	20738	1998	$20.00	NBA
Milwaukee Bucks (black)	20739	1998	$20.00	NBA
Minnesota	21193	1999	$16.00	University Barbie
Minnesota Timberwolves	20702	1998	$20.00	NBA
Minnesota Timberwolves (black)	20703	1998	$20.00	NBA
Mint Memories Barbie	20983	1999	$150.00	Victorian Tea Porcelain Collection
Miss America	3194	1972	$175.00	Kellogg Company
Miss America	9194	1973	$165.00	Kellogg Company
Miss America	9194	1974	$150.00	Kellogg Company
Miss Barbie	61747	1996	$35.00	Woolworth
Miss Barbie (sleep eye with 3 wigs)	1060	1964	$1,295.00	
Mississippi State	21190	1999	$16.00	University Barbie
Mississippi State (black)	21191	1999	$16.00	University Barbie
Mod Redux Barbie	C6262	2004	$70.00	Online Exclusive
Moja Barbie	50826	2001	$210.00	Byron Lars
Montana	21194	1999	$16.00	University Barbie
Montgomery Ward Anniversary Doll	3210	1972	$750.00	Montgomery Ward
Mood For Music	940	1963	$625.00	Dressed Boxed Dolls
Moon Goddess	14105	1996	$99.00	Bob Mackie
Moonlight Magic	10608	1993	$85.00	Toys "R" Us
Moonlight Magic (black)	10609	1993	$80.00	Toys "R" Us
Moonlight Rose	3549	1991	$32.00	Hill's
Moonlight Waltz	17763	1997	$48.00	Ballroom Beauties
Morning Sun Princess	27688	2000	$45.00	Celestial Collection
Moroccan Barbie	21507	1999	$18.00	Dolls of the World
Movie Star	25466	1999	$20.00	
Movin' Groovin'	17714	1997	$15.00	
Mrs. P.F.E. Albee	20330	1998	$70.00	Avon
Mrs. P.F.E. Albee	17690	1997	$75.00	Avon
Muffy Roberts Barbie	H6465	2005	$69.00	Barbie Fashion Model
Music Lovin'	9988	1986	$50.00	
My Fair Lady #1 (pink organza gown)	15501	1996	$75.00	Hollywood Legends
My Fair Lady #2 (ascot)	15497	1996	$100.00	Hollywood Legends
My Fair Lady #3 (flower girl)	15498	1996	$65.00	Hollywood Legends
My Fair Lady #4 (ball evening gown)	15500	1996	$100.00	Hollywood Legends
My First Ballerina	3839	1992	$20.00	
My First Ballerina	2516	1993	$20.00	
My First Ballerina	11294	1994	$15.00	
My First Ballerina (Asian)	11342	1994	$15.00	
My First Ballerina (black)	3861	1992	$20.00	
My First Ballerina (black)	2767	1993	$20.00	
My First Ballerina (black)	11340	1994	$15.00	
My First Ballerina (Hispanic)	2770	1993	$20.00	

Item	Number	Year	Value	Specials
My First Barbie	1875	1981	$25.00	
My First Barbie	1875	1983	$35.00	
My First Barbie	1788	1987	$20.00	
My First Barbie	1280	1988	$20.00	
My First Barbie	9942	1990	$20.00	
My First Barbie	96085	1990	$75.00	Deco-Pak
My First Barbie	1875	1974	$35.00	
My First Barbie	3839	1992	$20.00	
My First Barbie	2516	1993	$18.00	
My First Barbie	11294	1994	$15.00	
My First Barbie (Asian)	11342	1994	$20.00	
My First Barbie (black)	11340	1994	$15.00	
My First Barbie (black)	9858	1984	$30.00	
My First Barbie (black)	1801	1987	$20.00	
My First Barbie (black)	1281	1988	$20.00	
My First Barbie (black)	96085	1990	$55.00	Deco-Pak
My First Barbie (black)	9943	1990	$20.00	
My First Barbie (black)	2767	1993	$20.00	
My First Barbie (Hispanic)	5979	1987	$28.00	Zayre's
My First Barbie (Hispanic)	1282	1988	$20.00	
My First Barbie (Hispanic)	9944	1990	$25.00	
My First Barbie (Hispanic)	3860	1992	$20.00	
My First Barbie (Hispanic)	11341	1994	$15.00	
My First Princess	13064	1995	$15.00	
My First Princess (Asian)	13067	1995	$15.00	
My First Princess (black)	13065	1995	$15.00	
My First Princess (Hispanic)	13066	1995	$15.00	
My First Tea Party	14592	1997	$12.00	
My First Tea Party (Asian)	14876	1997	$12.00	
My First Tea Party (black)	14593	1997	$12.00	
My First Tea Party (Hispanic)	14875	1997	$12.00	
My Size	2517	1993	$115.00	
My Size (black)	11212	1993	$120.00	
My Size Angel Barbie	20493	1998	$105.00	
My Size Angel Barbie (black)	20494	1998	$105.00	
My Size Bride	12052	1994	$100.00	
My Size Bride (black)	12053	1994	$100.00	
My Size Bride Barbie (brunette)	14108	1995	$130.00	Toys "R" Us
My Size Bride Barbie (redhead)	15649	1996	$130.00	Toys "R" Us
My Size Butterfly	25863	2000	$135.00	
My Size Butterfly (black)	25864	2000	$135.00	
My Size Dancing	15909	1996	$105.00	
My Size Dancing (black)	15910	1996	$105.00	
My Size Princess	13767	1995	$100.00	
My Size Princess (black)	13768	1995	$100.00	
My Size Rapunzel	17801	1997	$100.00	
My Size Rapunzel (black)	17802	1997	$100.00	
My Size Redhead	15649	1996	$140.00	QVC
My Wardrobe Barbie	22962	1999	$28.00	Service Merchandise
N. Y. Knicks	20714	1998	$20.00	NBA
N. Y. Knicks (black)	20715	1998	$20.00	NBA
Naf Naf (Europe)	10997	1993	$40.00	
NASCAR #3	25636	2000	$35.00	
NASCAR 50th Anniversary Barbie	20442	1998	$25.00	NASCAR
NASCAR Official #94 Barbie (brunette)	22954	1999	$25.00	NASCAR

Item	Number	Year	Value	Specials
Native American #1	1753	1993	$32.00	Dolls of the World
Native American #2	11609	1994	$32.00	Dolls of the World
Native American #3	12699	1995	$25.00	Dolls of the World
Native American #4	15304	1996	$35.00	Dolls of the World
Native American #5 (box says fourth)	18558	1998	$20.00	Dolls of the World/Toys "R" Us
Navy	9693	1991	$27.00	Stars 'n Stripes
Navy (black)	9694	1991	$27.00	Stars 'n Stripes
Neptune Fantasy	4248	1992	$455.00	Bob Mackie
New Jersey Nets	20726	1998	$20.00	NBA
New Jersey Nets (black)	20727	1998	$20.00	NBA
New Living (auburn)	1116	1970	$200.00	
New Living (blonde)	1116	1969	$200.00	
New York Yankees Barbie	23881	1999	$28.00	Major League Baseball
New York Yankees Barbie (black)	24471	1999	$36.00	Major League Baseball
Newport #1	7807	1973	$175.00	
Newport #2	7807	1973	$175.00	
Nichelle Urban Hipster		2004	Retail	Model of the Moment
Nifty '50s Barbie	27675	2000	$65.00	Great Fashions of the 20th Century
Nigerian	7376	1990	$30.00	Dolls of the World
Night Dazzle	12191	1994	$55.00	JCPenney
Night Dazzle (brunette)	12191	1994	$185.00	Mattel Festival Doll
Night on the Town Barbie and River	B6708	2004	$29.00	My Scene
Night Sensation	2921	1991	$60.00	FAO Schwarz
Nighty Negligee	965	1963	$550.00	Dressed Boxed Dolls
Nne Barbie	B3423	2004	$90.00	Byron Lars
Noir et Blanc Barbie	B1992	2003	$65.00	Club Exclusive
Noir et Blanc Barbie (black)	B1993	2003	$100.00	Club Exclusive
North Carolina A & T	21167	1999	$16.00	University Barbie
North Carolina A & T (black)	21168	1999	$16.00	University Barbie
North Carolina State	17194	1997	$10.00	University Barbie
North Carolina State (black)	20127	1997	$9.00	University Barbie
Northwest Coast Native American	24671	2000	$25.00	Dolls of the World
Northwestern	19167	1998	$10.00	University Barbie
Northwestern (black)	19425	1998	$10.00	University Barbie
Norwegian #1	14450	1996	$37.00	Dolls of the World
Norwegian #2	14450	1996	$25.00	Dolls of the World
Nostalgic Barbie #1	62328	1996	$45.00	Nostalgic
Nostalgic Barbie #2	62329	1996	$45.00	Nostalgic
Nostalgic Barbie #3	62327	1996	$45.00	Nostalgic
Nostalgic Toys	25525	2000	$45.00	Cool Collecting Series
November Topaz Barbie	B2396	2003	$40.00	Birthstone Collection/Wal-Mart
November Topaz Barbie	C5329	2004	$40.00	Birthstone Collection
November Topaz Barbie (black)	C0581	2003	$40.00	Birthstone Collection/Wal-Mart
Nsync Barbie w/CD	50534	2000	$19.00	
Nutcracker	5472	1992	$79.00	Musical Ballet Series
Ocean Friends	15428	1996	$20.00	
Ocean Friends (black)	15429	1996	$20.00	
October Opal Barbie	B2395	2003	$40.00	Birthstone Collection/Wal-Mart
October Opal Barbie	C5328	2004	$40.00	Birthstone Collection
October Opal Barbie (black)	C0580	2003	$40.00	Birthstone Collection/Wal-Mart
Oklahoma	20125	1998	$11.00	University Barbie
Oklahoma State University	17752	1997	$10.00	University Barbie
Olympic Gymnast (black)	15124	1996	$20.00	
Olympic Gymnast (blonde)	15123	1996	$20.00	
Olympic Gymnast (redhead)	15125	1996	$35.00	Toys "R" Us

Item	Number	Year	Value	Specials
Olympic Skater	18501	1997	$15.00	
Olympic Skater (black)	18503	1997	$10.00	
Olympic Skating Star	4549	1987	$50.00	
Open Road Vintage Reproduction		2004	$80.00	Online Exclusive
Opening Night	10148	1993	$38.00	Classique
Orange Blossom	987	1963	$635.00	Dressed Boxed Dolls
Orange Pekoe	25507	2000	$500.00	Victorian Tea Porcelain Collection
Orchid Barbie, The	50319	2001	$76.00	Flowers in Fashion
Oreo Barbie	18511	1997	$20.00	Toys "R" Us
Oriental	3262	1981	$150.00	Dolls of the World
Original Arizona Jean Company III	19873	1998	$25.00	JCPenney
Orlando Magic (black)	20749	1998	$20.00	NBA
Oscar de la Renta Barbie	20376	1999	$40.00	
Oscar de la Renta Barbie	20376	1998	$60.00	Bloomingdale's
Paint & Dazzle (black)	10058	1993	$15.00	
Paint & Dazzle (blonde)	10039	1993	$15.00	
Paint & Dazzle (brunette)	10059	1993	$15.00	
Paint & Dazzle (redhead)	10057	1993	$15.00	
Pajama Fun Barbie	26883	1999	$13.00	Target
Paleontologist	17240	1997	$20.00	Toys "R" Us
Paleontologist (black)	17241	1997	$20.00	Toys "R" Us
Parisian	1600	1980	$90.00	Dolls of the World
Parisian #1	9843	1991	$35.00	Dolls of the World
Parisian #2 (Japan)	9843	1991	$38.00	Dolls of the World
Party in Pink	2909	1991	$30.00	Ames
Party Lace	4843	1989	$35.00	Hill's
Party Perfect	1876	1992	$34.00	Shopko/Venture
Party Pink	4629	1987	$25.00	Wal-Mart
Party Pink	7637	1989	$25.00	Winn Dixie
Party Premiere	2001	1992	$20.00	Supermarket
Party Pretty	5955	1990	$30.00	Target
Party Sensation	9025	1990	$55.00	Wholesale Clubs
Party Time	4798	1983	$20.00	
Party Time	12243	1994	$20.00	Toys "R" Us
Party Time (black)	14274	1994	$20.00	Toys "R" Us
Party Time (Hispanic)	12244	1994	$25.00	
Party Treats	4885	1989	$25.00	Toys "R" Us
Patriot	17312	1997	$25.00	American Stories Collection
Paul Frank Barbie		2004	Retail	Designer Dolls
Paul Frank Barbie (blonde)	B8954	2004	$60.00	Designer Dolls
Peace & Love '70s	27677	2000	$70.00	Great Fashions of the 20th Century
Peach Blossom	7009	1992	$40.00	Wholesale Clubs
Peach Pretty	4870	1989	$32.00	K-Mart
Peaches 'n Cream	7926	1985	$40.00	
Peaches 'n Cream (black)	9516	1985	$35.00	
Peacock	19365	1998	$59.00	Birds of Beauty Series
Pearl Beach	18576	1997	$10.00	
Pearl Beach Barbie Easter Basket	25381	1999	$15.00	Supermarket
Pen Friend	13558	1996	$20.00	Toys "R" Us
Penn State University	17698	1997	$10.00	University Barbie
Penn State University (black)	18344	1997	$10.00	University Barbie
Peppermint Obsession Barbie	J1743	2005	$35.00	Flavor Obsession
Peppermint Princess	13598	1995	$36.00	Winter Princess Collection
Pepsi Spirit	4869	1989	$75.00	Toys "R" Us
Perfume Pretty	4551	1988	$30.00	

Item	Number	Year	Value	Specials
Perfume Pretty (black)	4552	1988	$30.00	
Peruvian I	2995	1986	$36.00	Dolls of the World
Peruvian II	21506	1999	$18.00	Dolls of the World
Pet Doctor	14603	1996	$18.00	
Pet Doctor (black)	15302	1996	$18.00	
Pet Doctor (brunette)	16458	1996	$30.00	Target
Pet Doctor Barbie	G8815	2004	$20.00	
Pet Lovin'	23007	1999	$15.00	
Pet Lovin' (black)	23008	1999	$15.00	
Peter Rabbit 100 Year Celebration Barbie	53872	2002	$37.00	Keepsake Treasures
Phantom of the Opera	20377	1998	$150.00	FAO Schwarz
Philadelphia 76ers	20724	1998	$20.00	NBA
Philadelphia 76ers (black)	20725	1999	$20.00	NBA
Phoenix Suns Barbie	20710	1998	$20.00	NBA
Phoenix Suns Barbie (black)	20711	1998	$20.00	NBA
Picnic Pretty	3808	1992	$35.00	Osco Drugs
Picture Pockets Barbie	28701	2000	$10.00	Toys "R" Us
Pilgrim	12577	1995	$25.00	American Stories Collection
Pilot		2000	$15.00	
Pilot Barbie	18368	1998	$25.00	Toys "R" Us
Pilot Barbie	24017	1999	$12.00	
Pilot Barbie (black)	19384	1998	$25.00	Toys "R" Us
Pink & Pretty	3554	1982	$40.00	
Pink & Pretty Barbie Extra Special Modeling Set	5239	1982	$75.00	Department Store
Pink Ice	15141	1996	$100.00	Toys "R" Us
Pink Inspiration Barbie (black)	21722	1999	$30.00	Toys "R" Us
Pink Inspiration Barbie (blonde)	21914	1999	$30.00	Toys "R" Us
Pink Inspiration Barbie (brunette)	21721	1999	$30.00	Toys "R" Us
Pink Jubilee	3756	1989	$800.00	Jubilee Series
Pink Jubilee (25th anniversary Wal-Mart)	4589	1987	$50.00	Wal-Mart
Pink Reflections Barbie	19130	1998	$25.00	Sears
Pink Sensation	5410	1990	$25.00	Winn Dixie
Pink Splendor	16091	1996	$310.00	Ultra Limited Edition
Pioneer	12680	1995	$25.00	American Stories Collection
Pioneer #2	14756	1996	$25.00	American Stories Collection
Pisces Barbie		2005	$20.00	Zodiac
Pisces Barbie (black)		2005	$20.00	Zodiac
Pittsburgh	21169	1999	$16.00	University Barbie
Plantation Belle (blonde)	5351	1992	$315.00	Disney
Plantation Belle (redhead)	7526	1992	$140.00	Porcelain
Platinum	2703	1991	$289.00	Bob Mackie
Playtime	5336	1983	$20.00	
Plum Royal	23478	1999	$170.00	Byron Lars Runway Collection
Plus 3	9953	1977	$85.00	Ben Franklin
POG Barbie	13239	1995	$18.00	Toys "R" Us Canada
POG Fun	13239	1995	$20.00	Toys "R" Us
Police Officer	10688	1993	$75.00	Toys "R" Us
Police Officer (black)	10689	1993	$75.00	Toys "R" Us
Polish	18560	1997	$25.00	Dolls of the World
Polly Pockets	12412	1994	$20.00	Hill's
Polynesian	12700	1995	$25.00	Dolls of the World
Ponytails	18141	1997	$20.00	Military
Ponytails (black)	18142	1997	$20.00	Military
Poodle Parade	15280	1996	$42.00	Nostalgic
Portland Trailblazers	20720	1998	$20.00	NBA

Barbie® Dolls – Listed Alphabetically

Item	Number	Year	Value	Specials
Portland Trailblazers (black)	20721	1998	$20.00	NBA
Portrait in Blue Barbie	19355	1998	$15.00	Wal-Mart
Portrait in Blue Barbie (black)	19356	1998	$15.00	Wal-Mart
Portrait in Taffeta	15528	1996	$55.00	Couture Collection
Posable	8414	1965	$1,225.00	Montgomery Ward
Pretty Changes	2598	1980	$70.00	
Pretty Changes (lamp)	2598	1980	$80.00	
Pretty Changes Barbie (with free Barbie Play Perfume)	2598	1979	$90.00	Store Promotionals
Pretty Choices Barbie (black)	18018	1997	$20.00	Wal-Mart
Pretty Choices Barbie (blonde)	17971	1997	$20.00	Wal-Mart
Pretty Choices Barbie (brunette)	18019	1997	$20.00	Wal-Mart
Pretty Dreams 18"	13611	1995	$25.00	
Pretty Dreams 18" soft body (black)	13630	1995	$20.00	
Pretty Flowers Barbie (black)	24653	1999	$6.00	
Pretty Flowers Barbie (blonde)	24652	1999	$6.00	
Pretty Flowers Barbie (brunette)	24654	1999	$6.00	
Pretty Flowers Barbie (redhead)	24655	1999	$6.00	
Pretty Hearts	2901	1992	$25.00	Supermarket
Pretty Hearts	14473	1996	$10.00	
Pretty Hearts (black)	14474	1996	$10.00	
Pretty Hearts (Hispanic)	14475	1996	$10.00	
Pretty in Plaid	5413	1992	$30.00	Target
Pretty in Plaid (black)	21570	1998	$5.00	
Pretty in Plaid (blonde)	20666	1998	$5.00	
Pretty in Plaid (brunette)	20668	1998	$5.00	
Pretty in Plaid (redhead)	20667	1998	$5.00	
Pretty in Purple	3117	1992	$25.00	K-Mart
Pretty in Purple (black)	3121	1992	$25.00	K-Mart
Pretty Surprise	9823	1992	$20.00	
Princess	18404	1998	$10.00	
Princess	22891	1999	$15.00	
Princess	28264	2000	$11.00	
Princess	22894	1999	$15.00	
Princess (Asian)	18407	1998	$10.00	
Princess (Asian)	28267	2000	$11.00	
Princess (black)	18405	1998	$10.00	
Princess (black)	28265	2000	$11.00	
Princess (black)	22892	1999	$15.00	
Princess (brunette)	22893	1999	$15.00	
Princess (Hispanic)	18406	1998	$10.00	
Princess (Hispanic)	28266	2000	$11.00	
Princess and the Pea	28800	2000	$26.00	Princess Series
Princess Barbie (Asian)	23477	2000	$11.00	
Princess Barbie (black)	23475	2000	$11.00	
Princess Barbie (blonde)	23474	2000	$11.00	
Princess Barbie (brunette)	23476	2000	$11.00	
Princess Bride	28521	2000	$20.00	
Princess Bride (black)	28552	2000	$20.00	
Princess of Ancient Greece Barbie	B3461	2004	$20.00	Dolls of the World — Princess Collection
Princess of Ancient Mexico Barbie	C2203	2004	$20.00	Dolls of the World — Princess Collection
Princess of Cambodia Barbie	B3460	2004	$20.00	Dolls of the World — Princess Collection
Princess of China Barbie	53368	2002	$65.00	Dolls of the World — Princess Collection
Princess of England Barbie	B3459	2004	$20.00	Dolls of the World — Princess Collection
Princess of Holland Barbie	G8055	2005	$20.00	Dolls of the World — Princess Collection
Princess of Imperial Russia Barbie	G5861	2005	$20.00	Dolls of the World — Princess Collection

Item	Number	Year	Value	Specials
Princess of India Barbie	28374	2001	$165.00	Dolls of the World — Princess Collection
Princess of Ireland Barbie	53367	2002	$25.00	Dolls of the World — Princess Collection
Princess of Japan Barbie	B5731	2003	$23.00	Dolls of the World — Princess Collection
Princess of South Africa Barbie	56218	2003	$26.00	Dolls of the World — Princess Collection
Princess of the Danish Court Barbie	56216	2003	$22.00	Dolls of the World — Princess Collection
Princess of the French Court Barbie	28372	2001	$150.00	Dolls of the World — Princess Collection
Princess of the Hawaiian Islands Barbie	G8056	2005	$22.00	Dolls of the World — Princess Collection
Princess of the Incas Barbie	28373	2000	$115.00	Dolls of the World — Princess Collection
Princess of the Korean Court Barbie	B5870	2005	$20.00	Dolls of the World — Princess Collection
Princess of the Navajo Barbie	B8956	2004	$20.00	Dolls of the World — Princess Collection
Princess of the Nile Barbie	53369	2002	$40.00	Dolls of the World — Princess Collection
Princess of the Portuguese Empire Barbie	56217	2003	$22.00	Dolls of the World — Princess Collection
Princess of the Renaissance Barbie	G5860	2005	$20.00	Dolls of the World — Princess Collection
Princess of the Vikings Barbie	B6361	2003	$26.00	Dolls of the World — Princess Collection
Princess Sissy Barbie		1998	$35.00	Royal Houses of Europe
Promenade in the Park Barbie	18630	1998	$40.00	Great Fashions of the 20th Century
Provencale Barbie	50829	2002	$96.00	Barbie Fashion Model
Publicity Tour Party Barbie	27865	2001	$40.00	Hollywood Movie Star Collection
Puerto Rican	16754	1997	$18.00	Dolls of the World
Purdue	19868	1998	$11.00	University Barbie
Purple Passion	13555	1995	$35.00	Toys "R" Us
Purple Passion (black)	13554	1995	$30.00	Toys "R" Us
Puzzle Craze Barbie	20164	1998	$12.00	Wal-Mart
Puzzle Craze Barbie (black)	20165	1998	$12.00	Wal-Mart
Queen Elizabeth I Barbie	B3425	2004	$250.00	Women of Royalty
Queen of Hearts	12046	1994	$155.00	Bob Mackie
Queen of Sapphires	26926	2000	$85.00	Royal Jewel
Queen of the Prom Barbie		2001	$490.00	Collectors' Convention 2001
Quick Curl (blonde)	4220	1972	$80.00	
Quick Curl (with extra outfit)	4220	1973	$100.00	Store Promotional
Radiant 'n Rose	15140	1996	$55.00	Toys "R" Us
Radiant 'n Rose (black)	15061	1996	$55.00	Toys "R" Us
Radiant in Red	1276	1992	$45.00	Toys "R" Us
Radiant in Red (Hispanic)	4113	1992	$45.00	Toys "R" Us
Radiant Redhead Barbie	55501	2002	$150.00	Bob Mackie
Rain or Shine Barbie	29179	2000	$15.00	
Rainbow Princess	23474	1999	$12.00	
Rainbow Princess (black)	23475	1999	$11.00	
Rainbow Princess (brunette)	23476	1999	$12.00	
Rainbow Princess Barbie	26357	2000	$12.00	
Ralph Lauren Barbie	15950	1997	$60.00	Bloomingdale's
Rappin' Rockin'	3248	1992	$40.00	
Rapunzel	1869	1997	$50.00	
Rapunzel	16378	1997	$25.00	Fairy Tales
Rapunzel Barbie	53973	2002	$22.00	Princess
Ravishing in Rouge Barbie	52741	2001	$110.00	Barbie Fashion Model
Rayla The Cloud Queen Doll	G8401	2005	$20.00	
Red Hot Barbie (black)	56708	2003	$32.00	Diva Collection
Red Hot Barbie (white)	56707	2003	$35.00	Diva Collection
Red Romance	3161	1992	$25.00	Supermarket
Red Velvet Delight Haute Couture Barbie	None	1994	$220.00	Barbie Festival
Reflections of Light (Renoir)	23884	1999	$75.00	Artist Series
Regal Reflections	4116	1992	$200.00	Spiegel
Registered Nurse	991	1963	$760.00	Dressed Boxed Dolls
Rendezvous Barbie	20647	1998	$74.00	Masquerade Gala

Item	Number	Year	Value	Specials
Ribbons and Roses	13911	1995	$35.00	Sears
Rising Star Barbie	17864	1998	$38.00	Grand Ole Opry
Riviera Barbie	22974	1999	$10.00	
Rocker	1140	1986	$50.00	
Rocker (2nd issue)	3055	1987	$50.00	
Rockettes	2017	1993	$120.00	FAO Schwarz
Rocky Mountain Mod		2002	$210.00	Collectors' Convention 2002
Roller Skating	1880	1980	$60.00	
Rollerblade	2214	1992	$30.00	
Romantic Bride	1861	1993	$35.00	
Romantic Bride (black)	11054	1993	$35.00	
Romantic Interlude	17136	1997	$34.00	Classique
Romantic Interlude (black)	17137	1997	$36.00	Classique
Romantic Rose Bride (porcelain)	14541	1996	$140.00	Wedding Flower Collection
Romantic Wedding (white)	29438	2001	$36.00	The Bridal Collection
Romantic Wedding (black)	29439	2001	$36.00	The Bridal Collection
Rose Barbie	22337	1999	$30.00	A Garden of Flowers
Rose Barbie, The	29911	2001	$55.00	Flowers in Fashion
Rose Bride	15987	1996	$35.00	Wholesale Clubs
Rose Princess (black)	29189	2000	$13.00	
Rose Princess Barbie	56615	2004	$10.00	
Rose Series	28990	2000	$13.00	
Royal	1601	1980	$115.00	Dolls of the World
Royal Enchantment	14010	1995	$50.00	JCPenney
Royal Invitation	10969	1993	$85.00	Spiegel
Royal Romance	1858	1992	$80.00	Wholesale Clubs
Royal Splendor	10950	1993	$170.00	Presidential Porcelain
Ruby Radiance	15520	1997	$80.00	Bob Mackie Jewel Essence
Ruby Romance	13612	1995	$48.00	Service Merchandise
Ruffle Fun	12433	1995	$12.00	
Ruffle Fun (black)	12434	1995	$12.00	
Ruffle Fun (Hispanic)	12435	1995	$12.00	
Russell Stover Candies Special Edition Barbie (black)	17089	1997	$25.00	Russell Stover
Russell Stover Candies Special Edition Barbie (floral)	16351	1997	$25.00	Russell Stover
Russell Stover Candies Special Edition Barbie (pink)	17091	1997	$25.00	Russell Stover
Russell Stover Easter (checkered)	14617	1996	$25.00	Russell Stover
Russell Stover Easter (print)	14956	1996	$25.00	Russell Stover
Russell Stover Holiday	18199	1997	$25.00	Russell Stover
Russian	1916	1989	$30.00	Dolls of the World
Russian (reissue)	16500	1997	$17.00	Dolls of the World
Sacramento Kings	20746	1998	$20.00	NBA
Sacramento Kings (black)	20747	1998	$20.00	NBA
Safari	18970	1998	$30.00	Disney
Sagittarius Barbie		2005	$20.00	Zodiac
Sagittarius Barbie (black)		2005	$20.00	Zodiac
San Antonio Spurs	20722	1998	$20.00	NBA
San Antonio Spurs (black)	20723	1998	$20.00	NBA
San Diego State	21227	1999	$16.00	University Barbie
San Diego State (black)	21228	1999	$16.00	University Barbie
Santa's Helper Barbie	B6271	2004	$20.00	
Sapphire Dreams	13255	1995	$50.00	Toys "R" Us
Sapphire Sophisticate	16692	1997	$30.00	Toys "R" Us
Sapphire Sophisticate (black)	16693	1997	$20.00	Toys "R" Us
Sapphire Splendor	15523	1997	$80.00	Bob Mackie Jewel Essence

Item	Number	Year	Value	Specials
Sara Lee Barbie	60403	1993	$65.00	Sara Lee
Satin Nights	1886	1992	$70.00	Service Merchandise
Savvy Shopper	12152	1994	$50.00	Bloomingdale's
Scarlett (BBQ dress)	12997	1995	$47.00	Hollywood Legends
Scarlett (green velvet dress)	12045	1994	$48.00	Hollywood Legends
Scarlett (New Orleans dress)	13254	1995	$47.00	Hollywood Legends
Scarlett (red dress)	12815	1994	$60.00	Hollywood Legends
Scarlett O'Hara Doll, Barbecue at Twelve Oaks	29910	2001	$49.00	Gone with the Wind
Scarlett O'Hara Doll on Peachtree Street — The Drapery Dress	29771	2001	$52.00	Gone with the Wind
School Fun	2721	1991	$22.00	Toys "R" Us
School Fun (black)	4111	1992	$22.00	Toys "R" Us
School Spirit Barbie	10682	1993	$25.00	Toys "R" Us
School Spirit Barbie	15301	1996	$16.00	Supermarket
School Spirit Barbie	63569	1997	$40.00	Hudson's Bay Company Canada
School Spirit Barbie (black)	10683	1993	$25.00	Toys "R" Us
Schooltime Fun (black)	18488	1998	$10.00	Supermarket
Schooltime Fun Barbie	13741	1995	$15.00	Supermarket
Schooltime Fun Barbie	18487	1998	$10.00	Supermarket
Scorpio Barbie		2005	$20.00	Zodiac
Scorpio Barbie (black)		2005	$20.00	Zodiac
Scottish	3263	1981	$90.00	Dolls of the World
Scottish (reissue)	9845	1991	$45.00	Dolls of the World
Scuderia Ferrari Barbie		2000	$32.00	Barbie Loves Sports
Sea Holiday Barbie	5471	1993	$25.00	Toys "R" Us
Sea Pearl Mermaid	13940	1995	$20.00	Hill's
Sea Princess	15531	1996	$30.00	Service Merchandise
Sears 100th Anniversary Celebration	2998	1985	$100.00	Sears
Season's Greetings	12384	1994	$50.00	Wholesale Clubs
Seattle Supersonics	20718	1998	$20.00	NBA
Seattle Supersonics (black)	20719	1998	$20.00	NBA
Secret Hearts	7902	1993	$30.00	
Secret Hearts (black)	3836	1993	$20.00	
Secret Messages Barbie	26422	1999	$15.00	
Senior Prom	951	1964	$1,145.00	Dressed Boxed Dolls
Sensations	4931	1988	$50.00	
Sentimental Valentine	16536	1997	$30.00	Hallmark
September Sapphire Barbie	B2394	2003	$40.00	Birthstone Collection/Wal-Mart
September Sapphire Barbie	C5327	2004	$40.00	Birthstone Collection
September Sapphire Barbie (black)	C0579	2003	$40.00	Birthstone Collection/Wal-Mart
Serenade in Satin	17572	1997	$90.00	Couture Collection
Shampoo Magic (pink)	14457	1996	$15.00	
Shampoo Magic (yellow)	15098	1996	$15.00	
Share a Smile Barbie	17247	1997	$25.00	Toys "R" Us
Sheer Illusion Barbie #1	20662	1998	$92.00	Nolan Miller Designer Collection
Sheer Illusion Barbie #2	20662	1998	$70.00	Nolan Miller Designer Collection
Shopping Chic	14009	1995	$75.00	Spiegel
Shopping Chic (black)	15801	1996	$50.00	Spiegel
Shopping Fun Barbie	10051	1993	$25.00	Meijer
Shopping Spree Barbie #1	12749	1994	$38.00	FAO Schwarz
Shopping Spree Barbie #2	12749	1994	$35.00	FAO Schwarz
Shopping Time Barbie	18230	1997	$15.00	Wal-Mart
Shopping Time Barbie (black)	18231	1997	$15.00	Wal-Mart
Show 'n Ride	7799	1988	$40.00	Toys "R" Us
Show Parade Barbie with Star Stampin' Horse	15059	1997	$50.00	

Item	Number	Year	Value	Specials
Sidewalk Chalk Barbie	19784	1998	$20.00	Shopko/Venture
Sidewalk Chalk Barbie	19784	1998	$15.00	Hill's
Sign Language		2000	$18.00	Toys "R" Us
Silken Flame Barbie (blonde)	18449	1998	$24.00	Nostalgic
Silken Flame Barbie (blonde)	11099	1993	$330.00	Porcelain Disney
Silken Flame Barbie (brunette)	18448	1998	$24.00	Nostalgic
Silken Flame Barbie (brunette)	1249	1994	$130.00	Porcelain
Silver Royale	15952	1996	$75.00	Wholesale Clubs
Silver Screen	11652	1994	$100.00	FAO Schwarz
Silver Starlight	11305	1994	$190.00	Porcelain
Silver Sweetheart	12410	1994	$40.00	Sears
Sing & Dance	13179	1995	$20.00	
Sing & Dance (black)	13938	1995	$20.00	
Singapore Girl 1	None	1992	$100.00	Singapore Airlines
Singapore Girl 2	None	1994	$50.00	Singapore Airlines
Sisters Celebration Krissy and Barbie	28270	2000	$18.00	
Sit in Style Barbie	23421	1999	$10.00	
Sixties Fun Barbie (blonde)	17252	1997	$25.00	Wholesale Clubs
Sixties Fun Barbie (redhead)	17693	1997	$25.00	Wholesale Clubs
Skating Dream Barbie	17244	1997	$20.00	Wal-Mart
Skating Star	4547	1988	$65.00	Sears
Skating Star	15510	1996	$15.00	Wal-Mart
Skating Star	17244	1997	$10.00	Wal-Mart
Skating Star (black)	16691	1996	$15.00	Wal-Mart
Skating Star (Hispanic)	15511	1996	$15.00	Wal-Mart
Ski Fun	7511	1991	$30.00	
Sleep Over Party		2000	$40.00	QVC
Sleeping Beauty Barbie	20489	1999	$18.00	
Sleeping Beauty Barbie (black)	20490	1999	$18.00	
Slumber Party	12696	1995	$15.00	
Slumber Party (black)	12697	1995	$15.00	
Snap 'n Play	3550	1992	$20.00	
Snap 'n Play (black)	3556	1992	$20.00	
Snow Princess (blonde)	11875	1994	$60.00	Enchanted Seasons
Snow Princess (brunette)	12905	1994	$595.00	Mattel Festival Doll
Snow Sensation Barbie	23800	1999	$39.00	Avon
Snow Sensation Barbie (black)	23801	1999	$39.00	Avon
Soccer Barbie	20151	1999	$20.00	
Society Girl Barbie	56203	2002	$30.00	Style Set
Society Girl Barbie (black)	56204	2002	$32.00	Style Set
Society Hound Barbie	29057	2001	$85.00	Society Hound Collection
Soda Fountain Sweetheart	15762	1996	$88.00	Coca-Cola Fashion Classic Series
Solo in the Spotlight	7613	1990	$145.00	Nostalgic Porcelain
Solo in the Spotlight	982	1963	$845.00	Dressed Boxed Dolls
Solo in the Spotlight (blonde)	13534	1995	$25.00	Nostalgic Vinyl Series
Solo in the Spotlight (brunette)	13820	1995	$25.00	Nostalgic Vinyl Series
Something Extra	863	1992	$25.00	Meijer
Songbird	14320	1996	$25.00	
Songbird (black)	14486	1996	$25.00	
Sophisticated Lady	5313	1990	$140.00	Nostalgic Porcelain
Sophisticated Lady	24930	2000	$45.00	Collectors' Request
Sophisticated Wedding Barbie	53370	2002	$34.00	
Sophisticated Wedding Barbie (black)	53371	2002	$34.00	
South Carolina	21195	1999	$16.00	University Barbie
South Carolina (black)	21196	1999	$16.00	University Barbie

Item	Number	Year	Value	Specials
Southern Beauty	3284	1991	$25.00	Winn Dixie
Southern Belle	2586	1991	$40.00	Sears
Spa Getaway Barbie Gift Set	B1319	2004	$75.00	Barbie Fashion Model
Space Camp Barbie	22425	1999	$25.00	Toys "R" Us
Space Camp Barbie (black)	22426	1999	$25.00	Toys "R" Us
Spanish Barbie #1	4031	1983	$65.00	Dolls of the World
Spanish Barbie #2	4963	1992	$33.00	Dolls of the World
Spanish Barbie #3	24670	2000	$18.00	Dolls of the World
Spanish Teacher	29408	2000	$25.00	Toys "R" Us
Spanish Teacher (Hispanic)	29409	2000	$25.00	Toys "R" Us
Sparkle Beach	13132	1996	$10.00	
Sparkle Beauty	17251	1997	$30.00	Wholesale Club (BJ)
Sparkle Eyes	2482	1992	$30.00	
Sparkle Eyes Barbie (black)	5950	1992	$30.00	
Sparkle Eyes Barbie Dressing Room and Fashion Set	7131	1992	$55.00	Wholesale Clubs
Sparkling Splendor	10994	1993	$50.00	Service Merchandise
Special Expressions	4842	1989	$25.00	Woolworth
Special Expressions	5504	1990	$20.00	Woolworth
Special Expressions	2582	1991	$20.00	Woolworth
Special Expressions	3197	1992	$25.00	Woolworth
Special Expressions	10048	1993	$20.00	Woolworth
Special Expressions (black)	7346	1989	$25.00	Woolworth
Special Expressions (black)	5505	1990	$20.00	Woolworth
Special Expressions (black)	2583	1991	$20.00	Woolworth
Special Expressions (black)	3198	1992	$30.00	Woolworth
Special Expressions (black)	10049	1993	$18.00	Woolworth
Special Expressions (Hispanic)	3200	1992	$25.00	Woolworth
Special Expressions (Hispanic)	10050	1993	$18.00	Woolworth
Special Occasion Barbie		2003	Retail	
Special Occasion Barbie — Treasure Hunt Doll	B7565	2003	Retail	
Special Occasion Barbie I	15831	1996	$65.00	Mercantile Stores
Special Occasion Barbie II	18216	1997	$45.00	Mercantile Stores
Special Occasion Barbie II (black)	18217	1997	$45.00	Mercantile Stores
Specialty Deco-Pak Barbie	1511	1991	$75.00	Deco-Pak
Specialty Deco-Pak Barbie (black)	1534	1991	$55.00	Deco-Pak
Spellbound Lover Barbie		2005	Retail	Legends of Ireland
Spirit of the Earth Barbie	50707	2001	$60.00	Native Spirit Collection
Spirit of the Sky Barbie	B2367	2003	$60.00	Native Spirit Collection
Spirit of Water Barbie	53861	2002	$60.00	Native Spirit Collection
Splash 'n Color	16169	1996	$6.00	
Splash 'n Color (black)	16174	1997	$6.00	
Splash 'n Color (Hispanic)	16172	1997	$6.00	
Sport Star	1334	1979	$25.00	
Spots 'n Dots	10491	1993	$45.00	Toys "R" Us
Spring Blossom	15201	1996	$25.00	Avon
Spring Blossom (black)	15202	1996	$25.00	Avon
Spring Bouquet	3477	1993	$22.00	Supermarket
Spring Bouquet	12989	1995	$45.00	Enchanted Seasons
Spring in Tokyo Barbie	19430	1999	$34.00	City Seasons Collection
Spring in Tokyo Barbie (nostalgic face)	23499	1999	$40.00	City Seasons Collection
Spring Parade	7008	1992	$35.00	Toys "R" Us
Spring Parade (black)	2257	1992	$35.00	Toys "R" Us
Spring Petals (black)	16871	1997	$30.00	Avon
Spring Petals (blonde)	16746	1997	$30.00	Avon
Spring Petals (brunette)	16872	1997	$30.00	Avon

Item	Number	Year	Value	Specials
Spring Tea Party Barbie (black)	18657	1998	$30.00	Avon
Spring Tea Party Barbie (blonde)	18656	1998	$30.00	Avon
Spring Tea Party Barbie (brunette)	18656	1998	$30.00	Avon
Standard (brunette, straight leg)	1190	1967	$400.00	
Standard (redhead, straight leg)	1190	1967	$900.00	
Stanford	19870	1998	$11.00	University Barbie
Stanford (black)	20124	1998	$11.00	University Barbie
Star Dream	4550	1987	$50.00	Sears
Star Lily Bride (porcelain)	12953	1994	$150.00	Wedding Flower Collection
Star Splash	29260	2000	$13.00	
Star Splash (black)	29308	2000	$13.00	
Starlight Blue	3553	1989	$40.00	Lady Lovely Locks
Starlight Carousel Barbie	19708	1998	$18.00	K•B Toys
Starlight Dance	15461	1996	$32.00	Classique
Starlight Dance (black)	15819	1996	$32.00	Classique
Starlight Splendor	2704	1991	$500.00	Bob Mackie
Starlight Waltz	14070	1995	$35.00	Ballroom Beauties
Starlight Waltz (brunette, Disney)	14954	1995	$75.00	Ballroom Beauties
Starring Barbie in *King Kong*	56737	2003	$29.00	Pop Culture
Statue of Liberty	14664	1996	$100.00	FAO Schwarz
Steppin' Out	14110	1995	$22.00	Target
Steppin' Out Barbie – 1930s	21531	1999	$35.00	Great Fashions of the 20th Century
Sterling Silver Rose Barbie		2002	Retail	Bob Mackie
Sterling Wishes	3347	1991	$75.00	Spiegel
Sticker Craze (black)	19913	1998	$10.00	
Sticker Craze (blonde)	19224	1998	$10.00	
Sticker Craze (brunette)	19914	1998	$10.00	
Stolen Magic Barbie	G8072	2005	$115.00	Barbie Fashion Model
Strawberry Party Barbie	22895	1999	$15.00	Ames
Strawberry Sorbet Barbie	20317	1999	$25.00	Avon
Style	5315	1990	$35.00	Applause
Style	20766	1999	$10.00	K•B Toys
Style (black)	20767	1999	$10.00	K•B Toys
Style Magic	1283	1989	$30.00	
Style Magic (black)	1288	1989	$30.00	
Suburban Shopper Barbie	28378	2001	$70.00	Collectors' Request
Suite Retreat Barbie	G8078	2005	$40.00	Barbie Fashion Model
Suits Me Fine Fashion		2000	Retail	
Summer Daydreams Barbie	19739	1998	$55.00	Coca-Cola Fashion Classic Series
Summer in Rome Barbie	19431	1999	$35.00	City Seasons Collection
Summer in San Francisco Barbie (blonde) (FAO)	19363	1998	$95.00	City Seasons Collection
Summer in San Francisco Barbie (redhead) (FAO)	19363	1998	$675.00	City Seasons Collection
Summer Sophisticate	15591	1996	$43.00	Spiegel
Summer Splendor	15683	1997	$39.00	Enchanted Seasons
Summit	7027	1990	$15.00	
Summit (Asian)	7029	1990	$22.00	
Summit (black)	7028	1990	$15.00	
Summit (Hispanic)	7030	1990	$24.00	
Sun Gold Malibu	1067	1984	$25.00	
Sun Gold Malibu (black)	7745	1985	$20.00	
Sun Gold Malibu (Hispanic)	4970	1985	$25.00	
Sun Jewel	10953	1994	$10.00	
Sun Lovin' Malibu	1067	1979	$40.00	
Sun Sensation	1390	1992	$20.00	
Sun Sensation Barbie Spray & Play Fun	7149	1992	$60.00	Wholesale Clubs

Item	Number	Year	Value	Specials
Sun Valley	7806	1973	$95.00	
Sunday Best Barbie	B2520	2003	$48.00	Barbie Fashion Model
Sunflower Barbie	13488	1995	$20.00	Toys "R" Us
Sunflower Barbie (Van Gogh)	19366	1998	$68.00	Artist Series
Sunsational Malibu	1067	1981	$30.00	
Sunsational Malibu (Hispanic)	4970	1981	$40.00	
Super Dance	5838	1982	$40.00	
Super Gymnast	15821	1996	$20.00	K•B Toys
Super Gymnast Barbie (black)	23106	1999	$15.00	K•B Toys
Super Gymnast Barbie	23105	1999	$20.00	
Super Hair	3101	1987	$25.00	
Super Hair (black)	3296	1987	$20.00	
Super Size Barbie	9828	1977	$250.00	
Super Size Barbie (super hair)	2844	1979	$250.00	
Super Size Bridal Barbie	9975	1977	$295.00	Department Store
Super Size Bride	9975	1977	$295.00	Department Store
Super Talk! Barbie	14308	1995	$30.00	Toys "R" Us
Super Talk! Barbie (black)	14316	1995	$30.00	Toys "R" Us
SuperStar Barbie	1604	1988	$40.00	
SuperStar Barbie	10592	1993	$30.00	Wal-Mart
SuperStar Barbie (black)	1605	1988	$25.00	
SuperStar Barbie (black)	10711	1993	$40.00	Wal-Mart
SuperStar Barbie (with SuperStar Haircomb) #1	9720	1978	$60.00	Store Promotional
SuperStar Barbie (with SuperStar Haircomb) #2	9720	1978	$60.00	Store Promotional
SuperStar Barbie (with SuperStar Necklace)	9720	1977	$60.00	Store Promotional
SuperStar Barbie Fashion Change-abouts	2583	1978	$90.00	Tru Value
SuperStar Barbie in the Spotlight	2207	1977	$75.00	
SuperStar Barbie in the Spotlight	2586	1978	$110.00	Department Store
Supertalk	12290	1994	$40.00	
Supertalk (black)	12379	1994	$40.00	
Surf City	28417	2000	$5.00	
Surf City Barbie Doll and Play Set	28961	2000	$5.00	
Swan	27682	2000	$48.00	Birds of Beauty Series
Swan Lake	1648	1991	$88.00	Musical Ballet Series
Swedish Barbie	4032	1983	$54.00	Dolls of the World
Swedish Barbie	24672	2000	$18.00	Dolls of the World
Sweet 16	7796	1974	$73.00	Store Promotional
Sweet Daisy Barbie	15133	1996	$30.00	Military
Sweet Dreams	13611	1995	$20.00	
Sweet Dreams (black)	13630	1995	$20.00	
Sweet Lavender	2522	1992	$30.00	Woolworth
Sweet Lavender (black)	2225	1992	$30.00	Woolworth
Sweet Lavender (Hispanic)	3200	1992	$30.00	Woolworth
Sweet Magnolia	15622	1996	$18.00	Wal-Mart
Sweet Magnolia (black)	12265	1996	$18.00	Wal-Mart
Sweet Magnolia (Hispanic)	15654	1996	$18.00	Wal-Mart
Sweet Moments	17642	1997	$25.00	Wholesale Clubs
Sweet Romance	2917	1991	$30.00	
Sweet Roses	7635	1989	$30.00	Toys "R" Us
Sweet Spring	3208	1992	$22.00	Supermarket
Sweet Treats Barbie	20780	1998	$15.00	
Sweet Treats Barbie (black)	20955	1998	$15.00	
Sweet Valentine	14644	1995	$22.00	
Sweet Valentine	14880	1996	$35.00	Hallmark
Sweetheart (black)	18609	1998	$5.00	

Item	Number	Year	Value	Specials
Sweetheart (blonde)	18608	1998	$5.00	
Sweetheart (brunette)	18610	1998	$5.00	
Sweetheart (redhead)	18700	1998	$5.00	
Sweetheart Barbie	3161	1993	$35.00	Supermarket
Swim 'n Dive	11505	1993	$20.00	
Swim 'n Dive (black)	11734	1993	$20.00	
Swimming Champion Barbie	24590	1999	$15.00	
Swingin' Easy	955	1964	$637.00	Dressed Boxed Dolls
Swirl (ash blonde)	850	1964	$650.00	
Swirl (blonde)	850	1964	$650.00	
Swirl (brunette)	850	1964	$650.00	
Swirl (platinum)	850	1964	$1,300.00	
Swirl (redhead)	850	1964	$650.00	
Swiss	7541	1984	$48.00	Dolls of the World
Sydney 2000 Olympic Barbie Pin Collector	25644	2000	$25.00	Pop Culture
Sydney 2000 Olympic Barbie Pin Collector (black)	26302	2000	$25.00	Pop Culture
Symphony in Chiffon Barbie	20186	1998	$60.00	Barbie Couture Collection
Symphony in Chiffon Barbie (black)	21295	1998	$60.00	Barbie Couture Collection
Syracuse	19163	1998	$10.00	University Barbie
Syracuse (black)	19419	1998	$10.00	University Barbie
Tale of the Forest Princess, The, w/book	29458	2000	$25.00	
Tale of the Forest Princess, The, w/book (black)	29459	2000	$25.00	
Tales of Arabian Nights Barbie and Ken Gift Set	50827	2001	$76.00	Magic & Mystery
Talk With Me	17350	1997	$35.00	
Talk With Me (black)	17370	1997	$30.00	
Talking (blonde)	1115	1968	$400.00	
Talking (blonde)	1115	1970	$295.00	
Talking (brunette)	1115	1968	$400.00	
Talking (brunette)	1115	1970	$295.00	
Talking (redhead)	1115	1968	$400.00	
Talking (redhead)	1115	1970	$295.00	
Talking (Spanish, plastic box)	8348	1968	$285.00	
Tangerine Twist	17860	1997	$35.00	Fashion Savvy Collection
Tango (porcelain)	23451	1999	$300.00	Bob Mackie
Tano Barbie	G8050	2005	$80.00	Byron Lars
Target 35th Anniversary Barbie	16485	1997	$27.00	Target
Target 35th Anniversary Barbie (black)	17608	1997	$27.00	Target
Tatu Barbie	B2018	2003	$170.00	Byron Lars
Taurus Barbie		2005	$20.00	Zodiac
Taurus Barbie (black)		2005	$20.00	Zodiac
Teacher (black) (no panties)	13195	1995	$55.00	
Teacher (black) (painted panties)	13915	1995	$25.00	
Teacher (brunette)	13194	1996	$25.00	Supermarket
Teacher (Hispanic)	16210	1996	$25.00	
Teacher (no panties)	18914	1995	$60.00	
Teacher (painted panties)	13914	1996	$25.00	
Teddy Fun	15684	1996	$18.00	Hill's
Teen Talk	5745	1991	$50.00	
Teen Talk (ash blonde)	5745	1991	$50.00	
Teen Talk (black)	1612	1992	$30.00	
Teen Talk (brunette)	5745	1991	$50.00	
Teen Talk (redhead)	5745	1992	$50.00	
Teen Talk (strawberry blonde)	5745	1991	$50.00	
Teen Talk "Math Class is Tough"	5745	1992	$65.00	
Ten Speeder	7777	1973	$30.00	

Item	Number	Year	Value	Specials
Tennis Anyone?	941	1963	$610.00	Dressed Boxed Dolls
Teresa	G8470	2004	$6.00	
Texas Tech	21229	1999	$16.00	University Barbie
Texas Tech (black)	21230	1999	$16.00	University Barbie
Thai	18561	1998	$18.00	Dolls of the World
Theatre Date	959	1964	$660.00	Dressed Boxed Dolls
Theatre Elegance	12077	1994	$145.00	Spiegel
Todd Oldham Barbie	22205	1999	$54.00	Designer Collection
Tooth Fairy Barbie	11645	1995	$20.00	Wal-Mart
Tooth Fairy Barbie	17246	1998	$12.00	Wal-Mart
Tooth Fairy Barbie (blue)	11645	1994	$22.00	Wal-Mart
Toronto Raptors	20740	1998	$20.00	NBA
Toronto Raptors (black)	20741	1998	$20.00	NBA
Totally Hair	1112	1991	$35.00	
Totally Hair (black)	5948	1991	$25.00	
Totally Hair (brunette)	1117	1991	$35.00	
Totally Spring Barbie	C4480	2005	$16.00	
Totally Spring Barbie (black)	G5318	2005	$16.00	
Tour Guide Barbie — *Toy Story 2*	24015	1999	$30.00	Disney
Toyland Barbie	64176	1997	$40.00	Hudson's Bay Company Canada
Toys "R" Us 50th Anniversary Doll	20038	1998	$85.00	Toys "R" Us
Trace of Lace Barbie (brunette)	G7212	2005	$70.00	Barbie Fashion Model
Trace of Lace Barbie (blonde)	G7211	2005	$70.00	Barbie Fashion Model
Trade In Barbie (Twist 'n Turn, redhead)	1162	1967	$375.00	
Trail Blazin'	2783	1991	$25.00	Supermarket
Travel in Style	1544	1967	$240.00	Sears
Tree Trimming	22967	1999	$12.00	
Tree Trimming (black)	22968	1999	$12.00	
Trend Setter Barbie	B3442	2004	$50.00	Barbie Fashion Model
Trend Forecaster Barbie	22833	1999	$32.00	Clothes Minded Collection
Troll	10257	1993	$25.00	
Tropical	1017	1986	$20.00	
Tropical (black)	1022	1986	$20.00	
Tropical (Hispanic)	1646	1986	$25.00	
Tropical Splash	12446	1995	$10.00	
Twilight Gala Barbie	53862	2002	$72.00	Club Exclusive
Twilight Gala Barbie (black)	53870	2002	$86.00	Club Exclusive
Twinkle Lights	10390	1993	$50.00	
Twinkle Lights (black)	10521	1993	$40.00	
Twirlin' Make-Up (blonde)	18421	1998	$10.00	
Twirlin' Make-Up Barbie and Magic Hair Styler CD-Rom			Retail	
Twirling Ballerina	15086	1996	$15.00	
Twirling Ballerina (black)	15087	1996	$15.00	
Twirly Curls	5579	1983	$35.00	Department Store
Twirly Curls (black)	5723	1983	$35.00	
Twirly Curls (Hispanic)	5724	1983	$35.00	
Twist 'n Turn Barbie (brunette)	1160	1971	$500.00	
Twist 'n Turn Barbie (brunette, flip hair)	1160	1969	$500.00	
Twist 'n Turn Barbie (brunette, flip hair)	1160	1970	$500.00	
Twist 'n Turn Barbie (chocolate bon-bon, dark brown)	1160	1966	$500.00	
Twist 'n Turn Barbie (go-go co-co, brunette)	1160	1966	$550.00	
Twist 'n Turn Barbie (redhead)	1160	1966	$1,000.00	
Twist 'n Turn Barbie (summer sand, gray)	1160	1966	$550.00	
Twist 'n Turn Barbie (sun kissed, blonde)	1160	1966	$550.00	

Item	Number	Year	Value	Specials
Twist 'n Turn Barbie Smasheroo (brunette)	18941	1998	$50.00	Collectors' Request
Twist 'n Turn Barbie Smasheroo (redhead)	23258	1998	$50.00	Collectors' Request
Tye-Dye Barbie	20504	1999	$13.00	
Tye-Dye Barbie	20504	1998	$10.00	
Unicef	1920	1989	$20.00	Unicef
Unicef (Asian)	4774	1989	$24.00	Unicef
Unicef (black)	4770	1989	$18.00	
Unicef (Hispanic)	4782	1989	$24.00	
University of Arizona	17751	1997	$10.00	University Barbie
University of Arkansas (black)	17191	1998	$10.00	University Barbie
University of Arkansas	17191	1997	$10.00	University Barbie
University of Colorado	19169	1998	$10.00	University Barbie
University of Connecticut	19866	1998	$11.00	University Barbie
University of Florida	17700	1997	$10.00	University Barbie
University of Florida (black)	18343	1997	$10.00	University Barbie
University of Georgia	17192	1997	$10.00	University Barbie
University of Georgia (black)	18345	1997	$10.00	University Barbie
University of Illinois	17755	1997	$10.00	University Barbie
University of Kentucky	19153	1998	$11.00	University Barbie
University of Maryland	19867	1998	$11.00	University Barbie
University of Maryland (black)	20123	1998	$11.00	University Barbie
University of Miami	17794	1997	$10.00	University Barbie
University of Miami (black)	18348	1997	$10.00	University Barbie
University of Michigan	17398	1997	$10.00	University Barbie
University of Michigan (black)	18342	1997	$10.00	University Barbie
University of Mississippi	21232	1999	$16.00	University Barbie
University of Mississippi (black)	21233	1999	$16.00	University Barbie
University of Nebraska	17193	1997	$10.00	University Barbie
University of Tennessee	17554	1997	$10.00	University Barbie
University of Tennessee (black)	18347	1997	$10.00	University Barbie
University of Texas	17792	1997	$10.00	University Barbie
University of Texas (black)	20126	1998	$11.00	University Barbie
University of Virginia	17754	1997	$10.00	University Barbie
University of Virginia (black)	21216	1999	$16.00	University Barbie
University of Wisconsin	17195	1997	$10.00	University Barbie
UNLV	21234	1999	$16.00	University Barbie
Uptown Chic Barbie	11623	1994	$37.00	Classique
Uptown Chic Barbie	19632	1998	$32.00	Fashion Savvy Collection
Utah	21197	1999	$16.00	University Barbie
Utah Jazz Barbie	20708	1998	$20.00	NBA
Utah Jazz Barbie (black)	20709	1998	$20.00	NBA
Vacation Sensation (blue)	1675	1986	$50.00	Toys "R" Us
Vacation Sensation (pink)	1675	1988	$50.00	Toys "R" Us
Valentine Barbie	12675	1995	$22.00	Target
Valentine Barbie	15172	1996	$20.00	Target
Valentine Barbie	17649	1998	$12.00	Supermarket
Valentine Barbie (black)	17650	1998	$12.00	Supermarket
Valentine Date Barbie	18306	1998	$18.00	Target
Valentine Fun Barbie	16311	1997	$12.00	Supermarket
Valentine Fun Barbie (black)	16313	1997	$12.00	Supermarket
Valentine Romance Barbie	16059	1997	$18.00	Target
Valentine Style Barbie	20465	1999	$14.00	Target
Valentine Style Barbie (black)	22150	1999	$14.00	Target
Valentine Sweetheart	14644	1996	$15.00	Supermarket
Vancouver Grizzlies	20732	1998	$20.00	NBA

Item	Number	Year	Value	Specials
Vancouver Grizzlies (black)	20733	1998	$20.00	NBA
Vanderbilt	21160	1999	$16.00	University Barbie
Venetian Opulence	24501	2000	$90.00	Masquerade Gala
Vera Wang Awards Night Barbie	23027	1999	$89.00	Designer Collection
Vera Wang Barbie	19788	1998	$100.00	Designer Collection
Versace Barbie Doll	B3457	2004	$140.00	Versace
Versus Barbie	B9767	2004	$79.00	
Very Berry	26881	1999	$10.00	K-Mart
Very Velvet (brunette)	22249	1999	$30.00	
Very Velvet Barbie	20528	1998	$25.00	
Very Violet	1859	1992	$65.00	Wholesale Clubs
Victorian Barbie with Cedric Bear (blonde)	25526	2000	$50.00	Adult Collector Edition
Victorian Barbie with Cedric Bear (brunette)	25526	2000	$39.00	Victorian
Victorian Elegance	12579	1994	$35.00	Hallmark
Victorian Lady	14900	1996	$30.00	Great Eras Collection
Villanova	21172	1999	$16.00	University Barbie
Virginia Tech	19171	1998	$10.00	University Barbie
Virginia Tech (black)	19420	1998	$10.00	University Barbie
Virgo Barbie		2005	$20.00	Zodiac
Virgo Barbie (black)		2005	$20.00	Zodiac
Wacky Warehouse I	10309	1993	$55.00	Kool-Aid
Wacky Warehouse II	11763	1994	$45.00	Kool-Aid
Wacky Warehouse III	15620	1996	$35.00	Kool-Aid
Walk Lively (blonde)	1182	1972	$220.00	
Walking Barbie & Baby Sister Krissy	22232	1999	$18.00	
Walking Barbie & Baby Sister Krissy (black)	22307	1999	$18.00	
Walt Disney World 25th Anniversary	16525	1996	$35.00	Disney
Wash 'n Wear	29027	2000	$19.00	
Washington State	19869	1998	$11.00	University Barbie
Washington Wizards	20696	1998	$11.00	NBA
Washington Wizards (black)	20697	1998	$11.00	NBA
Water Lily (Monet)	17783	1997	$90.00	Artist Series
Water Rhapsody Barbie	19847	1998	$57.00	Essence of Nature
We Can Do Anything, Right Barbie!		1999	$410.00	Collectors' Convention 1999
Wedding Day	9608	1991	$35.00	
Wedding Day (blonde)	17119	1997	$25.00	Nostalgic Vinyl Series
Wedding Day (redhead)	17120	1997	$30.00	Nostalgic Vinyl Series
Wedding Fantasy	2125	1990	$45.00	
Wedding Fantasy (black)	7011	1989	$45.00	
Wedding Party	2641	1989	$275.00	Nostalgic Porcelain
Wedgwood Barbie	25641	2000	$110.00	Great Porcelain Houses
Wedgwood Barbie	25641	2000	$150.00	Wedgwood/Wal-Mart
Wedgwood Barbie	50823	2001	$79.00	Wedgwood
Wedgwood Barbie (black)	50824	2001	$79.00	Wedgwood
Weekend Barbie	23462	1999	$5.00	
West End Barbie	15513	1996	$45.00	Hamleys (England)
Western	1757	1981	$50.00	
Western Chic Barbie	55487	2002	$120.00	Pop Culture
Western Fun	9932	1990	$30.00	
Western Fun (black)	2930	1990	$30.00	
Western Plains	23205	1999	$40.00	Lifestyles of the West
Western Stampin'	10293	1993	$25.00	
Western Stampin' (black)	10539	1993	$25.00	
Western Stampin' Barbie Deluxe Play Set	10927	1993	$30.00	Wholesale Clubs

Item	Number	Year	Value	Specials
Western Stampin' Barbie with				
Western Star Horse (black)	13478	1995	$45.00	Toys "R" Us
Wet 'n Wild	4103	1990	$20.00	
Whispering Wind Barbie	22834	1999	$65.00	Essence of Nature
White Chocolate Obsession Barbie		2005		Flavor Obsession
Wig Wardrobe	971	1964	$475.00	
Wig Wardrobe (head and three wigs only)	871	1964	$450.00	
Wild Style Barbie	411	1992	$26.00	Target
Wild Style Barbie	19262	1998	$20.00	Toys "R" Us
Winner's Circle	17441	1997	$55.00	Spiegel
Winnie the Pooh Barbie	H6469	2005	$15.00	
Winter Belle	1637	1992	$20.00	
Winter Concert Barbie		2002	Retail	
Winter Dazzle Barbie	18456	1997	$30.00	General Mills
Winter Dazzle Barbie (black)	18457	1997	$30.00	General Mills
Winter Evening Barbie (blonde)	19218	1998	$25.00	Wholesale Clubs
Winter Evening Barbie (brunette)	19220	1998	$25.00	Wholesale Clubs
Winter Fantasy (brunette)	17666	1997	$25.00	Wholesale Clubs
Winter Fantasy Barbie	5946	1990	$90.00	FAO Schwarz
Winter Fantasy Barbie	B2519	2003	$45.00	Holiday Dolls
Winter Fantasy Barbie (black)	C0166	2003	$45.00	Holiday Dolls
Winter Fantasy Barbie (blonde)	15334	1996	$30.00	Sam's Club
Winter Fantasy Barbie (brunette)	15530	1996	$35.00	Sam's Club
Winter Fantasy II (black)	17747	1997	$25.00	Wholesale Clubs
Winter Fantasy II (blonde)	17249	1997	$25.00	Wholesale Clubs
Winter Fun	5949	1990	$40.00	Toys "R" Us
Winter in Montreal Barbie	22258	1999	$40.00	City Seasons Collection
Winter in New York	19429	1998	$50.00	City Seasons Collection
Winter Princess	10655	1993	$110.00	Winter Princess Collection
Winter Renaissance				
(Evening Elegance Series)	15570	1996	$40.00	JCPenney
Winter Rhapsody (black)	16354	1997	$35.00	Avon
Winter Rhapsody (blonde)	16353	1997	$35.00	Avon
Winter Rhapsody (brunette)	16873	1997	$35.00	Avon
Winter Royal	10658	1993	$75.00	Wholesale Clubs
Winter Splendor Barbie	19357	1998	$38.00	Avon
Winter Splendor Barbie (black)	19358	1998	$38.00	Avon
Winter Sports	13516	1995	$35.00	JCPenney
Winter Sports (catalog only)	9042	1975	$100.00	Sears
Winter Sports Barbie	13516	1995	$30.00	Toys "R" Us
Winter Velvet	15571	1996	$38.00	Avon
Winter Velvet (black)	15587	1996	$38.00	Avon
Winter's Eve	13613	1995	$30.00	Wholesale Clubs
Wizard of Oz-Dorothy with Toto	19364	2000	Retail	Porcelain Treasures Collection
Wizard of Oz-Wicked Witch	23880	2000	Retail	Porcelain Treasures Collection
WNBA Barbie	20205	1998	$16.00	WNBA
Wonder Woman	24638	2000	Retail	Warner Bros. Studio Store
Workin' Out (outfits vary)		1998	$11.00	Wholesale Club
Working Out Barbie	17317	1997	$15.00	
Working Woman Barbie	20548	1999	$25.00	
Working Woman Barbie (black)	20549	1999	$25.00	
World of Barbie, The		2003	$75.00	Collectors' Convention 2003
Wyoming	21246	1999	$16.00	University Barbie
Xavier	21173	1999	$16.00	University Barbie
Your Pen Pal Barbie	23221	1999	$20.00	Military

Item	Number	Year	Value	Specials
Your Pen Pal Barbie (black)	23222	1999	$20.00	Military
Yuletide Romance	15621	1996	$30.00	Hallmark

Barbie® Dolls

Listed by Stock Number

Number	Item	Year	Value	Specials
411	Wild Style Barbie	1992	$26.00	Target
820	Barbie in Mexico	1964	$820.00	Dressed Boxed Dolls
822	Barbie in Switzerland	1964	$820.00	Dressed Boxed Dolls
823	Barbie in Holland	1964	$820.00	Dressed Boxed Dolls
850	#1 Ponytail (blonde)	1959	$6,900.00	
850	#1 Ponytail (brunette)	1959	$7,000.00	
850	#2 Ponytail (blonde)	1959	$6,400.00	
850	#2 Ponytail (brunette)	1959	$6,400.00	
850	#3 Ponytail (blonde)	1960	$1,000.00	
850	#3 Ponytail (brunette)	1960	$1,100.00	
850	#4 Ponytail (blonde)	1960	$700.00	
850	#4 Ponytail (brunette)	1960	$700.00	
850	#5 Ponytail (blonde)	1961	$550.00	
850	#5 Ponytail (brunette)	1961	$550.00	
850	#5 Ponytail (titian)	1961	$675.00	
850	#6 Ponytail (ash blonde)	1962	$500.00	
850	#6 Ponytail (blonde)	1962	$500.00	
850	#6 Ponytail (brunette)	1962	$500.00	
850	#6 Ponytail (titian)	1962	$500.00	
850	#6 Ponytail (wheat blonde)	1962	$500.00	
850	#6 Ponytail (yellow blonde)	1962	$500.00	
850	Banquet Set Barbie Doll (blonde)	1994	$299.00	Barbie Festival
850	Banquet Set Barbie Doll (redhead)	1994	$299.00	Barbie Festival
850	Bubble Cut (blonde)	1961	$400.00	
850	Bubble Cut (blonde)	1962	$400.00	
850	Bubble Cut (brunette)	1961	$975.00	
850	Bubble Cut (brunette)	1961	$400.00	
850	Bubble Cut (brunette)	1962	$400.00	
850	Bubble Cut (Japanese, side part)	1965	$2,995.00	
850	Bubble Cut (side part)	1965	$445.00	
850	Bubble Cut (titian)	1961	$400.00	
850	Bubble Cut (titian)	1962	$400.00	
850	Bubble Cut (white ginger)	1961	$925.00	
850	Swirl (ash blonde)	1964	$650.00	
850	Swirl (blonde)	1964	$650.00	
850	Swirl (brunette)	1964	$650.00	
850	Swirl (platinum)	1964	$1,300.00	
850	Swirl (redhead)	1964	$650.00	
863	Something Extra	1992	$25.00	Meijer
870	Fashion Queen	1963	$450.00	
871	Wig Wardrobe (head and three wigs only)	1964	$450.00	
872	Cinderella	1964	$858.00	Dressed Boxed Dolls
873	Guinevere	1964	$645.00	Dressed Boxed Dolls
874	Arabian Nights	1964	$1,270.00	Dressed Boxed Dolls
931	Garden Party	1963	$600.00	Dressed Boxed Dolls
934	After Five	1963	$600.00	Dressed Boxed Dolls
940	Mood For Music	1963	$625.00	Dressed Boxed Dolls
941	Tennis Anyone?	1963	$610.00	Dressed Boxed Dolls

Number	Item	Year	Value	Specials
942	Ice Breaker	1964	$695.00	Dressed Boxed Dolls
944	Masquerade	1964	$635.00	Dressed Boxed Dolls
946	Dinner at Eight	1964	$595.00	Dressed Boxed Dolls
947	Bride's Dream	1964	$910.00	Dressed Boxed Dolls
951	Senior Prom	1964	$1,145.00	Dressed Boxed Dolls
954	Career Girl	1964	$858.00	Dressed Boxed Dolls
955	Swingin' Easy	1964	$637.00	Dressed Boxed Dolls
957	Knitting Pretty (pink version)	1964	$1,265.00	Dressed Boxed Dolls
957	Knitting Pretty (royal version)	1964	$635.00	Dressed Boxed Dolls
959	Theatre Date	1964	$660.00	Dressed Boxed Dolls
961	Evening Splendour	1964	$635.00	Dressed Boxed Dolls
965	Nighty Negligee	1963	$550.00	Dressed Boxed Dolls
971	Wig Wardrobe	1964	$475.00	
982	Solo in the Spotlight	1963	$845.00	Dressed Boxed Dolls
984	American Airlines Stewardess	1963	$700.00	Dressed Boxed Dolls
987	Orange Blossom	1963	$635.00	Dressed Boxed Dolls
991	Registered Nurse	1963	$760.00	Dressed Boxed Dolls
1017	Tropical	1986	$20.00	
1022	Tropical (black)	1986	$20.00	
1060	Miss Barbie (sleep eyes with 3 wigs)	1964	$1,295.00	
1067	Malibu	1975	$45.00	
1067	Malibu (baggie)	1972	$150.00	
1067	Malibu (Sunset)	1971	$65.00	
1067	Sun Gold Malibu	1984	$25.00	
1067	Sun Lovin' Malibu	1979	$40.00	
1067	Sunsational Malibu	1981	$30.00	
1070	American Girl (ash blonde)	1965	$1,500.00	
1070	American Girl (blonde)	1965	$1,500.00	
1070	American Girl (brown)	1965	$1,500.00	
1070	American Girl (brunette)	1965	$1,500.00	
1070	American Girl (brunette)	1966	$2,500.00	
1070	American Girl (color magic face)	1966	$3,000.00	
1070	American Girl (redhead)	1965	$2,500.00	
1070	American Girl (side part/blonde)	1966	$3,000.00	
1112	Totally Hair	1991	$35.00	
1115	Talking (blonde)	1968	$400.00	
1115	Talking (blonde)	1970	$295.00	
1115	Talking (brunette)	1968	$400.00	
1115	Talking (brunette)	1970	$295.00	
1115	Talking (redhead)	1968	$400.00	
1115	Talking (redhead)	1970	$295.00	
1116	Dramatic New Living (blonde)	1971	$195.00	
1116	Dramatic New Living (brunette)	1971	$250.00	
1116	Dramatic New Living (redhead)	1971	$150.00	
1116	Living	1970	$250.00	
1116	New Living (auburn)	1970	$200.00	
1116	New Living (blonde)	1969	$200.00	
1117	Totally Hair (brunette)	1991	$35.00	
1140	Rocker	1986	$50.00	
1144	Growin' Pretty Hair	1971	$375.00	
1150	Color Magic (cardboard box, blonde)	1967	$3,000.00	
1150	Color Magic (cardboard box, midnight black)	1967	$4,200.00	
1150	Color Magic (plastic box, blonde)	1966	$1,800.00	
1150	Color Magic (plastic box, midnight black)	1966	$3,000.00	
1152	Live Action on Stage	1971	$233.00	

Number	Item	Year	Value	Specials
1155	Live Action (baggie)	1973	$165.00	
1155	Live Action (blonde)	1971	$160.00	
1160	Twist 'n Turn Barbie (brunette)	1971	$500.00	
1160	Twist 'n Turn Barbie (brunette, flip hair)	1969	$500.00	
1160	Twist 'n Turn Barbie (brunette, flip hair)	1970	$500.00	
1160	Twist 'n Turn Barbie (chocolate bon-bon, dark brown)	1966	$500.00	
1160	Twist 'n Turn Barbie (go-go co-co, brunette)	1966	$550.00	
1160	Twist 'n Turn Barbie (redhead)	1966	$1,000.00	
1160	Twist 'n Turn Barbie (summer sand, gray)	1966	$550.00	
1160	Twist 'n Turn Barbie (sun kissed, blonde)	1966	$550.00	
1162	Trade In Barbie (Twist 'n Turn, redhead)	1967	$375.00	
1174	Hair Happenin's	1971	$1,075.00	
1182	Walk Lively (blonde)	1972	$220.00	
1189	Feelin' Fun (1st version)	1988	$30.00	
1190	Standard (brunette, straight leg)	1967	$400.00	
1190	Standard (redhead, straight leg)	1967	$900.00	
1195	Busy (Talking)	1972	$350.00	
1205	Gift Giving	1989	$35.00	
1207	Astronaut (black)	1986	$60.00	
1234	Army Desert Storm	1993	$24.00	Stars 'n Stripes
1249	Silken Flame Barbie (brunette)	1994	$130.00	Porcelain
1276	Radiant in Red	1992	$45.00	Toys "R" Us
1278	Evening Sensation	1992	$50.00	JCPenney
1280	My First Barbie	1988	$20.00	
1281	My First Barbie (black)	1988	$20.00	
1282	My First Barbie (Hispanic)	1988	$20.00	
1283	Style Magic	1989	$30.00	
1288	Style Magic (black)	1989	$30.00	
1290	Beauty Secrets Barbie, Pretty Reflections	1980	$75.00	Department Store
1292	Hispanic Barbie	1980	$60.00	
1293	Black Barbie Doll	1980	$75.00	
1334	Sport Star	1979	$25.00	
1350	Animal Lovin'	1988	$30.00	
1364	Blue Rhapsody	1991	$140.00	Service Merchandise
1372	Fun to Dress	1989	$15.00	
1373	Fun to Dress (black)	1989	$15.00	
1374	Frills & Fantasy	1988	$45.00	Wal-Mart
1390	Sun Sensation	1992	$20.00	
1429	Happy Holidays 1992	1992	$50.00	Happy Holidays Collection
1434	Mermaid	1992	$20.00	
1490	Cool 'n Sassy	1992	$25.00	Toys "R" Us
1511	Barbie Doll	1991	$80.00	McGlynn's Bakery
1511	Specialty Deco-Pak Barbie	1991	$75.00	Deco-Pak
1521	Benefit Ball	1992	$45.00	Classique
1534	Barbie Doll (black)	1991	$80.00	McGlynn's Bakery
1534	Specialty Deco-Pak Barbie (black)	1991	$55.00	Deco-Pak
1539	Madison Avenue	1992	$100.00	FAO Schwarz
1544	Travel in Style	1967	$240.00	Sears
1553	Crystal Rhapsody (blonde)	1992	$220.00	Presidential Porcelain
1585	Action Accents Set (auburn)	1969	$800.00	Sears
1600	Parisian	1980	$90.00	Dolls of the World
1601	Royal	1980	$115.00	Dolls of the World
1602	Italian	1980	$150.00	Dolls of the World
1603	Country Fair	1964	$595.00	Dressed Boxed Dolls

Number	Item	Year	Value	Specials
1604	SuperStar Barbie	1988	$40.00	
1605	SuperStar Barbie (black)	1988	$25.00	
1606	Garden Tea Party	1964	$595.00	Dressed Boxed Dolls
1609	Black Magic Ensemble	1964	$860.00	Dressed Boxed Dolls
1612	Teen Talk (black)	1992	$30.00	
1623	Dream Bride Barbie	1992	$60.00	
1637	Winter Belle	1992	$20.00	
1646	Tropical (Hispanic)	1986	$25.00	
1647	Dream Glow (Hispanic)	1986	$30.00	
1648	Swan Lake	1991	$88.00	Musical Ballet Series
1675	Vacation Sensation (blue)	1986	$50.00	Toys "R" Us
1675	Vacation Sensation (pink)	1988	$50.00	Toys "R" Us
1703	Happy Holidays 1988	1988	$390.00	Happy Holidays Collection
1703	Malibu Barbie – The Beach Party with Case	1980	$60.00	
1703	Malibu Barbie Beach Party, The	1980	$55.00	Department Store
1708	Blue Rhapsody	1986	$299.00	Porcelain
1737	Jewel Secrets	1987	$30.00	
1738	Funtime (purple watch)	1987	$30.00	Toys "R" Us
1739	Funtime (black)	1986	$30.00	Toys "R" Us
1753	Native American #1	1993	$32.00	Dolls of the World
1756	Jewel Secrets (black)	1987	$20.00	
1757	Horse Lovin'	1983	$40.00	
1757	Western	1981	$50.00	
1788	My First Barbie	1987	$20.00	
1801	My First Barbie (black)	1987	$20.00	
1858	Royal Romance	1992	$80.00	Wholesale Clubs
1859	Very Violet	1992	$65.00	Wholesale Clubs
1861	Romantic Bride	1993	$35.00	
1865	Evening Flame	1991	$150.00	Home Shopping Club
1869	Rapunzel	1997	$50.00	
1871	Happy Holidays 1991	1991	$65.00	Happy Holidays Collection
1874	Golden Dream	1981	$50.00	
1875	My First Barbie	1981	$25.00	
1875	My First Barbie	1983	$35.00	
1875	My First Barbie	1974	$35.00	
1876	Party Perfect	1992	$34.00	Shopko/Venture
1879	Blue Elegance	1992	$50.00	Hill's
1880	Roller Skating	1980	$60.00	
1882	Fashion Brights	1992	$20.00	Toys "R" Us
1886	Satin Nights	1992	$70.00	Service Merchandise
1916	Russian	1989	$30.00	Dolls of the World
1917	Mexican	1989	$25.00	Dolls of the World
1920	Unicef	1989	$20.00	Unicef
1922	Gift Giving	1986	$35.00	
1922	Happy Birthday	1981	$45.00	
1922	Happy Birthday (2nd issue)	1984	$25.00	
1922	Happy Birthday (3rd issue)	1984	$30.00	
1953	Garden Party	1989	$20.00	Wal-Mart
1998	Celebration Barbie	1986	$65.00	Sears
2000	Case with Doll (swirl ponytail)	1966	$800.00	
2001	Party Premiere	1992	$20.00	Supermarket
2017	Rockettes	1993	$120.00	FAO Schwarz
2066	Flight Time Barbie (Hispanic)	1990	$57.00	
2080	Friendship Barbie, Berlin Wall II	1991	$29.00	Friendship
2125	Wedding Fantasy	1990	$45.00	

Number	Item	Year	Value	Specials
2126	Magic Moves	1986	$60.00	
2127	Magic Moves (black)	1986	$40.00	
2207	SuperStar Barbie in the Spotlight	1977	$75.00	
2210	Fashion Photo	1978	$60.00	
2214	Rollerblade	1992	$30.00	
2225	Sweet Lavender (black)	1992	$30.00	Woolworth
2242	Dream Glow (black)	1986	$25.00	
2248	Dream Glow	1986	$25.00	
2249	Home Pretty	1990	$20.00	
2256	Italian (reissue)	1993	$36.00	Dolls of the World
2257	Spring Parade (black)	1992	$35.00	Toys "R" Us
2282	Anniversary Star	1992	$30.00	Wal-Mart
2289	Hawaiian SuperStar	1978	$175.00	
2306	Dream Princess	1992	$40.00	Sears
2308	Hollywood Hair	1993	$25.00	
2366	Jewel Jubilee	1991	$65.00	Wholesale Clubs
2374	Earring Magic (black)	1993	$20.00	
2396	Happy Holidays 1992 (black)	1992	$38.00	Happy Holidays Collection
2449	Astronaut	1986	$65.00	
2452	Denim 'n Lace	1992	$28.00	Ames
2482	Sparkle Eyes	1992	$30.00	
2516	My First Ballerina	1993	$20.00	
2516	My First Barbie	1993	$18.00	
2517	My Size	1993	$115.00	
2522	Sweet Lavender	1992	$30.00	Woolworth
2570	Fun to Dress (black)	1993	$15.00	
2582	Special Expressions	1991	$20.00	Woolworth
2583	Special Expressions (black)	1991	$20.00	Woolworth
2583	SuperStar Barbie Fashion Change-abouts	1978	$90.00	Tru Value
2586	Southern Belle	1991	$40.00	Sears
2586	SuperStar Barbie in the Spotlight	1978	$110.00	Department Store
2587	Golden Evening	1990	$45.00	Target
2597	Kissing (bangs style)	1979	$45.00	Department Store
2597	Kissing (extra dress)	1979	$45.00	Department Store
2598	Pretty Changes	1980	$70.00	
2598	Pretty Changes (lamp)	1980	$80.00	
2598	Pretty Changes Barbie (with free Barbie play perfume)	1979	$90.00	Store Promotional
2641	Wedding Party	1989	$275.00	Nostalgic Porcelain
2696	Happy Holidays 1991 (black)	1991	$40.00	Happy Holidays Collection
2702	Enchanted Evening	1991	$75.00	JCPenney
2703	Platinum	1991	$289.00	Bob Mackie
2704	Starlight Splendor	1991	$500.00	Bob Mackie
2713	Fashion Play (turquoise dress)	1991	$25.00	
2721	School Fun	1991	$22.00	Toys "R" Us
2730	Fashion Play	1992	$15.00	
2751	Barbie and the Beat	1990	$25.00	
2753	Malibu Fashion Combo	1978	$65.00	Catalog Showroom
2763	Fun to Dress (Hispanic)	1993	$15.00	
2767	My First Ballerina (black)	1993	$20.00	
2767	My First Barbie (black)	1993	$20.00	
2770	My First Ballerina (Hispanic)	1993	$20.00	
2783	Trail Blazin'	1991	$25.00	Supermarket
2844	Super Size Barbie (super hair)	1979	$250.00	
2901	Pretty Hearts	1992	$25.00	Supermarket

Number	Item	Year	Value	Specials
2909	Party in Pink	1991	$30.00	Ames
2917	Sweet Romance	1991	$30.00	
2921	Night Sensation	1991	$60.00	FAO Schwarz
2930	Western Fun (black)	1990	$30.00	
2954	Cute 'n Cool	1991	$30.00	Target
2954	Dayton Hudson Cute 'n Cool	1991	$25.00	
2995	Peruvian I	1986	$36.00	Dolls of the World
2996	Deluxe Tropical Barbie	1985	$30.00	
2996	Deluxe Tropical Barbie	1986	$40.00	Department Store
2997	Greek	1986	$38.00	Dolls of the World
2998	Sears 100th Anniversary Celebration	1985	$100.00	Sears
3022	Cool Times	1989	$25.00	
3055	Rocker (2nd issue)	1987	$50.00	
3101	Super Hair	1987	$25.00	
3117	Pretty in Purple	1992	$25.00	K-Mart
3121	Pretty in Purple (black)	1992	$25.00	K-Mart
3137	American Beauty Queen	1991	$35.00	
3142	Blossom Beauty	1991	$40.00	Shopko/Venture
3157	Caboodles	1993	$20.00	
3161	Red Romance	1992	$25.00	Supermarket
3161	Sweetheart Barbie	1993	$35.00	Supermarket
3188	German	1987	$50.00	Dolls of the World
3189	Icelandic	1987	$45.00	Dolls of the World
3194	Miss America	1972	$175.00	Kellogg Company
3196	Fantastica	1992	$60.00	Wholesale Clubs
3197	Kellogg Quick Curl	1974	$60.00	Kellogg Company
3197	Special Expressions	1992	$25.00	Woolworth
3198	Special Expressions (black)	1992	$30.00	Woolworth
3200	Special Expressions (Hispanic)	1992	$25.00	Woolworth
3200	Sweet Lavender (Hispanic)	1992	$30.00	Woolworth
3203	Dazzlin' Date	1992	$30.00	Target
3208	Sweet Spring	1992	$22.00	Supermarket
3210	Montgomery Ward Anniversary Doll	1972	$750.00	Montgomery Ward
3237	Beach Blast	1989	$15.00	
3240	Fun to Dress	1993	$15.00	
3245	American Beauty Queen (black)	1991	$35.00	
3248	Rappin' Rockin'	1992	$40.00	
3253	Beach Blast (black)	1989	$20.00	
3262	Oriental	1981	$150.00	Dolls of the World
3263	Scottish	1981	$90.00	Dolls of the World
3269	Forget-Me-Nots (baggie)	1972	$195.00	Kellogg Company
3274	Evening Sparkle	1990	$35.00	Hill's
3284	Southern Beauty	1991	$25.00	Winn Dixie
3296	Super Hair (black)	1987	$20.00	
3311	Busy Barbie	1972	$200.00	
3331	Dream Wardrobe Barbie	1992	$35.00	Wholesale Clubs
3347	Sterling Wishes	1991	$75.00	Spiegel
3360	Air Force	1991	$30.00	Stars 'n Stripes
3388	Birthday Party	1993	$30.00	
3406	Applause Barbie	1991	$35.00	Applause
3415	Enchanted Evening	1987	$228.00	Porcelain
3421	Feelin' Groovy	1987	$175.00	Department Store
3474	Fancy Frills	1992	$40.00	
3477	Spring Bouquet	1993	$22.00	Supermarket
3509	Dance Club with tape player	1989	$55.00	Child's World

Number	Item	Year	Value	Specials
3523	Happy Holidays 1989	1989	$125.00	Happy Holidays Collection
3533	Golden Dreams	1981	$70.00	Department Store
3533	Golden Dreams (2nd issue, big hair)	1981	$70.00	Department Store
3549	Moonlight Rose	1991	$32.00	Hill's
3550	Snap 'n Play	1992	$20.00	
3553	Starlight Blue	1989	$40.00	Lady Lovely Locks
3554	Pink & Pretty	1982	$40.00	
3556	Snap 'n Play (black)	1992	$20.00	
3596	Evening Enchantment	1989	$38.00	Sears
3602	Glitter Beach	1993	$15.00	
3626	Australian Barbie #1	1993	$32.00	Dolls of the World
3626	Australian Barbie #2	1993	$34.00	Dolls of the World
3677	Friendship Barbie, Berlin Wall III	1992	$25.00	Friendship
3678	Ballroom Beauty	1991	$30.00	Wal-Mart
3679	Birthday Surprise	1992	$40.00	
3702	Gibson Girl	1993	$45.00	Great Eras Collection
3717	Funtime (blue watch)	1987	$30.00	Toys "R" Us
3718	Funtime (pink watch)	1987	$30.00	Toys "R" Us
3722	Barbie for President (Presidential seal)	1991	$65.00	Toys "R" Us
3722	Barbie for President (white star)	1992	$40.00	Toys "R" Us
3756	Pink Jubilee	1989	$800.00	Jubilee Series
3808	Picnic Pretty	1992	$35.00	Osco Drugs
3817	Blossom Beautiful	1992	$225.00	Sears
3830	Bath Blast (black)	1993	$15.00	
3836	Secret Hearts (black)	1993	$20.00	
3839	My First Ballerina	1992	$20.00	
3839	My First Barbie	1992	$20.00	
3842	Fashion Play (black)	1992	$15.00	
3850	Doctor Barbie	1988	$55.00	
3850	Doctor Barbie	1990	$45.00	Toys "R" Us
3856	Magic Curl	1982	$55.00	
3860	Fashion Play (Hispanic)	1992	$15.00	
3860	My First Barbie (Hispanic)	1992	$20.00	
3861	My First Ballerina (black)	1992	$20.00	
3897	India	1982	$75.00	Dolls of the World
3898	Eskimo	1982	$65.00	Dolls of the World
3939	25th Anniversary	1972	$650.00	Montgomery Ward
3940	Barbie for President (black, Presidential seal)	1991	$45.00	Toys "R" Us
3963	Lavender Looks	1989	$35.00	Wal-Mart
3966	Army	1989	$25.00	American Beauty Collection
3989	Magic Curl (black)	1982	$40.00	
4031	Spanish Barbie #1	1983	$65.00	Dolls of the World
4032	Swedish Barbie	1983	$54.00	Dolls of the World
4043	Hair Fair	1967	$210.00	
4043	Hair Fair Set (re-issue)	1974	$125.00	
4044	Hair Fair	1971	$250.00	
4051	Birthday Surprise (black)	1992	$40.00	
4061	Island Fun	1988	$20.00	
4063	1920s Flapper Barbie	1993	$55.00	Great Eras Collection
4098	Happy Holidays 1990	1990	$65.00	Happy Holidays Collection
4103	Wet 'n Wild	1990	$20.00	
4110	Cool 'n Sassy (black)	1992	$25.00	Toys "R" Us
4111	School Fun (black)	1992	$22.00	Toys "R" Us
4112	Fashion Brights (black)	1992	$20.00	Toys "R" Us
4113	Radiant in Red (Hispanic)	1992	$45.00	Toys "R" Us

Number	Item	Year	Value	Specials
4116	Regal Reflections	1992	$200.00	Spiegel
4159	Bath Blast	1993	$15.00	
4220	Quick Curl (blonde)	1972	$80.00	
4220	Quick Curl (with extra outfit)	1973	$100.00	Store Promotional
4247	Empress Bride	1992	$460.00	Bob Mackie
4248	Neptune Fantasy	1992	$455.00	Bob Mackie
4385	Disney Special (with mouse hat)	1991	$45.00	Child's World
4439	California Barbie	1987	$20.00	
4439	California Dream	1988	$30.00	
4442	California Barbie (with Beach Boys record)	1987	$30.00	
4543	Happy Holidays 1990 (black)	1990	$40.00	Happy Holidays Collection
4547	Skating Star	1988	$65.00	Sears
4549	Olympic Skating Star	1987	$50.00	
4550	Star Dream	1987	$50.00	Sears
4551	Perfume Pretty	1988	$30.00	
4552	Perfume Pretty (black)	1988	$30.00	
4558	Fun to Dress	1988	$15.00	
4581	Malt Shop	1993	$35.00	Toys "R" Us
4583	Baseball	1993	$30.00	Target
4589	Pink Jubilee (25th anniversary Wal-Mart)	1987	$50.00	Wal-Mart
4598	Crystal	1984	$30.00	
4629	Party Pink	1987	$25.00	Wal-Mart
4647	Jamaican	1992	$28.00	Dolls of the World
4767	German Talking	1991	$55.00	
4770	Unicef (black)	1989	$18.00	
4774	Unicef (Asian)	1989	$24.00	Unicef
4782	Unicef (Hispanic)	1989	$24.00	
4798	Party Time	1983	$20.00	
4808	Feelin' Fun (2nd version)	1988	$20.00	
4808	Fun to Dress	1990	$15.00	
4809	Feelin' Fun (black)	1989	$20.00	
4809	Fun to Dress (Hispanic)	1992	$15.00	
4824	Animal Lovin' (black)	1988	$30.00	
4836	Dance Magic	1990	$25.00	
4839	Color 'n Curl Set (head only)	1965	$500.00	
4841	Hot Dancin' Set	1990	$40.00	
4842	Special Expressions	1989	$25.00	Woolworth
4843	Party Lace	1989	$35.00	Hill's
4859	Crystal (black)	1984	$30.00	
4869	Pepsi Spirit	1989	$75.00	Toys "R" Us
4870	Peach Pretty	1989	$32.00	K-Mart
4873	Benetton Shopping	1991	$30.00	
4885	Party Treats	1989	$25.00	Toys "R" Us
4928	Canadian	1988	$35.00	Dolls of the World
4929	Korean	1988	$35.00	Dolls of the World
4930	Mardi Gras	1988	$45.00	American Beauty Collection
4931	Sensations	1988	$50.00	
4939	Fun to Dress (black)	1990	$15.00	
4963	Spanish Barbie #2	1992	$33.00	Dolls of the World
4970	Sun Gold Malibu (Hispanic)	1985	$25.00	
4970	Sunsational Malibu (Hispanic)	1981	$40.00	
4973	English	1992	$37.00	Dolls of the World
4983	Ballerina	1983	$40.00	Mervyn's
4984	Ballerina (black)	1983	$60.00	Mervyn's
5239	Pink & Pretty Barbie Extra Special Modeling Set	1982	$75.00	Department Store

Number	Item	Year	Value	Specials
5274	Bath Magic	1992	$15.00	
5313	Fashion Jeans (black)	1982	$30.00	
5313	Sophisticated Lady	1990	$140.00	Nostalgic Porcelain
5315	Fashion Jeans	1982	$30.00	
5315	Style	1990	$35.00	Applause
5336	Playtime	1983	$20.00	
5351	Plantation Belle (blonde)	1992	$315.00	Disney
5405	Gold	1990	$500.00	Bob Mackie
5410	Pink Sensation	1990	$25.00	Winn Dixie
5413	Pretty in Plaid	1992	$30.00	Target
5471	Sea Holiday Barbie	1993	$25.00	Toys "R" Us
5472	Nutcracker	1992	$79.00	Musical Ballet Series
5475	Benefit Performance	1988	$235.00	Nostalgic Porcelain
5504	Special Expressions	1990	$20.00	Woolworth
5505	Special Expressions (black)	1990	$20.00	Woolworth
5506	Friendship Barbie, Berlin Wall I	1990	$24.00	Friendship
5579	Twirly Curls	1983	$35.00	Department Store
5588	Lavender Surprise (black)	1990	$35.00	Sears
5640	Angel Face	1983	$35.00	
5723	Twirly Curls (black)	1983	$35.00	
5724	Twirly Curls (Hispanic)	1983	$35.00	
5745	Teen Talk	1991	$50.00	
5745	Teen Talk (ash blonde)	1991	$50.00	
5745	Teen Talk (brunette)	1991	$50.00	
5745	Teen Talk (redhead)	1992	$50.00	
5745	Teen Talk (strawberry blonde)	1991	$50.00	
5745	Teen Talk, "Math Class is Tough"	1992	$65.00	
5756	Hot Looks	1992	$25.00	Ames
5766	Fashion Play	1990	$20.00	Woolworth
5816	Army Desert Storm (black)	1993	$24.00	Stars 'n Stripes
5838	Super Dance	1982	$40.00	
5854	Country Looks	1993	$25.00	Ames
5868	Dream Date	1983	$40.00	
5868	Dreamtime Barbie	1982	$20.00	
5940	Hawaiian Fun	1991	$20.00	
5946	Winter Fantasy Barbie	1990	$90.00	FAO Schwarz
5947	Cool Looks	1990	$25.00	Toys "R" Us
5948	Totally Hair (black)	1991	$25.00	
5949	Winter Fun	1990	$40.00	Toys "R" Us
5950	Sparkle Eyes Barbie (black)	1992	$30.00	
5953	Fashion Play (black)	1991	$15.00	
5954	Fashion Play (Hispanic)	1991	$15.00	
5955	Party Pretty	1990	$30.00	Target
5979	My First Barbie (Hispanic)	1987	$28.00	Zayre's
6279	Le Nouveau Theater de la Mode (Billy Boy) France	1985	$220.00	
7008	Spring Parade	1992	$35.00	Toys "R" Us
7009	Peach Blossom	1992	$40.00	Wholesale Clubs
7011	Wedding Fantasy (black)	1989	$45.00	
7014	Earring Magic	1993	$20.00	
7025	Great Shape	1984	$30.00	
7027	Summit	1990	$15.00	
7028	Summit (black)	1990	$15.00	
7029	Summit (Asian)	1990	$22.00	
7030	Summit (Hispanic)	1990	$24.00	
7057	Evening Elegance	1990	$75.00	JCPenney

Number	Item	Year	Value	Specials
7072	Loving You	1983	$55.00	
7080	Dance Magic (black)	1990	$25.00	
7093	Fabulous Fur	1986	$65.00	Mervyn's
7123	Costume Ball	1991	$30.00	
7131	Sparkle Eyes Barbie Dressing Room and Fashion Set	1992	$55.00	Wholesale Clubs
7134	Costume Ball (black)	1991	$30.00	
7149	Sun Sensation Barbie Spray & Play Fun	1992	$60.00	Wholesale Clubs
7193	Fashion Play (pink & white jumpsuit)	1983	$25.00	
7233	Gold Medal Swimmer	1975	$75.00	
7262	Gold Medal Skater	1975	$75.00	
7264	Gold Medal Skier	1975	$75.00	
7270	Free Moving	1974	$160.00	
7272	Barbie and Snowball Her Pet Dog	1990	$15.00	
7329	Malaysian	1991	$25.00	Dolls of the World
7330	Czechoslovakian	1991	$55.00	Dolls of the World
7335	Dream Fantasy	1990	$35.00	Wal-Mart
7346	Special Expressions (black)	1989	$25.00	Woolworth
7348	Ice Capades 50th Anniversary (black)	1990	$25.00	
7365	Ice Capades 50th Anniversary	1990	$50.00	
7373	Feelin' Fun (Hispanic)	1989	$20.00	
7373	Fun to Dress (Hispanic)	1990	$15.00	
7376	Nigerian	1990	$30.00	Dolls of the World
7438	Lisette Barbie	2001	$104.00	Barbie Fashion Model
7470	Hawaiian	1975	$50.00	Department Store
7470	Hawaiian (one-piece swimsuit)	1982	$50.00	Department Store
7470	Hawaiian (two-piece swimsuit)	1983	$40.00	Department Store
7476	Gold and Lace	1989	$35.00	Target
7511	Ski Fun	1991	$30.00	
7517	Irish	1984	$75.00	Dolls of the World
7526	Plantation Belle (redhead)	1992	$140.00	Porcelain
7541	Swiss	1984	$48.00	Dolls of the World
7549	Marine Corps	1992	$25.00	Stars 'n Stripes
7583	Loving You	1983	$50.00	
7594	Marine Corps (black)	1992	$25.00	Stars 'n Stripes
7613	Solo in the Spotlight	1990	$145.00	Nostalgic Porcelain
7635	Sweet Roses	1989	$30.00	Toys "R" Us
7637	Party Pink	1989	$25.00	Winn Dixie
7668	Fun to Dress (black)	1988	$15.00	
7669	Lilac and Lovely	1988	$45.00	Sears
7734	Golden Greetings	1989	$100.00	FAO Schwarz
7745	Sun Gold Malibu (black)	1985	$20.00	
7777	Ten Speeder	1973	$30.00	
7796	Sweet 16	1974	$73.00	Store Promotional
7799	Show 'n Ride	1988	$40.00	Toys "R" Us
7806	Sun Valley	1973	$95.00	
7807	Newport #1	1973	$175.00	
7807	Newport #2	1973	$175.00	
7834	Great Shape (black)	1984	$25.00	
7882	Barbie Babysits (yellow)	1974	$70.00	
7902	Secret Hearts	1993	$30.00	
7913	Happy Birthday (black)	1991	$35.00	
7914	Happy Birthday	1991	$36.00	
7926	Peaches 'n Cream	1985	$40.00	
7929	Day-to-Night	1985	$40.00	

Number	Item	Year	Value	Specials
7944	Day-to-Night (Hispanic)	1985	$40.00	
7945	Day-to-Night (black)	1985	$30.00	
7948	Birthday Party (black)	1993	$30.00	
7951	Bath Magic (black)	1992	$15.00	
8348	Talking (Spanish, plastic box)	1968	$285.00	
8414	Posable	1965	$1,225.00	Montgomery Ward
9025	Party Sensation	1990	$55.00	Wholesale Clubs
9042	Gold Medal Winter Sports	1975	$85.00	Sears
9042	Winter Sports (catalog only)	1975	$100.00	Sears
9044	Gold Medal Barbie and Her U.S. Olympic Wardrobe	1975	$90.00	Sears
9049	Lavender Surprise	1990	$32.00	Sears
9058	Dance Sensation	1984	$60.00	Toys "R" Us
9093	Ballerina (1st version)	1976	$70.00	
9093	Ballerina (2nd issue)	1979	$45.00	
9094	Brazilian	1990	$27.00	Dolls of the World
9099	Barbie and the All Stars	1990	$25.00	
9102	Beach Time	1985	$25.00	
9146	Barbie Celebration	1987	$30.00	
9180	Dream Time	1985	$25.00	Toys "R" Us
9180	Dreamtime Barbie	1988	$35.00	Toys "R" Us
9194	Miss America	1973	$165.00	Kellogg Company
9194	Miss America	1974	$150.00	Kellogg Company
9217	Deluxe Quick Curl	1976	$100.00	Jergens
9385	Disney Special (black)	1990	$45.00	Child's World
9404	Benetton	1991	$30.00	
9423	All American	1991	$28.00	Reebok
9429	Fashion Play	1987	$30.00	
9481	Japanese	1985	$70.00	Dolls of the World
9516	Peaches 'n Cream (black)	1985	$35.00	
9561	Happy Birthday (black)	1990	$35.00	
9584	Flight Time Barbie	1990	$35.00	
9599	Beautiful Bride	1976	$200.00	Department Store
9601	Bathtime Fun	1991	$15.00	Wal-Mart Wholesale Clubs
9603	Bathtime Fun (black)	1991	$15.00	Wal-Mart Wholesale Clubs
9608	Bridesmaid	1991	$30.00	
9608	Wedding Day	1991	$35.00	
9613	Ballerina Barbie on Tour	1976	$125.00	Department Store
9613	Ballerina Barbie on Tour (no wrist tag)	1979	$110.00	Department Store
9613	Ballerina Barbie on Tour (with wrist tag)	1979	$120.00	Department Store
9613	Ballerina Barbie on Tour (1st hair version)	1976	$140.00	
9613	Ballerina Barbie on Tour (2nd hair version)	1979	$90.00	
9629	Fashion Play	1991	$15.00	
9693	Navy	1991	$27.00	Stars 'n Stripes
9694	Navy (black)	1991	$27.00	Stars 'n Stripes
9720	SuperStar Barbie (with SuperStar Haircomb) #1	1978	$60.00	Store Promotional
9720	SuperStar Barbie (with SuperStar Haircomb) #2	1978	$60.00	Store Promotional
9720	SuperStar Barbie (with SuperStar Necklace)	1977	$60.00	Store Promotional
9725	Lights 'n Lace	1991	$30.00	
9805	Barbie and Her Super Fashion Fireworks #1	1997	$90.00	K-Mart/Kresge
9805	Barbie and Her Super Fashion Fireworks #2	1997	$90.00	K-Mart/Kresge
9805	Barbie and Her Super Fashion Fireworks #3	1997	$90.00	K-Mart/Kresge
9823	Pretty Surprise	1992	$20.00	
9828	Super Size Barbie	1977	$250.00	
9843	Parisian #1	1991	$35.00	Dolls of the World

Number	Item	Year	Value	Specials
9843	Parisian #2 (Japan)	1991	$38.00	Dolls of the World
9844	Eskimo (reissue)	1991	$32.00	Dolls of the World
9845	Scottish (reissue)	1991	$45.00	Dolls of the World
9847	Ice Capades	1991	$30.00	
9858	My First Barbie (black)	1984	$30.00	
9907	Beautiful Bride	1978	$175.00	Department Store
9910	Barbie in India	1993	$50.00	
9916	Flight Time Barbie (black)	1990	$30.00	
9932	Western Fun	1990	$30.00	
9942	My First Barbie	1990	$20.00	
9943	My First Barbie (black)	1990	$20.00	
9944	My First Barbie (Hispanic)	1990	$25.00	
9953	Plus 3	1977	$85.00	Ben Franklin
9973	Gay Parisienne (blonde)	1991	$350.00	Nostalgic Porcelain
9973	Gay Parisienne (brunette)	1991	$135.00	Nostalgic Porcelain
9975	Super Size Bride	1977	$295.00	Department Store
9975	Super Size Bridal Barbie	1977	$295.00	Department Store
9988	Music Lovin'	1986	$50.00	
10039	Paint & Dazzle (blonde)	1993	$15.00	
10048	Special Expressions	1993	$20.00	Woolworth
10049	Special Expressions (black)	1993	$18.00	Woolworth
10050	Special Expressions (Hispanic)	1993	$18.00	Woolworth
10051	Shopping Fun Barbie	1993	$25.00	Meijer
10057	Paint & Dazzle (redhead)	1993	$15.00	
10058	Paint & Dazzle (black)	1993	$15.00	
10059	Paint & Dazzle (brunette)	1993	$15.00	
10123	Little Debbie Barbie, Series I	1993	$60.00	Little Debbie Snacks
10148	Opening Night	1993	$38.00	Classique
10149	City Style Barbie	1993	$35.00	Classique
10149	City Style Barbie	1995	$105.00	Hudson's Bay Company Canada
10201	Crystal Rhapsody (brunette, Disney)	1992	$350.00	Presidential Porcelain
10202	Golf Date	1993	$30.00	Target
10217	Back to School	1993	$25.00	Supermarket
10246	Gold Sensation	1993	$180.00	Porcelain
10247	Disney Fun Barbie	1992	$50.00	Disney
10255	Earring Magic (brunette)	1993	$30.00	
10257	Troll	1993	$25.00	
10280	Holiday Hostess	1993	$40.00	Supermarket
10292	Enchanted Princess	1993	$50.00	Sears
10293	Western Stampin'	1993	$25.00	
10309	Wacky Warehouse I	1993	$55.00	Kool-Aid
10339	Festiva	1993	$50.00	Wholesale Clubs
10390	Twinkle Lights	1993	$50.00	
10393	Fountain Mermaid	1993	$20.00	
10412	Live Action (ranch)	1971	$100.00	Montgomery Ward
10456	Malibu Barbie & Her Ten-Speeder Set	1974	$95.00	Montgomery Ward
10491	Spots 'n Dots	1993	$45.00	Toys "R" Us
10521	Twinkle Lights (black)	1993	$40.00	
10522	Fountain Mermaid (black)	1993	$20.00	
10539	Western Stampin' (black)	1993	$25.00	
10592	SuperStar Barbie	1993	$30.00	Wal-Mart
10608	Moonlight Magic	1993	$85.00	Toys "R" Us
10609	Moonlight Magic (black)	1993	$80.00	Toys "R" Us
10610	Angel Lights	1993	$50.00	
10655	Winter Princess	1993	$110.00	Winter Princess Collection

Number	Item	Year	Value	Specials
10658	Winter Royal	1993	$75.00	Wholesale Clubs
10682	School Spirit Barbie	1993	$25.00	Toys "R" Us
10683	School Spirit Barbie (black)	1993	$25.00	Toys "R" Us
10684	Golden Winter	1993	$50.00	JCPenney
10688	Police Officer	1993	$75.00	Toys "R" Us
10689	Police Officer (black)	1993	$75.00	Toys "R" Us
10711	SuperStar Barbie (black)	1993	$40.00	Wal-Mart
10723	Disney Weekend	1993	$50.00	Disney
10724	Disney Weekend Barbie & Ken Deluxe	1993	$75.00	Disney Europe
10776	Dress 'n Fun	1994	$15.00	
10803	Masquerade Ball (scented)	1993	$275.00	Bob Mackie
10824	Happy Holidays 1993	1993	$48.00	Happy Holidays Collection
10911	Happy Holidays 1993 (black)	1993	$32.00	Happy Holidays Collection
10927	Western Stampin' Barbie Deluxe Play Set	1993	$30.00	Wholesale Clubs
10928	Hollywood Hair Barbie Deluxe Play Set	1993	$25.00	Wholesale Clubs
10950	Royal Splendor	1993	$170.00	Presidential Porcelain
10953	Sun Jewel	1994	$10.00	
10963	Locket Surprise	1994	$20.00	
10965	Glitter Hair (blonde)	1994	$20.00	
10966	Glitter Hair (brunette)	1994	$20.00	
10968	Glitter Hair (redhead)	1994	$20.00	
10969	Royal Invitation	1993	$85.00	Spiegel
10994	Sparkling Splendor	1993	$50.00	Service Merchandise
10997	Naf Naf (Europe)	1993	$40.00	
11054	Romantic Bride (black)	1993	$35.00	
11074	Camp	1994	$25.00	
11079	Bedtime	1993	$15.00	
11099	Silken Flame Barbie (blonde)	1993	$330.00	Porcelain Disney
11102	Dress 'n Fun (Hispanic)	1994	$15.00	
11104	Dutch	1994	$29.00	Dolls of the World
11160	Doctor Barbie (with black baby)	1994	$30.00	
11180	Chinese	1994	$23.00	Dolls of the World
11181	Kenyan	1994	$23.00	Dolls of the World
11182	B Mine Barbie	1994	$22.00	Supermarket
11184	Bedtime (black)	1993	$15.00	
11212	My Size (black)	1993	$120.00	
11224	Locket Surprise (black)	1994	$20.00	
11276	Easter Fun	1994	$25.00	Supermarket
11285	Caboodles Barbie with child-sized Caboodles case	1993	$35.00	JCPenney
11294	My First Ballerina	1994	$15.00	
11294	My First Barbie	1994	$15.00	
11305	Silver Starlight	1994	$190.00	Porcelain
11332	Glitter Hair (black)	1994	$15.00	
11333	Birthday	1994	$30.00	
11334	Birthday (black)	1994	$30.00	
11340	My First Ballerina (black)	1994	$15.00	
11340	My First Barbie (black)	1994	$15.00	
11341	My First Barbie (Hispanic)	1994	$15.00	
11342	My First Ballerina (Asian)	1994	$15.00	
11342	My First Barbie (Asian)	1994	$20.00	
11397	Egyptian Queen	1994	$48.00	Great Eras Collection
11478	1850s Southern Belle	1994	$42.00	Great Eras Collection
11505	Swim 'n Dive	1993	$20.00	
11546	Kraft Treasures	1994	$50.00	Kraft

Number	Item	Year	Value	Specials
11552	Air Force Thunderbirds	1994	$20.00	Stars 'n Stripes
11553	Air Force Thunderbirds (black)	1994	$20.00	Stars 'n Stripes
11590	35th Anniversary Barbie (blonde with arched eyebrows)	1994	$23.00	Nostalgic
11590	35th Anniversary Barbie (blonde with curved eyebrows)	1994	$28.00	Nostalgic
11591	35th Anniversary (redhead)	1994	$425.00	Mattel Festival Doll
11591	35th Anniversary Barbie Keepsake Collection	1994	$77.00	Nostalgic
11609	Native American #2	1994	$32.00	Dolls of the World
11622	Evening Extravaganza	1994	$40.00	Classique
11623	Uptown Chic Barbie	1994	$37.00	Classique
11638	Evening Extravaganza (black)	1994	$44.00	Classique
11645	Tooth Fairy Barbie	1995	$20.00	Wal-Mart
11645	Tooth Fairy Barbie (blue)	1994	$22.00	Wal-Mart
11646	Country & Western Star	1994	$30.00	Wal-Mart
11650	Disney Fun II	1994	$45.00	Disney
11652	Silver Screen	1994	$100.00	FAO Schwarz
11689	Bicyclin'	1994	$25.00	Toys "R" Us
11734	Swim 'n Dive (black)	1993	$20.00	
11763	Wacky Warehouse II	1994	$45.00	Kool-Aid
11782	35th Anniversary Barbie (brunette with arched eyebrows)	1994	$24.00	Nostalgic
11782	35th Anniversary Barbie (brunette with curved eyebrows)	1994	$36.00	Nostalgic
11814	Doctor Barbie (black, with white baby)	1994	$38.00	
11817	Bicyclin' (black)	1994	$25.00	Toys "R" Us
11831	Camp (black)	1994	$20.00	
11875	Snow Princess (blonde)	1994	$60.00	Enchanted Seasons
11902	Dance 'n Twirl	1994	$50.00	
11902	Dream Dancing	1994	$16.00	
11921	Gymnast (brunette)	1994	$35.00	Mattel Festival Doll
12005	City Sophisticate	1994	$50.00	Service Merchandise
12009	Gold Jubilee	1994	$345.00	Jubilee Series
12043	Dolls of the World Limited Edition Set	1994	$49.00	Dolls of the World
12045	Scarlett (green velvet dress)	1994	$48.00	Hollywood Legends
12046	Queen of Hearts	1994	$155.00	Bob Mackie
12052	My Size Bride	1994	$100.00	
12053	My Size Bride (black)	1994	$100.00	
12077	Theatre Elegance	1994	$145.00	Spiegel
12096	Country & Western Star (black)	1994	$30.00	Wal-Mart
12097	Country & Western Star (Hispanic)	1994	$30.00	Wal-Mart
12123	Evergreen Princess (blonde)	1994	$42.00	Winter Princess Collection
12123	Evergreen Princess (redhead)	1994	$151.00	Disney/Winter Princess (Theme)
12126	Gymnast (blonde)	1994	$14.00	
12143	Dance 'n Twirl (black)	1994	$45.00	
12143	Dream Dancing (black)	1994	$16.00	
12143	Dress 'n Fun (black)	1994	$15.00	
12149	Astronaut	1994	$45.00	Toys "R" Us
12150	Astronaut (black)	1994	$45.00	Toys "R" Us
12152	Savvy Shopper	1994	$50.00	Bloomingdale's
12153	Gymnast (black)	1994	$14.00	
12155	Happy Holidays 1994	1994	$50.00	Happy Holidays Collection
12155	Happy Holidays 1994 (brunette)	1994	$550.00	Mattel Festival Doll
12156	Happy Holidays 1994 (black)	1994	$36.00	Happy Holidays Collection
12184	Bedtime Barbie with Bed	1994	$30.00	Wholesale Clubs

Number	Item	Year	Value	Specials
12191	Night Dazzle	1994	$55.00	JCPenney
12191	Night Dazzle (brunette)	1994	$185.00	Mattel Festival Doll
12192	Holiday Dreams	1994	$30.00	Supermarket
12243	Party Time	1994	$20.00	Toys "R" Us
12244	Party Time (Hispanic)	1994	$25.00	
12265	Sweet Magnolia (black)	1996	$18.00	Wal-Mart
12271	Country Star Western Horse	1994	$25.00	Wal-Mart
12290	Supertalk	1994	$40.00	
12322	Emerald Elegance	1994	$35.00	Toys "R" Us
12322	Emerald Elegance	1994	$33.00	Society Style
12323	Emerald Elegance (black)	1994	$35.00	Toys "R" Us
12323	Emerald Elegance (black)	1994	$33.00	Society Style
12379	Supertalk (black)	1994	$40.00	
12384	Season's Greetings	1994	$50.00	Wholesale Clubs
12410	Silver Sweetheart	1994	$40.00	Sears
12412	Polly Pockets	1994	$20.00	Hill's
12432	Happy Holidays Barbie	1994	$65.00	Happy Holidays European
12433	Ruffle Fun	1995	$12.00	
12434	Ruffle Fun (black)	1995	$12.00	
12435	Ruffle Fun (Hispanic)	1995	$12.00	
12443	Bubble Angel	1995	$20.00	
12444	Bubble Angel (black)	1995	$15.00	
12446	Tropical Splash	1995	$10.00	
12577	Pilgrim	1995	$25.00	American Stories Collection
12578	Colonial	1995	$25.00	American Stories Collection
12579	Victorian Elegance	1994	$35.00	Hallmark
12639	Cut and Style (blonde)	1995	$20.00	
12642	Cut and Style (black)	1995	$20.00	
12643	Cut and Style (brunette)	1995	$20.00	
12644	Cut and Style (redhead)	1995	$20.00	
12670	35th Anniversary Festival Barbie	1994	$200.00	Barbie Festival
12675	Valentine Barbie	1995	$22.00	Target
12680	Pioneer	1995	$25.00	American Stories Collection
12696	Slumber Party	1995	$15.00	
12697	Slumber Party (black)	1995	$15.00	
12698	German (reissue)	1995	$22.00	Dolls of the World
12699	Native American #3	1995	$25.00	Dolls of the World
12700	Polynesian	1995	$25.00	Dolls of the World
12701	Barbie as Dorothy, 2nd Edition	1996	$75.00	Wizard of Oz
12701	Dorothy (Wizard of Oz)	1995	$72.00	Hollywood Legends
12749	Shopping Spree Barbie #1	1994	$38.00	FAO Schwarz
12749	Shopping Spree Barbie #2	1994	$35.00	FAO Schwarz
12791	Medieval Lady	1995	$36.00	Great Eras Collection
12792	Elizabethan Queen	1995	$40.00	Great Eras Collection
12793	Easter Party	1995	$20.00	Supermarket
12815	Scarlett (red dress)	1994	$60.00	Hollywood Legends
12825	Evening Pearl	1996	$140.00	Presidential Porcelain
12903	Doctor Barbie (brunette)	1994	$100.00	Mattel Festival Doll
12905	Snow Princess (brunette)	1994	$595.00	Mattel Festival Doll
12953	Star Lily Bride (porcelain)	1994	$150.00	Wedding Flower Collection
12954	Birthday	1995	$25.00	
12954	Happy Birthday	1994	$15.00	
12955	Birthday (black)	1995	$25.00	
12957	Disney Fun Barbie	1995	$55.00	Disney Europe
12957	Disney Weekend Barbie	1992	$60.00	Disney Europe

Number	Item	Year	Value	Specials
12989	Spring Bouquet	1995	$45.00	Enchanted Seasons
12997	Scarlett (BBQ dress)	1995	$47.00	Hollywood Legends
12998	Irish (reissue)	1995	$34.00	Dolls of the World
12999	Midnight Gala	1995	$34.00	Classique
13016	Barbie as Rapunzel	1995	$24.00	Children's Collector Series
13051	Butterfly Princess	1995	$25.00	
13052	Butterfly Princess (black)	1995	$25.00	
13064	My First Princess	1995	$15.00	
13065	My First Princess (black)	1995	$15.00	
13066	My First Princess (Hispanic)	1995	$15.00	
13067	My First Princess (Asian)	1995	$15.00	
13083	Dance Moves	1995	$15.00	
13086	Dance Moves (black)	1995	$15.00	
13132	Sparkle Beach	1996	$10.00	
13168	Christian Dior I	1995	$60.00	Designer Collection
13173	Evergreen Princess (redhead)	1994	$295.00	Mattel Festival Doll
13179	Sing & Dance	1995	$20.00	
13181	Barbie & Champion	1995	$45.00	Hill's
13194	Teacher (brunette)	1996	$25.00	Supermarket
13195	Teacher (black, no panties)	1995	$55.00	
13199	Baywatch	1995	$20.00	
13238	Butterfly Princess (Hispanic)	1995	$25.00	
13239	POG Barbie	1995	$18.00	Toys "R" Us Canada
13239	POG Fun	1995	$20.00	Toys "R" Us
13253	Birthday (Hispanic)	1995	$25.00	
13254	Scarlett (New Orleans dress)	1995	$47.00	Hollywood Legends
13255	Sapphire Dreams	1995	$50.00	Toys "R" Us
13257	Circus Star	1995	$70.00	FAO Schwarz
13258	Baywatch (black)	1995	$20.00	
13472	Fire Fighter (black)	1995	$40.00	Toys "R" Us
13478	Western Stampin' Barbie with Western Star Horse (black)	1995	$45.00	Toys "R" Us
13488	Sunflower Barbie	1995	$20.00	Toys "R" Us
13511	Hot Skatin'	1995	$20.00	
13512	Hot Skatin' (black)	1995	$18.00	
13516	Winter Sports	1995	$35.00	JCPenney
13516	Winter Sports Barbie	1995	$30.00	Toys "R" Us
13533	Disney Fun III	1995	$35.00	Disney
13534	Solo in the Spotlight (blonde)	1995	$25.00	Nostalgic Vinyl Series
13545	Happy Holidays Barbie	1995	$40.00	Happy Holidays International
13553	Fire Fighter	1995	$50.00	Toys "R" Us
13554	Purple Passion (black)	1995	$30.00	Toys "R" Us
13555	Purple Passion	1995	$35.00	Toys "R" Us
13558	International Pen Friend Barbie	1995	$18.00	Toys "R" Us
13558	Pen Friend	1996	$20.00	Toys "R" Us
13598	Peppermint Princess	1995	$36.00	Winter Princess Collection
13611	Pretty Dreams, 18"	1995	$25.00	
13611	Sweet Dreams	1995	$20.00	
13612	Ruby Romance	1995	$48.00	Service Merchandise
13613	Fifties Fun	1996	$35.00	Wholesale Clubs
13613	Winter's Eve	1995	$30.00	Wholesale Clubs
13614	Country Bride	1995	$20.00	Wal-Mart
13615	Country Bride (black)	1995	$20.00	Wal-Mart
13616	Country Bride (Hispanic)	1995	$20.00	Wal-Mart
13630	Pretty Dreams, 18", soft body (black)	1995	$20.00	

Number	Item	Year	Value	Specials
13630	Sweet Dreams (black)	1995	$20.00	
13675	Busy Gal	1995	$42.00	Nostalgic Vinyl Series
13676	Maria (Sound of Music)	1995	$36.00	Hollywood Legends
13741	Schooltime Fun Barbie	1995	$15.00	Supermarket
13767	My Size Princess	1995	$100.00	
13768	My Size Princess (black)	1995	$100.00	
13820	Solo in the Spotlight (brunette)	1995	$25.00	Nostalgic Vinyl Series
13911	Ribbons and Roses	1995	$35.00	Sears
13912	International Travel Barbie #2	1995	$50.00	Wessco
13912	International Travel I	1995	$40.00	Wessco
13914	Teacher (painted panties)	1996	$25.00	
13915	Teacher (black, painted panties)	1995	$25.00	
13938	Sing & Dance (black)	1995	$20.00	
13939	Dolls of the World Limited Edition Set	1995	$45.00	Dolls of the World
13940	Sea Pearl Mermaid	1995	$20.00	Hill's
13966	Caroling Fun	1995	$20.00	Supermarket
14009	Shopping Chic	1995	$75.00	Spiegel
14010	Governor's Ball Barbie	1996	$90.00	Hudson's Bay Company Canada
14010	Royal Enchantment	1995	$50.00	JCPenney
14024	Happy New Year	1995	$45.00	
14030	Flying Hero	1996	$15.00	
14056	Goddess of the Sun	1995	$95.00	Bob Mackie
14061	Jewel Splendor	1995	$90.00	FAO Schwarz
14070	Evening Glamour	1995	$75.00	Glamour Collection
14070	Starlight Waltz	1995	$35.00	Ballroom Beauties
14105	Moon Goddess	1996	$99.00	Bob Mackie
14106	Holiday Memories	1995	$30.00	Hallmark
14108	My Size Bride Barbie (brunette)	1995	$130.00	Toys "R" Us
14110	Steppin' Out	1995	$22.00	Target
14123	Happy Holidays 1995	1995	$28.00	Happy Holidays Collection
14124	Happy Holidays 1995 (black)	1995	$24.00	Happy Holidays Collection
14124	Happy Holidays with Ornament	1995	$80.00	JCPenney
14163	Japanese (reissue)	1996	$23.00	Dolls of the World
14274	Party Time (black)	1994	$20.00	Toys "R" Us
14278	Flying Hero (black)	1996	$20.00	
14308	Super Talk! Barbie	1995	$30.00	Toys "R" Us
14309	Doctor Barbie (white with 3 babies)	1995	$25.00	Toys "R" Us
14311	Holiday Jewel	1995	$100.00	Holiday Porcelain Series
14315	Doctor Barbie (black)	1995	$25.00	Toys "R" Us
14316	Super Talk! Barbie (black)	1995	$30.00	Toys "R" Us
14320	Songbird	1996	$25.00	
14449	Mexican (reissue)	1996	$23.00	Dolls of the World
14450	Norwegian #1	1996	$37.00	Dolls of the World
14450	Norwegian #2	1996	$25.00	Dolls of the World
14451	Indian	1996	$25.00	Dolls of the World
14452	Donna Karan NY (brunette)	1995	$85.00	Bloomingdale's
14457	Foam 'n Color (pink)	1996	$15.00	
14457	Shampoo Magic (pink)	1996	$15.00	
14473	Pretty Hearts	1996	$10.00	
14474	Pretty Hearts (black)	1996	$10.00	
14475	Pretty Hearts (Hispanic)	1996	$10.00	
14476	Barbie Style	1997	$20.00	
14479	Mattel Golden Anniversary	1995	$170.00	Porcelain
14486	Songbird (black)	1996	$25.00	
14541	Romantic Rose Bride (porcelain)	1996	$140.00	Wedding Flower Collection

Number	Item	Year	Value	Specials
14545	Donna Karan NY (blonde)	1995	$85.00	Bloomingdale's
14586	Jewel Hair Mermaid	1996	$15.00	
14587	Jewel Hair Mermaid (black)	1996	$15.00	
14592	My First Tea Party	1997	$12.00	
14593	My First Tea Party (black)	1997	$12.00	
14603	Pet Doctor	1996	$18.00	
14612	Civil War Nurse	1996	$25.00	American Stories Collection
14613	Easter Basket	1996	$18.00	Supermarket
14615	Chuck E Cheese	1996	$30.00	Chuck E Cheese Pizza
14616	Little Debbie Barbie, Series II (bent arms)	1996	$30.00	Little Debbie Snacks
14616	Little Debbie Barbie, Series II (straight arms)	1996	$25.00	Little Debbie Snacks
14617	Russell Stover Easter (checkered)	1996	$25.00	Russell Stover
14644	Sweet Valentine	1995	$22.00	
14644	Valentine Sweetheart	1996	$15.00	Supermarket
14649	Happy Birthday	1996	$20.00	
14662	Happy Birthday (black)	1996	$20.00	
14663	Happy Birthday (Hispanic)	1996	$20.00	
14664	Statue of Liberty	1996	$100.00	FAO Schwarz
14715	American Indian	1996	$25.00	American Stories Collection
14756	Pioneer #2	1996	$25.00	American Stories Collection
14875	My First Tea Party (Hispanic)	1997	$12.00	
14876	My First Tea Party (Asian)	1997	$12.00	
14879	Horse Lovin'	1996	$20.00	
14880	Sweet Valentine	1996	$35.00	Hallmark
14900	Victorian Lady	1996	$30.00	Great Eras Collection
14901	Glinda the Good Witch	1996	$68.00	Hollywood Legends
14954	Starlight Waltz (brunette, Disney)	1995	$75.00	Ballroom Beauties
14956	Russell Stover Easter (print)	1996	$25.00	Russell Stover
14960	Barbie as Little Bo Peep	1996	$55.00	Children's Collector Series
14992	Enchanted Evening (blonde)	1996	$25.00	Nostalgic Vinyl Series
15003	Graduation Class of '96	1996	$20.00	Supermarket
15005	Grecian Goddess	1996	$34.00	Great Eras Collection
15059	Show Parade Barbie with Star Stampin' Horse	1997	$50.00	
15061	Radiant 'n Rose (black)	1996	$55.00	Toys "R" Us
15086	Twirling Ballerina	1996	$15.00	
15087	Twirling Ballerina (black)	1996	$15.00	
15098	Foam 'n Color (yellow)	1996	$15.00	
15098	Shampoo Magic (yellow)	1996	$15.00	
15099	Foam 'n Color (blue)	1996	$15.00	
15121	Got Milk	1996	$20.00	Toys "R" Us
15122	Got Milk (black)	1996	$20.00	Toys "R" Us
15123	Olympic Gymnast (blonde)	1996	$20.00	
15124	Olympic Gymnast (black)	1996	$20.00	
15125	Olympic Gymnast (redhead)	1996	$35.00	Toys "R" Us
15133	Sweet Daisy Barbie	1996	$30.00	Military
15136	Crystal Splendor	1996	$25.00	Toys "R" Us
15137	Crystal Splendor (black)	1996	$25.00	Toys "R" Us
15139	Color 'n Wash My Hair Barbie	1997	$50.00	Avon
15140	Radiant 'n Rose	1996	$55.00	Toys "R" Us
15141	Pink Ice	1996	$100.00	Toys "R" Us
15172	Valentine Barbie	1996	$20.00	Target
15184	International Travel Barbie #1	1996	$45.00	Wessco
15186	Carnival Cruise Lines	1997	$30.00	Wessco
15201	Spring Blossom	1996	$25.00	Avon
15202	Spring Blossom (black)	1996	$25.00	Avon

Number	Item	Year	Value	Specials
15204	Autumn Glory	1996	$48.00	Enchanted Seasons
15280	Poodle Parade	1996	$42.00	Nostalgic
15283	Dolls of the World Limited Edition Set	1996	$40.00	Dolls of the World
15301	School Spirit Barbie	1996	$16.00	Supermarket
15302	Pet Doctor (black)	1996	$18.00	
15303	Ghanian	1996	$24.00	Dolls of the World
15304	Native American #4	1996	$35.00	Dolls of the World
15334	Winter Fantasy Barbie (blonde)	1996	$30.00	Sam's Club
15407	Enchanted Evening (brunette)	1996	$25.00	Nostalgic Vinyl Series
15428	Ocean Friends	1996	$20.00	
15429	Ocean Friends (black)	1996	$20.00	
15441	Arizona Jean Company I	1996	$25.00	JCPenney
15461	Starlight Dance	1996	$32.00	Classique
15473	In-Line Skating	1996	$25.00	
15497	My Fair Lady #2 (ascot)	1996	$100.00	Hollywood Legends
15498	My Fair Lady #3 (flower girl)	1996	$65.00	Hollywood Legends
15500	My Fair Lady #4 (ball/evening gown)	1996	$100.00	Hollywood Legends
15501	My Fair Lady #1 (pink organza gown)	1996	$75.00	Hollywood Legends
15510	Skating Star	1996	$15.00	Wal-Mart
15511	Skating Star (Hispanic)	1996	$15.00	Wal-Mart
15513	West End Barbie	1996	$45.00	Hamley's (England)
15519	Diamond Dazzle	1997	$100.00	Bob Mackie Jewel Essence
15520	Ruby Radiance	1997	$80.00	Bob Mackie Jewel Essence
15521	Emerald Embers	1997	$88.00	Bob Mackie Jewel Essence
15522	Amethyst Aura	1997	$90.00	Bob Mackie Jewel Essence
15523	Sapphire Splendor	1997	$80.00	Bob Mackie Jewel Essence
15528	Portrait in Taffeta	1996	$55.00	Couture Collection
15530	Winter Fantasy Barbie (brunette)	1996	$35.00	Sam's Club
15531	Sea Princess	1996	$30.00	Service Merchandise
15533	Evening Flame	1996	$30.00	Sears
15570	Winter Renaissance (Evening Elegance Series)	1996	$40.00	JCPenney
15571	Winter Velvet	1996	$38.00	Avon
15581	Holiday Season	1996	$16.00	Supermarket
15583	Holiday Season (black)	1996	$16.00	Supermarket
15587	Winter Velvet (black)	1996	$38.00	Avon
15591	Summer Sophisticate	1996	$43.00	Spiegel
15612	City Style Barbie	1996	$20.00	Target
15620	Wacky Warehouse III	1996	$35.00	Kool-Aid
15621	Yuletide Romance	1996	$30.00	Hallmark
15622	Sweet Magnolia	1996	$18.00	Wal-Mart
15646	Happy Holidays 1996	1996	$28.00	Happy Holidays Collection
15647	Happy Holidays 1996 (black)	1996	$28.00	Happy Holidays Collection
15648	Horse Lovin' SE	1997	$10.00	
15649	My Size Bride Barbie (redhead)	1996	$130.00	Toys "R" Us
15649	My Size (redhead)	1996	$140.00	QVC
15654	Sweet Magnolia (Hispanic)	1996	$18.00	Wal-Mart
15683	Summer Splendor	1997	$39.00	Enchanted Seasons
15684	Teddy Fun	1996	$18.00	Hill's
15685	Midnight Waltz (blonde)	1996	$35.00	Ballroom Beauties
15758	Andalucia	1996	$40.00	
15760	Holiday Caroler	1996	$70.00	Holiday Porcelain Series
15762	Soda Fountain Sweetheart	1996	$88.00	Coca-Cola Fashion Classic Series
15801	Shopping Chic (black)	1996	$50.00	Spiegel
15803	Doctor Barbie	1996	$30.00	Toys "R" Us
15804	Doctor Barbie (black)	1996	$30.00	Toys "R" Us

Number	Item	Year	Value	Specials
15814	Antique Rose	1996	$190.00	FAO Schwarz
15816	Happy Holidays Barbie	1996	$32.00	Happy Holidays International
15819	Starlight Dance (black)	1996	$32.00	Classique
15820	1950s Barbie	1996	$30.00	Sam's Club/Wholesale Club
15821	Super Gymnast	1996	$20.00	K•B Toys
15826	Jewel Princess (blonde)	1996	$25.00	Winter Princess Collection
15831	Special Occasion Barbie I	1996	$65.00	Mercantile Stores
15846	Barbie as Empress Sissy	1996	$55.00	Royal House of Europe
15909	My Size Dancing	1996	$105.00	
15910	My Size Dancing (black)	1996	$105.00	
15911	Angel Princess	1997	$24.00	
15912	Angel Princess (black)	1997	$24.00	
15948	Escada	1996	$48.00	Designer Collection
15950	Ralph Lauren Barbie	1997	$60.00	Bloomingdale's
15952	Silver Royale	1996	$75.00	Wholesale Clubs
15987	Rose Bride	1996	$35.00	Wholesale Clubs
15998	Birthday	1997	$20.00	
15999	Birthday (black)	1997	$20.00	
16000	Birthday (Hispanic)	1997	$20.00	
16005	Jewelry Fun My First Barbie	1997	$10.00	
16006	Jewelry Fun My First Barbie (black)	1997	$10.00	
16007	Jewelry Fun My First Barbie (Hispanic)	1997	$10.00	
16008	Jewelry Fun My First Barbie (Asian)	1997	$10.00	
16013	Christian Dior II	1997	$68.00	Designer Collection
16059	Valentine Romance Barbie	1997	$18.00	Target
16063	Flower Fun	1997	$6.00	
16064	Flower Fun (black)	1997	$6.00	
16065	Flower Fun (Hispanic)	1997	$6.00	
16079	Barbie Millicent Roberts Matinee Today	1996	$40.00	Barbie Millicent Roberts
16091	Pink Splendor	1996	$310.00	Ultra Limited Edition
16093	Happy New Year	1997	$44.00	
16131	Bubbling Mermaid	1997	$15.00	
16132	Bubbling Mermaid (black)	1997	$15.00	
16158	International Travel II	1996	$50.00	Wessco
16169	Splash 'n Color	1996	$6.00	
16172	Splash 'n Color (Hispanic)	1997	$6.00	
16174	Splash 'n Color (black)	1997	$6.00	
16210	Teacher (Hispanic)	1996	$25.00	
16211	Calvin Klein Jeans Barbie	1996	$55.00	Bloomingdale's
16211	Calvin Klein Jeans Barbie	1996	$70.00	Hudson's Bay Company Canada
16289	City Shopper	1996	$40.00	Macy's
16290	Barbie at Bloomingdale's	1996	$35.00	Bloomingdale's
16311	Valentine Fun Barbie	1997	$12.00	Supermarket
16313	Valentine Fun Barbie (black)	1997	$12.00	Supermarket
16315	Easter Barbie	1997	$15.00	Supermarket
16317	Easter Barbie (black)	1997	$15.00	Supermarket
16351	Russell Stover Candies Special Edition Barbie (floral)	1997	$25.00	Russell Stover
16352	Little Debbie Barbie Series III	1998	$22.00	Little Debbie Snacks
16353	Winter Rhapsody (blonde)	1997	$35.00	Avon
16354	Winter Rhapsody (black)	1997	$35.00	Avon
16378	Rapunzel	1997	$25.00	Fairy Tales
16449	Gap Barbie	1996	$60.00	Gap Stores
16450	Gap Barbie (black)	1996	$60.00	Gap Stores
16458	Pet Doctor (brunette)	1996	$30.00	Target

Number	Item	Year	Value	Specials
16485	35th Anniversary Target	1997	$25.00	Target
16485	Target 35th Anniversary Barbie	1997	$27.00	Target
16487	Graduation Class of '97	1997	$15.00	Supermarket
16489	Graduation Barbie Class of '97 (black)	1997	$15.00	Supermarket
16491	Birthday Surprise	1997	$15.00	Supermarket
16495	Arctic	1996	$25.00	Dolls of the World
16498	Grand Premier	1997	$79.00	Barbie Collector's Club
16499	French	1997	$25.00	Dolls of the World
16500	Russian (reissue)	1997	$17.00	Dolls of the World
16525	Walt Disney World 25th Anniversary	1996	$35.00	Disney
16536	Sentimental Valentine	1997	$30.00	Hallmark
16691	Skating Star (black)	1996	$15.00	Wal-Mart
16692	Sapphire Sophisticate	1997	$30.00	Toys "R" Us
16693	Sapphire Sophisticate (black)	1997	$20.00	Toys "R" Us
16705	Midnight Waltz (brunette)	1996	$52.00	Ballroom Beauties
16707	French Lady	1997	$28.00	Great Eras Collection
16708	Chinese Empress Barbie	1997	$32.00	Great Eras Collection
16708	Chinese Empress Barbie	1997	$88.00	Hong Kong Commemorative Edition
16746	Spring Petals (blonde)	1997	$30.00	Avon
16754	Puerto Rican	1997	$18.00	Dolls of the World
16871	Spring Petals (black)	1997	$30.00	Avon
16872	Spring Petals (brunette)	1997	$30.00	Avon
16873	Winter Rhapsody (brunette)	1997	$35.00	Avon
16900	Barbie as Cinderella	1996	$24.00	Children's Collector Series
16962	Blushing Orchid Bride (porcelain)	1997	$125.00	Wedding Flower Collection
17031	In The Limelight (black)	1997	$140.00	Byron Lars Runway Collection
17032	Blossom Beauty	1997	$20.00	
17033	Blossom Beauty (black)	1997	$20.00	
17040	Bill Blass	1997	$80.00	Designer Collection
17047	Hula Hair	1997	$18.00	
17048	Hula Hair (black)	1997	$18.00	
17056	Barbie as the Sugar Plum Fairy from *The Nutcracker*	1997	$29.00	Classic Ballet Series
17058	Disney Fun IV	1997	$35.00	Disney
17089	Russell Stover Candies Special Edition Barbie (black)	1997	$25.00	Russell Stover
17091	Russell Stover Candies Special Edition Barbie (pink)	1997	$25.00	Russell Stover
17094	Holiday Traditions	1997	$45.00	Hallmark
17099	Back to School	1997	$10.00	Supermarket
17100	Back to School (black)	1997	$10.00	Supermarket
17116	Barbie & Ginger	1997	$35.00	
17119	Wedding Day (blonde)	1997	$25.00	Nostalgic Vinyl Series
17120	Wedding Day (redhead)	1997	$30.00	Nostalgic Vinyl Series
17125	Blue Starlight	1997	$35.00	Sears
17136	Romantic Interlude	1997	$34.00	Classique
17137	Romantic Interlude (black)	1997	$36.00	Classique
17153	Dream Bride Barbie	1997	$35.00	Service Merchandise
17155	Marilyn Monroe (white dress)	1997	$50.00	Hollywood Legends
17191	University of Arkansas (black)	1998	$10.00	University Barbie
17191	University of Arkansas	1997	$10.00	University Barbie
17192	University of Georgia	1997	$10.00	University Barbie
17193	University of Nebraska	1997	$10.00	University Barbie
17194	North Carolina State	1997	$10.00	University Barbie
17195	University of Wisconsin	1997	$10.00	University Barbie
17235	Evening Majesty	1997	$40.00	JCPenney

Number	Item	Year	Value	Specials
17236	Holiday Treats Barbie	1997	$15.00	Supermarket
17237	City Style Barbie	1997	$15.00	Target
17240	Paleontologist	1997	$20.00	Toys "R" Us
17241	Paleontologist (black)	1997	$20.00	Toys "R" Us
17244	Skating Dream Barbie	1997	$20.00	Wal-Mart
17244	Skating Star	1997	$10.00	Wal-Mart
17245	35th Anniversary Wal-Mart	1997	$25.00	Wal-Mart
17246	Tooth Fairy Barbie	1998	$12.00	Wal-Mart
17247	Share a Smile Barbie	1997	$25.00	Toys "R" Us
17248	101 Dalmatians	1997	$25.00	Toys "R" Us
17249	Winter Fantasy II (blonde)	1997	$25.00	Wholesale Clubs
17251	Sparkle Beauty	1997	$30.00	Wholesale Club (BJ)
17252	Sixties Fun Barbie (blonde)	1997	$25.00	Wholesale Clubs
17255	Dentist (blonde)	1997	$20.00	
17298	Barbie at FAO	1997	$30.00	FAO Schwarz
17312	Patriot	1997	$25.00	American Stories Collection
17313	American Indian II	1997	$28.00	American Stories Collection
17317	Working Out Barbie	1997	$15.00	
17320	Birthday Surprise Barbie (black)	1997	$15.00	Supermarket
17341	After the Walk	1997	$48.00	Coca-Cola Fashion Classic Series
17350	Talk With Me	1997	$35.00	
17369	Barbie & Ginger (black)	1997	$35.00	
17370	Talk With Me (black)	1997	$30.00	
17382	Fashion Luncheon	1997	$49.00	Nostalgic Vinyl Series
17398	University of Michigan	1997	$10.00	University Barbie
17441	Winner's Circle	1997	$55.00	Spiegel
17443	Emerald Enchantment	1997	$55.00	Toys "R" Us
17451	Marilyn Monroe (pink dress)	1997	$55.00	Hollywood Legends
17452	Marilyn Monroe (red dress)	1997	$60.00	Hollywood Legends
17478	Dentist (black)	1997	$20.00	
17487	Cool Shoppin'	1997	$20.00	
17488	Cool Shoppin' (black)	1997	$20.00	
17554	University of Tennessee	1997	$10.00	University Barbie
17556	Lily	1997	$125.00	FAO Schwarz
17567	Barbie Millicent Roberts Perfectly Suited	1997	$35.00	Barbie Millicent Roberts
17572	Serenade in Satin	1997	$90.00	Couture Collection
17590	Easy Chic Barbie	1996	$750.00	Harrods England
17601	101 Dalmatians (black)	1997	$25.00	Toys "R" Us
17603	Anne Klein Barbie	1997	$40.00	Macy's
17608	35th Anniversary Target (black)	1997	$25.00	Target
17608	Target 35th Anniversary Barbie (black)	1997	$27.00	Target
17616	35th Anniversary Wal-Mart (black)	1997	$25.00	Wal-Mart
17618	Holiday Treats Barbie (black)	1997	$15.00	Supermarket
17641	Billions of Dreams	1997	$199.00	Ultra Limited Edition
17642	Sweet Moments	1997	$25.00	Wholesale Clubs
17649	Valentine Barbie	1998	$12.00	Supermarket
17650	Valentine Barbie (black)	1998	$12.00	Supermarket
17651	Easter Style Barbie	1998	$12.00	Supermarket
17652	Easter Style Barbie (black)	1998	$12.00	Supermarket
17666	Winter Fantasy (brunette)	1997	$25.00	Wholesale Clubs
17690	Mrs. P.F.E. Albee	1997	$75.00	Avon
17692	Harley-Davidson Barbie #1	1997	$450.00	Toys "R" Us
17693	Sixties Fun Barbie (redhead)	1997	$25.00	Wholesale Clubs
17695	Ladybug Fun	1997	$18.00	Ames
17698	Penn State University	1997	$10.00	University Barbie

Number	Item	Year	Value	Specials
17699	Auburn University	1997	$10.00	University Barbie
17700	University of Florida	1997	$10.00	University Barbie
17707	Dentist (brunette)	1997	$20.00	
17714	Movin' Groovin'	1997	$15.00	
17747	Winter Fantasy II (black)	1997	$25.00	Wholesale Clubs
17749	Georgetown University	1997	$10.00	University Barbie
17750	Duke University	1997	$10.00	University Barbie
17751	University of Arizona	1997	$10.00	University Barbie
17752	Oklahoma State University	1997	$10.00	University Barbie
17753	Clemson University	1997	$10.00	University Barbie
17754	University of Virginia	1997	$10.00	University Barbie
17755	University of Illinois	1997	$10.00	University Barbie
17757	George Washington Barbie	1997	$50.00	FAO Schwarz
17763	Moonlight Waltz	1997	$48.00	Ballroom Beauties
17780	Midnight Princess Barbie (blonde)	1997	$25.00	Winter Princess Collection
17782	Country Rose	1997	$42.00	Grand Ole Opry
17783	Water Lily (Monet)	1997	$90.00	Artist Series
17792	University of Texas	1997	$10.00	University Barbie
17794	University of Miami	1997	$10.00	University Barbie
17801	My Size Rapunzel	1997	$100.00	
17802	My Size Rapunzel (black)	1997	$100.00	
17830	Graduation Class of '98	1998	$10.00	Supermarket
17831	Graduation Barbie Class of '98 (black)	1998	$10.00	Supermarket
17832	Happy Holidays 1997 (blonde)	1997	$64.00	Happy Holidays Collection
17833	Happy Holidays 1997 (black)	1997	$20.00	Happy Holidays Collection
17857	Hollywood Nails Barbie	1999	$12.00	
17860	Tangerine Twist	1997	$35.00	Fashion Savvy Collection
17864	Country Rose	1997	$50.00	Sam's Club/Wholesale Club
17864	Rising Star Barbie	1998	$38.00	Grand Ole Opry
17933	Dream Bride Barbie (black)	1997	$25.00	Service Merchandise
17934	Madame Du Barbie	1997	$225.00	Bob Mackie
17971	Pretty Choices Barbie (blonde)	1997	$20.00	Wal-Mart
18012	Holiday Treats Fiesta Barbie (Hispanic)	1997	$15.00	Supermarket
18018	Pretty Choices Barbie (black)	1997	$20.00	Wal-Mart
18019	Pretty Choices Barbie (brunette)	1997	$20.00	Wal-Mart
18020	Arizona Jean Company II	1997	$25.00	JCPenney
18091	Fair Valentine Barbie	1998	$30.00	Hallmark
18141	Ponytails	1997	$20.00	Military
18142	Ponytails (black)	1997	$20.00	Military
18167	Hula-Hoop	1997	$16.00	Hill's
18199	Russell Stover Holiday	1997	$25.00	Russell Stover
18216	Special Occasion Barbie II	1997	$45.00	Mercantile Stores
18217	Special Occasion Barbie II (black)	1997	$45.00	Mercantile Stores
18218	Chic	1999	$5.00	K•B Toys
18230	Shopping Time Barbie	1997	$15.00	Wal-Mart
18231	Shopping Time Barbie (black)	1997	$15.00	Wal-Mart
18292	Birthday (brunette)	1998	$20.00	
18306	Valentine Date Barbie	1998	$18.00	Target
18326	Holiday Ball	1997	$65.00	Holiday Porcelain Series
18341	Georgetown University (black)	1997	$10.00	University Barbie
18342	University of Michigan (black)	1997	$10.00	University Barbie
18343	University of Florida (black)	1997	$10.00	University Barbie
18344	Penn State University (black)	1997	$10.00	University Barbie
18345	University of Georgia (black)	1997	$10.00	University Barbie
18346	Auburn University (black)	1997	$9.00	University Barbie

Number	Item	Year	Value	Specials
18347	University of Tennessee (black)	1997	$10.00	University Barbie
18348	University of Miami (black)	1997	$10.00	University Barbie
18349	Clemson University (black)	1997	$9.00	University Barbie
18350	Children's Day Barbie	1998	$15.00	K•B Toys
18350	Children's Day Barbie	1998	$15.00	Children's Day
18351	Birthday Party Barbie	1998	$12.00	Supermarket
18352	Birthday Party Barbie (black)	1998	$12.00	Supermarket
18368	Pilot Barbie	1998	$25.00	Toys "R" Us
18404	Princess	1998	$10.00	
18405	Princess (black)	1998	$10.00	
18406	Princess (Hispanic)	1998	$10.00	
18407	Princess (Asian)	1998	$10.00	
18421	Twirlin' Make-Up (blonde)	1998	$10.00	
18448	Silken Flame Barbie (brunette)	1998	$24.00	Nostalgic
18449	Silken Flame Barbie (blonde)	1998	$24.00	Nostalgic
18456	Winter Dazzle Barbie	1997	$30.00	General Mills
18457	Winter Dazzle Barbie (black)	1997	$30.00	General Mills
18486	Midnight Princess Barbie (brunette)	1997	$86.00	W.D.W. Teddy Bear & Doll Con.
18487	Schooltime Fun Barbie	1998	$10.00	Supermarket
18488	Schooltime Fun (black)	1998	$10.00	Supermarket
18501	Olympic Skater	1997	$15.00	
18503	Olympic Skater (black)	1997	$10.00	
18506	March of Dimes Walk America Barbie	1998	$20.00	K-Mart
18507	March of Dimes Walk America Barbie (black)	1998	$20.00	K-Mart
18509	Barbie as the Swan Queen from *Swan Lake*	1997	$22.00	Classic Ballet Series
18510	Barbie as the Swan Queen from *Swan Lake* (black)	1997	$22.00	Classic Ballet Series
18511	Oreo Barbie	1997	$20.00	Toys "R" Us
18558	Native American #5 (box says fourth)	1998	$20.00	Dolls of the World/Toys "R" Us
18559	Chilean	1997	$25.00	Dolls of the World
18560	Polish	1997	$25.00	Dolls of the World
18561	Thai	1998	$18.00	Dolls of the World
18576	Pearl Beach	1997	$10.00	
18586	Barbie as Sleeping Beauty	1998	$25.00	Children's Collector Series
18594	Fantasy Ball Barbie	1997	$20.00	K•B Toys
18594	Glamour Barbie	1997	$15.00	K•B Toys
18595	Fantasy Ball Barbie (black)	1997	$20.00	K•B Toys
18595	Glamour Barbie (black)	1997	$15.00	K•B Toys
18608	Sweetheart (blonde)	1998	$5.00	
18609	Sweetheart (black)	1998	$5.00	
18610	Sweetheart (brunette)	1998	$5.00	
18630	Promenade in the Park Barbie	1998	$40.00	Great Fashions of the 20th Century
18651	Holiday Voyage Barbie	1998	$40.00	Hallmark
18656	Spring Tea Party Barbie (blonde)	1998	$30.00	Avon
18656	Spring Tea Party Barbie (brunette)	1998	$30.00	Avon
18657	Spring Tea Party Barbie (black)	1998	$30.00	Avon
18667	Illusion Barbie	1997	$80.00	Masquerade Gala
18667	Masquerade Ball	1997	$235.00	Bob Mackie
18700	Sweetheart (redhead)	1998	$5.00	
18888	Bead Blast (blonde)	1997	$15.00	
18889	Bead Blast (black)	1997	$15.00	
18890	Bead Blast (redhead)	1997	$15.00	
18891	Bead Blast (brunette)	1997	$15.00	
18892	Café Society Barbie	1998	$68.00	Barbie Collector's Club
18894	Harpist Angel Barbie	1998	$45.00	Angels of Music
18895	I'm a Toys "R" Us Kid (50th Anniversary)	1998	$30.00	Toys "R" Us

Number	Item	Year	Value	Specials
18909	Festive Season Barbie	1998	$14.00	Supermarket
18910	Festive Season Barbie (black)	1998	$14.00	Supermarket
18914	Teacher (no panties)	1995	$60.00	
18941	Twist 'n Turn Barbie Smasheroo (brunette)	1998	$50.00	Collectors' Request
18952	City Style Barbie	1998	$16.00	Target
18952	City Style Barbie	1999	$14.00	Target
18970	Disney Fun Barbie	1998	$27.00	Disney
18970	Safari	1998	$30.00	Disney
18979	Charity Ball Barbie	1998	$30.00	Toys "R" Us
18980	Flip 'n Dive Barbie	1998	$20.00	
19016	Dinner Date (blonde)	1998	$15.00	Wholesale Clubs
19037	Dinner Date (redhead)	1998	$20.00	Wholesale Clubs
19047	Color with Me Barbie	1998	$15.00	Supermarket
19130	Pink Reflections Barbie	1998	$25.00	Sears
19132	Charity Ball Barbie (black)	1998	$30.00	Toys "R" Us
19152	Brigham Young University	1998	$10.00	University Barbie
19153	University of Kentucky	1998	$11.00	University Barbie
19155	East Carolina University	1998	$10.00	University Barbie
19156	Kansas State	1998	$10.00	University Barbie
19159	Georgia Tech	1998	$10.00	University Barbie
19161	Florida State University	1998	$10.00	University Barbie
19162	Arizona State University	1998	$10.00	University Barbie
19163	Syracuse	1998	$10.00	University Barbie
19167	Northwestern	1998	$10.00	University Barbie
19169	University of Colorado	1998	$10.00	University Barbie
19170	Alabama	1998	$10.00	University Barbie
19171	Virginia Tech	1998	$10.00	University Barbie
19218	Winter Evening Barbie (blonde)	1998	$25.00	Wholesale Clubs
19220	Winter Evening Barbie (brunette)	1998	$25.00	Wholesale Clubs
19224	Sticker Craze (blonde)	1998	$10.00	
19262	Wild Style Barbie	1998	$20.00	Toys "R" Us
19268	Horse Ridin'	1998	$10.00	
19269	Horse Ridin' Barbie (black)	1997	$13.00	
19280	Ice Cream Barbie	1998	$16.00	Ames
19355	Portrait in Blue Barbie	1998	$15.00	Wal-Mart
19356	Portrait in Blue Barbie (black)	1998	$15.00	Wal-Mart
19357	Winter Splendor Barbie	1998	$38.00	Avon
19358	Winter Splendor Barbie (black)	1998	$38.00	Avon
19360	Barbie and *The Tale of Peter Rabbit*	1998	$28.00	Keepsake Treasures
19361	Evening Sophisticate Barbie	1998	$30.00	Classique
19363	Summer in San Francisco Barbie (blonde) (FAO)	1998	$95.00	City Seasons Collection
19363	Summer in San Francisco Barbie (redhead) (FAO)	1998	$675.00	City Seasons Collection
19364	Wizard of Oz-Dorothy with Toto	2000	Retail	Porcelain Treasures Collection
19365	Peacock	1998	$59.00	Birds of Beauty Series
19366	Sunflower Barbie (Van Gogh)	1998	$68.00	Artist Series
19367	Autumn in Paris	1998	$35.00	City Seasons
19384	Pilot Barbie (black)	1998	$25.00	Toys "R" Us
19419	Syracuse (black)	1998	$10.00	University Barbie
19420	Virginia Tech (black)	1998	$10.00	University Barbie
19422	Alabama (black)	1998	$10.00	University Barbie
19425	Northwestern (black)	1998	$10.00	University Barbie
19426	East Carolina University (black)	1998	$10.00	University Barbie
19427	Georgia Tech (black)	1998	$10.00	University Barbie
19428	Generation Girl Barbie	1999	$20.00	
19429	Winter in New York	1998	$50.00	City Seasons Collection

Number	Item	Year	Value	Specials
19430	Spring in Tokyo Barbie	1999	$34.00	City Seasons Collection
19431	Summer in Rome Barbie	1999	$35.00	City Seasons Collection
19592	Making Friends	1998	$18.00	Military
19593	Making Friends (black)	1998	$18.00	Military
19626	Coca-Cola Picnic Barbie	1998	$15.00	Supermarket
19627	Coca-Cola Picnic Barbie (black)	1998	$15.00	Supermarket
19631	Dance 'Till Dawn Barbie	1998	$40.00	Great Fashions of the 20th Century
19632	Uptown Chic Barbie	1998	$32.00	Fashion Savvy Collection
19633	Angel of Joy Barbie	1998	$45.00	Timeless Sentiments
19665	Duke University (black)	1997	$9.00	University Barbie
19708	Starlight Carousel Barbie	1998	$18.00	K•B Toys
19717	Club Wedd Barbie (blonde)	1998	$20.00	Target
19718	Club Wedd Barbie (brunette)	1998	$20.00	Target
19739	Summer Daydreams Barbie	1998	$55.00	Coca-Cola Fashion Classic Series
19777	Evening Symphony Barbie	1998	$25.00	Service Merchandise
19783	Evening Enchantment Barbie	1998	$35.00	JCPenney
19783	Evening Enchantment Barbie	1998	$45.00	Evening Elegance
19784	Sidewalk Chalk Barbie	1998	$20.00	Shopko/Venture
19784	Sidewalk Chalk Barbie	1998	$15.00	Hill's
19788	Vera Wang Barbie	1998	$100.00	Designer Collection
19791	Barbie Millicent Roberts Pinstripe Power	1998	$30.00	Barbie Millicent Roberts
19792	Holiday Sensation	1999	$35.00	Holiday Homecoming Series
19816	Imperial Elegance	1998	$290.00	Fabergé Porcelain
19847	Water Rhapsody Barbie	1998	$57.00	Essence of Nature
19848	Cinnabar Sensation (black)	1998	$76.00	Byron Lars Runway Collection
19866	University of Connecticut	1998	$11.00	University Barbie
19867	University of Maryland	1998	$11.00	University Barbie
19868	Purdue	1998	$11.00	University Barbie
19869	Washington State	1998	$11.00	University Barbie
19870	Stanford	1998	$11.00	University Barbie
19873	Original Arizona Jean Company III	1998	$25.00	JCPenney
19913	Sticker Craze (black)	1998	$10.00	
19914	Sticker Craze (brunette)	1998	$10.00	
19928	70s Disco Barbie (blonde)	1998	$25.00	Wholesale Clubs
19929	70s Disco Barbie (brunette)	1998	$25.00	Wholesale Clubs
20017	Beyond Pink	1998	$15.00	
20017	Birthday (blonde)	1998	$20.00	
20022	Bronze Sensation Barbie	1998	$55.00	Wholesale Clubs
20038	Golden Anniversary Barbie	1998	$90.00	Toys "R" Us
20038	Toys "R" Us 50th Anniversary Doll	1998	$85.00	Toys "R" Us
20044	Indiana	1998	$15.00	University Barbie
20122	Cool Blue Barbie	1998	$15.00	
20123	University of Maryland (black)	1998	$11.00	University Barbie
20124	Stanford (black)	1998	$11.00	University Barbie
20125	Oklahoma	1998	$11.00	University Barbie
20126	University of Texas (black)	1998	$11.00	University Barbie
20127	North Carolina State (black)	1997	$9.00	University Barbie
20128	Holiday Gift Barbie	1998	$90.00	Holiday Porcelain Series
20151	Soccer Barbie	1999	$20.00	
20164	Puzzle Craze Barbie	1998	$12.00	Wal-Mart
20165	Puzzle Craze Barbie (black)	1998	$12.00	Wal-Mart
20186	Symphony in Chiffon Barbie	1998	$60.00	Barbie Couture Collection
20200	Happy Holidays 1998	1998	$25.00	Happy Holidays Collection
20201	Happy Holidays 1998 (black)	1998	$25.00	Happy Holidays Collection
20204	Definitely Diamonds Barbie	1998	$55.00	Jewelry Collection Series

Number	Item	Year	Value	Specials
20204	Definitely Diamonds Barbie	1998	$110.00	Service Merchandise
20205	WNBA Barbie	1998	$16.00	WNBA
20317	Strawberry Sorbet Barbie	1999	$25.00	Avon
20318	Lemon-Lime Sorbet Barbie	1999	$25.00	Avon
20319	Fruit Fantasy Barbie (brunette)	1999	$30.00	Avon
20330	Mrs. P.F.E. Albee	1998	$70.00	Avon
20333	Giggles 'n Swing Barbie & Kelly	2000	$15.00	
20339	Make-A-Valentine Barbie	1999	$10.00	Supermarket
20340	Make-A-Valentine Barbie (black)	1999	$10.00	Supermarket
20359	Butterfly Art	1998	$10.00	
20363	Disney's Animal Kingdom Barbie	1998	$28.00	Disney
20367	Iowa	1998	$15.00	University Barbie
20376	Oscar de la Renta Barbie	1999	$40.00	
20376	Oscar de la Renta Barbie	1998	$60.00	Bloomingdale's
20377	Phantom of the Opera	1998	$150.00	FAO Schwarz
20416	Happy Holidays 1997 (all variations) (brunette)	1997	$20.00	Happy Holidays Collection
20423	Club Wedd Barbie (black)	1998	$20.00	Target
20441	Harley-Davidson Barbie #2	1998	$150.00	Toys "R" Us
20442	NASCAR 50th Anniversary Barbie	1998	$25.00	NASCAR
20465	Valentine Style Barbie	1999	$14.00	Target
20489	Sleeping Beauty Barbie	1999	$18.00	
20490	Sleeping Beauty Barbie (black)	1999	$18.00	
20493	My Size Angel Barbie	1998	$105.00	
20494	My Size Angel Barbie (black)	1998	$105.00	
20504	Tye-Dye Barbie	1998	$10.00	
20504	Tye-Dye Barbie	1999	$13.00	
20528	Very Velvet Barbie	1998	$25.00	
20534	Giggles 'n Swing Barbie & Kelly (black)	2000	$15.00	
20535	Florida Vacation	1998	$10.00	
20542	Easter Surprise Barbie	1999	$10.00	Supermarket
20543	Easter Surprise Barbie (black)	1999	$10.00	Supermarket
20548	Working Woman Barbie	1999	$25.00	
20549	Working Woman Barbie (black)	1999	$25.00	
20551	Harpist Angel Barbie (black)	1998	$45.00	Angels of Music
20647	Rendezvous Barbie	1998	$74.00	Masquerade Gala
20648	Fantasy Goddess of Asia	1998	$100.00	Bob Mackie International Beauty
20649	Anniversary Edition Golden Qi-Pao Barbie	1998	$75.00	Hong Kong Commemorative Edition
20662	Sheer Illusion Barbie #1	1998	$92.00	Nolan Miller Designer Collection
20662	Sheer Illusion Barbie #2	1998	$70.00	Nolan Miller Designer Collection
20666	Pretty in Plaid (blonde)	1998	$5.00	
20667	Pretty in Plaid (redhead)	1998	$5.00	
20668	I Love Barbie	1999	$5.00	
20668	Pretty in Plaid (brunette)	1998	$5.00	
20676	Ballerina Dreams Barbie	1999	$14.00	Supermarket
20692	Chicago Bulls	1998	$20.00	NBA
20693	Chicago Bulls (black)	1998	$20.00	NBA
20694	Miami Heat	1998	$20.00	NBA
20695	Miami Heat (black)	1998	$20.00	NBA
20696	Washington Wizards	1998	$11.00	NBA
20697	Washington Wizards (black)	1998	$11.00	NBA
20698	Charlotte Hornets	1998	$20.00	NBA
20699	Charlotte Hornets (black)	1998	$20.00	NBA
20702	Minnesota Timberwolves	1998	$20.00	NBA
20703	Minnesota Timberwolves (black)	1998	$20.00	NBA
20704	L. A. Lakers	1998	$25.00	NBA

Number	Item	Year	Value	Specials
20705	L. A. Lakers (black)	1998	$20.00	NBA
20706	Detroit Pistons	1998	$20.00	NBA
20707	Detroit Pistons (black)	1998	$20.00	NBA
20708	Utah Jazz Barbie	1998	$20.00	NBA
20709	Utah Jazz Barbie (black)	1998	$20.00	NBA
20710	Phoenix Suns Barbie	1998	$20.00	NBA
20711	Phoenix Suns Barbie (black)	1998	$20.00	NBA
20714	N. Y. Knicks	1998	$20.00	NBA
20715	N. Y. Knicks (black)	1998	$20.00	NBA
20716	Boston Celtics	1998	$20.00	NBA
20717	Boston Celtics (black)	1998	$20.00	NBA
20718	Seattle Supersonics	1998	$20.00	NBA
20719	Seattle Supersonics (black)	1998	$20.00	NBA
20720	Portland Trailblazers	1998	$20.00	NBA
20721	Portland Trailblazers (black)	1998	$20.00	NBA
20722	San Antonio Spurs	1998	$20.00	NBA
20723	San Antonio Spurs (black)	1998	$20.00	NBA
20724	Philadelphia 76ers	1998	$20.00	NBA
20725	Philadelphia 76ers (black)	1999	$20.00	NBA
20726	New Jersey Nets	1998	$20.00	NBA
20727	New Jersey Nets (black)	1998	$20.00	NBA
20728	Dallas Mavericks	1998	$20.00	NBA
20729	Dallas Mavericks (black)	1998	$20.00	NBA
20730	Denver Nuggets	1998	$20.00	NBA
20731	Denver Nuggets (black)	1998	$20.00	NBA
20732	Vancouver Grizzlies	1998	$20.00	NBA
20733	Vancouver Grizzlies (black)	1998	$20.00	NBA
20734	Atlanta Hawks	1998	$20.00	NBA
20735	Atlanta Hawks (black)	1998	$20.00	NBA
20736	Cleveland Cavaliers	1998	$20.00	NBA
20737	Cleveland Cavaliers (black)	1998	$20.00	NBA
20738	Milwaukee Bucks	1998	$20.00	NBA
20739	Milwaukee Bucks (black)	1998	$20.00	NBA
20740	Toronto Raptors	1998	$20.00	NBA
20741	Toronto Raptors (black)	1998	$20.00	NBA
20742	Golden State Warriors	1998	$20.00	NBA
20743	Golden State Warriors (black)	1998	$20.00	NBA
20744	L. A. Clippers	1998	$20.00	NBA
20745	L. A. Clippers (black)	1998	$20.00	NBA
20746	Sacramento Kings	1998	$20.00	NBA
20747	Sacramento Kings (black)	1998	$20.00	NBA
20749	Orlando Magic (black)	1998	$20.00	NBA
20766	Style	1999	$10.00	K•B Toys
20767	Style (black)	1999	$10.00	K•B Toys
20780	Sweet Treats Barbie	1998	$15.00	
20782	Fashion Avenue Barbie	1998	$15.00	K•B Toys
20851	Barbie as Marzipan from *The Nutcracker*	1999	$26.00	Classic Ballet Series
20866	Golden Qi-Pao Barbie	1998	$65.00	Spiegel
20929	Angel of Joy Barbie (black)	1998	$45.00	Timeless Sentiments
20955	Sweet Treats Barbie (black)	1998	$15.00	
20983	Mint Memories Barbie	1999	$150.00	Victorian Tea Porcelain Collection
20989	Disney's Animal Kingdom Barbie (black)	1998	$28.00	Disney
21040	I'm a Toys "R" Us Kid Barbie (black)	1998	$25.00	Toys "R" Us
21128	Birthday Wishes Barbie	1999	$26.00	Birthday Wishes Series
21130	Barbie as Snow White	1999	$28.00	Children's Collector Series

Number	Item	Year	Value	Specials
21159	Army	1999	$14.00	University Barbie
21160	Vanderbilt	1999	$16.00	University Barbie
21166	Air Force Academy	1999	$14.00	University Barbie
21167	North Carolina A & T	1999	$16.00	University Barbie
21168	North Carolina A & T (black)	1999	$16.00	University Barbie
21169	Pittsburgh	1999	$16.00	University Barbie
21172	Villanova	1999	$16.00	University Barbie
21173	Xavier	1999	$16.00	University Barbie
21189	Boston College	1999	$16.00	University Barbie
21190	Mississippi State	1999	$16.00	University Barbie
21191	Mississippi State (black)	1999	$16.00	University Barbie
21192	Massachusetts	1999	$16.00	University Barbie
21193	Minnesota	1999	$16.00	University Barbie
21194	Montana	1999	$16.00	University Barbie
21195	South Carolina	1999	$16.00	University Barbie
21196	South Carolina (black)	1999	$16.00	University Barbie
21197	Utah	1999	$16.00	University Barbie
21216	University of Virginia (black)	1999	$16.00	University Barbie
21219	LSU	1999	$16.00	University Barbie
21220	LSU (black)	1999	$16.00	University Barbie
21226	Boston University	1999	$16.00	University Barbie
21227	San Diego State	1999	$16.00	University Barbie
21228	San Diego State (black)	1999	$16.00	University Barbie
21229	Texas Tech	1999	$16.00	University Barbie
21230	Texas Tech (black)	1999	$16.00	University Barbie
21231	Cincinnati	1999	$16.00	University Barbie
21232	University of Mississippi	1999	$16.00	University Barbie
21233	University of Mississippi (black)	1999	$16.00	University Barbie
21234	UNLV	1999	$16.00	University Barbie
21245	Marshall	1999	$16.00	University Barbie
21246	Wyoming	1999	$16.00	University Barbie
21295	Symphony in Chiffon Barbie (black)	1998	$60.00	Barbie Couture Collection
21375	101 Dalmatians Barbie (strawberry blonde)	1999	$20.00	Toys "R" Us
21377	101 Dalmatians Barbie (brunette)	1999	$20.00	Toys "R" Us
21384	40th Anniversary Barbie (blonde)	1999	$45.00	40th Anniversary Collection
21386	Fruit Fantasy Barbie (blonde)	1999	$25.00	Avon
21414	Heartstring Angel Barbie	1999	$60.00	Angels of Music
21506	Peruvian II	1999	$18.00	Dolls of the World
21507	Moroccan Barbie	1999	$18.00	Dolls of the World
21509	Birthday Wishes Barbie (black)	1999	$26.00	Birthday Wishes Series
21510	Commuter Set Barbie	1999	$50.00	Collectors' Request
21531	Steppin' Out Barbie – 1930s	1999	$35.00	Great Fashions of the 20th Century
21553	Austrian Barbie	1999	$18.00	Dolls of the World
21570	Pretty in Plaid (black)	1998	$5.00	
21632	Barbie Loves Tweety	1999	$35.00	Warner Bros. Studio Store
21721	Pink Inspiration Barbie (brunette)	1999	$30.00	Toys "R" Us
21722	Pink Inspiration Barbie (black)	1999	$30.00	Toys "R" Us
21740	Barbie Had a Little Lamb	1999	$25.00	Nursery Rhyme
21911	Far Out Barbie	1999	$40.00	Twist 'n Turn Collection
21914	Pink Inspiration Barbie (blonde)	1999	$30.00	Toys "R" Us
21915	Heartstring Angel Barbie (black)	1999	$60.00	Angels of Music
21923	Crystal Jubilee Barbie	1999	$155.00	Jubilee Series
21933	Alice in Wonderland	1998	$16.00	Disney Classics
22044	Fantasy Goddess of Africa	1999	$280.00	Bob Mackie International Beauty
22069	Crystal Glitter (blonde)	1999	$15.00	

Number	Item	Year	Value	Specials
22070	Crystal Glitter (black)	1999	$15.00	
22071	Crystal Glitter (brunette)	1999	$15.00	
22071	Crystal Glitter (redhead)	1999	$15.00	
22087	Bubble Fairy	1998	$20.00	
22150	Valentine Style Barbie (black)	1999	$14.00	Target
22162	Fabulous Forties Barbie	2000	$55.00	Great Fashions of the 20th Century
22202	Avon Representative Barbie	1999	$50.00	Avon
22203	Avon Representative Barbie (black)	1999	$40.00	Avon
22204	Avon Representative Barbie (Hispanic)	1999	$50.00	Avon
22205	Todd Oldham Barbie	1999	$54.00	Designer Collection
22232	Walking Barbie & Baby Sister Krissy	1999	$18.00	
22249	Very Velvet (brunette)	1999	$30.00	
22256	Harley-Davidson Barbie #3	1999	$95.00	Toys "R" Us
22257	Autumn in London	1999	$30.00	City Seasons Collection
22258	Winter in Montreal Barbie	1999	$40.00	City Seasons Collection
22307	Walking Barbie & Baby Sister Krissy (black)	1999	$18.00	
22336	40th Anniversary Barbie (black)	1999	$45.00	40th Anniversary Collection
22337	Rose Barbie	1999	$30.00	A Garden of Flowers
22357	Bath Boutique Barbie (blonde)	1999	$15.00	
22358	Bath Boutique Barbie (black)	1999	$15.00	
22359	Bath Boutique Barbie (brunette)	1999	$15.00	
22360	Club Wedd Barbie (blonde)	1999	$20.00	Target
22361	Club Wedd Barbie (black)	1999	$20.00	Target
22362	Club Wedd Barbie (brunette)	1999	$20.00	Target
22425	Space Camp Barbie	1999	$25.00	Toys "R" Us
22426	Space Camp Barbie (black)	1999	$25.00	Toys "R" Us
22831	Coca-Cola Barbie (blonde)	1999	$60.00	Coca-Cola Series
22831	Coca-Cola Drive-In Waitress	1999	$60.00	American Classics
22832	Golden Hollywood Barbie	1999	$95.00	FAO Schwarz
22832	MGM 75th Anniversary Barbie	1999	$70.00	
22833	Trend Forecaster Barbie	1999	$32.00	Clothes Minded Collection
22834	Whispering Wind Barbie	1999	$65.00	Essence of Nature
22836	Embassy Waltz Barbie	1999	$60.00	Barbie Collector's Club
22857	Chicago Cubs Fan Barbie	1999	$85.00	Chicago Cubs
22882	Happenin' Hair Barbie	1999	$12.00	
22891	Princess	1999	$15.00	
22892	Princess (black)	1999	$15.00	
22893	Princess (brunette)	1999	$15.00	
22894	Princess	1999	$15.00	
22895	Strawberry Party Barbie	1999	$15.00	Ames
22902	Celebration Cake Barbie (blonde)	1999	$20.00	
22902	Happy Birthday	1999	$20.00	
22903	Celebration Cake Barbie (black)	1999	$20.00	
22903	Happy Birthday (black)	1999	$20.00	
22904	Celebration Cake Barbie (brunette)	1999	$20.00	
22904	Happy Birthday (brunette)	1999	$20.00	
22906	Birthday Party Barbie (black)	1999	$20.00	
22907	Birthday Party Barbie	1999	$20.00	
22954	NASCAR Official #94 Barbie (brunette)	1999	$25.00	NASCAR
22957	Flamingo Barbie	1999	$55.00	Birds of Beauty Series
22961	Golden Allure Barbie	1999	$32.00	Home Shopping Club
22962	My Wardrobe Barbie	1999	$28.00	Service Merchandise
22964	Coca-Cola Brand Party Barbie	1999	$12.00	Supermarket
22967	Tree Trimming	1999	$12.00	
22968	Tree Trimming (black)	1999	$12.00	

Number	Item	Year	Value	Specials
22974	Riviera Barbie	1999	$10.00	
22976	Golden Waltz Barbie (blonde)	1999	$25.00	Wholesale Clubs
23007	Pet Lovin'	1999	$15.00	
23008	Pet Lovin' (black)	1999	$15.00	
23027	Vera Wang Awards Night Barbie	1999	$89.00	Designer Collection
23041	40th Anniversary Bumblebee Gala Barbie	1999	$80.00	40th Anniversary Collection
23105	Super Gymnast Barbie	1999	$20.00	
23106	Super Gymnast Barbie (black)	1999	$15.00	K•B Toys
23205	Western Plains	1999	$40.00	Lifestyles of the West
23220	Golden Waltz Barbie (redhead)	1999	$30.00	Wholesale Clubs
23221	Your Pen Pal Barbie	1999	$20.00	Military
23222	Your Pen Pal Barbie (black)	1999	$20.00	Military
23239	Jewel Skating Barbie	1999	$12.00	Wal-Mart
23240	Jewel Skating Barbie (black)	1999	$12.00	Wal-Mart
23258	Twist 'n Turn Barbie Smasheroo (redhead)	1998	$50.00	Collectors' Request
23273	Le Papillon Barbie	1999	$175.00	FAO Schwarz
23275	Magna Doodle Barbie	1999	$15.00	Ames
23276	Le Papillon Barbie	1999	$214.00	Bob Mackie Custom Limited Edition
23420	Cinnabar Sensation	1998	$76.00	Byron Lars Runway Collection
23421	Sit in Style Barbie	1999	$10.00	
23451	Tango (porcelain)	1999	$300.00	Bob Mackie
23462	Weekend Barbie	1999	$5.00	
23474	Princess Barbie (blonde)	2000	$11.00	
23474	Rainbow Princess	1999	$12.00	
23475	Princess Barbie (black)	2000	$11.00	
23475	Rainbow Princess (black)	1999	$11.00	
23476	Princess Barbie (brunette)	2000	$11.00	
23476	Rainbow Princess (brunette)	1999	$12.00	
23477	Princess Barbie (Asian)	2000	$11.00	
23478	Plum Royal	1999	$170.00	Byron Lars Runway Collection
23495	Evening Illusion Barbie	1999	$72.00	Nolan Miller Designer Collection
23499	Spring in Tokyo Barbie (nostalgic face)	1999	$40.00	City Seasons Collection
23740	Florida Vacation Beach Time Fun Barbie	1999	$22.00	Wholesale Clubs
23800	Snow Sensation Barbie	1999	$39.00	Avon
23801	Snow Sensation Barbie (black)	1999	$39.00	Avon
23877	Golden Hollywood Barbie (black)	1999	$95.00	FAO Schwarz
23880	Wizard of Oz-Wicked Witch	2000	Retail	Porcelain Treasures Collection
23881	New York Yankees Barbie	1999	$28.00	Major League Baseball
23882	Los Angeles Dodgers Barbie	1999	$27.00	Major League Baseball
23883	Chicago Cubs Barbie	1999	$29.00	Major League Baseball
23884	Reflections of Light (Renoir)	1999	$75.00	Artist Series
23934	Coca-Cola Barbie (brunette) Walt Disney World	1999	$198.00	Coca-Cola Series
23995	Millennium Princess Barbie (black)	1999	$45.00	Millennium Collection
24015	Tour Guide Barbie — *Toy Story 2*	1999	$30.00	Disney
24017	Pilot Barbie	1999	$12.00	
24154	Millennium Princess Barbie	1999	$45.00	Millennium Collection
24240	Angel of Peace	1999	$40.00	Timeless Sentiments
24241	Angel of Peace (black)	1999	$40.00	Timeless Sentiments
24252	The Charleston Barbie	2001	$250.00	Bob Mackie
24471	New York Yankees Barbie (black)	1999	$36.00	Major League Baseball
24472	Los Angeles Dodgers Barbie (black)	1999	$32.00	Major League Baseball
24473	Chicago Cubs Barbie (black)	1999	$35.00	Major League Baseball
24494	Hanae Mori Barbie	2000	$75.00	
24501	Venetian Opulence	2000	$90.00	Masquerade Gala

Number	Item	Year	Value	Specials
24505	Millennium Bride	2000	$285.00	Millennium Collection
24557	Hollywood Nails (black)	1999	$15.00	
24590	Swimming Champion Barbie	1999	$15.00	
24614	Hawaii Barbie	1999	$5.00	
24635	Givenchy Barbie	2000	$60.00	
24636	Mann's Chinese Theatre	2000	$48.00	FAO Schwarz
24637	Coca-Cola Barbie #2 (brunette)	2000	$60.00	American Classics
24637	Coca-Cola Barbie (Sweetheart)	2000	$40.00	Coca-Cola Series
24638	Barbie as Wonder Woman	2000	$18.00	Barbie Loves Pop Culture
24638	Wonder Woman	2000	Retail	Warner Bros. Studio Store
24652	Pretty Flowers Barbie (blonde)	1999	$6.00	
24653	Pretty Flowers Barbie (black)	1999	$6.00	
24654	Pretty Flowers Barbie (brunette)	1999	$6.00	
24655	Pretty Flowers Barbie (redhead)	1999	$6.00	
24658	Corduroy Cool (blonde)	1999	$15.00	
24659	Corduroy Cool Barbie (brunette)	1999	$9.00	
24667	Birthday Wishes Barbie #2	2000	$24.00	Birthday Wishes Series
24668	Birthday Wishes Barbie #2 (black)	2000	$24.00	Birthday Wishes Series
24668	Birthday Wishes Barbie (black)	2000	$25.00	
24670	Spanish Barbie #3	2000	$18.00	Dolls of the World
24671	Northwest Coast Native American	2000	$25.00	Dolls of the World
24672	Swedish Barbie	2000	$18.00	Dolls of the World
24673	Barbie as Beauty	2000	$30.00	Children's Collector Series
24746	Cool Looks Fashion Designer CD-ROM	1999	$28.00	Meijer
24748	Magic Hair Styler CD-ROM	1999	$28.00	Meijer
24788	Horse Riding Barbie with Riding Club CD-ROM	1999	$28.00	Meijer
24842	40th Anniversary Barbie (brunette)	1999	$150.00	Collectors Convention 1999
24930	Sophisticated Lady	2000	$45.00	Collectors' Request
24998	Mann's Chinese Theatre (black)	2000	$60.00	FAO Schwarz
25381	Pearl Beach Barbie Easter Basket	1999	$15.00	Supermarket
25466	Movie Star	1999	$20.00	
25507	Orange Pekoe	2000	$500.00	Victorian Tea Porcelain Collection
25525	Cool Collecting	2000	$36.00	
25525	Nostalgic Toys	2000	$45.00	Cool Collecting Series
25526	Victorian Barbie with Cedric Bear (blonde)	2000	$50.00	Adult Collector Edition
25526	Victorian Barbie with Cedric Bear (brunette)	2000	$39.00	Victorian
25636	Ferrari Barbie	2000	$47.00	Sports
25636	Ferrari Barbie	2001	$35.00	Sports
25636	NASCAR #3	2000	$35.00	
25639	Fairy of the Forest	2000	$42.00	Enchanted World of Fairies
25639	Forest Fairy	2000	$40.00	Fairy Series
25641	Wedgwood Barbie	2000	$110.00	Great Porcelain Houses
25641	Wedgwood Barbie	2000	$150.00	Wedgwood/Wal-Mart
25642	Barbie as Snowflake from *The Nutcracker*	2000	$27.00	Classic Ballet Series
25644	Sydney 2000 Olympic Barbie Pin Collector	2000	$25.00	Pop Culture
25680	Empress of Emeralds	2000	$100.00	QVC/Royal Jewel
25740	Millennium Grad w/blue gown (black)	2000	$5.00	Supermarket
25750	Millennium Grad w/black gown (black)	2000	$5.00	Supermarket
25766	Generation Girl Barbie Dance Party	2000	$20.00	
25812	Barbie as Dorothy	2000	$25.00	Wizard of Oz
25812	Barbie as Dorothy	1999	$18.00	Wizard of Oz
25813	Barbie as Glinda	2000	$25.00	Wizard of Oz
25813	Barbie as Glinda	1999	$18.00	Wizard of Oz
25837	Barbie Sign Language	1999	$20.00	
25859	Fantasy Goddess of the Americas	2000	$135.00	Bob Mackie International Beauty

Number	Item	Year	Value	Specials
25863	My Size Butterfly	2000	$135.00	
25864	My Size Butterfly (black)	2000	$135.00	
25871	Bowling Champ Barbie	2000	$30.00	Sports
25887	Cool Skating Barbie	2000	$20.00	
26068	Club Couture	2000	$70.00	Barbie Collector's Club
26107	Corduroy Cool (black)	1999	$15.00	
26251	Glam 'n Groom	2000	$15.00	Dressed Boxed Dolls
26284	Barbie for President (black)	2000	Retail	Career
26288	Barbie for President	2000	Retail	Career
26302	Sydney 2000 Olympic Barbie Pin Collector (black)	2000	$25.00	Pop Culture
26327	Dancing Fire Barbie	2000	$60.00	Essence of Nature
26357	Rainbow Princess Barbie	2000	$12.00	
26394	Barbie Sign Language (black)	1999	$20.00	
26422	Secret Messages Barbie	1999	$15.00	
26425	Cool Clips Barbie	2000	$14.00	
26425	Day in the Sun (blonde)	2001	$35.00	Hollywood Movie Star Collection
26426	Day in the Sun (brunette)	2001	$70.00	Hollywood Movie Star Collection
26464	Country Charm	2000	$25.00	Cracker Barrel Restaurant
26774	Ballet Lessons	1999	$11.00	
26775	Ballet Lessons (black)	2000	$50.00	
26837	Magical Mermaids Barbie & Krissy	2000	$25.00	
26838	Magical Mermaids Barbie & Krissy (black)	2000	$25.00	
26881	Very Berry	1999	$10.00	K-Mart
26883	Pajama Fun Barbie	1999	$13.00	Target
26914	Hollywood Premiere	2000	$36.00	Hollywood Movie Star Collection
26926	Queen of Sapphires	2000	$85.00	Royal Jewel
26929	Delphine Barbie	2000	$95.00	Fashion Model
26930	Lingerie (blonde)	2000	$255.00	Fashion Model
26931	Lingerie (brunette)	2000	$265.00	Fashion Model
26932	Lunch at the Club Fashion	2000	$77.00	Barbie Fashion Model
26933	Garden Party Fashion	2000	$90.00	Barbie Fashion Model
26935	Indigo Obsession Barbie	2000	$165.00	Byron Lars Runway Collection
26972	Countess of Rubies Barbie	2001	$80.00	Jewel Collection
26980	Coca-Cola Soda Fountain	2000	$140.00	Coca-Cola Series
27028	Imperial Splendor	2000	$310.00	Fabergé Porcelain
27271	Glam 'n Groom Barbie	1999	$9.00	
27286	Goddess of Beauty and Love	2000	Retail	Inspirational Series
27374	Dream Wedding	2000	$16.00	
27409	Barbie 2000	2000	$48.00	
27410	Barbie 2000 (black)	2000	$48.00	
27673	Holiday Treasures Barbie	2000	$78.00	Club Exclusive
27674	Millennium Wedding (black)	2000	$36.00	The Bridal Collection
27674	Millennium Wedding (white)	2000	$36.00	The Bridal Collection
27675	Nifty '50s Barbie	2000	$65.00	Great Fashions of the 20th Century
27676	Groovy '60s Barbie	2000	$38.00	Great Fashions of the 20th Century
27677	Peace & Love '70s	2000	$70.00	Great Fashions of the 20th Century
27682	Swan	2000	$48.00	Birds of Beauty Series
27683	In the Pink Barbie	2001	$140.00	Barbie Fashion Model
27684	Between Takes Barbie	2000	$50.00	Hollywood Movie Star Collection
27687	Midnight Moon Princess	2000	$50.00	Celestial Collection
27688	Morning Sun Princess	2000	$45.00	Celestial Collection
27690	Evening Star Princess	2000	$45.00	Celestial Collection
27765	Millennium Wedding (Hispanic)	2000	$45.00	The Bridal Collection
27788	Fashion Wardrobe	2000	Retail	
27789	Fashion Wardrobe (black)	2000	Retail	

Number	Item	Year	Value	Specials
27865	Publicity Tour Party Barbie	2001	$40.00	Hollywood Movie Star Collection
28066	Jewel Girl	2000	Retail	
28080	Holiday Angel	2000	$32.00	
28080	Holiday Angel Barbie #2 (black)	2001	$34.00	Holiday Angel
28081	Holiday Angel (black)	2000	$30.00	
28081	Holiday Angel Barbie #2	2001	$36.00	Holiday Angel
28112	Goddess of Spring	2000	Retail	Inspirational Series
28264	Princess	2000	$11.00	
28265	Princess (black)	2000	$11.00	
28266	Princess (Hispanic)	2000	$11.00	
28267	Princess (Asian)	2000	$11.00	
28269	Celebration Barbie	2000	$34.00	Holiday Dolls
28270	Celebration Barbie (black)	2001	$45.00	
28270	Sisters Celebration Krissy and Barbie	2000	$18.00	
28314	Hip 2 Be Square (black)	2000	$6.00	
28316	Hip 2 Be Square (redhead)	2000	$6.00	
28372	Princess of the French Court Barbie	2001	$150.00	Dolls of the World — Princess Collection
28373	Princess of the Incas Barbie	2000	$115.00	Dolls of the World — Princess Collection
28374	Princess of India Barbie	2001	$165.00	Dolls of the World — Princess Collection
28375	Barbie as Flower Ballerina from *The Nutcracker*	2001	$25.00	Classic Ballet Series
28378	Suburban Shopper Barbie	2001	$70.00	Collectors' Request
28417	Surf City	2000	$5.00	
28434	Birthday Wishes Barbie #3	2000	$27.00	Birthday Wishes Series
28435	Birthday Wishes Barbie #3 (black)	2000	$27.00	
28435	Birthday Wishes Barbie (black)	2001	$27.00	
28521	Princess Bride	2000	$20.00	
28533	Grand Entrance Barbie	2001	$45.00	Grand Entrance
28534	Ferrari Barbie #2	2001	$50.00	Barbie Loves Sports
28552	Princess Bride (black)	2000	$20.00	
28612	Kitty Fun (blonde)	2000	$16.00	
28624	Kitty Fun (black)	2000	$15.00	
28701	Picture Pockets Barbie	2000	$10.00	Toys "R" Us
28796	Midnight Tuxedo Barbie	2001	$77.00	Club Exclusive
28798	Barbie and *Curious George*	2001	$28.00	Keepsake Treasures
28799	Fairy of the Garden	2001	$45.00	Enchanted World of Fairies
28800	Princess and the Pea	2000	$26.00	Princess Series
28866	Kitty Fun (brunette)	2000	$16.00	
28961	Surf City Barbie Doll and Play Set	2000	$5.00	
28990	Rose Series	2000	$13.00	
29002	Flower Power	2000	$9.00	
29003	Flower Power (black)	2000	$9.00	
29027	Wash 'n Wear	2000	$19.00	
29057	Society Hound Barbie	2001	$85.00	Society Hound Collection
29179	Rain or Shine Barbie	2000	$15.00	
29189	Rose Princess (black)	2000	$13.00	
29195	Ballet Star	2000	$11.00	
29196	Ballet Star (black)	2000	$12.00	
29207	Harley-Davidson Barbie	2000	$70.00	
29208	Harley-Davidson Barbie	2001	$100.00	
29260	Star Splash	2000	$13.00	
29307	Midnight Tuxedo Barbie (black)	2001	$400.00	Club Exclusive
29308	Star Splash (black)	2000	$13.00	
29332	Country Charm (black)	2000	$25.00	Cracker Barrel Restaurant
29345	Flying Butterfly Barbie	2000	$13.00	
29399	Fashion Designer	2000	$22.00	

Number	Item	Year	Value	Specials
29408	Spanish Teacher	2000	$25.00	Toys "R" Us
29409	Spanish Teacher (Hispanic)	2000	$25.00	Toys "R" Us
29410	Hip 2 Be Square (blonde)	2000	$8.00	Value Pack
29421	Burberry Barbie	2001	$70.00	Designer Burberry
29426	Bedtime Stories w/book	2000	$25.00	Toys "R" Us
29427	Bedtime Stories w/book (black)	2000	$25.00	Toys "R" Us
29438	Romantic Wedding (white)	2001	$36.00	The Bridal Collection
29439	Romantic Wedding (black)	2001	$36.00	The Bridal Collection
29458	The Tale of the Forest Princess w/book	2000	$25.00	
29459	The Tale of the Forest Princess w/book (black)	2000	$25.00	
29461	Children's Doctor	2000	$20.00	
29605	Goldilocks and The Three Bears	2001	$30.00	Storybook Favorites/Kelly
29651	Lingerie Barbie #3	2001	$100.00	Barbie Fashion Model
29652	Blush Becomes Her Fashion	2001	$75.00	Barbie Fashion Model
29653	Boulevard Fashion	2001	$60.00	Barbie Fashion Model
29654	Dusk to Dawn Barbie Gift Set	2001	$145.00	Barbie Fashion Model
29662	Grand Entrance Barbie (black)	2001	$45.00	Grand Entrance
29663	Hip 2 Be Square (brunette)	2000	$8.00	Value Pack
29771	Scarlett O'Hara Doll on Peachtree Street — The Drapery Dress	2001	$52.00	Gone with the Wind
29905	Lighter Than Air Barbie	2001	$120.00	Prima Ballerina
29910	Scarlett O'Hara Doll, Barbecue at Twelve Oaks	2001	$49.00	Gone with the Wind
29911	The Rose Barbie	2001	$55.00	Flowers in Fashion
29912	The Calla Lily Barbie	2002	$57.00	Flowers in Fashion
29913	Barbie as Jeannie from *I Dream of Jeannie*	2001	$40.00	Barbie Loves Pop Culture
40389	Color 'n Curl Set (molded Barbie head only)	1965	$585.00	
50319	The Orchid Barbie	2001	$76.00	Flowers in Fashion
50534	Nsync Barbie w/CD	2000	$19.00	
50576	Grand Hotel	2001	$20.00	Toys "R" Us
50707	Spirit of the Earth Barbie	2001	$60.00	Native Spirit Collection
50723	Jo from *Little Women*	2001	$15.00	When I Read, I Dream
50724	Fern from *Charlotte's Web*	2001	$15.00	When I Read, I Dream
50726	Anne from *Anne of Green Gables*	2002	$14.00	When I Read, I Dream
50823	Wedgwood Barbie	2001	$79.00	Wedgwood
50824	Wedgwood Barbie (black)	2001	$79.00	Wedgwood
50825	Hollywood Cast Party Barbie	2001	$65.00	Hollywood Movie Star Collection/ FAO Schwarz
50826	Moja Barbie	2001	$210.00	Byron Lars
50827	Tales of Arabian Nights Barbie and Ken Gift Set	2001	$76.00	Magic & Mystery
50829	Provencale Barbie	2002	$96.00	Barbie Fashion Model
50840	Fantasy Goddess of the Arctic	2001	$140.00	Bob Mackie
50841	Barbie 2001	2001	$102.00	
50842	Barbie 2001 (black)	2001	$70.00	
52639	Baking Fun Barbie	2004	$12.00	
52739	Gone Platinum Barbie	2002	$40.00	Diva Collection
52741	Ravishing in Rouge Barbie	2001	$110.00	Barbie Fashion Model
52834	Home for the Holidays Barbie	2001	$34.00	
52899	Little Red Riding Hood and The Wolf	2002	$22.00	Storybook Favorites/Kelly
52900	Heidi	2002	$10.00	When I Read, I Dream
53367	Princess of Ireland Barbie	2002	$25.00	Dolls of the World — Princess Collection
53368	Princess of China Barbie	2002	$65.00	Dolls of the World — Princess Collection
53369	Princess of the Nile Barbie	2002	$40.00	Dolls of the World — Princess Collection
53370	Sophisticated Wedding Barbie	2002	$34.00	
53371	Sophisticated Wedding Barbie (black)	2002	$34.00	
53510	Barbie as Samantha from *Bewitched*	2002	$30.00	Barbie Loves Pop Culture

Number	Item	Year	Value	Specials
53511	Fire and Ice Barbie	2002	$45.00	Pop Culture
53841	Grand Entrance Barbie #2	2002	$30.00	Grand Entrance
53842	Grand Entrance Barbie #2 (black)	2002	$30.00	Grand Entrance
53861	Spirit of Water Barbie	2002	$60.00	Native Spirit Collection
53862	Twilight Gala Barbie	2002	$72.00	Club Exclusives
53863	Fire and Ice Barbie (black)	2002	$45.00	Pop Culture
53867	Barbie as Swan Ballerina	2002	$24.00	Classic Ballet Series
53868	Gone Platinum Barbie (black)	2002	$40.00	Diva Collection
53870	Twilight Gala Barbie (black)	2002	$86.00	Club Exclusives
53872	Peter Rabbit 100 Year Celebration Barbie	2002	$37.00	Keepsake Treasures
53935	The Iris Barbie	2002	$70.00	Flowers in Fashion
53973	Rapunzel Barbie	2002	$22.00	Princess
53974	Coca-Cola Barbie (Cheerleader)	2001	$46.00	Coca-Cola Series
53975	Barbie 2002	2002	$44.00	
53976	Barbie 2002 (black)	2002	$38.00	
53978	Enchanted Mermaid Barbie	2002	$200.00	
53991	Marie Antoinette Barbie	2003	$250.00	Women of Royalty
54185	Gold 'n Glamour Barbie	2002	$42.00	Collectors' Request
55387	Mademoiselle Isabelle Barbie	2002	$79.00	Portrait Collection
55426	All That Glitters Barbie	2002	$27.00	Diva Collection
55487	Western Chic Barbie	2002	$120.00	Pop Culture
55496	Marie Therese Barbie	2002	$64.00	Barbie Fashion Model
55497	Continental Holiday Barbie Gift Set	2002	$100.00	Barbie Fashion Model
55498	Lingerie Barbie #4 (blonde)	2002	$54.00	Barbie Fashion Model
55501	Radiant Redhead Barbie	2002	$150.00	Bob Mackie
55558	Barbie and Snoopy	2002	$60.00	
56061	Malibu Barbie	2002	$24.00	Pop Culture
56120	Lingerie Barbie #5 (black)	2002	$50.00	Barbie Fashion Model
56203	Society Girl Barbie	2002	$30.00	Style Set
56204	Society Girl Barbie (black)	2002	$32.00	Style Set
56216	Princess of the Danish Court Barbie	2003	$22.00	Dolls of the World — Princess Collection
56217	Princess of the Portuguese Empire Barbie	2003	$22.00	Dolls of the World — Princess Collection
56218	Princess of South Africa Barbie	2003	$26.00	Dolls of the World — Princess Collection
56615	Rose Princess Barbie	2004	$10.00	
56705	Barbie as That Girl	2003	$40.00	Barbie Loves Pop Culture
56707	Red Hot Barbie (white)	2003	$35.00	Diva Collection
56708	Red Hot Barbie (black)	2003	$32.00	Diva Collection
56737	Starring Barbie in *King Kong*	2003	$29.00	Pop Culture
56948	Lingerie Barbie #6	2003	$42.00	Barbie Fashion Model
57578	Barbie as Peppermint Candy Cane from *The Nutcracker*	2003	$33.00	Classic Ballet Series
57610	Gay Parisienne Barbie (blonde)	2003	$200.00	Collectors' Request
60403	Sara Lee Barbie	1993	$65.00	Sara Lee
61747	Miss Barbie	1996	$35.00	Woolworth
62327	Nostalgic Barbie #3	1996	$45.00	Nostalgic
62328	Nostalgic Barbie #1	1996	$45.00	Nostalgic
62329	Nostalgic Barbie #2	1996	$45.00	Nostalgic
62889	Arcadian Court Barbie	1996	$85.00	Hudson's Bay Company Canada
63569	School Spirit Barbie	1997	$40.00	Hudson's Bay Company Canada
63987	Barbie on Bay	1997	$35.00	Hudson's Bay Company Canada
64176	Toyland Barbie	1997	$40.00	Hudson's Bay Company Canada
64347	JAL Barbie	1997	$150.00	Japan Air Lines
96085	My First Barbie	1990	$75.00	Deco-Pak
96085	My First Barbie (black)	1990	$55.00	Deco-Pak
25-1992	Earring Magic Barbie Doll Software Pak	1993	$30.00	Radio Shack

Number	Item	Year	Value	Specials
9973-9999	Gay Parisienne (redhead/porcelain)	1991	$350.00	Disney
B0144	Barbie 2003	2003	$65.00	
B0145	Barbie 2003 (black)	2003	$65.00	
B0146	Capucine Barbie	2003	$100.00	Barbie Fashion Model
B0147	A Model Life Barbie Gift Set	2003	$80.00	
B0149	Exotic Beauty Barbie	2003	$26.00	Style Set
B0150	Exotic Beauty Barbie (black)	2003	$54.00	Style Set
B0150	James Bond 007 Ken and Barbie Gift Set	2003	$55.00	Barbie Loves Pop Culture
B0445	45th Anniversary Barbie by Robert Best (black)	2004	$50.00	Barbie Fashion Model
B0585	Brunette Brilliance Barbie	2003	$100.00	Bob Mackie
B0836	Designer Spotlight by Katiana Jimenez	2003	$450.00	Designer Spotlight
B1319	Spa Getaway Barbie Gift Set	2004	$75.00	Barbie Fashion Model
B1992	Noir et Blanc Barbie	2003	$65.00	Club Exclusive
B1993	Noir et Blanc Barbie (black)	2003	$100.00	Club Exclusive
B2017	Diana Ross by Bob Mackie	2004	$32.00	Celebrities
B2018	Tatu Barbie	2003	$170.00	Byron Lars
B23431	Joyeux Barbie (redhead)	2003	$320.00	Barbie Fashion Model
B2367	Spirit of the Sky Barbie	2003	$60.00	Native Spirit Collection
B2394	September Sapphire Barbie	2003	$40.00	Birthstone Collection/Wal-Mart
B2395	October Opal Barbie	2003	$40.00	Birthstone Collection/Wal-Mart
B2396	November Topaz Barbie	2003	$40.00	Birthstone Collection/Wal-Mart
B2397	December Turquoise Barbie	2003	$40.00	Birthstone Collection/Wal-Mart
B2510	Grease Barbie	2003	$100.00	Barbie Loves Pop Culture
B2511	The Bard Barbie Doll	2004	$60.00	Legends of Ireland
B2512	Bohemian Glamour Barbie	2003	$39.00	Style Set
B2513	Kate Spade Barbie	2004	$79.00	Kate Spade
B2518	French Quarter Barbie Fashion	2003	$29.00	Barbie Collector's Club
B2519	Winter Fantasy Barbie	2003	$45.00	Holiday Dolls
B2520	Sunday Best Barbie	2003	$48.00	Barbie Fashion Model
B2521	Giorgio Armani Barbie	2003	$135.00	Giorgio Armani
B2523	1 Modern Circle Barbie	2003	$30.00	1 Modern Circle
B2527	1 Modern Circle Barbie	2004	$33.00	1 Modern Circle
B3409	January Garnet Barbie	2003	$40.00	Birthstone Collection/Wal-Mart
B3410	February Amethyst Barbie	2003	$40.00	Birthstone Collection/Wal-Mart
B3411	March Aquamarine Barbie	2003	$40.00	Birthstone Collection/Wal-Mart
B3412	April Diamond Barbie	2003	$40.00	Birthstone Collection/Wal-Mart
B3413	May Emerald Barbie	2003	$40.00	Birthstone Collection/Wal-Mart
B3414	June Pearl Barbie	2003	$40.00	Birthstone Collection/Wal-Mart
B3415	July Ruby Barbie	2003	$40.00	Birthstone Collection/Wal-Mart
B3416	August Peridot Barbie	2003	$40.00	Birthstone Collection/Wal-Mart
B3417	Lounge Kitties Leopard	2004	$70.00	Lounge Kitties
B3422	Duchess Emma Barbie	2004	$80.00	Portrait Collection
B3423	Nne Barbie	2004	$90.00	Byron Lars
B3425	Queen Elizabeth I Barbie	2004	$250.00	Women of Royalty
B3426	Hollywood Divine Barbie (brunette)	2004	$70.00	Barbie Fan Club Exclusive
B3430	Joyeux Barbie	2003	$115.00	Barbie Fashion Model
B3431	Chinoiserie Red Moon Barbie	2004	$50.00	Barbie Fashion Model
B3437	Color Magic Barbie (brunette)	2004	$40.00	Collectors' Request
B3437	Color Magic Barbie (blonde)	2004	$175.00	Collectors' Request
B3437	Color Magic Barbie (redhead)	2004	$210.00	Collectors' Request
B3442	Trend Setter Barbie	2004	$50.00	Barbie Fashion Model
B3449	Barbie and Ken as Arwen and Aragorn from *The Lord of the Rings*	2004	$180.00	Hollywood
B3452	45th Anniversary Barbie by Bob Mackie (blonde)	2004	$50.00	
B3453	45th Anniversary Barbie by Bob Mackie (black)	2004	$60.00	

Number	Item	Year	Value	Specials
B3454	45th Anniversary Barbie by Bob Mackie (black hair)	2004	$150.00	
B3456	Faerie Queen Barbie (brunette)	2004	$185.00	Legends of Ireland
B3456	Faerie Queen Barbie	2004	$50.00	Legends of Ireland
B3457	Versace Barbie Doll	2004	$140.00	Versace
B3459	Princess of England Barbie	2004	$20.00	Dolls of the World — Princess Collection
B3460	Princess of Cambodia Barbie	2004	$20.00	Dolls of the World — Princess Collection
B3461	Princess of Ancient Greece Barbie	2004	$20.00	Dolls of the World — Princess Collection
B4425	Chataine Barbie	2003	$425.00	Barbie Fashion Model
B4773	Grease Barbie #2	2004	$30.00	Barbie Loves Pop Culture
B5655	Barbie as Juliet	2004	$30.00	Classic Ballet Series
B5731	Princess of Japan Barbie	2003	$23.00	Dolls of the World — Princess Collection
B5838	Barbie as Catwoman	2004	$20.00	Barbie Loves Pop Culture
B5870	Princess of the Korean Court Barbie	2005	$20.00	Dolls of the World — Princess Collection
B6271	Santa's Helper Barbie	2004	$20.00	
B6361	Princess of the Vikings Barbie	2003	$26.00	Dolls of the World — Princess Collection
B6708	Night on the Town Barbie and River	2004	$29.00	My Scene
B7565	Special Occasion Barbie — Treasure Hunt Doll	2003	Retail	
B8946	Badgley Mischka Bride Barbie	2004	$139.00	Designer Dolls
B8954	Paul Frank Barbie (blonde)	2004	$60.00	Designer Dolls
B8955	45th Anniversary Barbie by Robert Best	2004	$49.00	Barbie Fashion Model
B8956	Princess of the Navajo Barbie	2004	$20.00	Dolls of the World — Princess Collection
B9284	Barbie as Elle Woods from *Legally Blonde 2*	2003	$35.00	Barbie Loves Pop Culture
B9767	Versus Barbie	2004	$79.00	
B9797	Carolina Herrera Bride Barbie	2005	$140.00	Designer Dolls
C0166	Winter Fantasy Barbie (black)	2003	$45.00	Holiday Dolls
C0575	May Emerald Barbie (black)	2003	$40.00	Birthstone Collection/Wal-Mart
C0576	June Pearl Barbie (black)	2003	$40.00	Birthstone Collection/Wal-Mart
C0577	July Ruby Barbie (black)	2003	$40.00	Birthstone Collection/Wal-Mart
C0578	August Peridot Barbie (black)	2003	$40.00	Birthstone Collection/Wal-Mart
C0579	September Sapphire Barbie (black)	2003	$40.00	Birthstone Collection/Wal-Mart
C0580	October Opal Barbie (black)	2003	$40.00	Birthstone Collection/Wal-Mart
C0581	November Topaz Barbie (black)	2003	$40.00	Birthstone Collection/Wal-Mart
C0582	December Turquoise Barbie (black)	2003	$40.00	Birthstone Collection/Wal-Mart
C0583	January Garnet Barbie (black)	2003	$40.00	Birthstone Collection/Wal-Mart
C0584	February Amethyst Barbie (black)	2003	$40.00	Birthstone Collection/Wal-Mart
C0585	March Aquamarine Barbie (black)	2003	$40.00	Birthstone Collection/Wal-Mart
C0586	April Diamond Barbie (black)	2003	$40.00	Birthstone Collection/Wal-Mart
C2203	Princess of Ancient Mexico Barbie	2004	$20.00	Dolls of the World — Princess Collection
C2478	Lounge Kitties Tiger	2004	$36.00	Lounge Kitties
C3553	Lounge Kitties Panther	2004	$36.00	Lounge Kitties
C3699	Barbie Loves Patrick	2005	$15.00	
C3819	Barbie as Titania	2004	$27.00	Classic Ballet Series
C4212	Cruisin' the Boardwalk Barbie and River	2004	$33.00	My Scene
C4480	Totally Spring Barbie	2005	$16.00	
C4558	Batik Princess Barbie	2004	$25.00	Online Exclusive
C4656	45th Anniversary Barbie and Ken Gift Set	2004	$97.00	Barbie Fashion Model/FAO Schwarz
C5323	May Emerald Barbie	2004	$40.00	Birthstone Collection
C5324	June Pearl Barbie	2004	$40.00	Birthstone Collection
C5325	July Ruby Barbie	2004	$40.00	Birthstone Collection
C5327	September Sapphire Barbie	2004	$40.00	Birthstone Collection
C5328	October Opal Barbie	2004	$40.00	Birthstone Collection
C5329	November Topaz Barbie	2004	$40.00	Birthstone Collection
C5330	December Turquoise Barbie	2004	$40.00	Birthstone Collection
C5331	January Garnet Barbie	2004	$40.00	Birthstone Collection

Number	Item	Year	Value	Specials
C5332	February Amethyst Barbie	2004	$40.00	Birthstone Collection
C5333	March Aquamarine Barbie	2004	$40.00	Birthstone Collection
C6228	Birthday Wishes Barbie, Violet	2004	$37.00	
C6229	Birthday Wishes Barbie, Red	2004	$24.00	
C6261	A Nod for Mod Barbie	2004	$80.00	Barbie Fan Club Exclusive
C6262	Mod Redux Barbie	2004	$70.00	Online Exclusive
C6463	Cali Girl Teresa	2004	$8.00	
G3673	Fashion Show Barbie	2004	$23.00	
G3675	Fashion Show Teresa	2004	$23.00	
G5318	Totally Spring Barbie (black)	2005	$16.00	
G5860	Princess of the Renaissance Barbie	2005	$20.00	Dolls of the World — Princess Collection
G5861	Princess of Imperial Russia Barbie	2005	$20.00	Dolls of the World — Princess Collection
G6261	Crystal Fairytopia Barbie	2005	$17.00	
G6262	Jewelia Fairytopia Barbie	2005	$17.00	
G7211	Trace of Lace Barbie (blonde)	2005	$70.00	Barbie Fashion Model
G7212	Trace of Lace Barbie (brunette)	2005	$70.00	Barbie Fashion Model
G7915	Hard Rock Café Barbie	2004	$105.00	Pop Culture
G8050	Tano Barbie	2005	$80.00	Byron Lars
G8051	Empress Josephine Barbie	2005	$250.00	Women of Royalty/Avon
G8055	Princess of Holland Barbie	2005	$20.00	Dolls of the World — Princess Collection
G8056	Princess of the Hawaiian Islands Barbie	2005	$22.00	Dolls of the World — Princess Collection
G8058	Holiday Barbie by Bob Mackie (blonde)	2005	$40.00	
G8061	Birthday Wishes Barbie (black)	2005	$30.00	
G8064	Cynthia Rowley Barbie	2005	$80.00	Cynthia Rowley
G8065	Fairytopia Enchantress Barbie	2004	$35.00	
G8072	Stolen Magic Barbie	2005	$115.00	Barbie Fashion Model
G8078	Suite Retreat Barbie	2005	$40.00	Barbie Fashion Model
G8079	Juicy Couture Barbie Doll	2005	$100.00	Juicy Couture
G8399	Barbie as Princess Annika	2005	$20.00	
G8401	Rayla The Cloud Queen Doll	2005	$20.00	
G8469	Barbie	2004	$6.00	
G8470	Teresa	2004	$6.00	
G8490	Happy Birthday Barbie	2004	$16.00	
G8815	Barbie Pet Doctor	2004	$16.00	
G8815	Pet Doctor Barbie	2004	$20.00	
G8878	Chocolate Obsession Barbie	2005	$35.00	Flavor Obsession
G8887	Martina McBride Barbie	2005	$23.00	
G8889	Happy Go Lightly Barbie	2005	$70.00	Barbie Fashion Model
G8890	Evening Splendor Barbie	2005	$50.00	Collectors' Request
H0178	Holiday Barbie by Bob Mackie (ethnic)	2005	$40.00	
H0187	Lilly Pulitzer Barbie and Stacie Doll Gift Set	2005	$50.00	
H1179	Barbie as Galadriel from *The Lord of the Rings*	2004	$40.00	Hollywood
H1699	Elektra Barbie	2005	$15.00	
H1703	Barbie Loves Shrek	2005	$17.00	
H6465	Muffy Roberts Barbie	2005	$69.00	Barbie Fashion Model
H6466	Ferrari Barbie	2005	$105.00	
H6468	Mickey Mouse Barbie	2005	$15.00	
H6469	Winnie the Pooh Barbie	2005	$15.00	
H6482	Fashion Fun Barbie	2005	$8.00	
H7614	Archie Comics Betty Barbie	2005	$20.00	
H7615	Archie Comics Veronica Barbie	2005	$20.00	
H7616	Harley Quinn Barbie	2005	$24.00	
J0927	Carnival Barbie	2005	$20.00	Festivals of the World
J0928	Chinese New Year Barbie	2005	$20.00	Festivals of the World
J0933	Citrus Obsession Barbie	2005	$35.00	Flavor Obsession

Number	Item	Year	Value	Specials
J0963	Hard Rock Café Barbie	2005	$70.00	Pop Culture
J1743	Peppermint Obsession Barbie	2005	$35.00	Flavor Obsession

Barbie Dolls

Listed by Year

Year	Item	Number	Value	Specials
1959	#1 Ponytail (blonde)	850	$6,900.00	
1959	#1 Ponytail (brunette)	850	$7,000.00	
1959	#2 Ponytail (blonde)	850	$6,400.00	
1959	#2 Ponytail (brunette)	850	$6,400.00	
1960	#3 Ponytail (blonde)	850	$1,000.00	
1960	#3 Ponytail (brunette)	850	$1,100.00	
1960	#4 Ponytail (blonde)	850	$700.00	
1960	#4 Ponytail (brunette)	850	$700.00	
1961	#5 Ponytail (blonde)	850	$550.00	
1961	#5 Ponytail (brunette)	850	$550.00	
1961	#5 Ponytail (titian)	850	$675.00	
1961	Bubble Cut (blonde)	850	$400.00	
1961	Bubble Cut (brunette)	850	$975.00	
1961	Bubble Cut (brunette)	850	$400.00	
1961	Bubble Cut (titian)	850	$400.00	
1961	Bubble Cut (white ginger)	850	$925.00	
1962	#6 Ponytail (ash blonde)	850	$500.00	
1962	#6 Ponytail (blonde)	850	$500.00	
1962	#6 Ponytail (brunette)	850	$500.00	
1962	#6 Ponytail (titian)	850	$500.00	
1962	#6 Ponytail (wheat blonde)	850	$500.00	
1962	#6 Ponytail (yellow blonde)	850	$500.00	
1962	Bubble Cut (blonde)	850	$400.00	
1962	Bubble Cut (brunette)	850	$400.00	
1962	Bubble Cut (titian)	850	$400.00	
1963	After Five	934	$600.00	Dressed Boxed Dolls
1963	American Airlines Stewardess	984	$700.00	Dressed Boxed Dolls
1963	Fashion Queen	870	$450.00	
1963	Garden Party	931	$600.00	Dressed Boxed Dolls
1963	Mood For Music	940	$625.00	Dressed Boxed Dolls
1963	Nighty Negligee	965	$550.00	Dressed Boxed Dolls
1963	Orange Blossom	987	$635.00	Dressed Boxed Dolls
1963	Registered Nurse	991	$760.00	Dressed Boxed Dolls
1963	Solo in the Spotlight	982	$845.00	Dressed Boxed Dolls
1963	Tennis Anyone?	941	$610.00	Dressed Boxed Dolls
1964	Arabian Nights	874	$1,270.00	Dressed Boxed Dolls
1964	Barbie in Holland	823	$820.00	Dressed Boxed Dolls
1964	Barbie in Mexico	820	$820.00	Dressed Boxed Dolls
1964	Barbie in Switzerland	822	$820.00	Dressed Boxed Dolls
1964	Black Magic Ensemble	1609	$860.00	Dressed Boxed Dolls
1964	Bride's Dream	947	$910.00	Dressed Boxed Dolls
1964	Career Girl	954	$858.00	Dressed Boxed Dolls
1964	Cinderella	872	$858.00	Dressed Boxed Dolls
1964	Country Fair	1603	$595.00	Dressed Boxed Dolls
1964	Dinner at Eight	946	$595.00	Dressed Boxed Dolls
1964	Evening Splendour	961	$635.00	Dressed Boxed Dolls
1964	Garden Tea Party	1606	$595.00	Dressed Boxed Dolls
1964	Guinevere	873	$645.00	Dressed Boxed Dolls

Year	Item	Number	Value	Specials
1964	Ice Breaker	942	$695.00	Dressed Boxed Dolls
1964	Knitting Pretty (pink version)	957	$1,265.00	Dressed Boxed Dolls
1964	Knitting Pretty (royal version)	957	$635.00	Dressed Boxed Dolls
1964	Masquerade	944	$635.00	Dressed Boxed Dolls
1964	Miss Barbie (sleep eyes with 3 wigs)	1060	$1,295.00	
1964	Senior Prom	951	$1,145.00	Dressed Boxed Dolls
1964	Swingin' Easy	955	$637.00	Dressed Boxed Dolls
1964	Swirl (ash blonde)	850	$650.00	
1964	Swirl (blonde)	850	$650.00	
1964	Swirl (brunette)	850	$650.00	
1964	Swirl (platinum)	850	$1,300.00	
1964	Swirl (redhead)	850	$650.00	
1964	Theatre Date	959	$660.00	Dressed Boxed Dolls
1964	Wig Wardrobe	971	$475.00	
1964	Wig Wardrobe (head and three wigs only)	871	$450.00	
1965	American Girl (ash blonde)	1070	$1,500.00	
1965	American Girl (blonde)	1070	$1,500.00	
1965	American Girl (brown)	1070	$1,500.00	
1965	American Girl (brunette)	1070	$1,500.00	
1965	American Girl (redhead)	1070	$2,500.00	
1965	Bubble Cut (Japanese, side part)	850	$2,995.00	
1965	Bubble Cut (side part)	850	$445.00	
1965	Color 'n Curl Set (molded Barbie head only)	40389	$585.00	
1965	Color 'n Curl Set (head only)	4839	$500.00	
1965	Posable	8414	$1,225.00	Montgomery Ward
1966	American Girl (brunette)	1070	$2,500.00	
1966	American Girl (color magic face)	1070	$3,000.00	
1966	American Girl (side part/blonde)	1070	$3,000.00	
1966	Case with Doll (swirl ponytail)	2000	$800.00	
1966	Color Magic (plastic box, blonde)	1150	$1,800.00	
1966	Color Magic (plastic box, midnight black)	1150	$3,000.00	
1966	Twist 'n Turn Barbie (chocolate bon-bon, dark brown)	1160	$500.00	
1966	Twist 'n Turn Barbie (go-go co-co, brunette)	1160	$550.00	
1966	Twist 'n Turn Barbie (redhead)	1160	$1,000.00	
1966	Twist 'n Turn Barbie (summer sand, gray)	1160	$550.00	
1966	Twist 'n Turn Barbie (sun kissed, blonde)	1160	$550.00	
1967	Color Magic (cardboard box, blonde)	1150	$3,000.00	
1967	Color Magic (cardboard box, midnight black)	1150	$4,200.00	
1967	Hair Fair	4043	$210.00	
1967	Standard (brunette, straight leg)	1190	$400.00	
1967	Standard (redhead, straight leg)	1190	$900.00	
1967	Trade In Barbie (Twist 'n Turn, redhead)	1162	$375.00	
1967	Travel in Style	1544	$240.00	Sears
1968	Talking (blonde)	1115	$400.00	
1968	Talking (brunette)	1115	$400.00	
1968	Talking (redhead)	1115	$400.00	
1968	Talking (Spanish, plastic box)	8348	$285.00	
1969	Action Accents Set (auburn)	1585	$800.00	Sears
1969	New Living (blonde)	1116	$200.00	
1969	Twist 'n Turn Barbie (brunette, flip hair)	1160	$500.00	
1970	Living	1116	$250.00	
1970	New Living (auburn)	1116	$200.00	
1970	Talking (blonde)	1115	$295.00	
1970	Talking (brunette)	1115	$295.00	

Year	Item	Number	Value	Specials
1970	Talking (redhead)	1115	$295.00	
1970	Twist 'n Turn Barbie (brunette, flip hair)	1160	$500.00	
1971	Dramatic New Living (blonde)	1116	$195.00	
1971	Dramatic New Living (brunette)	1116	$250.00	
1971	Dramatic New Living (redhead)	1116	$150.00	
1971	Growin' Pretty Hair	1144	$375.00	
1971	Hair Fair	4044	$250.00	
1971	Hair Happenin's	1174	$1,075.00	
1971	Live Action (blonde)	1155	$160.00	
1971	Live Action (ranch)	10412	$100.00	Montgomery Ward
1971	Live Action on Stage	1152	$233.00	
1971	Malibu (Sunset)	1067	$65.00	
1971	Twist 'n Turn Barbie (brunette)	1160	$500.00	
1972	25th Anniversary	3939	$650.00	Montgomery Ward
1972	Busy (Talking)	1195	$350.00	
1972	Busy Barbie	3311	$200.00	
1972	Forget-Me-Nots (baggie)	3269	$195.00	Kellogg Company
1972	Malibu (baggie)	1067	$150.00	
1972	Miss America	3194	$175.00	Kellogg Company
1972	Montgomery Ward Anniversary Doll	3210	$750.00	Montgomery Ward
1972	Quick Curl (blonde)	4220	$80.00	
1972	Walk Lively (blonde)	1182	$220.00	
1973	Live Action (baggie)	1155	$165.00	
1973	Miss America	9194	$165.00	Kellogg Company
1973	Newport #1	7807	$175.00	
1973	Newport #2	7807	$175.00	
1973	Quick Curl (with extra outfit)	4220	$100.00	Store Promotional
1973	Sun Valley	7806	$95.00	
1973	Ten Speeder	7777	$30.00	
1974	Barbie Babysits (yellow)	7882	$70.00	
1974	Free Moving	7270	$160.00	
1974	Hair Fair Set (re-issue)	4043	$125.00	
1974	Kellogg Quick Curl	3197	$60.00	Kellogg Company
1974	Malibu Barbie & Her Ten-Speeder Set	10456	$95.00	Montgomery Ward
1974	Miss America	9194	$150.00	Kellogg Company
1974	My First Barbie	1875	$35.00	
1974	Sweet 16	7796	$73.00	Store Promotional
1975	Gold Medal Barbie and Her U.S. Olympic Wardrobe	9044	$90.00	Sears
1975	Gold Medal Skater	7262	$75.00	
1975	Gold Medal Skier	7264	$75.00	
1975	Gold Medal Swimmer	7233	$75.00	
1975	Gold Medal Winter Sports	9042	$85.00	Sears
1975	Hawaiian	7470	$50.00	Department Store
1975	Malibu	1067	$45.00	
1975	Winter Sports (catalog only)	9042	$100.00	Sears
1976	Ballerina Barbie (1st version)	9093	$70.00	
1976	Ballerina Barbie on Tour	9613	$125.00	Department Store
1976	Ballerina on Tour (1st hair version)	9613	$140.00	
1976	Beautiful Bride	9599	$200.00	Department Store
1976	Deluxe Quick Curl	9217	$100.00	Jergens
1977	Plus 3	9953	$85.00	Ben Franklin
1977	Super Size Barbie	9828	$250.00	
1977	Super Size Bride	9975	$295.00	Department Store
1977	Super Size Bridal Barbie	9975	$295.00	Department Store

Year	Item	Number	Value	Specials
1977	SuperStar Barbie (with SuperStar Necklace)	9720	$60.00	Store Promotional
1977	SuperStar Barbie in the Spotlight	2207	$75.00	
1978	Beautiful Bride	9907	$175.00	Department Store
1978	Fashion Photo	2210	$60.00	
1978	Hawaiian SuperStar	2289	$175.00	
1978	Malibu Fashion Combo	2753	$65.00	Catalog Showroom
1978	SuperStar Barbie (with SuperStar Haircomb) #1	9720	$60.00	Store Promotional
1978	SuperStar Barbie (with SuperStar Haircomb) #2	9720	$60.00	Store Promotional
1978	SuperStar Barbie Fashion Change-abouts	2583	$90.00	Tru Value
1978	SuperStar Barbie in the Spotlight	2586	$110.00	Department Store
1979	Ballerina Barbie(2nd issue)	9093	$45.00	
1979	Ballerina Barbie on Tour (no wrist tag)	9613	$110.00	Department Store
1979	Ballerina Barbie on Tour (with wrist tag)	9613	$120.00	Department Store
1979	Ballerina on Tour (2nd hair version)	9613	$90.00	
1979	Kissing (bangs style)	2597	$45.00	Department Store
1979	Kissing (extra dress)	2597	$45.00	Department Store
1979	Pretty Changes Barbie (with free Barbie play perfume)	2598	$90.00	Store Promotional
1979	Sport Star	1334	$25.00	
1979	Sun Lovin' Malibu	1067	$40.00	
1979	Super Size Barbie (super hair)	2844	$250.00	
1980	Beauty Secrets Barbie, Pretty Reflections	1290	$75.00	Department Store
1980	Black Barbie Doll	1293	$75.00	
1980	Hispanic Barbie	1292	$60.00	
1980	Italian	1602	$150.00	Dolls of the World
1980	Malibu Barbie – The Beach Party with Case	1703	$60.00	
1980	Malibu Barbie Beach Party, The	1703	$55.00	Department Store
1980	Parisian	1600	$90.00	Dolls of the World
1980	Pretty Changes	2598	$70.00	
1980	Pretty Changes (lamp)	2598	$80.00	
1980	Roller Skating	1880	$60.00	
1980	Royal	1601	$115.00	Dolls of the World
1981	Golden Dream	1874	$50.00	
1981	Golden Dreams	3533	$70.00	Department Store
1981	Golden Dreams (2nd issue, big hair)	3533	$70.00	Department Store
1981	Happy Birthday	1922	$45.00	
1981	My First Barbie	1875	$25.00	
1981	Oriental	3262	$150.00	Dolls of the World
1981	Scottish	3263	$90.00	Dolls of the World
1981	Sunsational Malibu	1067	$30.00	
1981	Sunsational Malibu (Hispanic)	4970	$40.00	
1981	Western	1757	$50.00	
1982	Dreamtime Barbie	5868	$20.00	
1982	Eskimo	3898	$65.00	Dolls of the World
1982	Fashion Jeans	5315	$30.00	
1982	Fashion Jeans (black)	5313	$30.00	
1982	Hawaiian (one-piece swimsuit)	7470	$50.00	Department Store
1982	India	3897	$75.00	Dolls of the World
1982	Magic Curl	3856	$55.00	
1982	Magic Curl (black)	3989	$40.00	
1982	Pink & Pretty	3554	$40.00	
1982	Pink & Pretty Barbie Extra Special Modeling Set	5239	$75.00	Department Store
1982	Super Dance	5838	$40.00	
1983	Angel Face	5640	$35.00	
1983	Ballerina	4983	$40.00	Mervyn's

Year	Item	Number	Value	Specials
1983	Ballerina (black)	4984	$60.00	Mervyn's
1983	Dream Date	5868	$40.00	
1983	Fashion Play (pink & white jumpsuit)	7193	$25.00	
1983	Hawaiian (two-piece swimsuit)	7470	$40.00	Department Store
1983	Horse Lovin'	1757	$40.00	
1983	Loving You	7072	$55.00	
1983	Loving You	7583	$50.00	
1983	My First Barbie	1875	$35.00	
1983	Party Time	4798	$20.00	
1983	Playtime	5336	$20.00	
1983	Spanish Barbie #1	4031	$65.00	Dolls of the World
1983	Swedish Barbie	4032	$54.00	Dolls of the World
1983	Twirly Curls	5579	$35.00	Department Store
1983	Twirly Curls (black)	5723	$35.00	
1983	Twirly Curls (Hispanic)	5724	$35.00	
1984	Crystal	4598	$30.00	
1984	Crystal (black)	4859	$30.00	
1984	Dance Sensation	9058	$60.00	Toys "R" Us
1984	Great Shape	7025	$30.00	
1984	Great Shape (black)	7834	$25.00	
1984	Happy Birthday (2nd issue)	1922	$25.00	
1984	Happy Birthday (3rd issue)	1922	$30.00	
1984	Irish	7517	$75.00	Dolls of the World
1984	My First Barbie (black)	9858	$30.00	
1984	Sun Gold Malibu	1067	$25.00	
1984	Swiss	7541	$48.00	Dolls of the World
1985	Beach Time	9102	$25.00	
1985	Day-to-Night	7929	$40.00	
1985	Day-to-Night (black)	7945	$30.00	
1985	Day-to-Night (Hispanic)	7944	$40.00	
1985	Deluxe Tropical Barbie	2996	$30.00	
1985	Dream Time	9180	$25.00	Toys "R" Us
1985	Japanese	9481	$70.00	Dolls of the World
1985	Le Nouveau Theater de la Mode (Billy Boy) France	6279	$220.00	
1985	Peaches 'n Cream	7926	$40.00	
1985	Peaches 'n Cream (black)	9516	$35.00	
1985	Sears 100th Anniversary Celebration	2998	$100.00	Sears
1985	Sun Gold Malibu (black)	7745	$20.00	
1985	Sun Gold Malibu (Hispanic)	4970	$25.00	
1986	Astronaut	2449	$65.00	
1986	Astronaut (black)	1207	$60.00	
1986	Blue Rhapsody	1708	$299.00	Porcelain
1986	Celebration Barbie	1998	$65.00	Sears
1986	Deluxe Tropical Barbie	2996	$40.00	Department Store
1986	Dream Glow	2248	$25.00	
1986	Dream Glow (black)	2242	$25.00	
1986	Dream Glow (Hispanic)	1647	$30.00	
1986	Fabulous Fur	7093	$65.00	Mervyn's
1986	Funtime (black)	1739	$30.00	Toys "R" Us
1986	Gift Giving	1922	$35.00	
1986	Greek	2997	$38.00	Dolls of the World
1986	Magic Moves	2126	$60.00	
1986	Magic Moves (black)	2127	$40.00	
1986	Music Lovin'	9988	$50.00	

Year	Item	Number	Value	Specials
1986	Peruvian I	2995	$36.00	Dolls of the World
1986	Rocker	1140	$50.00	
1986	Tropical	1017	$20.00	
1986	Tropical (black)	1022	$20.00	
1986	Tropical (Hispanic)	1646	$25.00	
1986	Vacation Sensation (blue)	1675	$50.00	Toys "R" Us
1987	Barbie Celebration	9146	$30.00	
1987	California Barbie	4439	$20.00	
1987	California Barbie (with Beach Boys record)	4442	$30.00	
1987	Enchanted Evening	3415	$228.00	Porcelain
1987	Fashion Play	9429	$30.00	
1987	Feelin' Groovy	3421	$175.00	Department Store
1987	Funtime (blue watch)	3717	$30.00	Toys "R" Us
1987	Funtime (pink watch)	3718	$30.00	Toys "R" Us
1987	Funtime (purple watch)	1738	$30.00	Toys "R" Us
1987	German	3188	$50.00	Dolls of the World
1987	Icelandic	3189	$45.00	Dolls of the World
1987	Jewel Secrets	1737	$30.00	
1987	Jewel Secrets (black)	1756	$20.00	
1987	My First Barbie	1788	$20.00	
1987	My First Barbie (black)	1801	$20.00	
1987	My First Barbie (Hispanic)	5979	$28.00	Zayre's
1987	Olympic Skating Star	4549	$50.00	
1987	Party Pink	4629	$25.00	Wal-Mart
1987	Pink Jubilee (25th Anniversary Wal-Mart)	4589	$50.00	Wal-Mart
1987	Rocker (2nd issue)	3055	$50.00	
1987	Star Dream	4550	$50.00	Sears
1987	Super Hair	3101	$25.00	
1987	Super Hair (black)	3296	$20.00	
1988	Animal Lovin'	1350	$30.00	
1988	Animal Lovin' (black)	4824	$30.00	
1988	Benefit Performance	5475	$235.00	Nostalgic Porcelain
1988	California Dream	4439	$30.00	
1988	Canadian	4928	$35.00	Dolls of the World
1988	Doctor Barbie	3850	$55.00	
1988	Dreamtime Barbie	9180	$35.00	Toys "R" Us
1988	Feelin' Fun (2nd version)	4808	$20.00	
1988	Feelin' Fun (1st version)	1189	$30.00	
1988	Frills & Fantasy	1374	$45.00	Wal-Mart
1988	Fun to Dress	4558	$15.00	
1988	Fun to Dress (black)	7668	$15.00	
1988	Happy Holidays 1988	1703	$390.00	Happy Holidays Collection
1988	Island Fun	4061	$20.00	
1988	Korean	4929	$35.00	Dolls of the World
1988	Lilac and Lovely	7669	$45.00	Sears
1988	Mardi Gras	4930	$45.00	American Beauty Collection
1988	My First Barbie	1280	$20.00	
1988	My First Barbie (black)	1281	$20.00	
1988	My First Barbie (Hispanic)	1282	$20.00	
1988	Perfume Pretty	4551	$30.00	
1988	Perfume Pretty (black)	4552	$30.00	
1988	Sensations	4931	$50.00	
1988	Show 'n Ride	7799	$40.00	Toys "R" Us
1988	Skating Star	4547	$65.00	Sears
1988	SuperStar Barbie	1604	$40.00	

Year	Item	Number	Value	Specials
1988	SuperStar Barbie (black)	1605	$25.00	
1988	Vacation Sensation (pink)	1675	$50.00	Toys "R" Us
1989	Army	3966	$25.00	American Beauty Collection
1989	Beach Blast	3237	$15.00	
1989	Beach Blast (black)	3253	$20.00	
1989	Cool Times	3022	$25.00	
1989	Dance Club with Tape Player	3509	$55.00	Child's World
1989	Evening Enchantment	3596	$38.00	Sears
1989	Feelin' Fun (black)	4809	$20.00	
1989	Feelin' Fun (Hispanic)	7373	$20.00	
1989	Fun to Dress	1372	$15.00	
1989	Fun to Dress (black)	1373	$15.00	
1989	Garden Party	1953	$20.00	Wal-Mart
1989	Gift Giving	1205	$35.00	
1989	Gold and Lace	7476	$35.00	Target
1989	Golden Greetings	7734	$100.00	FAO Schwarz
1989	Happy Holidays 1989	3523	$125.00	Happy Holidays Collection
1989	Lavender Looks	3963	$35.00	Wal-Mart
1989	Mexican	1917	$25.00	Dolls of the World
1989	Party Lace	4843	$35.00	Hill's
1989	Party Pink	7637	$25.00	Winn Dixie
1989	Party Treats	4885	$25.00	Toys "R" Us
1989	Peach Pretty	4870	$32.00	K-Mart
1989	Pepsi Spirit	4869	$75.00	Toys "R" Us
1989	Pink Jubilee	3756	$800.00	Jubilee Series
1989	Russian	1916	$30.00	Dolls of the World
1989	Special Expressions	4842	$25.00	Woolworth
1989	Special Expressions (black)	7346	$25.00	Woolworth
1989	Starlight Blue	3553	$40.00	Lady Lovely Locks
1989	Style Magic	1283	$30.00	
1989	Style Magic (black)	1288	$30.00	
1989	Sweet Roses	7635	$30.00	Toys "R" Us
1989	Unicef	1920	$20.00	Unicef
1989	Unicef (Asian)	4774	$24.00	Unicef
1989	Unicef (black)	4770	$18.00	
1989	Unicef (Hispanic)	4782	$24.00	
1989	Wedding Fantasy (black)	7011	$45.00	
1989	Wedding Party	2641	$275.00	Nostalgic Porcelain
1990	Barbie and Snowball Her Pet Dog	7272	$15.00	
1990	Barbie and the All Stars	9099	$25.00	
1990	Barbie and the Beat	2751	$25.00	
1990	Brazilian	9094	$27.00	Dolls of the World
1990	Cool Looks	5947	$25.00	Toys "R" Us
1990	Dance Magic	4836	$25.00	
1990	Dance Magic (black)	7080	$25.00	
1990	Disney Special (black)	9385	$45.00	Child's World
1990	Doctor Barbie	3850	$45.00	Toys "R" Us
1990	Dream Fantasy	7335	$35.00	Wal-Mart
1990	Evening Elegance	7057	$75.00	JCPenney
1990	Evening Sparkle	3274	$35.00	Hill's
1990	Fashion Play	5766	$20.00	Woolworth
1990	Flight Time Barbie	9584	$35.00	
1990	Flight Time Barbie (black)	9916	$30.00	
1990	Flight Time Barbie (Hispanic)	2066	$57.00	
1990	Friendship Barbie, Berlin Wall I	5506	$24.00	Friendship

Year	Item	Number	Value	Specials
1990	Fun to Dress	4808	$15.00	
1990	Fun to Dress (black)	4939	$15.00	
1990	Fun to Dress (Hispanic)	7373	$15.00	
1990	Gold	5405	$500.00	Bob Mackie
1990	Golden Evening	2587	$45.00	Target
1990	Happy Birthday (black)	9561	$35.00	
1990	Happy Holidays 1990	4098	$65.00	Happy Holidays Collection
1990	Happy Holidays 1990 (black)	4543	$40.00	Happy Holidays Collection
1990	Home Pretty	2249	$20.00	
1990	Hot Dancin' Set	4841	$40.00	
1990	Ice Capades 50th Anniversary	7365	$50.00	
1990	Ice Capades 50th Anniversary (black)	7348	$25.00	
1990	Lavender Surprise	9049	$32.00	Sears
1990	Lavender Surprise (black)	5588	$35.00	Sears
1990	My First Barbie	9942	$20.00	
1990	My First Barbie	96085	$75.00	Deco-Pak
1990	My First Barbie (black)	96085	$55.00	Deco-Pak
1990	My First Barbie (black)	9943	$20.00	
1990	My First Barbie (Hispanic)	9944	$25.00	
1990	Nigerian	7376	$30.00	Dolls of the World
1990	Party Pretty	5955	$30.00	Target
1990	Party Sensation	9025	$55.00	Wholesale Clubs
1990	Pink Sensation	5410	$25.00	Winn Dixie
1990	Solo in the Spotlight	7613	$145.00	Nostalgic Porcelain
1990	Sophisticated Lady	5313	$140.00	Nostalgic Porcelain
1990	Special Expressions	5504	$20.00	Woolworth
1990	Special Expressions (black)	5505	$20.00	Woolworth
1990	Style	5315	$35.00	Applause
1990	Summit	7027	$15.00	
1990	Summit (Asian)	7029	$22.00	
1990	Summit (black)	7028	$15.00	
1990	Summit (Hispanic)	7030	$24.00	
1990	Wedding Fantasy	2125	$45.00	
1990	Western Fun	9932	$30.00	
1990	Western Fun (black)	2930	$30.00	
1990	Wet 'n Wild	4103	$20.00	
1990	Winter Fantasy Barbie	5946	$90.00	FAO Schwarz
1990	Winter Fun	5949	$40.00	Toys "R" Us
1991	Air Force	3360	$30.00	Stars 'n Stripes
1991	All American	9423	$28.00	Reebok
1991	American Beauty Queen	3137	$35.00	
1991	American Beauty Queen (black)	3245	$35.00	
1991	Applause Barbie	3406	$35.00	Applause
1991	Ballroom Beauty	3678	$30.00	Wal-Mart
1991	Barbie Doll	1511	$80.00	McGlynn's Bakery
1991	Barbie Doll (black)	1534	$80.00	McGlynn's Bakery
1991	Barbie for President (black, Presidential seal)	3940	$45.00	Toys "R" Us
1991	Barbie for President (Presidential seal)	3722	$65.00	Toys "R" Us
1991	Bathtime Fun	9601	$15.00	Wal-Mart Wholesale Clubs
1991	Bathtime Fun (black)	9603	$15.00	Wal-Mart Wholesale Clubs
1991	Benetton	9404	$30.00	
1991	Benetton Shopping	4873	$30.00	
1991	Blossom Beauty	3142	$40.00	Shopko/Venture
1991	Blue Rhapsody	1364	$140.00	Service Merchandise
1991	Bridesmaid	9608	$30.00	

Year	Item	Number	Value	Specials
1991	Costume Ball	7123	$30.00	
1991	Costume Ball (black)	7134	$30.00	
1991	Cute 'n Cool	2954	$30.00	Target
1991	Czechoslovakian	7330	$55.00	Dolls of the World
1991	Dayton Hudson Cute 'n Cool	2954	$25.00	
1991	Disney Special (with mouse hat)	4385	$45.00	Child's World
1991	Enchanted Evening	2702	$75.00	JCPenney
1991	Eskimo (reissue)	9844	$32.00	Dolls of the World
1991	Evening Flame	1865	$150.00	Home Shopping Club
1991	Fashion Play	9629	$15.00	
1991	Fashion Play (black)	5953	$15.00	
1991	Fashion Play (Hispanic)	5954	$15.00	
1991	Fashion Play (turquoise dress)	2713	$25.00	
1991	Friendship Barbie, Berlin Wall II	2080	$29.00	Friendship
1991	Gay Parisienne (blonde)	9973	$350.00	Nostalgic Porcelain
1991	Gay Parisienne (brunette)	9973	$135.00	Nostalgic Porcelain
1991	Gay Parisienne (redhead/porcelain)	9973-9999	$350.00	Disney
1991	German Talking	4767	$55.00	
1991	Happy Birthday	7914	$36.00	
1991	Happy Birthday (black)	7913	$35.00	
1991	Happy Holidays 1991	1871	$65.00	Happy Holidays Collection
1991	Happy Holidays 1991 (black)	2696	$40.00	Happy Holidays Collection
1991	Hawaiian Fun	5940	$20.00	
1991	Ice Capades	9847	$30.00	
1991	Jewel Jubilee	2366	$65.00	Wholesale Clubs
1991	Lights 'n Lace	9725	$30.00	
1991	Malaysian	7329	$25.00	Dolls of the World
1991	Marine Biologist (black)		$15.00	Career
1991	Moonlight Rose	3549	$32.00	Hill's
1991	Navy	9693	$27.00	Stars 'n Stripes
1991	Navy (black)	9694	$27.00	Stars 'n Stripes
1991	Night Sensation	2921	$60.00	FAO Schwarz
1991	Parisian #1	9843	$35.00	Dolls of the World
1991	Parisian #2 (Japan)	9843	$38.00	Dolls of the World
1991	Party in Pink	2909	$30.00	Ames
1991	Platinum	2703	$289.00	Bob Mackie
1991	School Fun	2721	$22.00	Toys "R" Us
1991	Scottish (reissue)	9845	$45.00	Dolls of the World
1991	Ski Fun	7511	$30.00	
1991	Southern Beauty	3284	$25.00	Winn Dixie
1991	Southern Belle	2586	$40.00	Sears
1991	Special Expressions	2582	$20.00	Woolworth
1991	Special Expressions (black)	2583	$20.00	Woolworth
1991	Specialty Deco-Pak Barbie	1511	$75.00	Deco-Pak
1991	Specialty Deco-Pak Barbie (black)	1534	$55.00	Deco-Pak
1991	Starlight Splendor	2704	$500.00	Bob Mackie
1991	Sterling Wishes	3347	$75.00	Spiegel
1991	Swan Lake	1648	$88.00	Musical Ballet Series
1991	Sweet Romance	2917	$30.00	
1991	Teen Talk	5745	$50.00	
1991	Teen Talk (ash blonde)	5745	$50.00	
1991	Teen Talk (brunette)	5745	$50.00	
1991	Teen Talk (strawberry blonde)	5745	$50.00	
1991	Totally Hair	1112	$35.00	
1991	Totally Hair (black)	5948	$25.00	

Year	Item	Number	Value	Specials
1991	Totally Hair (brunette)	1117	$35.00	
1991	Trail Blazin'	2783	$25.00	Supermarket
1991	Wedding Day	9608	$35.00	
1992	Anniversary Star	2282	$30.00	Wal-Mart
1992	Barbie for President (white star)	3722	$40.00	Toys "R" Us
1992	Bath Magic	5274	$15.00	
1992	Bath Magic (black)	7951	$15.00	
1992	Benefit Ball	1521	$45.00	Classique
1992	Birthday Surprise	3679	$40.00	
1992	Birthday Surprise (black)	4051	$40.00	
1992	Blossom Beautiful	3817	$225.00	Sears
1992	Blue Elegance	1879	$50.00	Hill's
1992	Cool 'n Sassy	1490	$25.00	Toys "R" Us
1992	Cool 'n Sassy (black)	4110	$25.00	Toys "R" Us
1992	Crystal Rhapsody (blonde)	1553	$220.00	Presidential Porcelain
1992	Crystal Rhapsody (brunette, Disney)	10201	$350.00	Presidential Porcelain
1992	Dazzlin' Date	3203	$30.00	Target
1992	Denim 'n Lace	2452	$28.00	Ames
1992	Disney Fun Barbie	10247	$50.00	Disney
1992	Disney Weekend Barbie	12957	$60.00	Disney Europe
1992	Dream Bride Barbie	1623	$60.00	
1992	Dream Princess	2306	$40.00	Sears
1992	Dream Wardrobe Barbie	3331	$35.00	Wholesale Clubs
1992	Empress Bride	4247	$460.00	Bob Mackie
1992	English	4973	$37.00	Dolls of the World
1992	Evening Sensation	1278	$50.00	JCPenney
1992	Fancy Frills	3474	$40.00	
1992	Fantastica	3196	$60.00	Wholesale Clubs
1992	Fashion Brights	1882	$20.00	Toys "R" Us
1992	Fashion Brights (black)	4112	$20.00	Toys "R" Us
1992	Fashion Play	2730	$15.00	
1992	Fashion Play (black)	3842	$15.00	
1992	Fashion Play (Hispanic)	3860	$15.00	
1992	Friendship Barbie, Berlin Wall III	3677	$25.00	Friendship
1992	Fun to Dress (Hispanic)	4809	$15.00	
1992	Happy Holidays 1992	1429	$50.00	Happy Holidays Collection
1992	Happy Holidays 1992 (black)	2396	$38.00	Happy Holidays Collection
1992	Hot Looks	5756	$25.00	Ames
1992	Jamaican	4647	$28.00	Dolls of the World
1992	Madison Avenue	1539	$100.00	FAO Schwarz
1992	Marine Corps	7549	$25.00	Stars 'n Stripes
1992	Marine Corps (black)	7594	$25.00	Stars 'n Stripes
1992	Mermaid	1434	$20.00	
1992	My First Ballerina	3839	$20.00	
1992	My First Ballerina (black)	3861	$20.00	
1992	My First Barbie	3839	$20.00	
1992	My First Barbie (Hispanic)	3860	$20.00	
1992	Neptune Fantasy	4248	$455.00	Bob Mackie
1992	Nutcracker	5472	$79.00	Musical Ballet Series
1992	Party Perfect	1876	$34.00	Shopko/Venture
1992	Party Premiere	2001	$20.00	Supermarket
1992	Peach Blossom	7009	$40.00	Wholesale Clubs
1992	Picnic Pretty	3808	$35.00	Osco Drugs
1992	Plantation Belle (blonde)	5351	$315.00	Disney
1992	Plantation Belle (redhead)	7526	$140.00	Porcelain

Year	Item	Number	Value	Specials
1992	Pretty Hearts	2901	$25.00	Supermarket
1992	Pretty in Plaid	5413	$30.00	Target
1992	Pretty in Purple	3117	$25.00	K-Mart
1992	Pretty in Purple (black)	3121	$25.00	K-Mart
1992	Pretty Surprise	9823	$20.00	
1992	Radiant in Red	1276	$45.00	Toys "R" Us
1992	Radiant in Red (Hispanic)	4113	$45.00	Toys "R" Us
1992	Rappin' Rockin'	3248	$40.00	
1992	Red Romance	3161	$25.00	Supermarket
1992	Regal Reflections	4116	$200.00	Spiegel
1992	Rollerblade	2214	$30.00	
1992	Royal Romance	1858	$80.00	Wholesale Clubs
1992	Satin Nights	1886	$70.00	Service Merchandise
1992	School Fun (black)	4111	$22.00	Toys "R" Us
1992	Singapore Girl 1	None	$100.00	Singapore Airlines
1992	Snap 'n Play	3550	$20.00	
1992	Snap 'n Play (black)	3556	$20.00	
1992	Something Extra	863	$25.00	Meijer
1992	Spanish Barbie #2	4963	$33.00	Dolls of the World
1992	Sparkle Eyes	2482	$30.00	
1992	Sparkle Eyes Barbie (black)	5950	$30.00	
1992	Sparkle Eyes Barbie Dressing Room and Fashion Set	7131	$55.00	Wholesale Clubs
1992	Special Expressions	3197	$25.00	Woolworth
1992	Special Expressions (black)	3198	$30.00	Woolworth
1992	Special Expressions (Hispanic)	3200	$25.00	Woolworth
1992	Spring Parade	7008	$35.00	Toys "R" Us
1992	Spring Parade (black)	2257	$35.00	Toys "R" Us
1992	Sun Sensation	1390	$20.00	
1992	Sun Sensation Barbie Spray & Play Fun	7149	$60.00	Wholesale Clubs
1992	Sweet Lavender	2522	$30.00	Woolworth
1992	Sweet Lavender (black)	2225	$30.00	Woolworth
1992	Sweet Lavender (Hispanic)	3200	$30.00	Woolworth
1992	Sweet Spring	3208	$22.00	Supermarket
1992	Teen Talk (black)	1612	$30.00	
1992	Teen Talk (redhead)	5745	$50.00	
1992	Teen Talk, "Math Class is Tough"	5745	$65.00	
1992	Very Violet	1859	$65.00	Wholesale Clubs
1992	Wild Style Barbie	411	$26.00	Target
1992	Winter Belle	1637	$20.00	
1993	1920s Flapper Barbie	4063	$55.00	Great Eras Collection
1993	Angel Lights	10610	$50.00	
1993	Army Desert Storm	1234	$24.00	Stars 'n Stripes
1993	Army Desert Storm (black)	5816	$24.00	Stars 'n Stripes
1993	Australian Barbie #1	3626	$32.00	Dolls of the World
1993	Australian Barbie #2	3626	$34.00	Dolls of the World
1993	Back to School	10217	$25.00	Supermarket
1993	Barbie in India	9910	$50.00	
1993	Baseball	4583	$30.00	Target
1993	Bath Blast	4159	$15.00	
1993	Bath Blast (black)	3830	$15.00	
1993	Bedtime	11079	$15.00	
1993	Bedtime (black)	11184	$15.00	
1993	Birthday Party	3388	$30.00	
1993	Birthday Party (black)	7948	$30.00	

Year	Item	Number	Value	Specials
1993	Caboodles	3157	$20.00	
1993	Caboodles Barbie with Child-Sized Caboodles case	11285	$35.00	JCPenney
1993	City Style Barbie	10149	$35.00	Classique
1993	Country Looks	5854	$25.00	Ames
1993	Disney Weekend	10723	$50.00	Disney
1993	Disney Weekend Barbie & Ken Deluxe	10724	$75.00	Disney Europe
1993	Earring Magic	7014	$20.00	
1993	Earring Magic (black)	2374	$20.00	
1993	Earring Magic (brunette)	10255	$30.00	
1993	Earring Magic Barbie Doll Software Pak	25-1992	$30.00	Radio Shack
1993	Enchanted Princess	10292	$50.00	Sears
1993	Festiva	10339	$50.00	Wholesale Clubs
1993	Fountain Mermaid	10393	$20.00	
1993	Fountain Mermaid (black)	10522	$20.00	
1993	Fun to Dress	3240	$15.00	
1993	Fun to Dress (black)	2570	$15.00	
1993	Fun to Dress (Hispanic)	2763	$15.00	
1993	Gibson Girl	3702	$45.00	Great Eras Collection
1993	Glitter Beach	3602	$15.00	
1993	Gold Sensation	10246	$180.00	Porcelain
1993	Golden Winter	10684	$50.00	JCPenney
1993	Golf Date	10202	$30.00	Target
1993	Happy Holidays 1993	10824	$48.00	Happy Holidays Collection
1993	Happy Holidays 1993 (black)	10911	$32.00	Happy Holidays Collection
1993	Holiday Hostess	10280	$40.00	Supermarket
1993	Hollywood Hair	2308	$25.00	
1993	Hollywood Hair Barbie Deluxe Play Set	10928	$25.00	Wholesale Clubs
1993	Italian (reissue)	2256	$36.00	Dolls of the World
1993	Little Debbie Barbie Series I	10123	$60.00	Little Debbie Snacks
1993	Malt Shop	4581	$35.00	Toys "R" Us
1993	Masquerade Ball (scented)	10803	$275.00	Bob Mackie
1993	Moonlight Magic	10608	$85.00	Toys "R" Us
1993	Moonlight Magic (black)	10609	$80.00	Toys "R" Us
1993	My First Ballerina	2516	$20.00	
1993	My First Ballerina (black)	2767	$20.00	
1993	My First Ballerina (Hispanic)	2770	$20.00	
1993	My First Barbie	2516	$18.00	
1993	My First Barbie (black)	2767	$20.00	
1993	My Size	2517	$115.00	
1993	My Size (black)	11212	$120.00	
1993	Naf Naf (Europe)	10997	$40.00	
1993	Native American #1	1753	$32.00	Dolls of the World
1993	Opening Night	10148	$38.00	Classique
1993	Paint & Dazzle (black)	10058	$15.00	
1993	Paint & Dazzle (blonde)	10039	$15.00	
1993	Paint & Dazzle (brunette)	10059	$15.00	
1993	Paint & Dazzle (redhead)	10057	$15.00	
1993	Police Officer	10688	$75.00	Toys "R" Us
1993	Police Officer (black)	10689	$75.00	Toys "R" Us
1993	Rockettes	2017	$120.00	FAO Schwarz
1993	Romantic Bride	1861	$35.00	
1993	Romantic Bride (black)	11054	$35.00	
1993	Royal Invitation	10969	$85.00	Spiegel
1993	Royal Splendor	10950	$170.00	Presidential Porcelain

Year	Item	Number	Value	Specials
1993	Sara Lee Barbie	60403	$65.00	Sara Lee
1993	School Spirit Barbie	10682	$25.00	Toys "R" Us
1993	School Spirit Barbie (black)	10683	$25.00	Toys "R" Us
1993	Sea Holiday Barbie	5471	$25.00	Toys "R" Us
1993	Secret Hearts	7902	$30.00	
1993	Secret Hearts (black)	3836	$20.00	
1993	Shopping Fun Barbie	10051	$25.00	Meijer
1993	Silken Flame Barbie (blonde)	11099	$330.00	Porcelain Disney
1993	Sparkling Splendor	10994	$50.00	Service Merchandise
1993	Special Expressions	10048	$20.00	Woolworth
1993	Special Expressions (black)	10049	$18.00	Woolworth
1993	Special Expressions (Hispanic)	10050	$18.00	Woolworth
1993	Spots 'n Dots	10491	$45.00	Toys "R" Us
1993	Spring Bouquet	3477	$22.00	Supermarket
1993	SuperStar Barbie	10592	$30.00	Wal-Mart
1993	SuperStar Barbie (black)	10711	$40.00	Wal-Mart
1993	Sweetheart Barbie	3161	$35.00	Supermarket
1993	Swim 'n Dive	11505	$20.00	
1993	Swim 'n Dive (black)	11734	$20.00	
1993	Troll	10257	$25.00	
1993	Twinkle Lights	10390	$50.00	
1993	Twinkle Lights (black)	10521	$40.00	
1993	Wacky Warehouse I	10309	$55.00	Kool-Aid
1993	Western Stampin'	10293	$25.00	
1993	Western Stampin' (black)	10539	$25.00	
1993	Western Stampin' Barbie Deluxe Play Set	10927	$30.00	Wholesale Clubs
1993	Winter Princess	10655	$110.00	Winter Princess Collection
1993	Winter Royal	10658	$75.00	Wholesale Clubs
1994	1850s Southern Belle	11478	$42.00	Great Eras Collection
1994	35th Anniversary (redhead)	11591	$425.00	Mattel Festival Doll
1994	35th Anniversary Barbie (blonde with arched eyebrows)	11590	$23.00	Nostalgic
1994	35th Anniversary Barbie (blonde with curved eyebrows)	11590	$28.00	Nostalgic
1994	35th Anniversary Barbie (brunette with arched eyebrows)	11782	$24.00	Nostalgic
1994	35th Anniversary Barbie (brunette with curved eyebrows)	11782	$36.00	Nostalgic
1994	35th Anniversary Barbie Keepsake Collection	11591	$77.00	Nostalgic
1994	35th Anniversary Festival Barbie	12670	$200.00	Barbie Festival
1994	Air Force Thunderbirds	11552	$20.00	Stars 'n Stripes
1994	Air Force Thunderbirds (black)	11553	$20.00	Stars 'n Stripes
1994	Astronaut	12149	$45.00	Toys "R" Us
1994	Astronaut (black)	12150	$45.00	Toys "R" Us
1994	B Mine Barbie	11182	$22.00	Supermarket
1994	Banquet Set Barbie Doll (blonde)	850	$299.00	Barbie Festival
1994	Banquet Set Barbie Doll (redhead)	850	$299.00	Barbie Festival
1994	Bedtime Barbie with Bed	12184	$30.00	Wholesale Clubs
1994	Bicyclin'	11689	$25.00	Toys "R" Us
1994	Bicyclin' (black)	11817	$25.00	Toys "R" Us
1994	Birthday	11333	$30.00	
1994	Birthday (black)	11334	$30.00	
1994	Camp	11074	$25.00	
1994	Camp (black)	11831	$20.00	
1994	Chinese	11180	$23.00	Dolls of the World

Year	Item	Number	Value	Specials
1994	City Sophisticate	12005	$50.00	Service Merchandise
1994	Country & Western Star	11646	$30.00	Wal-Mart
1994	Country & Western Star (black)	12096	$30.00	Wal-Mart
1994	Country & Western Star (Hispanic)	12097	$30.00	Wal-Mart
1994	Country Star Western Horse	12271	$25.00	Wal-Mart
1994	Dance 'n Twirl	11902	$50.00	
1994	Dance 'n Twirl (black)	12143	$45.00	
1994	Disney Fun II	11650	$45.00	Disney
1994	Doctor Barbie (black, with white baby)	11814	$38.00	
1994	Doctor Barbie (brunette)	12903	$100.00	Mattel Festival Doll
1994	Doctor Barbie (with black baby)	11160	$30.00	
1994	Dolls of the World Limited Edition Set	12043	$49.00	Dolls of the World
1994	Dream Dancing	11902	$16.00	
1994	Dream Dancing (black)	12143	$16.00	
1994	Dress 'n Fun	10776	$15.00	
1994	Dress 'n Fun (black)	12143	$15.00	
1994	Dress 'n Fun (Hispanic)	11102	$15.00	
1994	Dutch	11104	$29.00	Dolls of the World
1994	Easter Fun	11276	$25.00	Supermarket
1994	Egyptian Queen	11397	$48.00	Great Eras Collection
1994	Emerald Elegance	12322	$35.00	Toys "R" Us
1994	Emerald Elegance	12322	$33.00	Society Style
1994	Emerald Elegance (black)	12323	$35.00	Toys "R" Us
1994	Emerald Elegance (black)	12323	$33.00	Society Style
1994	Evening Extravaganza	11622	$40.00	Classique
1994	Evening Extravaganza (black)	11638	$44.00	Classique
1994	Evergreen Princess (blonde)	12123	$42.00	Winter Princess Collection
1994	Evergreen Princess (redhead)	13173	$295.00	Mattel Festival Doll
1994	Evergreen Princess (redhead)	12123	$151.00	Disney/Winter Princess (Theme)
1994	Glitter Hair (black)	11332	$15.00	
1994	Glitter Hair (blonde)	10965	$20.00	
1994	Glitter Hair (brunette)	10966	$20.00	
1994	Glitter Hair (redhead)	10968	$20.00	
1994	Gold Jubilee	12009	$345.00	Jubilee Series
1994	Gymnast (black)	12153	$14.00	
1994	Gymnast (blonde)	12126	$14.00	
1994	Gymnast (brunette)	11921	$35.00	Mattel Festival Doll
1994	Happy Birthday	12954	$15.00	
1994	Happy Holidays 1994	12155	$50.00	Happy Holidays Collection
1994	Happy Holidays 1994 (black)	12156	$36.00	Happy Holidays Collection
1994	Happy Holidays 1994 (brunette)	12155	$550.00	Mattel Festival Doll
1994	Happy Holidays Barbie	12432	$65.00	Happy Holidays European
1994	Holiday Dreams	12192	$30.00	Supermarket
1994	International Haute Couture Rainbow Barbie	None	$199.00	Barbie Festival
1994	Kenyan	11181	$23.00	Dolls of the World
1994	Kraft Treasures	11546	$50.00	Kraft
1994	Locket Surprise	10963	$20.00	
1994	Locket Surprise (black)	11224	$20.00	
1994	My First Ballerina	11294	$15.00	
1994	My First Ballerina (Asian)	11342	$15.00	
1994	My First Ballerina (black)	11340	$15.00	
1994	My First Barbie	11294	$15.00	
1994	My First Barbie (Asian)	11342	$20.00	
1994	My First Barbie (black)	11340	$15.00	
1994	My First Barbie (Hispanic)	11341	$15.00	

Year	Item	Number	Value	Specials
1994	My Size Bride	12052	$100.00	
1994	My Size Bride (black)	12053	$100.00	
1994	Native American #2	11609	$32.00	Dolls of the World
1994	Night Dazzle	12191	$55.00	JCPenney
1994	Night Dazzle (brunette)	12191	$185.00	Mattel Festival Doll
1994	Party Time	12243	$20.00	Toys "R" Us
1994	Party Time (black)	14274	$20.00	Toys "R" Us
1994	Party Time (Hispanic)	12244	$25.00	
1994	Polly Pockets	12412	$20.00	Hill's
1994	Queen of Hearts	12046	$155.00	Bob Mackie
1994	Red Velvet Delight Haute Couture Barbie	None	$220.00	Barbie Festival
1994	Savvy Shopper	12152	$50.00	Bloomingdale's
1994	Scarlett (green velvet dress)	12045	$48.00	Hollywood Legends
1994	Scarlett (red dress)	12815	$60.00	Hollywood Legends
1994	Season's Greetings	12384	$50.00	Wholesale Clubs
1994	Shopping Spree Barbie #1	12749	$38.00	FAO Schwarz
1994	Shopping Spree Barbie #2	12749	$35.00	FAO Schwarz
1994	Silken Flame Barbie (brunette)	1249	$130.00	Porcelain
1994	Silver Screen	11652	$100.00	FAO Schwarz
1994	Silver Starlight	11305	$190.00	Porcelain
1994	Silver Sweetheart	12410	$40.00	Sears
1994	Singapore Girl 2	None	$50.00	Singapore Airlines
1994	Snow Princess (blonde)	11875	$60.00	Enchanted Seasons
1994	Snow Princess (brunette)	12905	$595.00	Mattel Festival Doll
1994	Star Lily Bride (porcelain)	12953	$150.00	Wedding Flower Collection
1994	Sun Jewel	10953	$10.00	
1994	Supertalk	12290	$40.00	
1994	Supertalk (black)	12379	$40.00	
1994	Theatre Elegance	12077	$145.00	Spiegel
1994	Tooth Fairy Barbie (blue)	11645	$22.00	Wal-Mart
1994	Uptown Chic Barbie	11623	$37.00	Classique
1994	Victorian Elegance	12579	$35.00	Hallmark
1994	Wacky Warehouse II	11763	$45.00	Kool-Aid
1995	Barbie & Champion	13181	$45.00	Hill's
1995	Barbie as Rapunzel	13016	$24.00	Children's Collector Series
1995	Baywatch	13199	$20.00	
1995	Baywatch (black)	13258	$20.00	
1995	Birthday	12954	$25.00	
1995	Birthday (black)	12955	$25.00	
1995	Birthday (Hispanic)	13253	$25.00	
1995	Bubble Angel	12443	$20.00	
1995	Bubble Angel (black)	12444	$15.00	
1995	Busy Gal	13675	$42.00	Nostalgic Vinyl Series
1995	Butterfly Princess	13051	$25.00	
1995	Butterfly Princess (black)	13052	$25.00	
1995	Butterfly Princess (Hispanic)	13238	$25.00	
1995	Caroling Fun	13966	$20.00	Supermarket
1995	Christian Dior I	13168	$60.00	Designer Collection
1995	Circus Star	13257	$70.00	FAO Schwarz
1995	City Style Barbie	10149	$105.00	Hudson's Bay Company Canada
1995	Colonial	12578	$25.00	American Stories Collection
1995	Country Bride	13614	$20.00	Wal-Mart
1995	Country Bride (black)	13615	$20.00	Wal-Mart
1995	Country Bride (Hispanic)	13616	$20.00	Wal-Mart
1995	Cut and Style (black)	12642	$20.00	

Year	Item	Number	Value	Specials
1995	Cut and Style (blonde)	12639	$20.00	
1995	Cut and Style (brunette)	12643	$20.00	
1995	Cut and Style (redhead)	12644	$20.00	
1995	Dance Moves	13083	$15.00	
1995	Dance Moves (black)	13086	$15.00	
1995	Disney Fun Barbie	12957	$55.00	Disney Europe
1995	Disney Fun III	13533	$35.00	Disney
1995	Doctor Barbie (black)	14315	$25.00	Toys "R" Us
1995	Doctor Barbie (white with 3 babies)	14309	$25.00	Toys "R" Us
1995	Dolls of the World Limited Edition Set	13939	$45.00	Dolls of the World
1995	Donna Karan NY (blonde)	14545	$85.00	Bloomingdale's
1995	Donna Karan NY (brunette)	14452	$85.00	Bloomingdale's
1995	Dorothy (Wizard of Oz)	12701	$72.00	Hollywood Legends
1995	Easter Party	12793	$20.00	Supermarket
1995	Elizabethan Queen	12792	$40.00	Great Eras Collection
1995	Evening Glamour	14070	$75.00	Glamour Collection
1995	Fire Fighter	13553	$50.00	Toys "R" Us
1995	Fire Fighter (black)	13472	$40.00	Toys "R" Us
1995	German (reissue)	12698	$22.00	Dolls of the World
1995	Goddess of the Sun	14056	$95.00	Bob Mackie
1995	Happy Holidays 1995	14123	$28.00	Happy Holidays Collection
1995	Happy Holidays 1995 (black)	14124	$24.00	Happy Holidays Collection
1995	Happy Holidays Barbie	13545	$40.00	Happy Holidays International
1995	Happy Holidays With Ornament	14124	$80.00	JCPenney
1995	Happy New Year	14024	$45.00	
1995	Holiday Jewel	14311	$100.00	Holiday Porcelain Series
1995	Holiday Memories	14106	$30.00	Hallmark
1995	Hot Skatin'	13511	$20.00	
1995	Hot Skatin' (black)	13512	$18.00	
1995	International Pen Friend Barbie	13558	$18.00	Toys "R" Us
1995	International Travel Barbie #2	13912	$50.00	Wessco
1995	International Travel I	13912	$40.00	Wessco
1995	Irish (reissue)	12998	$34.00	Dolls of the World
1995	Jewel Splendor	14061	$90.00	FAO Schwarz
1995	Maria (Sound of Music)	13676	$36.00	Hollywood Legends
1995	Mattel Golden Anniversary	14479	$170.00	Porcelain
1995	Medieval Lady	12791	$36.00	Great Eras Collection
1995	Midnight Gala	12999	$34.00	Classique
1995	My First Princess	13064	$15.00	
1995	My First Princess (Asian)	13067	$15.00	
1995	My First Princess (black)	13065	$15.00	
1995	My First Princess (Hispanic)	13066	$15.00	
1995	My Size Bride Barbie (brunette)	14108	$130.00	Toys "R" Us
1995	My Size Princess	13767	$100.00	
1995	My Size Princess (black)	13768	$100.00	
1995	Native American #3	12699	$25.00	Dolls of the World
1995	Peppermint Princess	13598	$36.00	Winter Princess Collection
1995	Pilgrim	12577	$25.00	American Stories Collection
1995	Pioneer	12680	$25.00	American Stories Collection
1995	POG Barbie	13239	$18.00	Toys "R" Us Canada
1995	POG Fun	13239	$20.00	Toys "R" Us
1995	Polynesian	12700	$25.00	Dolls of the World
1995	Pretty Dreams 18"	13611	$25.00	
1995	Pretty Dreams 18" soft body (black)	13630	$20.00	
1995	Purple Passion	13555	$35.00	Toys "R" Us

Year	Item	Number	Value	Specials
1995	Purple Passion (black)	13554	$30.00	Toys "R" Us
1995	Ribbons and Roses	13911	$35.00	Sears
1995	Royal Enchantment	14010	$50.00	JCPenney
1995	Ruby Romance	13612	$48.00	Service Merchandise
1995	Ruffle Fun	12433	$12.00	
1995	Ruffle Fun (black)	12434	$12.00	
1995	Ruffle Fun (Hispanic)	12435	$12.00	
1995	Sapphire Dreams	13255	$50.00	Toys "R" Us
1995	Scarlett (BBQ dress)	12997	$47.00	Hollywood Legends
1995	Scarlett (New Orleans dress)	13254	$47.00	Hollywood Legends
1995	Schooltime Fun Barbie	13741	$15.00	Supermarket
1995	Sea Pearl Mermaid	13940	$20.00	Hill's
1995	Shopping Chic	14009	$75.00	Spiegel
1995	Sing & Dance	13179	$20.00	
1995	Sing & Dance (black)	13938	$20.00	
1995	Slumber Party	12696	$15.00	
1995	Slumber Party (black)	12697	$15.00	
1995	Solo in the Spotlight (blonde)	13534	$25.00	Nostalgic Vinyl Series
1995	Solo in the Spotlight (brunette)	13820	$25.00	Nostalgic Vinyl Series
1995	Spring Bouquet	12989	$45.00	Enchanted Seasons
1995	Starlight Waltz	14070	$35.00	Ballroom Beauties
1995	Starlight Waltz (brunette, Disney)	14954	$75.00	Ballroom Beauties
1995	Steppin' Out	14110	$22.00	Target
1995	Sunflower Barbie	13488	$20.00	Toys "R" Us
1995	Super Talk! Barbie	14308	$30.00	Toys "R" Us
1995	Super Talk! Barbie (black)	14316	$30.00	Toys "R" Us
1995	Sweet Dreams	13611	$20.00	
1995	Sweet Dreams (black)	13630	$20.00	
1995	Sweet Valentine	14644	$22.00	
1995	Teacher (black, no panties)	13195	$55.00	
1995	Teacher (black, painted panties)	13915	$25.00	
1995	Teacher (no panties)	18914	$60.00	
1995	Tooth Fairy Barbie	11645	$20.00	Wal-Mart
1995	Tropical Splash	12446	$10.00	
1995	Valentine Barbie	12675	$22.00	Target
1995	Western Stampin' Barbie with Western Star Horse (black)	13478	$45.00	Toys "R" Us
1995	Winter Sports	13516	$35.00	JCPenney
1995	Winter Sports Barbie	13516	$30.00	Toys "R" Us
1995	Winter's Eve	13613	$30.00	Wholesale Clubs
1996	1950s Barbie	15820	$30.00	Sam's Club/Wholesale Club
1996	American Indian	14715	$25.00	American Stories
1996	Andalucia	15758	$40.00	
1996	Antique Rose	15814	$190.00	FAO Schwarz
1996	Arcadian Court Barbie	62889	$85.00	Hudson's Bay Company Canada
1996	Arctic	16495	$25.00	Dolls of the World
1996	Arizona Jean Company I	15441	$25.00	JCPenney
1996	Autumn Glory	15204	$48.00	Enchanted Seasons
1996	Barbie as Cinderella	16900	$24.00	Children's Collector Series
1996	Barbie as Dorothy, 2nd Edition	12701	$75.00	Wizard of Oz
1996	Barbie as Empress Sissy	15846	$55.00	Royal House of Europe
1996	Barbie as Little Bo Peep	14960	$55.00	Children's Collector Series
1996	Barbie at Bloomingdale's	16290	$35.00	Bloomingdale's
1996	Barbie Millicent Roberts Matinee Today	16079	$40.00	Barbie Millicent Roberts
1996	Calvin Klein Jeans Barbie	16211	$55.00	Bloomingdale's

Year	Item	Number	Value	Specials
1996	Calvin Klein Jeans Barbie	16211	$70.00	Hudson's Bay Company Canada
1996	Chuck E Cheese	14615	$30.00	Chuck E Cheese Pizza
1996	City Shopper	16289	$40.00	Macy's
1996	City Style Barbie	15612	$20.00	Target
1996	Civil War Nurse	14612	$25.00	American Stories Collection
1996	Crystal Splendor	15136	$25.00	Toys "R" Us
1996	Crystal Splendor (black)	15137	$25.00	Toys "R" Us
1996	Doctor Barbie	15803	$30.00	Toys "R" Us
1996	Doctor Barbie (black)	15804	$30.00	Toys "R" Us
1996	Dolls of the World Limited Edition Set	15283	$40.00	Dolls of the World
1996	Easter Basket	14613	$18.00	Supermarket
1996	Easy Chic Barbie	17590	$750.00	Harrod's England
1996	Enchanted Evening (blonde)	14992	$25.00	Nostalgic Vinyl Series
1996	Enchanted Evening (brunette)	15407	$25.00	Nostalgic Vinyl Series
1996	Escada	15948	$48.00	Designer Collection
1996	Evening Flame	15533	$30.00	Sears
1996	Evening Pearl	12825	$140.00	Presidential Porcelain
1996	Fifties Fun	13613	$35.00	Wholesale Clubs
1996	Flying Hero	14030	$15.00	
1996	Flying Hero (black)	14278	$20.00	
1996	Foam 'n Color (blue)	15099	$15.00	
1996	Foam 'n Color (pink)	14457	$15.00	
1996	Foam 'n Color (yellow)	15098	$15.00	
1996	Gap Barbie	16449	$60.00	Gap Stores
1996	Gap Barbie (black)	16450	$60.00	Gap Stores
1996	Ghanian	15303	$24.00	Dolls of the World
1996	Glinda the Good Witch	14901	$68.00	Hollywood Legends
1996	Got Milk	15121	$20.00	Toys "R" Us
1996	Got Milk (black)	15122	$20.00	Toys "R" Us
1996	Governor's Ball Barbie	14010	$90.00	Hudson's Bay Company Canada
1996	Graduation Class of '96	15003	$20.00	Supermarket
1996	Grecian Goddess	15005	$34.00	Great Eras Collection
1996	Happy Birthday	14649	$20.00	
1996	Happy Birthday (black)	14662	$20.00	
1996	Happy Birthday (Hispanic)	14663	$20.00	
1996	Happy Holidays 1996	15646	$28.00	Happy Holidays Collection
1996	Happy Holidays 1996 (black)	15647	$28.00	Happy Holidays Collection
1996	Happy Holidays Barbie	15816	$32.00	Happy Holidays International
1996	Holiday Caroler	15760	$70.00	Holiday Porcelain Series
1996	Holiday Season	15581	$16.00	Supermarket
1996	Holiday Season (black)	15583	$16.00	Supermarket
1996	Horse Lovin'	14879	$20.00	
1996	Indian	14451	$25.00	Dolls of the World
1996	In-Line Skating	15473	$25.00	
1996	International Travel Barbie #1	15184	$45.00	Wessco
1996	International Travel II	16158	$50.00	Wessco
1996	Japanese (reissue)	14163	$23.00	Dolls of the World
1996	Jewel Hair Mermaid	14586	$15.00	
1996	Jewel Hair Mermaid (black)	14587	$15.00	
1996	Jewel Princess (blonde)	15826	$25.00	Winter Princess Collection
1996	Little Debbie Barbie Series II (bent arms)	14616	$30.00	Little Debbie Snacks
1996	Little Debbie Barbie Series II (straight arms)	14616	$25.00	Little Debbie Snacks
1996	Mexican (reissue)	14449	$23.00	Dolls of the World
1996	Midnight Waltz (blonde)	15685	$35.00	Ballroom Beauties
1996	Midnight Waltz (brunette)	16705	$52.00	Ballroom Beauties

Year	Item	Number	Value	Specials
1996	Miss Barbie	61747	$35.00	Woolworth
1996	Moon Goddess	14105	$99.00	Bob Mackie
1996	My Fair Lady #1 (pink organza gown)	15501	$75.00	Hollywood Legends
1996	My Fair Lady #2 (ascot)	15497	$100.00	Hollywood Legends
1996	My Fair Lady #3 (flower girl)	15498	$65.00	Hollywood Legends
1996	My Fair Lady #4 (ball evening gown)	15500	$100.00	Hollywood Legends
1996	My Size Bride Barbie (redhead)	15649	$130.00	Toys "R" Us
1996	My Size Dancing	15909	$105.00	
1996	My Size Dancing (black)	15910	$105.00	
1996	My Size Redhead	15649	$140.00	QVC
1996	Native American #4	15304	$35.00	Dolls of the World
1996	Norwegian #1	14450	$37.00	Dolls of the World
1996	Norwegian #2	14450	$25.00	Dolls of the World
1996	Nostalgic Barbie #1	62328	$45.00	Nostalgic
1996	Nostalgic Barbie #2	62329	$45.00	Nostalgic
1996	Nostalgic Barbie #3	62327	$45.00	Nostalgic
1996	Ocean Friends	15428	$20.00	
1996	Ocean Friends (black)	15429	$20.00	
1996	Olympic Gymnast (black)	15124	$20.00	
1996	Olympic Gymnast (blonde)	15123	$20.00	
1996	Olympic Gymnast (redhead)	15125	$35.00	Toys "R" Us
1996	Pen Friend	13558	$20.00	Toys "R" Us
1996	Pet Doctor	14603	$18.00	
1996	Pet Doctor (black)	15302	$18.00	
1996	Pet Doctor (brunette)	16458	$30.00	Target
1996	Pink Ice	15141	$100.00	Toys "R" Us
1996	Pink Splendor	16091	$310.00	Ultra Limited Edition
1996	Pioneer #2	14756	$25.00	American Stories Collection
1996	Poodle Parade	15280	$42.00	Nostalgic
1996	Portrait in Taffeta	15528	$55.00	Couture Collection
1996	Pretty Hearts	14473	$10.00	
1996	Pretty Hearts (black)	14474	$10.00	
1996	Pretty Hearts (Hispanic)	14475	$10.00	
1996	Radiant 'n Rose	15140	$55.00	Toys "R" Us
1996	Radiant 'n Rose (black)	15061	$55.00	Toys "R" Us
1996	Romantic Rose Bride (porcelain)	14541	$140.00	Wedding Flower Collection
1996	Rose Bride	15987	$35.00	Wholesale Clubs
1996	Russell Stover Easter (checkered)	14617	$25.00	Russell Stover
1996	Russell Stover Easter (print)	14956	$25.00	Russell Stover
1996	School Spirit Barbie	15301	$16.00	Supermarket
1996	Sea Princess	15531	$30.00	Service Merchandise
1996	Shampoo Magic (pink)	14457	$15.00	
1996	Shampoo Magic (yellow)	15098	$15.00	
1996	Shopping Chic (black)	15801	$50.00	Spiegel
1996	Silver Royale	15952	$75.00	Wholesale Clubs
1996	Skating Star	15510	$15.00	Wal-Mart
1996	Skating Star (black)	16691	$15.00	Wal-Mart
1996	Skating Star (Hispanic)	15511	$15.00	Wal-Mart
1996	Soda Fountain Sweetheart	15762	$88.00	Coca-Cola Fashion Classic Series
1996	Songbird	14320	$25.00	
1996	Songbird (black)	14486	$25.00	
1996	Sparkle Beach	13132	$10.00	
1996	Special Occasion Barbie I	15831	$65.00	Mercantile Stores
1996	Splash 'n Color	16169	$6.00	
1996	Spring Blossom	15201	$25.00	Avon

Year	Item	Number	Value	Specials
1996	Spring Blossom (black)	15202	$25.00	Avon
1996	Starlight Dance	15461	$32.00	Classique
1996	Starlight Dance (black)	15819	$32.00	Classique
1996	Statue of Liberty	14664	$100.00	FAO Schwarz
1996	Summer Sophisticate	15591	$43.00	Spiegel
1996	Super Gymnast	15821	$20.00	K•B Toys
1996	Sweet Daisy Barbie	15133	$30.00	Military
1996	Sweet Magnolia	15622	$18.00	Wal-Mart
1996	Sweet Magnolia (black)	12265	$18.00	Wal-Mart
1996	Sweet Magnolia (Hispanic)	15654	$18.00	Wal-Mart
1996	Sweet Valentine	14880	$35.00	Hallmark
1996	Teacher (brunette)	13194	$25.00	Supermarket
1996	Teacher (Hispanic)	16210	$25.00	
1996	Teacher (painted panties)	13914	$25.00	
1996	Teddy Fun	15684	$18.00	Hill's
1996	Twirling Ballerina	15086	$15.00	
1996	Twirling Ballerina (black)	15087	$15.00	
1996	Valentine Barbie	15172	$20.00	Target
1996	Valentine Sweetheart	14644	$15.00	Supermarket
1996	Victorian Lady	14900	$30.00	Great Eras Collection
1996	Wacky Warehouse III	15620	$35.00	Kool-Aid
1996	Walt Disney World 25th Anniversary	16525	$35.00	Disney
1996	West End Barbie	15513	$45.00	Hamley's (England)
1996	Winter Fantasy Barbie (blonde)	15334	$30.00	Sam's Club
1996	Winter Fantasy Barbie (brunette)	15530	$35.00	Sam's Club
1996	Winter Renaissance (Evening Elegance Series)	15570	$40.00	JCPenney
1996	Winter Velvet	15571	$38.00	Avon
1996	Winter Velvet (black)	15587	$38.00	Avon
1996	Yuletide Romance	15621	$30.00	Hallmark
1997	101 Dalmatians	17248	$25.00	Toys "R" Us
1997	101 Dalmatians (black)	17601	$25.00	Toys "R" Us
1997	35th Anniversary Target	16485	$25.00	Target
1997	35th Anniversary Target (black)	17608	$25.00	Target
1997	35th Anniversary Wal-Mart	17245	$25.00	Wal-Mart
1997	35th Anniversary Wal-Mart (black)	17616	$25.00	Wal-Mart
1997	After the Walk	17341	$48.00	Coca-Cola Fashion Classic Series
1997	American Indian II	17313	$28.00	American Stories
1997	Amethyst Aura	15522	$90.00	Bob Mackie Jewel Essence
1997	Angel Princess	15911	$24.00	
1997	Angel Princess (black)	15912	$24.00	
1997	Anne Klein Barbie	17603	$40.00	Macy's
1997	Arizona Jean Company II	18020	$25.00	JCPenney
1997	Auburn University	17699	$10.00	University Barbie
1997	Auburn University (black)	18346	$9.00	University Barbie
1997	Back to School	17099	$10.00	Supermarket
1997	Back to School (black)	17100	$10.00	Supermarket
1997	Barbie & Ginger	17116	$35.00	
1997	Barbie & Ginger (black)	17369	$35.00	
1997	Barbie and Her Super Fashion Fireworks #1	9805	$90.00	K-Mart/Kresge
1997	Barbie and Her Super Fashion Fireworks #2	9805	$90.00	K-Mart/Kresge
1997	Barbie and Her Super Fashion Fireworks #3	9805	$90.00	K-Mart/Kresge
1997	Barbie as the Sugar Plum Fairy from *The Nutcracker*	17056	$29.00	Classic Ballet Series
1997	Barbie as the Swan Queen from *Swan Lake*	18509	$22.00	Classic Ballet Series
1997	Barbie as the Swan Queen from *Swan Lake* (black)	18510	$22.00	Classic Ballet Series
1997	Barbie at FAO	17298	$30.00	FAO Schwarz

Year	Item	Number	Value	Specials
1997	Barbie Millicent Roberts Perfectly Suited	17567	$35.00	Barbie Millicent Roberts
1997	Barbie on Bay	63987	$35.00	Hudson's Bay Company Canada
1997	Barbie Style	14476	$20.00	
1997	Bead Blast (black)	18889	$15.00	
1997	Bead Blast (blonde)	18888	$15.00	
1997	Bead Blast (brunette)	18891	$15.00	
1997	Bead Blast (redhead)	18890	$15.00	
1997	Bill Blass	17040	$80.00	Designer Collection
1997	Billions of Dreams	17641	$199.00	Ultra Limited Edition
1997	Birthday	15998	$20.00	
1997	Birthday (black)	15999	$20.00	
1997	Birthday (Hispanic)	16000	$20.00	
1997	Birthday Surprise	16491	$15.00	Supermarket
1997	Birthday Surprise Barbie (black)	17320	$15.00	Supermarket
1997	Blossom Beauty	17032	$20.00	
1997	Blossom Beauty (black)	17033	$20.00	
1997	Blue Starlight	17125	$35.00	Sears
1997	Blushing Orchid Bride (porcelain)	16962	$125.00	Wedding Flower Collection
1997	Bubbling Mermaid	16131	$15.00	
1997	Bubbling Mermaid (black)	16132	$15.00	
1997	Carnival Cruise Lines	15186	$30.00	Wessco
1997	Chilean	18559	$25.00	Dolls of the World
1997	Chinese Empress Barbie	16708	$32.00	Great Eras Collection
1997	Chinese Empress Barbie	16708	$88.00	Hong Kong Commemorative Edition
1997	Christian Dior II	16013	$68.00	Designer Collection
1997	City Style Barbie	17237	$15.00	Target
1997	Clemson University	17753	$10.00	University Barbie
1997	Clemson University (black)	18349	$9.00	University Barbie
1997	Color 'n Wash My Hair Barbie	15139	$50.00	Avon
1997	Cool Shoppin'	17487	$20.00	
1997	Cool Shoppin' (black)	17488	$20.00	
1997	Country Rose	17782	$42.00	Grand Ole Opry
1997	Country Rose	17864	$50.00	Sam's Club/Wholesale Club
1997	Dentist (black)	17478	$20.00	
1997	Dentist (blonde)	17255	$20.00	
1997	Dentist (brunette)	17707	$20.00	
1997	Diamond Dazzle	15519	$100.00	Bob Mackie Jewel Essence
1997	Disney Fun IV	17058	$35.00	Disney
1997	Dream Bride Barbie	17153	$35.00	Service Merchandise
1997	Dream Bride Barbie (black)	17933	$25.00	Service Merchandise
1997	Duke University	17750	$10.00	University Barbie
1997	Duke University (black)	19665	$9.00	University Barbie
1997	Easter Barbie	16315	$15.00	Supermarket
1997	Easter Barbie (black)	16317	$15.00	Supermarket
1997	Emerald Embers	15521	$88.00	Bob Mackie Jewel Essence
1997	Emerald Enchantment	17443	$55.00	Toys "R" Us
1997	Evening Majesty	17235	$40.00	JCPenney
1997	Fantasy Ball Barbie	18594	$20.00	K•B Toys
1997	Fantasy Ball Barbie (black)	18595	$20.00	K•B Toys
1997	Fashion Luncheon	17382	$49.00	Nostalgic Vinyl Series
1997	Flower Fun	16063	$6.00	
1997	Flower Fun (black)	16064	$6.00	
1997	Flower Fun (Hispanic)	16065	$6.00	
1997	French	16499	$25.00	Dolls of the World
1997	French Lady	16707	$28.00	Great Eras Collection

Year	Item	Number	Value	Specials
1997	George Washington Barbie	17757	$50.00	FAO Schwarz
1997	Georgetown University	17749	$10.00	University Barbie
1997	Georgetown University (black)	18341	$10.00	University Barbie
1997	Glamour Barbie	18594	$15.00	K•B Toys
1997	Glamour Barbie (black)	18595	$15.00	K•B Toys
1997	Graduation Barbie Class of '97 (black)	16489	$15.00	Supermarket
1997	Graduation Class of '97	16487	$15.00	Supermarket
1997	Grand Premier	16498	$79.00	Barbie Collector's Club
1997	Happy Holidays 1997 (all variations) (brunette)	20416	$20.00	Happy Holidays Collection
1997	Happy Holidays 1997 (black)	17833	$20.00	Happy Holidays Collection
1997	Happy Holidays 1997 (blonde)	17832	$64.00	Happy Holidays Collection
1997	Happy New Year	16093	$44.00	
1997	Harley-Davidson Barbie #1	17692	$450.00	Toys "R" Us
1997	Holiday Ball	18326	$65.00	Holiday Porcelain Series
1997	Holiday Traditions	17094	$45.00	Hallmark
1997	Holiday Treats Barbie	17236	$15.00	Supermarket
1997	Holiday Treats Barbie (black)	17618	$15.00	Supermarket
1997	Holiday Treats Fiesta Barbie (Hispanic)	18012	$15.00	Supermarket
1997	Horse Lovin' SE	15648	$10.00	
1997	Horse Ridin' Barbie (black)	19269	$13.00	
1997	Hula Hair	17047	$18.00	
1997	Hula Hair (black)	17048	$18.00	
1997	Hula-Hoop	18167	$16.00	Hill's
1997	Illusion Barbie	18667	$80.00	Masquerade Gala
1997	In The Limelight (black)	17031	$140.00	Byron Lars Runway Collection
1997	JAL Barbie	64347	$150.00	Japan Air Lines
1997	Jewelry Fun My First Barbie	16005	$10.00	
1997	Jewelry Fun My First Barbie (Asian)	16008	$10.00	
1997	Jewelry Fun My First Barbie (black)	16006	$10.00	
1997	Jewelry Fun My First Barbie (Hispanic)	16007	$10.00	
1997	Ladybug Fun	17695	$18.00	Ames
1997	Lily	17556	$125.00	FAO Schwarz
1997	Madame Du Barbie	17934	$225.00	Bob Mackie
1997	Marilyn Monroe (pink dress)	17451	$55.00	Hollywood Legends
1997	Marilyn Monroe (red dress)	17452	$60.00	Hollywood Legends
1997	Marilyn Monroe (white dress)	17155	$50.00	Hollywood Legends
1997	Masquerade Ball	18667	$235.00	Bob Mackie
1997	Midnight Princess Barbie (blonde)	17780	$25.00	Winter Princess Collection
1997	Midnight Princess Barbie (brunette)	18486	$86.00	W.D.W. Teddy Bear & Doll Con.
1997	Moonlight Waltz	17763	$48.00	Ballroom Beauties
1997	Movin' Groovin'	17714	$15.00	
1997	Mrs. P.F.E. Albee	17690	$75.00	Avon
1997	My First Tea Party	14592	$12.00	
1997	My First Tea Party (Asian)	14876	$12.00	
1997	My First Tea Party (black)	14593	$12.00	
1997	My First Tea Party (Hispanic)	14875	$12.00	
1997	My Size Rapunzel	17801	$100.00	
1997	My Size Rapunzel (black)	17802	$100.00	
1997	North Carolina State	17194	$10.00	University Barbie
1997	North Carolina State (black)	20127	$9.00	University Barbie
1997	Oklahoma State University	17752	$10.00	University Barbie
1997	Olympic Skater	18501	$15.00	
1997	Olympic Skater (black)	18503	$10.00	
1997	Oreo Barbie	18511	$20.00	Toys "R" Us
1997	Paleontologist	17240	$20.00	Toys "R" Us

Year	Item	Number	Value	Specials
1997	Paleontologist (black)	17241	$20.00	Toys "R" Us
1997	Patriot	17312	$25.00	American Stories Collection
1997	Pearl Beach	18576	$10.00	
1997	Penn State University	17698	$10.00	University Barbie
1997	Penn State University (black)	18344	$10.00	University Barbie
1997	Polish	18560	$25.00	Dolls of the World
1997	Ponytails	18141	$20.00	Military
1997	Ponytails (black)	18142	$20.00	Military
1997	Pretty Choices Barbie (black)	18018	$20.00	Wal-Mart
1997	Pretty Choices Barbie (blonde)	17971	$20.00	Wal-Mart
1997	Pretty Choices Barbie (brunette)	18019	$20.00	Wal-Mart
1997	Puerto Rican	16754	$18.00	Dolls of the World
1997	Ralph Lauren Barbie	15950	$60.00	Bloomingdale's
1997	Rapunzel	1869	$50.00	
1997	Rapunzel	16378	$25.00	Fairy Tales
1997	Romantic Interlude	17136	$34.00	Classique
1997	Romantic Interlude (black)	17137	$36.00	Classique
1997	Ruby Radiance	15520	$80.00	Bob Mackie Jewel Essence
1997	Russell Stover Candies Special Edition Barbie (black)	17089	$25.00	Russell Stover
1997	Russell Stover Candies Special Edition Barbie (floral)	16351	$25.00	Russell Stover
1997	Russell Stover Candies Special Edition Barbie (pink)	17091	$25.00	Russell Stover
1997	Russell Stover Holiday	18199	$25.00	Russell Stover
1997	Russian (reissue)	16500	$17.00	Dolls of the World
1997	Sapphire Sophisticate	16692	$30.00	Toys "R" Us
1997	Sapphire Sophisticate (black)	16693	$20.00	Toys "R" Us
1997	Sapphire Splendor	15523	$80.00	Bob Mackie Jewel Essence
1997	School Spirit Barbie	63569	$40.00	Hudson's Bay Company Canada
1997	Sentimental Valentine	16536	$30.00	Hallmark
1997	Serenade in Satin	17572	$90.00	Couture Collection
1997	Share a Smile Barbie	17247	$25.00	Toys "R" Us
1997	Shopping Time Barbie	18230	$15.00	Wal-Mart
1997	Shopping Time Barbie (black)	18231	$15.00	Wal-Mart
1997	Show Parade Barbie with Star Stampin' Horse	15059	$50.00	
1997	Sixties Fun Barbie (blonde)	17252	$25.00	Wholesale Clubs
1997	Sixties Fun Barbie (redhead)	17693	$25.00	Wholesale Clubs
1997	Skating Dream Barbie	17244	$20.00	Wal-Mart
1997	Skating Star	17244	$10.00	Wal-Mart
1997	Sparkle Beauty	17251	$30.00	Wholesale Club (BJ)
1997	Special Occasion Barbie II	18216	$45.00	Mercantile Stores
1997	Special Occasion Barbie II (black)	18217	$45.00	Mercantile Stores
1997	Splash 'n Color (black)	16174	$6.00	
1997	Splash 'n Color (Hispanic)	16172	$6.00	
1997	Spring Petals (black)	16871	$30.00	Avon
1997	Spring Petals (blonde)	16746	$30.00	Avon
1997	Spring Petals (brunette)	16872	$30.00	Avon
1997	Summer Splendor	15683	$39.00	Enchanted Seasons
1997	Sweet Moments	17642	$25.00	Wholesale Clubs
1997	Talk With Me	17350	$35.00	
1997	Talk With Me (black)	17370	$30.00	
1997	Tangerine Twist	17860	$35.00	Fashion Savvy Collection
1997	Target 35th Anniversary Barbie	16485	$27.00	Target
1997	Target 35th Anniversary Barbie (black)	17608	$27.00	Target

Year	Item	Number	Value	Specials
1997	Toyland Barbie	64176	$40.00	Hudson's Bay Company Canada
1997	University of Arizona	17751	$10.00	University Barbie
1997	University of Arkansas	17191	$10.00	University Barbie
1997	University of Florida	17700	$10.00	University Barbie
1997	University of Florida (black)	18343	$10.00	University Barbie
1997	University of Georgia	17192	$10.00	University Barbie
1997	University of Georgia (black)	18345	$10.00	University Barbie
1997	University of Illinois	17755	$10.00	University Barbie
1997	University of Miami	17794	$10.00	University Barbie
1997	University of Miami (black)	18348	$10.00	University Barbie
1997	University of Michigan	17398	$10.00	University Barbie
1997	University of Michigan (black)	18342	$10.00	University Barbie
1997	University of Nebraska	17193	$10.00	University Barbie
1997	University of Tennessee	17554	$10.00	University Barbie
1997	University of Tennessee (black)	18347	$10.00	University Barbie
1997	University of Texas	17792	$10.00	University Barbie
1997	University of Virginia	17754	$10.00	University Barbie
1997	University of Wisconsin	17195	$10.00	University Barbie
1997	Valentine Fun Barbie	16311	$12.00	Supermarket
1997	Valentine Fun Barbie (black)	16313	$12.00	Supermarket
1997	Valentine Romance Barbie	16059	$18.00	Target
1997	Water Lily (Monet)	17783	$90.00	Artist Series
1997	Wedding Day (blonde)	17119	$25.00	Nostalgic Vinyl Series
1997	Wedding Day (redhead)	17120	$30.00	Nostalgic Vinyl Series
1997	Winner's Circle	17441	$55.00	Spiegel
1997	Winter Dazzle Barbie	18456	$30.00	General Mills
1997	Winter Dazzle Barbie (black)	18457	$30.00	General Mills
1997	Winter Fantasy (brunette)	17666	$25.00	Wholesale Clubs
1997	Winter Fantasy II (black)	17747	$25.00	Wholesale Clubs
1997	Winter Fantasy II (blonde)	17249	$25.00	Wholesale Clubs
1997	Winter Rhapsody (black)	16354	$35.00	Avon
1997	Winter Rhapsody (blonde)	16353	$35.00	Avon
1997	Winter Rhapsody (brunette)	16873	$35.00	Avon
1997	Working Out Barbie	17317	$15.00	
1998	70s Disco Barbie (blonde)	19928	$25.00	Wholesale Clubs
1998	70s Disco Barbie (brunette)	19929	$25.00	Wholesale Clubs
1998	Alabama	19170	$10.00	University Barbie
1998	Alabama (black)	19422	$10.00	University Barbie
1998	Alice in Wonderland	21933	$16.00	Disney Classics
1998	Angel of Joy Barbie	19633	$45.00	Timeless Sentiments
1998	Angel of Joy Barbie (black)	20929	$45.00	Timeless Sentiments
1998	Anniversary Edition Golden Qi-Pao Barbie	20649	$75.00	Hong Kong Commemorative Edition
1998	Arizona State University	19162	$10.00	University Barbie
1998	Atlanta Hawks	20734	$20.00	NBA
1998	Atlanta Hawks (black)	20735	$20.00	NBA
1998	Autumn in Paris	19367	$35.00	City Seasons Collection
1998	Barbie and *The Tale of Peter Rabbit*	19360	$28.00	Keepsake Treasures
1998	Barbie as Sleeping Beauty	18586	$25.00	Children's Collector Series
1998	Barbie Millicent Roberts Pinstripe Power	19791	$30.00	Barbie Millicent Roberts
1998	Beyond Pink	20017	$15.00	
1998	Birthday (blonde)	20017	$20.00	
1998	Birthday (brunette)	18292	$20.00	
1998	Birthday Party Barbie	18351	$12.00	Supermarket
1998	Birthday Party Barbie (black)	18352	$12.00	Supermarket
1998	Boston Celtics	20716	$20.00	NBA

Year	Item	Number	Value	Specials
1998	Boston Celtics (black)	20717	$20.00	NBA
1998	Brigham Young University	19152	$10.00	University Barbie
1998	Bronze Sensation Barbie	20022	$55.00	Wholesale Clubs
1998	Bubble Fairy	22087	$20.00	
1998	Butterfly Art	20359	$10.00	
1998	Café Society Barbie	18892	$68.00	Barbie Collector's Club
1998	Charity Ball Barbie	18979	$30.00	Toys "R" Us
1998	Charity Ball Barbie (black)	19132	$30.00	Toys "R" Us
1998	Charlotte Hornets	20698	$20.00	NBA
1998	Charlotte Hornets (black)	20699	$20.00	NBA
1998	Chicago Bulls	20692	$20.00	NBA
1998	Chicago Bulls (black)	20693	$20.00	NBA
1998	Children's Day Barbie	18350	$15.00	K•B Toys
1998	Children's Day Barbie	18350	$15.00	Children's Day
1998	Cinnabar Sensation	23420	$76.00	Byron Lars Runway Collection
1998	Cinnabar Sensation (black)	19848	$76.00	Byron Lars Runway Collection
1998	City Style Barbie	18952	$16.00	Target
1998	Cleveland Cavaliers	20736	$20.00	NBA
1998	Cleveland Cavaliers (black)	20737	$20.00	NBA
1998	Club Wedd Barbie (black)	20423	$20.00	Target
1998	Club Wedd Barbie (blonde)	19717	$20.00	Target
1998	Club Wedd Barbie (brunette)	19718	$20.00	Target
1998	Coca-Cola Picnic Barbie	19626	$15.00	Supermarket
1998	Coca-Cola Picnic Barbie (black)	19627	$15.00	Supermarket
1998	Color with Me Barbie	19047	$15.00	Supermarket
1998	Cool Blue Barbie	20122	$15.00	
1998	Dallas Mavericks	20728	$20.00	NBA
1998	Dallas Mavericks (black)	20729	$20.00	NBA
1998	Dance 'Till Dawn Barbie	19631	$40.00	Great Fashions of the 20th Century
1998	Definitely Diamonds	20204	$55.00	Jewelry Collection Series
1998	Definitely Diamonds Barbie	20204	$110.00	Service Merchandise
1998	Denver Nuggets	20730	$20.00	NBA
1998	Denver Nuggets (black)	20731	$20.00	NBA
1998	Detroit Pistons	20706	$20.00	NBA
1998	Detroit Pistons (black)	20707	$20.00	NBA
1998	Dinner Date (blonde)	19016	$15.00	Wholesale Clubs
1998	Dinner Date (redhead)	19037	$20.00	Wholesale Clubs
1998	Disney Fun Barbie	18970	$27.00	Disney
1998	Disney's Animal Kingdom Barbie	20363	$28.00	Disney
1998	Disney's Animal Kingdom Barbie (black)	20989	$28.00	Disney
1998	East Carolina University	19155	$10.00	University Barbie
1998	East Carolina University (black)	19426	$10.00	University Barbie
1998	Easter Style Barbie	17651	$12.00	Supermarket
1998	Easter Style Barbie (black)	17652	$12.00	Supermarket
1998	Evening Enchantment Barbie	19783	$35.00	JCPenney
1998	Evening Enchantment Barbie	19783	$45.00	Evening Elegance
1998	Evening Sophisticate Barbie	19361	$30.00	Classique
1998	Evening Symphony Barbie	19777	$25.00	Service Merchandise
1998	Fair Valentine Barbie	18091	$30.00	Hallmark
1998	Fantasy Goddess of Asia	20648	$100.00	Bob Mackie International Beauty
1998	Fashion Avenue Barbie	20782	$15.00	K•B Toys
1998	Festive Season Barbie	18909	$14.00	Supermarket
1998	Festive Season Barbie (black)	18910	$14.00	Supermarket
1998	Flip 'n Dive Barbie	18980	$20.00	
1998	Florida State University	19161	$10.00	University Barbie

Year	Item	Number	Value	Specials
1998	Florida Vacation	20535	$10.00	
1998	Georgia Tech	19159	$10.00	University Barbie
1998	Georgia Tech (black)	19427	$10.00	University Barbie
1998	Golden Anniversary Barbie	20038	$90.00	Toys "R" Us
1998	Golden Qi-Pao Barbie	20866	$65.00	Spiegel
1998	Golden State Warriors (black)	20743	$20.00	NBA
1998	Golden State Warriors	20742	$20.00	NBA
1998	Graduation Barbie Class of '98 (black)	17831	$10.00	Supermarket
1998	Graduation Class of '98	17830	$10.00	Supermarket
1998	Happy Holidays 1998	20200	$25.00	Happy Holidays Collection
1998	Happy Holidays 1998 (black)	20201	$25.00	Happy Holidays Collection
1998	Harley-Davidson Barbie #2	20441	$150.00	Toys "R" Us
1998	Harpist Angel Barbie	18894	$45.00	Angels of Music
1998	Harpist Angel Barbie (black)	20551	$45.00	Angels of Music
1998	Holiday Gift Barbie	20128	$90.00	Holiday Porcelain Series
1998	Holiday Voyage Barbie	18651	$40.00	Hallmark
1998	Horse Ridin'	19268	$10.00	
1998	I'm a Toys "R" Us Kid (50th Anniversary)	18895	$30.00	Toys "R" Us
1998	I'm a Toys "R" Us Kid Barbie (black)	21040	$25.00	Toys "R" Us
1998	Ice Cream Barbie	19280	$16.00	Ames
1998	Imperial Elegance	19816	$290.00	Fabergé Porcelain
1998	Indiana	20044	$15.00	University Barbie
1998	Iowa	20367	$15.00	University Barbie
1998	Kansas State	19156	$10.00	University Barbie
1998	L. A. Clippers	20744	$20.00	NBA
1998	L. A. Clippers (black)	20745	$20.00	NBA
1998	L. A. Lakers	20704	$25.00	NBA
1998	L. A. Lakers (black)	20705	$20.00	NBA
1998	Little Debbie Barbie, Series III	16352	$22.00	Little Debbie Snacks
1998	Making Friends	19592	$18.00	Military
1998	Making Friends (black)	19593	$18.00	Military
1998	March of Dimes Walk America Barbie	18506	$20.00	K-Mart
1998	March of Dimes Walk America Barbie (black)	18507	$20.00	K-Mart
1998	Miami Heat	20694	$20.00	NBA
1998	Miami Heat (black)	20695	$20.00	NBA
1998	Milwaukee Bucks	20738	$20.00	NBA
1998	Milwaukee Bucks (black)	20739	$20.00	NBA
1998	Minnesota Timberwolves	20702	$20.00	NBA
1998	Minnesota Timberwolves (black)	20703	$20.00	NBA
1998	Mrs. P.F.E. Albee	20330	$70.00	Avon
1998	My Size Angel Barbie	20493	$105.00	
1998	My Size Angel Barbie (black)	20494	$105.00	
1998	N. Y. Knicks	20714	$20.00	NBA
1998	N. Y. Knicks (black)	20715	$20.00	NBA
1998	NASCAR 50th Anniversary Barbie	20442	$25.00	NASCAR
1998	Native American #5 (box says fourth)	18558	$20.00	Dolls of the World/Toys "R" Us
1998	New Jersey Nets	20726	$20.00	NBA
1998	New Jersey Nets (black)	20727	$20.00	NBA
1998	Northwestern	19167	$10.00	University Barbie
1998	Northwestern (black)	19425	$10.00	University Barbie
1998	Oklahoma	20125	$11.00	University Barbie
1998	Original Arizona Jean Company III	19873	$25.00	JCPenney
1998	Orlando Magic (black)	20749	$20.00	NBA
1998	Oscar de la Renta Barbie	20376	$60.00	Bloomingdale's
1998	Peacock	19365	$59.00	Birds of Beauty Series

Year	Item	Number	Value	Specials
1998	Phantom of the Opera	20377	$150.00	FAO Schwarz
1998	Philadelphia 76ers	20724	$20.00	NBA
1998	Phoenix Suns Barbie	20710	$20.00	NBA
1998	Phoenix Suns Barbie (black)	20711	$20.00	NBA
1998	Pilot Barbie	18368	$25.00	Toys "R" Us
1998	Pilot Barbie (black)	19384	$25.00	Toys "R" Us
1998	Pink Reflections Barbie	19130	$25.00	Sears
1998	Portland Trailblazers	20720	$20.00	NBA
1998	Portland Trailblazers (black)	20721	$20.00	NBA
1998	Portrait in Blue Barbie	19355	$15.00	Wal-Mart
1998	Portrait in Blue Barbie (black)	19356	$15.00	Wal-Mart
1998	Pretty in Plaid (black)	21570	$5.00	
1998	Pretty in Plaid (blonde)	20666	$5.00	
1998	Pretty in Plaid (brunette)	20668	$5.00	
1998	Pretty in Plaid (redhead)	20667	$5.00	
1998	Princess	18404	$10.00	
1998	Princess (Asian)	18407	$10.00	
1998	Princess (black)	18405	$10.00	
1998	Princess (Hispanic)	18406	$10.00	
1998	Princess Sissy Barbie		$35.00	Royal Houses of Europe
1998	Promenade in the Park Barbie	18630	$40.00	Great Fashions of the 20th Century
1998	Purdue	19868	$11.00	University Barbie
1998	Puzzle Craze Barbie	20164	$12.00	Wal-Mart
1998	Puzzle Craze Barbie (black)	20165	$12.00	Wal-Mart
1998	Rendezvous Barbie	20647	$74.00	Masquerade Gala
1998	Rising Star Barbie	17864	$38.00	Grand Ole Opry
1998	Sacramento Kings	20746	$20.00	NBA
1998	Sacramento Kings (black)	20747	$20.00	NBA
1998	Safari	18970	$30.00	Disney
1998	San Antonio Spurs	20722	$20.00	NBA
1998	San Antonio Spurs (black)	20723	$20.00	NBA
1998	Schooltime Fun (black)	18488	$10.00	Supermarket
1998	Schooltime Fun Barbie	18487	$10.00	Supermarket
1998	Seattle Supersonics	20718	$20.00	NBA
1998	Seattle Supersonics (black)	20719	$20.00	NBA
1998	Sheer Illusion Barbie #1	20662	$92.00	Nolan Miller Designer Collection
1998	Sheer Illusion Barbie #2	20662	$70.00	Nolan Miller Designer Collection
1998	Sidewalk Chalk Barbie	19784	$20.00	Shopko/Venture
1998	Sidewalk Chalk Barbie	19784	$15.00	Hill's
1998	Silken Flame Barbie (blonde)	18449	$24.00	Nostalgic
1998	Silken Flame Barbie (brunette)	18448	$24.00	Nostalgic
1998	Spring Tea Party Barbie (black)	18657	$30.00	Avon
1998	Spring Tea Party Barbie (blonde)	18656	$30.00	Avon
1998	Spring Tea Party Barbie (brunette)	18656	$30.00	Avon
1998	Stanford	19870	$11.00	University Barbie
1998	Stanford (black)	20124	$11.00	University Barbie
1998	Starlight Carousel Barbie	19708	$18.00	K•B Toys
1998	Sticker Craze (black)	19913	$10.00	
1998	Sticker Craze (blonde)	19224	$10.00	
1998	Sticker Craze (brunette)	19914	$10.00	
1998	Summer Daydreams Barbie	19739	$55.00	Coca-Cola Fashion Classic Series
1998	Summer in San Francisco Barbie (blonde) (FAO)	19363	$95.00	City Seasons Collection
1998	Summer in San Francisco Barbie (redhead) (FAO)	19363	$675.00	City Seasons Collection
1998	Sunflower Barbie (Van Gogh)	19366	$68.00	Artist Series
1998	Sweet Treats Barbie	20780	$15.00	

Year	Item	Number	Value	Specials
1998	Sweet Treats Barbie (black)	20955	$15.00	
1998	Sweetheart (black)	18609	$5.00	
1998	Sweetheart (blonde)	18608	$5.00	
1998	Sweetheart (brunette)	18610	$5.00	
1998	Sweetheart (redhead)	18700	$5.00	
1998	Symphony in Chiffon Barbie	20186	$60.00	Barbie Couture Collection
1998	Symphony in Chiffon Barbie (black)	21295	$60.00	Barbie Couture Collection
1998	Syracuse	19163	$10.00	University Barbie
1998	Syracuse (black)	19419	$10.00	University Barbie
1998	Thai	18561	$18.00	Dolls of the World
1998	Tooth Fairy Barbie	17246	$12.00	Wal-Mart
1998	Toronto Raptors	20740	$20.00	NBA
1998	Toronto Raptors (black)	20741	$20.00	NBA
1998	Toys "R" Us 50th Anniversary Doll	20038	$85.00	Toys "R" Us
1998	Twirlin' Make-Up (blonde)	18421	$10.00	
1998	Twist 'n Turn Barbie Smasheroo (brunette)	18941	$50.00	Collectors' Request
1998	Twist 'n Turn Barbie Smasheroo (redhead)	23258	$50.00	Collectors' Request
1998	Tye-Dye Barbie	20504	$10.00	
1998	University of Arkansas (black)	17191	$10.00	University Barbie
1998	University of Colorado	19169	$10.00	University Barbie
1998	University of Connecticut	19866	$11.00	University Barbie
1998	University of Kentucky	19153	$11.00	University Barbie
1998	University of Maryland	19867	$11.00	University Barbie
1998	University of Maryland (black)	20123	$11.00	University Barbie
1998	University of Texas (black)	20126	$11.00	University Barbie
1998	Uptown Chic Barbie	19632	$32.00	Fashion Savvy Collection
1998	Utah Jazz Barbie	20708	$20.00	NBA
1998	Utah Jazz Barbie (black)	20709	$20.00	NBA
1998	Valentine Barbie	17649	$12.00	Supermarket
1998	Valentine Barbie (black)	17650	$12.00	Supermarket
1998	Valentine Date Barbie	18306	$18.00	Target
1998	Vancouver Grizzlies	20732	$20.00	NBA
1998	Vancouver Grizzlies (black)	20733	$20.00	NBA
1998	Vera Wang Barbie	19788	$100.00	Designer Collection
1998	Very Velvet Barbie	20528	$25.00	
1998	Virginia Tech	19171	$10.00	University Barbie
1998	Virginia Tech (black)	19420	$10.00	University Barbie
1998	Washington State	19869	$11.00	University Barbie
1998	Washington Wizards	20696	$11.00	NBA
1998	Washington Wizards (black)	20697	$11.00	NBA
1998	Water Rhapsody Barbie	19847	$57.00	Essence of Nature
1998	Wild Style Barbie	19262	$20.00	Toys "R" Us
1998	Winter Evening Barbie (blonde)	19218	$25.00	Wholesale Clubs
1998	Winter Evening Barbie (brunette)	19220	$25.00	Wholesale Clubs
1998	Winter in New York	19429	$50.00	City Seasons Collection
1998	Winter Splendor Barbie	19357	$38.00	Avon
1998	Winter Splendor Barbie (black)	19358	$38.00	Avon
1998	WNBA Barbie	20205	$16.00	WNBA
1998	Workin' Out (outfits vary)		$11.00	Wholesale Club
1999	101 Dalmatians Barbie (brunette)	21377	$20.00	Toys "R" Us
1999	101 Dalmatians Barbie (strawberry blonde)	21375	$20.00	Toys "R" Us
1999	40th Anniversary Barbie (black)	22336	$45.00	40th Anniversary Collection
1999	40th Anniversary Barbie (blonde)	21384	$45.00	40th Anniversary Collection
1999	40th Anniversary Barbie (brunette)	24842	$150.00	Collectors' Convention 1999
1999	40th Anniversary Bumblebee Gala Barbie	23041	$80.00	40th Anniversary Collection

Year	Item	Number	Value	Specials
1999	Air Force Academy	21166	$14.00	University Barbie
1999	Angel of Peace	24240	$40.00	Timeless Sentiments
1999	Angel of Peace (black)	24241	$40.00	Timeless Sentiments
1999	Army	21159	$14.00	University Barbie
1999	Austrian Barbie	21553	$18.00	Dolls of the World
1999	Autumn in London	22257	$30.00	City Seasons Collection
1999	Avon Representative Barbie	22202	$50.00	Avon
1999	Avon Representative Barbie (black)	22203	$40.00	Avon
1999	Avon Representative Barbie (Hispanic)	22204	$50.00	Avon
1999	Ballerina Dreams Barbie	20676	$14.00	Supermarket
1999	Ballet Lessons	26774	$11.00	
1999	Barbie as Dorothy	25812	$18.00	Wizard of Oz
1999	Barbie as Glinda	25813	$18.00	Wizard of Oz
1999	Barbie as Marzipan from *The Nutcracker*	20851	$26.00	Classic Ballet Series
1999	Barbie as Snow White	21130	$28.00	Children's Collector Series
1999	Barbie Had a Little Lamb	21740	$25.00	Nursery Rhyme
1999	Barbie Loves Tweety	21632	$35.00	Warner Bros. Studio Store
1999	Barbie Sign Language	25837	$20.00	
1999	Barbie Sign Language (black)	26394	$20.00	
1999	Bath Boutique Barbie (brunette)	22359	$15.00	
1999	Bath Boutique Barbie (black)	22358	$15.00	
1999	Bath Boutique Barbie (blonde)	22357	$15.00	
1999	Birthday Party Barbie	22907	$20.00	
1999	Birthday Party Barbie (black)	22906	$20.00	
1999	Birthday Wishes Barbie	21128	$26.00	Birthday Wishes Series
1999	Birthday Wishes Barbie (black)	21509	$26.00	Birthday Wishes Series
1999	Boston College	21189	$16.00	University Barbie
1999	Boston University	21226	$16.00	University Barbie
1999	Celebration Cake Barbie (black)	22903	$20.00	
1999	Celebration Cake Barbie (blonde)	22902	$20.00	
1999	Celebration Cake Barbie (brunette)	22904	$20.00	
1999	Chic	18218	$5.00	K•B Toys
1999	Chicago Cubs Barbie	23883	$29.00	Major League Baseball
1999	Chicago Cubs Barbie (black)	24473	$35.00	Major League Baseball
1999	Chicago Cubs Fan Barbie	22857	$85.00	Chicago Cubs
1999	Cincinnati	21231	$16.00	University Barbie
1999	City Style Barbie	18952	$14.00	Target
1999	Club Wedd Barbie (black)	22361	$20.00	Target
1999	Club Wedd Barbie (blonde)	22360	$20.00	Target
1999	Club Wedd Barbie (brunette)	22362	$20.00	Target
1999	Coca-Cola Barbie (blonde)	22831	$60.00	Coca-Cola Series
1999	Coca-Cola Barbie (brunette) Walt Disney World	23934	$198.00	Coca-Cola Series
1999	Coca-Cola Brand Party Barbie	22964	$12.00	Supermarket
1999	Coca-Cola Drive-In Waitress	22831	$60.00	American Classics
1999	Commuter Set Barbie	21510	$50.00	Collectors' Request
1999	Cool Looks Fashion Designer CD-ROM	24746	$28.00	Meijer
1999	Cool Skating Barbie		$20.00	
1999	Corduroy Cool (black)	26107	$15.00	
1999	Corduroy Cool (blonde)	24658	$15.00	
1999	Corduroy Cool Barbie (brunette)	24659	$9.00	
1999	Crystal Glitter (black)	22070	$15.00	
1999	Crystal Glitter (blonde)	22069	$15.00	
1999	Crystal Glitter (brunette)	22071	$15.00	
1999	Crystal Glitter (redhead)	22071	$15.00	
1999	Crystal Jubilee Barbie	21923	$155.00	Jubilee Series

Year	Item	Number	Value	Specials
1999	Easter Surprise Barbie	20542	$10.00	Supermarket
1999	Easter Surprise Barbie (black)	20543	$10.00	Supermarket
1999	Embassy Waltz Barbie	22836	$60.00	Barbie Collector's Club
1999	Evening Illusion Barbie	23495	$72.00	Nolan Miller Designer Collection
1999	Fantasy Goddess of Africa	22044	$280.00	Bob Mackie International Beauty
1999	Far Out Barbie	21911	$40.00	Twist 'n Turn Collection
1999	Flamingo Barbie	22957	$55.00	Birds of Beauty Series
1999	Florida Vacation Beach Time Fun Barbie	23740	$22.00	Wholesale Clubs
1999	Fruit Fantasy Barbie (blonde)	21386	$25.00	Avon
1999	Fruit Fantasy Barbie (brunette)	20319	$30.00	Avon
1999	Generation Girl Barbie	19428	$20.00	
1999	Glam 'n Groom Barbie	27271	$9.00	
1999	Golden Allure Barbie	22961	$32.00	Home Shopping Club
1999	Golden Hollywood Barbie	22832	$95.00	FAO Schwarz
1999	Golden Hollywood Barbie (black)	23877	$95.00	FAO Schwarz
1999	Golden Waltz Barbie (blonde)	22976	$25.00	Wholesale Clubs
1999	Golden Waltz Barbie (redhead)	23220	$30.00	Wholesale Clubs
1999	Happenin' Hair Barbie	22882	$12.00	
1999	Happy Birthday	22902	$20.00	
1999	Happy Birthday (black)	22903	$20.00	
1999	Happy Birthday (brunette)	22904	$20.00	
1999	Harley-Davidson Barbie #3	22256	$95.00	Toys "R" Us
1999	Hawaii Barbie	24614	$5.00	
1999	Heartstring Angel Barbie	21414	$60.00	Angels of Music
1999	Heartstring Angel Barbie (black)	21915	$60.00	Angels of Music
1999	Holiday Sensation	19792	$35.00	Holiday Homecoming Series
1999	Holiday Treasures Barbie		$120.00	
1999	Hollywood Nails (black)	24557	$15.00	
1999	Hollywood Nails Barbie	17857	$12.00	
1999	Horse Riding Barbie with Riding Club CD-ROM	24788	$28.00	Meijer
1999	I Love Barbie	20668	$5.00	
1999	Jewel Princess (brunette)		$95.00	Disney/Winter Princess
1999	Jewel Skating Barbie	23239	$12.00	Wal-Mart
1999	Jewel Skating Barbie (black)	23240	$12.00	Wal-Mart
1999	Le Papillon Barbie	23276	$214.00	Bob Mackie Custom Limited Edition
1999	Le Papillon Barbie	23273	$175.00	FAO Schwarz
1999	Lemon-Lime Sorbet Barbie	20318	$25.00	Avon
1999	Los Angeles Dodgers Barbie	23882	$27.00	Major League Baseball
1999	Los Angeles Dodgers Barbie (black)	24472	$32.00	Major League Baseball
1999	LSU	21219	$16.00	University Barbie
1999	LSU (black)	21220	$16.00	University Barbie
1999	Magic Hair Styler CD-ROM	24748	$28.00	Meijer
1999	Magna Doodle Barbie	23275	$15.00	Ames
1999	Make-A-Valentine Barbie	20339	$10.00	Supermarket
1999	Make-A-Valentine Barbie (black)	20340	$10.00	Supermarket
1999	Marine Biologist		$15.00	Career
1999	Marshall	21245	$16.00	University Barbie
1999	Massachusetts	21192	$16.00	University Barbie
1999	MGM 75th Anniversary Barbie	22832	$70.00	
1999	Millennium Princess Barbie	24154	$45.00	Millennium Collection
1999	Millennium Princess Barbie (black)	23995	$45.00	Millennium Collection
1999	Minnesota	21193	$16.00	University Barbie
1999	Mint Memories Barbie	20983	$150.00	Victorian Tea Porcelain Collection
1999	Mississippi State	21190	$16.00	University Barbie
1999	Mississippi State (black)	21191	$16.00	University Barbie

Year	Item	Number	Value	Specials
1999	Montana	21194	$16.00	University Barbie
1999	Moroccan Barbie	21507	$18.00	Dolls of the World
1999	Movie Star	25466	$20.00	
1999	My Wardrobe Barbie	22962	$28.00	Service Merchandise
1999	NASCAR Official #94 Barbie (brunette)	22954	$25.00	NASCAR
1999	New York Yankees Barbie	23881	$28.00	Major League Baseball
1999	New York Yankees Barbie (black)	24471	$36.00	Major League Baseball
1999	North Carolina A & T	21167	$16.00	University Barbie
1999	North Carolina A & T (black)	21168	$16.00	University Barbie
1999	Oscar de la Renta Barbie	20376	$40.00	
1999	Pajama Fun Barbie	26883	$13.00	Target
1999	Pearl Beach Barbie Easter Basket	25381	$15.00	Supermarket
1999	Peruvian II	21506	$18.00	Dolls of the World
1999	Pet Lovin'	23007	$15.00	
1999	Pet Lovin' (black)	23008	$15.00	
1999	Philadelphia 76ers (black)	20725	$20.00	NBA
1999	Pilot Barbie	24017	$12.00	
1999	Pink Inspiration Barbie (black)	21722	$30.00	Toys "R" Us
1999	Pink Inspiration Barbie (blonde)	21914	$30.00	Toys "R" Us
1999	Pink Inspiration Barbie (brunette)	21721	$30.00	Toys "R" Us
1999	Pittsburgh	21169	$16.00	University Barbie
1999	Plum Royal	23478	$170.00	Byron Lars Runway Collection
1999	Pretty Flowers Barbie (black)	24653	$6.00	
1999	Pretty Flowers Barbie (blonde)	24652	$6.00	
1999	Pretty Flowers Barbie (brunette)	24654	$6.00	
1999	Pretty Flowers Barbie (redhead)	24655	$6.00	
1999	Princess	22891	$15.00	
1999	Princess	22894	$15.00	
1999	Princess (black)	22892	$15.00	
1999	Princess (brunette)	22893	$15.00	
1999	Rainbow Princess	23474	$12.00	
1999	Rainbow Princess (black)	23475	$11.00	
1999	Rainbow Princess (brunette)	23476	$12.00	
1999	Reflections of Light (Renoir)	23884	$75.00	Artist Series
1999	Riviera Barbie	22974	$10.00	
1999	Rose Barbie	22337	$30.00	A Garden of Flowers
1999	San Diego State	21227	$16.00	University Barbie
1999	San Diego State (black)	21228	$16.00	University Barbie
1999	Secret Messages Barbie	26422	$15.00	
1999	Sit in Style Barbie	23421	$10.00	
1999	Sleeping Beauty Barbie	20489	$18.00	
1999	Sleeping Beauty Barbie (black)	20490	$18.00	
1999	Snow Sensation Barbie	23800	$39.00	Avon
1999	Snow Sensation Barbie (black)	23801	$39.00	Avon
1999	Soccer Barbie	20151	$20.00	
1999	South Carolina	21195	$16.00	University Barbie
1999	South Carolina (black)	21196	$16.00	University Barbie
1999	Space Camp Barbie	22425	$25.00	Toys "R" Us
1999	Space Camp Barbie (black)	22426	$25.00	Toys "R" Us
1999	Spring in Tokyo Barbie	19430	$34.00	City Seasons Collection
1999	Spring in Tokyo Barbie (nostalgic face)	23499	$40.00	City Seasons Collection
1999	Steppin' Out Barbie – 1930s	21531	$35.00	Great Fashions of the 20th Century
1999	Strawberry Party Barbie	22895	$15.00	Ames
1999	Strawberry Sorbet Barbie	20317	$25.00	Avon
1999	Style	20766	$10.00	K•B Toys

Year	Item	Number	Value	Specials
1999	Style (black)	20767	$10.00	K•B Toys
1999	Summer in Rome Barbie	19431	$35.00	City Seasons Collection
1999	Super Gymnast Barbie (black)	23106	$15.00	K•B Toys
1999	Super Gymnast Barbie	23105	$20.00	
1999	Swimming Champion Barbie	24590	$15.00	
1999	Tango (porcelain)	23451	$300.00	Bob Mackie
1999	Texas Tech	21229	$16.00	University Barbie
1999	Texas Tech (black)	21230	$16.00	University Barbie
1999	Todd Oldham Barbie	22205	$54.00	Designer Collection
1999	Tour Guide Barbie — *Toy Story 2*	24015	$30.00	Disney
1999	Tree Trimming	22967	$12.00	
1999	Tree Trimming (black)	22968	$12.00	
1999	Trend Forecaster Barbie	22833	$32.00	Clothes Minded Collection
1999	Tye-Dye Barbie	20504	$13.00	
1999	University of Mississippi	21232	$16.00	University Barbie
1999	University of Mississippi (black)	21233	$16.00	University Barbie
1999	University of Virginia (black)	21216	$16.00	University Barbie
1999	UNLV	21234	$16.00	University Barbie
1999	Utah	21197	$16.00	University Barbie
1999	Valentine Style Barbie	20465	$14.00	Target
1999	Valentine Style Barbie (black)	22150	$14.00	Target
1999	Vanderbilt	21160	$16.00	University Barbie
1999	Vera Wang Awards Night Barbie	23027	$89.00	Designer Collection
1999	Very Berry	26881	$10.00	K-Mart
1999	Very Velvet (brunette)	22249	$30.00	
1999	Villanova	21172	$16.00	University Barbie
1999	Walking Barbie & Baby Sister Krissy	22232	$18.00	
1999	Walking Barbie & Baby Sister Krissy (black)	22307	$18.00	
1999	We Can Do Anything, Right Barbie!		$410.00	Collectors' Convention 1999
1999	Weekend Barbie	23462	$5.00	
1999	Western Plains	23205	$40.00	Lifestyles of the West
1999	Whispering Wind Barbie	22834	$65.00	Essence of Nature
1999	Winter in Montreal Barbie	22258	$40.00	City Seasons Collection
1999	Working Woman Barbie	20548	$25.00	
1999	Working Woman Barbie (black)	20549	$25.00	
1999	Wyoming	21246	$16.00	University Barbie
1999	Xavier	21173	$16.00	University Barbie
1999	Your Pen Pal Barbie	23221	$20.00	Military
1999	Your Pen Pal Barbie (black)	23222	$20.00	Military
2000	Ballet Lessons (black)	26775	$50.00	
2000	Ballet Star	29195	$11.00	
2000	Ballet Star (black)	29196	$12.00	
2000	Barbie 2000	27409	$48.00	
2000	Barbie 2000 (black)	27410	$48.00	
2000	Barbie as Beauty	24673	$30.00	Children's Collector Series
2000	Barbie as Dorothy	25812	$25.00	Wizard of Oz
2000	Barbie as Glinda	25813	$25.00	Wizard of Oz
2000	Barbie as Snowflake from *The Nutcracker*	25642	$27.00	Classic Ballet Series
2000	Barbie as Wonder Woman	24638	$18.00	Barbie Loves Pop Culture
2000	Barbie for President	26288	Retail	Career
2000	Barbie for President (black)	26284	Retail	Career
2000	Barbie for President (Hispanic)		Retail	Career/Online Exclusive
2000	Bedtime Stories w/book	29426	$25.00	Toys "R" Us
2000	Bedtime Stories w/book (black)	29427	$25.00	Toys "R" Us
2000	Between Takes Barbie	27684	$50.00	Hollywood Movie Star Collection

Year	Item	Number	Value	Specials
2000	Birthday Wishes Barbie #2	24667	$24.00	Birthday Wishes Series
2000	Birthday Wishes Barbie #2 (black)	24668	$24.00	Birthday Wishes Series
2000	Birthday Wishes Barbie #3	28434	$27.00	Birthday Wishes Series
2000	Birthday Wishes Barbie #3 (black)	28435	$27.00	
2000	Birthday Wishes Barbie (black)	24668	$25.00	
2000	Blushing Bride		$30.00	Avon
2000	Blushing Bride (black)		$30.00	
2000	Bowling Champ Barbie	25871	$30.00	Sports
2000	Bride Barbie (brunette)		$60.00	My Design Friend of Barbie
2000	Bride Barbie (redhead)		$60.00	My Design Friend of Barbie
2000	Celebration Barbie	28269	$34.00	Holiday Dolls
2000	Celebration Barbie (black)	28270	$34.00	
2000	Children's Doctor	29461	$20.00	
2000	Club Couture	26068	$70.00	Barbie Collector's Club
2000	Coca-Cola Barbie #2 (brunette)	24637	$60.00	American Classics
2000	Coca-Cola Barbie (Sweetheart)	24637	$40.00	Coca-Cola Series
2000	Coca-Cola Soda Fountain	26980	$140.00	Coca-Cola Series
2000	Convention 2000 Barbie Democrat (black)		$120.00	
2000	Convention 2000 Barbie Democrat (blonde)		$95.00	
2000	Convention 2000 Barbie Democrat (brunette)		$110.00	
2000	Convention 2000 Barbie Republican (black)		$130.00	
2000	Convention 2000 Barbie Republican (blonde)		$97.00	
2000	Convention 2000 Barbie Republican (brunette)		$115.00	
2000	Cool Clips Barbie	26425	$14.00	
2000	Cool Collecting	25525	$36.00	
2000	Cool Skating Barbie	25887	$20.00	
2000	Country Charm	26464	$25.00	Cracker Barrel Restaurant
2000	Country Charm (black)	29332	$25.00	Cracker Barrel Restaurant
2000	Dancing Fire Barbie	26327	$60.00	Essence of Nature
2000	Delphine Barbie	26929	$95.00	Fashion Model
2000	Dorothy with Toto Porcelain #1		Retail	Wizard of Oz
2000	Dream Wedding	27374	$16.00	
2000	Empress of Emeralds	25680	$100.00	QVC/Royal Jewel
2000	Evening Star Princess	27690	$45.00	Celestial Collection
2000	Fabulous Forties Barbie	22162	$55.00	Great Fashions of the 20th Century
2000	Fairy of the Forest	25639	$42.00	Enchanted World of Fairies
2000	Fantasy Goddess of the Americas	25859	$135.00	Bob Mackie International Beauty
2000	Fashion Designer	29399	$22.00	
2000	Fashion Wardrobe	27788	Retail	
2000	Fashion Wardrobe (black)	27789	Retail	
2000	Ferrari Barbie	25636	$47.00	Sports
2000	Flower Power	29002	$9.00	
2000	Flower Power (black)	29003	$9.00	
2000	Flying Butterfly Barbie	29345	$13.00	
2000	Forest Fairy	25639	$40.00	Fairy Series
2000	Garden Party Fashion	26933	$90.00	Barbie Fashion Model
2000	Generation Girl Barbie Dance Party	25766	$20.00	
2000	Giggles 'n Swing Barbie & Kelly	20333	$15.00	
2000	Giggles 'n Swing Barbie & Kelly (black)	20534	$15.00	
2000	Givenchy Barbie	24635	$60.00	
2000	Glam 'n Groom	26251	$15.00	Dressed Boxed Dolls
2000	Goddess of Beauty and Love	27286	Retail	Inspirational Series
2000	Goddess of Beauty Barbie		$82.00	Goddess Collection
2000	Goddess of Spring	28112	Retail	Inspirational Series
2000	Goddess of Spring Barbie		$79.00	Goddess Collection

Year	Item	Number	Value	Specials
2000	Goddess of the Americas	25859	$189.00	
2000	Graduation Barbie		$55.00	My Design Friend of Barbie
2000	Graduation Barbie (black)		$55.00	My Design Friend of Barbie
2000	Groovy '60s Barbie	27676	$38.00	Great Fashions of the 20th Century
2000	Hanae Mori Barbie	24494	$75.00	
2000	Harley-Davidson Barbie	29207	$70.00	
2000	Hip 2 Be Square (black)	28314	$6.00	
2000	Hip 2 Be Square (blonde)	29410	$8.00	Value Pack
2000	Hip 2 Be Square (brunette)	29663	$8.00	Value Pack
2000	Hip 2 Be Square (redhead)	28316	$6.00	
2000	Holiday Angel	28080	$32.00	
2000	Holiday Angel (black)	28081	$30.00	
2000	Holiday Treasures Barbie	27673	$78.00	Club Exclusive
2000	Hollywood Premiere	26914	$36.00	Hollywood Movie Star Collection
2000	Imperial Splendor	27028	$310.00	Fabergé Porcelain
2000	Indigo Obsession Barbie	26935	$165.00	Byron Lars Runway Collection
2000	Jewel Girl	28066	Retail	
2000	Kitty Fun (black)	28624	$15.00	
2000	Kitty Fun (blonde)	28612	$16.00	
2000	Kitty Fun (brunette)	28866	$16.00	
2000	Lady Liberty		$225.00	Bob Mackie Custom Limited Edition
2000	Lady Liberty		$225.00	
2000	Lingerie (blonde)	26930	$255.00	Fashion Model
2000	Lingerie (brunette)	26931	$265.00	Fashion Model
2000	Lunch at the Club Fashion	26932	$77.00	Barbie Fashion Model
2000	Magical Mermaids Barbie & Krissy	26837	$25.00	
2000	Magical Mermaids Barbie & Krissy (black)	26838	$25.00	
2000	Mann's Chinese Theatre	24636	$48.00	FAO Schwarz
2000	Mann's Chinese Theatre (black)	24998	$60.00	FAO Schwarz
2000	Midnight Moon Princess	27687	$50.00	Celestial Collection
2000	Millennium Bride	24505	$285.00	Millennium Collection
2000	Millennium Grad w/black gown (black)	25750	$5.00	Supermarket
2000	Millennium Grad w/blue gown (black)	25740	$5.00	Supermarket
2000	Millennium Wedding (black)	27674	$36.00	The Bridal Collection
2000	Millennium Wedding (Hispanic)	27765	$45.00	The Bridal Collection
2000	Millennium Wedding (white)	27674	$36.00	The Bridal Collection
2000	Morning Sun Princess	27688	$45.00	Celestial Collection
2000	My Size Butterfly	25863	$135.00	
2000	My Size Butterfly (black)	25864	$135.00	
2000	NASCAR #3	25636	$35.00	
2000	Nifty '50s Barbie	27675	$65.00	Great Fashions of the 20th Century
2000	Northwest Coast Native American	24671	$25.00	Dolls of the World
2000	Nostalgic Toys	25525	$45.00	Cool Collecting Series
2000	Nsync Barbie w/CD	50534	$19.00	
2000	Orange Pekoe	25507	$500.00	Victorian Tea Porcelain Collection
2000	Peace & Love '70s	27677	$70.00	Great Fashions of the 20th Century
2000	Picture Pockets Barbie	28701	$10.00	Toys "R" Us
2000	Pilot		$15.00	
2000	Princess	28264	$11.00	
2000	Princess (Asian)	28267	$11.00	
2000	Princess (black)	28265	$11.00	
2000	Princess (Hispanic)	28266	$11.00	
2000	Princess and the Pea	28800	$26.00	Princess Series
2000	Princess Barbie (Asian)	23477	$11.00	
2000	Princess Barbie (black)	23475	$11.00	

Year	Item	Number	Value	Specials
2000	Princess Barbie (blonde)	23474	$11.00	
2000	Princess Barbie (brunette)	23476	$11.00	
2000	Princess Bride	28521	$20.00	
2000	Princess Bride (black)	28552	$20.00	
2000	Princess of the Incas Barbie	28373	$115.00	Princess Collection/Dolls of the World
2000	Queen of Sapphires	26926	$85.00	Royal Jewel
2000	Rain or Shine Barbie	29179	$15.00	
2000	Rainbow Princess Barbie	26357	$12.00	
2000	Rose Princess (black)	29189	$13.00	
2000	Rose Series	28990	$13.00	
2000	Scuderia Ferrari Barbie		$32.00	Barbie Loves Sports
2000	Sign Language		$18.00	Toys "R" Us
2000	Sisters Celebration Krissy and Barbie	28270	$18.00	
2000	Sleep Over Party		$40.00	QVC
2000	Sophisticated Lady	24930	$45.00	Collectors' Request
2000	Spanish Barbie #3	24670	$18.00	Dolls of the World
2000	Spanish Teacher	29408	$25.00	Toys "R" Us
2000	Spanish Teacher (Hispanic)	29409	$25.00	Toys "R" Us
2000	Star Splash	29260	$13.00	
2000	Star Splash (black)	29308	$13.00	
2000	Suits Me Fine Fashion		Retail	
2000	Surf City	28417	$5.00	
2000	Surf City Barbie Doll and Play Set	28961	$5.00	
2000	Swan	27682	$48.00	Birds of Beauty Series
2000	Swedish Barbie	24672	$18.00	Dolls of the World
2000	Sydney 2000 Olympic Barbie Pin Collector	25644	$25.00	Pop Culture
2000	Sydney 2000 Olympic Barbie Pin Collector (black)	26302	$25.00	Pop Culture
2000	The Addams Family Gift Set	27276	$88.00	
2000	The Tale of the Forest Princess w/book	29458	$25.00	
2000	The Tale of the Forest Princess w/book (black)	29459	$25.00	
2000	Venetian Opulence	24501	$90.00	Masquerade Gala
2000	Victorian Barbie with Cedric Bear (blonde)	25526	$50.00	Adult Collector Edition
2000	Victorian Barbie with Cedric Bear (brunette)	25526	$39.00	Victorian
2000	Wash 'n Wear	29027	$19.00	
2000	Wedgwood Barbie	25641	$110.00	Great Porcelain Houses
2000	Wedgwood Barbie	25641	$150.00	Wedgwood/Wal-Mart
2000	Wizard of Oz-Dorothy with Toto	19364	Retail	Porcelain Treasures Collection
2000	Wizard of Oz-Wicked Witch	23880	Retail	Porcelain Treasures Collection
2000	Wonder Woman	24638	Retail	Warner Bros. Studio Store
2001	Barbie 2001	50841	$102.00	
2001	Barbie 2001 (black)	50842	$70.00	
2001	Barbie and *Curious George*	28798	$28.00	Keepsake Treasures
2001	Barbie as Flower Ballerina from *The Nutcracker*	28375	$25.00	Classic Ballet Series
2001	Barbie as Jeannie from *I Dream of Jeannie*	29913	$40.00	Barbie Loves Pop Culture
2001	Birthday Wishes Barbie (black)	28435	$27.00	
2001	Blush Becomes Her Fashion	29652	$75.00	Barbie Fashion Model
2001	Boulevard Fashion	29653	$60.00	Barbie Fashion Model
2001	Burberry Barbie	29421	$70.00	Designer Burberry
2001	Celebration Barbie (black)	28270	$45.00	
2001	Coca-Cola Barbie (Cheerleader)	53974	$46.00	Coca-Cola Series
2001	Countess of Rubies Barbie	26972	$80.00	Jewel Collection
2001	Day in the Sun (blonde)	26425	$35.00	Hollywood Movie Star Collection
2001	Day in the Sun (brunette)	26426	$70.00	Hollywood Movie Star Collection
2001	Duchess of Diamonds Barbie		Retail	Jewel Collection
2001	Dusk to Dawn Barbie Gift Set	29654	$145.00	Barbie Fashion Model

Year	Item	Number	Value	Specials
2001	Fairy of the Garden	28799	$45.00	Enchanted World of Fairies
2001	Fantasy Goddess of the Arctic	50840	$140.00	Bob Mackie
2001	Fashion Editor Barbie		$110.00	Barbie Fashion Model
2001	Fern from *Charlotte's Web*	50724	$15.00	When I Read, I Dream
2001	Ferrari Barbie	25636	$35.00	Sports
2001	Ferrari Barbie #2	28534	$50.00	Barbie Loves Sports
2001	Glamour Gal Betty Boop		Retail	Pop Culture
2001	Goddess of Wisdom Barbie		$119.00	Goddess Collection
2001	Goldilocks and The Three Bears	29605	$30.00	Storybook Favorites/Kelly
2001	Grand Entrance Barbie	28533	$45.00	Grand Entrance
2001	Grand Entrance Barbie (black)	29662	$45.00	Grand Entrance
2001	Grand Hotel	50576	$20.00	Toys "R" Us
2001	Harley-Davidson Barbie	29208	$100.00	
2001	Holiday Angel Barbie #2	28081	$36.00	Holiday Angel
2001	Holiday Angel Barbie #2 (black)	28080	$34.00	Holiday Angel
2001	Holiday Treasures Barbie		$110.00	
2001	Hollywood Cast Party Barbie	50825	$65.00	Hollywood Movie Star Collection/ FAO Schwarz
2001	Home for the Holidays Barbie	52834	$34.00	
2001	In the Pink Barbie	27683	$140.00	Barbie Fashion Model
2001	Jo from *Little Women*	50723	$15.00	When I Read, I Dream
2001	Lighter Than Air Barbie	29905	$120.00	Prima Ballerina
2001	Lingerie Barbie #3	29651	$100.00	Barbie Fashion Model
2001	Lisette Barbie	7438	$104.00	Barbie Fashion Model
2001	Midnight Tuxedo Barbie	28796	$77.00	Club Exclusive
2001	Midnight Tuxedo Barbie (black)	29307	$400.00	Club Exclusive
2001	Moja Barbie	50826	$210.00	Byron Lars
2001	Princess of India Barbie	28374	$165.00	Dolls of the World — Princess Collection
2001	Princess of the French Court Barbie	28372	$150.00	Dolls of the World — Princess Collection
2001	Publicity Tour Party Barbie	27865	$40.00	Hollywood Movie Star Collection
2001	Queen of the Prom Barbie		$490.00	Collectors' Convention 2001
2001	Ravishing in Rouge Barbie	52741	$110.00	Barbie Fashion Model
2001	Romantic Wedding (white)	29438	$36.00	The Bridal Collection
2001	Romantic Wedding (black)	29439	$36.00	The Bridal Collection
2001	Scarlett O'Hara Doll, Barbecue at Twelve Oaks	29910	$49.00	Gone with the Wind
2001	Scarlett O'Hara Doll on Peachtree Street — The Drapery Dress	29771	$52.00	Gone with the Wind
2001	Society Hound Barbie	29057	$85.00	Society Hound Collection
2001	Spirit of the Earth Barbie	50707	$60.00	Native Spirit Collection
2001	Suburban Shopper Barbie	28378	$70.00	Collectors' Request
2001	Tales of Arabian Nights Barbie and Ken Gift Set	50827	$76.00	Magic & Mystery
2001	The Charleston Barbie	24252	$250.00	Bob Mackie
2001	The Munsters Gift Set	50544	$235.00	Barbie Loves Pop Culture
2001	The Orchid Barbie	50319	$76.00	Flowers in Fashion
2001	The Rose Barbie	29911	$55.00	Flowers in Fashion
2001	Wedgwood Barbie	50823	$79.00	Wedgwood
2001	Wedgwood Barbie (black)	50824	$79.00	Wedgwood
2002	All That Glitters Barbie	55426	$27.00	Diva Collection
2002	Anne from *Anne of Green Gables*	50726	$14.00	When I Read, I Dream
2002	Barbie 2002	53975	$44.00	
2002	Barbie 2002 (black)	53976	$38.00	
2002	Barbie and Snoopy	55558	$60.00	
2002	Barbie as Samantha from *Bewitched*	53510	$30.00	Barbie Loves Pop Culture
2002	Barbie as Swan Ballerina	53867	$24.00	Classic Ballet Series
2002	Classic Grace Barbie		Retail	Prima Ballerina

Year	Item	Number	Value	Specials
2002	Coca-Cola Barbie (Majorette)		$35.00	Coca-Cola Series
2002	Continental Holiday Barbie Gift Set	55497	$100.00	Barbie Fashion Model
2002	Enchanted Mermaid Barbie	53978	$200.00	
2002	Fashion Designer Barbie		$95.00	Barbie Fashion Model
2002	Fire and Ice Barbie	53511	$45.00	Pop Culture
2002	Fire and Ice Barbie (black)	53863	$45.00	Pop Culture
2002	Gold 'n Glamour Barbie	54185	$42.00	Collectors' Request
2002	Gone Platinum Barbie (black)	53868	$40.00	Diva Collection
2002	Gone Platinum Barbie	52739	$40.00	Diva Collection
2002	Grand Entrance Barbie #2	53841	$30.00	Grand Entrance
2002	Grand Entrance Barbie #2 (black)	53842	$30.00	Grand Entrance
2002	Heidi	52900	$10.00	When I Read, I Dream
2002	Holiday Celebration Barbie		$65.00	
2002	Holiday Celebration Barbie (black)		$65.00	
2002	Lingerie Barbie #4 (blonde)	55498	$54.00	Barbie Fashion Model
2002	Lingerie Barbie #5 (black)	56120	$50.00	Barbie Fashion Model
2002	Little Red Riding Hood and The Wolf	52899	$22.00	Storybook Favorites/Kelly
2002	Mademoiselle Isabelle Barbie	55387	$79.00	Portrait Collection
2002	Malibu Barbie	56061	$24.00	Pop Culture
2002	Marie Therese Barbie	55496	$64.00	Barbie Fashion Model
2002	Mbili Barbie		$135.00	Byron Lars
2002	Peter Rabbit 100 Year Celebration Barbie	53872	$37.00	Keepsake Treasures
2002	Princess of China Barbie	53368	$65.00	Dolls of the World — Princess Collection
2002	Princess of Ireland Barbie	53367	$25.00	Dolls of the World — Princess Collection
2002	Princess of the Nile Barbie	53369	$40.00	Dolls of the World — Princess Collection
2002	Provencale Barbie	50829	$96.00	Barbie Fashion Model
2002	Radiant Redhead Barbie	55501	$150.00	Bob Mackie
2002	Rapunzel Barbie	53973	$22.00	Princess
2002	Rocky Mountain Mod		$210.00	Collectors' Convention 2002
2002	Society Girl Barbie (black)	56204	$32.00	Style Set
2002	Society Girl Barbie	56203	$30.00	Style Set
2002	Sophisticated Wedding Barbie	53370	$34.00	
2002	Sophisticated Wedding Barbie (black)	53371	$34.00	
2002	Spirit of Water Barbie	53861	$60.00	Native Spirit Collection
2002	Sterling Silver Rose Barbie		Retail	Bob Mackie
2002	The Calla Lily Barbie	29912	$57.00	Flowers in Fashion
2002	The Iris Barbie	53935	$70.00	Flowers in Fashion
2002	Twilight Gala Barbie	53862	$72.00	Club Exclusive
2002	Twilight Gala Barbie (black)	53870	$86.00	Club Exclusive
2002	Western Chic Barbie	55487	$120.00	Pop Culture
2002	Winter Concert Barbie		Retail	
2003	1 Modern Circle Barbie	B2523	$30.00	1 Modern Circle
2003	A Model Life Barbie Gift Set	B0147	$80.00	
2003	April Diamond Barbie	B3412	$40.00	Birthstone Collection/Wal-Mart
2003	April Diamond Barbie (black)	C0586	$40.00	Birthstone Collection/Wal-Mart
2003	August Peridot Barbie	B3416	$40.00	Birthstone Collection/Wal-Mart
2003	August Peridot Barbie (black)	C0578	$40.00	Birthstone Collection/Wal-Mart
2003	Barbie 2003	B0144	$65.00	
2003	Barbie 2003 (black)	B0145	$65.00	
2003	Barbie 2003 (redhead)		$125.00	
2003	Barbie as Elle Woods from *Legally Blonde 2*	B9284	$35.00	Barbie Loves Pop Culture
2003	Barbie as Peppermint Candy Cane from *The Nutcracker*	57578	$33.00	Classic Ballet Series
2003	Barbie as That Girl	56705	$40.00	Barbie Loves Pop Culture
2003	Bohemian Glamour Barbie	B2512	$39.00	Style Set

Year	Item	Number	Value	Specials
2003	Brunette Brilliance Barbie	B0585	$100.00	Bob Mackie
2003	Capucine Barbie	B0146	$100.00	Barbie Fashion Model
2003	Chataine Barbie	B4425	$425.00	Barbie Fashion Model
2003	City Smart Barbie		$510.00	Barbie Fashion Model
2003	December Turquoise Barbie	B2397	$40.00	Birthstone Collection/Wal-Mart
2003	December Turquoise Barbie (black)	C0582	$40.00	Birthstone Collection/Wal-Mart
2003	Designer Spotlight by Katiana Jimenez	B0836	$450.00	Designer Spotlight
2003	Exotic Beauty Barbie	B0149	$26.00	Style Set
2003	Exotic Beauty Barbie (black)	B0150	$54.00	Style Set
2003	February Amethyst Barbie	B3410	$40.00	Birthstone Collection/Wal-Mart
2003	February Amethyst Barbie (black)	C0584	$40.00	Birthstone Collection/Wal-Mart
2003	French Quarter Barbie Fashion	B2518	$29.00	Barbie Collector's Club
2003	Gay Parisienne Barbie (blonde)	57610	$200.00	Collectors' Request
2003	Gay Parisienne Barbie (brunette)		$37.00	Collectors' Request
2003	Gay Parisienne Barbie (redhead)		$185.00	Collectors' Request
2003	Giorgio Armani Barbie	B2521	$135.00	Giorgio Armani
2003	Grease Barbie	B2510	$100.00	Barbie Loves Pop Culture
2003	James Bond 007 Ken and Barbie Gift Set	B0150	$55.00	Barbie Loves Pop Culture
2003	January Garnet Barbie	B3409	$40.00	Birthstone Collection/Wal-Mart
2003	January Garnet Barbie (black)	C0583	$40.00	Birthstone Collection/Wal-Mart
2003	Joyeux Barbie	B3430	$115.00	Barbie Fashion Model
2003	Joyeux Barbie (redhead)	B23431	$320.00	Barbie Fashion Model
2003	Jude Deveraux The Raider Barbie and Ken Gift Set		$50.00	Romance Novels
2003	July Ruby Barbie	B3415	$40.00	Birthstone Collection/Wal-Mart
2003	July Ruby Barbie (black)	C0577	$40.00	Birthstone Collection/Wal-Mart
2003	June Pearl Barbie	B3414	$40.00	Birthstone Collection/Wal-Mart
2003	June Pearl Barbie (black)	C0576	$40.00	Birthstone Collection/Wal-Mart
2003	Lady Camille Barbie		Retail	Portrait Collection
2003	Lingerie Barbie #6	56948	$42.00	Barbie Fashion Model
2003	March Aquamarine Barbie	B3411	$40.00	Birthstone Collection/Wal-Mart
2003	March Aquamarine Barbie (black)	C0585	$40.00	Birthstone Collection/Wal-Mart
2003	Marie Antoinette Barbie	53991	$250.00	Women of Royalty
2003	May Emerald Barbie	B3413	$40.00	Birthstone Collection/Wal-Mart
2003	May Emerald Barbie (black)	C0575	$40.00	Birthstone Collection/Wal-Mart
2003	Noir et Blanc Barbie	B1992	$65.00	Club Exclusive
2003	Noir et Blanc Barbie (black)	B1993	$100.00	Club Exclusive
2003	November Topaz Barbie	B2396	$40.00	Birthstone Collection/Wal-Mart
2003	November Topaz Barbie (black)	C0581	$40.00	Birthstone Collection/Wal-Mart
2003	October Opal Barbie	B2395	$40.00	Birthstone Collection/Wal-Mart
2003	October Opal Barbie (black)	C0580	$40.00	Birthstone Collection/Wal-Mart
2003	Princess of Japan Barbie	B5731	$23.00	Dolls of the World — Princess Collection
2003	Princess of South Africa Barbie	56218	$26.00	Dolls of the World — Princess Collection
2003	Princess of the Danish Court Barbie	56216	$22.00	Dolls of the World — Princess Collection
2003	Princess of the Portuguese Empire Barbie	56217	$22.00	Dolls of the World — Princess Collection
2003	Princess of the Vikings Barbie	B6361	$26.00	Dolls of the World — Princess Collection
2003	Red Hot Barbie (black)	56708	$32.00	Diva Collection
2003	Red Hot Barbie (white)	56707	$35.00	Diva Collection
2003	September Sapphire Barbie	B2394	$40.00	Birthstone Collection/Wal-Mart
2003	September Sapphire Barbie (black)	C0579	$40.00	Birthstone Collection/Wal-Mart
2003	Special Occasion Barbie		Retail	
2003	Special Occasion Barbie — Treasure Hunt Doll	B7565	Retail	
2003	Spirit of the Sky Barbie	B2367	$60.00	Native Spirit Collection
2003	Starring Barbie in *King Kong*	56737	$29.00	Pop Culture
2003	Sunday Best Barbie	B2520	$48.00	Barbie Fashion Model
2003	Tatu Barbie	B2018	$170.00	Byron Lars

Year	Item	Number	Value	Specials
2003	The Waltz Barbie and Ken Gift Set	B2655	$100.00	
2003	The World of Barbie		$75.00	Collectors' Convention 2003
2003	Winter Fantasy Barbie	B2519	$45.00	Holiday Dolls
2003	Winter Fantasy Barbie (black)	C0166	$45.00	Holiday Dolls
2004	1 Modern Circle Barbie	B2527	$33.00	1 Modern Circle
2004	45th Anniversary Barbie and Ken Gift Set	C4656	$97.00	Barbie Fashion Model/FAO Schwarz
2004	45th Anniversary Barbie by Bob Mackie (black hair)	B3454	$150.00	
2004	45th Anniversary Barbie by Bob Mackie (black)	B3453	$60.00	
2004	45th Anniversary Barbie by Bob Mackie (blonde)	B3452	$50.00	
2004	45th Anniversary Barbie by Robert Best	B8955	$49.00	Barbie Fashion Model
2004	45th Anniversary Barbie by Robert Best (black)	B0445	$50.00	Barbie Fashion Model
2004	A Nod for Mod Barbie	C6261	$80.00	Barbie Fan Club Exclusive
2004	Badgley Mischka Bride Barbie	B8946	$139.00	Designer Dolls
2004	Baking Fun Barbie	52639	$12.00	
2004	Barbie	G8469	$6.00	
2004	Barbie and Ken as Arwen and Aragorn from *The Lord of the Rings*	B3449	$180.00	Hollywood
2004	Barbie as Catwoman	B5838	$20.00	Barbie Loves Pop Culture
2004	Barbie as Galadriel from *The Lord of the Rings*	H1179	$40.00	Hollywood
2004	Barbie as Juliet	B5655	$30.00	Classic Ballet Series
2004	Barbie as Titania	C3819	$27.00	Classic Ballet Series
2004	Barbie Pet Doctor	G8815	$16.00	
2004	Batik Princess Barbie	C4558	$25.00	Online Exclusive
2004	Beautiful Bride Barbie		$15.00	
2004	Birthday Wishes Barbie (black)		$24.00	
2004	Birthday Wishes Barbie, Aqua		$19.00	
2004	Birthday Wishes Barbie, Green		$24.00	
2004	Birthday Wishes Barbie, Lavender		$19.00	
2004	Birthday Wishes Barbie, Pink		$19.00	
2004	Birthday Wishes Barbie, Red	C6229	$24.00	
2004	Birthday Wishes Barbie, Violet	C6228	$37.00	
2004	Birthday Wishes Barbie, Yellow		$19.00	
2004	Cali Girl Teresa	C6463	$8.00	
2004	Chinoiserie Red Midnight Barbie		$175.00	Barbie Fashion Model
2004	Chinoiserie Red Moon Barbie	B3431	$50.00	Barbie Fashion Model
2004	Chinoiserie Red Sunset Barbie		$115.00	Online Exclusive
2004	Color Magic Barbie (brunette)	B3437	$40.00	Collectors' Request
2004	Color Magic Barbie (blonde)	B3437	$175.00	Collectors' Request
2004	Color Magic Barbie (redhead)	B3437	$210.00	Collectors' Request
2004	Cruisin the Boardwalk Barbie and River	C4212	$33.00	My Scene
2004	Daria Celebutante		Retail	Model of the Moment
2004	David's Bridal Unforgettable Barbie		Retail	David's Bridal
2004	David's Bridal Unforgettable Barbie (black)		Retail	David's Bridal
2004	David's Bridal Unforgettable Barbie (Hispanic)		Retail	David's Bridal
2004	December Turquoise Barbie	C5330	$40.00	Birthstone Collection
2004	Designer Spotlight by Heather Fonseca		Retail	Designer Spotlight
2004	Diana Ross by Bob Mackie	B2017	$32.00	Celebrities
2004	Duchess Emma Barbie	B3422	$80.00	Portrait Collection
2004	Exotic Intrigue Barbie		Retail	Avon
2004	Exotic Intrigue Barbie (black)		Retail	Avon
2004	Exotic Intrigue Barbie (Hispanic)		Retail	Avon
2004	Faerie Queen Barbie (brunette)	B3456	$185.00	Legends of Ireland
2004	Faerie Queen Barbie	B3456	$50.00	Legends of Ireland
2004	Fairytopia Enchantress Barbie	G8065	$35.00	

Year	Item	Number	Value	Specials
2004	Fashion Show Barbie	G3673	$23.00	
2004	Fashion Show Teresa	G3675	$23.00	
2004	February Amethyst Barbie	C5332	$40.00	Birthstone Collection
2004	Grease Barbie #2	B4773	$30.00	Barbie Loves Pop Culture
2004	Happy Birthday Barbie	G8490	$16.00	
2004	Hard Rock Café Barbie	G7915	$105.00	Pop Culture
2004	Holiday Barbie		$39.00	
2004	Holiday Barbie (black)		$39.00	
2004	Hollywood Divine Barbie (blonde)		$65.00	Barbie Fan Club Exclusive
2004	Hollywood Divine Barbie (brunette)	B3426	$70.00	Barbie Fan Club Exclusive
2004	January Garnet Barbie	C5331	$40.00	Birthstone Collection
2004	July Ruby Barbie	C5325	$40.00	Birthstone Collection
2004	June Pearl Barbie	C5324	$40.00	Birthstone Collection
2004	Kate Spade Barbie	B2513	$79.00	Kate Spade
2004	Lounge Kitties Leopard	B3417	$70.00	Lounge Kitties
2004	Lounge Kitties Panther	C3553	$36.00	Lounge Kitties
2004	Lounge Kitties Tiger	C2478	$36.00	Lounge Kitties
2004	March Aquamarine Barbie	C5333	$40.00	Birthstone Collection
2004	May Emerald Barbie	C5323	$40.00	Birthstone Collection
2004	Mod Redux Barbie	C6262	$70.00	Online Exclusives
2004	Nichelle Urban Hipster		Retail	Model of the Moment
2004	Night on the Town Barbie and River	B6708	$29.00	My Scene
2004	Nne Barbie	B3423	$90.00	Byron Lars
2004	November Topaz Barbie	C5329	$40.00	Birthstone Collection
2004	October Opal Barbie	C5328	$40.00	Birthstone Collection
2004	Open Road Vintage Reproduction		$80.00	Online Exclusive
2004	Paul Frank Barbie		Retail	Designer Dolls
2004	Paul Frank Barbie (blonde)	B8954	$60.00	Designer Dolls
2004	Pet Doctor Barbie	G8815	$20.00	
2004	Princess of Ancient Greece Barbie	B3461	$20.00	Dolls of the World — Princess Collection
2004	Princess of Ancient Mexico Barbie	C2203	$20.00	Dolls of the World — Princess Collection
2004	Princess of Cambodia Barbie	B3460	$20.00	Dolls of the World — Princess Collection
2004	Princess of England Barbie	B3459	$20.00	Dolls of the World — Princess Collection
2004	Princess of the Navajo Barbie	B8956	$20.00	Dolls of the World — Princess Collection
2004	Queen Elizabeth I Barbie	B3425	$250.00	Women of Royalty
2004	Rose Princess Barbie	56615	$10.00	
2004	Santa's Helper Barbie	B6271	$20.00	
2004	September Sapphire Barbie	C5327	$40.00	Birthstone Collection
2004	Spa Getaway Barbie Gift Set	B1319	$75.00	Barbie Fashion Model
2004	Teresa	G8470	$6.00	
2004	The Bard Barbie Doll	B2511	$60.00	Legends of Ireland
2004	Trend Setter Barbie	B3442	$50.00	Barbie Fashion Model
2004	Versace Barbie Doll	B3457	$140.00	Versace
2004	Versus Barbie	B9767	$79.00	
2005	Aquarius Barbie		$20.00	Zodiac
2005	Aquarius Barbie (black)		$20.00	Zodiac
2005	Archie Comics Betty Barbie	H7614	$20.00	
2005	Archie Comics Veronica Barbie	H7615	$20.00	
2005	Aries Barbie		$20.00	Zodiac
2005	Barbie as Princess Annika	G8399	$20.00	
2005	Barbie Loves Patrick	C3699	$15.00	
2005	Barbie Loves Shrek	H1703	$17.00	
2005	Birthday Wishes Barbie (black)	G8061	$30.00	
2005	Birthday Wishes Barbie, Peach		$30.00	
2005	Cancer Barbie		$20.00	Zodiac

Year	Item	Number	Value	Specials
2005	Cancer Barbie (black)		$20.00	Zodiac
2005	Capricorn Barbie		$20.00	Zodiac/FAO Schwarz
2005	Capricorn Barbie (black)		$20.00	Zodiac
2005	Carnival Barbie	J0927	$20.00	Festivals of the World
2005	Carolina Herrera Bride Barbie	B9797	$140.00	Designer Dolls
2005	Chinese New Year Barbie	J0928	$20.00	Festivals of the World
2005	Chocolate Obsession Barbie	G8878	$35.00	Flavor Obsession
2005	Citrus Obsession Barbie	J0933	$35.00	Flavor Obsession
2005	Crystal Fairytopia Barbie	G6261	$17.00	
2005	Cynthia Rowley Barbie	G8064	$80.00	Cynthia Rowley
2005	Daria Shopping Queen		Retail	Model of the Moment
2005	David's Bridal Eternal Barbie		Retail	David's Bridal
2005	David's Bridal Eternal Barbie (black)		Retail	David's Bridal
2005	David's Bridal Eternal Barbie (Hispanic)		Retail	David's Bridal
2005	Elektra Barbie	H1699	$15.00	
2005	Empress Josephine Barbie	G8051	$250.00	Women of Royalty/Avon
2005	Evening Splendor Barbie	G8890	$50.00	Collectors' Request
2005	Fashion Fun Barbie	H6482	$8.00	
2005	Ferrari Barbie	H6466	$105.00	
2005	Gemini Barbie		$20.00	Zodiac
2005	Gemini Barbie (black)		$20.00	Zodiac
2005	Happy Go Lightly Barbie	G8889	$70.00	Barbie Fashion Model
2005	Hard Rock Café Barbie	J0963	$70.00	Pop Culture
2005	Harley Quinn Barbie	H7616	$24.00	
2005	Holiday Barbie by Bob Mackie (blonde)	G8058	$40.00	
2005	Holiday Barbie by Bob Mackie (ethnic)	H0178	$40.00	
2005	Inuit Legend Barbie		Retail	World Culture Collection
2005	Jewelia Fairytopia Barbie	G6262	$17.00	
2005	Judith Leiber Barbie		Retail	Designer Dolls
2005	Juicy Couture Barbie Doll	G8079	$100.00	Juicy Couture
2005	Leo Barbie		$20.00	Zodiac
2005	Leo Barbie (black)		$20.00	Zodiac
2005	Libra Barbie		$20.00	Zodiac
2005	Libra Barbie (black)		$20.00	Zodiac
2005	Lilly Pulitzer Barbie and Stacie Doll Gift Set	H0187	$50.00	
2005	Lone Star Great Barbie		Retail	Barbie Fan Club Exclusive
2005	Martina McBride Barbie	G8887	$23.00	
2005	Mickey Mouse Barbie	H6468	$15.00	
2005	Muffy Roberts Barbie	H6465	$69.00	Barbie Fashion Model
2005	Peppermint Obsession Barbie	J1743	$35.00	Flavor Obsession
2005	Pisces Barbie		$20.00	Zodiac
2005	Pisces Barbie (black)		$20.00	Zodiac
2005	Princess of Holland Barbie	G8055	$20.00	Dolls of the World — Princess Collection
2005	Princess of Imperial Russia Barbie	G5861	$20.00	Dolls of the World — Princess Collection
2005	Princess of the Hawaiian Islands Barbie	G8056	$22.00	Dolls of the World — Princess Collection
2005	Princess of the Korean Court Barbie	B5870	$20.00	Dolls of the World — Princess Collection
2005	Princess of the Renaissance Barbie	G5860	$20.00	Dolls of the World — Princess Collection
2005	Rayla The Cloud Queen Doll	G8401	$20.00	
2005	Sagittarius Barbie		$20.00	Zodiac
2005	Sagittarius Barbie (black)		$20.00	Zodiac
2005	Scorpio Barbie		$20.00	Zodiac
2005	Scorpio Barbie (black)		$20.00	Zodiac
2005	Spellbound Lover Barbie		Retail	Legends of Ireland
2005	Stolen Magic Barbie	G8072	$115.00	Barbie Fashion Model
2005	Suite Retreat Barbie	G8078	$40.00	Barbie Fashion Model

Year	Item	Number	Value	Specials
2005	Tano Barbie	G8050	$80.00	Byron Lars
2005	Taurus Barbie		$20.00	Zodiac
2005	Taurus Barbie (black)		$20.00	Zodiac
2005	Totally Spring Barbie	C4480	$16.00	
2005	Totally Spring Barbie (black)	G5318	$16.00	
2005	Trace of Lace Barbie (brunette)	G7212	$70.00	Barbie Fashion Model
2005	Trace of Lace Barbie (blonde)	G7211	$70.00	Barbie Fashion Model
2005	Virgo Barbie		$20.00	Zodiac
2005	Virgo Barbie (black)		$20.00	Zodiac
2005	White Chocolate Obsession Barbie		Retail	Flavor Obsession
2005	Winnie the Pooh Barbie	H6469	$15.00	

Barbie® Dolls

Listed by Store/Collection

Store/Collection	Item	Number	Year	Value
1 Modern Circle	1 Modern Circle Barbie	B2523	2003	$30.00
1 Modern Circle	1 Modern Circle Barbie	B2527	2004	$33.00
40th Anniversary Collection	40th Anniversary Barbie (black)	22336	1999	$45.00
40th Anniversary Collection	40th Anniversary Barbie (blonde)	21384	1999	$45.00
40th Anniversary Collection	40th Anniversary Bumblebee Gala Barbie	23041	1999	$80.00
A Garden of Flowers	Rose Barbie	22337	1999	$30.00
Adult Collector Edition	Victorian Barbie with Cedric Bear (blonde)	25526	2000	$50.00
American Beauty Collection	Army	3966	1989	$25.00
American Beauty Collection	Mardi Gras	4930	1988	$45.00
American Classics	Coca-Cola Barbie #2 (brunette)	24637	2000	$60.00
American Classics	Coca-Cola Drive-In Waitress	22831	1999	$60.00
American Stories Collection	American Indian	14715	1996	$25.00
American Stories Collection	American Indian II	17313	1997	$28.00
American Stories Collection	Civil War Nurse	14612	1996	$25.00
American Stories Collection	Colonial	12578	1995	$25.00
American Stories Collection	Patriot	17312	1997	$25.00
American Stories Collection	Pilgrim	12577	1995	$25.00
American Stories Collection	Pioneer	12680	1995	$25.00
American Stories Collection	Pioneer #2	14756	1996	$25.00
Ames	Country Looks	5854	1993	$25.00
Ames	Denim 'n Lace	2452	1992	$28.00
Ames	Hot Looks	5756	1992	$25.00
Ames	Ice Cream Barbie	19280	1998	$16.00
Ames	Ladybug Fun	17695	1997	$18.00
Ames	Magna Doodle Barbie	23275	1999	$15.00
Ames	Party in Pink	2909	1991	$30.00
Ames	Strawberry Party Barbie	22895	1999	$15.00
Angels of Music	Harpist Angel Barbie	18894	1998	$45.00
Angels of Music	Harpist Angel Barbie (black)	20551	1998	$45.00
Angels of Music	Heartstring Angel Barbie	21414	1999	$60.00
Angels of Music	Heartstring Angel Barbie (black)	21915	1999	$60.00
Applause	Applause Barbie	3406	1991	$35.00
Applause	Style	5315	1990	$35.00
Artist Series	Reflections of Light (Renoir)	23884	1999	$75.00
Artist Series	Sunflower Barbie (Van Gogh)	19366	1998	$68.00
Artist Series	Water Lily (Monet)	17783	1997	$90.00
Avon	Avon Representative Barbie	22202	1999	$50.00
Avon	Avon Representative Barbie (black)	22203	1999	$40.00
Avon	Avon Representative Barbie (Hispanic)	22204	1999	$50.00
Avon	Blushing Bride		2000	$30.00
Avon	Color 'n Wash My Hair Barbie	15139	1997	$50.00
Avon	Exotic Intrigue Barbie		2004	Retail
Avon	Exotic Intrigue Barbie (black)		2004	Retail
Avon	Exotic Intrigue Barbie (Hispanic)		2004	Retail
Avon	Fruit Fantasy Barbie (blonde)	21386	1999	$25.00
Avon	Fruit Fantasy Barbie (brunette)	20319	1999	$30.00
Avon	Lemon-Lime Sorbet Barbie	20318	1999	$25.00
Avon	Mrs. P.F.E. Albee	20330	1998	$70.00

Store/Collection	Item	Number	Year	Value
Avon	Mrs. P.F.E. Albee	17690	1997	$75.00
Avon	Snow Sensation Barbie	23800	1999	$39.00
Avon	Snow Sensation Barbie (black)	23801	1999	$39.00
Avon	Spring Blossom	15201	1996	$25.00
Avon	Spring Blossom (black)	15202	1996	$25.00
Avon	Spring Petals (black)	16871	1997	$30.00
Avon	Spring Petals (blonde)	16746	1997	$30.00
Avon	Spring Petals (brunette)	16872	1997	$30.00
Avon	Spring Tea Party Barbie (black)	18657	1998	$30.00
Avon	Spring Tea Party Barbie (blonde)	18656	1998	$30.00
Avon	Spring Tea Party Barbie (brunette)	18656	1998	$30.00
Avon	Strawberry Sorbet Barbie	20317	1999	$25.00
Avon	Winter Rhapsody (black)	16354	1997	$35.00
Avon	Winter Rhapsody (blonde)	16353	1997	$35.00
Avon	Winter Rhapsody (brunette)	16873	1997	$35.00
Avon	Winter Splendor Barbie	19357	1998	$38.00
Avon	Winter Splendor Barbie (black)	19358	1998	$38.00
Avon	Winter Velvet	15571	1996	$38.00
Avon	Winter Velvet (black)	15587	1996	$38.00
Ballroom Beauties	Midnight Waltz (blonde)	15685	1996	$35.00
Ballroom Beauties	Midnight Waltz (brunette)	16705	1996	$52.00
Ballroom Beauties	Moonlight Waltz	17763	1997	$48.00
Ballroom Beauties	Starlight Waltz	14070	1995	$35.00
Ballroom Beauties	Starlight Waltz (brunette, Disney)	14954	1995	$75.00
Barbie Collectors' Club	Café Society Barbie	18892	1998	$68.00
Barbie Collectors' Club	Club Couture	26068	2000	$70.00
Barbie Collectors' Club	Embassy Waltz Barbie	22836	1999	$60.00
Barbie Collectors' Club	French Quarter Barbie Fashion	B2518	2003	$29.00
Barbie Collectors' Club	Grand Premier	16498	1997	$79.00
Barbie Couture Collection	Symphony in Chiffon Barbie	20186	1998	$60.00
Barbie Couture Collection	Symphony in Chiffon Barbie (black)	21295	1998	$60.00
Barbie Fan Club Exclusive	A Nod for Mod Barbie	C6261	2004	$80.00
Barbie Fan Club Exclusive	Hollywood Divine Barbie (blonde)		2004	$65.00
Barbie Fan Club Exclusive	Hollywood Divine Barbie (brunette)	B3426	2004	$70.00
Barbie Fan Club Exclusive	Lone Star Great Barbie		2005	Retail
Barbie Fashion Model/FAO Schwarz	45th Anniversary Barbie and Ken Gift Set	C4656	2004	$97.00
Barbie Fashion Model	45th Anniversary Barbie by Robert Best	B8955	2004	$49.00
Barbie Fashion Model	45th Anniversary Barbie by Robert Best (black)	B0445	2004	$50.00
Barbie Fashion Model	Blush Becomes Her Fashion	29652	2001	$75.00
Barbie Fashion Model	Boulevard Fashion	29653	2001	$60.00
Barbie Fashion Model	Capucine Barbie	B0146	2003	$100.00
Barbie Fashion Model	Chataine Barbie	B4425	2003	$425.00
Barbie Fashion Model	Chinoiserie Red Midnight Barbie		2004	$175.00
Barbie Fashion Model	Chinoiserie Red Moon Barbie	B3431	2004	$50.00
Barbie Fashion Model	City Smart Barbie		2003	$510.00
Barbie Fashion Model	Continental Holiday Barbie Gift Set	55497	2002	$100.00
Barbie Fashion Model	Dusk to Dawn Barbie Gift Set	29654	2001	$145.00
Barbie Fashion Model	Fashion Designer Barbie		2002	$95.00
Barbie Fashion Model	Fashion Editor Barbie		2001	$110.00
Barbie Fashion Model	Garden Party Fashion	26933	2000	$90.00
Barbie Fashion Model	Happy Go Lightly Barbie	G8889	2005	$70.00
Barbie Fashion Model	In the Pink Barbie	27683	2001	$140.00
Barbie Fashion Model	Joyeux Barbie	B3430	2003	$115.00
Barbie Fashion Model	Joyeux Barbie (redhead)	B23431	2003	$320.00
Barbie Fashion Model	Lingerie Barbie #3	29651	2001	$100.00

Store/Collection	Item	Number	Year	Value
Barbie Fashion Model	Lingerie Barbie #4 (blonde)	55498	2002	$54.00
Barbie Fashion Model	Lingerie Barbie #5 (black)	56120	2002	$50.00
Barbie Fashion Model	Lingerie Barbie #6	56948	2003	$42.00
Barbie Fashion Model	Lisette Barbie	7438	2001	$104.00
Barbie Fashion Model	Lunch at the Club Fashion	26932	2000	$77.00
Barbie Fashion Model	Marie Therese Barbie	55496	2002	$64.00
Barbie Fashion Model	Muffy Roberts Barbie	H6465	2005	$69.00
Barbie Fashion Model	Provencale Barbie	50829	2002	$96.00
Barbie Fashion Model	Ravishing in Rouge Barbie	52741	2001	$110.00
Barbie Fashion Model	Spa Getaway Barbie Gift Set	B1319	2004	$75.00
Barbie Fashion Model	Stolen Magic Barbie	G8072	2005	$115.00
Barbie Fashion Model	Suite Retreat Barbie	G8078	2005	$40.00
Barbie Fashion Model	Sunday Best Barbie	B2520	2003	$48.00
Barbie Fashion Model	Trace of Lace Barbie (brunette)	G7212	2005	$70.00
Barbie Fashion Model	Trace of Lace Barbie (blonde)	G7211	2005	$70.00
Barbie Fashion Model	Trend Setter Barbie	B3442	2004	$50.00
Barbie Festival	35th Anniversary Festival Barbie	12670	1994	$200.00
Barbie Festival	Banquet Set Barbie Doll (blonde)	850	1994	$299.00
Barbie Festival	Banquet Set Barbie Doll (redhead)	850	1994	$299.00
Barbie Festival	International Haute Couture Rainbow Barbie	None	1994	$199.00
Barbie Festival	Red Velvet Delight Haute Couture Barbie	None	1994	$220.00
Barbie Loves Pop Culture	Barbie as Catwoman	B5838	2004	$20.00
Barbie Loves Pop Culture	Barbie as Elle Woods from *Legally Blonde 2*	B9284	2003	$35.00
Barbie Loves Pop Culture	Barbie as Jeannie from *I Dream of Jeannie*	29913	2001	$40.00
Barbie Loves Pop Culture	Barbie as Samantha from *Bewitched*	53510	2002	$30.00
Barbie Loves Pop Culture	Barbie as That Girl	56705	2003	$40.00
Barbie Loves Pop Culture	Barbie as Wonder Woman	24638	2000	$18.00
Barbie Loves Pop Culture	Grease Barbie	B2510	2003	$100.00
Barbie Loves Pop Culture	Grease Barbie #2	B4773	2004	$30.00
Barbie Loves Pop Culture	James Bond 007 Ken and Barbie Gift Set	B0150	2003	$55.00
Barbie Loves Pop Culture	The Munsters Gift Set	50544	2001	$235.00
Barbie Loves Sports	Ferrari Barbie #2	28534	2001	$50.00
Barbie Loves Sports	Scuderia Ferrari Barbie		2000	$32.00
Barbie Millicent Roberts	Barbie Millicent Roberts Matinee Today	16079	1996	$40.00
Barbie Millicent Roberts	Barbie Millicent Roberts Perfectly Suited	17567	1997	$35.00
Barbie Millicent Roberts	Barbie Millicent Roberts Pinstripe Power	19791	1998	$30.00
Ben Franklin	Plus 3	9953	1977	$85.00
Birds of Beauty Series	Peacock	19365	1998	$59.00
Birds of Beauty Series	Flamingo Barbie	22957	1999	$55.00
Birds of Beauty Series	Swan	27682	2000	$48.00
Birthday Wishes Series	Birthday Wishes Barbie	21128	1999	$26.00
Birthday Wishes Series	Birthday Wishes Barbie #2	24667	2000	$24.00
Birthday Wishes Series	Birthday Wishes Barbie #2 (black)	24668	2000	$24.00
Birthday Wishes Series	Birthday Wishes Barbie #3	28434	2000	$27.00
Birthday Wishes Series	Birthday Wishes Barbie (black)	21509	1999	$26.00
Birthstone Collection	December Turquoise Barbie	C5330	2004	$40.00
Birthstone Collection	February Amethyst Barbie	C5332	2004	$40.00
Birthstone Collection	January Garnet Barbie	C5331	2004	$40.00
Birthstone Collection	July Ruby Barbie	C5325	2004	$40.00
Birthstone Collection	June Pearl Barbie	C5324	2004	$40.00
Birthstone Collection	March Aquamarine Barbie	C5333	2004	$40.00
Birthstone Collection	May Emerald Barbie	C5323	2004	$40.00
Birthstone Collection	November Topaz Barbie	C5329	2004	$40.00
Birthstone Collection	October Opal Barbie	C5328	2004	$40.00
Birthstone Collection	September Sapphire Barbie	C5327	2004	$40.00

Store/Collection	Item	Number	Year	Value
Birthstone Collection/Wal-Mart	April Diamond Barbie	B3412	2003	$40.00
Birthstone Collection/Wal-Mart	April Diamond Barbie (black)	C0586	2003	$40.00
Birthstone Collection/Wal-Mart	August Peridot Barbie	B3416	2003	$40.00
Birthstone Collection/Wal-Mart	August Peridot Barbie (black)	C0578	2003	$40.00
Birthstone Collection/Wal-Mart	December Turquoise Barbie	B2397	2003	$40.00
Birthstone Collection/Wal-Mart	December Turquoise Barbie (black)	C0582	2003	$40.00
Birthstone Collection/Wal-Mart	February Amethyst Barbie	B3410	2003	$40.00
Birthstone Collection/Wal-Mart	February Amethyst Barbie (black)	C0584	2003	$40.00
Birthstone Collection/Wal-Mart	January Garnet Barbie	B3409	2003	$40.00
Birthstone Collection/Wal-Mart	January Garnet Barbie (black)	C0583	2003	$40.00
Birthstone Collection/Wal-Mart	July Ruby Barbie	B3415	2003	$40.00
Birthstone Collection/Wal-Mart	July Ruby Barbie (black)	C0577	2003	$40.00
Birthstone Collection/Wal-Mart	June Pearl Barbie	B3414	2003	$40.00
Birthstone Collection/Wal-Mart	June Pearl Barbie (black)	C0576	2003	$40.00
Birthstone Collection/Wal-Mart	March Aquamarine Barbie	B3411	2003	$40.00
Birthstone Collection/Wal-Mart	March Aquamarine Barbie (black)	C0585	2003	$40.00
Birthstone Collection/Wal-Mart	May Emerald Barbie	B3413	2003	$40.00
Birthstone Collection/Wal-Mart	May Emerald Barbie (black)	C0575	2003	$40.00
Birthstone Collection/Wal-Mart	November Topaz Barbie	B2396	2003	$40.00
Birthstone Collection/Wal-Mart	November Topaz Barbie (black)	C0581	2003	$40.00
Birthstone Collection/Wal-Mart	October Opal Barbie	B2395	2003	$40.00
Birthstone Collection/Wal-Mart	October Opal Barbie (black)	C0580	2003	$40.00
Birthstone Collection/Wal-Mart	September Sapphire Barbie	B2394	2003	$40.00
Birthstone Collection/Wal-Mart	September Sapphire Barbie (black)	C0579	2003	$40.00
Bloomingdale's	Barbie at Bloomingdale's	16290	1996	$35.00
Bloomingdale's	Calvin Klein Jeans Barbie	16211	1996	$55.00
Bloomingdale's	Donna Karan NY (blonde)	14545	1995	$85.00
Bloomingdale's	Donna Karan NY (brunette)	14452	1995	$85.00
Bloomingdale's	Oscar de la Renta Barbie	20376	1998	$60.00
Bloomingdale's	Ralph Lauren Barbie	15950	1997	$60.00
Bloomingdale's	Savvy Shopper	12152	1994	$50.00
Bob Mackie	Brunette Brilliance Barbie	B0585	2003	$100.00
Bob Mackie	Empress Bride	4247	1992	$460.00
Bob Mackie	Fantasy Goddess of the Arctic	50840	2001	$140.00
Bob Mackie	Goddess of the Sun	14056	1995	$95.00
Bob Mackie	Gold	5405	1990	$500.00
Bob Mackie	Madame Du Barbie	17934	1997	$225.00
Bob Mackie	Masquerade Ball	18667	1997	$235.00
Bob Mackie	Masquerade Ball (scented)	10803	1993	$275.00
Bob Mackie	Moon Goddess	14105	1996	$99.00
Bob Mackie	Neptune Fantasy	4248	1992	$455.00
Bob Mackie	Platinum	2703	1991	$289.00
Bob Mackie	Queen of Hearts	12046	1994	$155.00
Bob Mackie	Radiant Redhead Barbie	55501	2002	$150.00
Bob Mackie	Starlight Splendor	2704	1991	$500.00
Bob Mackie	Sterling Silver Rose Barbie		2002	Retail
Bob Mackie	Tango (porcelain)	23451	1999	$300.00
Bob Mackie	The Charleston Barbie	24252	2001	$250.00
Bob Mackie Custom Limited Edition	Lady Liberty		2000	$225.00
Bob Mackie Custom Limited Edition	Le Papillon Barbie	23276	1999	$214.00
Bob Mackie International Beauty	Fantasy Goddess of Africa	22044	1999	$280.00
Bob Mackie International Beauty	Fantasy Goddess of Asia	20648	1998	$100.00
Bob Mackie International Beauty	Fantasy Goddess of the Americas	25859	2000	$135.00
Bob Mackie Jewel Essence	Amethyst Aura	15522	1997	$90.00
Bob Mackie Jewel Essence	Diamond Dazzle	15519	1997	$100.00

Store/Collection	Item	Number	Year	Value
Bob Mackie Jewel Essence	Emerald Embers	15521	1997	$88.00
Bob Mackie Jewel Essence	Ruby Radiance	15520	1997	$80.00
Bob Mackie Jewel Essence	Sapphire Splendor	15523	1997	$80.00
The Bridal Collection	Millennium Wedding (black)	27674	2000	$36.00
The Bridal Collection	Millennium Wedding (hispanic)	27765	2000	$45.00
The Bridal Collection	Millennium Wedding (white)	27674	2000	$36.00
The Bridal Collection	Romantic Wedding (white)	29438	2001	$36.00
The Bridal Collection	Romantic Wedding (black)	29439	2001	$36.00
Byron Lars	Mbili Barbie		2002	$135.00
Byron Lars	Moja Barbie	50826	2001	$210.00
Byron Lars	Nne Barbie	B3423	2004	$90.00
Byron Lars	Tano Barbie	G8050	2005	$80.00
Byron Lars	Tatu Barbie	B2018	2003	$170.00
Byron Lars Runway Collection	Cinnabar Sensation	23420	1998	$76.00
Byron Lars Runway Collection	Cinnabar Sensation (black)	19848	1998	$76.00
Byron Lars Runway Collection	In The Limelight (black)	17031	1997	$140.00
Byron Lars Runway Collection	Indigo Obsession Barbie	26935	2000	$165.00
Byron Lars Runway Collection	Plum Royal	23478	1999	$170.00
Career	Barbie for President	26288	2000	Retail
Career	Barbie for President (black)	26284	2000	Retail
Career/Online Exclusive	Barbie for President (Hispanic)		2000	Retail
Career	Marine Biologist		1999	$15.00
Career	Marine Biologist (black)		1991	$15.00
Catalog Showroom	Malibu Fashion Combo	2753	1978	$65.00
Celebrities	Diana Ross by Bob Mackie	B2017	2004	$32.00
Celestial Collection	Evening Star Princess	27690	2000	$45.00
Celestial Collection	Midnight Moon Princess	27687	2000	$50.00
Celestial Collection	Morning Sun Princess	27688	2000	$45.00
Chicago Cubs	Chicago Cubs Fan Barbie	22857	1999	$85.00
Child's World	Dance Club with tape player	3509	1989	$55.00
Child's World	Disney Special (black)	9385	1990	$45.00
Child's World	Disney Special (with mouse hat)	4385	1991	$45.00
Children's Collector Series	Barbie as Beauty	24673	2000	$30.00
Children's Collector Series	Barbie as Cinderella	16900	1996	$24.00
Children's Collector Series	Barbie as Little Bo Peep	14960	1996	$55.00
Children's Collector Series	Barbie as Rapunzel	13016	1995	$24.00
Children's Collector Series	Barbie as Sleeping Beauty	18586	1998	$25.00
Children's Collector Series	Barbie as Snow White	21130	1999	$28.00
Children's Day	Children's Day Barbie	18350	1998	$15.00
Chuck E Cheese Pizza	Chuck E Cheese	14615	1996	$30.00
City Seasons Collection	Autumn in London	22257	1999	$30.00
City Seasons Collection	Autumn in Paris	19367	1998	$35.00
City Seasons Collection	Spring in Tokyo Barbie	19430	1999	$34.00
City Seasons Collection	Spring in Tokyo Barbie (nostalgic face)	23499	1999	$40.00
City Seasons Collection	Summer in Rome Barbie	19431	1999	$35.00
City Seasons Collection	Summer in San Francisco Barbie (blonde) (FAO)	19363	1998	$95.00
City Seasons Collection	Summer in San Francisco Barbie (redhead) (FAO)	19363	1998	$675.00
City Seasons Collection	Winter in Montreal Barbie	22258	1999	$40.00
City Seasons Collection	Winter in New York	19429	1998	$50.00
Classic Ballet Series	Barbie as Flower Ballerina from *The Nutcracker*	28375	2001	$25.00
Classic Ballet Series	Barbie as Juliet	B5655	2004	$30.00
Classic Ballet Series	Barbie as Marzipan from *The Nutcracker*	20851	1999	$26.00
Classic Ballet Series	Barbie as Peppermint Candy Cane from *The Nutcracker*	57578	2003	$33.00
Classic Ballet Series	Barbie as Snowflake from *The Nutcracker*	25642	2000	$27.00

Store/Collection	Item	Number	Year	Value
Classic Ballet Series	Barbie as the Sugar Plum Fairy from *The Nutcracker*	17056	1997	$29.00
Classic Ballet Series	Barbie as Swan Ballerina	53867	2002	$24.00
Classic Ballet Series	Barbie as the Swan Queen from *Swan Lake*	18509	1997	$22.00
Classic Ballet Series	Barbie as the Swan Queen from *Swan Lake* (black)	18510	1997	$22.00
Classic Ballet Series	Barbie as Titania	C3819	2004	$27.00
Classique	Benefit Ball	1521	1992	$45.00
Classique	City Style Barbie	10149	1993	$35.00
Classique	Evening Extravaganza	11622	1994	$40.00
Classique	Evening Extravaganza (black)	11638	1994	$44.00
Classique	Evening Sophisticate Barbie	19361	1998	$30.00
Classique	Midnight Gala	12999	1995	$34.00
Classique	Opening Night	10148	1993	$38.00
Classique	Romantic Interlude	17136	1997	$34.00
Classique	Romantic Interlude (black)	17137	1997	$36.00
Classique	Starlight Dance	15461	1996	$32.00
Classique	Starlight Dance (black)	15819	1996	$32.00
Classique	Uptown Chic Barbie	11623	1994	$37.00
Clothes Minded Collection	Trend Forecaster Barbie	22833	1999	$32.00
Club Exclusive	Holiday Treasures Barbie	27673	2000	$78.00
Club Exclusive	Midnight Tuxedo Barbie	28796	2001	$77.00
Club Exclusive	Midnight Tuxedo Barbie (black)	29307	2001	$400.00
Club Exclusive	Noir et Blanc Barbie	B1992	2003	$65.00
Club Exclusive	Noir et Blanc Barbie (black)	B1993	2003	$100.00
Club Exclusive	Twilight Gala Barbie	53862	2002	$72.00
Club Exclusive	Twilight Gala Barbie (black)	53870	2002	$86.00
Coca-Cola Fashion Classic Series	After the Walk	17341	1997	$48.00
Coca-Cola Fashion Classic Series	Soda Fountain Sweetheart	15762	1996	$88.00
Coca-Cola Fashion Classic Series	Summer Daydreams Barbie	19739	1998	$55.00
Coca-Cola Series	Coca-Cola Barbie (blonde)	22831	1999	$60.00
Coca-Cola Series	Coca-Cola Barbie (brunette), Walt Disney World	23934	1999	$198.00
Coca-Cola Series	Coca-Cola Barbie (Cheerleader)	53974	2001	$46.00
Coca-Cola Series	Coca-Cola Barbie (Majorette)		2002	$35.00
Coca-Cola Series	Coca-Cola Soda Fountain	26980	2000	$140.00
Collectors' Convention 1999	40th Anniversary Barbie (brunette)	24842	1999	$150.00
Collectors' Convention 1999	We Can Do Anything, Right Barbie!		1999	$410.00
Collectors' Convention 2001	Queen of the Prom Barbie		2001	$490.00
Collectors' Convention 2002	Rocky Mountain Mod		2002	$210.00
Collectors' Convention 2003	The World of Barbie		2003	$75.00
Collectors' Request	Color Magic Barbie (brunette)	B3437	2004	$40.00
Collectors' Request	Color Magic Barbie (blonde)	B3437	2004	$175.00
Collectors' Request	Color Magic Barbie (redhead)		2004	$210.00
Collectors' Request	Commuter Set Barbie	21510	1999	$50.00
Collectors' Request	Evening Splendor Barbie	G8890	2005	$50.00
Collectors' Request	Gay Parisienne Barbie (blonde)	57610	2003	$200.00
Collectors' Request	Gay Parisienne Barbie (brunette)		2003	$37.00
Collectors' Request	Gay Parisienne Barbie (redhead)		2003	$185.00
Collectors' Request	Gold 'n Glamour Barbie	54185	2002	$42.00
Collectors' Request	Sophisticated Lady	24930	2000	$45.00
Collectors' Request	Suburban Shopper Barbie	28378	2001	$70.00
Collectors' Request	Twist 'n Turn Barbie Smasheroo (brunette)	18941	1998	$50.00
Collectors' Request	Twist 'n Turn Barbie Smasheroo (redhead)	23258	1998	$50.00
Cool Collecting Series	Nostalgic Toys	25525	2000	$45.00
Couture Collection	Portrait in Taffeta	15528	1996	$55.00
Couture Collection	Serenade in Satin	17572	1997	$90.00
Cracker Barrel Restaurant	Country Charm	26464	2000	$25.00

Store/Collection	Item	Number	Year	Value
Cracker Barrel Restaurant	Country Charm (black)	29332	2000	$25.00
Cynthia Rowley	Cynthia Rowley Barbie	G8064	2005	$80.00
David's Bridal	David's Bridal Eternal Barbie		2005	Retail
David's Bridal	David's Bridal Eternal Barbie (black)		2005	Retail
David's Bridal	David's Bridal Eternal Barbie (Hispanic)		2005	Retail
David's Bridal	David's Bridal Unforgettable Barbie		2004	Retail
David's Bridal	David's Bridal Unforgettable Barbie (black)		2004	Retail
David's Bridal	David's Bridal Unforgettable Barbie (Hispanic)		2004	Retail
Deco-Pak	My First Barbie	96085	1990	$75.00
Deco-Pak	My First Barbie (black)	96085	1990	$55.00
Deco-Pak	Specialty Deco-Pak Barbie	1511	1991	$75.00
Deco-Pak	Specialty Deco-Pak Barbie (black)	1534	1991	$55.00
Department Store	Ballerina Barbie on Tour	9613	1976	$125.00
Department Store	Ballerina Barbie on Tour (no wrist tag)	9613	1979	$110.00
Department Store	Ballerina Barbie on Tour (with wrist tag)	9613	1979	$120.00
Department Store	Beautiful Bride	9599	1976	$200.00
Department Store	Beautiful Bride	9907	1978	$175.00
Department Store	Beauty Secrets Barbie, Pretty Reflections	1290	1980	$75.00
Department Store	Deluxe Tropical Barbie	2996	1986	$40.00
Department Store	Feelin' Groovy	3421	1987	$175.00
Department Store	Golden Dreams	3533	1981	$70.00
Department Store	Golden Dreams (2nd issue, big hair)	3533	1981	$70.00
Department Store	Hawaiian	7470	1975	$50.00
Department Store	Hawaiian (one-piece swimsuit)	7470	1982	$50.00
Department Store	Hawaiian (two-piece swimsuit)	7470	1983	$40.00
Department Store	Kissing (bangs style)	2597	1979	$45.00
Department Store	Kissing (extra dress)	2597	1979	$45.00
Department Store	Malibu Barbie Beach Party, The	1703	1980	$55.00
Department Store	Pink & Pretty Barbie Extra Special Modeling Set	5239	1982	$75.00
Department Store	Super Size Bride	9975	1977	$295.00
Department Store	Super Size Bridal Barbie	9975	1977	$295.00
Department Store	SuperStar Barbie in the Spotlight	2586	1978	$110.00
Department Store	Twirly Curls	5579	1983	$35.00
Designer Burberry	Burberry Barbie	29421	2001	$70.00
Designer Collection	Bill Blass	17040	1997	$80.00
Designer Collection	Christian Dior I	13168	1995	$60.00
Designer Collection	Christian Dior II	16013	1997	$68.00
Designer Collection	Escada	15948	1996	$48.00
Designer Collection	Todd Oldham Barbie	22205	1999	$54.00
Designer Collection	Vera Wang Awards Night Barbie	23027	1999	$89.00
Designer Collection	Vera Wang Barbie	19788	1998	$100.00
Designer Dolls	Badgley Mischka Bride Barbie	B8946	2004	$139.00
Designer Dolls	Carolina Herrera Bride Barbie	B9797	2005	$140.00
Designer Dolls	Judith Leiber Barbie		2005	Retail
Designer Dolls	Paul Frank Barbie		2004	Retail
Designer Dolls	Paul Frank Barbie (blonde)	B8954	2004	$60.00
Designer Spotlight	Designer Spotlight by Heather Fonseca		2004	Retail
Designer Spotlight	Designer Spotlight by Katiana Jimenez	B0836	2003	$450.00
Disney	Disney Fun Barbie	10247	1992	$50.00
Disney	Disney Fun Barbie	18970	1998	$27.00
Disney	Disney Fun II	11650	1994	$45.00
Disney	Disney Fun III	13533	1995	$35.00
Disney	Disney Fun IV	17058	1997	$35.00
Disney	Disney Weekend	10723	1993	$50.00
Disney	Disney's Animal Kingdom Barbie	20363	1998	$28.00

Store/Collection	Item	Number	Year	Value
Disney	Disney's Animal Kingdom Barbie (black)	20989	1998	$28.00
Disney	Gay Parisienne (redhead/porcelain)	9973-9999	1991	$350.00
Disney	Plantation Belle (blonde)	5351	1992	$315.00
Disney	Safari	18970	1998	$30.00
Disney	Tour Guide Barbie — *Toy Story 2*	24015	1999	$30.00
Disney	Walt Disney World 25th Anniversary	16525	1996	$35.00
Disney Classics	Alice in Wonderland	21933	1998	$16.00
Disney Europe	Disney Fun Barbie	12957	1995	$55.00
Disney Europe	Disney Weekend Barbie	12957	1992	$60.00
Disney Europe	Disney Weekend Barbie & Ken Deluxe	10724	1993	$75.00
Disney/Winter Princess	Jewel Princess (brunette)		1999	$95.00
Disney/Winter Princess (Theme)	Evergreen Princess (redhead)	12123	1994	$151.00
Diva Collection	All That Glitters Barbie	55426	2002	$27.00
Diva Collection	Gone Platinum Barbie (black)	53868	2002	$40.00
Diva Collection	Gone Platinum Barbie	52739	2002	$40.00
Diva Collection	Red Hot Barbie (black)	56708	2003	$32.00
Diva Collection	Red Hot Barbie (white)	56707	2003	$35.00
Dolls of the World	Arctic	16495	1996	$25.00
Dolls of the World	Australian Barbie #1	3626	1993	$32.00
Dolls of the World	Australian Barbie #2	3626	1993	$34.00
Dolls of the World	Austrian Barbie	21553	1999	$18.00
Dolls of the World	Brazilian	9094	1990	$27.00
Dolls of the World	Canadian	4928	1988	$35.00
Dolls of the World	Chilean	18559	1997	$25.00
Dolls of the World	Chinese	11180	1994	$23.00
Dolls of the World	Czechoslovakian	7330	1991	$55.00
Dolls of the World	Dolls of the World Limited Edition Set	12043	1994	$49.00
Dolls of the World	Dolls of the World Limited Edition Set	13939	1995	$45.00
Dolls of the World	Dolls of the World Limited Edition Set	15283	1996	$40.00
Dolls of the World	Dutch	11104	1994	$29.00
Dolls of the World	English	4973	1992	$37.00
Dolls of the World	Eskimo	3898	1982	$65.00
Dolls of the World	Eskimo (reissue)	9844	1991	$32.00
Dolls of the World	French	16499	1997	$25.00
Dolls of the World	German	3188	1987	$50.00
Dolls of the World	German (reissue)	12698	1995	$22.00
Dolls of the World	Ghanian	15303	1996	$24.00
Dolls of the World	Greek	2997	1986	$38.00
Dolls of the World	Icelandic	3189	1987	$45.00
Dolls of the World	India	3897	1982	$75.00
Dolls of the World	Indian	14451	1996	$25.00
Dolls of the World	Irish	7517	1984	$75.00
Dolls of the World	Irish (reissue)	12998	1995	$34.00
Dolls of the World	Italian	1602	1980	$150.00
Dolls of the World	Italian (reissue)	2256	1993	$36.00
Dolls of the World	Jamaican	4647	1992	$28.00
Dolls of the World	Japanese	9481	1985	$70.00
Dolls of the World	Japanese (reissue)	14163	1996	$23.00
Dolls of the World	Kenyan	11181	1994	$23.00
Dolls of the World	Korean	4929	1988	$35.00
Dolls of the World	Malaysian	7329	1991	$25.00
Dolls of the World	Mexican	1917	1989	$25.00
Dolls of the World	Mexican (reissue)	14449	1996	$23.00
Dolls of the World	Moroccan Barbie	21507	1999	$18.00
Dolls of the World	Native American #1	1753	1993	$32.00

Store/Collection	Item	Number	Year	Value
Dolls of the World	Native American #2	11609	1994	$32.00
Dolls of the World	Native American #3	12699	1995	$25.00
Dolls of the World	Native American #4	15304	1996	$35.00
Dolls of the World/Toys "R" Us	Native American #5 (box says fourth)	18558	1998	$20.00
Dolls of the World	Nigerian	7376	1990	$30.00
Dolls of the World	Northwest Coast Native American	24671	2000	$25.00
Dolls of the World	Norwegian #1	14450	1996	$37.00
Dolls of the World	Norwegian #2	14450	1996	$25.00
Dolls of the World	Oriental	3262	1981	$150.00
Dolls of the World	Parisian	1600	1980	$90.00
Dolls of the World	Parisian #1	9843	1991	$35.00
Dolls of the World	Parisian #2 (Japan)	9843	1991	$38.00
Dolls of the World	Peruvian I	2995	1986	$36.00
Dolls of the World	Peruvian II	21506	1999	$18.00
Dolls of the World	Polish	18560	1997	$25.00
Dolls of the World	Polynesian	12700	1995	$25.00
Dolls of the World	Puerto Rican	16754	1997	$18.00
Dolls of the World	Royal	1601	1980	$115.00
Dolls of the World	Russian	1916	1989	$30.00
Dolls of the World	Russian (reissue)	16500	1997	$17.00
Dolls of the World	Scottish	3263	1981	$90.00
Dolls of the World	Scottish (reissue)	9845	1991	$45.00
Dolls of the World	Spanish Barbie #1	4031	1983	$65.00
Dolls of the World	Spanish Barbie #2	4963	1992	$33.00
Dolls of the World	Spanish Barbie #3	24670	2000	$18.00
Dolls of the World	Swedish Barbie	4032	1983	$54.00
Dolls of the World	Swedish Barbie	24672	2000	$18.00
Dolls of the World	Swiss	7541	1984	$48.00
Dolls of the World	Thai	18561	1998	$18.00
Dolls of the World — Princess Collection,	Princess of the Navajo Barbie	B8956	2004	$20.00
Dolls of the World — Princess Collection,	Princess of Ancient Greece Barbie	B3461	2004	$20.00
Dolls of the World — Princess Collection,	Princess of Ancient Mexico Barbie	C2203	2004	$20.00
Dolls of the World — Princess Collection,	Princess of Cambodia Barbie	B3460	2004	$20.00
Dolls of the World — Princess Collection,	Princess of China Barbie	53368	2002	$65.00
Dolls of the World — Princess Collection,	Princess of England Barbie	B3459	2004	$20.00
Dolls of the World — Princess Collection,	Princess of Holland Barbie	G8055	2005	$20.00
Dolls of the World — Princess Collection,	Princess of Imperial Russia Barbie	G5861	2005	$20.00
Dolls of the World — Princess Collection,	Princess of India Barbie	28374	2001	$165.00
Dolls of the World — Princess Collection,	Princess of Ireland Barbie	53367	2002	$25.00
Dolls of the World — Princess Collection,	Princess of Japan Barbie	B5731	2003	$23.00
Dolls of the World — Princess Collection,	Princess of South Africa Barbie	56218	2003	$26.00
Dolls of the World — Princess Collection,	Princess of the Danish Court Barbie	56216	2003	$22.00
Dolls of the World — Princess Collection,	Princess of the French Court Barbie	28372	2001	$150.00
Dolls of the World — Princess Collection,	Princess of the Hawaiian Islands Barbie	G8056	2005	$22.00
Dolls of the World — Princess Collection,	Princess of the Korean Court Barbie	B5870	2005	$20.00
Dolls of the World — Princess Collection,	Princess of the Nile Barbie	53369	2002	$40.00
Dolls of the World — Princess Collection,	Princess of the Portuguese Empire Barbie	56217	2003	$22.00
Dolls of the World — Princess Collection,	Princess of the Renaissance Barbie	G5860	2005	$20.00
Dolls of the World — Princess Collection,	Princess of the Vikings Barbie	B6361	2003	$26.00
Dressed Boxed Dolls	After Five	934	1963	$600.00
Dressed Boxed Dolls	American Airlines Stewardess	984	1963	$700.00
Dressed Boxed Dolls	Arabian Nights	874	1964	$1,270.00
Dressed Boxed Dolls	Barbie in Holland	823	1964	$820.00
Dressed Boxed Dolls	Barbie in Mexico	820	1964	$820.00
Dressed Boxed Dolls	Barbie in Switzerland	822	1964	$820.00

Store/Collection	Item	Number	Year	Value
Dressed Boxed Dolls	Black Magic Ensemble	1609	1964	$860.00
Dressed Boxed Dolls	Bride's Dream	947	1964	$910.00
Dressed Boxed Dolls	Career Girl	954	1964	$858.00
Dressed Boxed Dolls	Cinderella	872	1964	$858.00
Dressed Boxed Dolls	Country Fair	1603	1964	$595.00
Dressed Boxed Dolls	Dinner at Eight	946	1964	$595.00
Dressed Boxed Dolls	Evening Splendour	961	1964	$635.00
Dressed Boxed Dolls	Garden Party	931	1963	$600.00
Dressed Boxed Dolls	Garden Tea Party	1606	1964	$595.00
Dressed Boxed Dolls	Glam 'n Groom	26251	2000	$15.00
Dressed Boxed Dolls	Guinevere	873	1964	$645.00
Dressed Boxed Dolls	Ice Breaker	942	1964	$695.00
Dressed Boxed Dolls	Knitting Pretty (pink version)	957	1964	$1,265.00
Dressed Boxed Dolls	Knitting Pretty (royal version)	957	1964	$635.00
Dressed Boxed Dolls	Masquerade	944	1964	$635.00
Dressed Boxed Dolls	Mood For Music	940	1963	$625.00
Dressed Boxed Dolls	Nighty Negligee	965	1963	$550.00
Dressed Boxed Dolls	Orange Blossom	987	1963	$635.00
Dressed Boxed Dolls	Registered Nurse	991	1963	$760.00
Dressed Boxed Dolls	Senior Prom	951	1964	$1,145.00
Dressed Boxed Dolls	Solo in the Spotlight	982	1963	$845.00
Dressed Boxed Dolls	Swingin' Easy	955	1964	$637.00
Dressed Boxed Dolls	Tennis Anyone?	941	1963	$610.00
Dressed Boxed Dolls	Theatre Date	959	1964	$660.00
Enchanted Seasons	Autumn Glory	15204	1996	$48.00
Enchanted Seasons	Snow Princess (blonde)	11875	1994	$60.00
Enchanted Seasons	Spring Bouquet	12989	1995	$45.00
Enchanted Seasons	Summer Splendor	15683	1997	$39.00
Enchanted World of Fairies	Fairy of the Forest	25639	2000	$42.00
Enchanted World of Fairies	Fairy of the Garden	28799	2001	$45.00
Essence of Nature	Dancing Fire Barbie	26327	2000	$60.00
Essence of Nature	Water Rhapsody Barbie	19847	1998	$57.00
Essence of Nature	Whispering Wind Barbie	22834	1999	$65.00
Evening Elegance	Evening Enchantment Barbie	19783	1998	$45.00
Fabergé Porcelain	Imperial Elegance	19816	1998	$290.00
Fabergé Porcelain	Imperial Splendor	27028	2000	$310.00
Fairy Series	Forest Fairy	25639	2000	$40.00
Fairy Tales	Rapunzel	16378	1997	$25.00
FAO Schwarz	Antique Rose	15814	1996	$190.00
FAO Schwarz	Barbie at FAO	17298	1997	$30.00
FAO Schwarz	Circus Star	13257	1995	$70.00
FAO Schwarz	George Washington Barbie	17757	1997	$50.00
FAO Schwarz	Golden Greetings	7734	1989	$100.00
FAO Schwarz	Golden Hollywood Barbie	22832	1999	$95.00
FAO Schwarz	Golden Hollywood Barbie (black)	23877	1999	$95.00
FAO Schwarz	Jewel Splendor	14061	1995	$90.00
FAO Schwarz	Le Papillon Barbie	23273	1999	$175.00
FAO Schwarz	Lily	17556	1997	$125.00
FAO Schwarz	Madison Avenue	1539	1992	$100.00
FAO Schwarz	Mann's Chinese Theatre	24636	2000	$48.00
FAO Schwarz	Mann's Chinese Theatre (black)	24998	2000	$60.00
FAO Schwarz	Night Sensation	2921	1991	$60.00
FAO Schwarz	Phantom of the Opera	20377	1998	$150.00
FAO Schwarz	Rockettes	2017	1993	$120.00
FAO Schwarz	Shopping Spree Barbie #1	12749	1994	$38.00

Store/Collection	Item	Number	Year	Value
FAO Schwarz	Shopping Spree Barbie #2	12749	1994	$35.00
FAO Schwarz	Silver Screen	11652	1994	$100.00
FAO Schwarz	Statue of Liberty	14664	1996	$100.00
FAO Schwarz	Winter Fantasy Barbie	5946	1990	$90.00
Fashion Model	Delphine Barbie	26929	2000	$95.00
Fashion Model	Lingerie (blonde)	26930	2000	$255.00
Fashion Model	Lingerie (brunette)	26931	2000	$265.00
Fashion Savvy Collection	Tangerine Twist	17860	1997	$35.00
Fashion Savvy Collection	Uptown Chic Barbie	19632	1998	$32.00
Festivals of the World	Carnival Barbie	J0927	2005	$20.00
Festivals of the World	Chinese New Year Barbie	J0928	2005	$20.00
Flavor Obsession	Chocolate Obsession Barbie	G8878	2005	$35.00
Flavor Obsession	Citrus Obsession Barbie	J0933	2005	$35.00
Flavor Obsession	Peppermint Obsession Barbie	J1743	2005	$35.00
Flavor Obsession	White Chocolate Obsession Barbie		2005	Retail
Flowers in Fashion	The Calla Lily Barbie	29912	2002	$57.00
Flowers in Fashion	The Iris Barbie	53935	2002	$70.00
Flowers in Fashion	The Orchid Barbie	50319	2001	$76.00
Flowers in Fashion	The Rose Barbie	29911	2001	$55.00
Friendship	Friendship Barbie, Berlin Wall I	5506	1990	$24.00
Friendship	Friendship Barbie, Berlin Wall II	2080	1991	$29.00
Friendship	Friendship Barbie, Berlin Wall III	3677	1992	$25.00
Gap Stores	Gap Barbie	16449	1996	$60.00
Gap Stores	Gap Barbie (black)	16450	1996	$60.00
General Mills	Winter Dazzle Barbie	18456	1997	$30.00
General Mills	Winter Dazzle Barbie (black)	18457	1997	$30.00
Giorgio Armani	Giorgio Armani Barbie	B2521	2003	$135.00
Glamour Collection	Evening Glamour	14070	1995	$75.00
Goddess Collection	Goddess of Beauty Barbie		2000	$82.00
Goddess Collection	Goddess of Spring Barbie		2000	$79.00
Goddess Collection	Goddess of Wisdom Barbie		2001	$119.00
Gone with the Wind	Scarlett O'Hara Doll, Barbecue at Twelve Oaks	29910	2001	$49.00
Gone with the Wind	Scarlett O'Hara Doll on Peachtree Street — The Drapery Dress	29771	2001	$52.00
Grand Entrance	Grand Entrance Barbie	28533	2001	$45.00
Grand Entrance	Grand Entrance Barbie #2	53841	2002	$30.00
Grand Entrance	Grand Entrance Barbie #2 (black)	53842	2002	$30.00
Grand Entrance	Grand Entrance Barbie (black)	29662	2001	$45.00
Grand Ole Opry	Country Rose	17782	1997	$42.00
Grand Ole Opry	Rising Star Barbie	17864	1998	$38.00
Great Eras Collection	1850s Southern Belle	11478	1994	$42.00
Great Eras Collection	1920s Flapper Barbie	4063	1993	$55.00
Great Eras Collection	Chinese Empress Barbie	16708	1997	$32.00
Great Eras Collection	Egyptian Queen	11397	1994	$48.00
Great Eras Collection	Elizabethan Queen	12792	1995	$40.00
Great Eras Collection	French Lady	16707	1997	$28.00
Great Eras Collection	Gibson Girl	3702	1993	$45.00
Great Eras Collection	Grecian Goddess	15005	1996	$34.00
Great Eras Collection	Medieval Lady	12791	1995	$36.00
Great Eras Collection	Victorian Lady	14900	1996	$30.00
Great Fashions of the 20th Century	Dance 'Till Dawn Barbie	19631	1998	$40.00
Great Fashions of the 20th Century	Fabulous Forties Barbie	22162	2000	$55.00
Great Fashions of the 20th Century	Groovy '60s Barbie	27676	2000	$38.00
Great Fashions of the 20th Century	Nifty '50s Barbie	27675	2000	$65.00
Great Fashions of the 20th Century	Peace & Love '70s	27677	2000	$70.00

Store/Collection	Item	Number	Year	Value
Great Fashions of the 20th Century	Promenade in the Park Barbie	18630	1998	$40.00
Great Fashions of the 20th Century	Steppin' Out Barbie – 1930s	21531	1999	$35.00
Great Porcelain Houses	Wedgwood Barbie	25641	2000	$110.00
Hallmark	Fair Valentine Barbie	18091	1998	$30.00
Hallmark	Holiday Memories	14106	1995	$30.00
Hallmark	Holiday Traditions	17094	1997	$45.00
Hallmark	Holiday Voyage Barbie	18651	1998	$40.00
Hallmark	Sentimental Valentine	16536	1997	$30.00
Hallmark	Sweet Valentine	14880	1996	$35.00
Hallmark	Victorian Elegance	12579	1994	$35.00
Hallmark	Yuletide Romance	15621	1996	$30.00
Hamley's (England)	West End Barbie	15513	1996	$45.00
Happy Holidays Collection	Happy Holidays 1988	1703	1988	$390.00
Happy Holidays Collection	Happy Holidays 1989	3523	1989	$125.00
Happy Holidays Collection	Happy Holidays 1990	4098	1990	$65.00
Happy Holidays Collection	Happy Holidays 1990 (black)	4543	1990	$40.00
Happy Holidays Collection	Happy Holidays 1991	1871	1991	$65.00
Happy Holidays Collection	Happy Holidays 1991 (black)	2696	1991	$40.00
Happy Holidays Collection	Happy Holidays 1992	1429	1992	$50.00
Happy Holidays Collection	Happy Holidays 1992 (black)	2396	1992	$38.00
Happy Holidays Collection	Happy Holidays 1993	10824	1993	$48.00
Happy Holidays Collection	Happy Holidays 1993 (black)	10911	1993	$32.00
Happy Holidays Collection	Happy Holidays 1994	12155	1994	$50.00
Happy Holidays Collection	Happy Holidays 1994 (black)	12156	1994	$36.00
Happy Holidays Collection	Happy Holidays 1995	14123	1995	$28.00
Happy Holidays Collection	Happy Holidays 1995 (black)	14124	1995	$24.00
Happy Holidays Collection	Happy Holidays 1996	15646	1996	$28.00
Happy Holidays Collection	Happy Holidays 1996 (black)	15647	1996	$28.00
Happy Holidays Collection	Happy Holidays 1997 (all variations) (brunette)	20416	1997	$20.00
Happy Holidays Collection	Happy Holidays 1997 (black)	17833	1997	$20.00
Happy Holidays Collection	Happy Holidays 1997 (blonde)	17832	1997	$64.00
Happy Holidays Collection	Happy Holidays 1998	20200	1998	$25.00
Happy Holidays Collection	Happy Holidays 1998 (black)	20201	1998	$25.00
Happy Holidays European	Happy Holidays Barbie	12432	1994	$65.00
Happy Holidays International	Happy Holidays Barbie	13545	1995	$40.00
Happy Holidays International	Happy Holidays Barbie	15816	1996	$32.00
Harrod's England	Easy Chic Barbie	17590	1996	$750.00
Hill's	Barbie & Champion	13181	1995	$45.00
Hill's	Blue Elegance	1879	1992	$50.00
Hill's	Evening Sparkle	3274	1990	$35.00
Hill's	Hula-Hoop	18167	1997	$16.00
Hill's	Moonlight Rose	3549	1991	$32.00
Hill's	Party Lace	4843	1989	$35.00
Hill's	Polly Pockets	12412	1994	$20.00
Hill's	Sea Pearl Mermaid	13940	1995	$20.00
Hill's	Sidewalk Chalk Barbie	19784	1998	$15.00
Hill's	Teddy Fun	15684	1996	$18.00
Holiday Angel	Holiday Angel Barbie #2	28081	2001	$36.00
Holiday Angel	Holiday Angel Barbie #2 (black)	28080	2001	$34.00
Holiday Dolls	Celebration Barbie	28269	2000	$34.00
Holiday Dolls	Winter Fantasy Barbie	B2519	2003	$45.00
Holiday Dolls	Winter Fantasy Barbie (black)	C0166	2003	$45.00
Holiday Homecoming Series	Holiday Sensation	19792	1999	$35.00
Holiday Porcelain Series	Holiday Ball	18326	1997	$65.00
Holiday Porcelain Series	Holiday Caroler	15760	1996	$70.00

Store/Collection	Item	Number	Year	Value
Holiday Porcelain Series	Holiday Gift Barbie	20128	1998	$90.00
Holiday Porcelain Series	Holiday Jewel	14311	1995	$100.00
Hollywood	Barbie and Ken as Arwen and Aragorn from *The Lord of the Rings*	B3449	2004	$180.00
Hollywood	Barbie as Galadriel from *The Lord of the Rings*	H1179	2004	$40.00
Hollywood Legends	Dorothy (Wizard of Oz)	12701	1995	$72.00
Hollywood Legends	Glinda the Good Witch	14901	1996	$68.00
Hollywood Legends	Maria (*The Sound of Music*)	13676	1995	$36.00
Hollywood Legends	Marilyn Monroe (pink dress)	17451	1997	$55.00
Hollywood Legends	Marilyn Monroe (red dress)	17452	1997	$60.00
Hollywood Legends	Marilyn Monroe (white dress)	17155	1997	$50.00
Hollywood Legends	My Fair Lady #1 (pink organza gown)	15501	1996	$75.00
Hollywood Legends	My Fair Lady #2 (ascot)	15497	1996	$100.00
Hollywood Legends	My Fair Lady #3 (flower girl)	15498	1996	$65.00
Hollywood Legends	My Fair Lady #4 (ball evening gown)	15500	1996	$100.00
Hollywood Legends	Scarlett (BBQ dress)	12997	1995	$47.00
Hollywood Legends	Scarlett (green velvet dress)	12045	1994	$48.00
Hollywood Legends	Scarlett (New Orleans dress)	13254	1995	$47.00
Hollywood Legends	Scarlett (red dress)	12815	1994	$60.00
Hollywood Movie Star Collection	Between Takes Barbie	27684	2000	$50.00
Hollywood Movie Star Collection	Day in the Sun (blonde)	26425	2001	$35.00
Hollywood Movie Star Collection	Day in the Sun (brunette)	26426	2001	$70.00
Hollywood Movie Star Collection	Hollywood Premiere Barbie	26914	2000	$36.00
Hollywood Movie Star Collection	Publicity Tour Party Barbie	27865	2001	$40.00
Hollywood Movie Star Collection/ FAO Schwarz	Hollywood Cast Party Barbie	50825	2001	$65.00
Home Shopping Club	Evening Flame	1865	1991	$150.00
Home Shopping Club	Golden Allure Barbie	22961	1999	$32.00
Hong Kong Commemorative Edition	Anniversary Edition Golden Qi-Pao Barbie	20649	1998	$75.00
Hong Kong Commemorative Edition	Chinese Empress Barbie	16708	1997	$88.00
Hudson's Bay Company Canada	Arcadian Court Barbie	62889	1996	$85.00
Hudson's Bay Company Canada	Barbie on Bay	63987	1997	$35.00
Hudson's Bay Company Canada	Calvin Klein Jeans Barbie	16211	1996	$70.00
Hudson's Bay Company Canada	City Style Barbie	10149	1995	$105.00
Hudson's Bay Company Canada	Governor's Ball Barbie	14010	1996	$90.00
Hudson's Bay Company Canada	School Spirit Barbie	63569	1997	$40.00
Hudson's Bay Company Canada	Toyland Barbie	64176	1997	$40.00
Inspirational Series	Goddess of Beauty and Love	27286	2000	Retail
Inspirational Series	Goddess of Spring	28112	2000	Retail
JCPenney	Arizona Jean Company I	15441	1996	$25.00
JCPenney	Arizona Jean Company II	18020	1997	$25.00
JCPenney	Caboodles Barbie with Child-Sized Caboodles case	11285	1993	$35.00
JCPenney	Enchanted Evening	2702	1991	$75.00
JCPenney	Evening Elegance	7057	1990	$75.00
JCPenney	Evening Enchantment Barbie	19783	1998	$35.00
JCPenney	Evening Majesty	17235	1997	$40.00
JCPenney	Evening Sensation	1278	1992	$50.00
JCPenney	Golden Winter	10684	1993	$50.00
JCPenney	Happy Holidays with Ornament	14124	1995	$80.00
JCPenney	Night Dazzle	12191	1994	$55.00
JCPenney	Original Arizona Jean Company III	19873	1998	$25.00
JCPenney	Royal Enchantment	14010	1995	$50.00
JCPenney	Winter Renaissance (Evening Elegance Series)	15570	1996	$40.00
JCPenney	Winter Sports	13516	1995	$35.00
Japan Air Lines	JAL Barbie	64347	1997	$150.00

Store/Collection	Item	Number	Year	Value
Jergens	Deluxe Quick Curl	9217	1976	$100.00
Jewel Collection	Countess of Rubies Barbie	26972	2001	$80.00
Jewel Collection	Duchess of Diamonds Barbie		2001	Retail
Jewelry Collection Series	Definitely Diamonds Barbie	20204	1998	$55.00
Jubilee Series	Crystal Jubilee Barbie	21923	1999	$155.00
Jubilee Series	Gold Jubilee	12009	1994	$345.00
Jubilee Series	Pink Jubilee	3756	1989	$800.00
Juicy Couture	Juicy Couture Barbie Dolls	G8079	2005	$100.00
K•B Toys	Chic	18218	1999	$5.00
K•B Toys	Children's Day Barbie	18350	1998	$15.00
K•B Toys	Fantasy Ball Barbie	18594	1997	$20.00
K•B Toys	Fantasy Ball Barbie (black)	18595	1997	$20.00
K•B Toys	Fashion Avenue Barbie	20782	1998	$15.00
K•B Toys	Glamour Barbie	18594	1997	$15.00
K•B Toys	Glamour Barbie (black)	18595	1997	$15.00
K•B Toys	Starlight Carousel Barbie	19708	1998	$18.00
K•B Toys	Style	20766	1999	$10.00
K•B Toys	Style (black)	20767	1999	$10.00
K•B Toys	Super Gymnast Barbie	15821	1996	$20.00
K•B Toys	Super Gymnast Barbie (black)	23106	1999	$15.00
Kate Spade	Kate Spade Barbie	B2513	2004	$79.00
Keepsake Treasures	Barbie and *The Tale of Peter Rabbit*	19360	1998	$28.00
Keepsake Treasures	Peter Rabbit 100 Year Celebration Barbie	53872	2002	$37.00
Keepsake Treasures	Barbie and *Curious George*	28798	2001	$28.00
Kellogg Company	Forget-Me-Nots (baggie)	3269	1972	$195.00
Kellogg Company	Kellogg Quick Curl	3197	1974	$60.00
Kellogg Company	Miss America	3194	1972	$175.00
Kellogg Company	Miss America	9194	1973	$165.00
Kellogg Company	Miss America	9194	1974	$150.00
K-Mart	March of Dimes Walk America Barbie	18506	1998	$20.00
K-Mart	March of Dimes Walk America Barbie (black)	18507	1998	$20.00
K-Mart	Peach Pretty	4870	1989	$32.00
K-Mart	Pretty in Purple	3117	1992	$25.00
K-Mart	Pretty in Purple (black)	3121	1992	$25.00
K-Mart	Very Berry	26881	1999	$10.00
K-Mart/Kresge	Barbie and Her Super Fashion Fireworks #1	9805	1997	$90.00
K-Mart/Kresge	Barbie and Her Super Fashion Fireworks #2	9805	1997	$90.00
K-Mart/Kresge	Barbie and Her Super Fashion Fireworks #3	9805	1997	$90.00
Kool-Aid	Wacky Warehouse I	10309	1993	$55.00
Kool-Aid	Wacky Warehouse II	11763	1994	$45.00
Kool-Aid	Wacky Warehouse III	15620	1996	$35.00
Kraft	Kraft Treasures	11546	1994	$50.00
Lady Lovely Locks	Starlight Blue	3553	1989	$40.00
Legends of Ireland	Faerie Queen Barbie (brunette)	B3456	2004	$185.00
Legends of Ireland	Faerie Queen Barbie	B3456	2004	$50.00
Legends of Ireland	Spellbound Lover Barbie		2005	Retail
Legends of Ireland	The Bard Barbie Doll	B2511	2004	$60.00
Lifestyles of the West	Western Plains	23205	1999	$40.00
Little Debbie Snacks	Little Debbie Barbie, Series I	10123	1993	$60.00
Little Debbie Snacks	Little Debbie Barbie, Series II (bent arms)	14616	1996	$30.00
Little Debbie Snacks	Little Debbie Barbie, Series II (straight arms)	14616	1996	$25.00
Little Debbie Snacks	Little Debbie Barbie, Series III	16352	1998	$22.00
Lounge Kitties	Lounge Kitties Panther	C3553	2004	$36.00
Macy's	Anne Klein Barbie	17603	1997	$40.00
Macy's	City Shopper	16289	1996	$40.00

Store/Collection	Item	Number	Year	Value
Magic & Mystery	Tales of Arabian Nights Barbie and Ken Gift Set	50827	2001	$76.00
Major League Baseball	Chicago Cubs Barbie	23883	1999	$29.00
Major League Baseball	Chicago Cubs Barbie (black)	24473	1999	$35.00
Major League Baseball	Los Angeles Dodgers Barbie	23882	1999	$27.00
Major League Baseball	Los Angeles Dodgers Barbie (black)	24472	1999	$32.00
Major League Baseball	New York Yankees Barbie	23881	1999	$28.00
Major League Baseball	New York Yankees Barbie (black)	24471	1999	$36.00
Masquerade Gala	Illusion Barbie	18667	1997	$80.00
Masquerade Gala	Rendezvous Barbie	20647	1998	$74.00
Masquerade Gala	Venetian Opulence	24501	2000	$90.00
Mattel Festival Doll	35th Anniversary (redhead)	11591	1994	$425.00
Mattel Festival Doll	Doctor Barbie (brunette)	12903	1994	$100.00
Mattel Festival Doll	Evergreen Princess (redhead)	13173	1994	$295.00
Mattel Festival Doll	Gymnast (brunette)	11921	1994	$35.00
Mattel Festival Doll	Happy Holidays 1994 (brunette)	12155	1994	$550.00
Mattel Festival Doll	Night Dazzle (brunette)	12191	1994	$185.00
Mattel Festival Doll	Snow Princess (brunette)	12905	1994	$595.00
McGlynn's Bakery	Barbie Doll	1511	1991	$80.00
McGlynn's Bakery	Barbie Doll (black)	1534	1991	$80.00
Meijer	Cool Looks Fashion Designer CD-ROM	24746	1999	$28.00
Meijer	Horse Riding Barbie with Riding Club CD-ROM	24788	1999	$28.00
Meijer	Magic Hair Styler CD-ROM	24748	1999	$28.00
Meijer	Shopping Fun Barbie	10051	1993	$25.00
Meijer	Something Extra	863	1992	$25.00
Mercantile Stores	Special Occasion Barbie I	15831	1996	$65.00
Mercantile Stores	Special Occasion Barbie II	18216	1997	$45.00
Mercantile Stores	Special Occasion Barbie II (black)	18217	1997	$45.00
Mervyn's	Ballerina	4983	1983	$40.00
Mervyn's	Ballerina (black)	4984	1983	$60.00
Mervyn's	Fabulous Fur	7093	1986	$65.00
Military	Making Friends	19592	1998	$18.00
Military	Making Friends (black)	19593	1998	$18.00
Military	Ponytails	18141	1997	$20.00
Military	Ponytails (black)	18142	1997	$20.00
Military	Sweet Daisy Barbie	15133	1996	$30.00
Military	Your Pen Pal Barbie	23221	1999	$20.00
Military	Your Pen Pal Barbie (black)	23222	1999	$20.00
Millennium Collection	Millennium Bride	24505	2000	$285.00
Millennium Collection	Millennium Princess Barbie	24154	1999	$45.00
Millennium Collection	Millennium Princess Barbie (black)	23995	1999	$45.00
Model of the Moment	Daria Celebutante		2004	Retail
Model of the Moment	Daria Shopping Queen		2005	Retail
Model of the Moment	Nichelle Urban Hipster		2004	Retail
Montgomery Ward	25th Anniversary	3939	1972	$650.00
Montgomery Ward	Live Action (ranch)	10412	1971	$100.00
Montgomery Ward	Malibu Barbie & Her Ten-Speeder Set	10456	1974	$95.00
Montgomery Ward	Montgomery Ward Anniversary Doll	3210	1972	$750.00
Montgomery Ward	Posable	8414	1965	$1,225.00
Musical Ballet Series	Nutcracker	5472	1992	$79.00
Musical Ballet Series	Swan Lake	1648	1991	$88.00
My Design Friend of Barbie	Bride Barbie (brunette)		2000	$60.00
My Design Friend of Barbie	Bride Barbie (redhead)		2000	$60.00
My Design Friend of Barbie	Graduation Barbie		2000	$55.00
My Design Friend of Barbie	Graduation Barbie (black)		2000	$55.00
My Scene	Cruisin' the Boardwalk Barbie and River	C4212	2004	$33.00

Store/Collection	Item	Number	Year	Value
My Scene	Night on the Town Barbie and River	B6708	2004	$29.00
NASCAR	NASCAR 50th Anniversary Barbie	20442	1998	$25.00
NASCAR	NASCAR Official #94 Barbie (brunette)	22954	1999	$25.00
Native Spirit Collection	Spirit of the Earth Barbie	50707	2001	$60.00
Native Spirit Collection	Spirit of the Sky Barbie	B2367	2003	$60.00
Native Spirit Collection	Spirit of Water Barbie	53861	2002	$60.00
NBA	Atlanta Hawks	20734	1998	$20.00
NBA	Atlanta Hawks (black)	20735	1998	$20.00
NBA	Boston Celtics	20716	1998	$20.00
NBA	Boston Celtics (black)	20717	1998	$20.00
NBA	Charlotte Hornets	20698	1998	$20.00
NBA	Charlotte Hornets (black)	20699	1998	$20.00
NBA	Chicago Bulls	20692	1998	$20.00
NBA	Chicago Bulls (black)	20693	1998	$20.00
NBA	Cleveland Cavaliers	20736	1998	$20.00
NBA	Cleveland Cavaliers (black)	20737	1998	$20.00
NBA	Dallas Mavericks	20728	1998	$20.00
NBA	Dallas Mavericks (black)	20729	1998	$20.00
NBA	Denver Nuggets	20730	1998	$20.00
NBA	Denver Nuggets (black)	20731	1998	$20.00
NBA	Detroit Pistons	20706	1998	$20.00
NBA	Detroit Pistons (black)	20707	1998	$20.00
NBA	Golden State Warriors (black)	20743	1998	$20.00
NBA	Golden State Warriors	20742	1998	$20.00
NBA	L. A. Clippers	20744	1998	$20.00
NBA	L. A. Clippers (black)	20745	1998	$20.00
NBA	L. A. Lakers	20704	1998	$25.00
NBA	L. A. Lakers (black)	20705	1998	$20.00
NBA	Miami Heat	20694	1998	$20.00
NBA	Miami Heat (black)	20695	1998	$20.00
NBA	Milwaukee Bucks	20738	1998	$20.00
NBA	Milwaukee Bucks (black)	20739	1998	$20.00
NBA	Minnesota Timberwolves	20702	1998	$20.00
NBA	Minnesota Timberwolves (black)	20703	1998	$20.00
NBA	N. Y. Knicks	20714	1998	$20.00
NBA	N. Y. Knicks (black)	20715	1998	$20.00
NBA	New Jersey Nets	20726	1998	$20.00
NBA	New Jersey Nets (black)	20727	1998	$20.00
NBA	Orlando Magic (black)	20749	1998	$20.00
NBA	Philadelphia 76ers	20724	1998	$20.00
NBA	Philadelphia 76ers (black)	20725	1999	$20.00
NBA	Phoenix Suns Barbie	20710	1998	$20.00
NBA	Phoenix Suns Barbie (black)	20711	1998	$20.00
NBA	Portland Trailblazers	20720	1998	$20.00
NBA	Portland Trailblazers (black)	20721	1998	$20.00
NBA	Sacramento Kings	20746	1998	$20.00
NBA	Sacramento Kings (black)	20747	1998	$20.00
NBA	San Antonio Spurs	20722	1998	$20.00
NBA	San Antonio Spurs (black)	20723	1998	$20.00
NBA	Seattle Supersonics	20718	1998	$20.00
NBA	Seattle Supersonics (black)	20719	1998	$20.00
NBA	Toronto Raptors	20740	1998	$20.00
NBA	Toronto Raptors (black)	20741	1998	$20.00
NBA	Utah Jazz Barbie	20708	1998	$20.00
NBA	Utah Jazz Barbie (black)	20709	1998	$20.00

Store/Collection	Item	Number	Year	Value
NBA	Vancouver Grizzlies	20732	1998	$20.00
NBA	Vancouver Grizzlies (black)	20733	1998	$20.00
NBA	Washington Wizards	20696	1998	$11.00
NBA	Washington Wizards (black)	20697	1998	$11.00
Nolan Miller Designer Collection	Evening Illusion Barbie	23495	1999	$72.00
Nolan Miller Designer Collection	Sheer Illusion Barbie #1	20662	1998	$92.00
Nolan Miller Designer Collection	Sheer Illusion Barbie #2	20662	1998	$70.00
Nostalgic	35th Anniversary Barbie (blonde with arched eyebrows)	11590	1994	$23.00
Nostalgic	35th Anniversary Barbie (blonde with curved eyebrows)	11590	1994	$28.00
Nostalgic	35th Anniversary Barbie (brunette with arched eyebrows)	11782	1994	$24.00
Nostalgic	35th Anniversary Barbie (brunette with curved eyebrows)	11782	1994	$36.00
Nostalgic	35th Anniversary Barbie Keepsake Collection	11591	1994	$77.00
Nostalgic	Nostalgic Barbie #1	62328	1996	$45.00
Nostalgic	Nostalgic Barbie #2	62329	1996	$45.00
Nostalgic	Nostalgic Barbie #3	62327	1996	$45.00
Nostalgic	Poodle Parade	15280	1996	$42.00
Nostalgic	Silken Flame Barbie (blonde)	18449	1998	$24.00
Nostalgic	Silken Flame Barbie (brunette)	18448	1998	$24.00
Nostalgic Porcelain	Benefit Performance	5475	1988	$235.00
Nostalgic Porcelain	Gay Parisienne (blonde)	9973	1991	$350.00
Nostalgic Porcelain	Gay Parisienne (brunette)	9973	1991	$135.00
Nostalgic Porcelain	Solo in the Spotlight	7613	1990	$145.00
Nostalgic Porcelain	Sophisticated Lady	5313	1990	$140.00
Nostalgic Porcelain	Wedding Party	2641	1989	$275.00
Nostalgic Vinyl Series	Busy Gal	13675	1995	$42.00
Nostalgic Vinyl Series	Enchanted Evening (blonde)	14992	1996	$25.00
Nostalgic Vinyl Series	Enchanted Evening (brunette)	15407	1996	$25.00
Nostalgic Vinyl Series	Fashion Luncheon	17382	1997	$49.00
Nostalgic Vinyl Series	Solo in the Spotlight (blonde)	13534	1995	$25.00
Nostalgic Vinyl Series	Solo in the Spotlight (brunette)	13820	1995	$25.00
Nostalgic Vinyl Series	Wedding Day (blonde)	17119	1997	$25.00
Nostalgic Vinyl Series	Wedding Day (redhead)	17120	1997	$30.00
Nursery Rhyme	Barbie Had a Little Lamb	21740	1999	$25.00
Online Exclusive	Batik Princess Barbie	C4558	2004	$25.00
Online Exclusive	Chinoiserie Red Sunset Barbie		2004	$115.00
Online Exclusive	Open Road Vintage Reproduction		2004	$80.00
Online Exclusive	Mod Redux Barbie	C6262	2004	$70.00
Osco Drugs	Picnic Pretty	3808	1992	$35.00
Pop Culture	Fire and Ice Barbie	53511	2002	$45.00
Pop Culture	Fire and Ice Barbie (black)	53863	2002	$45.00
Pop Culture	Glamour Gal Betty Boop		2001	Retail
Pop Culture	Hard Rock Café Barbie	G7915	2004	$105.00
Pop Culture	Hard Rock Café Barbie	J0963	2005	$70.00
Pop Culture	Malibu Barbie	56061	2002	$24.00
Pop Culture	Starring Barbie in *King Kong*	56737	2003	$29.00
Pop Culture	Sydney 2000 Olympic Barbie Pin Collector	25644	2000	$25.00
Pop Culture	Sydney 2000 Olympic Barbie Pin Collector (black)	26302	2000	$25.00
Pop Culture	Western Chic Barbie	55487	2002	$120.00
Porcelain	Blue Rhapsody	1708	1986	$299.00
Porcelain	Enchanted Evening	3415	1987	$228.00
Porcelain	Gold Sensation	10246	1993	$180.00

Store/Collection	Item	Number	Year	Value
Porcelain	Mattel Golden Anniversary	14479	1995	$170.00
Porcelain	Plantation Belle (redhead)	7526	1992	$140.00
Porcelain	Silken Flame Barbie (brunette)	1249	1994	$130.00
Porcelain	Silver Starlight	11305	1994	$190.00
Porcelain Disney	Silken Flame Barbie (blonde)	11099	1993	$330.00
Porcelain Treasures Collection	Wizard of Oz-Dorothy with Toto	19364	2000	Retail
Porcelain Treasures Collection	Wizard of Oz-Wicked Witch	23880	2000	Retail
Portrait Collection	Duchess Emma Barbie	B3422	2004	$80.00
Portrait Collection	Lady Camille Barbie		2003	Retail
Portrait Collection	Mademoiselle Isabelle Barbie	55387	2002	$79.00
Presidential Porcelain	Crystal Rhapsody (blonde)	1553	1992	$220.00
Presidential Porcelain	Crystal Rhapsody (brunette, Disney)	10201	1992	$350.00
Presidential Porcelain	Evening Pearl	12825	1996	$140.00
Presidential Porcelain	Royal Splendor	10950	1993	$170.00
Prima Ballerina	Classic Grace Barbie		2002	Retail
Prima Ballerina	Lighter Than Air Barbie	29905	2001	$120.00
Princess	Rapunzel Barbie	53973	2002	$22.00
Princess Collection/Dolls of the World	Princess of the Incas Barbie	28373	2000	$115.00
Princess Series	Princess and the Pea	28800	2000	$26.00
QVC	My Size Redhead	15649	1996	$140.00
QVC	Sleep Over Party		2000	$40.00
QVC/Royal Jewel	Empress of Emeralds	25680	2000	$100.00
Radio Shack	Earring Magic Barbie Doll Software Pak	25-1992	1993	$30.00
Reebok	All American	9423	1991	$28.00
Romance Novels	Jude Deveraux The Raider Barbie and Ken Gift Set		2003	$50.00
Royal House of Europe	Barbie as Empress Sissy	15846	1996	$55.00
Royal Houses of Europe	Princess Sissy Barbie		1998	$35.00
Royal Jewel	Queen of Sapphires	26926	2000	$85.00
Russell Stover	Russell Stover Candies Special Edition Barbie (black)	17089	1997	$25.00
Russell Stover	Russell Stover Candies Special Edition Barbie (floral)	16351	1997	$25.00
Russell Stover	Russell Stover Candies Special Edition Barbie (pink)	17091	1997	$25.00
Russell Stover	Russell Stover Easter (checkered)	14617	1996	$25.00
Russell Stover	Russell Stover Easter (print)	14956	1996	$25.00
Russell Stover	Russell Stover Holiday	18199	1997	$25.00
Sam's Club	Winter Fantasy Barbie (blonde)	15334	1996	$30.00
Sam's Club	Winter Fantasy Barbie (brunette)	15530	1996	$35.00
Sam's Club/Wholesale Club	1950s Barbie	15820	1996	$30.00
Sam's Club/Wholesale Club	Country Rose	17864	1997	$50.00
Sara Lee	Sara Lee Barbie	60403	1993	$65.00
Sears	Action Accents Set (auburn)	1585	1969	$800.00
Sears	Blossom Beautiful	3817	1992	$225.00
Sears	Blue Starlight	17125	1997	$35.00
Sears	Celebration Barbie	1998	1986	$65.00
Sears	Dream Princess	2306	1992	$40.00
Sears	Enchanted Princess	10292	1993	$50.00
Sears	Evening Enchantment	3596	1989	$38.00
Sears	Evening Flame	15533	1996	$30.00
Sears	Gold Medal Barbie and Her U.S. Olympic Wardrobe	9044	1975	$90.00
Sears	Gold Medal Winter Sports	9042	1975	$85.00
Sears	Lavender Surprise	9049	1990	$32.00
Sears	Lavender Surprise (black)	5588	1990	$35.00
Sears	Lilac and Lovely	7669	1988	$45.00
Sears	Pink Reflections Barbie	19130	1998	$25.00
Sears	Ribbons and Roses	13911	1995	$35.00
Sears	Sears 100th Anniversary Celebration	2998	1985	$100.00

Store/Collection	Item	Number	Year	Value
Sears	Silver Sweetheart	12410	1994	$40.00
Sears	Skating Star	4547	1988	$65.00
Sears	Southern Belle	2586	1991	$40.00
Sears	Star Dream	4550	1987	$50.00
Sears	Travel in Style	1544	1967	$240.00
Sears	Winter Sports (catalog only)	9042	1975	$100.00
Service Merchandise	Blue Rhapsody	1364	1991	$140.00
Service Merchandise	City Sophisticate	12005	1994	$50.00
Service Merchandise	Definitely Diamonds Barbie	20204	1998	$110.00
Service Merchandise	Dream Bride Barbie	17153	1997	$35.00
Service Merchandise	Dream Bride Barbie (black)	17933	1997	$25.00
Service Merchandise	Evening Symphony Barbie	19777	1998	$25.00
Service Merchandise	My Wardrobe Barbie	22962	1999	$28.00
Service Merchandise	Ruby Romance	13612	1995	$48.00
Service Merchandise	Satin Nights	1886	1992	$70.00
Service Merchandise	Sea Princess	15531	1996	$30.00
Service Merchandise	Sparkling Splendor	10994	1993	$50.00
Shopko/Venture	Blossom Beauty	3142	1991	$40.00
Shopko/Venture	Party Perfect	1876	1992	$34.00
Shopko/Venture	Sidewalk Chalk Barbie	19784	1998	$20.00
Singapore Airlines	Singapore Girl 1	None	1992	$100.00
Singapore Airlines	Singapore Girl 2	None	1994	$50.00
Society Hound Collection	Society Hound Barbie	29057	2001	$85.00
Society Style	Emerald Elegance (black)	12323	1994	$33.00
Society Style	Emerald Elegance	12322	1994	$33.00
Spiegel	Golden Qi-Pao Barbie	20866	1998	$65.00
Spiegel	Regal Reflections	4116	1992	$200.00
Spiegel	Royal Invitation	10969	1993	$85.00
Spiegel	Shopping Chic	14009	1995	$75.00
Spiegel	Shopping Chic (black)	15801	1996	$50.00
Spiegel	Sterling Wishes	3347	1991	$75.00
Spiegel	Summer Sophisticate	15591	1996	$43.00
Spiegel	Theatre Elegance	12077	1994	$145.00
Spiegel	Winner's Circle	17441	1997	$55.00
Sports	Bowling Champ Barbie	25871	2000	$30.00
Sports	Ferrari Barbie	25636	2000	$47.00
Sports	Ferrari Barbie	25636	2001	$35.00
Stars 'n Stripes	Air Force	3360	1991	$30.00
Stars 'n Stripes	Air Force Thunderbirds	11552	1994	$20.00
Stars 'n Stripes	Air Force Thunderbirds (black)	11553	1994	$20.00
Stars 'n Stripes	Army Desert Storm	1234	1993	$24.00
Stars 'n Stripes	Army Desert Storm (black)	5816	1993	$24.00
Stars 'n Stripes	Marine Corps	7549	1992	$25.00
Stars 'n Stripes	Marine Corps (black)	7594	1992	$25.00
Stars 'n Stripes	Navy	9693	1991	$27.00
Stars 'n Stripes	Navy (black)	9694	1991	$27.00
Store Promotional	Pretty Changes Barbie (with free Barbie play perfume)	2598	1979	$90.00
Store Promotional	Quick Curl (with extra outfit)	4220	1973	$100.00
Store Promotional	SuperStar Barbie (with SuperStar Haircomb) #1	9720	1978	$60.00
Store Promotional	SuperStar Barbie (with SuperStar Haircomb) #2	9720	1978	$60.00
Store Promotional	SuperStar Barbie (with SuperStar Necklace)	9720	1977	$60.00
Store Promotional	Sweet 16	7796	1974	$73.00
Storybook Favorites/Kelly	Goldilocks and The Three Bears	29605	2001	$30.00
Storybook Favorites/Kelly	Little Red Riding Hood and the Wolf	52899	2002	$22.00
Style Set	Bohemian Glamour Barbie	B2512	2003	$39.00

Store/Collection	Item	Number	Year	Value
Style Set	Exotic Beauty Barbie	B0149	2003	$26.00
Style Set	Exotic Beauty Barbie (black)	B0150	2003	$54.00
Style Set	Society Girl Barbie	56203	2002	$30.00
Style Set	Society Girl Barbie (black)	56204	2002	$32.00
Supermarket	B Mine Barbie	11182	1994	$22.00
Supermarket	Back to School	10217	1993	$25.00
Supermarket	Back to School	17099	1997	$10.00
Supermarket	Back to School (black)	17100	1997	$10.00
Supermarket	Ballerina Dreams Barbie	20676	1999	$14.00
Supermarket	Birthday Party Barbie	18351	1998	$12.00
Supermarket	Birthday Party Barbie (black)	18352	1998	$12.00
Supermarket	Birthday Surprise	16491	1997	$15.00
Supermarket	Birthday Surprise Barbie (black)	17320	1997	$15.00
Supermarket	Caroling Fun	13966	1995	$20.00
Supermarket	Coca-Cola Brand Party Barbie	22964	1999	$12.00
Supermarket	Coca-Cola Picnic Barbie	19626	1998	$15.00
Supermarket	Coca-Cola Picnic Barbie (black)	19627	1998	$15.00
Supermarket	Color with Me Barbie	19047	1998	$15.00
Supermarket	Easter Barbie	16315	1997	$15.00
Supermarket	Easter Barbie (black)	16317	1997	$15.00
Supermarket	Easter Basket	14613	1996	$18.00
Supermarket	Easter Fun	11276	1994	$25.00
Supermarket	Easter Party	12793	1995	$20.00
Supermarket	Easter Style Barbie	17651	1998	$12.00
Supermarket	Easter Style Barbie (black)	17652	1998	$12.00
Supermarket	Easter Surprise Barbie	20542	1999	$10.00
Supermarket	Easter Surprise Barbie (black)	20543	1999	$10.00
Supermarket	Festive Season Barbie	18909	1998	$14.00
Supermarket	Festive Season Barbie (black)	18910	1998	$14.00
Supermarket	Graduation Barbie Class of '97 (black)	16489	1997	$15.00
Supermarket	Graduation Barbie Class of '98 (black)	17831	1998	$10.00
Supermarket	Graduation Class of '96	15003	1996	$20.00
Supermarket	Graduation Class of '97	16487	1997	$15.00
Supermarket	Graduation Class of '98	17830	1998	$10.00
Supermarket	Holiday Dreams	12192	1994	$30.00
Supermarket	Holiday Hostess	10280	1993	$40.00
Supermarket	Holiday Season	15581	1996	$16.00
Supermarket	Holiday Season (black)	15583	1996	$16.00
Supermarket	Holiday Treats Barbie	17236	1997	$15.00
Supermarket	Holiday Treats Barbie (black)	17618	1997	$15.00
Supermarket	Holiday Treats Fiesta Barbie (Hispanic)	18012	1997	$15.00
Supermarket	Make-A-Valentine Barbie	20339	1999	$10.00
Supermarket	Make-A-Valentine Barbie (black)	20340	1999	$10.00
Supermarket	Millennium Grad w/black gown (black)	25750	2000	$5.00
Supermarket	Millennium Grad w/blue gown (black)	25740	2000	$5.00
Supermarket	Party Premiere	2001	1992	$20.00
Supermarket	Pearl Beach Barbie Easter Basket	25381	1999	$15.00
Supermarket	Pretty Hearts	2901	1992	$25.00
Supermarket	Red Romance	3161	1992	$25.00
Supermarket	School Spirit Barbie	15301	1996	$16.00
Supermarket	Schooltime Fun (black)	18488	1998	$10.00
Supermarket	Schooltime Fun Barbie	13741	1995	$15.00
Supermarket	Schooltime Fun Barbie	18487	1998	$10.00
Supermarket	Spring Bouquet	3477	1993	$22.00
Supermarket	Sweet Spring	3208	1992	$22.00

Store/Collection	Item	Number	Year	Value
Supermarket	Sweetheart Barbie	3161	1993	$35.00
Supermarket	Teacher (brunette)	13194	1996	$25.00
Supermarket	Trail Blazin'	2783	1991	$25.00
Supermarket	Valentine Barbie	17649	1998	$12.00
Supermarket	Valentine Barbie (black)	17650	1998	$12.00
Supermarket	Valentine Fun Barbie	16311	1997	$12.00
Supermarket	Valentine Fun Barbie (black)	16313	1997	$12.00
Supermarket	Valentine Sweetheart	14644	1996	$15.00
Target	35th Anniversary Target	16485	1997	$25.00
Target	35th Anniversary Target (black)	17608	1997	$25.00
Target	Baseball	4583	1993	$30.00
Target	City Style Barbie	15612	1996	$20.00
Target	City Style Barbie	17237	1997	$15.00
Target	City Style Barbie	18952	1998	$16.00
Target	City Style Barbie	18952	1999	$14.00
Target	Club Wedd Barbie (black)	20423	1998	$20.00
Target	Club Wedd Barbie (black)	22361	1999	$20.00
Target	Club Wedd Barbie (blonde)	19717	1998	$20.00
Target	Club Wedd Barbie (blonde)	22360	1999	$20.00
Target	Club Wedd Barbie (brunette)	19718	1998	$20.00
Target	Club Wedd Barbie (brunette)	22362	1999	$20.00
Target	Cute 'n Cool	2954	1991	$30.00
Target	Dazzlin' Date	3203	1992	$30.00
Target	Gold and Lace	7476	1989	$35.00
Target	Golden Evening	2587	1990	$45.00
Target	Golf Date	10202	1993	$30.00
Target	Pajama Fun Barbie	26883	1999	$13.00
Target	Party Pretty	5955	1990	$30.00
Target	Pet Doctor (brunette)	16458	1996	$30.00
Target	Pretty in Plaid	5413	1992	$30.00
Target	Steppin' Out	14110	1995	$22.00
Target	Target 35th Anniversary Barbie	16485	1997	$27.00
Target	Target 35th Anniversary Barbie (black)	17608	1997	$27.00
Target	Valentine Barbie	12675	1995	$22.00
Target	Valentine Barbie	15172	1996	$20.00
Target	Valentine Date Barbie	18306	1998	$18.00
Target	Valentine Romance Barbie	16059	1997	$18.00
Target	Valentine Style Barbie	20465	1999	$14.00
Target	Valentine Style Barbie (black)	22150	1999	$14.00
Target	Wild Style Barbie	411	1992	$26.00
Timeless Sentiments	Angel of Joy Barbie	19633	1998	$45.00
Timeless Sentiments	Angel of Joy Barbie (black)	20929	1998	$45.00
Timeless Sentiments	Angel of Peace	24240	1999	$40.00
Timeless Sentiments	Angel of Peace (black)	24241	1999	$40.00
Toys "R" Us	101 Dalmatians	17248	1997	$25.00
Toys "R" Us	101 Dalmatians (black)	17601	1997	$25.00
Toys "R" Us	101 Dalmatians Barbie (brunette)	21377	1999	$20.00
Toys "R" Us	101 Dalmatians Barbie (strawberry blonde)	21375	1999	$20.00
Toys "R" Us	Astronaut	12149	1994	$45.00
Toys "R" Us	Astronaut (black)	12150	1994	$45.00
Toys "R" Us	Barbie for President (black, Presidential seal)	3940	1991	$45.00
Toys "R" Us	Barbie for President (Presidential seal)	3722	1991	$65.00
Toys "R" Us	Barbie for President (white star)	3722	1992	$40.00
Toys® R Us	Bedtime Stories w/book	29426	2000	$25.00
Toys "R" Us	Bedtime Stories w/book (black)	29427	2000	$25.00

Store/Collection	Item	Number	Year	Value
Toys "R" Us	Bicyclin'	11689	1994	$25.00
Toys "R" Us	Bicyclin' (black)	11817	1994	$25.00
Toys "R" Us	Charity Ball Barbie	18979	1998	$30.00
Toys "R" Us	Charity Ball Barbie (black)	19132	1998	$30.00
Toys "R" Us	Cool 'n Sassy	1490	1992	$25.00
Toys "R" Us	Cool 'n Sassy (black)	4110	1992	$25.00
Toys "R" Us	Cool Looks	5947	1990	$25.00
Toys "R" Us	Crystal Splendor	15136	1996	$25.00
Toys "R" Us	Crystal Splendor (black)	15137	1996	$25.00
Toys "R" Us	Dance Sensation	9058	1984	$60.00
Toys "R" Us	Doctor Barbie	3850	1990	$45.00
Toys "R" Us	Doctor Barbie	15803	1996	$30.00
Toys "R" Us	Doctor Barbie (black)	14315	1995	$25.00
Toys "R" Us	Doctor Barbie (black)	15804	1996	$30.00
Toys "R" Us	Doctor Barbie (white with 3 babies)	14309	1995	$25.00
Toys "R" Us	Dream Time	9180	1985	$25.00
Toys "R" Us	Dreamtime Barbie	9180	1988	$35.00
Toys "R" Us	Emerald Elegance	12322	1994	$35.00
Toys "R" Us	Emerald Elegance (black)	12323	1994	$35.00
Toys "R" Us	Emerald Enchantment	17443	1997	$55.00
Toys "R" Us	Fashion Brights	1882	1992	$20.00
Toys "R" Us	Fashion Brights (black)	4112	1992	$20.00
Toys "R" Us	Fire Fighter	13553	1995	$50.00
Toys "R" Us	Fire Fighter (black)	13472	1995	$40.00
Toys "R" Us	Funtime (black)	1739	1986	$30.00
Toys "R" Us	Funtime (blue watch)	3717	1987	$30.00
Toys "R" Us	Funtime (pink watch)	3718	1987	$30.00
Toys "R" Us	Funtime (purple watch)	1738	1987	$30.00
Toys "R" Us	Golden Anniversary Barbie	20038	1998	$90.00
Toys "R" Us	Got Milk	15121	1996	$20.00
Toys "R" Us	Got Milk (black)	15122	1996	$20.00
Toys "R" Us	Grand Hotel	50576	2001	$20.00
Toys "R" Us	Harley-Davidson Barbie #1	17692	1997	$450.00
Toys "R" Us	Harley-Davidson Barbie #2	20441	1998	$150.00
Toys "R" Us	Harley-Davidson Barbie #3	22256	1999	$95.00
Toys "R" Us	I'm a Toys "R" Us Kid (50th Anniversary)	18895	1998	$30.00
Toys "R" Us	I'm a Toys "R" Us Kid Barbie (black)	21040	1998	$25.00
Toys "R" Us	International Pen Friend Barbie	13558	1995	$18.00
Toys "R" Us	Malt Shop	4581	1993	$35.00
Toys "R" Us	Moonlight Magic	10608	1993	$85.00
Toys "R" Us	Moonlight Magic (black)	10609	1993	$80.00
Toys "R" Us	My Size Bride Barbie (brunette)	14108	1995	$130.00
Toys "R" Us	My Size Bride Barbie (redhead)	15649	1996	$130.00
Toys "R" Us	Olympic Gymnast (redhead)	15125	1996	$35.00
Toys "R" Us	Oreo Barbie	18511	1997	$20.00
Toys "R" Us	Paleontologist	17240	1997	$20.00
Toys "R" Us	Paleontologist (black)	17241	1997	$20.00
Toys "R" Us	Party Time	12243	1994	$20.00
Toys "R" Us	Party Time (black)	14274	1994	$20.00
Toys "R" Us	Party Treats	4885	1989	$25.00
Toys "R" Us	Pen Friend	13558	1996	$20.00
Toys "R" Us	Pepsi Spirit	4869	1989	$75.00
Toys "R" Us	Picture Pockets Barbie	28701	2000	$10.00
Toys "R" Us	Pilot Barbie	18368	1998	$25.00
Toys "R" Us	Pilot Barbie (black)	19384	1998	$25.00

Store/Collection	Item	Number	Year	Value
Toys "R" Us	Pink Ice	15141	1996	$100.00
Toys "R" Us	Pink Inspiration Barbie (black)	21722	1999	$30.00
Toys "R" Us	Pink Inspiration Barbie (blonde)	21914	1999	$30.00
Toys "R" Us	Pink Inspiration Barbie (brunette)	21721	1999	$30.00
Toys "R" Us	POG Fun	13239	1995	$20.00
Toys "R" Us	Police Officer	10688	1993	$75.00
Toys "R" Us	Police Officer (black)	10689	1993	$75.00
Toys "R" Us	Purple Passion	13555	1995	$35.00
Toys "R" Us	Purple Passion (black)	13554	1995	$30.00
Toys "R" Us	Radiant 'n Rose	15140	1996	$55.00
Toys "R" Us	Radiant 'n Rose (black)	15061	1996	$55.00
Toys "R" Us	Radiant in Red	1276	1992	$45.00
Toys "R" Us	Radiant in Red (Hispanic)	4113	1992	$45.00
Toys "R" Us	Sapphire Dreams	13255	1995	$50.00
Toys "R" Us	Sapphire Sophisticate	16692	1997	$30.00
Toys "R" Us	Sapphire Sophisticate (black)	16693	1997	$20.00
Toys "R" Us	School Fun	2721	1991	$22.00
Toys "R" Us	School Fun (black)	4111	1992	$22.00
Toys "R" Us	School Spirit Barbie	10682	1993	$25.00
Toys "R" Us	School Spirit Barbie (black)	10683	1993	$25.00
Toys "R" Us	Sea Holiday Barbie	5471	1993	$25.00
Toys "R" Us	Share a Smile Barbie	17247	1997	$25.00
Toys "R" Us	Show 'n Ride	7799	1988	$40.00
Toys "R" Us	Sign Language		2000	$18.00
Toys "R" Us	Space Camp Barbie	22425	1999	$25.00
Toys "R" Us	Space Camp Barbie (black)	22426	1999	$25.00
Toys "R" Us	Spanish Teacher	29408	2000	$25.00
Toys "R" Us	Spanish Teacher (Hispanic)	29409	2000	$25.00
Toys "R" Us	Spots 'n Dots	10491	1993	$45.00
Toys "R" Us	Spring Parade	7008	1992	$35.00
Toys "R" Us	Spring Parade (black)	2257	1992	$35.00
Toys "R" Us	Sunflower Barbie	13488	1995	$20.00
Toys "R" Us	Super Talk! Barbie	14308	1995	$30.00
Toys "R" Us	Super Talk! Barbie (black)	14316	1995	$30.00
Toys "R" Us	Sweet Roses	7635	1989	$30.00
Toys "R" Us	Toys "R" Us 50th Anniversary Doll	20038	1998	$85.00
Toys "R" Us	Vacation Sensation (blue)	1675	1986	$50.00
Toys "R" Us	Vacation Sensation (pink)	1675	1988	$50.00
Toys "R" Us	Western Stampin' Barbie with Western Star Horse (black)	13478	1995	$45.00
Toys "R" Us	Wild Style Barbie	19262	1998	$20.00
Toys "R" Us	Winter Fun	5949	1990	$40.00
Toys "R" Us	Winter Sports Barbie	13516	1995	$30.00
Toys "R" Us Canada	POG Barbie	13239	1995	$18.00
Tru Value	SuperStar Barbie Fashion Change-abouts	2583	1978	$90.00
Twist 'n Turn Collection	Far Out Barbie	21911	1999	$40.00
Ultra Limited Edition	Billions of Dreams	17641	1997	$199.00
Ultra Limited Edition	Pink Splendor	16091	1996	$310.00
Unicef	Unicef	1920	1989	$20.00
Unicef	Unicef (Asian)	4774	1989	$24.00
University Barbie	Air Force Academy	21166	1999	$14.00
University Barbie	Alabama	19170	1998	$10.00
University Barbie	Alabama (black)	19422	1998	$10.00
University Barbie	Arizona State University	19162	1998	$10.00
University Barbie	Army	21159	1999	$14.00
University Barbie	Auburn University	17699	1997	$10.00

Store/Collection	Item	Number	Year	Value
University Barbie	Auburn University (black)	18346	1997	$9.00
University Barbie	Boston College	21189	1999	$16.00
University Barbie	Boston University	21226	1999	$16.00
University Barbie	Brigham Young University	19152	1998	$10.00
University Barbie	Cincinnati	21231	1999	$16.00
University Barbie	Clemson University	17753	1997	$10.00
University Barbie	Clemson University (black)	18349	1997	$9.00
University Barbie	Duke University	17750	1997	$10.00
University Barbie	Duke University (black)	19665	1997	$9.00
University Barbie	East Carolina University	19155	1998	$10.00
University Barbie	East Carolina University (black)	19426	1998	$10.00
University Barbie	Florida State University	19161	1998	$10.00
University Barbie	Georgetown University	17749	1997	$10.00
University Barbie	Georgetown University (black)	18341	1997	$10.00
University Barbie	Georgia Tech	19159	1998	$10.00
University Barbie	Georgia Tech (black)	19427	1998	$10.00
University Barbie	Indiana	20044	1998	$15.00
University Barbie	Iowa	20367	1998	$15.00
University Barbie	Kansas State	19156	1998	$10.00
University Barbie	LSU	21219	1999	$16.00
University Barbie	LSU (black)	21220	1999	$16.00
University Barbie	Marshall	21245	1999	$16.00
University Barbie	Massachusetts	21192	1999	$16.00
University Barbie	Minnesota	21193	1999	$16.00
University Barbie	Mississippi State	21190	1999	$16.00
University Barbie	Mississippi State (black)	21191	1999	$16.00
University Barbie	Montana	21194	1999	$16.00
University Barbie	North Carolina A & T	21167	1999	$16.00
University Barbie	North Carolina A & T (black)	21168	1999	$16.00
University Barbie	North Carolina State	17194	1997	$10.00
University Barbie	North Carolina State (black)	20127	1997	$9.00
University Barbie	Northwestern	19167	1998	$10.00
University Barbie	Northwestern (black)	19425	1998	$10.00
University Barbie	Oklahoma	20125	1998	$11.00
University Barbie	Oklahoma State University	17752	1997	$10.00
University Barbie	Penn State University	17698	1997	$10.00
University Barbie	Penn State University (black)	18344	1997	$10.00
University Barbie	Pittsburgh	21169	1999	$16.00
University Barbie	Purdue	19868	1998	$11.00
University Barbie	San Diego State	21227	1999	$16.00
University Barbie	San Diego State (black)	21228	1999	$16.00
University Barbie	South Carolina	21195	1999	$16.00
University Barbie	South Carolina (black)	21196	1999	$16.00
University Barbie	Stanford	19870	1998	$11.00
University Barbie	Stanford (black)	20124	1998	$11.00
University Barbie	Syracuse	19163	1998	$10.00
University Barbie	Syracuse (black)	19419	1998	$10.00
University Barbie	Texas Tech	21229	1999	$16.00
University Barbie	Texas Tech (black)	21230	1999	$16.00
University Barbie	University of Arizona	17751	1997	$10.00
University Barbie	University of Arkansas (black)	17191	1998	$10.00
University Barbie	University of Arkansas	17191	1997	$10.00
University Barbie	University of Colorado	19169	1998	$10.00
University Barbie	University of Connecticut	19866	1998	$11.00
University Barbie	University of Florida	17700	1997	$10.00

Store/Collection	Item	Number	Year	Value
University Barbie	University of Florida (black)	18343	1997	$10.00
University Barbie	University of Georgia	17192	1997	$10.00
University Barbie	University of Georgia (black)	18345	1997	$10.00
University Barbie	University of Illinois	17755	1997	$10.00
University Barbie	University of Kentucky	19153	1998	$11.00
University Barbie	University of Maryland	19867	1998	$11.00
University Barbie	University of Maryland (black)	20123	1998	$11.00
University Barbie	University of Miami	17794	1997	$10.00
University Barbie	University of Miami (black)	18348	1997	$10.00
University Barbie	University of Michigan	17398	1997	$10.00
University Barbie	University of Michigan (black)	18342	1997	$10.00
University Barbie	University of Mississippi	21232	1999	$16.00
University Barbie	University of Mississippi (black)	21233	1999	$16.00
University Barbie	University of Nebraska	17193	1997	$10.00
University Barbie	University of Tennessee	17554	1997	$10.00
University Barbie	University of Tennessee (black)	18347	1997	$10.00
University Barbie	University of Texas	17792	1997	$10.00
University Barbie	University of Texas (black)	20126	1998	$11.00
University Barbie	University of Virginia	17754	1997	$10.00
University Barbie	University of Virginia (black)	21216	1999	$16.00
University Barbie	University of Wisconsin	17195	1997	$10.00
University Barbie	UNLV	21234	1999	$16.00
University Barbie	Utah	21197	1999	$16.00
University Barbie	Vanderbilt	21160	1999	$16.00
University Barbie	Villanova	21172	1999	$16.00
University Barbie	Virginia Tech	19171	1998	$10.00
University Barbie	Virginia Tech (black)	19420	1998	$10.00
University Barbie	Washington State	19869	1998	$11.00
University Barbie	Wyoming	21246	1999	$16.00
University Barbie	Xavier	21173	1999	$16.00
Value Pack	Hip 2 Be Square (blonde)	29410	2000	$8.00
Value Pack	Hip 2 Be Square (brunette)	29663	2000	$8.00
Versace	Versace Barbie Doll	B3457	2004	$140.00
Victorian	Victorian Barbie with Cedric Bear (brunette)	25526	2000	$39.00
Victorian Tea Porcelain Collection	Mint Memories Barbie	20983	1999	$150.00
Victorian Tea Porcelain Collection	Orange Pekoe	25507	2000	$500.00
W.D.W. Teddy Bear & Doll Con.	Midnight Princess Barbie (brunette)	18486	1997	$86.00
Wal-Mart	35th Anniversary Wal-Mart	17245	1997	$25.00
Wal-Mart	35th Anniversary Wal-Mart (black)	17616	1997	$25.00
Wal-Mart	Anniversary Star	2282	1992	$30.00
Wal-Mart	Ballroom Beauty	3678	1991	$30.00
Wal-Mart	Country & Western Star	11646	1994	$30.00
Wal-Mart	Country & Western Star (black)	12096	1994	$30.00
Wal-Mart	Country & Western Star (Hispanic)	12097	1994	$30.00
Wal-Mart	Country Bride	13614	1995	$20.00
Wal-Mart	Country Bride (black)	13615	1995	$20.00
Wal-Mart	Country Bride (Hispanic)	13616	1995	$20.00
Wal-Mart	Country Star Western Horse	12271	1994	$25.00
Wal-Mart	Dream Fantasy	7335	1990	$35.00
Wal-Mart	Frills & Fantasy	1374	1988	$45.00
Wal-Mart	Garden Party	1953	1989	$20.00
Wal-Mart	Jewel Skating Barbie	23239	1999	$12.00
Wal-Mart	Jewel Skating Barbie (black)	23240	1999	$12.00
Wal-Mart	Lavender Looks	3963	1989	$35.00
Wal-Mart	Party Pink	4629	1987	$25.00

Store/Collection	Item	Number	Year	Value
Wal-Mart	Pink Jubilee (25th anniversary Wal-Mart)	4589	1987	$50.00
Wal-Mart	Portrait in Blue Barbie	19355	1998	$15.00
Wal-Mart	Portrait in Blue Barbie (black)	19356	1998	$15.00
Wal-Mart	Pretty Choices Barbie (black)	18018	1997	$20.00
Wal-Mart	Pretty Choices Barbie (blonde)	17971	1997	$20.00
Wal-Mart	Pretty Choices Barbie (brunette)	18019	1997	$20.00
Wal-Mart	Puzzle Craze Barbie	20164	1998	$12.00
Wal-Mart	Puzzle Craze Barbie (black)	20165	1998	$12.00
Wal-Mart	Shopping Time Barbie	18230	1997	$15.00
Wal-Mart	Shopping Time Barbie (black)	18231	1997	$15.00
Wal-Mart	Skating Dream Barbie	17244	1997	$20.00
Wal-Mart	Skating Star	15510	1996	$15.00
Wal-Mart	Skating Star	17244	1997	$10.00
Wal-Mart	Skating Star (black)	16691	1996	$15.00
Wal-Mart	Skating Star (Hispanic)	15511	1996	$15.00
Wal-Mart	SuperStar Barbie	10592	1993	$30.00
Wal-Mart	SuperStar Barbie (black)	10711	1993	$40.00
Wal-Mart	Sweet Magnolia	15622	1996	$18.00
Wal-Mart	Sweet Magnolia (black)	12265	1996	$18.00
Wal-Mart	Sweet Magnolia (Hispanic)	15654	1996	$18.00
Wal-Mart	Tooth Fairy Barbie	11645	1995	$20.00
Wal-Mart	Tooth Fairy Barbie	17246	1998	$12.00
Wal-Mart	Tooth Fairy Barbie (blue)	11645	1994	$22.00
Wal-Mart Wholesale Clubs	Bathtime Fun	9601	1991	$15.00
Wal-Mart Wholesale Clubs	Bathtime Fun (black)	9603	1991	$15.00
Warner Bros. Studio Store	Barbie Loves Tweety	21632	1999	$35.00
Warner Bros. Studio Store	Wonder Woman	24638	2000	Retail
Wedding Flower Collection	Blushing Orchid Bride (porcelain)	16962	1997	$125.00
Wedding Flower Collection	Romantic Rose Bride (porcelain)	14541	1996	$140.00
Wedding Flower Collection	Star Lily Bride (porcelain)	12953	1994	$150.00
Wedgwood	Wedgwood Barbie	50823	2001	$79.00
Wedgwood	Wedgwood Barbie (black)	50824	2001	$79.00
Wedgwood/Wal-Mart	Wedgwood Barbie	25641	2000	$150.00
Wessco	Carnival Cruise Lines	15186	1997	$30.00
Wessco	International Travel Barbie #1	15184	1996	$45.00
Wessco	International Travel Barbie #2	13912	1995	$50.00
Wessco	International Travel I	13912	1995	$40.00
Wessco	International Travel II	16158	1996	$50.00
When I Read, I Dream	Anne from *Anne of Green Gables*	50726	2002	$14.00
When I Read, I Dream	Fern from *Charlotte's Web*	50724	2001	$15.00
When I Read, I Dream	Heidi	52900	2002	$10.00
When I Read, I Dream	Jo from *Little Women*	50723	2001	$15.00
Wholesale Club (BJ)	Sparkle Beauty	17251	1997	$30.00
Wholesale Clubs	70s Disco Barbie (blonde)	19928	1998	$25.00
Wholesale Clubs	70s Disco Barbie (brunette)	19929	1998	$25.00
Wholesale Clubs	Bedtime Barbie with Bed	12184	1994	$30.00
Wholesale Clubs	Bronze Sensation Barbie	20022	1998	$55.00
Wholesale Clubs	Dinner Date (blonde)	19016	1998	$15.00
Wholesale Clubs	Dinner Date (redhead)	19037	1998	$20.00
Wholesale Clubs	Dream Wardrobe Barbie	3331	1992	$35.00
Wholesale Clubs	Fantastica	3196	1992	$60.00
Wholesale Clubs	Festiva	10339	1993	$50.00
Wholesale Clubs	Fifties Fun	13613	1996	$35.00
Wholesale Clubs	Florida Vacation Beach Time Fun Barbie	23740	1999	$22.00
Wholesale Clubs	Golden Waltz Barbie (blonde)	22976	1999	$25.00

Store/Collection	Item	Number	Year	Value
Wholesale Clubs	Golden Waltz Barbie (redhead)	23220	1999	$30.00
Wholesale Clubs	Hollywood Hair Barbie Deluxe Play Set	10928	1993	$25.00
Wholesale Clubs	Jewel Jubilee	2366	1991	$65.00
Wholesale Clubs	Party Sensation	9025	1990	$55.00
Wholesale Clubs	Peach Blossom	7009	1992	$40.00
Wholesale Clubs	Rose Bride	15987	1996	$35.00
Wholesale Clubs	Royal Romance	1858	1992	$80.00
Wholesale Clubs	Season's Greetings	12384	1994	$50.00
Wholesale Clubs	Silver Royale	15952	1996	$75.00
Wholesale Clubs	Sixties Fun Barbie (blonde)	17252	1997	$25.00
Wholesale Clubs	Sixties Fun Barbie (redhead)	17693	1997	$25.00
Wholesale Clubs	Sparkle Eyes Barbie Dressing Room and Fashion Set	7131	1992	$55.00
Wholesale Clubs	Sun Sensation Barbie Spray & Play Fun	7149	1992	$60.00
Wholesale Clubs	Sweet Moments	17642	1997	$25.00
Wholesale Clubs	Very Violet	1859	1992	$65.00
Wholesale Clubs	Western Stampin' Barbie Deluxe Play Set	10927	1993	$30.00
Wholesale Clubs	Winter Evening Barbie (blonde)	19218	1998	$25.00
Wholesale Clubs	Winter Evening Barbie (brunette)	19220	1998	$25.00
Wholesale Clubs	Winter Fantasy (brunette)	17666	1997	$25.00
Wholesale Clubs	Winter Fantasy II (black)	17747	1997	$25.00
Wholesale Clubs	Winter Fantasy II (blonde)	17249	1997	$25.00
Wholesale Clubs	Winter Royal	10658	1993	$75.00
Wholesale Clubs	Winter's Eve	13613	1995	$30.00
Wholesale Clubs	Workin' Out (outfits vary)		1998	$11.00
Winn Dixie	Party Pink	7637	1989	$25.00
Winn Dixie	Pink Sensation	5410	1990	$25.00
Winn Dixie	Southern Beauty	3284	1991	$25.00
Winter Princess Collection	Evergreen Princess (blonde)	12123	1994	$42.00
Winter Princess Collection	Jewel Princess (blonde)	15826	1996	$25.00
Winter Princess Collection	Midnight Princess Barbie (blonde)	17780	1997	$25.00
Winter Princess Collection	Peppermint Princess	13598	1995	$36.00
Winter Princess Collection	Winter Princess	10655	1993	$110.00
Wizard of Oz	Barbie as Dorothy	25812	2000	$25.00
Wizard of Oz	Barbie as Dorothy	25812	1999	$18.00
Wizard of Oz	Barbie as Dorothy, 2nd Edition	12701	1996	$75.00
Wizard of Oz	Barbie as Glinda	25813	2000	$25.00
Wizard of Oz	Barbie as Glinda	25813	1999	$18.00
Wizard of Oz	Dorothy with Toto Porcelain #1		2000	Retail
WNBA	WNBA Barbie	20205	1998	$16.00
Women of Royalty	Marie Antoinette Barbie	53991	2003	$250.00
Women of Royalty	Queen Elizabeth I Barbie	B3425	2004	$250.00
Women of Royalty/Avon	Empress Josephine Barbie	G8051	2005	$250.00
Woolworth	Fashion Play	5766	1990	$20.00
Woolworth	Miss Barbie	61747	1996	$35.00
Woolworth	Special Expressions	4842	1989	$25.00
Woolworth	Special Expressions	5504	1990	$20.00
Woolworth	Special Expressions	2582	1991	$20.00
Woolworth	Special Expressions	3197	1992	$25.00
Woolworth	Special Expressions	10048	1993	$20.00
Woolworth	Special Expressions (black)	7346	1989	$25.00
Woolworth	Special Expressions (black)	5505	1990	$20.00
Woolworth	Special Expressions (black)	2583	1991	$20.00
Woolworth	Special Expressions (black)	3198	1992	$30.00
Woolworth	Special Expressions (black)	10049	1993	$18.00
Woolworth	Special Expressions (Hispanic)	3200	1992	$25.00

Store/Collection	Item	Number	Year	Value
Woolworth	Special Expressions (Hispanic)	10050	1993	$18.00
Woolworth	Sweet Lavender	2522	1992	$30.00
Woolworth	Sweet Lavender (black)	2225	1992	$30.00
Woolworth	Sweet Lavender (Hispanic)	3200	1992	$30.00
World Culture Collection	Inuit Legend Barbie		2005	Retail
Zayre's	My First Barbie (Hispanic)	5979	1987	$28.00
Zodiac	Aquarius Barbie		2005	$20.00
Zodiac	Aquarius Barbie (black)		2005	$20.00
Zodiac	Aries Barbie		2005	$20.00
Zodiac	Aries Barbie (black)		2005	$20.00
Zodiac	Cancer Barbie		2005	$20.00
Zodiac	Cancer Barbie (black)		2005	$20.00
Zodiac	Capricorn Barbie		2005	$20.00
Zodiac/FAO Schwarz	Capricorn Barbie (black)		2005	$20.00
Zodiac	Gemini Barbie		2005	$20.00
Zodiac	Gemini Barbie (black)		2005	$20.00
Zodiac	Leo Barbie		2005	$20.00
Zodiac	Leo Barbie (black)		2005	$20.00
Zodiac	Libra Barbie		2005	$20.00
Zodiac	Libra Barbie (black)		2005	$20.00
Zodiac	Pisces Barbie		2005	$20.00
Zodiac	Pisces Barbie (black)		2005	$20.00
Zodiac	Sagittarius Barbie		2005	$20.00
Zodiac	Sagittarius Barbie (black)		2005	$20.00
Zodiac	Scorpio Barbie		2005	$20.00
Zodiac	Scorpio Barbie (black)		2005	$20.00
Zodiac	Taurus Barbie		2005	$20.00
Zodiac	Taurus Barbie (black)		2005	$20.00
Zodiac	Virgo Barbie		2005	$20.00
Zodiac	Virgo Barbie (black)		2005	$20.00

Ken Dolls

Listed Alphabetically

Item	Number	Year	Value	Specials
30th Anniversary Ken	1110	1991	$80.00	Porcelain
Air Force Ken	11554	1994	$30.00	Stars 'n Stripes
Air Force Ken (black)	11555	1994	$20.00	Stars 'n Stripes
All American Ken	9424	1991	$15.00	
All Star Ken	3553	1982	$25.00	
All Stars Ken	9361	1990	$25.00	
Animal Lovin' Ken	1351	1989	$20.00	
Arabian Nights	774	1964	$420.00	Dressed Boxed Dolls
Army Ken	1237	1993	$40.00	Stars 'n Stripes
Army Ken (black)	5619	1993	$38.00	Stars 'n Stripes
Baywatch Ken	13200	1995	$20.00	
Baywatch Ken (black)	13259	1995	$20.00	Elvis Presley
Beach Blast Ken	3238	1989	$15.00	
Beach Fun Ken	2683	1998	$30.00	
Beach Time Ken	9103	1984	$20.00	Frank Sinatra Collection
Benetton Ken	9406	1991	$30.00	
Benetton Shopping Ken	4876	1992	$50.00	
Big Brother Ken and Baby Brother Tommy	17055	1997	$20.00	
Big Brother Ken and Baby Brother Tommy (black)	17588	1997	$20.00	
Busy Ken	3314	1972	$175.00	
Busy Ken Talking	1196	1972	$200.00	
Butterfly Art Ken	22995	1999	$15.00	
California Dream Ken	4441	1988	$15.00	
California Ken	4441	1988	$25.00	
Camp Ken	11075	1994	$25.00	
Campus Hero	770	1963	$350.00	Dressed Boxed Dolls
Casuals	782	1963	$350.00	Dressed Boxed Dolls
Cool Lookin' Ken	20778	1998	$10.00	
Cool School Ken	23941	1999	$11.00	
Cool Shavin' Ken	15469	1996	$12.00	
Cool Times Ken	3215	1989	$18.00	
Costume Ball Ken	7154	1990	$25.00	
Costume Ball Ken (black)	7160	1991	$20.00	
Crystal Ken	4898	1984	$20.00	
Crystal Ken (black)	9036	1984	$20.00	
Dance Club Ken	3511	1989	$20.00	
Dance Magic Ken	7081	1990	$15.00	
Dance Magic Ken (black)	7082	1990	$15.00	
Day to Night Ken	9019	1985	$25.00	
Day to Night Ken (black)	9018	1985	$25.00	
Doctor Ken	4118	1987	$25.00	
Dr. Ken	793	1964	$380.00	Dressed Boxed Dolls
Dr. Ken & Little Patient Tommy	18898	1998	$14.00	
Dr. Ken & Little Patient Tommy (black)	18899	1998	$14.00	
Dream Date Ken	4077	1983	$30.00	
Dream Glow Ken	2250	1986	$25.00	
Dream Glow Ken (black)	2421	1986	$25.00	
Earring Magic Ken	2290	1993	$25.00	

Item	Number	Year	Value	Specials
Elvis in the Eagle Jumpsuit	28570	2000	$40.00	Timeless Treasures/Elvis Presley
Fashion Jeans Ken	5316	1982	$25.00	
Flight Time Ken	9600	1990	$30.00	
Florida Vacation Ken	20496	1998	$6.00	
Frank Sinatra, The Recording Years	26419	2000	$40.00	Timeless Treasures/Frank Sinatra
Fraternity Meeting	1408	1964	$410.00	Dressed Boxed Dolls
Free Moving Ken	7280	1975	$65.00	
Funtime Ken	7194	1975	$75.00	
Glitter Beach Ken	4904	1993	$15.00	
Gold Medal Skier Ken	7261	1975	$100.00	
Great Date Ken	14837	1996	$15.00	
Great Date Ken	14837	1997	$15.00	
Great Shape Ken	7318	1984	$15.00	
Harley-Davidson Ken #1	22255	1999	$60.00	Toys "R" Us
Harley-Davidson Ken #2	22235	2000	$50.00	Toys "R" Us
Hawaii Ken	24616	1999	$5.00	
Hawaiian Fun Ken	5941	1991	$15.00	
Hawaiian Ken	2960	1981	$45.00	Department Store
Hawaiian Ken	7495	1983	$25.00	Department Store
Hawaiian Ken	7495	1984	$25.00	
Hollywood Hair Ken	4829	1993	$20.00	
Horse Lovin' Ken	3600	1983	$30.00	
Hot Skatin' Ken	13513	1995	$15.00	
Ice Capades Ken	7375	1990	$13.00	
In-Line Skating Ken	15474	1996	$20.00	FAO Schwarz
Island Fun Ken	4060	1988	$13.00	
James Dean American Legend	27786	2000	$40.00	
Jewel Secrets Ken	1719	1987	$40.00	
Jewel Secrets Ken (black)	3232	1987	$20.00	
Ken (baggie, non talking)	1111	1973	$60.00	
Ken (baggie, talking body—live action head)	1159	1974	$60.00	
Ken as Cowardly Lion	25814	2000	$25.00	
Ken as Professor Higgins	15499	1996	$60.00	Hollywood Legends Collection
Ken as Rhett Butler	12741	1995	$60.00	Gone With the Wind
Ken as Scarecrow	25816	2000	$20.00	Hollywood Legends Collection
Ken as the Cowardly Lion	16573	1997	$180.00	Hollywood Legends Collection
Ken as the Scarecrow	16497	1996	$150.00	Hollywood Legends Collection
Ken as the Tin Man	14902	1996	$90.00	Hollywood Legends Collection
Ken as Tin Man	25815	2000	$25.00	
Ken Doll (bendable leg, blonde)	1020	1965	$350.00	
Ken Doll (bendable leg, brunette)	1020	1965	$350.00	
Ken Doll (flocked, brunette)	750	1961	$250.00	
Ken Doll (flocked, blonde)	750	1961	$200.00	
Ken Doll (painted blonde)	750	1962	$120.00	
Ken Doll (painted brunette)	750	1962	$120.00	
Ken Doll (¾" shorter, painted blonde)	750	1963	$135.00	
Ken in Holland	777	1964	$375.00	Dressed Boxed Dolls
Ken in Mexico	778	1964	$370.00	Dressed Boxed Dolls
Ken in Switzerland	776	1964	$380.00	Dressed Boxed Dolls
King Arthur	773	1964	$450.00	Dressed Boxed Dolls
Live Action Ken	1159	1971	$100.00	
Live Action Ken (baggie)	1159	1973	$50.00	
Live Action on Stage Ken	1172	1971	$120.00	
Locket Surprise Ken	10964	1994	$15.00	
Malibu Ken (darker skin, new box)	1088	1976	$80.00	

Item	Number	Year	Value	Specials
Malibu Ken (new rose box)	1088	1976	$80.00	
Malibu Ken (Sunset)	1088	1971	$60.00	
Marine Corps Ken	7574	1992	$40.00	Stars 'n Stripes
Marine Corps Ken (black)	5352	1992	$40.00	Stars 'n Stripes
Mod Hair Ken	4224	1973	$110.00	
Mod Hair Ken	4234	1974	$175.00	Montgomery Ward
Movie Date Ken	28731	2000	$10.00	
Movie Date Ken (black)	29261	2000	$12.00	
Music Lovin' Ken	2388	1985	$20.00	
My First Ken	1389	1989	$20.00	
My First Ken	1503	1993	$12.00	
My First Ken	3841	1992	$11.00	
My First Ken	9940	1991	$14.00	
My First Ken (black)	3876	1993	$12.00	
My First Ken (black)	1807	1992	$10.00	
My First Ken Prince	9940	1990	$13.00	
Now Look Ken (longer hair)	9342	1976	$75.00	
Now Look Ken (shorter hair)	9342	1976	$75.00	
Ocean Friends Ken	15430	1996	$13.00	
Olympic Skater Ken	18502	1997	$12.00	
Olympic Skater Ken (black)	18504	1997	$12.00	
Partytime Ken	9927	1977	$50.00	
Pearl Beach Ken	18577	1997	$10.00	
Perfume Giving Ken	4554	1988	$15.00	
Perfume Giving Ken (black)	4555	1988	$20.00	
Prince Ken	18080	1997	$20.00	
Prince Ken	20491	1999	$25.00	
Rainbow Prince Ken	61537	1999	$12.00	
Rainbow Prince Ken	26359	2000	$15.00	
Rappin' Rockin' Ken	4903	1992	$15.00	
Rock Star Ken	15469	1996	$50.00	
Rocker Ken	3131	1986	$25.00	
Rocker Ken (revised)	3131	1987	$40.00	
Roller Skating Ken	1881	1981	$25.00	
Rollerblade Ken	2215	1992	$20.00	
Rose Prince Ken	29807	2000	$13.00	
Sailor	796	1964	$300.00	Dressed Boxed Dolls
Sea Holiday Ken	5474	1993	$25.00	FAO Schwarz
Secret Hearts Ken	7988	1993	$15.00	
Shave 'N Style	23788	1999	$20.00	
Shave 'N Style (black)	23937	1999	$12.00	
Shaving Fun Ken	12956	1995	$25.00	
Ski Fun Ken	7512	1992	$19.00	
Sleeping Beauty Prince Ken	20491	1998	$20.00	
Sparkle Beach Ken	14350	1996	$6.00	
Sparkle Surprise Ken	3149	1992	$15.00	
Splash 'n Color Ken	16170	1996	$10.00	Splash 'n Color
Sport & Shave Ken	1294	1980	$20.00	
Sun Charm Ken	9934	1989	$25.00	
Sun Gold Malibu Ken	1088	1984	$25.00	
Sun Gold Malibu Ken (black)	3849	1985	$20.00	
Sun Gold Malibu Ken (Hispanic)	4971	1984	$20.00	
Sun Jewel Ken	10954	1994	$10.00	
Sun Lovin' Malibu Ken	1088	1979	$20.00	
Sun Sensation Ken	1392	1992	$10.00	

Item	Number	Year	Value	Specials
Sun Valley Ken	7809	1974	$80.00	
Sunsational Ken (black rooted hair)	3849	1982	$50.00	
Sunsational Malibu Ken	1088	1982	$30.00	
Sunsational Malibu Ken (black)	3849	1982	$30.00	
Sunsational Malibu Ken (Hispanic)	4971	1983	$35.00	
Super Sport Ken	5839	1982	$14.00	
SuperStar Ken	1535	1989	$15.00	
SuperStar Ken (black)	1550	1989	$20.00	
SuperStar Ken (with ring, 1st issue)	2211	1978	$50.00	
SuperStar Ken (without ring, 2nd issue)	2211	1978	$35.00	
Surf City Ken	28422	2000	$5.00	
Sweetheart Ken	25678	2000	$60.00	**Coca-Cola Series**
Talking Ken (blue outfit)	1111	1969	$110.00	
Talking Ken (Spanish)	8372	1969	$100.00	
The Prince	772	1964	$430.00	**Dressed Boxed Dolls**
Time For Tennis	790	1963	$300.00	**Dressed Boxed Dolls**
Totally Cool Ken (1st version)	19209	1998	$10.00	
Totally Cool Ken (2nd version)	19387	1998	$10.00	
Totally Hair Ken	1115	1992	$15.00	
Touchdown	799	1964	$275.00	**Dressed Boxed Dolls**
Tropical Ken	1020	1986	$12.00	
Tropical Ken (black)	1023	1986	$15.00	
Tropical Splash Ken	12447	1995	$15.00	
Walk Lively Ken	1184	1972	$150.00	
Wedding Day Ken	9609	1991	$25.00	**Midge Wedding Party**
Western Fun Ken	9934	1990	$20.00	
Western Ken	3600	1981	$20.00	
Western Stampin' Ken	10294	1993	$25.00	
Wet 'n Wild Ken	4104	1990	$11.00	
Winter Sport Ken	13515	1995	$15.00	

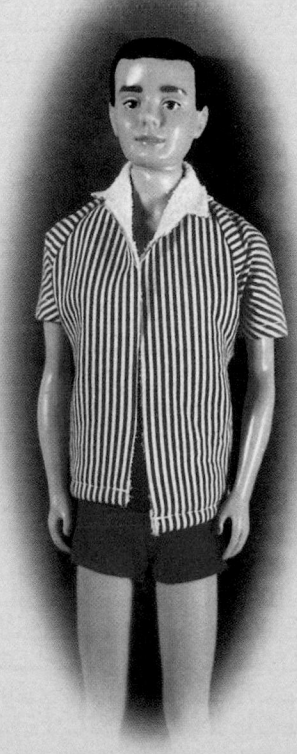

Ken® Dolls

Number	Item	Year	Value	Specials
750	Ken Doll (flocked brunette)	1961	$250.00	
750	Ken Doll (flocked, blonde)	1961	$200.00	
750	Ken Doll (painted blonde)	1962	$120.00	
750	Ken Doll (painted brunette)	1962	$120.00	
750	Ken Doll (¾" shorter, painted blonde)	1963	$135.00	
770	Campus Hero	1963	$350.00	Dressed Boxed Dolls
772	The Prince	1964	$430.00	Dressed Boxed Dolls
773	King Arthur	1964	$450.00	Dressed Boxed Dolls
774	Arabian Nights	1964	$420.00	Dressed Boxed Dolls
776	Ken in Switzerland	1964	$380.00	Dressed Boxed Dolls
777	Ken in Holland	1964	$375.00	Dressed Boxed Dolls
778	Ken in Mexico	1964	$370.00	Dressed Boxed Dolls
782	Casuals	1963	$350.00	Dressed Boxed Dolls
790	Time For Tennis	1963	$300.00	Dressed Boxed Dolls
793	Dr. Ken	1964	$380.00	Dressed Boxed Dolls
796	Sailor	1964	$300.00	Dressed Boxed Dolls
799	Touchdown	1964	$275.00	Dressed Boxed Dolls
1020	Ken Doll (bendable leg, blonde)	1965	$350.00	
1020	Ken Doll (bendable leg, brunette)	1965	$350.00	
1020	Tropical Ken	1986	$12.00	
1023	Tropical Ken (black)	1986	$15.00	
1088	Malibu Ken (darker skin, new box)	1976	$80.00	
1088	Malibu Ken (new rose box)	1976	$80.00	
1088	Malibu Ken (Sunset)	1971	$60.00	
1088	Sun Gold Malibu Ken	1984	$25.00	
1088	Sun Lovin' Malibu Ken	1979	$20.00	
1088	Sunsational Malibu Ken	1982	$30.00	
1110	30th Anniversary Ken	1991	$80.00	Porcelain
1111	Ken (baggie, non talking)	1973	$60.00	
1111	Talking Ken (blue outfit)	1969	$110.00	
1115	Totally Hair Ken	1992	$15.00	
1159	Ken (baggie, talking body-live action head)	1974	$60.00	
1159	Live Action Ken	1971	$100.00	
1159	Live Action Ken (baggie)	1973	$50.00	
1172	Live Action on Stage Ken	1971	$120.00	
1184	Walk Lively Ken	1972	$150.00	
1196	Busy Ken Talking	1972	$200.00	
1237	Army Ken	1993	$40.00	Stars 'n Stripes
1294	Sport & Shave Ken	1980	$20.00	
1351	Animal Lovin' Ken	1989	$20.00	
1389	My First Ken	1989	$20.00	
1392	Sun Sensation Ken	1992	$10.00	
1408	Fraternity Meeting	1964	$410.00	Dressed Boxed Dolls
1503	My First Ken	1993	$12.00	
1535	SuperStar Ken	1989	$15.00	
1550	SuperStar Ken (black)	1989	$20.00	
1719	Jewel Secrets Ken	1987	$40.00	
1807	My First Ken (black)	1992	$10.00	

Number	Item	Year	Value	Specials
1881	Roller Skating Ken	1981	$25.00	
2211	SuperStar Ken (with ring, 1st issue)	1978	$50.00	
2211	SuperStar Ken (without ring, 2nd issue)	1978	$35.00	
2215	Rollerblade Ken	1992	$20.00	
2250	Dream Glow Ken	1986	$25.00	
2290	Earring Magic Ken	1993	$25.00	
2388	Music Lovin' Ken	1985	$20.00	
2421	Dream Glow Ken (black)	1986	$25.00	
2683	Beach Fun Ken	1998	$30.00	
2960	Hawaiian Ken	1981	$45.00	Department Store
3131	Rocker Ken	1986	$25.00	
3131	Rocker Ken (revised)	1987	$40.00	
3149	Sparkle Surprise Ken	1992	$15.00	
3215	Cool Times Ken	1989	$18.00	
3232	Jewel Secrets Ken (black)	1987	$20.00	
3238	Beach Blast Ken	1989	$15.00	
3314	Busy Ken	1972	$175.00	
3511	Dance Club Ken	1989	$20.00	
3553	All Star Ken	1982	$25.00	
3600	Horse Lovin' Ken	1983	$30.00	
3600	Western Ken	1981	$20.00	
3841	My First Ken	1992	$11.00	
3849	Sun Gold Malibu Ken (black)	1985	$20.00	
3849	Sunsational Ken (black rooted hair)	1982	$50.00	
3849	Sunsational Malibu Ken (black)	1982	$30.00	
3876	My First Ken (black)	1993	$12.00	
4060	Island Fun Ken	1988	$13.00	
4077	Dream Date Ken	1983	$30.00	
4104	Wet 'n Wild Ken	1990	$11.00	
4118	Doctor Ken	1987	$25.00	
4224	Mod Hair Ken	1973	$110.00	
4234	Mod Hair Ken	1974	$175.00	Montgomery Ward
4441	California Dream Ken	1988	$15.00	
4441	California Ken	1988	$25.00	
4554	Perfume Giving Ken	1988	$15.00	
4555	Perfume Giving Ken (black)	1988	$20.00	
4829	Hollywood Hair Ken	1993	$20.00	
4876	Benetton Shopping Ken	1992	$50.00	
4898	Crystal Ken	1984	$20.00	
4903	Rappin' Rockin' Ken	1992	$15.00	
4904	Glitter Beach Ken	1993	$15.00	
4971	Sun Gold Malibu Ken (Hispanic)	1984	$20.00	
4971	Sunsational Malibu Ken (Hispanic)	1983	$35.00	
5316	Fashion Jeans Ken	1982	$25.00	
5352	Marine Corps Ken (black)	1992	$40.00	Stars 'n Stripes
5474	Sea Holiday Ken	1993	$25.00	FAO Schwarz
5619	Army Ken (black)	1993	$38.00	Stars 'n Stripes
5839	Super Sport Ken	1982	$14.00	
5941	Hawaiian Fun Ken	1991	$15.00	
7081	Dance Magic Ken	1990	$15.00	
7082	Dance Magic Ken (black)	1990	$15.00	
7154	Costume Ball Ken	1990	$25.00	
7160	Costume Ball Ken (black)	1991	$20.00	
7194	Funtime Ken	1975	$75.00	
7261	Gold Medal Skier Ken	1975	$100.00	

Number	Item	Year	Value	Specials
7280	Free Moving Ken	1975	$65.00	
7318	Great Shape Ken	1984	$15.00	
7375	Ice Capades Ken	1990	$13.00	
7495	Hawaiian Ken	1983	$25.00	Department Store
7495	Hawaiian Ken	1984	$25.00	
7512	Ski Fun Ken	1992	$19.00	
7574	Marine Corps Ken	1992	$40.00	Stars 'n Stripes
7809	Sun Valley Ken	1974	$80.00	
7988	Secret Hearts Ken	1993	$15.00	
8372	Talking Ken (Spanish)	1969	$100.00	
9018	Day to Night Ken (black)	1985	$25.00	
9019	Day to Night Ken	1985	$25.00	
9036	Crystal Ken (black)	1984	$20.00	
9103	Beach Time Ken	1984	$20.00	Frank Sinatra Collection
9342	Now Look Ken (longer hair)	1976	$75.00	
9342	Now Look Ken (shorter hair)	1976	$75.00	
9361	All Stars Ken	1990	$25.00	
9406	Benetton Ken	1991	$30.00	
9424	All American Ken	1991	$15.00	
9600	Flight Time Ken	1990	$30.00	
9609	Wedding Day Ken	1991	$25.00	Midge Wedding Party
9927	Partytime Ken	1977	$50.00	
9934	Sun Charm Ken	1989	$25.00	
9934	Western Fun Ken	1990	$20.00	
9940	My First Ken	1991	$14.00	
9940	My First Ken Prince	1990	$13.00	
10294	Western Stampin' Ken	1993	$25.00	
10954	Sun Jewel Ken	1994	$10.00	
10964	Locket Surprise Ken	1994	$15.00	
11075	Camp Ken	1994	$25.00	
11554	Air Force Ken	1994	$30.00	Stars 'n Stripes
11555	Air Force Ken (black)	1994	$20.00	Stars 'n Stripes
12447	Tropical Splash Ken	1995	$15.00	
12741	Ken as Rhett Butler	1995	$60.00	Gone With the Wind
12956	Shaving Fun Ken	1995	$25.00	
13200	Baywatch Ken	1995	$20.00	
13259	Baywatch Ken (black)	1995	$20.00	Elvis Presley
13513	Hot Skatin' Ken	1995	$15.00	
13515	Winter Sport Ken	1995	$15.00	
14350	Sparkle Beach Ken	1996	$6.00	
14837	Great Date Ken	1996	$15.00	
14837	Great Date Ken	1997	$15.00	
14902	Ken as the Tin Man	1996	$90.00	Hollywood Legends Collection
15430	Ocean Friends Ken	1996	$13.00	
15469	Cool Shavin' Ken	1996	$12.00	
15469	Rock Star Ken	1996	$50.00	
15474	In-Line Skating Ken	1996	$20.00	FAO Schwarz
15499	Ken as Professor Higgins	1996	$60.00	Hollywood Legends Collection
16170	Splash 'n Color Ken	1996	$10.00	Splash 'n Color
16497	Ken as the Scarecrow	1996	$150.00	Hollywood Legends Collection
16573	Ken as the Cowardly Lion	1997	$180.00	Hollywood Legends Collection
17055	Big Brother Ken and Baby Brother Tommy	1997	$20.00	
17588	Big Brother Ken and Baby Brother Tommy (black)	1997	$20.00	
18080	Prince Ken	1997	$20.00	
18502	Olympic Skater Ken	1997	$12.00	

Number	Item	Year	Value	Specials
18504	Olympic Skater Ken (black)	1997	$12.00	
18577	Pearl Beach Ken	1997	$10.00	
18898	Dr. Ken & Little Patient Tommy	1998	$14.00	
18899	Dr. Ken & Little Patient Tommy (black)	1998	$14.00	
19209	Totally Cool Ken (1st version)	1998	$10.00	
19387	Totally Cool Ken (2nd version)	1998	$10.00	
20491	Prince Ken	1999	$25.00	
20491	Sleeping Beauty Prince Ken	1998	$20.00	
20496	Florida Vacation Ken	1998	$6.00	
20778	Cool Lookin' Ken	1998	$10.00	
22235	Harley-Davidson Ken #2	2000	$50.00	Toys "R" Us
22255	Harley-Davidson Ken #1	1999	$60.00	Toys "R" Us
22995	Butterfly Art Ken	1999	$15.00	
23788	Shave 'N Style	1999	$20.00	
23937	Shave 'N Style (black)	1999	$12.00	
23941	Cool School Ken	1999	$11.00	
24616	Hawaii Ken	1999	$5.00	
25678	Sweetheart Ken	2000	$60.00	Coca-Cola Series
25814	Ken as Cowardly Lion	2000	$25.00	
25815	Ken as Tin Man	2000	$25.00	
25816	Ken as Scarecrow	2000	$20.00	Hollywood Legends Collection
26359	Rainbow Prince Ken	2000	$15.00	
26419	Frank Sinatra, The Recording Years	2000	$40.00	Timeless Treasures/Frank Sinatra
27786	James Dean American Legend	2000	$40.00	
28422	Surf City Ken	2000	$5.00	
28570	Elvis in the Eagle Jumpsuit	2000	$40.00	Timeless Treasures/Elvis Presley
28731	Movie Date Ken	2000	$10.00	
29261	Movie Date Ken (black)	2000	$12.00	
29807	Rose Prince Ken	2000	$13.00	
61537	Rainbow Prince Ken	1999	$12.00	

Ken Dolls

Listed by Year

Year	Item	Number	Value	Specials
1961	Ken Doll (flocked, brunette)	750	$250.00	
1961	Ken Doll (flocked, blonde)	750	$200.00	
1962	Ken Doll (painted blonde)	750	$120.00	
1962	Ken Doll (painted brunette)	750	$120.00	
1963	Ken Doll (¾" shorter, painted blonde)	750	$135.00	
1963	Campus Hero	770	$350.00	Dressed Boxed Dolls
1963	Casuals	782	$350.00	Dressed Boxed Dolls
1963	Time For Tennis	790	$300.00	Dressed Boxed Dolls
1964	The Prince	772	$430.00	Dressed Boxed Dolls
1964	King Arthur	773	$450.00	Dressed Boxed Dolls
1964	Arabian Nights	774	$420.00	Dressed Boxed Dolls
1964	Ken in Switzerland	776	$380.00	Dressed Boxed Dolls
1964	Ken in Holland	777	$375.00	Dressed Boxed Dolls
1964	Ken in Mexico	778	$370.00	Dressed Boxed Dolls
1964	Dr. Ken	793	$380.00	Dressed Boxed Dolls
1964	Sailor	796	$300.00	Dressed Boxed Dolls
1964	Touchdown	799	$275.00	Dressed Boxed Dolls
1964	Fraternity Meeting	1408	$410.00	Dressed Boxed Dolls
1965	Ken Doll (bendable leg, blonde)	1020	$350.00	
1965	Ken Doll (bendable leg, brunette)	1020	$350.00	
1969	Talking Ken (blue outfit)	1111	$110.00	
1969	Talking Ken (Spanish)	8372	$100.00	
1971	Malibu Ken (Sunset)	1088	$60.00	
1971	Live Action Ken	1159	$100.00	
1971	Live Action on Stage Ken	1172	$120.00	
1972	Walk Lively Ken	1184	$150.00	
1972	Busy Ken Talking	1196	$200.00	
1972	Busy Ken	3314	$175.00	
1973	Ken (baggie, non talking)	1111	$60.00	
1973	Live Action Ken (baggie)	1159	$50.00	
1973	Mod Hair Ken	4224	$110.00	
1974	Ken (baggie, talking body-live action head)	1159	$60.00	
1974	Mod Hair Ken	4234	$175.00	Montgomery Ward
1974	Sun Valley Ken	7809	$80.00	
1975	Funtime Ken	7194	$75.00	
1975	Gold Medal Skier Ken	7261	$100.00	
1975	Free Moving Ken	7280	$65.00	
1976	Malibu Ken (darker skin, new box)	1088	$80.00	
1976	Malibu Ken (new rose box)	1088	$80.00	
1976	Now Look Ken (longer hair)	9342	$75.00	
1976	Now Look Ken (shorter hair)	9342	$75.00	
1977	Partytime Ken	9927	$50.00	
1978	SuperStar Ken (with ring, 1st issue)	2211	$50.00	
1978	SuperStar Ken (without ring, 2nd issue)	2211	$35.00	
1979	Sun Lovin' Malibu Ken	1088	$20.00	
1980	Sport & Shave Ken	1294	$20.00	
1981	Roller Skating Ken	1881	$25.00	
1981	Hawaiian Ken	2960	$45.00	Department Store

Year	Item	Number	Value	Specials
1981	Western Ken	3600	$20.00	
1982	Sunsational Malibu Ken	1088	$30.00	
1982	All Star Ken	3553	$25.00	
1982	Sunsational Ken (black rooted hair)	3849	$50.00	
1982	Sunsational Malibu Ken (black)	3849	$30.00	
1982	Fashion Jeans Ken	5316	$25.00	
1982	Super Sport Ken	5839	$14.00	
1983	Horse Lovin' Ken	3600	$30.00	
1983	Dream Date Ken	4077	$30.00	
1983	Sunsational Malibu Ken (Hispanic)	4971	$35.00	
1983	Hawaiian Ken	7495	$25.00	Department Store
1984	Sun Gold Malibu Ken	1088	$25.00	
1984	Crystal Ken	4898	$20.00	
1984	Sun Gold Malibu Ken (Hispanic)	4971	$20.00	
1984	Great Shape Ken	7318	$15.00	
1984	Hawaiian Ken	7495	$25.00	
1984	Crystal Ken (black)	9036	$20.00	
1984	Beach Time Ken	9103	$20.00	Frank Sinatra Collection
1985	Music Lovin' Ken	2388	$20.00	
1985	Sun Gold Malibu Ken (black)	3849	$20.00	
1985	Day to Night Ken (black)	9018	$25.00	
1985	Day to Night Ken	9019	$25.00	
1986	Tropical Ken	1020	$12.00	
1986	Tropical Ken (black)	1023	$15.00	
1986	Dream Glow Ken	2250	$25.00	
1986	Dream Glow Ken (black)	2421	$25.00	
1986	Rocker Ken	3131	$25.00	
1987	Jewel Secrets Ken	1719	$40.00	
1987	Rocker Ken (revised)	3131	$40.00	
1987	Jewel Secrets Ken (black)	3232	$20.00	
1987	Doctor Ken	4118	$25.00	
1988	Island Fun Ken	4060	$13.00	
1988	California Dream Ken	4441	$15.00	
1988	California Ken	4441	$25.00	
1988	Perfume Giving Ken	4554	$15.00	
1988	Perfume Giving Ken (black)	4555	$20.00	
1989	Animal Lovin' Ken	1351	$20.00	
1989	My First Ken	1389	$20.00	
1989	SuperStar Ken	1535	$15.00	
1989	SuperStar Ken (black)	1550	$20.00	
1989	Cool Times Ken	3215	$18.00	
1989	Beach Blast Ken	3238	$15.00	
1989	Dance Club Ken	3511	$20.00	
1989	Sun Charm Ken	9934	$25.00	
1990	Wet 'n Wild Ken	4104	$11.00	
1990	Dance Magic Ken	7081	$15.00	
1990	Dance Magic Ken (black)	7082	$15.00	
1990	Costume Ball Ken	7154	$25.00	
1990	Ice Capades Ken	7375	$13.00	
1990	All Stars Ken	9361	$25.00	
1990	Flight Time Ken	9600	$30.00	
1990	Western Fun Ken	9934	$20.00	
1990	My First Ken Prince	9940	$13.00	
1991	30th Anniversary Ken	1110	$80.00	Porcelain
1991	Hawaiian Fun Ken	5941	$15.00	

Year	Item	Number	Value	Specials
1991	Costume Ball Ken (black)	7160	$20.00	
1991	Benetton Ken	9406	$30.00	
1991	All American Ken	9424	$15.00	
1991	Wedding Day Ken	9609	$25.00	Midge Wedding Party
1991	My First Ken	9940	$14.00	
1992	Totally Hair Ken	1115	$15.00	
1992	Sun Sensation Ken	1392	$10.00	
1992	My First Ken (black)	1807	$10.00	
1992	Rollerblade Ken	2215	$20.00	
1992	Sparkle Surprise Ken	3149	$15.00	
1992	My First Ken	3841	$11.00	
1992	Benetton Shopping Ken	4876	$50.00	
1992	Rappin' Rockin' Ken	4903	$15.00	
1992	Marine Corps Ken (black)	5352	$40.00	Stars 'n Stripes
1992	Ski Fun Ken	7512	$19.00	
1992	Marine Corps Ken	7574	$40.00	Stars 'n Stripes
1993	Army Ken	1237	$40.00	Stars 'n Stripes
1993	My First Ken	1503	$12.00	
1993	Earring Magic Ken	2290	$25.00	
1993	My First Ken (black)	3876	$12.00	
1993	Hollywood Hair Ken	4829	$20.00	
1993	Glitter Beach Ken	4904	$15.00	
1993	Sea Holiday Ken	5474	$25.00	FAO Schwarz
1993	Army Ken (black)	5619	$38.00	Stars 'n Stripes
1993	Secret Hearts Ken	7988	$15.00	
1993	Western Stampin' Ken	10294	$25.00	
1994	Sun Jewel Ken	10954	$10.00	
1994	Locket Surprise Ken	10964	$15.00	
1994	Camp Ken	11075	$25.00	
1994	Air Force Ken	11554	$30.00	Stars 'n Stripes
1994	Air Force Ken (black)	11555	$20.00	Stars 'n Stripes
1995	Tropical Splash Ken	12447	$15.00	
1995	Ken as Rhett Butler	12741	$60.00	Gone With the Wind
1995	Shaving Fun Ken	12956	$25.00	
1995	Baywatch Ken	13200	$20.00	
1995	Baywatch Ken (black)	13259	$20.00	Elvis Presley
1995	Hot Skatin' Ken	13513	$15.00	
1995	Winter Sport Ken	13515	$15.00	
1996	Sparkle Beach Ken	14350	$6.00	
1996	Great Date Ken	14837	$15.00	
1996	Ken as the Tin Man	14902	$90.00	Hollywood Legends Collection
1996	Ocean Friends Ken	15430	$13.00	
1996	Cool Shavin' Ken	15469	$12.00	
1996	Rock Star Ken	15469	$50.00	
1996	In-Line Skating Ken	15474	$20.00	FAO Schwarz
1996	Ken as Professor Higgins	15499	$60.00	Hollywood Legends Collection
1996	Splash 'n Color Ken	16170	$10.00	Splash 'n Color
1996	Ken as the Scarecrow	16497	$150.00	Hollywood Legends Collection
1997	Great Date Ken	14837	$15.00	
1997	Ken as the Cowardly Lion	16573	$180.00	Hollywood Legends Collection
1997	Big Brother Ken and Baby Brother Tommy	17055	$20.00	
1997	Big Brother Ken and Baby Brother Tommy (black)	17588	$20.00	
1997	Prince Ken	18080	$20.00	
1997	Olympic Skater Ken	18502	$12.00	
1997	Olympic Skater Ken (black)	18504	$12.00	

Year	Item	Number	Value	Specials
1997	Pearl Beach Ken	18577	$10.00	
1998	Beach Fun Ken	2683	$30.00	
1998	Dr. Ken & Little Patient Tommy	18898	$14.00	
1998	Dr. Ken & Little Patient Tommy (black)	18899	$14.00	
1998	Totally Cool Ken (1st version)	19209	$10.00	
1998	Totally Cool Ken (2nd version)	19387	$10.00	
1998	Sleeping Beauty Prince Ken	20491	$20.00	
1998	Florida Vacation Ken	20496	$6.00	
1998	Cool Lookin' Ken	20778	$10.00	
1999	Prince Ken	20491	$25.00	
1999	Harley-Davidson Ken #1	22255	$60.00	Toys "R" Us
1999	Butterfly Art Ken	22995	$15.00	
1999	Shave 'N Style	23788	$20.00	
1999	Shave 'N Style (black)	23937	$12.00	
1999	Cool School Ken	23941	$11.00	
1999	Hawaii Ken	24616	$5.00	
1999	Rainbow Prince Ken	61537	$12.00	
2000	Harley-Davidson Ken #2	22235	$50.00	Toys "R" Us
2000	Sweetheart Ken	25678	$60.00	Coca-Cola Series
2000	Ken as Cowardly Lion	25814	$25.00	
2000	Ken as Tin Man	25815	$25.00	
2000	Ken as Scarecrow	25816	$20.00	Hollywood Legends Collection
2000	Rainbow Prince Ken	26359	$15.00	
2000	Frank Sinatra, The Recording Years	26419	$40.00	Timeless Treasures/Frank Sinatra
2000	James Dean American Legend	27786	$40.00	
2000	Surf City Ken	28422	$5.00	
2000	Elvis in the Eagle Jumpsuit	28570	$40.00	Timeless Treasures/Elvis Presley
2000	Movie Date Ken	28731	$10.00	
2000	Movie Date Ken (black)	29261	$12.00	
2000	Rose Prince Ken	29807	$13.00	

Skipper Dolls

Listed Alphabetically

Item	Number	Year	Value	Specials
30th Anniversary Skipper	11396	1994	$160.00	Porcelain
Babs (Baggie Busy Steffie)	7888	1974	$170.00	
Babysitter Skipper	12071	1994	$15.00	
Babysitter Skipper	9433	1991	$20.00	
Babysitter Skipper (black)	1599	1991	$20.00	
Babysitter Skipper (black)	12072	1994	$10.00	
Bathtime Fun Skipper	7970	1992	$20.00	Target
Baton Twirling Skipper	3931	1993	$15.00	
Baton Twirling Skipper (black)	7498	1993	$15.00	
Beach Blast Skipper	3242	1989	$20.00	
Beauty Pageant Skipper	9324	1991	$25.00	Toys "R" Us
California Dream Skipper	4440	1988	$25.00	
Camp Skipper	11076	1994	$20.00	
Cheerleader Teen Fun Skipper	5893	1988	$25.00	
Cool Crimp Skipper	11179	1994	$20.00	
Cool Crimp Skipper (black)	11547	1994	$20.00	
Cool Sitter Skipper	26756	1998	$10.00	
Cool Sitter Skipper (black)	20375	1998	$10.00	
Cool Sitter Teen Skipper	20334	1998	$15.00	
Cool Sitter Teen Skipper (black)	20335	1998	$15.00	
Cool Tops Skipper	4989	1990	$20.00	
Cool Tops Skipper (black)	5441	1990	$20.00	
Deluxe Quick Curl Skipper	9428	1975	$100.00	
Dream Date Skipper	4817	1990	$25.00	Toys "R" Us
Dream Date Skipper	1075	1990	$30.00	Toys "R" Us
Dream Date Skipper (black)	4849	1990	$25.00	Toys "R" Us
Extreme Green Skipper	19666	1998	$15.00	
Fashion Party Skipper	29938	2000	$14.00	
Florida Vacation Skipper	20495	1998	$6.00	
Flower Girl	1904	1964	$360.00	Dressed Boxed Dolls
Funtime Skipper	7193	1975	$25.00	
Glitter Beach Skipper	4920	1993	$15.00	
Gold Medal Skipper	7379	1976	$80.00	
Great Shape Skipper	7417	1984	$30.00	
Growing Up Skipper (long pale blonde)	7259	1975	$100.00	
Growing Up Skipper (short golden blonde)	7259	1975	$100.00	
Hawaiian Fun Skipper	5942	1991	$20.00	
Hollywood Hair Skipper	2309	1993	$25.00	
Homecoming Queen Skipper	1950	1989	$35.00	
Homecoming Queen Skipper (black)	2390	1989	$35.00	
Horse Lovin' Skipper	5029	1983	$35.00	
Hot Stuff Skipper	7927	1985	$25.00	
Island Fun Skipper	4064	1988	$15.00	
Jewel Secrets Skipper	3133	1987	$50.00	
Living Skipper (dramatic)	1117	1970	$125.00	
Malibu Skipper	1069	1978	$50.00	
Malibu Skipper (baggie)	1117	1973	$30.00	
Malibu Skipper (new box)	1069	1975	$55.00	

Item	Number	Year	Value	Specials
Malibu Skipper (new rose box)	1069	1976	$55.00	
Malibu Sunset Skipper	1069	1971	$570.00	
Masquerade	1903	1964	$350.00	Dressed Boxed Dolls
Mermaid Skipper and the Sea Twins	10506	1993	$20.00	
Music Lovin' Skipper	2854	1985	$50.00	
Pajama Fun Skipper	24592	1999	$13.00	
Party Teen Skipper	5899	1988	$25.00	
Pearl Beach Skipper	19223	1997	$10.00	
Pepsi Spirit Skipper	4867	1989	$60.00	Toys "R" Us
Pet Pals Skipper	2709	1992	$25.00	
Pet Pals Skipper (black)	4049	1992	$25.00	
Phone Fun Skipper	14312	1996	$15.00	
Phone Fun Skipper (black)	14313	1996	$15.00	
Pizza Party Skipper	12920	1995	$12.00	
Pizza Party Skipper (black)	12942	1995	$10.00	
Pose 'n Play Skipper (baggie)	1117	1973	$90.00	
Pose 'n Play Skipper (swing-a-round)	1179	1972	$275.00	
Quick Curl Skipper	4223	1973	$90.00	
Red Sensation	1901	1964	$325.00	Dressed Boxed Dolls
School Days	1921	1964	$350.00	Dressed Boxed Dolls
Silk 'N Fancy	1902	1964	$325.00	Dressed Boxed Dolls
Skating Fun	1908	1964	$345.00	Dressed Boxed Dolls
Skipper Doll (bendable leg re-issue)	1030	1967	$425.00	
Skipper Doll (bendable leg, blonde)	1030	1965	$250.00	
Skipper Doll (bendable leg, brunette)	1030	1965	$250.00	
Skipper Doll (bendable leg, titian)	1030	1965	$350.00	
Skipper Doll (blonde, straight leg)	950	1964	$200.00	
Skipper Doll (brunette, straight leg)	950	1964	$200.00	
Skipper Doll (straight leg, reissue)	950	1971	$475.00	
Skipper Doll (straight leg, titian)	950	1964	$200.00	
Sparkle Beach Skipper	14352	1996	$10.00	
Splash 'n Color Skipper	16171	1996	$6.00	Splash 'n Color
Style Magic Skipper	1915	1989	$30.00	
Sun Gold Malibu Skipper	1069	1984	$25.00	
Sun Jewel Skipper	19055	1994	$10.00	
Sun Lovin' Malibu Skipper	1069	1979	$30.00	
Sun Sensation Skipper	1446	1992	$20.00	
Sunsational Malibu Skipper	1069	1982	$30.00	
Sunsational Malibu Skipper	1069	1984	$30.00	
Sunset Malibu Skipper	1069	1975	$70.00	
Super Teen Skipper	2756	1980	$40.00	
Teen Skipper	17351	1997	$15.00	
Teen Skipper (black)	17602	1997	$10.00	
Teen Sweetheart Skipper	4855	1988	$25.00	
TeenTime Skipper	1951	1989	$25.00	
Totally Hair Skipper	1430	1991	$30.00	Toys "R" Us
Totally Yo-Yo Skipper	22228	1999	$10.00	
Trade-In Special Living Skipper	1147	1970	$130.00	
Tropical Skipper	1021	1986	$20.00	
Tropical Splash Skipper	12448	1995	$15.00	
Twist 'n Turn Skipper (blonde)	1105	1968	$300.00	
Twist 'n Turn Skipper (blonde)	1105	1969	$275.00	
Western Skipper	5029	1982	$40.00	
Wet 'n Wild Skipper	4138	1990	$20.00	
Workout Teen Fun Skipper	5899	1988	$25.00	

Skipper Dolls

Listed by Stock Number

Number	Item	Year	Value	Specials
950	Skipper Doll (blonde, straight leg)	1964	$200.00	
950	Skipper Doll (brunette, straight leg)	1964	$200.00	
950	Skipper Doll (straight leg, reissue)	1971	$475.00	
950	Skipper Doll (straight leg, titian)	1964	$200.00	
1021	Tropical Skipper	1986	$20.00	
1030	Skipper Doll (bendable leg re-issue)	1967	$425.00	
1030	Skipper Doll (bendable leg, blonde)	1965	$250.00	
1030	Skipper Doll (bendable leg, brunette)	1965	$250.00	
1030	Skipper Doll (bendable leg, titian)	1965	$350.00	
1069	Malibu Skipper	1978	$50.00	
1069	Malibu Skipper (new box)	1975	$55.00	
1069	Malibu Skipper (new rose box)	1976	$55.00	
1069	Malibu Sunset Skipper	1971	$570.00	
1069	Sun Gold Malibu Skipper	1984	$25.00	
1069	Sun Lovin' Malibu Skipper	1979	$30.00	
1069	Sunsational Malibu Skipper	1982	$30.00	
1069	Sunsational Malibu Skipper	1984	$30.00	
1069	Sunset Malibu Skipper	1975	$70.00	
1075	Dream Date Skipper	1990	$30.00	Toys "R" Us
1105	Twist 'n Turn Skipper (blonde)	1968	$300.00	
1105	Twist 'n Turn Skipper (blonde)	1969	$275.00	
1117	Living Skipper (dramatic)	1970	$125.00	
1117	Malibu Skipper (baggie)	1973	$30.00	
1117	Pose 'n Play Skipper (baggie)	1973	$90.00	
1147	Trade-In Special Living Skipper	1970	$130.00	
1179	Pose 'n Play Skipper (swing-a-round)	1972	$275.00	
1430	Totally Hair Skipper	1991	$30.00	Toys "R" Us
1446	Sun Sensation Skipper	1992	$20.00	
1599	Babysitter Skipper (black)	1991	$20.00	
1901	Red Sensation	1964	$325.00	Dressed Boxed Dolls
1902	Silk 'N Fancy	1964	$325.00	Dressed Boxed Dolls
1903	Masquerade	1964	$350.00	Dressed Boxed Dolls
1904	Flower Girl	1964	$360.00	Dressed Boxed Dolls
1908	Skating Fun	1964	$345.00	Dressed Boxed Dolls
1915	Style Magic Skipper	1989	$30.00	
1921	School Days	1964	$350.00	Dressed Boxed Dolls
1950	Homecoming Queen Skipper	1989	$35.00	
1951	TeenTime Skipper	1989	$25.00	
2309	Hollywood Hair Skipper	1993	$25.00	
2390	Homecoming Queen Skipper (black)	1989	$35.00	
2709	Pet Pals Skipper	1992	$25.00	
2756	Super Teen Skipper	1980	$40.00	
2854	Music Lovin' Skipper	1985	$50.00	
3133	Jewel Secrets Skipper	1987	$50.00	
3242	Beach Blast Skipper	1989	$20.00	
3931	Baton Twirling Skipper	1993	$15.00	
4049	Pet Pals Skipper (black)	1992	$25.00	
4064	Island Fun Skipper	1988	$15.00	

Number	Item	Year	Value	Specials
4138	Wet 'n Wild Skipper	1990	$20.00	
4223	Quick Curl Skipper	1973	$90.00	
4440	California Dream Skipper	1988	$25.00	
4817	Dream Date Skipper	1990	$25.00	Toys "R" Us
4849	Dream Date Skipper (black)	1990	$25.00	Toys "R" Us
4855	Teen Sweetheart Skipper	1988	$25.00	
4867	Pepsi Spirit Skipper	1989	$60.00	Toys "R" Us
4920	Glitter Beach Skipper	1993	$15.00	
4989	Cool Tops Skipper	1990	$20.00	
5029	Horse Lovin' Skipper	1983	$35.00	
5029	Western Skipper	1982	$40.00	
5441	Cool Tops Skipper (black)	1990	$20.00	
5893	Cheerleader Teen Fun Skipper	1988	$25.00	
5899	Party Teen Skipper	1988	$25.00	
5899	Workout Teen Fun Skipper	1988	$25.00	
5942	Hawaiian Fun Skipper	1991	$20.00	
7193	Funtime Skipper	1975	$25.00	
7259	Growing Up Skipper (long pale blonde)	1975	$100.00	
7259	Growing Up Skipper (short golden blonde)	1975	$100.00	
7379	Gold Medal Skipper	1976	$80.00	
7417	Great Shape Skipper	1984	$30.00	
7498	Baton Twirling Skipper (black)	1993	$15.00	
7888	Babs (Baggie Busy Steffie)	1974	$170.00	
7927	Hot Stuff Skipper	1985	$25.00	
7970	Bathtime Fun Skipper	1992	$20.00	Target
9324	Beauty Pageant Skipper	1991	$25.00	Toys "R" Us
9428	Deluxe Quick Curl Skipper	1975	$100.00	
9433	Babysitter Skipper	1991	$20.00	
10506	Mermaid Skipper and the Sea Twins	1993	$20.00	
11076	Camp Skipper	1994	$20.00	
11179	Cool Crimp Skipper	1994	$20.00	
11396	30th Anniversary Skipper	1994	$160.00	Porcelain
11547	Cool Crimp Skipper (black)	1994	$20.00	
12071	Babysitter Skipper	1994	$15.00	
12072	Babysitter Skipper (black)	1994	$10.00	
12448	Tropical Splash Skipper	1995	$15.00	
12920	Pizza Party Skipper	1995	$12.00	
12942	Pizza Party Skipper (black)	1995	$10.00	
14312	Phone Fun Skipper	1996	$15.00	
14313	Phone Fun Skipper (black)	1996	$15.00	
14352	Sparkle Beach Skipper	1996	$10.00	
16171	Splash 'n Color Skipper	1996	$6.00	Splash 'n Color
17351	Teen Skipper	1997	$15.00	
17602	Teen Skipper (black)	1997	$10.00	
19055	Sun Jewel Skipper	1994	$10.00	
19223	Pearl Beach Skipper	1997	$10.00	
19666	Extreme Green Skipper	1998	$15.00	
20334	Cool Sitter Teen Skipper	1998	$15.00	
20335	Cool Sitter Teen Skipper (black)	1998	$15.00	
20375	Cool Sitter Skipper (black)	1998	$10.00	
20495	Florida Vacation Skipper	1998	$6.00	
22228	Totally Yo-Yo Skipper	1999	$10.00	
24592	Pajama Fun Skipper	1999	$13.00	
26756	Cool Sitter Skipper	1998	$10.00	
29938	Fashion Party Skipper	2000	$14.00	

Skipper Dolls

Listed by Year

Year	Item	Number	Value	Specials
1964	Flower Girl	1904	$360.00	Dressed Boxed Dolls
1964	Masquerade	1903	$350.00	Dressed Boxed Dolls
1964	Red Sensation	1901	$325.00	Dressed Boxed Dolls
1964	School Days	1921	$350.00	Dressed Boxed Dolls
1964	Silk 'N Fancy	1902	$325.00	Dressed Boxed Dolls
1964	Skating Fun	1908	$345.00	Dressed Boxed Dolls
1964	Skipper Doll (blonde, straight leg)	950	$200.00	
1964	Skipper Doll (brunette, straight leg)	950	$200.00	
1964	Skipper Doll (straight leg, titian)	950	$200.00	
1965	Skipper Doll (bendable leg, blonde)	1030	$250.00	
1965	Skipper Doll (bendable leg, brunette)	1030	$250.00	
1965	Skipper Doll (bendable leg, titian)	1030	$350.00	
1967	Skipper Doll (bendable leg re-issue)	1030	$425.00	
1968	Twist 'n Turn Skipper (blonde)	1105	$300.00	
1969	Twist 'n Turn Skipper (blonde)	1105	$275.00	
1970	Living Skipper (dramatic)	1117	$125.00	
1970	Trade-In Special Living Skipper	1147	$130.00	
1971	Malibu Sunset Skipper	1069	$570.00	
1971	Skipper Doll (straight leg, reissue)	950	$475.00	
1972	Pose 'n Play Skipper (swing-a-round)	1179	$275.00	
1973	Malibu Skipper (baggie)	1117	$30.00	
1973	Pose 'n Play Skipper (baggie)	1117	$90.00	
1973	Quick Curl Skipper	4223	$90.00	
1974	Babs (Baggie Busy Steffie)	7888	$170.00	
1975	Deluxe Quick Curl Skipper	9428	$100.00	
1975	Funtime Skipper	7193	$25.00	
1975	Growing Up Skipper (long pale blonde)	7259	$100.00	
1975	Growing Up Skipper (short golden blonde)	7259	$100.00	
1975	Malibu Skipper (new box)	1069	$55.00	
1975	Sunset Malibu Skipper	1069	$70.00	
1976	Gold Medal Skipper	7379	$80.00	
1976	Malibu Skipper (new rose box)	1069	$55.00	
1978	Malibu Skipper	1069	$50.00	
1979	Sun Lovin' Malibu Skipper	1069	$30.00	
1980	Super Teen Skipper	2756	$40.00	
1982	Sunsational Malibu Skipper	1069	$30.00	
1982	Western Skipper	5029	$40.00	
1983	Horse Lovin' Skipper	5029	$35.00	
1984	Great Shape Skipper	7417	$30.00	
1984	Sun Gold Malibu Skipper	1069	$25.00	
1984	Sunsational Malibu Skipper	1069	$30.00	
1985	Hot Stuff Skipper	7927	$25.00	
1985	Music Lovin' Skipper	2854	$50.00	
1986	Tropical Skipper	1021	$20.00	
1987	Jewel Secrets Skipper	3133	$50.00	
1988	California Dream Skipper	4440	$25.00	
1988	Cheerleader Teen Fun Skipper	5893	$25.00	
1988	Island Fun Skipper	4064	$15.00	

Year	Item	Number	Value	Specials
1988	Party Teen Skipper	5899	$25.00	
1988	Teen Sweetheart Skipper	4855	$25.00	
1988	Workout Teen Fun Skipper	5899	$25.00	
1989	Beach Blast Skipper	3242	$20.00	
1989	Homecoming Queen Skipper	1950	$35.00	
1989	Homecoming Queen Skipper (black)	2390	$35.00	
1989	Pepsi Spirit Skipper	4867	$60.00	Toys "R" Us
1989	Style Magic Skipper	1915	$30.00	
1989	TeenTime Skipper	1951	$25.00	
1990	Cool Tops Skipper	4989	$20.00	
1990	Cool Tops Skipper (black)	5441	$20.00	
1990	Dream Date Skipper	4817	$25.00	Toys "R" Us
1990	Dream Date Skipper	1075	$30.00	Toys "R" Us
1990	Dream Date Skipper (black)	4849	$25.00	Toys "R" Us
1990	Wet 'n Wild Skipper	4138	$20.00	
1991	Babysitter Skipper	9433	$20.00	
1991	Babysitter Skipper (black)	1599	$20.00	
1991	Beauty Pageant Skipper	9324	$25.00	Toys "R" Us
1991	Hawaiian Fun Skipper	5942	$20.00	
1991	Totally Hair Skipper	1430	$30.00	Toys "R" Us
1992	Bathtime Fun Skipper	7970	$20.00	Target
1992	Pet Pals Skipper	2709	$25.00	
1992	Pet Pals Skipper (black)	4049	$25.00	
1992	Sun Sensation Skipper	1446	$20.00	
1993	Baton Twirling Skipper	3931	$15.00	
1993	Baton Twirling Skipper (black)	7498	$15.00	
1993	Glitter Beach Skipper	4920	$15.00	
1993	Hollywood Hair Skipper	2309	$25.00	
1993	Mermaid Skipper and the Sea Twins	10506	$20.00	
1994	30th Anniversary Skipper	11396	$160.00	Porcelain
1994	Babysitter Skipper	12071	$15.00	
1994	Babysitter Skipper (black)	12072	$10.00	
1994	Camp Skipper	11076	$20.00	
1994	Cool Crimp Skipper	11179	$20.00	
1994	Cool Crimp Skipper (black)	11547	$20.00	
1994	Sun Jewel Skipper	19055	$10.00	
1995	Pizza Party Skipper	12920	$12.00	
1995	Pizza Party Skipper (black)	12942	$10.00	
1995	Tropical Splash Skipper	12448	$15.00	
1996	Phone Fun Skipper	14312	$15.00	
1996	Phone Fun Skipper (black)	14313	$15.00	
1996	Sparkle Beach Skipper	14352	$10.00	
1996	Splash 'n Color Skipper	16171	$6.00	Splash 'n Color
1997	Pearl Beach Skipper	19223	$10.00	
1997	Teen Skipper	17351	$15.00	
1997	Teen Skipper (black)	17602	$10.00	
1998	Cool Sitter Skipper	26756	$10.00	
1998	Cool Sitter Skipper (black)	20375	$10.00	
1998	Cool Sitter Teen Skipper	20334	$15.00	
1998	Cool Sitter Teen Skipper (black)	20335	$15.00	
1998	Extreme Green Skipper	19666	$15.00	
1998	Florida Vacation Skipper	20495	$6.00	
1999	Pajama Fun Skipper	24592	$13.00	
1999	Totally Yo-Yo Skipper	22228	$10.00	
2000	Fashion Party Skipper	29938	$14.00	

Family & Friends Dolls

Listed Alphabetically

Item	Number	Year	Value	Specials	Doll
101 Dalmatians Teresa	17602	1997	$20.00	Toys "R" Us	Teresa
30th Anniversary Francie	14608	1996	$65.00		Francie
30th Anniversary Midge (porcelain)	7957	1993	$140.00		Midge
35th Anniversary Teresa	17617	1997	$25.00	Wal-Mart	Teresa
African Dress Deidre	18655	1998	$5.00		Deidre
All American Christie	9425	1991	$25.00		Christie
All American Kira	9427	1991	$25.00	Reebok	Kira
All American Teresa	9426	1991	$25.00		Teresa
All Star Christie	9352	1990	$25.00		Christie
All Star Midge	9360	1990	$30.00		Midge
All Star Teresa	9353	1990	$30.00		Teresa
Allan (bendable leg)	1010	1965	$550.00		Allan
Allan (straight leg, redhead)	1000	1964	$150.00		Allan
Amusement Park Kelly	28391	2000	$5.00		Kelly
Amusement Park Marisa	29200	2000	$5.00	Kelly Club	Marisa
Amusement Park Ryan	28392	2000	$5.00	Kelly Club	Ryan
Animal Lovin' Ginger		1998	$40.00		Ginger
Animal Lovin' Nikki	1352	1989	$30.00		Nikki
Asha	1752	1991	$25.00	Toys "R" Us	Asha
Asha I	12676	1994	$20.00	Toys "R" Us	Asha
Asha II	13532	1995	$20.00	Toys "R" Us	Asha
Asha III	15139	1996	$20.00	Toys "R" Us	Asha
Awesome Skateboard Janet	24991	1999	$13.00		Janet
Awesome Skateboard Stacie	24644	1999	$14.00		Stacie
Awesome Skateboard Whitney	24990	1999	$13.00		Whitney
Baby Krissy Layette	26572	1999	$10.00		Krissy
Baby Krissy Layette (black)	26806	1999	$10.00		Krissy
Baby Sister Kelly	12489	1995	$12.00		Kelly
Baby Sister Kelly (black)	13256	1995	$12.00		Kelly
Babysitter Courtney	9434	1991	$20.00		Courtney
Babysitter Kevin	9324	1991	$18.00		Kevin
Babysitter Christie	9434	1991	$20.00		Christie
Baker Chelsie	24594	1999	$5.00	Kelly Club	Chelsie
Ballerina Cara	9528	1976	$80.00		Cara
Ballerina Deidre	18914	1998	$5.00		Deidre
Ballerina Melody	18654	1998	$5.00		Melody
Baker Nia	24605	1999	$5.00		Nia
Basketball Kevin	4713	1993	$25.00		Kevin
Bath Time Fun Kelly	14552	1996	$10.00		Kelly
Bath Time Fun Kelly (black)	14553	1996	$10.00		Kelly
Baywatch Teresa	13201	1995	$40.00		Teresa
Beach Blast Christie	3253	1989	$20.00		Christie
Beach Blast Miko	3244	1989	$20.00		Miko
Beach Blast Shani	5774	1991	$20.00		Shani
Beach Blast Steven	3251	1989	$20.00		Steven
Beach Blast Teresa	3249	1989	$20.00		Teresa
Beach Dazzle Asha	5777	1992	$10.00	Toys "R" Us	Asha
Beach Dazzle Nichelle	5775	1992	$15.00	Toys "R" Us	Nichelle

Item	Number	Year	Value	Specials	Doll
Beach Dazzle Plus 2 Fashions Shani		1992	$37.00	Sears	Shani
Beach Dazzle Shani	3633	1988	$20.00		Shani
Beach Dazzle Shani	5774	1992	$15.00	Toys "R" Us	Shani
Beach Dazzle Shani	N/A	1992	$40.00	Sears	Shani
Beach Streak Asha	3457	1993	$10.00	Toys "R" Us	Asha
Beach Streak Jamal	3802	1993	$15.00	Toys "R" Us	Jamal
Beach Streak Nichelle	3456	1993	$15.00	Toys "R" Us	Nichelle
Beach Streak Shani	3428	1993	$15.00	Toys "R" Us	Shani
Beautiful Bride Tracy	4103	1982	$40.00		Tracy
Beauty Secrets Christie	1295	1980	$50.00		Christie
Becky	14850	1996	$5.00	Li'l Friends of Kelly	Becky
Becky	14853	1996	$6.00	Li'l Friends of Kelly	Becky
Benetton Christie	9407	1991	$30.00		Christie
Benetton Kira	9409	1990	$30.00		Kira
Benetton Marina	9409	1991	$40.00		Marina
Benetton Shopping Christie	4887	1992	$35.00		Christie
Benetton Shopping Marina	4898	1992	$65.00		Marina
Benetton Shopping Teresa	4880	1992	$80.00		Teresa
Benetton Teresa	9408	1991	$50.00		Teresa
Beyond Pink Christie	20019	1998	$15.00		Christie
Beyond Pink Teresa	20018	1998	$10.00		Teresa
Bicyclin' Janet	16735	1997	$15.00		Janet
Bicyclin' Stacie	16734	1997	$15.00		Stacie
Bicyclin' Whitney	16736	1997	$15.00		Whitney
Biker Baby Belinda	24602	1999	$5.00	Kelly Club	Belinda
Birthday Deidre	17323	1998	$5.00		Deidre
Blossom Beauty Teresa	17035	1997	$20.00		Teresa
Bowling Party Janet	22014	1999	$13.00		Janet
Bowling Party Stacie	22013	1999	$13.00		Stacie
Bowling Party Whitney	22015	1999	$13.00		Whitney
Brad Doll (bendable leg)	1142	1970	$200.00		Brad
Brad Doll (bendable leg, darker skin)	1142	1971	$200.00		Brad
Brandy	24502	1999	$17.00	Friends of Barbie	Brandy
Bubble Fairy Christie	2088	1999	$10.00		Christie
Bubble Fairy Teresa	22089	1999	$11.00		Teresa
Buffy and Mrs. Beasley	3577	1968	$200.00		Buffy
Busy Francie	3313	1972	$425.00		Francie
Busy Steffie	3312	1972	$350.00		Steffie
Busy Talking Steffie	1186	1972	$375.00		Steffie
Butterfly Art Christie	20360	1998	$10.00		Christie
Butterfly Art Kira	20362	1998	$10.00		Kira
Butterfly Art Steven	22996	1999	$10.00		Steven
Butterfly Art Teresa	20361	1998	$11.00		Teresa
Butterfly Catcher Chelsie	18911	1998	$5.00		Chelsie
Butterfly Princess Teresa	13238	1995	$20.00		Teresa
California Christie	4443	1987	$30.00		Christie
California Dream Christie	4443	1988	$25.00		Christie
California Dream Midge	4442	1988	$25.00		Midge
California Dream Teresa	5503	1988	$25.00		Teresa
California Midge	4442	1987	$30.00		Midge
California Teresa	5503	1988	$20.00		Teresa
Camp Midge	11077	1994	$20.00		Midge
Camp Teresa	11078	1994	$20.00		Teresa
Carla	7377	1976	$100.00		Carla
Casey (baggie)	9000	1975	$150.00		Casey

Item	Number	Year	Value	Specials	Doll
Casey (TNT) (blonde)	1180	1967	$350.00		Casey
Casey (TNT) (brunette)	1180	1967	$350.00		Casey
Cheerleader Jazzie	3631	1989	$25.00		Jazzie
Cheerleading Christie	3933	1993	$20.00		Christie
Cheerleading Courtney	3933	1993	$20.00		Courtney
Chelsie	14852	1997	$6.00	Li'l Friends of Kelly	Chelsie
Chelsie	16004	1996	$6.00	Li'l Friends of Kelly	Chelsie
Chelsie Artist	20854	1998	$5.00	Li'l Friends of Kelly	Chelsie
Cher	29049	2000	$40.00	Timeless Treasures	Cher
Chris (blonde)	3570	1967	$250.00		Chris
Chris (brunette)	3570	1967	$250.00		Chris
Club California Christie	4443	1988	$30.00		Christie
Coat Deidre	18318	1998	$5.00		Deidre
Cookin' Goodies Tutti	3559	1967	$300.00		Tutti
Cool Blading Christie	26230	2000	$15.00		Christie
Cool Blading Teresa	26231	2000	Retail		Teresa
Cool Clips Christie	26426	2000	$14.00		Christie
Cool Clips Teresa	26427	2000	$17.00		Teresa
Cool Crimp Christie	11548	1994	$15.00		Christie
Cool Crimp Courtney	11548	1994	$20.00		Courtney
Cool Crimp Kevin	11549	1994	$20.00		Kevin
Cool Skating Christie	16230	1999	$20.00		Christie
Cool Skating Christie	26230	2000	$15.00		Christie
Cool Skating Teresa	26231	1999	$20.00		Teresa
Cool Skating Teresa	26424	2000	$15.00		Teresa
Cool Teen Courtney	19668	1998	$10.00		Courtney
Cool Teen Nikki	19667`	1998	$15.00		Nikki
Cool Times Christie	3217	1989	$25.00		Christie
Cool Times Midge	3216	1989	$25.00		Midge
Cool Times Teresa	3218	1989	$25.00		Teresa
Cool Tops Christie	7079	1990	$20.00		Christie
Cool Tops Courtney	7079	1990	$20.00		Courtney
Cool Tops Kevin	9351	1990	$20.00		Kevin
Country Western Star Teresa	12097	1994	$30.00		Teresa
Cowgirl Chelsie	20856	1998	$5.00		Chelsie
Cowgirl Deidre	20861	1998	$5.00	Li'l Friends of Kelly	Deidre
Cowgirl Kelly	50733	2001	$20.00	Toys "R" Us	Kelly
Cuddle Soft Kelly	23966	1999	$45.00		Kelly
Cuddly Soft Kelly	23966	1999	$45.00		Kelly
Cuddly Soft Kelly (black)	23967`	1999	$45.00		Kelly
Dance Club Devon	3513	1989	$55.00		Devon
Dance Club Kayla	3512	1989	$65.00		Kayla
Dance Moves Midge	13085	1995	$25.00		Midge
Dance Moves Teresa	13084	1995	$15.00		Teresa
Deidra	16466	1996	$5.00	Li'l Friends of Kelly	Deidre
Deidra	17323	1997	$6.00	Li'l Friends of Kelly	Deidre
Deluxe Quick Curl Cara	9220	1976	$75.00		Cara
Deluxe Quick Curl P.J.	9218	1976	$130.00		P.J.
Diving Midge	18982	1998	$10.00		Midge
Dream Date P.J.	5869	1983	$40.00		P.J.
Dress-Up Deidre	21641	1998	$5.00	Kelly Club	Deidre
Earring Magic Midge	10256	1993	$25.00		Midge
Eatin' Fun Kelly	18582	1997	$8.00		Kelly
Eatin' Fun Kelly (black)	18596	1997	$8.00		Kelly
Fashion Party Courtney	29104	2000	$14.00		Courtney

Item	Number	Year	Value	Specials	Doll
Fashion Party Nikki		2000	$14.00		Nikki
Fashion Photo Christie	2324	1978	$70.00		Christie
Fashion Photo P.J.	2323	1978	$90.00		P.J.
Flashlight Fun Janet	19670	1998	$12.00		Janet
Flashlight Fun Stacie	19669	1998	$15.00		Stacie
Flashlight Fun Whitney	19671	1998	$15.00		Whitney
Flip 'n Dive Christie	18981	1998	$15.00		Christie
Flip 'n Dive Teresa	18983	1998	$20.00		Teresa
Florida Vacation Christie	20536	1998	$10.00		Christie
Florida Vacation Midge	20538	1998	$6.00		Midge
Florida Vacation Steven	20497	1999	$5.00		Steven
Florida Vacation Teresa	20537	1998	$6.00		Teresa
Flying Butterfly Teresa	50347	2000	$13.00		Teresa
Flying Hero Kira	14032	1996	$20.00		Kira
Flying Hero Teresa	14031	1996	$20.00		Teresa
Francie (1st issue, black, red oxidized)	1100	1967	$1,600.00		Francie
Francie (2nd issue, black, dark brown)	1100	1967	$1,300.00		Francie
Francie (baggie)	7699	1975	$125.00		Francie
Francie (bendable leg, blonde)	1130	1966	$375.00		Francie
Francie (bendable leg, brunette)	1130	1966	$375.00		Francie
Francie (no bangs, blonde)	1170	1971	$1,500.00		Francie
Francie (no bangs, brunette)	1170	1971	$1,500.00		Francie
Francie (straight leg, blonde)	1140	1966	$350.00		Francie
Francie (straight leg, brunette)	1140	1966	$350.00		Francie
Free Moving Cara	7283	1975	$125.00		Cara
Free Moving Curtis	7282	1975	$175.00		Curtis
Free Moving P.J.	7281	1975	$90.00		P.J.
Gad About Francie	14608	1996	$45.00		Francie
Gardener Jenny	18653	1998	$5.00		Jenny
Gardening Melody	22206	1998	$5.00		Melody
Generation Girl Ana (3 versions)	20972	1998	$20.00	Generation Girls	Ana
Generation Girl Blaine	26111	2000	$20.00	Generation Girls	Blaine
Generation Girl Chelsie	20967	1999	$15.00	Generation Girls	Chelsie
Generation Girl Chelsie	26848	2000	$20.00	Generation Girls	Chelsie
Generation Girl Lara	25769	2000	$20.00	Generation Girls	Lara
Generation Girl Lara	20968	1999	$20.00	Generation Girls	Lara
Generation Girl Mari	26112	2000	$20.00	Generation Girls	Mari
Generation Girl Mari w/book	25112	1999	$20.00	Generation Girls	Mari
Generation Girl Nichelle	20966	1999	$15.00	Generation Girls	Nichelle
Generation Girl Nichelle	25767	1999	$20.00	Generation Girls	Nichelle
Generation Girl Nichelle	25767	2000	$20.00	Generation Girls	Nichelle
Generation Girl Tori	20969	1999	$15.00	Generation Girls	Tori
Generation Girl Tori	25768	1999	$20.00	Generation Girls	Tori
Generation Girl Tori	25768	2000	$20.00	Generation Girls	Tori
Generation Girl Tori w/book	48573	1999	$20.00	Generation Girls	Tori
Glam 'n Groom	26253	2000	$15.00		Teresa
Glam 'n Groom Christie	26252	2000	$15.00		Christie
Glitter Beach Christie	4907	1993	$12.00		Christie
Glitter Beach Jazzie	4935	1993	$12.00		Jazzie
Glitter Beach Kira	4924	1993	$15.00		Kira
Glitter Beach Steven	4918	1993	$12.00		Steven
Glitter Beach Teresa	4921	1993	$12.00		Teresa
Gold Medal Gymnast P.J.	7263	1975	$120.00		P.J.
Golden Dream Christie	3249	1981	$45.00		Christie
Goldilocks and the Three Bears	29605	2000	$19.00		Kelly

Item	Number	Year	Value	Specials	Doll
Golfer Liana	24601	1999	$5.00	Kelly Club	Liana
Grand Gala Teresa	17239	1997	$20.00	Toys "R" Us	Teresa
Growin' Pretty Hair Francie	1129	1970	$275.00		Francie
Growin' Pretty Hair Francie (extra hair piece)	1074	1971	$300.00		Francie
Growing Up Ginger	9222	1976	$150.00		Ginger
Gym Marisa	18992	1998	$5.00		Marisa
Gymnast Janet	14611	1996	$12.00		Janet
Gymnast P.J.	7263	1974	$50.00		P.J.
Gymnast Stacie	14609	1996	$12.00		Stacie
Gymnast Stacie	16568	1996	$20.00	JCPenney	Stacie
Gymnast Whitney	14610	1996	$12.00		Whitney
Hair Happenin's Francie	1122	1970	$400.00		Francie
Haircut Tommy	22012	1999	$6.00		Tommy
Haircut Tommy (black)	22017	1999	$6.00		Tommy
Hansel & Gretel	28539	2000	$19.00		Kelly & Tommy
Happenin' Hair Christie	22883	1999	$12.00		Christie
Happenin' Hair Teresa	22884	1999	$12.00		Teresa
Happy Meal Janet	11477	1994	$25.00		Janet
Happy Meal Stacie	11474	1994	$25.00		Stacie
Happy Meal Todd	11475	1994	$25.00		Todd
Happy Meal Whitney	11476	1994	$25.00		Whitney
Hawaii Christie	24615	1999	$5.00		Christie
Hawaii Midge	24617	1999	$5.00		Midge
Hawaii Steven	24620	1999	$5.00		Steven
Hawaii Steven	24620	2000	$5.00		Steven
Hawaii Teresa	24618	1999	$5.00		Teresa
Hawaiian Fun Christie	5944	1991	$20.00		Christie
Hawaiian Fun Jazzie	9294	1991	$20.00		Jazzie
Hawaiian Fun Kira	5943	1991	$20.00		Kira
Hawaiian Fun Steven	5945	1991	$20.00		Steven
High School Chelsie	3698	1989	$30.00		Chelsie
High School Dude	3637	1989	$30.00		Dude
High School Jazzie	3635	1989	$30.00		Jazzie
High School Stacie	3636	1989	$25.00		Stacie
Hollywood Hair Teresa	2316	1993	$30.00		Teresa
Hollywood Nails Christie		1999	$12.00		Christie
Hollywood Nails Teresa	24244	1999	$12.00		Teresa
Hot Skatin' Midge	13393	1995	$20.00		Midge
Hula Hair Teresa	17049	1997	$15.00		Teresa
I Dream of Jeannie	29913	2000	$50.00		Jeannie
I'm the School Photographer Becky	20202	1998	$15.00		Becky
In-Line Skating Midge	15475	1996	$20.00	FAO Schwarz	Midge
Island Fun Christie	4092	1988	$20.00		Christie
Island Fun Miko	4065	1988	$20.00		Miko
Island Fun Steven	4093	1988	$20.00		Steven
Island Fun Teresa	4117	1988	$20.00		Teresa
Jamal	7795	1992	$30.00	Toys "R" Us	Jamal
Jenny	16467	1996	$5.00	Li'l Friends of Kelly	Jenny
Jenny Hawaiian	20858	1998	$5.00	Li'l Friends of Kelly	Jenny
Jenny Sunflower	18913	1998	$5.00	Li'l Friends of Kelly	Jenny
Jester Jenny	24598	1999	$5.00		Jenny
Jewel Hair Mermaid Midge	14589	1996	$20.00		Midge
Jewel Hair Mermaid Teresa	14588	1996	$20.00		Teresa
Jewel Secrets Whitney	3179	1987	$55.00		Whitney
Kayla Back to School	20855	1998	$5.00	Li'l Friends of Kelly	Kayla

Item	Number	Year	Value	Specials	Doll
Kayla Dress Up	20859	1998	$5.00	Li'l Friends of Kelly	Kayla
Keeya African Dress (Kwanzaa)	18917	1998	$5.00	Li'l Friends of Kelly	Keeya
Keeya Back to School	21642	1998	$5.00	Li'l Friends of Kelly	Keeya
Kelly	12489	1995	$10.00	Li'l Sisters of Barbie	Kelly
Kelly & Ginger	19810	1998	$25.00		Kelly
Kelly (black)	13256	1995	$10.00		Kelly
Kelly as Lullaby Munchkin	25818	1999	$6.00	Wizard of Oz	Kelly
Kelly Superslide	24645	1999	$15.00		Kelly
Kelly Superslide (black)	24749	1999	$15.00		Kelly
Kevin	9325	1991	$25.00		Kevin
Kissing Christie	2955	1980	$65.00		Christie
Kwanzaa Kayla	24606	2000	$5.00		Kayla
Lemonade Stand Maria	24593	1999	$5.00	Kelly Club	Maria
Lemonade Stand Tamika	24604	1999	$5.00	Kelly Club	Tamika
Lights 'n Lace Christie	9728	1991	$30.00		Christie
Lights 'n Lace Teresa	9727	1991	$30.00		Teresa
Little Swimmer Marisa	24600	1999	$5.00	Kelly Club	Marisa
Live Action Christie	1175	1971	$240.00		Christie
Live Action on Stage P.J.	1153	1971	$225.00		P.J.
Live Action P.J. (baggie)	1156	1973	$125.00		P.J.
Live Action P.J. (no stage) (mint)	1156	1971	$100.00		P.J.
Living Fluff	1143	1971	$225.00		Fluff
Locket Surprise Kayla	11209	1994	$20.00		Kayla
Love 'n Care Kelly	27039	2000	$10.00		Kelly
Malibu Christie	7745	1973	$60.00		Christie
Malibu Christie	7745	1978	$50.00		Christie
Malibu Francie	1068	1973	$45.00		Francie
Malibu Francie	1068	1978	$30.00		Francie
Malibu Francie (new box)	1068	1975	$110.00		Francie
Malibu Francie (new rose box)	1068	1976	$55.00		Francie
Malibu P.J. (new box)	1187	1975	$110.00		P.J.
Malibu P.J. (new rose box)	7281	1976	$75.00		P.J.
Malibu Sunset Christie	7745	1973	$53.00		Christie
Malibu Sunset Francie	1068	1971	$60.00		Francie
Malibu Sunset P.J.	1187	1971	$80.00		P.J.
Malibu SunSet Christie (new box)	7745	1975	$85.00		Christie
Malibu SunSet Christie (new rose box)	7745	1976	$85.00		Christie
Maria Flower Girl	20857	1999	$5.00	Li'l Friends of Kelly	Maria
Marisa	16002	1996	$5.00	Li'l Friends of Kelly	Marisa
Me and My Dog Tutti	3558	1966	$300.00		Tutti
Melody	14854	1993	$10.00	Li'l Friends of Kelly	Melody
Melody	16003	1996	$5.00	Li'l Friends of Kelly	Melody
Melody	16003	1997	$6.00	Li'l Friends of Kelly	Melody
Melody Bunny	18912	1998	$5.00	Li'l Friends of Kelly	Melody
Melody in Pink Tutti #1	3555	1966	$275.00		Tutti
Melody in Pink Tutti #2 (different dress)	3555	1966	$275.00	Li'l Friends of Kelly	Tutti
Mickey's Toontown Stacie	11587	1993	$35.00	Disney	Stacie
Midge (bendable leg, blonde)	1080	1965	$500.00		Midge
Midge (bendable leg, brunette)	1080	1965	$550.00		Midge
Midge (straight leg, blonde)	860	1963	$225.00		Midge
Midge (straight leg, brunette)	860	1963	$225.00		Midge
Midge (straight leg, no freckles)	860	1963	$400.00		Midge
Midge (straight leg, titian)	860	1963	$225.00		Midge
Midge (straight leg, with teeth)	860	1963	$350.00		Midge
Millennium Princess Teresa	25504	1999	$40.00	Toys "R" Us	Teresa

Item	Number	Year	Value	Specials	Doll
Movie Star Christie	26428	1999	$20.00		Christie
Movie Star Teresa		2000	$15.00		Teresa
Movin' Groovin' Kira	17717	1997	$12.00		Kira
Movin' Groovin' Teresa	17716	1997	$14.00		Teresa
Movin' Groovin' Christie	17715	1997	$15.00		Christie
New 'n Groovy Talking P.J.	1113	1969	$150.00		P.J.
Nia Playtime	20860	1998	$5.00	Li'l Friends of Kelly	Nia
Nichelle	1751	1991	$25.00	Toys "R" Us	Nichelle
Night Night Sleep Tight Tutti	3553	1966	$275.00		Tutti
Nsync Christie w/CD	50535	2000	$19.00		Christie
Nsync Teresa w/CD	50536	2000	$19.00		Teresa
Nurse Whitney	4405	1987	$80.00		Whitney
Ocean Friends Kira	15431	1996	$15.00		Kira
Ocean Friends Marina	15431	1996	$20.00		Marina
Pajama Fun Courtney	24992	1999	$13.00		Courtney
Pajama Fun Nikki	24993	1999	$13.00		Nikki
Paralympic Champion Becky	24662	1999	$20.00		Becky
Partners in Print	1293	1967	$500.00		Francie
Party Dress Marisa	18036	1998	$5.00		Marisa
Party 'n Play Stacie	5411	1993	$20.00		Stacie
Party 'n Play Stacie (black)	4115	1993	$20.00		Stacie
Party 'n Play Todd	7903	1993	$20.00		Todd
Partytime Teresa	12244	1994	$25.00	Toys "R" Us	Teresa
Pearl Beach Christie	18578	1997	$5.00		Christie
Pearl Beach Christie Easter Basket	25381	1999	$15.00	Supermarket	Christie
Pearl Beach Kira	18580	1997	$10.00		Kira
Pearl Beach Steven	18581	1997	$10.00		Steven
Pearl Beach Teresa	18579	1997	$10.00		Teresa
Pearl Beach Teresa Easter Basket	25381	1999	$15.00	Supermarket	Teresa
Perfect Pink Teresa	19668	1998	$15.00		Teresa
Perfume Pretty Whitney	4557	1988	$40.00		Whitney
Pet Pals Christie	2710	1992	$20.00		Christie
Pet Pals Courtney	2710	1992	$25.00		Courtney
Pet Pals Kevin	2711	1992	$25.00		Kevin
Phone Fun Christie	14314	1996	$10.00		Christie
Phone Fun Courtney	14314	1996	$15.00		Courtney
Picnic Deidre	16466	1998	$5.00		Deidre
Picture Pockets Christie	28702	2000	$9.00		Christie
Picture Pockets Kira	28704	2000	$10.00		Kira
Picture Pockets Teresa	28703	2000	$10.00	Toys "R" Us	Teresa
Pilot Tommy	24595	1999	$5.00	Kelly Club	Tommy
Pink and Pretty Christie	3555	1982	$50.00		Christie
Pizza Party Christie	12943	1995	$15.00		Christie
Pizza Party Courtney	12943	1995	$12.00		Courtney
Pizza Party Kevin	12944	1995	$15.00		Kevin
Polly Pocket Janet	12984	1995	$12.00		Janet
Polly Pocket Stacie	12982	1995	$15.00		Stacie
Polly Pocket Whitney	12983	1995	$15.00		Whitney
Pool Fun Chelsie	17054	1997	$10.00		Chelsie
Pool Fun Kelly	17052	1997	$10.00		Kelly
Pool Fun Kelly (black)	17589	1997	$10.00		Kelly
Pool Fun Marisa	17053	1997	$10.00		Marisa
Pose 'n Play Tiff	1199	1972	$350.00		Tiff
Potty Training Kelly	16066	1996	$10.00		Kelly
Potty Training Kelly (black)	16067	1996	$10.00		Kelly

Item	Number	Year	Value	Specials	Doll
Pretty Reflections Christie	1295	1979	$85.00		Christie
Prince Ken	20491	1998	$18.00		Ken
Prince Tommy	24597	1999	$5.00		Tommy
Princess Kelly	24596	1999	$5.00		Kelly
Princess Kelly	25599	2000	$5.00		Kelly
Princess Kelly (black)		1999	$5.00		Kelly
Purple Panic Christie	19667	1998	$15.00		Christie
Puzzle Craze Teresa	20166	1998	$10.00	Wal-Mart	Teresa
Quick Curl Cara	7291	1975	$100.00		Cara
Quick Curl Francie	4222	1973	$175.00		Francie
Quick Curl Kelley	4221	1973	$160.00		Kelley
Quick Curl Miss America	8697	1976	$125.00		Miss America
Quick Curl Miss America (blonde)	8697	1974	$125.00		Miss America
Quick Curl Miss America (brunette)	8697	1973	$125.00		Miss America
Quinceanera Teresa	11928	1994	$25.00		Teresa
Raggedy Ann and Andy	24639	1999	$20.00		Kelly & Tommy
Rain or Shine Christie		2000	$15.00		Christie
Rain or Shine Teresa	29181	2000	$15.00		Teresa
Rappin' Rockin' Christie	3265	1992	$45.00		Christie
Rappin' Rockin' Teresa	3270	1992	$45.00		Teresa
Ricky (redhead, straight leg)	1090	1965	$150.00		Ricky
Rocker Dana	1196	1986	$40.00		Dana
Rocker Dana (revised)	3158	1987	$35.00		Dana
Rocker Dancin' Action Dana	3158	1986	$35.00		Dana
Rocker Dancin' Action Dee Dee	3160	1986	$35.00		Dee Dee
Rocker Dancin' Action Diva	3159	1986	$35.00		Diva
Rocker Dee Dee	1141	1986	$40.00		Dee Dee
Rocker Dee Dee (revised)	3160	1987	$35.00		Dee Dee
Rocker Derek	2428	1986	$60.00		Derek
Rocker Derek (revised)	3173	1987	$60.00		Derek
Rocker Diva	2427	1986	$55.00		Diva
Rocker Diva (revised)	3159	1987	$50.00		Diva
Rollerblade Christie	2217	1992	$30.00		Christie
Rollerblade Kira	2218	1992	$30.00		Kira
Rollerblade Teresa	2216	1992	$30.00		Teresa
Rosie O'Donnell	22016	1999	$25.00	Friends of Barbie	Rosie
Sailor Deidre	18319	1998	$5.00		Deidre
Sailor Melody	18035	1998	$5.00		Melody
Sailor Tommy	18037	1998	$6.00		Tommy
Senior Prom Midge (35th Anniversary)	18976	1998	$45.00	Toys "R" Us	Midge
Scott	1019	1980	$80.00		Scott
Scrub-a-dub-dub Krissy	26897	2000	$9.00		Krissy
Scrub-a-dub-dub Krissy (black)	27244	2000	$9.00		Krissy
Sea Holiday Midge	5476	1993	$40.00		Midge
Secret Messages Christie	26423	1999	$12.00		Christie
Secret Messages Teresa	26424	1999	$12.00		Teresa
Shani	1750	1991	$30.00	Toys "R" US	Shani
Share a Smile Becky	15761	1997	$25.00	Toys "R" Us	Becky
Share A Smile Christie	17372	1997	$20.00	Toys "R" Us	Christie
Shopping Time Teresa	18232	1997	$15.00	Wal-Mart	Teresa
Sit in Style Christie	23422	1999	$8.00		Christie
Sit in Style Kira	23424	1999	$8.00		Kira
Sit in Style Teresa	23423	1999	$8.00		Teresa
Ski Fun Midge	7513	1991	$30.00	Toys "R" Us	Midge
Skooter (bendable leg, blonde)	1120	1966	$300.00		Skooter

Item	Number	Year	Value	Specials	Doll
Skooter (bendable leg, titian)	1120	1966	$300.00		Skooter
Skooter (straight leg, blonde)	1040	1965	$150.00		Skooter
Skooter (straight leg, brunette)	1040	1965	$150.00		Skooter
Skooter (straight leg, titian)	1040	1965	$150.00		Skooter
Slumber Party Midge	13236	1995	$15.00		Midge
Slumber Party Teresa	13235	1995	$12.00		Teresa
Soccer Christie	20351	1999	$15.00		Christie
Soccer Kira	20352	1999	$15.00		Kira
Soccer Teresa	20207	1999	$17.00		Teresa
Songbird Teresa	14484	1996	$20.00		Teresa
Songbird Teresa (2nd version)	14484	1997	$15.00		Teresa
Soul Train Asha	10291	1993	$20.00	Toys "R" Us	Asha
Soul Train Jamal	10288	1993	$20.00	Toys "R" Us	Jamal
Soul Train Nichelle	10290	1993	$20.00	Toys "R" Us	Nichelle
Soul Train Shani	10289	1993	$25.00	Toys "R" Us	Shani
Sparkle Beach Christie	14355	1996	$10.00		Christie
Sparkle Beach Kira	14351	1996	$10.00		Kira
Sparkle Beach Steven	14353	1996	$10.00		Steven
Sparkle Beach Teresa	14354	1996	$10.00		Teresa
Splash 'n Color Christie	16174	1996	$6.00		Christie
Splash 'n Color Kira	16173	1996	$6.00		Kira
Splash 'n Color Kira	16173	1997	$10.00		Kira
Splash 'n Color Steven	16175	1996	$6.00		Steven
Splash 'n Color Teresa	16172	1996	$6.00		Teresa
Spots and Dots Teresa	10885	1993	$45.00	Toys "R" Us	Teresa
Stacie	4240	1992	$20.00		Stacie
Style Magic Christie	1288	1989	$30.00		Christie
Style Magic Whitney (brown)	1290	1989	$35.00		Whitney
Style Magic Whitney (brunette)	1288	1989	$35.00		Whitney
Sun Gold Malibu P.J.	1187	1984	$30.00		P.J.
Sun Jewel Kira	19056	1994	$10.00		Kira
Sun Jewel Shani	19058	1994	$10.00		Shani
Sun Jewel Steven	19059	1994	$10.00		Steven
Sun Jewel Teresa	19057	1994	$10.00		Teresa
Sun Lovin' Jazzie	4088	1990	$30.00		Jazzie
Sun Lovin' Malibu Christie	7745	1979	$40.00		Christie
Sun Lovin' Malibu P.J.	1187	1979	$40.00		P.J.
Sun Sensation Christie	1393	1992	$20.00		Christie
Sun Sensation Jazzie	5473	1992	$20.00		Jazzie
Sun Sensation Kira	1447	1992	$20.00		Kira
Sun Sensation Steven	1396	1992	$20.00		Steven
Sunflower Teresa	13489	1994	$20.00	Toys "R" Us	Teresa
Sunsational Christie	7745	1984	$35.00		Christie
Sunsational Malibu Christie	7745	1982	$30.00		Christie
Sunsational Malibu P.J.	1187	1982	$40.00		P.J.
Super Power Kira	14032	1995	$15.00		Kira
Super Size Christie	9839	1977	$250.00		Christie
Super Slide Kelly (black)	24749	2000	$10.00		Kelly
Super Teen Scott	1019	1979	$40.00		Scott
SuperStar Christie	9950	1978	$75.00		Christie
Surf City Christie	28418	2000	$5.00		Christie
Surf City Kira	28420	2000	$5.00		Kira
Surf City Midge	28421	2000	$5.00		Midge
Surf City Steven	28423	2000	$5.00		Steven
Surf City Teresa	28419	2000	$5.00		Teresa

Item	Number	Year	Value	Specials	Doll
Sweet Roses P.J.	7455	1984	$35.00		P.J.
Swim Suit Jazzie	3632	1989	$25.00		Jazzie
Swimming Champion Christie	25488	1999	$17.00		Christie
Swimming Champion Teresa	25489	1999	$15.00		Teresa
Swing-a-Ling Tutti	3560	1967	$300.00		Tutti
Talking Brad	1114	1970	$200.00		Brad
Talking Brad (darker skin)	1114	1971	$200.00		Brad
Talking Christie (brunette)	1126	1968	$250.00		Christie
Talking Christie (darker skin)	1126	1971	$200.00		Christie
Talking Christie (new window box)	1126	1969	$250.00		Christie
Talking Julia	1128	1969	$225.00		Julia
Talking Julia (darker skin)	1128	1971	$225.00		Julia
Talking P.J.	1113	1969	$325.00		P.J.
Talking P.J. (baggie, non-talking)	1113	1973	$110.00		P.J.
Talking Stacey (blonde)	1125	1968	$300.00		Stacey
Talking Stacey (titian)	1125	1968	$350.00		Stacey
Talking Stacey (titian)	1125	1970	$550.00		Stacey
Tamika Picnicker	18916	1998	$5.00	Li'l Friends of Kelly	Tamika
Teen Courtney	17354	1997	$15.00		Courtney
Teen Dance Jazzie	3634	1989	$40.00		Jazzie
Teen Nikki	17353	1997	$15.00		Nikki
Teen Scene Jazzie	5507	1991	$30.00		Jazzie
Teen Scene Sidney	20969	1999	$15.00		Sidney
Teen Time Christie	1952	1989	$30.00		Christie
TeenTime Courtney	1952	1989	$25.00		Courtney
Tennis Desiree	24607	1999	$5.00	Kelly Club	Deidre
Tennis Lorena	24603	1999	$5.00	Kelly Club	Lorena
The Beat Christie (Barbie & The Beat)	2754	1990	$25.00		Christie
The Beat Midge	2752	1990	$35.00		Midge
The Sensations Becky	4977	1988	$40.00		Becky
The Sensations Belinda	4976	1988	$40.00		Belinda
The Sensations Bopsy	4967	1988	$40.00		Bopsy
Tiny Steps Kelly	22226	1999	$11.00		Kelly
Tiny Steps Kelly (black)	22227	1999	$10.00		Kelly
Todd (titian)	3590	1967	$225.00		Todd
Todd Handsome Groom	4253	1983	$40.00		Todd
Tommy as Lollipop Munchkin	25819	1999	$6.00	Wizard of Oz	Tommy
Tommy as Mayor Munchkin	25817	1999	$6.00	Wizard of Oz	Tommy
Tommy Fireman	20852	1998	$5.00	Li'l Friends of Kelly	Tommy
Tommy Winter Fun	20853	1999	$5.00	Li'l Friends of Kelly	Tommy
Totally Hair Christie	1433	1991	$25.00	Toys "R" Us	Christie
Totally Hair Courtney	1433	1991	$25.00		Courtney
Totally Hair Whitney	7735	1992	$25.00	Toys "R" Us	Whitney
Totally Yo-Yo Courtney	22230	1999	$13.00		Courtney
Totally Yo-Yo Nikki	22229	1999	$13.00		Nikki
Tropical Miko	2056	1986	$20.00		Miko
Tropical Splash Christie	12451	1995	$10.00		Christie
Tropical Splash Kira	12449	1995	$10.00		Kira
Tropical Splash Steven	12452	1995	$10.00		Steven
Tropical Splash Teresa	12450	1995	$10.00		Teresa
Truly Scrumptious – Standard	1108	1969	$245.00		Truly
Truly Scrumptious – Talking	1107	1969	$270.00		Truly
Tutti (blonde)	3550	1966	$165.00		Tutti
Tutti (blonde, different dress)	3580	1967	$130.00		Tutti
Tutti (brunette)	3550	1966	$165.00		Tutti

Item	Number	Year	Value	Specials	Doll
Tutti (brunette, different dress)	3580	1967	$130.00		Tutti
Twiggy (TNT)	1185	1967	$350.00		Twiggy
Twirling Ballerina Teresa	15299	1996	$20.00		Teresa
Twirling Make-up Christie	18422	1998	$10.00		Christie
Twirling Make-up Teresa	18423	1998	$9.00		Teresa
Twist 'n Turn Christie	1119	1970	$350.00		Christie
Twist 'n Turn Francie (blonde)	1170	1967	$400.00		Francie
Twist 'n Turn Francie (blonde)	1170	1969	$325.00		Francie
Twist 'n Turn Francie (brunette)	1170	1967	$400.00		Francie
Twist 'n Turn Julia	1127	1969	$325.00		Julia
Twist 'n Turn P.J.	1118	1970	$225.00		P.J.
Twist 'n Turn Stacey (blonde)	1165	1968	$400.00		Stacey
Twist 'n Turn Stacey (blonde)	1165	1969	$500.00		Stacey
Twist 'n Turn Stacey (blonde)	1165	1970	$425.00		Stacey
Twist 'n Turn Stacey (titian)	1165	1968	$400.00		Stacey
Tye-Dye Christie	20505	1998	$10.00		Christie
Tye-Dye Teresa	20506	1998	$13.00		Teresa
Very Velvet Christie	20529	1998	$10.00		Christie
Very Velvet Kira	20531	1998	$20.00		Kira
Very Velvet Teresa	20530	1998	$20.00		Teresa
Walk Lively Miss America	3200	1972	$200.00		Miss America
Walk Lively Steffie	1183	1972	$350.00		Steffie
Walking Barbie & Baby Sister Krissy	22232	1999	$18.00		Krissy
Walking Barbie & Baby Sister Krissy (black)	22307	1999	$18.00		Krissy
Walking Jamie (blonde)	1132	1970	$400.00		Jamie
Walking My Dolly Tutti	3552	1966	$300.00		Tutti
Wedding Day Alan (2 box versions)	9607	1991	$30.00		Alan
Wedding Day Midge	9606	1991	$35.00		Midge
Western Fun Nia	9933	1990	$60.00		Nia
Western Stampin' Tara Lynn	10295	1993	$65.00		Tara Lynn
Wet 'n Wild Christie	4121	1990	$15.00		Christie
Wet 'n Wild Kira	4120	1990	$15.00		Kira
Wet 'n Wild Steven	4137	1990	$15.00		Steven
Wet 'n Wild Teresa	4136	1990	$15.00		Teresa
Wet 'n Wild Whitney	4136	1990	$15.00		Whitney
Wig Wardrobe Molded (head only)	1009	1965	$550.00		Midge
Wild Bunch Francie	17607	1997	$45.00		Francie
Wild Style Teresa	19263	1998	$20.00	Toys "R" Us	Teresa
Winter Coat Chelsie	18034	1999	$5.00		Chelsie
Winter Sport Midge	13514	1995	$35.00	Toys "R" Us	Midge
Wizard Melody	24599	1999	$5.00		Melody
WNBA Basketball Kira	20349	1998	$15.00		Kira
WNBA Basketball Teresa	20350	1998	$15.00		Teresa
WNBA Basketball Christie	20206	1998	$15.00		Christie
Workin' Out Christie	17319	1997	$15.00		Christie
Workin' Out Teresa	17318	1997	$10.00		Teresa
Workout Jazzie	3633	1989	$30.00		Jazzie
Yellowstone Kelley	7808	1974	$328.00		Kelley

Family & Friends Dolls

Listed by Doll

Doll	Item	Number	Year	Value	Specials
Alan	Wedding Day Alan (2 box versions)	9607	1991	$30.00	
Allan	Allan (bendable leg)	1010	1965	$550.00	
Allan	Allan (straight leg, redhead)	1000	1964	$150.00	
Ana	Generation Girl Ana (3 versions)	20972	1998	$20.00	Generation Girls
Asha	Asha	1752	1991	$25.00	Toys "R" Us
Asha	Asha I	12676	1994	$20.00	Toys "R" Us
Asha	Asha II	13532	1995	$20.00	Toys "R" Us
Asha	Asha III	15139	1996	$20.00	Toys "R" Us
Asha	Beach Dazzle Asha	5777	1992	$10.00	Toys "R" Us
Asha	Beach Streak Asha	3457	1993	$10.00	Toys "R" Us
Asha	Soul Train Asha	10291	1993	$20.00	Toys "R" Us
Becky	Becky	14850	1996	$5.00	Li'l Friends of Kelly
Becky	Becky	14853	1996	$6.00	Li'l Friends of Kelly
Becky	I'm the School Photographer Becky	20202	1998	$15.00	
Becky	Paralympic Champion Becky	24662	1999	$20.00	
Becky	Share a Smile Becky	15761	1997	$25.00	Toys "R" Us
Becky	The Sensations Becky	4977	1988	$40.00	
Belinda	Biker Baby Belinda	24602	1999	$5.00	Kelly Club
Belinda	The Sensations Belinda	4976	1988	$40.00	
Blaine	Generation Girl Blaine	26111	2000	$20.00	Generation Girls
Bopsy	The Sensations Bopsy	4967	1988	$40.00	
Brad	Brad Doll (bendable leg)	1142	1970	$200.00	
Brad	Brad Doll (bendable leg, darker skin)	1142	1971	$200.00	
Brad	Talking Brad	1114	1970	$200.00	
Brad	Talking Brad (darker skin)	1114	1971	$200.00	
Brandy	Brandy	24502	1999	$17.00	Friends of Barbie
Buffy	Buffy and Mrs. Beasley	3577	1968	$200.00	
Cara	Ballerina Cara	9528	1976	$80.00	
Cara	Deluxe Quick Curl Cara	9220	1976	$75.00	
Cara	Free Moving Cara	7283	1975	$125.00	
Cara	Quick Curl Cara	7291	1975	$100.00	
Carla	Carla	7377	1976	$100.00	
Casey	Casey (baggie)	9000	1975	$150.00	
Casey	Casey (TNT) (blonde)	1180	1967	$350.00	
Casey	Casey (TNT) (brunette)	1180	1967	$350.00	
Chelsie	Baker Chelsie	24594	1999	$5.00	Kelly Club
Chelsie	Butterfly Catcher Chelsie	18911	1998	$5.00	
Chelsie	Chelsie	14852	1997	$6.00	Li'l Friends of Kelly
Chelsie	Chelsie	16004	1996	$6.00	Li'l Friends of Kelly
Chelsie	Chelsie Artist	20854	1998	$5.00	Li'l Friends of Kelly
Chelsie	Cowgirl Chelsie	20856	1998	$5.00	
Chelsie	Generation Girl Chelsie	20967	1999	$15.00	Generation Girls
Chelsie	Generation Girl Chelsie	26848	2000	$20.00	Generation Girls
Chelsie	High School Chelsie	3698	1989	$30.00	
Chelsie	Pool Fun Chelsie	17054	1997	$10.00	
Chelsie	Winter Coat Chelsie	18034	1999	$5.00	
Cher	Cher	29049	2000	$40.00	Timeless Treasures
Chris	Chris (blonde)	3570	1967	$250.00	

Doll	Item	Number	Year	Value	Specials
Chris	Chris (brunette)	3570	1967	$250.00	
Christie	All American Christie	9425	1991	$25.00	
Christie	All Star Christie	9352	1990	$25.00	
Christie	Babysitter Christie	9434	1991	$20.00	
Christie	Beach Blast Christie	3253	1989	$20.00	
Christie	Beauty Secrets Christie	1295	1980	$50.00	
Christie	Benetton Christie	9407	1991	$30.00	
Christie	Benetton Shopping Christie	4887	1992	$35.00	
Christie	Beyond Pink Christie	20019	1998	$15.00	
Christie	Bubble Fairy Christie	2088	1999	$10.00	
Christie	Butterfly Art Christie	20360	1998	$10.00	
Christie	California Christie	4443	1987	$30.00	
Christie	California Dream Christie	4443	1988	$25.00	
Christie	Cheerleading Christie	3933	1993	$20.00	
Christie	Club California Christie	4443	1988	$30.00	
Christie	Cool Blading Christie	26230	2000	$15.00	
Christie	Cool Clips Christie	26426	2000	$14.00	
Christie	Cool Crimp Christie	11548	1994	$15.00	
Christie	Cool Skating Christie	16230	1999	$20.00	
Christie	Cool Skating Christie	26230	2000	$15.00	
Christie	Cool Times Christie	3217	1989	$25.00	
Christie	Cool Tops Christie	7079	1990	$20.00	
Christie	Fashion Photo Christie	2324	1978	$70.00	
Christie	Flip 'n Dive Christie	18981	1998	$15.00	
Christie	Florida Vacation Christie	20536	1998	$10.00	
Christie	Glam 'n Groom Christie	26252	2000	$15.00	
Christie	Glitter Beach Christie	4907	1993	$12.00	
Christie	Golden Dream Christie	3249	1981	$45.00	
Christie	Happenin' Hair Christie	22883	1999	$12.00	
Christie	Hawaii Christie	24615	1999	$5.00	
Christie	Hawaiian Fun Christie	5944	1991	$20.00	
Christie	Hollywood Nails Christie		1999	$12.00	
Christie	Island Fun Christie	4092	1988	$20.00	
Christie	Kissing Christie	2955	1980	$65.00	
Christie	Lights 'n Lace Christie	9728	1991	$30.00	
Christie	Live Action Christie	1175	1971	$240.00	
Christie	Malibu Christie	7745	1973	$60.00	
Christie	Malibu Christie	7745	1978	$50.00	
Christie	Malibu Sunset Christie	7745	1973	$53.00	
Christie	Malibu Sunset Christie (new box)	7745	1975	$85.00	
Christie	Malibu Sunset Christie (new rose box)	7745	1976	$85.00	
Christie	Movie Star Christie	26428	1999	$20.00	
Christie	Movin' Groovin' Christie	17715	1997	$15.00	
Christie	Nsync Christie w/CD	50535	2000	$19.00	
Christie	Pearl Beach Christie	18578	1997	$5.00	
Christie	Pearl Beach Christie Easter Basket	25381	1999	$15.00	Supermarket
Christie	Pet Pals Christie	2710	1992	$20.00	
Christie	Phone Fun Christie	14314	1996	$10.00	
Christie	Picture Pockets Christie	28702	2000	$9.00	
Christie	Pink and Pretty Christie	3555	1982	$50.00	
Christie	Pizza Party Christie	12943	1995	$15.00	
Christie	Pretty Reflections Christie	1295	1979	$85.00	
Christie	Purple Panic Christie	19667	1998	$15.00	
Christie	Rain or Shine Christie		2000	$15.00	
Christie	Rappin' Rockin' Christie	3265	1992	$45.00	

Doll	Item	Number	Year	Value	Specials
Christie	Rollerblade Christie	2217	1992	$30.00	
Christie	Secret Messages Christie	26423	1999	$12.00	
Christie	Share A Smile Christie	17372	1997	$20.00	Toys "R" Us
Christie	Sit in Style Christie	23422	1999	$8.00	
Christie	Soccer Christie	20351	1999	$15.00	
Christie	Sparkle Beach Christie	14355	1996	$10.00	
Christie	Splash 'n Color Christie	16174	1996	$6.00	
Christie	Style Magic Christie	1288	1989	$30.00	
Christie	Sun Lovin' Malibu Christie	7745	1979	$40.00	
Christie	Sun Sensation Christie	1393	1992	$20.00	
Christie	Sunsational Christie	7745	1984	$35.00	
Christie	Sensational Malibu Christie	7745	1982	$30.00	
Christie	Super Size Christie	9839	1977	$250.00	
Christie	SuperStar Christie	9950	1978	$75.00	
Christie	Surf City Christie	28418	2000	$5.00	
Christie	Swimming Champion Christie	25488	1999	$17.00	
Christie	Talking Christie (brunette)	1126	1968	$250.00	
Christie	Talking Christie (darker skin)	1126	1971	$200.00	
Christie	Talking Christie (new window box)	1126	1969	$250.00	
Christie	Teen Time Christie	1952	1989	$30.00	
Christie	The Beat Christie (Barbie & The Beat)	2754	1990	$25.00	
Christie	Totally Hair Christie	1433	1991	$25.00	Toys "R" Us
Christie	Tropical Splash Christie	12451	1995	$10.00	
Christie	Twirling Make-up Christie	18422	1998	$10.00	
Christie	Twist 'n Turn Christie	1119	1970	$350.00	
Christie	Tye-Dye Christie	20505	1998	$10.00	
Christie	Very Velvet Christie	20529	1998	$10.00	
Christie	Wet 'n Wild Christie	4121	1990	$15.00	
Christie	WNBA Basketball Christie	20206	1998	$15.00	
Christie	Workin' Out Christie	17319	1997	$15.00	
Christie	Sunsational Christie	7745	1984	$35.00	
Courtney	Babysitter Courtney	9434	1991	$20.00	
Courtney	Cheerleading Courtney	3933	1993	$20.00	
Courtney	Cool Crimp Courtney	11548	1994	$20.00	
Courtney	Cool Teen Courtney	19668	1998	$10.00	
Courtney	Cool Tops Courtney	7079	1990	$20.00	
Courtney	Fashion Party Courtney	29104	2000	$14.00	
Courtney	Pajama Fun Courtney	24992	1999	$13.00	
Courtney	Pet Pals Courtney	2710	1992	$25.00	
Courtney	Phone Fun Courtney	14314	1996	$15.00	
Courtney	Pizza Party Courtney	12943	1995	$12.00	
Courtney	Teen Courtney	17354	1997	$15.00	
Courtney	TeenTime Courtney	1952	1989	$25.00	
Courtney	Totally Hair Courtney	1433	1991	$25.00	
Courtney	Totally Yo-Yo Courtney	22230	1999	$13.00	
Curtis	Free Moving Curtis	7282	1975	$175.00	
Dana	Rocker Dana	1196	1986	$40.00	
Dana	Rocker Dana (revised)	3158	1987	$35.00	
Dana	Rocker Dancin' Action Dana	3158	1986	$35.00	
Dee Dee	Rocker Dancin' Action Dee Dee	3160	1986	$35.00	
Dee Dee	Rocker Dee Dee	1141	1986	$40.00	
Dee Dee	Rocker Dee Dee (revised)	3160	1987	$35.00	
Deidra	Deidra	16466	1996	$5.00	Li'l Friends of Kelly
Deidra	Deidra	17323	1997	$6.00	Li'l Friends of Kelly
Deidre	African Dress Deidre	18655	1998	$5.00	

Doll	Item	Number	Year	Value	Specials
Deidre	Ballerina Deidre	18914	1998	$5.00	
Deidre	Birthday Deidre	17323	1998	$5.00	
Deidre	Coat Deidre	18318	1998	$5.00	
Deidre	Cowgirl Deidre	20861	1998	$5.00	Li'l Friends of Kelly
Deidre	Dress-Up Deidre	21641	1998	$5.00	Kelly Club
Deidre	Picnic Deidre	16466	1998	$5.00	
Deidre	Sailor Deidre	18319	1998	$5.00	
Deidre	Tennis Deidre	24607	1999	$5.00	Kelly Club
Derek	Rocker Derek	2428	1986	$60.00	
Derek	Rocker Derek (revised)	3173	1987	$60.00	
Devon	Dance Club Devon	3513	1989	$55.00	
Diva	Rocker Dancin' Action Diva	3159	1986	$35.00	
Diva	Rocker Diva	2427	1986	$55.00	
Diva	Rocker Diva (revised)	3159	1987	$50.00	
Dude	High School Dude	3637	1989	$30.00	
Fluff	Living Fluff	1143	1971	$225.00	
Francie	30th Anniversary Francie	14608	1996	$65.00	
Francie	Busy Francie	3313	1972	$425.00	
Francie	Francie (1st issue, black, red oxidized)	1100	1967	$1,600.00	
Francie	Francie (2nd issue, black, dark brown)	1100	1967	$1,300.00	
Francie	Francie (baggie)	7699	1975	$125.00	
Francie	Francie (bendable leg, blonde)	1130	1966	$375.00	
Francie	Francie (bendable leg, brunette)	1130	1966	$375.00	
Francie	Francie (no bangs, blonde)	1170	1971	$1,500.00	
Francie	Francie (no bangs, brunette)	1170	1971	$1,500.00	
Francie	Francie (straight leg, blonde)	1140	1966	$350.00	
Francie	Francie (straight leg, brunette)	1140	1966	$350.00	
Francie	Gad About Francie	14608	1996	$45.00	
Francie	Growin' Pretty Hair Francie	1129	1970	$275.00	
Francie	Growin' Pretty Hair Francie (extra hair piece)	1074	1971	$300.00	
Francie	Hair Happenin's Francie	1122	1970	$400.00	
Francie	Malibu Francie	1068	1973	$45.00	
Francie	Malibu Francie	1068	1978	$30.00	
Francie	Malibu Francie (new box)	1068	1975	$110.00	
Francie	Malibu Francie (new rose box)	1068	1976	$55.00	
Francie	Malibu Sunset Francie	1068	1971	$60.00	
Francie	Partners in Print	1293	1967	$500.00	
Francie	Quick Curl Francie	4222	1973	$175.00	
Francie	Twist 'n Turn Francie (blonde)	1170	1967	$400.00	
Francie	Twist 'n Turn Francie (blonde)	1170	1969	$325.00	
Francie	Twist 'n Turn Francie (brunette)	1170	1967	$400.00	
Francie	Wild Bunch Francie	17607	1997	$45.00	
Ginger	Animal Lovin' Ginger		1998	$40.00	
Ginger	Growing Up Ginger	9222	1976	$150.00	
Jamal	Beach Streak Jamal	3802	1993	$15.00	Toys "R" Us
Jamal	Jamal	7795	1992	$30.00	Toys "R" Us
Jamal	Soul Train Jamal	10288	1993	$20.00	Toys "R" Us
Jamie	Walking Jamie (blonde)	1132	1970	$400.00	
Janet	Awesome Skateboard Janet	24991	1999	$13.00	
Janet	Bicyclin' Janet	16735	1997	$15.00	
Janet	Bowling Party Janet	22014	1999	$13.00	
Janet	Flashlight Fun Janet	19670	1998	$12.00	
Janet	Gymnast Janet	14611	1996	$12.00	
Janet	Happy Meal Janet	11477	1994	$25.00	
Janet	Polly Pocket Janet	12984	1995	$12.00	

Doll	Item	Number	Year	Value	Specials
Jazzie	Cheerleader Jazzie	3631	1989	$25.00	
Jazzie	Glitter Beach Jazzie	4935	1993	$12.00	
Jazzie	Hawaiian Fun Jazzie	9294	1991	$20.00	
Jazzie	High School Jazzie	3635	1989	$30.00	
Jazzie	Sun Lovin' Jazzie	4088	1990	$30.00	
Jazzie	Sun Sensation Jazzie	5473	1992	$20.00	
Jazzie	Swim Suit Jazzie	3632	1989	$25.00	
Jazzie	Teen Dance Jazzie	3634	1989	$40.00	
Jazzie	Teen Scene Jazzie	5507	1991	$30.00	
Jazzie	Workout Jazzie	3633	1989	$30.00	
Jeannie	I Dream of Jeannie	29913	2000	$50.00	
Jenny	Gardener Jenny	18653	1998	$5.00	
Jenny	Jenny	16467	1996	$5.00	Li'l Friends of Kelly
Jenny	Jenny Hawaiian	20858	1998	$5.00	Li'l Friends of Kelly
Jenny	Jenny Sunflower	18913	1998	$5.00	Li'l Friends of Kelly
Jenny	Jester Jenny	24598	1999	$5.00	
Julia	Talking Julia	1128	1969	$225.00	
Julia	Talking Julia (darker skin)	1128	1971	$225.00	
Julia	Twist 'n Turn Julia	1127	1969	$325.00	
Kayla	Dance Club Kayla	3512	1989	$65.00	
Kayla	Kayla Back to School	20855	1998	$5.00	Li'l Friends of Kelly
Kayla	Kayla Dress Up	20859	1998	$5.00	Li'l Friends of Kelly
Kayla	Kwanzaa Kayla	24606	2000	$5.00	
Kayla	Locket Surprise Kayla	11209	1994	$20.00	
Keeya	Keeya African Dress (Kwanzaa)	18917	1998	$5.00	Li'l Friends of Kelly
Keeya	Keeya Back to School	21642	1998	$5.00	Li'l Friends of Kelly
Kelley	Quick Curl Kelley	4221	1973	$160.00	
Kelley	Yellowstone Kelley	7808	1974	$328.00	
Kelly	Amusement Park Kelly	28391	2000	$5.00	
Kelly	Baby Sister Kelly	12489	1995	$12.00	
Kelly	Baby Sister Kelly (black)	13256	1995	$12.00	
Kelly	Bath Time Fun Kelly	14552	1996	$10.00	
Kelly	Bath Time Fun Kelly (black)	14553	1996	$10.00	
Kelly	Cowgirl Kelly	50733	2001	$20.00	Toys "R" Us
Kelly	Cuddle Soft Kelly	23966	1999	$45.00	
Kelly	Cuddly Soft Kelly	23966	1999	$45.00	
Kelly	Cuddly Soft Kelly (black)	23967	1999	$45.00	
Kelly	Eatin' Fun Kelly	18582	1997	$8.00	
Kelly	Eatin' Fun Kelly (black)	18596	1997	$8.00	
Kelly	Goldilocks and the Three Bears	29605	2000	$19.00	
Kelly	Kelly	12489	1995	$10.00	Li'l Sisters of Barbie
Kelly	Kelly & Ginger	19810	1998	$25.00	
Kelly	Kelly (black)	13256	1995	$10.00	
Kelly	Kelly as Lullaby Munchkin	25818	1999	$6.00	Wizard of Oz
Kelly	Kelly Superslide	24645	1999	$15.00	
Kelly	Love 'n Care	27039	2000	$10.00	
Kelly	Pool Fun Kelly	17052	1997	$10.00	
Kelly	Pool Fun Kelly (black)	17589	1997	$10.00	
Kelly	Potty Training Kelly	16066	1996	$10.00	
Kelly	Potty Training Kelly (black)	16067	1996	$10.00	
Kelly	Princess Kelly	24596	1999	$5.00	
Kelly	Princess Kelly	25599	2000	$5.00	
Kelly	Princess Kelly (black)		1999	$5.00	
Kelly	Super Slide Kelly (black)	24749	2000	$10.00	
Kelly	Tiny Steps Kelly	22226	1999	$11.00	

Doll	Item	Number	Year	Value	Specials
Kelly	Tiny Steps Kelly (black)	22227	1999	$10.00	
Kelly & Tommy	Hansel & Gretel	28539	2000	$19.00	
Kelly & Tommy	Raggedy Ann and Andy	24639	1999	$20.00	
Ken	Prince Ken	20491	1998	$18.00	
Kevin	Babysitter Kevin	9324	1991	$18.00	
Kevin	Basketball Kevin	4713	1993	$25.00	
Kevin	Cool Crimp Kevin	11549	1994	$20.00	
Kevin	Cool Tops Kevin	9351	1990	$20.00	
Kevin	Pet Pals Kevin	2711	1992	$25.00	
Kevin	Pizza Party Kevin	12944	1995	$15.00	
Kevin	Kevin	9325	1991	$25.00	
Kira	All American Kira	9427	1991	$25.00	Reebok
Kira	Benetton Kira	9409	1990	$30.00	
Kira	Butterfly Art Kira	20362	1998	$10.00	
Kira	Flying Hero Kira	14032	1996	$20.00	
Kira	Glitter Beach Kira	4924	1993	$15.00	
Kira	Hawaiian Fun Kira	5943	1991	$20.00	
Kira	Movin' Groovin' Kira	17717	1997	$12.00	
Kira	Ocean Friends Kira	15431	1996	$15.00	
Kira	Pearl Beach Kira	18580	1997	$10.00	
Kira	Picture Pockets Kira	28704	2000	$10.00	Toys "R" Us
Kira	Rollerblade Kira	2218	1992	$30.00	
Kira	Sit in Style Kira	23424	1999	$8.00	
Kira	Soccer Kira	20352	1999	$15.00	
Kira	Sparkle Beach Kira	14351	1996	$10.00	
Kira	Splash 'n Color Kira	16173	1996	$6.00	
Kira	Splash 'n Color Kira	16173	1997	$10.00	
Kira	Sun Jewel Kira	19056	1994	$10.00	
Kira	Sun Sensation Kira	1447	1992	$20.00	
Kira	Super Power Kira	14032	1995	$15.00	
Kira	Surf City Kira	28420	2000	$5.00	
Kira	Tropical Splash Kira	12449	1995	$10.00	
Kira	Very Velvet Kira	20531	1998	$20.00	
Kira	Wet 'n Wild Kira	4120	1990	$15.00	
Kira	WNBA Basketball Kira	20349	1998	$15.00	
Krissy	Baby Krissy Layette	26572	1999	$10.00	
Krissy	Baby Krissy Layette (black)	26806	1999	$10.00	
Krissy	Scrub-a-dub-dub Krissy	26897	2000	$9.00	
Krissy	Scrub-a-dub-dub Krissy (black)	27244	2000	$9.00	
Krissy	Walking Barbie & Baby Sister Krissy	22232	1999	$18.00	
Krissy	Walking Barbie & Baby Sister Krissy (black)	22307	1999	$18.00	
Lara	Generation Girl Lara	25769	2000	$20.00	Generation Girls
Lara	Generation Girl Lara	20968	1999	$20.00	Generation Girls
Liana	Golfer Liana	24601	1999	$5.00	Kelly Club
Lorena	Tennis Lorena	24603	1999	$5.00	Kelly Club
Mari	Generation Girl Mari	26112	2000	$20.00	Generation Girls
Mari	Generation Girl Mari w/book	25112	1999	$20.00	Generation Girls
Maria	Lemonade Stand Maria	24593	1999	$5.00	Kelly Club
Maria	Maria Flower Girl	20857	1999	$5.00	Li'l Friends of Kelly
Marina	Benetton Marina	9409	1991	$40.00	
Marina	Benetton Shopping Marina	4898	1992	$65.00	
Marina	Ocean Friends Marina	15431	1996	$20.00	
Marisa	Amusement Park Marisa	29200	2000	$5.00	Kelly Club
Marisa	Gym Marisa	18992	1998	$5.00	
Marisa	Little Swimmer Marisa	24600	1999	$5.00	Kelly Club

Doll	Item	Number	Year	Value	Specials
Marisa	Marisa	16002	1996	$5.00	Li'l Friends of Kelly
Marisa	Party Dress Marisa	18036	1998	$5.00	
Marisa	Pool Fun Marisa	17053	1997	$10.00	
Melody	Ballerina Melody	18654	1998	$5.00	
Melody	Gardening Melody	22206	1998	$5.00	
Melody	Melody	14854	1993	$10.00	Li'l Friends of Kelly
Melody	Melody	16003	1996	$5.00	Li'l Friends of Kelly
Melody	Melody	16003	1997	$6.00	Li'l Friends of Kelly
Melody	Melody Bunny	18912	1998	$5.00	Li'l Friends of Kelly
Melody	Sailor Melody	18035	1998	$5.00	
Melody	Wizard Melody	24599	1999	$5.00	
Midge	30th Anniversary Midge (porcelain)	7957	1993	$140.00	
Midge	All Star Midge	9360	1990	$30.00	
Midge	California Dream Midge	4442	1988	$25.00	
Midge	California Midge	4442	1987	$30.00	
Midge	Camp Midge	11077	1994	$20.00	
Midge	Cool Times Midge	3216	1989	$25.00	
Midge	Dance Moves Midge	13085	1995	$25.00	
Midge	Diving Midge	18982	1998	$10.00	
Midge	Earring Magic Midge	10256	1993	$25.00	
Midge	Florida Vacation Midge	20538	1998	$6.00	
Midge	Hawaii Midge	24617	1999	$5.00	
Midge	Hot Skatin' Midge	13393	1995	$20.00	
Midge	In-Line Skating Midge	15475	1996	$20.00	FAO Schwarz
Midge	Jewel Hair Mermaid Midge	14589	1996	$20.00	
Midge	Midge (bendable leg, blonde)	1080	1965	$500.00	
Midge	Midge (bendable leg, brunette)	1080	1965	$550.00	
Midge	Midge (blonde, straight leg)	860	1963	$225.00	
Midge	Midge (brunette, straight leg)	860	1963	$225.00	
Midge	Midge (no freckles, straight leg)	860	1963	$400.00	
Midge	Midge (titian, straight leg)	860	1963	$225.00	
Midge	Midge (with teeth, straight leg)	860	1963	$350.00	
Midge	Sea Holiday Midge	5476	1993	$40.00	
Midge	Senior Prom Midge (35th Anniversary)	18976	1998	$45.00	Toys "R" Us
Midge	Ski Fun Midge	7513	1991	$30.00	Toys "R" Us
Midge	Slumber Party Midge	13236	1995	$15.00	
Midge	Surf City Midge	28421	2000	$5.00	
Midge	The Beat Midge	2752	1990	$35.00	
Midge	Wedding Day Midge	9606	1991	$35.00	
Midge	Wig Wardrobe Molded (head only)	1009	1965	$550.00	
Midge	Winter Sport Midge	13514	1995	$35.00	Toys "R" Us
Miko	Beach Blast Miko	3244	1989	$20.00	
Miko	Island Fun Miko	4065	1988	$20.00	
Miko	Tropical Miko	2056	1986	$20.00	
Miss America	Quick Curl Miss America	8697	1976	$125.00	
Miss America	Quick Curl Miss America (blonde)	8697	1974	$125.00	
Miss America	Quick Curl Miss America (brunette)	8697	1973	$125.00	
Miss America	Walk Lively Miss America	3200	1972	$200.00	
Nia	Baker Nia	24605	1999	$5.00	
Nia	Nia Playtime	20860	1998	$5.00	Li'l Friends of Kelly
Nia	Western Fun Nia	9933	1990	$60.00	
Nichelle	Beach Dazzle Nichelle	5775	1992	$15.00	Toys "R" Us
Nichelle	Beach Streak Nichelle	3456	1993	$15.00	Toys "R" Us
Nichelle	Generation Girl Nichelle	20966	1999	$15.00	Generation Girls
Nichelle	Generation Girl Nichelle	25767	1999	$20.00	Generation Girls

Doll	Item	Number	Year	Value	Specials
Nichelle	Generation Girl Nichelle	25767	2000	$20.00	Generation Girls
Nichelle	Nichelle	1751	1991	$25.00	Toys "R" Us
Nichelle	Soul Train Nichelle	10290	1993	$20.00	Toys "R" Us
Nikki	Animal Lovin' Nikki	1352	1989	$30.00	
Nikki	Cool Teen Nikki	19667	1998	$15.00	
Nikki	Fashion Party Nikki		2000	$14.00	
Nikki	Pajama Fun Nikki	24993	1999	$13.00	
Nikki	Teen Nikki	17353	1997	$15.00	
Nikki	Totally Yo-Yo Nikki	22229	1999	$13.00	
P.J.	Deluxe Quick Curl P.J.	9218	1976	$130.00	
P.J.	Dream Date P.J.	5869	1983	$40.00	
P.J.	Fashion Photo P.J.	2323	1978	$90.00	
P.J.	Free Moving P.J.	7281	1975	$90.00	
P.J.	Gold Medal Gymnast P.J.	7263	1975	$120.00	
P.J.	Gymnast P.J.	7263	1974	$50.00	
P.J.	Live Action on Stage P.J.	1153	1971	$225.00	
P.J.	Live Action P.J. (baggie)	1156	1973	$125.00	
P.J.	Live Action P.J. (no stage) (mint)	1156	1971	$100.00	
P.J.	Malibu P.J. (new box)	1187	1975	$110.00	
P.J.	Malibu P.J. (new rose box)	7281	1976	$75.00	
P.J.	Malibu Sunset P.J.	1187	1971	$80.00	
P.J.	New 'n Groovy Talking P.J.	1113	1969	$150.00	
P.J.	Sun Gold Malibu P.J.	1187	1984	$30.00	
P.J.	Sun Lovin' Malibu P.J.	1187	1979	$40.00	
P.J.	Sunsational Malibu P.J.	1187	1982	$40.00	
P.J.	Sweet Roses P.J.	7455	1984	$35.00	
P.J.	Talking P.J.	1113	1969	$325.00	
P.J.	Talking P.J. (baggie, non-talking)	1113	1973	$110.00	
P.J.	Twist 'n Turn P.J.	1118	1970	$225.00	
Ricky	Ricky (redhead, straight leg)	1090	1965	$150.00	
Rosie	Rosie O'Donnell	22016	1999	$25.00	Friends of Barbie
Ryan	Amusement Park Ryan	28392	2000	$5.00	Kelly Club
Scott	Scott	1019	1980	$80.00	
Scott	Super Teen Scott	1019	1979	$40.00	
Shani	Beach Blast Shani	5774	1991	$20.00	
Shani	Beach Dazzle Plus 2 Fashions Shani		1992	$37.00	Sears
Shani	Beach Dazzle Shani	3633	1988	$20.00	
Shani	Beach Dazzle Shani	5774	1992	$15.00	Toys "R" Us
Shani	Beach Dazzle Shani	N/A	1992	$40.00	Sears
Shani	Beach Streak Shani	3428	1993	$15.00	Toys "R" Us
Shani	Shani	1750	1991	$30.00	Toys "R" Us
Shani	Soul Train Shani	10289	1993	$25.00	Toys "R" Us
Shani	Sun Jewel Shani	19058	1994	$10.00	
Skooter	Skooter (bendable leg, blonde)	1120	1966	$300.00	
Skooter	Skooter (bendable leg, titian)	1120	1966	$300.00	
Skooter	Skooter (straight leg, blonde)	1040	1965	$150.00	
Sidney	Teen Scene Sidney	20969	1999	$15.00	
Skooter	Skooter (straight leg, brunette)	1040	1965	$150.00	
Skooter	Skooter (straight leg, titian)	1040	1965	$150.00	
Stacey	Talking Stacey (blonde)	1125	1968	$300.00	
Stacey	Talking Stacey (titian)	1125	1968	$350.00	
Stacey	Talking Stacey (titian)	1125	1970	$550.00	
Stacey	Twist 'n Turn Stacey (blonde)	1165	1968	$400.00	
Stacey	Twist 'n Turn Stacey (blonde)	1165	1969	$500.00	
Stacey	Twist 'n Turn Stacey (blonde)	1165	1970	$425.00	

Doll	Item	Number	Year	Value	Specials
Stacey	Twist 'n Turn Stacey (titian)	1165	1968	$400.00	
Stacie	Awesome Skateboard Stacie	24644	1999	$11.00	
Stacie	Bicyclin' Stacie	16734	1997	$15.00	
Stacie	Bowling Party Stacie	22013	1999	$13.00	
Stacie	Flashlight Fun Stacie	19669	1998	$15.00	
Stacie	Gymnast Stacie	14609	1996	$12.00	
Stacie	Gymnast Stacie	16568	1996	$20.00	JCPenney
Stacie	Happy Meal Stacie	11474	1994	$25.00	
Stacie	High School Stacie	3636	1989	$25.00	
Stacie	Mickey's Toontown Stacie	11587	1993	$35.00	Disney
Stacie	Party 'n Play Stacie	5411	1993	$20.00	
Stacie	Party 'n Play Stacie (black)	4115	1993	$20.00	
Stacie	Polly Pocket Stacie	12982	1995	$15.00	
Stacie	Stacie	4240	1992	$20.00	
Steffie	Busy Steffie	3312	1972	$350.00	
Steffie	Busy Talking Steffie	1186	1972	$375.00	
Steffie	Walk Lively Steffie	1183	1972	$350.00	
Steven	Beach Blast Steven	3251	1989	$20.00	
Steven	Butterfly Art Steven	22996	1999	$10.00	
Steven	Florida Vacation Steven	20497	1999	$5.00	
Steven	Glitter Beach Steven	4918	1993	$12.00	
Steven	Hawaii Steven	24620	1999	$5.00	
Steven	Hawaii Steven	24620	2000	$5.00	
Steven	Hawaiian Fun Steven	5945	1991	$20.00	
Steven	Island Fun Steven	4093	1988	$20.00	
Steven	Pearl Beach Steven	18581	1997	$10.00	
Steven	Sparkle Beach Steven	14353	1996	$10.00	
Steven	Splash 'n Color Steven	16175	1996	$6.00	
Steven	Sun Jewel Steven	19059	1994	$10.00	
Steven	Sun Sensation Steven	1396	1992	$20.00	
Steven	Surf City Steven	28423	2000	$5.00	
Steven	Tropical Splash Steven	12452	1995	$10.00	
Steven	Wet 'n Wild Steven	4137	1990	$15.00	
Tamika	Lemonade Stand Tamika	24604	1999	$5.00	Kelly Club
Tamika	Tamika Picnicker	18916	1998	$5.00	Li'l Friends of Kelly
Tara Lynn	Western Stampin' Tara Lynn	10295	1993	$65.00	
Teresa	101 Dalmatians Teresa	17602	1997	$20.00	Toys "R" Us
Teresa	35th Anniversary Teresa	17617	1997	$25.00	Wal-Mart
Teresa	All American Teresa	9426	1991	$25.00	
Teresa	All Star Teresa	9353	1990	$30.00	
Teresa	Baywatch Teresa	13201	1995	$40.00	
Teresa	Beach Blast Teresa	3249	1989	$20.00	
Teresa	Benetton Shopping Teresa	4880	1992	$80.00	
Teresa	Benetton Teresa	9408	1991	$50.00	
Teresa	Beyond Pink Teresa	20018	1998	$10.00	
Teresa	Blossom Beauty Teresa	17035	1997	$20.00	
Teresa	Bubble Fairy Teresa	22089	1999	$11.00	
Teresa	Butterfly Art Teresa	20361	1998	$11.00	
Teresa	Butterfly Princess Teresa	13238	1995	$20.00	
Teresa	California Dream Teresa	5503	1988	$25.00	
Teresa	California Teresa	5503	1988	$20.00	
Teresa	Camp Teresa	11078	1994	$20.00	
Teresa	Cool Blading Teresa	26231	2000	Retail	
Teresa	Cool Clips Teresa	26427	2000	$17.00	
Teresa	Cool Skating Teresa	26231	1999	$20.00	

Doll	Item	Number	Year	Value	Specials
Teresa	Cool Skating Teresa	26424	2000	$15.00	
Teresa	Cool Times Teresa	3218	1989	$25.00	
Teresa	Country Western Star Teresa	12097	1994	$30.00	
Teresa	Dance Moves Teresa	13084	1995	$15.00	
Teresa	Flip 'n Dive Teresa	18983	1998	$20.00	
Teresa	Florida Vacation Teresa	20537	1998	$6.00	
Teresa	Flying Butterfly Teresa	50347	2000	$13.00	
Teresa	Flying Hero Teresa	14031	1996	$20.00	
Teresa	Glam 'n Groom	26253	2000	$15.00	
Teresa	Glitter Beach Teresa	4921	1993	$12.00	
Teresa	Grand Gala Teresa	17239	1997	$20.00	Toys "R" Us
Teresa	Happenin' Hair Teresa	22884	1999	$12.00	
Teresa	Hawaii Teresa	24618	1999	$5.00	
Teresa	Hollywood Hair Teresa	2316	1993	$30.00	
Teresa	Hollywood Nails Teresa	24244	1999	$12.00	
Teresa	Hula Hair Teresa	17049	1997	$15.00	
Teresa	Island Fun Teresa	4117	1988	$20.00	
Teresa	Jewel Hair Mermaid Teresa	14588	1996	$20.00	
Teresa	Lights 'n Lace Teresa	9727	1991	$30.00	
Teresa	Millennium Princess Teresa	25504	1999	$40.00	Toys "R" Us
Teresa	Movie Star Teresa		2000	$15.00	
Teresa	Movin' Groovin' Teresa	17716	1997	$14.00	
Teresa	Nsync Teresa w/CD	50536	2000	$19.00	
Teresa	Partytime Teresa	12244	1994	$25.00	Toys "R" Us
Teresa	Pearl Beach Teresa	18579	1997	$10.00	
Teresa	Pearl Beach Teresa Easter Basket	25381	1999	$15.00	Supermarket
Teresa	Perfect Pink Teresa	19668	1998	$15.00	
Teresa	Picture Pockets Teresa	28703	2000	$10.00	Toys "R" Us
Teresa	Puzzle Craze Teresa	20166	1998	$10.00	Wal-Mart
Teresa	Quinceanera Teresa	11928	1994	$25.00	
Teresa	Rain or Shine Teresa	29181	2000	$15.00	
Teresa	Rappin' Rockin' Teresa	3270	1992	$45.00	
Teresa	Rollerblade Teresa	2216	1992	$30.00	
Teresa	Secret Messages Teresa	26424	1999	$12.00	
Teresa	Shopping Time Teresa	18232	1997	$15.00	Wal-Mart
Teresa	Sit in Style Teresa	23423	1999	$8.00	
Teresa	Slumber Party Teresa	13235	1995	$12.00	
Teresa	Soccer Teresa	20207	1999	$17.00	
Teresa	Songbird Teresa	14484	1996	$20.00	
Teresa	Songbird Teresa (2nd version)	14484	1997	$15.00	
Teresa	Sparkle Beach Teresa	14354	1996	$10.00	
Teresa	Splash 'n Color Teresa	16172	1996	$6.00	
Teresa	Spots and Dots Teresa	10885	1993	$45.00	Toys "R" Us
Teresa	Sun Jewel Teresa	19057	1994	$10.00	
Teresa	Sunflower Teresa	13489	1994	$20.00	Toys "R" Us
Teresa	Surf City Teresa	28419	2000	$5.00	
Teresa	Swimming Champion Teresa	25489	1999	$15.00	
Teresa	Tropical Splash Teresa	12450	1995	$10.00	
Teresa	Twirling Ballerina Teresa	15299	1996	$20.00	
Teresa	Twirling Make-up Teresa	18423	1998	$9.00	
Teresa	Tye-Dye Teresa	20506	1998	$13.00	
Teresa	Very Velvet Teresa	20530	1998	$20.00	
Teresa	Wet 'n Wild Teresa	4136	1990	$15.00	
Teresa	Wild Style Teresa	19263	1998	$20.00	Toys "R" Us
Teresa	WNBA Basketball Teresa	20350	1998	$15.00	

Doll	Item	Number	Year	Value	Specials
Teresa	Workin' Out Teresa	17318	1997	$10.00	
Tiff	Pose 'n Play Tiff	1199	1972	$350.00	
Todd	Happy Meal Todd	11475	1994	$25.00	
Todd	Party 'n Play Todd	7903	1993	$20.00	
Todd	Todd (titian)	3590	1967	$225.00	
Todd	Todd Handsome Groom	4253	1983	$40.00	
Tommy	Haircut Tommy	22012	1999	$6.00	
Tommy	Haircut Tommy (black)	22017	1999	$6.00	
Tommy	Pilot Tommy	24595	1999	$5.00	Kelly Club
Tommy	Prince Tommy	24597	1999	$5.00	
Tommy	Sailor Tommy	18037	1998	$6.00	
Tommy	Tommy as Lollipop Munchkin	25819	1999	$6.00	Wizard of Oz
Tommy	Tommy as Mayor Munchkin	25817	1999	$6.00	Wizard of Oz
Tommy	Tommy Fireman	20852	1998	$5.00	Li'l Friends of Kelly
Tommy	Tommy Winter Fun	20853	1999	$5.00	Li'l Friends of Kelly
Tori	Generation Girl Tori	20969	1999	$15.00	Generation Girls
Tori	Generation Girl Tori	25768	1999	$20.00	Generation Girls
Tori	Generation Girl Tori	25768	2000	$20.00	Generation Girls
Tori	Generation Girl Tori w/book	48573	1999	$20.00	Generation Girls
Tracy	Beautiful Bride Tracy	4103	1982	$40.00	
Truly	Truly Scrumptious – Standard	1108	1969	$245.00	
Truly	Truly Scrumptious – Talking	1107	1969	$270.00	
Tutti	Cookin' Goodies Tutti	3559	1967	$300.00	
Tutti	Me and My Dog Tutti	3558	1966	$300.00	
Tutti	Melody in Pink Tutti #1	3555	1966	$275.00	
Tutti	Melody in Pink Tutti #2 (different dress)	3555	1966	$275.00	Li'l Friends of Kelly
Tutti	Night Night Sleep Tight Tutti	3553	1966	$275.00	
Tutti	Swing-a-Ling Tutti	3560	1967	$300.00	
Tutti	Tutti (blonde)	3550	1966	$165.00	
Tutti	Tutti (blonde, different dress)	3580	1967	$130.00	
Tutti	Tutti (brunette)	3550	1966	$165.00	
Tutti	Tutti (brunette, different dress)	3580	1967	$130.00	
Tutti	Walking My Dolly Tutti	3552	1966	$300.00	
Twiggy	Twiggy (TNT)	1185	1967	$350.00	
Whitney	Awesome Skateboard Whitney	24990	1999	$13.00	
Whitney	Bicyclin' Whitney	16736	1997	$15.00	
Whitney	Bowling Party Whitney	22015	1999	$13.00	
Whitney	Flashlight Fun Whitney	19671	1998	$15.00	
Whitney	Gymnast Whitney	14610	1996	$12.00	
Whitney	Happy Meal Whitney	11476	1994	$25.00	
Whitney	Jewel Secrets Whitney	3179	1987	$55.00	
Whitney	Nurse Whitney	4405	1987	$80.00	
Whitney	Perfume Pretty Whitney	4557	1988	$40.00	
Whitney	Polly Pocket Whitney	12983	1995	$15.00	
Whitney	Style Magic Whitney (brown)	1290	1989	$35.00	
Whitney	Style Magic Whitney (brunette)	1288	1989	$35.00	
Whitney	Totally Hair Whitney	7735	1992	$25.00	Toys "R" Us
Whitney	Wet 'n Wild Whitney	4136	1990	$15.00	

Family & Friends Dolls

Listed by Stock Number

Number	Item	Year	Value	Specials	Doll
860	Midge (blonde, straight leg)	1963	$225.00		Midge
860	Midge (brunette, straight leg)	1963	$225.00		Midge
860	Midge (no freckles, straight leg)	1963	$400.00		Midge
860	Midge (titian, straight leg)	1963	$225.00		Midge
860	Midge (with teeth, straight leg)	1963	$350.00		Midge
1000	Allan (straight leg, redhead)	1964	$150.00		Allan
1009	Wig Wardrobe Molded (head only)	1965	$550.00		Midge
1010	Allan (bendable leg)	1965	$550.00		Allan
1019	Scott	1980	$80.00		Scott
1019	Super Teen Scott	1979	$40.00		Scott
1040	Skooter (straight leg, blonde)	1965	$150.00		Skooter
1040	Skooter (straight leg, brunette)	1965	$150.00		Skooter
1040	Skooter (straight leg, titian)	1965	$150.00		Skooter
1068	Malibu Francie	1973	$45.00		Francie
1068	Malibu Francie	1978	$30.00		Francie
1068	Malibu Francie (new box)	1975	$110.00		Francie
1068	Malibu Francie (new rose box)	1976	$55.00		Francie
1068	Malibu Sunset Francie	1971	$60.00		Francie
1074	Growin' Pretty Hair Francie (extra hair piece)	1971	$300.00		Francie
1080	Midge (bendable leg, blonde)	1965	$500.00		Midge
1080	Midge (bendable leg, brownette)	1965	$550.00		Midge
1090	Ricky (redhead, straight leg)	1965	$150.00		Ricky
1100	Francie (1st issue, black, red oxidized)	1967	$1,600.00		Francie
1100	Francie (2nd issue, black, dark brown)	1967	$1,300.00		Francie
1107	Truly Scrumptious – Talking	1969	$270.00		Truly
1108	Truly Scrumptious – Standard	1969	$245.00		Truly
1113	New 'n Groovy Talking P.J.	1969	$150.00		P.J.
1113	Talking P.J.	1969	$325.00		P.J.
1113	Talking P.J. (baggie, non-talking)	1973	$110.00		P.J.
1114	Talking Brad	1970	$200.00		Brad
1114	Talking Brad (darker skin)	1971	$200.00		Brad
1118	Twist 'n Turn P.J.	1970	$225.00		P.J.
1119	Twist 'n Turn Christie	1970	$350.00		Christie
1120	Skooter (bendable leg, blonde)	1966	$300.00		Skooter
1120	Skooter (bendable leg, titian)	1966	$300.00		Skooter
1122	Hair Happenin's Francie	1970	$400.00		Francie
1125	Talking Stacey (blonde)	1968	$300.00		Stacey
1125	Talking Stacey (titian)	1968	$350.00		Stacey
1125	Talking Stacey (titian)	1970	$550.00		Stacey
1126	Talking Christie (brunette)	1968	$250.00		Christie
1126	Talking Christie (darker skin)	1971	$200.00		Christie
1126	Talking Christie (new window box)	1969	$250.00		Christie
1127	Twist 'n Turn Julia	1969	$325.00		Julia
1128	Talking Julia	1969	$225.00		Julia
1128	Talking Julia (darker skin)	1971	$225.00		Julia
1129	Growin' Pretty Hair Francie	1970	$275.00		Francie
1130	Francie (bendable leg, blonde)	1966	$375.00		Francie
1130	Francie (bendable leg, brunette)	1966	$375.00		Francie

Number	Item	Year	Value	Specials	Doll
1132	Walking Jamie (blonde)	1970	$400.00		Jamie
1140	Francie (straight leg, blonde)	1966	$350.00		Francie
1140	Francie (straight leg, brunette)	1966	$350.00		Francie
1141	Rocker Dee Dee	1986	$40.00		Dee Dee
1142	Brad Doll (bendable leg)	1970	$200.00		Brad
1142	Brad Doll (bendable leg, darker skin)	1971	$200.00		Brad
1143	Living Fluff	1971	$225.00		Fluff
1153	Live Action on Stage P.J.	1971	$225.00		P.J.
1156	Live Action P.J. (baggie)	1973	$125.00		P.J.
1156	Live Action P.J. (no stage) (mint)	1971	$100.00		P.J.
1165	Twist 'n Turn Stacey (blonde)	1968	$400.00		Stacey
1165	Twist 'n Turn Stacey (blonde)	1969	$500.00		Stacey
1165	Twist 'n Turn Stacey (blonde)	1970	$425.00		Stacey
1165	Twist 'n Turn Stacey (titian)	1968	$400.00		Stacey
1170	Francie (no bangs, blonde)	1971	$1,500.00		Francie
1170	Francie (no bangs, brunette)	1971	$1,500.00		Francie
1170	Twist 'n Turn Francie (blonde)	1967	$400.00		Francie
1170	Twist 'n Turn Francie (blonde)	1969	$325.00		Francie
1170	Twist 'n Turn Francie (brunette)	1967	$400.00		Francie
1175	Live Action Christie	1971	$240.00		Christie
1180	Casey (TNT) (blonde)	1967	$350.00		Casey
1180	Casey (TNT) (brunette)	1967	$350.00		Casey
1183	Walk Lively Steffie	1972	$350.00		Steffie
1185	Twiggy (TNT)	1967	$350.00		Twiggy
1186	Busy Talking Steffie	1972	$375.00		Steffie
1187	Malibu P.J. (new box)	1975	$110.00		P.J.
1187	Malibu Sunset P.J.	1971	$80.00		P.J.
1187	Sun Gold Malibu P.J.	1984	$30.00		P.J.
1187	Sun Lovin' Malibu P.J.	1979	$40.00		P.J.
1187	Sunsational Malibu P.J.	1982	$40.00		P.J.
1196	Rocker Dana	1986	$40.00		Dana
1199	Pose 'n Play Tiff	1972	$350.00		Tiff
1288	Style Magic Christie	1989	$30.00		Christie
1288	Style Magic Whitney (brunette)	1989	$35.00		Whitney
1290	Style Magic Whitney (brown)	1989	$35.00		Whitney
1293	Partners in Print	1967	$500.00		Francie
1295	Beauty Secrets Christie	1980	$50.00		Christie
1295	Pretty Reflections Christie	1979	$85.00		Christie
1352	Animal Lovin' Nikki	1989	$30.00		Nikki
1393	Sun Sensation Christie	1992	$20.00		Christie
1396	Sun Sensation Steven	1992	$20.00		Steven
1433	Totally Hair Christie	1991	$25.00	Toys "R" Us	Christie
1433	Totally Hair Courtney	1991	$25.00		Courtney
1447	Sun Sensation Kira	1992	$20.00		Kira
1750	Shani	1991	$30.00	Toys "R" Us	Shani
1751	Nichelle	1991	$25.00	Toys "R" Us	Nichelle
1752	Asha	1991	$25.00	Toys "R" Us	Asha
1952	Teen Time Christie	1989	$30.00		Christie
1952	Teen Time Courtney	1989	$25.00		Courtney
2056	Tropical Miko	1986	$20.00		Miko
2088	Bubble Fairy Christie	1999	$10.00		Christie
2216	Rollerblade Teresa	1992	$30.00		Teresa
2217	Rollerblade Christie	1992	$30.00		Christie
2218	Rollerblade Kira	1992	$30.00		Kira
2316	Hollywood Hair Teresa	1993	$30.00		Teresa

Number	Item	Year	Value	Specials	Doll
2323	Fashion Photo P.J.	1978	$90.00		P.J.
2324	Fashion Photo Christie	1978	$70.00		Christie
2427	Rocker Diva	1986	$55.00		Diva
2428	Rocker Derek	1986	$60.00		Derek
2710	Pet Pals Christie	1992	$20.00		Christie
2710	Pet Pals Courtney	1992	$25.00		Courtney
2711	Pet Pals Kevin	1992	$25.00		Kevin
2752	The Beat Midge	1990	$35.00		Midge
2754	The Beat Christie (Barbie & The Beat)	1990	$25.00		Christie
2955	Kissing Christie	1980	$65.00		Christie
3158	Rocker Dana (revised)	1987	$35.00		Dana
3158	Rocker Dancin' Action Dana	1986	$35.00		Dana
3159	Rocker Dancin' Action Diva	1986	$35.00		Diva
3159	Rocker Diva (revised)	1987	$50.00		Diva
3160	Rocker Dancin' Action Dee Dee	1986	$35.00		Dee Dee
3160	Rocker Dee Dee (revised)	1987	$35.00		Dee Dee
3173	Rocker Derek (revised)	1987	$60.00		Derek
3179	Jewel Secrets Whitney	1987	$55.00		Whitney
3200	Walk Lively Miss America	1972	$200.00		Miss America
3216	Cool Times Midge	1989	$25.00		Midge
3217	Cool Times Christie	1989	$25.00		Christie
3218	Cool Times Teresa	1989	$25.00		Teresa
3244	Beach Blast Miko	1989	$20.00		Miko
3249	Beach Blast Teresa	1989	$20.00		Teresa
3249	Golden Dream Christie	1981	$45.00		Christie
3251	Beach Blast Steven	1989	$20.00		Steven
3253	Beach Blast Christie	1989	$20.00		Christie
3265	Rappin' Rockin' Christie	1992	$45.00		Christie
3270	Rappin' Rockin' Teresa	1992	$45.00		Teresa
3312	Busy Steffie	1972	$350.00		Steffie
3313	Busy Francie	1972	$425.00		Francie
3428	Beach Streak Shani	1993	$15.00	Toys "R" Us	Shani
3456	Beach Streak Nichelle	1993	$15.00	Toys "R" Us	Nichelle
3457	Beach Streak Asha	1993	$10.00	Toys "R" Us	Asha
3512	Dance Club Kayla	1989	$65.00		Kayla
3513	Dance Club Devon	1989	$55.00		Devon
3550	Tutti (blonde)	1966	$165.00		Tutti
3550	Tutti (brunette)	1966	$165.00		Tutti
3552	Walking My Dolly Tutti	1966	$300.00		Tutti
3553	Night Night Sleep Tight Tutti	1966	$275.00		Tutti
3555	Melody in Pink Tutti #1	1966	$275.00		Tutti
3555	Melody in Pink Tutti #2 (different dress)	1966	$275.00	Li'l Friends of Kelly	Tutti
3555	Pink and Pretty Christie	1982	$50.00		Christie
3558	Me and My Dog Tutti	1966	$300.00		Tutti
3559	Cookin' Goodies Tutti	1967	$300.00		Tutti
3560	Swing-a-Ling Tutti	1967	$300.00		Tutti
3570	Chris (blonde)	1967	$250.00		Chris
3570	Chris (brunette)	1967	$250.00		Chris
3577	Buffy and Mrs. Beasley	1968	$200.00		Buffy
3580	Tutti (blonde, different dress)	1967	$130.00		Tutti
3580	Tutti (brunette, different dress)	1967	$130.00		Tutti
3590	Todd (titian)	1967	$225.00		Todd
3631	Cheerleader Jazzie	1989	$25.00		Jazzie
3632	Swim Suit Jazzie	1989	$25.00		Jazzie
3633	Beach Dazzle Shani	1988	$20.00		Shani

Number	Item	Year	Value	Specials	Doll
3633	Workout Jazzie	1989	$30.00		Jazzie
3634	Teen Dance Jazzie	1989	$40.00		Jazzie
3635	High School Jazzie	1989	$30.00		Jazzie
3636	High School Stacie	1989	$25.00		Stacie
3637	High School Dude	1989	$30.00		Dude
3698	High School Chelsie	1989	$30.00		Chelsie
3802	Beach Streak Jamal	1993	$15.00	Toys "R" Us	Jamal
3933	Cheerleading Christie	1993	$20.00		Christie
3933	Cheerleading Courtney	1993	$20.00		Courtney
4065	Island Fun Miko	1988	$20.00		Miko
4088	Sun Lovin' Jazzie	1990	$30.00		Jazzie
4092	Island Fun Christie	1988	$20.00		Christie
4093	Island Fun Steven	1988	$20.00		Steven
4103	Beautiful Bride Tracy	1982	$40.00		Tracy
4115	Party 'n Play Stacie (black)	1993	$20.00		Stacie
4117	Island Fun Teresa	1988	$20.00		Teresa
4120	Wet 'n Wild Kira	1990	$15.00		Kira
4121	Wet 'n Wild Christie	1990	$15.00		Christie
4136	Wet 'n Wild Teresa	1990	$15.00		Teresa
4136	Wet 'n Wild Whitney	1990	$15.00		Whitney
4137	Wet 'n Wild Steven	1990	$15.00		Steven
4221	Quick Curl Kelley	1973	$160.00		Kelley
4222	Quick Curl Francie	1973	$175.00		Francie
4240	Stacie	1992	$20.00		Stacie
4253	Todd Handsome Groom	1983	$40.00		Todd
4405	Nurse Whitney	1987	$80.00		Whitney
4442	California Dream Midge	1988	$25.00		Midge
4442	California Midge	1987	$30.00		Midge
4443	California Christie	1987	$30.00		Christie
4443	California Dream Christie	1988	$25.00		Christie
4443	Club California Christie	1988	$30.00		Christie
4557	Perfume Pretty Whitney	1988	$40.00		Whitney
4713	Basketball Kevin	1993	$25.00		Kevin
4880	Benetton Shopping Teresa	1992	$80.00		Teresa
4887	Benetton Shopping Christie	1992	$35.00		Christie
4898	Benetton Shopping Marina	1992	$65.00		Marina
4907	Glitter Beach Christie	1993	$12.00		Christie
4918	Glitter Beach Steven	1993	$12.00		Steven
4921	Glitter Beach Teresa	1993	$12.00		Teresa
4924	Glitter Beach Kira	1993	$15.00		Kira
4935	Glitter Beach Jazzie	1993	$12.00		Jazzie
4967	The Sensations Bopsy	1988	$40.00		Bopsy
4976	The Sensations Belinda	1988	$40.00		Belinda
4977	The Sensations Becky	1988	$40.00		Becky
5411	Party 'n Play Stacie	1993	$20.00		Stacie
5473	Sun Sensation Jazzie	1992	$20.00		Jazzie
5476	Sea Holiday Midge	1993	$40.00		Midge
5503	California Dream Teresa	1988	$25.00		Teresa
5503	California Teresa	1988	$20.00		Teresa
5507	Teen Scene Jazzie	1991	$30.00		Jazzie
5774	Beach Blast Shani	1991	$20.00		Shani
5774	Beach Dazzle Shani	1992	$15.00	Toys "R" Us	Shani
5775	Beach Dazzle Nichelle	1992	$15.00	Toys "R" Us	Nichelle
5777	Beach Dazzle Asha	1992	$10.00	Toys "R" Us	Asha
5869	Dream Date P.J.	1983	$40.00		P.J.

Number	Item	Year	Value	Specials	Doll
5943	Hawaiian Fun Kira	1991	$20.00		Kira
5944	Hawaiian Fun Christie	1991	$20.00		Christie
5945	Hawaiian Fun Steven	1991	$20.00		Steven
7079	Cool Tops Christie	1990	$20.00		Christie
7079	Cool Tops Courtney	1990	$20.00		Courtney
7263	Gold Medal Gymnast P.J.	1975	$120.00		P.J.
7263	Gymnast P.J.	1974	$50.00		P.J.
7281	Free Moving P.J.	1975	$90.00		P.J.
7281	Malibu P.J. (new rose box)	1976	$75.00		P.J.
7282	Free Moving Curtis	1975	$175.00		Curtis
7283	Free Moving Cara	1975	$125.00		Cara
7291	Quick Curl Cara	1975	$100.00		Cara
7377	Carla	1976	$100.00		Carla
7455	Sweet Roses P.J.	1984	$35.00		P.J.
7513	Ski Fun Midge	1991	$30.00	Toys "R" Us	Midge
7699	Francie (baggie)	1975	$125.00		Francie
7735	Totally Hair Whitney	1992	$25.00	Toys "R" Us	Whitney
7745	Malibu Christie	1973	$60.00		Christie
7745	Malibu Christie	1978	$50.00		Christie
7745	Malibu Sunset Christie	1973	$53.00		Christie
7745	Malibu Sunset Christie (new box)	1975	$85.00		Christie
7745	Malibu Sunset Christie (new rose box)	1976	$85.00		Christie
7745	Sun Lovin' Malibu Christie	1979	$40.00		Christie
7745	Sunsational Christie	1984	$35.00		Christie
7745	Sunsational Malibu Christie	1982	$30.00		Christie
7795	Jamal	1992	$30.00	Toys "R" Us	Jamal
7808	Yellowstone Kelley	1974	$328.00		Kelley
7903	Party 'n Play Todd	1993	$20.00		Todd
7957	30th Anniversary Midge (porcelain)	1993	$140.00		Midge
8697	Quick Curl Miss America	1976	$125.00		Miss America
8697	Quick Curl Miss America (blonde)	1974	$125.00		Miss America
8697	Quick Curl Miss America (brunette)	1973	$125.00		Miss America
9000	Casey (baggie)	1975	$150.00		Casey
9218	Deluxe Quick Curl P.J.	1976	$130.00		P.J.
9220	Deluxe Quick Curl Cara	1976	$75.00		Cara
9222	Growing Up Ginger	1976	$150.00		Ginger
9294	Hawaiian Fun Jazzie	1991	$20.00		Jazzie
9324	Babysitter Kevin	1991	$18.00		Kevin
9325	Kevin	1991	$25.00		Kevin
9351	Cool Tops Kevin	1990	$20.00		Kevin
9352	All Star Christie	1990	$25.00		Christie
9353	All Star Teresa	1990	$30.00		Teresa
9360	All Star Midge	1990	$30.00		Midge
9407	Benetton Christie	1991	$30.00		Christie
9408	Benetton Teresa	1991	$50.00		Teresa
9409	Benetton Kira	1990	$30.00		Kira
9409	Benetton Marina	1991	$40.00		Marina
9425	All American Christie	1991	$25.00		Christie
9426	All American Teresa	1991	$25.00		Teresa
9427	All American Kira	1991	$25.00	Reebok	Kira
9434	Babysitter Courtney	1991	$20.00		Courtney
9434	Babysitter Christie	1991	$20.00		Christie
9528	Ballerina Cara	1976	$80.00		Cara
9606	Wedding Day Midge	1991	$35.00		Midge
9607	Wedding Day Alan (2 box versions)	1991	$30.00		Alan

Number	Item	Year	Value	Specials	Doll
9727	Lights 'n Lace Teresa	1991	$30.00		Teresa
9728	Lights 'n Lace Christie	1991	$30.00		Christie
9839	Super Size Christie	1977	$250.00		Christie
9933	Western Fun Nia	1990	$60.00		Nia
9950	SuperStar Christie	1978	$75.00		Christie
10256	Earring Magic Midge	1993	$25.00		Midge
10288	Soul Train Jamal	1993	$20.00	Toys "R" Us	Jamal
10289	Soul Train Shani	1993	$25.00	Toys "R" Us	Shani
10290	Soul Train Nichelle	1993	$20.00	Toys "R" Us	Nichelle
10291	Soul Train Asha	1993	$20.00	Toys "R" Us	Asha
10295	Western Stampin' Tara Lynn	1993	$65.00		Tara Lynn
10885	Spots and Dots Teresa	1993	$45.00	Toys "R" Us	Teresa
11077	Camp Midge	1994	$20.00		Midge
11078	Camp Teresa	1994	$20.00		Teresa
11209	Locket Surprise Kayla	1994	$20.00		Kayla
11474	Happy Meal Stacie	1994	$25.00		Stacie
11475	Happy Meal Todd	1994	$25.00		Todd
11476	Happy Meal Whitney	1994	$25.00		Whitney
11477	Happy Meal Janet	1994	$25.00		Janet
11548	Cool Crimp Christie	1994	$15.00		Christie
11548	Cool Crimp Courtney	1994	$20.00		Courtney
11549	Cool Crimp Kevin	1994	$20.00		Kevin
11587	Mickey's Toontown Stacie	1993	$35.00	Disney	Stacie
11928	Quinceanera Teresa	1994	$25.00		Teresa
12097	Country Western Star Teresa	1994	$30.00		Teresa
12244	Partytime Teresa	1994	$25.00	Toys "R" Us	Teresa
12449	Tropical Splash Kira	1995	$10.00		Kira
12450	Tropical Splash Teresa	1995	$10.00		Teresa
12451	Tropical Splash Christie	1995	$10.00		Christie
12452	Tropical Splash Steven	1995	$10.00		Steven
12489	Baby Sister Kelly	1995	$12.00		Kelly
12489	Kelly	1995	$10.00	Li'l Sisters of Barbie	Kelly
12676	Asha I	1994	$20.00	Toys "R" Us	Asha
12943	Pizza Party Christie	1995	$15.00		Christie
12943	Pizza Party Courtney	1995	$12.00		Courtney
12944	Pizza Party Kevin	1995	$15.00		Kevin
12982	Polly Pocket Stacie	1995	$15.00		Stacie
12983	Polly Pocket Whitney	1995	$15.00		Whitney
12984	Polly Pocket Janet	1995	$12.00		Janet
13084	Dance Moves Teresa	1995	$15.00		Teresa
13085	Dance Moves Midge	1995	$25.00		Midge
13201	Baywatch Teresa	1995	$40.00		Teresa
13235	Slumber Party Teresa	1995	$12.00		Teresa
13236	Slumber Party Midge	1995	$15.00		Midge
13238	Butterfly Princess Teresa	1995	$20.00		Teresa
13256	Baby Sister Kelly (black)	1995	$12.00		Kelly
13256	Kelly (black)	1995	$10.00		Kelly
13393	Hot Skatin' Midge	1995	$20.00		Midge
13489	Sunflower Teresa	1994	$20.00	Toys "R" Us	Teresa
13514	Winter Sport Midge	1995	$35.00	Toys "R" Us	Midge
13532	Asha II	1995	$20.00	Toys "R" Us	Asha
14031	Flying Hero Teresa	1996	$20.00		Teresa
14032	Flying Hero Kira	1996	$20.00		Kira
14032	Super Power Kira	1995	$15.00		Kira
14314	Phone Fun Christie	1996	$10.00		Christie

Number	Item	Year	Value	Specials	Doll
14314	Phone Fun Courtney	1996	$15.00		Courtney
14351	Sparkle Beach Kira	1996	$10.00		Kira
14353	Sparkle Beach Steven	1996	$10.00		Steven
14354	Sparkle Beach Teresa	1996	$10.00		Teresa
14355	Sparkle Beach Christie	1996	$10.00		Christie
14484	Songbird Teresa	1996	$20.00		Teresa
14484	Songbird Teresa (2nd version)	1997	$15.00		Teresa
14552	Bath Time Fun Kelly	1996	$10.00		Kelly
14553	Bath Time Fun Kelly (black)	1996	$10.00		Kelly
14588	Jewel Hair Mermaid Teresa	1996	$20.00		Teresa
14589	Jewel Hair Mermaid Midge	1996	$20.00		Midge
14608	30th Anniversary Francie	1996	$65.00		Francie
14608	Gad About Francie	1996	$45.00		Francie
14609	Gymnast Stacie	1996	$12.00		Stacie
14610	Gymnast Whitney	1996	$12.00		Whitney
14611	Gymnast Janet	1996	$12.00		Janet
14850	Becky	1996	$5.00	Li'l Friends of Kelly	Becky
14852	Chelsie	1997	$6.00	Li'l Friends of Kelly	Chelsie
14853	Becky	1996	$6.00	Li'l Friends of Kelly	Becky
14854	Melody	1993	$10.00	Li'l Friends of Kelly	Melody
15139	Asha III	1996	$20.00	Toys "R" Us	Asha
15299	Twirling Ballerina Teresa	1996	$20.00		Teresa
15431	Ocean Friends Kira	1996	$15.00		Kira
15431	Ocean Friends Marina	1996	$20.00		Marina
15475	In-Line Skating Midge	1996	$20.00	FAO Schwarz	Midge
15761	Share a Smile Becky	1997	$25.00	Toys "R" Us	Becky
16002	Marisa	1996	$5.00	Li'l Friends of Kelly	Marisa
16003	Melody	1996	$5.00	Li'l Friends of Kelly	Melody
16003	Melody	1997	$6.00	Li'l Friends of Kelly	Melody
16004	Chelsie	1996	$6.00	Li'l Friends of Kelly	Chelsie
16066	Potty Training Kelly	1996	$10.00		Kelly
16067	Potty Training Kelly (black)	1996	$10.00		Kelly
16172	Splash 'n Color Teresa	1996	$6.00		Teresa
16173	Splash 'n Color Kira	1996	$6.00		Kira
16173	Splash 'n Color Kira	1997	$10.00		Kira
16174	Splash 'n Color Christie	1996	$6.00		Christie
16175	Splash 'n Color Steven	1996	$6.00		Steven
16230	Cool Skating Christie	1999	$20.00		Christie
16466	Deidra	1996	$5.00	Li'l Friends of Kelly	Deidra
16466	Picnic Deidre	1998	$5.00		Deidre
16467	Jenny	1996	$5.00	Li'l Friends of Kelly	Jenny
16568	Gymnast Stacie	1996	$20.00	J.C. Penney	Stacie
16734	Bicyclin' Stacie	1997	$15.00		Stacie
16735	Bicyclin' Janet	1997	$15.00		Janet
16736	Bicyclin' Whitney	1997	$15.00		Whitney
17035	Blossom Beauty Teresa	1997	$20.00		Teresa
17049	Hula Hair Teresa	1997	$15.00		Teresa
17052	Pool Fun Kelly	1997	$10.00		Kelly
17053	Pool Fun Marisa	1997	$10.00		Marisa
17054	Pool Fun Chelsie	1997	$10.00		Chelsie
17239	Grand Gala Teresa	1997	$20.00	Toys "R" Us	Teresa
17318	Workin' Out Teresa	1997	$10.00		Teresa
17319	Workin' Out Christie	1997	$15.00		Christie
17323	Birthday Deidre	1998	$5.00		Deidre
17323	Deidra	1997	$6.00	Li'l Friends of Kelly	Deidra

Number	Item	Year	Value	Specials	Doll
17353	Teen Nikki	1997	$15.00		Nikki
17354	Teen Courtney	1997	$15.00		Courtney
17372	Share A Smile Christie	1997	$20.00	Toys "R" Us	Christie
17589	Pool Fun Kelly (black)	1997	$10.00		Kelly
17602	101 Dalmatians Teresa	1997	$20.00	Toys "R" Us	Teresa
17607	Wild Bunch Francie	1997	$45.00		Francie
17617	35th Anniversary Teresa	1997	$25.00	Wal-Mart	Teresa
17715	Movin' Groovin' Christie	1997	$15.00		Christie
17716	Movin' Groovin' Teresa	1997	$14.00		Teresa
17717	Movin' Groovin' Kira	1997	$12.00		Kira
18034	Winter Coat Chelsie	1999	$5.00		Chelsie
18035	Sailor Melody	1998	$5.00		Melody
18036	Party Dress Marisa	1998	$5.00		Marisa
18037	Sailor Tommy	1998	$6.00		Tommy
18232	Shopping Time Teresa	1997	$15.00	Wal-Mart	Teresa
18318	Coat Deidre	1998	$5.00		Deidre
18319	Sailor Deidre	1998	$5.00		Deidre
18422	Twirling Make-up Christie	1998	$10.00		Christie
18423	Twirling Make-up Teresa	1998	$9.00		Teresa
18578	Pearl Beach Christie	1997	$5.00		Christie
18579	Pearl Beach Teresa	1997	$10.00		Teresa
18580	Pearl Beach Kira	1997	$10.00		Kira
18581	Pearl Beach Steven	1997	$10.00		Steven
18582	Eatin' Fun Kelly	1997	$8.00		Kelly
18596	Eatin' Fun Kelly (black)	1997	$8.00		Kelly
18653	Gardener Jenny	1998	$5.00		Jenny
18654	Ballerina Melody	1998	$5.00		Melody
18655	African Dress Deidre	1998	$5.00		Deidre
18911	Butterfly Catcher Chelsie	1998	$5.00		Chelsie
18912	Melody Bunny	1998	$5.00	Li'l Friends of Kelly	Melody
18913	Jenny Sunflower	1998	$5.00	Li'l Friends of Kelly	Jenny
18914	Ballerina Deidre	1998	$5.00		Deidre
18916	Tamika Picnicker	1998	$5.00	Li'l Friends of Kelly	Tamika
18917	Keeya African Dress (Kwanzaa)	1998	$5.00	Li'l Friends of Kelly	Keeya
18976	Senior Prom Midge (35th Anniversary)	1998	$45.00	Toys "R" Us	Midge
18981	Flip 'n Dive Christie	1998	$15.00		Christie
18982	Diving Midge	1998	$10.00		Midge
18983	Flip 'n Dive Teresa	1998	$20.00		Teresa
18992	Gym Marisa	1998	$5.00		Marisa
19056	Sun Jewel Kira	1994	$10.00		Kira
19057	Sun Jewel Teresa	1994	$10.00		Teresa
19058	Sun Jewel Shani	1994	$10.00		Shani
19059	Sun Jewel Steven	1994	$10.00		Steven
19263	Wild Style Teresa	1998	$20.00	Toys "R" Us	Teresa
19667	Cool Teen Nikki	1998	$15.00		Nikki
19667	Purple Panic Christie	1998	$15.00		Christie
19668	Cool Teen Courtney	1998	$10.00		Courtney
19668	Perfect Pink Teresa	1998	$15.00		Teresa
19669	Flashlight Fun Stacie	1998	$15.00		Stacie
19670	Flashlight Fun Janet	1998	$12.00		Janet
19671	Flashlight Fun Whitney	1998	$15.00		Whitney
19810	Kelly & Ginger	1998	$25.00		Kelly
20018	Beyond Pink Teresa	1998	$10.00		Teresa
20019	Beyond Pink Christie	1998	$15.00		Christie
20166	Puzzle Craze Teresa	1998	$10.00	Wal-Mart	Teresa

Number	Item	Year	Value	Specials	Doll
20202	I'm the School Photographer Becky	1998	$15.00		Becky
20206	WNBA Basketball Christie	1998	$15.00		Christie
20207	Soccer Teresa	1999	$17.00		Teresa
20349	WNBA Basketball Kira	1998	$15.00		Kira
20350	WNBA Basketball Teresa	1998	$15.00		Teresa
20351	Soccer Christie	1999	$15.00		Christie
20352	Soccer Kira	1999	$15.00		Kira
20360	Butterfly Art Christie	1998	$10.00		Christie
20361	Butterfly Art Teresa	1998	$11.00		Teresa
20362	Butterfly Art Kira	1998	$10.00		Kira
20491	Prince Ken	1998	$18.00		Ken
20497	Florida Vacation Steven	1999	$5.00		Steven
20505	Tye-Dye Christie	1998	$10.00		Christie
20506	Tye-Dye Teresa	1998	$13.00		Teresa
20529	Very Velvet Christie	1998	$10.00		Christie
20530	Very Velvet Teresa	1998	$20.00		Teresa
20531	Very Velvet Kira	1998	$20.00		Kira
20536	Florida Vacation Christie	1998	$10.00		Christie
20537	Florida Vacation Teresa	1998	$6.00		Teresa
20538	Florida Vacation Midge	1998	$6.00		Midge
20852	Tommy Fireman	1998	$5.00	Li'l Friends of Kelly	Tommy
20853	Tommy Winter Fun	1999	$5.00	Li'l Friends of Kelly	Tommy
20854	Chelsie Artist	1998	$5.00	Li'l Friends of Kelly	Chelsie
20855	Kayla Back to School	1998	$5.00	Li'l Friends of Kelly	Kayla
20856	Cowgirl Chelsie	1998	$5.00		Chelsie
20857	Maria Flower Girl	1999	$5.00	Li'l Friends of Kelly	Maria
20858	Jenny Hawaiian	1998	$5.00	Li'l Friends of Kelly	Jenny
20859	Kayla Dress Up	1998	$5.00	Li'l Friends of Kelly	Kayla
20860	Nia Playtime	1998	$5.00	Li'l Friends of Kelly	Nia
20861	Cowgirl Deidre	1998	$5.00	Li'l Friends of Kelly	Deidre
20966	Generation Girl Nichelle	1999	$15.00	Generation Girls	Nichelle
20967	Generation Girl Chelsie	1999	$15.00	Generation Girls	Chelsie
20968	Generation Girl Lara	1999	$20.00	Generation Girls	Lara
20969	Generation Girl Tori	1999	$15.00	Generation Girls	Tori
20969	Teen Scene Sidney	1999	$15.00		Sidney
20972	Generation Girl Ana (3 versions)	1998	$20.00		Ana
21641	Dress-Up Deidre	1998	$5.00	Kelly Club	Deidre
21642	Keeya Back to School	1998	$5.00	Li'l Friends of Kelly	Keeya
22012	Haircut Tommy	1999	$6.00		Tommy
22013	Bowling Party Stacie	1999	$13.00		Stacie
22014	Bowling Party Janet	1999	$13.00		Janet
22015	Bowling Party Whitney	1999	$13.00		Whitney
22016	Rosie O'Donnell	1999	$25.00	Friends of Barbie	Rosie
22017	Haircut Tommy (black)	1999	$6.00		Tommy
22089	Bubble Fairy Teresa	1999	$11.00		Teresa
22206	Gardening Melody	1998	$5.00		Melody
22226	Tiny Steps Kelly	1999	$11.00		Kelly
22227	Tiny Steps Kelly (black)	1999	$10.00		Kelly
22229	Totally Yo-Yo Nikki	1999	$13.00		Nikki
22230	Totally Yo-Yo Courtney	1999	$13.00		Courtney
22232	Walking Barbie & Baby Sister Krissy	1999	$18.00		Krissy
22307	Walking Barbie & Baby Sister Krissy (black)	1999	$18.00		Krissy
22883	Happenin' Hair Christie	1999	$12.00		Christie
22884	Happenin' Hair Teresa	1999	$12.00		Teresa
22996	Butterfly Art Steven	1999	$10.00		Steven

Number	Item	Year	Value	Specials	Doll
23422	Sit in Style Christie	1999	$8.00		Christie
23423	Sit in Style Teresa	1999	$8.00		Teresa
23424	Sit in Style Kira	1999	$8.00		Kira
23966	Cuddle Soft Kelly	1999	$45.00		Kelly
23966	Cuddly Soft Kelly	1999	$45.00		Kelly
23967	Cuddly Soft Kelly (black)	1999	$45.00		Kelly
24244	Hollywood Nails Teresa	1999	$12.00		Teresa
24502	Brandy	1999	$17.00	Friends of Barbie	Brandy
24593	Lemonade Stand Maria	1999	$5.00	Kelly Club	Maria
24594	Baker Chelsie	1999	$5.00	Kelly Club	Chelsie
24595	Pilot Tommy	1999	$5.00	Kelly Club	Tommy
24596	Princess Kelly	1999	$5.00		Kelly
24597	Prince Tommy	1999	$5.00		Tommy
24598	Jester Jenny	1999	$5.00		Jenny
24599	Wizard Melody	1999	$5.00		Melody
24600	Little Swimmer Marisa	1999	$5.00	Kelly Club	Marisa
24601	Golfer Liana	1999	$5.00	Kelly Club	Liana
24602	Biker Baby Belinda	1999	$5.00	Kelly Club	Belinda
24603	Tennis Lorena	1999	$5.00	Kelly Club	Lorena
24604	Lemonade Stand Tamika	1999	$5.00	Kelly Club	Tamika
24605	Baker Nia	1999	$5.00		Nia
24606	Kwanzaa Kayla	2000	$5.00		Kayla
24607	Tennis Deidre	1999	$5.00	Kelly Club	Deidre
24615	Hawaii Christie	1999	$5.00		Christie
24617	Hawaii Midge	1999	$5.00		Midge
24618	Hawaii Teresa	1999	$5.00		Teresa
24620	Hawaii Steven	1999	$5.00		Steven
24620	Hawaii Steven	2000	$5.00		Steven
24639	Raggedy Ann and Andy	1999	$20.00		Kelly & Tommy
24644	Awesome Skateboard Stacie	1999	$11.00		Stacie
24645	Kelly Superslide	1999	$15.00		Kelly
24662	Paralympic Champion Becky	1999	$20.00		Becky
24749	Super Slide Kelly (black)	2000	$10.00		Kelly
24990	Awesome Skateboard Whitney	1999	$13.00		Whitney
24991	Awesome Skateboard Janet	1999	$13.00		Janet
24992	Pajama Fun Courtney	1999	$13.00		Courtney
24993	Pajama Fun Nikki	1999	$13.00		Nikki
25112	Generation Girl Mari w/book	1999	$20.00	Generation Girls	Mari
25381	Pearl Beach Christie Easter Basket	1999	$15.00	Supermarket	Christie
25381	Pearl Beach Teresa Easter Basket	1999	$15.00	Supermarket	Teresa
25488	Swimming Champion Christie	1999	$17.00		Christie
25489	Swimming Champion Teresa	1999	$15.00		Teresa
25504	Millennium Princess Teresa	1999	$40.00	Toys "R" Us	Teresa
25599	Princess Kelly	2000	$5.00		Kelly
25767	Generation Girl Nichelle	1999	$20.00	Generation Girls	Nichelle
25767	Generation Girl Nichelle	2000	$20.00	Generation Girls	Nichelle
25768	Generation Girl Tori	1999	$20.00	Generation Girls	Tori
25768	Generation Girl Tori	2000	$20.00	Generation Girls	Tori
25769	Generation Girl Lara	2000	$20.00	Generation Girls	Lara
25817	Tommy as Mayor Munchkin	1999	$6.00	Wizard of Oz	Tommy
25818	Kelly as Lullaby Munchkin	1999	$6.00	Wizard of Oz	Kelly
25819	Tommy as Lollipop Munchkin	1999	$6.00	Wizard of Oz	Tommy
26111	Generation Girl Blaine	2000	$20.00	Generation Girls	Blaine
26112	Generation Girl Mari	2000	$20.00	Generation Girls	Mari
26230	Cool Blading Christie	2000	$15.00		Christie

Number	Item	Year	Value	Specials	Doll
26230	Cool Skating Christie	2000	$15.00		Christie
26231	Cool Blading Teresa	2000	Retail		Teresa
26231	Cool Skating Teresa	1999	$20.00		Teresa
26252	Glam 'n Groom Christie	2000	$15.00		Christie
26253	Glam 'n Groom	2000	$15.00		Teresa
26423	Secret Messages Christie	1999	$12.00		Christie
26424	Cool Skating Teresa	2000	$15.00		Teresa
26424	Secret Messages Teresa	1999	$15.00		Teresa
26426	Cool Clips Christie	2000	$14.00		Christie
26427	Cool Clips Teresa	2000	$17.00		Teresa
26428	Movie Star Christie	1999	$20.00		Christie
26572	Baby Krissy Layette	1999	$10.00		Krissy
26806	Baby Krissy Layette (black)	1999	$10.00		Krissy
26848	Generation Girl Chelsie	2000	$20.00	Generation Girls	Chelsie
26897	Scrub-a-dub-dub Krissy	2000	$9.00		Krissy
27039	Love 'n Care Kelly	2000	$10.00		Kelly
27244	Scrub-a-dub-dub Krissy (black)	2000	$9.00		Krissy
28391	Amusement Park Kelly	2000	$5.00		Kelly
28392	Amusement Park Ryan	2000	$5.00	Kelly Club	Ryan
28418	Surf City Christie	2000	$5.00		Christie
28419	Surf City Teresa	2000	$5.00		Teresa
28420	Surf City Kira	2000	$5.00		Kira
28421	Surf City Midge	2000	$5.00		Midge
28423	Surf City Steven	2000	$5.00		Steven
28539	Hansel & Gretel	2000	$19.00		Kelly & Tommy
28702	Picture Pockets Christie	2000	$9.00		Christie
28703	Picture Pockets Teresa	2000	$10.00	Toys "R" Us	Teresa
28704	Picture Pockets Kira	2000	$10.00	Toys "R" Us	Kira
29049	Cher	2000	$40.00	Timeless Treasures	Cher
29104	Fashion Party Courtney	2000	$14.00		Courtney
29181	Rain or Shine Teresa	2000	$15.00		Teresa
29200	Amusement Park Marisa	2000	$5.00	Kelly Club	Marisa
29605	Goldilocks and the Three Bears	2000	$19.00		Kelly
29913	I Dream of Jeannie	2000	$50.00		Jeannie
48573	Generation Girl Tori w/book	1999	$20.00	Generation Girls	Tori
50347	Flying Butterfly Teresa	2000	$13.00		Teresa
50535	Nsync Christie w/CD	2000	$19.00		Christie
50536	Nsync Teresa w/CD	2000	$19.00		Teresa
50733	Cowgirl Kelly	2001	$20.00	Toys "R" Us	Kelly

Family & Friends Dolls

Listed by Year

Year	Item	Number	Value	Specials	Doll
1963	Midge (blonde, straight leg)	860	$225.00		Midge
1963	Midge (brunette, straight leg)	860	$225.00		Midge
1963	Midge (no freckles, straight leg)	860	$400.00		Midge
1963	Midge (titian, straight leg)	860	$225.00		Midge
1963	Midge (with teeth, straight leg)	860	$350.00		Midge
1964	Allan (straight leg, redhead)	1000	$150.00		Allan
1965	Allan (bendable leg)	1010	$550.00		Allan
1965	Midge (bendable leg, blonde)	1080	$500.00		Midge
1965	Midge (bendable leg, brunette)	1080	$550.00		Midge
1965	Ricky (redhead, straight leg)	1090	$150.00		Ricky
1965	Skooter (straight leg, blonde)	1040	$150.00		Skooter
1965	Skooter (straight leg, brunette)	1040	$150.00		Skooter
1965	Skooter (straight leg, titian)	1040	$150.00		Skooter
1965	Wig Wardrobe Molded (head only)	1009	$550.00		Midge
1966	Francie (bendable leg, blonde)	1130	$375.00		Francie
1966	Francie (bendable leg, brunette)	1130	$375.00		Francie
1966	Francie (straight leg, blonde)	1140	$350.00		Francie
1966	Francie (straight leg, brunette)	1140	$350.00		Francie
1966	Me and My Dog Tutti	3558	$300.00		Tutti
1966	Melody in Pink Tutti #1	3555	$275.00		Tutti
1966	Melody in Pink Tutti #2 (different dress)	3555	$275.00	Li'l Friends of Kelly	Tutti
1966	Night Night Sleep Tight Tutti	3553	$275.00		Tutti
1966	Skooter (bendable leg, blonde)	1120	$300.00		Skooter
1966	Skooter (bendable leg, titian)	1120	$300.00		Skooter
1966	Tutti (blonde)	3550	$165.00		Tutti
1966	Tutti (brunette)	3550	$165.00		Tutti
1966	Walking My Dolly Tutti	3552	$300.00		Tutti
1967	Casey (TNT) (blonde)	1180	$350.00		Casey
1967	Casey (TNT) (brunette)	1180	$350.00		Casey
1967	Chris (blonde)	3570	$250.00		Chris
1967	Chris (brunette)	3570	$250.00		Chris
1967	Cookin' Goodies Tutti	3559	$300.00		Tutti
1967	Francie (1st issue, black, red oxidized)	1100	$1,600.00		Francie
1967	Francie (2nd issue, black, dark brown)	1100	$1,300.00		Francie
1967	Partners in Print	1293	$500.00		Francie
1967	Swing-a-Ling Tutti	3560	$300.00		Tutti
1967	Todd (titian)	3590	$225.00		Todd
1967	Tutti (blonde, different dress)	3580	$130.00		Tutti
1967	Tutti (brunette, different dress)	3580	$130.00		Tutti
1967	Twiggy (TNT)	1185	$350.00		Twiggy
1967	Twist 'n Turn Francie (blonde)	1170	$400.00		Francie
1967	Twist 'n Turn Francie (brunette)	1170	$400.00		Francie
1968	Buffy and Mrs. Beasley	3577	$200.00		Buffy
1968	Talking Christie (brunette)	1126	$250.00		Christie
1968	Talking Stacey (blonde)	1125	$300.00		Stacey
1968	Talking Stacey (titian)	1125	$350.00		Stacey
1968	Twist 'n Turn Stacey (blonde)	1165	$400.00		Stacey
1968	Twist 'n Turn Stacey (titian)	1165	$400.00		Stacey

Year	Item	Number	Value	Specials	Doll
1969	New 'n Groovy Talking P.J.	1113	$150.00		P.J.
1969	Talking Christie (new window box)	1126	$250.00		Christie
1969	Talking Julia	1128	$225.00		Julia
1969	Talking P.J.	1113	$325.00		P.J.
1969	Truly Scrumptious – Standard	1108	$245.00		Truly
1969	Truly Scrumptious – Talking	1107	$270.00		Truly
1969	Twist 'n Turn Francie (blonde)	1170	$325.00		Francie
1969	Twist 'n Turn Julia	1127	$325.00		Julia
1969	Twist 'n Turn Stacey (blonde)	1165	$500.00		Stacey
1970	Brad Doll (bendable leg)	1142	$200.00		Brad
1970	Growin' Pretty Hair Francie	1129	$275.00		Francie
1970	Hair Happenin's Francie	1122	$400.00		Francie
1970	Talking Brad	1114	$200.00		Brad
1970	Talking Stacey (titian)	1125	$550.00		Stacey
1970	Twist 'n Turn Christie	1119	$350.00		Christie
1970	Twist 'n Turn P.J.	1118	$225.00		P.J.
1970	Twist 'n Turn Stacey (blonde)	1165	$425.00		Stacey
1970	Walking Jamie (blonde)	1132	$400.00		Jamie
1971	Brad Doll (bendable leg, darker skin)	1142	$200.00		Brad
1971	Francie (no bangs, blonde)	1170	$1,500.00		Francie
1971	Francie (no bangs, brunette)	1170	$1,500.00		Francie
1971	Growin' Pretty Hair Francie (extra hair piece)	1074	$300.00		Francie
1971	Live Action Christie	1175	$240.00		Christie
1971	Live Action on Stage P.J.	1153	$225.00		P.J.
1971	Live Action P.J. (no stage) (mint)	1156	$100.00		P.J.
1971	Living Fluff	1143	$225.00		Fluff
1971	Malibu Sunset Francie	1068	$60.00		Francie
1971	Malibu Sunset P.J.	1187	$80.00		P.J.
1971	Talking Brad (darker skin)	1114	$200.00		Brad
1971	Talking Christie (darker skin)	1126	$200.00		Christie
1971	Talking Julia (darker skin)	1128	$225.00		Julia
1972	Busy Francie	3313	$425.00		Francie
1972	Busy Steffie	3312	$350.00		Steffie
1972	Busy Talking Steffie	1186	$375.00		Steffie
1972	Pose 'n Play Tiff	1199	$350.00		Tiff
1972	Walk Lively Miss America	3200	$200.00		Miss America
1972	Walk Lively Steffie	1183	$350.00		Steffie
1973	Live Action P.J. (baggie)	1156	$125.00		P.J.
1973	Malibu Christie	7745	$53.00		Christie
1973	Malibu Francie	1068	$45.00		Francie
1973	Malibu Sunset Christie	7745	$53.00		Christie
1973	Quick Curl Francie	4222	$175.00		Francie
1973	Quick Curl Kelley	4221	$160.00		Kelley
1973	Quick Curl Miss America (brunette)	8697	$125.00		Miss America
1973	Talking P.J. (baggie, non-talking)	1113	$110.00		P.J.
1974	Gymnast P.J.	7263	$50.00		P.J.
1974	Quick Curl Miss America (blonde)	8697	$125.00		Miss America
1974	Yellowstone Kelley	7808	$328.00		Kelley
1975	Casey (baggie)	9000	$150.00		Casey
1975	Francie (baggie)	7699	$125.00		Francie
1975	Free Moving Cara	7283	$125.00		Cara
1975	Free Moving Curtis	7282	$175.00		Curtis
1975	Free Moving P.J.	7281	$90.00		P.J.
1975	Gold Medal Gymnast P.J.	7263	$120.00		P.J.
1975	Malibu Francie (new box)	1068	$110.00		Francie

Year	Item	Number	Value	Specials	Doll
1975	Malibu P.J. (new box)	1187	$110.00		P.J.
1975	Malibu Sunset Christie (new box)	7745	$85.00		Christie
1975	Quick Curl Cara	7291	$100.00		Cara
1976	Ballerina Cara	9528	$80.00		Cara
1976	Carla	7377	$100.00		Carla
1976	Deluxe Quick Curl Cara	9220	$75.00		Cara
1976	Deluxe Quick Curl P.J.	9218	$130.00		P.J.
1976	Growing Up Ginger	9222	$150.00		Ginger
1976	Malibu Francie (new rose box)	1068	$55.00		Francie
1976	Malibu P.J. (new rose box)	7281	$75.00		P.J.
1976	Malibu Sunset Christie (new rose box)	7745	$85.00		Christie
1976	Quick Curl Miss America	8697	$125.00		Miss America
1977	Super Size Christie	9839	$250.00		Christie
1978	Fashion Photo Christie	2324	$70.00		Christie
1978	Fashion Photo P.J.	2323	$90.00		P.J.
1978	Malibu Christie	7745	$50.00		Christie
1978	Malibu Francie	1068	$30.00		Francie
1978	SuperStar Christie	9950	$75.00		Christie
1979	Pretty Reflections Christie	1295	$85.00		Christie
1979	Sun Lovin' Malibu Christie	7745	$40.00		Christie
1979	Sun Lovin' Malibu P.J.	1187	$40.00		P.J.
1979	Super Teen Scott	1019	$40.00		Scott
1980	Beauty Secrets Christie	1295	$50.00		Christie
1980	Kissing Christie	2955	$65.00		Christie
1980	Scott	1019	$80.00		Scott
1981	Golden Dream Christie	3249	$45.00		Christie
1982	Beautiful Bride Tracy	4103	$40.00		Tracy
1982	Pink and Pretty Christie	3555	$50.00		Christie
1982	Sunsational Malibu Christie	7745	$30.00		Christie
1982	Sunsational Malibu P.J.	1187	$40.00		P.J.
1983	Dream Date P.J.	5869	$40.00		P.J.
1983	Todd Handsome Groom	4253	$40.00		Todd
1984	Sun Gold Malibu P.J.	1187	$30.00		P.J.
1984	Sunsational Christie	7745	$35.00		Christie
1984	Sweet Roses P.J.	7455	$35.00		P.J.
1986	Rocker Dana	1196	$40.00		Dana
1986	Rocker Dancin' Action Dana	3158	$35.00		Dana
1986	Rocker Dancin' Action Dee Dee	3160	$35.00		Dee Dee
1986	Rocker Dancin' Action Diva	3159	$35.00		Diva
1986	Rocker Dee Dee	1141	$40.00		Dee Dee
1986	Rocker Derek	2428	$60.00		Derek
1986	Rocker Diva	2427	$55.00		Diva
1986	Tropical Miko	2056	$20.00		Miko
1987	California Christie	4443	$30.00		Christie
1987	California Midge	4442	$30.00		Midge
1987	Jewel Secrets Whitney	3179	$55.00		Whitney
1987	Nurse Whitney	4405	$80.00		Whitney
1987	Rocker Dana (revised)	3158	$35.00		Dana
1987	Rocker Dee Dee (revised)	3160	$35.00		Dee Dee
1987	Rocker Derek (revised)	3173	$60.00		Derek
1987	Rocker Diva (revised)	3159	$50.00		Diva
1988	Beach Dazzle Shani	3633	$20.00		Shani
1988	California Dream Christie	4443	$25.00		Christie
1988	California Dream Midge	4442	$25.00		Midge
1988	California Dream Teresa	5503	$25.00		Teresa

Year	Item	Number	Value	Specials	Doll
1988	California Teresa	5503	$20.00		Teresa
1988	Club California Christie	4443	$30.00		Christie
1988	Island Fun Christie	4092	$20.00		Christie
1988	Island Fun Miko	4065	$20.00		Miko
1988	Island Fun Steven	4093	$20.00		Steven
1988	Island Fun Teresa	4117	$20.00		Teresa
1988	Perfume Pretty Whitney	4557	$40.00		Whitney
1988	The Sensations Becky	4977	$40.00		Becky
1988	The Sensations Belinda	4976	$40.00		Belinda
1988	The Sensations Bopsy	4967	$40.00		Bopsy
1989	Animal Lovin' Nikki	1352	$30.00		Nikki
1989	Beach Blast Christie	3253	$20.00		Christie
1989	Beach Blast Miko	3244	$20.00		Miko
1989	Beach Blast Steven	3251	$20.00		Steven
1989	Beach Blast Teresa	3249	$20.00		Teresa
1989	Cheerleader Jazzie	3631	$25.00		Jazzie
1989	Cool Times Christie	3217	$25.00		Christie
1989	Cool Times Midge	3216	$25.00		Midge
1989	Cool Times Teresa	3218	$25.00		Teresa
1989	Dance Club Devon	3513	$55.00		Devon
1989	Dance Club Kayla	3512	$65.00		Kayla
1989	High School Chelsie	3698	$30.00		Chelsie
1989	High School Dude	3637	$30.00		Dude
1989	High School Jazzie	3635	$30.00		Jazzie
1989	High School Stacie	3636	$25.00		Stacie
1989	Style Magic Christie	1288	$30.00		Christie
1989	Style Magic Whitney (brown)	1290	$35.00		Whitney
1989	Style Magic Whitney (brunette)	1288	$35.00		Whitney
1989	Swim Suit Jazzie	3632	$25.00		Jazzie
1989	Teen Dance Jazzie	3634	$40.00		Jazzie
1989	Teen Time Christie	1952	$30.00		Christie
1989	TeenTime Courtney	1952	$25.00		Courtney
1989	Workout Jazzie	3633	$30.00		Jazzie
1990	All Star Christie	9352	$25.00		Christie
1990	All Star Midge	9360	$30.00		Midge
1990	All Star Teresa	9353	$30.00		Teresa
1990	Benetton Kira	9409	$30.00		Kira
1990	Cool Tops Christie	7079	$20.00		Christie
1990	Cool Tops Courtney	7079	$20.00		Courtney
1990	Cool Tops Kevin	9351	$20.00		Kevin
1990	Sun Lovin' Jazzie	4088	$30.00		Jazzie
1990	The Beat Christie (Barbie & The Beat)	2754	$25.00		Christie
1990	The Beat Midge	2752	$35.00		Midge
1990	Western Fun Nia	9933	$60.00		Nia
1990	Wet 'n Wild Christie	4121	$15.00		Christie
1990	Wet 'n Wild Kira	4120	$15.00		Kira
1990	Wet 'n Wild Steven	4137	$15.00		Steven
1990	Wet 'n Wild Teresa	4136	$15.00		Teresa
1990	Wet 'n Wild Whitney	4136	$15.00		Whitney
1991	All American Christie	9425	$25.00		Christie
1991	All American Kira	9427	$25.00	Reebok	Kira
1991	All American Teresa	9426	$25.00		Teresa
1991	Asha	1752	$25.00	Toys "R" Us	Asha
1991	Babysitter Courtney	9434	$20.00		Courtney
1991	Babysitter Kevin	9324	$18.00		Kevin

Year	Item	Number	Value	Specials	Doll
1991	Babysitter Christie	9434	$20.00		Christie
1991	Beach Blast Shani	5774	$20.00		Shani
1991	Benetton Christie	9407	$30.00		Christie
1991	Benetton Marina	9409	$40.00		Marina
1991	Benetton Teresa	9408	$50.00		Teresa
1991	Hawaiian Fun Christie	5944	$20.00		Christie
1991	Hawaiian Fun Jazzie	9294	$20.00		Jazzie
1991	Hawaiian Fun Kira	5943	$20.00		Kira
1991	Hawaiian Fun Steven	5945	$20.00		Steven
1991	Kevin	9325	$25.00		Kevin
1991	Lights 'n Lace Christie	9728	$30.00		Christie
1991	Lights 'n Lace Teresa	9727	$30.00		Teresa
1991	Nichelle	1751	$25.00	Toys "R" Us	Nichelle
1991	Shani	1750	$30.00	Toys "R" Us	Shani
1991	Ski Fun Midge	7513	$30.00	Toys "R" Us	Midge
1991	Teen Scene Jazzie	5507	$30.00		Jazzie
1991	Totally Hair Christie	1433	$25.00	Toys "R" Us	Christie
1991	Totally Hair Courtney	1433	$25.00		Courtney
1991	Wedding Day Alan (2 box versions)	9607	$30.00		Alan
1991	Wedding Day Midge	9606	$35.00		Midge
1992	Beach Dazzle Asha	5777	$10.00	Toys "R" Us	Asha
1992	Beach Dazzle Nichelle	5775	$15.00	Toys "R" Us	Nichelle
1992	Beach Dazzle Plus 2 Fashions Shani		$37.00	Sears	Shani
1992	Beach Dazzle Shani	5774	$15.00	Toys "R" Us	Shani
1992	Beach Dazzle Shani		$40.00	Sears	Shani
1992	Benetton Shopping Christie	4887	$35.00		Christie
1992	Benetton Shopping Marina	4898	$65.00		Marina
1992	Benetton Shopping Teresa	4880	$80.00		Teresa
1992	Jamal	7795	$30.00	Toys "R" Us	Jamal
1992	Pet Pals Christie	2710	$20.00		Christie
1992	Pet Pals Courtney	2710	$25.00		Courtney
1992	Pet Pals Kevin	2711	$25.00		Kevin
1992	Rappin' Rockin' Christie	3265	$45.00		Christie
1992	Rappin' Rockin' Teresa	3270	$45.00		Teresa
1992	Rollerblade Christie	2217	$30.00		Christie
1992	Rollerblade Kira	2218	$30.00		Kira
1992	Rollerblade Teresa	2216	$30.00		Teresa
1992	Stacie	4240	$20.00		Stacie
1992	Sun Sensation Christie	1393	$20.00		Christie
1992	Sun Sensation Jazzie	5473	$20.00		Jazzie
1992	Sun Sensation Kira	1447	$20.00		Kira
1992	Sun Sensation Steven	1396	$20.00		Steven
1992	Totally Hair Whitney	7735	$25.00	Toys "R" Us	Whitney
1993	30th Anniversary Midge (porcelain)	7957	$140.00		Midge
1993	Basketball Kevin	4713	$25.00		Kevin
1993	Beach Streak Asha	3457	$10.00	Toys "R" Us	Asha
1993	Beach Streak Jamal	3802	$15.00	Toys "R" Us	Jamal
1993	Beach Streak Nichelle	3456	$15.00	Toys "R" Us	Nichelle
1993	Beach Streak Shani	3428	$15.00	Toys "R" Us	Shani
1993	Cheerleading Christie	3933	$20.00		Christie
1993	Cheerleading Courtney	3933	$20.00		Courtney
1993	Earring Magic Midge	10256	$25.00		Midge
1993	Glitter Beach Christie	4907	$12.00		Christie
1993	Glitter Beach Jazzie	4935	$12.00		Jazzie
1993	Glitter Beach Kira	4924	$15.00		Kira

Year	Item	Number	Value	Specials	Doll
1993	Glitter Beach Steven	4918	$12.00		Steven
1993	Glitter Beach Teresa	4921	$12.00		Teresa
1993	Hollywood Hair Teresa	2316	$30.00		Teresa
1993	Melody	14854	$10.00	Li'l Friends of Kelly	Melody
1993	Mickey's Toontown Stacie	11587	$35.00	Disney	Stacie
1993	Party 'n Play Stacie	5411	$20.00		Stacie
1993	Party 'n Play Stacie (black)	4115	$20.00		Stacie
1993	Party 'n Play Todd	7903	$20.00		Todd
1993	Sea Holiday Midge	5476	$40.00		Midge
1993	Soul Train Asha	10291	$20.00	Toys "R" Us	Asha
1993	Soul Train Jamal	10288	$20.00	Toys "R" Us	Jamal
1993	Soul Train Nichelle	10290	$20.00	Toys "R" Us	Nichelle
1993	Soul Train Shani	10289	$25.00	Toys "R" Us	Shani
1993	Spots and Dots Teresa	10885	$45.00	Toys "R" Us	Teresa
1993	Western Stampin' Tara Lynn	10295	$65.00		Tara Lynn
1994	Asha I	12676	$20.00	Toys "R" Us	Asha
1994	Camp Midge	11077	$20.00		Midge
1994	Camp Teresa	11078	$20.00		Teresa
1994	Cool Crimp Christie	11548	$15.00		Christie
1994	Cool Crimp Courtney	11548	$20.00		Courtney
1994	Cool Crimp Kevin	11549	$20.00		Kevin
1994	Country Western Star Teresa	12097	$30.00		Teresa
1994	Happy Meal Janet	11477	$25.00		Janet
1994	Happy Meal Stacie	11474	$25.00		Stacie
1994	Happy Meal Todd	11475	$25.00		Todd
1994	Happy Meal Whitney	11476	$25.00		Whitney
1994	Locket Surprise Kayla	11209	$20.00		Kayla
1994	Partytime Teresa	12244	$25.00	Toys "R" Us	Teresa
1994	Quinceanera Teresa	11928	$25.00		Teresa
1994	Sun Jewel Kira	19056	$10.00		Kira
1994	Sun Jewel Shani	19058	$10.00		Shani
1994	Sun Jewel Steven	19059	$10.00		Steven
1994	Sun Jewel Teresa	19057	$10.00		Teresa
1994	Sunflower Teresa	13489	$20.00	Toys "R" Us	Teresa
1995	Asha II	13532	$20.00	Toys "R" Us	Asha
1995	Baby Sister Kelly	12489	$12.00		Kelly
1995	Baby Sister Kelly (black)	13256	$12.00		Kelly
1995	Baywatch Teresa	13201	$40.00		Teresa
1995	Butterfly Princess Teresa	13238	$20.00		Teresa
1995	Dance Moves Midge	13085	$25.00		Midge
1995	Dance Moves Teresa	13084	$15.00		Teresa
1995	Hot Skatin' Midge	13393	$20.00		Midge
1995	Kelly	12489	$10.00	Li'l Sisters of Barbie	Kelly
1995	Kelly (black)	13256	$10.00		Kelly
1995	Pizza Party Christie	12943	$15.00		Christie
1995	Pizza Party Courtney	12943	$12.00		Courtney
1995	Pizza Party Kevin	12944	$15.00		Kevin
1995	Polly Pocket Janet	12984	$12.00		Janet
1995	Polly Pocket Stacie	12982	$15.00		Stacie
1995	Polly Pocket Whitney	12983	$15.00		Whitney
1995	Slumber Party Midge	13236	$15.00		Midge
1995	Slumber Party Teresa	13235	$12.00		Teresa
1995	Super Power Kira	14032	$15.00		Kira
1995	Tropical Splash Christie	12451	$10.00		Christie
1995	Tropical Splash Kira	12449	$10.00		Kira

Year	Item	Number	Value	Specials	Doll
1995	Tropical Splash Steven	12452	$10.00		Steven
1995	Tropical Splash Teresa	12450	$10.00		Teresa
1995	Winter Sport Midge	13514	$35.00	Toys "R" Us	Midge
1996	30th Anniversary Francie	14608	$65.00		Francie
1996	Asha III	15139	$20.00	Toys "R" Us	Asha
1996	Bath Time Fun Kelly	14552	$10.00		Kelly
1996	Bath Time Fun Kelly (black)	14553	$10.00		Kelly
1996	Becky	14850	$5.00	Li'l Friends of Kelly	Becky
1996	Becky	14853	$6.00	Li'l Friends of Kelly	Becky
1996	Chelsie	16004	$6.00	Li'l Friends of Kelly	Chelsie
1996	Deidra	16466	$5.00	Li'l Friends of Kelly	Deidra
1996	Flying Hero Kira	14032	$20.00		Kira
1996	Flying Hero Teresa	14031	$20.00		Teresa
1996	Gad About Francie	14608	$45.00		Francie
1996	Gymnast Janet	14611	$12.00		Janet
1996	Gymnast Stacie	14609	$12.00		Stacie
1996	Gymnast Stacie	16568	$20.00	JCPenney	Stacie
1996	Gymnast Whitney	14610	$12.00		Whitney
1996	In-Line Skating Midge	15475	$20.00	FAO Schwarz	Midge
1996	Jenny	16467	$5.00	Li'l Friends of Kelly	Jenny
1996	Jewel Hair Mermaid Midge	14589	$20.00		Midge
1996	Jewel Hair Mermaid Teresa	14588	$20.00		Teresa
1996	Marisa	16002	$5.00	Li'l Friends of Kelly	Marisa
1996	Melody	16003	$5.00	Li'l Friends of Kelly	Melody
1996	Ocean Friends Kira	15431	$15.00		Kira
1996	Ocean Friends Marina	15431	$20.00		Marina
1996	Phone Fun Christie	14314	$10.00		Christie
1996	Phone Fun Courtney	14314	$15.00		Courtney
1996	Potty Training Kelly	16066	$10.00		Kelly
1996	Potty Training Kelly (black)	16067	$10.00		Kelly
1996	Songbird Teresa	14484	$20.00		Teresa
1996	Sparkle Beach Christie	14355	$10.00		Christie
1996	Sparkle Beach Kira	14351	$10.00		Kira
1996	Sparkle Beach Steven	14353	$10.00		Steven
1996	Sparkle Beach Teresa	14354	$10.00		Teresa
1996	Splash 'n Color Christie	16174	$6.00		Christie
1996	Splash 'n Color Kira	16173	$6.00		Kira
1996	Splash 'n Color Steven	16175	$6.00		Steven
1996	Splash 'n Color Teresa	16172	$6.00		Teresa
1996	Twirling Ballerina Teresa	15299	$20.00		Teresa
1997	101 Dalmatians Teresa	17602	$20.00	Toys "R" Us	Teresa
1997	35th Anniversary Teresa	17617	$25.00	Wal-Mart	Teresa
1997	Bicyclin' Janet	16735	$15.00		Janet
1997	Bicyclin' Stacie	16734	$15.00		Stacie
1997	Bicyclin' Whitney	16736	$15.00		Whitney
1997	Blossom Beauty Teresa	17035	$20.00		Teresa
1997	Chelsie	14852	$6.00	Li'l Friends of Kelly	Chelsie
1997	Deidra	17323	$6.00	Li'l Friends of Kelly	Deidra
1997	Eatin' Fun Kelly	18582	$8.00		Kelly
1997	Eatin' Fun Kelly (black)	18596	$8.00		Kelly
1997	Grand Gala Teresa	17239	$20.00	Toys "R" Us	Teresa
1997	Hula Hair Teresa	17049	$15.00		Teresa
1997	Melody	16003	$6.00	Li'l Friends of Kelly	Melody
1997	Movin' Groovin' Kira	17717	$12.00		Kira
1997	Movin' Groovin' Teresa	17716	$14.00		Teresa

Year	Item	Number	Value	Specials	Doll
1997	Movin' Groovin' Christie	17715	$15.00		Christie
1997	Pearl Beach Christie	18578	$5.00		Christie
1997	Pearl Beach Kira	18580	$10.00		Kira
1997	Pearl Beach Steven	18581	$10.00		Steven
1997	Pearl Beach Teresa	18579	$10.00		Teresa
1997	Pool Fun Chelsie	17054	$10.00		Chelsie
1997	Pool Fun Kelly	17052	$10.00		Kelly
1997	Pool Fun Kelly (black)	17589	$10.00		Kelly
1997	Pool Fun Marisa	17053	$10.00		Marisa
1997	Share a Smile Becky	15761	$25.00	Toys "R" Us	Becky
1997	Share A Smile Christie	17372	$20.00	Toys "R" Us	Christie
1997	Shopping Time Teresa	18232	$15.00	Wal-Mart	Teresa
1997	Songbird Teresa (2nd version)	14484	$15.00		Teresa
1997	Splash 'n Color Kira	16173	$10.00		Kira
1997	Teen Courtney	17354	$15.00		Courtney
1997	Teen Nikki	17353	$15.00		Nikki
1997	Wild Bunch Francie	17607	$45.00		Francie
1997	Workin' Out Christie	17319	$15.00		Christie
1997	Workin' Out Teresa	17318	$10.00		Teresa
1998	African Dress Deidre	18655	$5.00		Deidre
1998	Animal Lovin' Ginger		$40.00		Ginger
1998	Ballerina Deidre	18914	$5.00		Deidre
1998	Ballerina Melody	18654	$5.00		Melody
1998	Beyond Pink Christie	20019	$15.00		Christie
1998	Beyond Pink Teresa	20018	$10.00		Teresa
1998	Birthday Deidre	17323	$5.00		Deidre
1998	Butterfly Art Christie	20360	$10.00		Christie
1998	Butterfly Art Kira	20362	$10.00		Kira
1998	Butterfly Art Teresa	20361	$11.00		Teresa
1998	Butterfly Catcher Chelsie	18911	$5.00		Chelsie
1998	Chelsie Artist	20854	$5.00	Li'l Friends of Kelly	Chelsie
1998	Coat Deidre	18318	$5.00		Deidre
1998	Cool Teen Courtney	19668	$10.00		Courtney
1998	Cool Teen Nikki	19667	$15.00		Nikki
1998	Cowgirl Chelsie	20856	$5.00		Chelsie
1998	Cowgirl Deidre	20861	$5.00	Li'l Friends of Kelly	Deidre
1998	Diving Midge	18982	$10.00		Midge
1998	Dress-Up Deidre	21641	$5.00	Kelly Club	Deidre
1998	Flashlight Fun Janet	19670	$12.00		Janet
1998	Flashlight Fun Stacie	19669	$15.00		Stacie
1998	Flashlight Fun Whitney	19671	$15.00		Whitney
1998	Flip 'n Dive Christie	18981	$15.00		Christie
1998	Flip 'n Dive Teresa	18983	$20.00		Teresa
1998	Florida Vacation Christie	20536	$10.00		Christie
1998	Florida Vacation Midge	20538	$6.00		Midge
1998	Florida Vacation Teresa	20537	$6.00		Teresa
1998	Gardener Jenny	18653	$5.00		Jenny
1998	Gardening Melody	22206	$5.00		Melody
1998	Generation Girl Ana (3 versions)	20972	$20.00		Ana
1998	Gym Marisa	18992	$5.00		Marisa
1998	I'm the School Photographer Becky	20202	$15.00		Becky
1998	Jenny Hawaiian	20858	$5.00	Li'l Friends of Kelly	Jenny
1998	Jenny Sunflower	18913	$5.00	Li'l Friends of Kelly	Jenny
1998	Kayla Back to School	20855	$5.00	Li'l Friends of Kelly	Kayla
1998	Kayla Dress Up	20859	$5.00	Li'l Friends of Kelly	Kayla

Year	Item	Number	Value	Specials	Doll
1998	Keeya African Dress (Kwanzaa)	18917	$5.00	Li'l Friends of Kelly	Keeya
1998	Keeya Back to School	21642	$5.00	Li'l Friends of Kelly	Keeya
1998	Kelly & Ginger	19810	$25.00		Kelly
1998	Melody Bunny	18912	$5.00	Li'l Friends of Kelly	Melody
1998	Nia Playtime	20860	$5.00	Li'l Friends of Kelly	Nia
1998	Party Dress Marisa	18036	$5.00		Marisa
1998	Perfect Pink Teresa	19668	$15.00		Teresa
1998	Picnic Deidre	16466	$5.00		Deidre
1998	Prince Ken	20491	$18.00		Ken
1998	Purple Panic Christie	19667	$15.00		Christie
1998	Puzzle Craze Teresa	20166	$10.00	Wal-Mart	Teresa
1998	Sailor Deidre	18319	$5.00		Deidre
1998	Sailor Melody	18035	$5.00		Melody
1998	Sailor Tommy	18037	$6.00		Tommy
1998	Senior Prom Midge (35th Anniversary)	18976	$45.00	Toys "R" Us	Midge
1998	Tamika Picnicker	18916	$5.00	Li'l Friends of Kelly	Tamika
1998	Tommy Fireman	20852	$5.00	Li'l Friends of Kelly	Tommy
1998	Twirling Make-up Christie	18422	$10.00		Christie
1998	Twirling Make-up Teresa	18423	$9.00		Teresa
1998	Tye-Dye Christie	20505	$10.00		Christie
1998	Tye-Dye Teresa	20506	$13.00		Teresa
1998	Very Velvet Christie	20529	$10.00		Christie
1998	Very Velvet Kira	20531	$20.00		Kira
1998	Very Velvet Teresa	20530	$20.00		Teresa
1998	Wild Style Teresa	19263	$20.00	Toys "R" Us	Teresa
1998	WNBA Basketball Kira	20349	$15.00		Kira
1998	WNBA Basketball Teresa	20350	$15.00		Teresa
1998	WNBA Basketball Christie	20206	$15.00		Christie
1999	Awesome Skateboard Janet	24991	$13.00		Janet
1999	Awesome Skateboard Stacie	24644	$11.00		Stacie
1999	Awesome Skateboard Whitney	24990	$13.00		Whitney
1999	Baby Krissy Layette	26572	$10.00		Krissy
1999	Baby Krissy Layette (black)	26806	$10.00		Krissy
1999	Baker Chelsie	24594	$5.00	Kelly Club	Chelsie
1999	Baker Nia	24605	$5.00		Nia
1999	Biker Baby Belinda	24602	$5.00	Kelly Club	Belinda
1999	Bowling Party Janet	22014	$13.00		Janet
1999	Bowling Party Stacie	22013	$13.00		Stacie
1999	Bowling Party Whitney	22015	$13.00		Whitney
1999	Brandy	24502	$17.00	Friends of Barbie	Brandy
1999	Bubble Fairy Christie	2088	$10.00		Christie
1999	Bubble Fairy Teresa	22089	$11.00		Teresa
1999	Butterfly Art Steven	22996	$10.00		Steven
1999	Cool Skating Christie	16230	$20.00		Christie
1999	Cool Skating Teresa	26231	$20.00		Teresa
1999	Cuddle Soft Kelly	23966	$45.00		Kelly
1999	Cuddly Soft Kelly	23966	$45.00		Kelly
1999	Cuddly Soft Kelly (black)	23967	$45.00		Kelly
1999	Florida Vacation Steven	20497	$5.00		Steven
1999	Generation Girl Chelsie	20967	$15.00	Generation Girls	Chelsie
1999	Generation Girl Lara	20968	$20.00	Generation Girls	Lara
1999	Generation Girl Mari w/book	25112	$20.00	Generation Girls	Mari
1999	Generation Girl Nichelle	20966	$15.00	Generation Girls	Nichelle
1999	Generation Girl Nichelle	25767	$20.00	Generation Girls	Nichelle
1999	Generation Girl Tori	20969	$15.00	Generation Girls	Tori

Year	Item	Number	Value	Specials	Doll
1999	Generation Girl Tori	25768	$20.00	Generation Girls	Tori
1999	Generation Girl Tori w/book	48573	$20.00	Generation Girls	Tori
1999	Golfer Liana	24601	$5.00	Kelly Club	Liana
1999	Haircut Tommy	22012	$6.00		Tommy
1999	Haircut Tommy (black)	22017	$6.00		Tommy
1999	Happenin' Hair Christie	22883	$12.00		Christie
1999	Happenin' Hair Teresa	22884	$12.00		Teresa
1999	Hawaii Christie	24615	$5.00		Christie
1999	Hawaii Midge	24617	$5.00		Midge
1999	Hawaii Steven	24620	$5.00		Steven
1999	Hawaii Teresa	24618	$5.00		Teresa
1999	Hollywood Nails Christie		$12.00		Christie
1999	Hollywood Nails Teresa	24244	$12.00		Teresa
1999	Jester Jenny	24598	$5.00		Jenny
1999	Kelly as Lullaby Munchkin	25818	$6.00	Wizard of Oz	Kelly
1999	Kelly Superslide	24645	$15.00		Kelly
1999	Kelly Superslide (black)	24749	$15.00		Kelly
1999	Lemonade Stand Maria	24593	$5.00	Kelly Club	Maria
1999	Lemonade Stand Tamika	24604	$5.00	Kelly Club	Tamika
1999	Little Swimmer Marisa	24600	$5.00	Kelly Club	Marisa
1999	Maria Flower Girl	20857	$5.00	Li'l Friends of Kelly	Maria
1999	Millennium Princess Teresa	25504	$40.00	Toys "R" Us	Teresa
1999	Movie Star Christie	26428	$20.00		Christie
1999	Pajama Fun Courtney	24992	$13.00		Courtney
1999	Pajama Fun Nikki	24993	$13.00		Nikki
1999	Paralympic Champion Becky	24662	$20.00		Becky
1999	Pearl Beach Christie Easter Basket	25381	$15.00	Supermarket	Christie
1999	Pearl Beach Teresa Easter Basket	25381	$15.00	Supermarket	Teresa
1999	Pilot Tommy	24595	$5.00	Kelly Club	Tommy
1999	Prince Tommy	24597	$5.00		Tommy
1999	Princess Kelly	24596	$5.00		Kelly
1999	Princess Kelly (black)		$5.00		Kelly
1999	Raggedy Ann and Andy	24639	$20.00		Kelly & Tommy
1999	Rosie O'Donnell	22016	$25.00	Friends of Barbie	Rosie
1999	Secret Messages Christie	26423	$12.00		Christie
1999	Secret Messages Teresa	26424	$12.00		Teresa
1999	Sit in Style Christie	23422	$8.00		Christie
1999	Sit in Style Kira	23424	$8.00		Kira
1999	Sit in Style Teresa	23423	$8.00		Teresa
1999	Soccer Christie	20351	$15.00		Christie
1999	Soccer Kira	20352	$15.00		Kira
1999	Soccer Teresa	20207	$17.00		Teresa
1999	Swimming Champion Christie	25488	$17.00		Christie
1999	Swimming Champion Teresa	25489	$15.00		Teresa
1999	Teen Scene Sidney	20969	$15.00		Sidney
1999	Tennis Deidre	24607	$5.00	Kelly Club	Deidre
1999	Tennis Lorena	24603	$5.00	Kelly Club	Lorena
1999	Tiny Steps Kelly	22226	$11.00		Kelly
1999	Tiny Steps Kelly (black)	22227	$10.00		Kelly
1999	Tommy as Lollipop Munchkin	25819	$6.00	Wizard of Oz	Tommy
1999	Tommy as Mayor Munchkin	25817	$6.00	Wizard of Oz	Tommy
1999	Tommy Winter Fun	20853	$5.00	Li'l Friends of Kelly	Tommy
1999	Totally Yo-Yo Courtney	22230	$13.00		Courtney
1999	Totally Yo-Yo Nikki	22229	$13.00		Nikki
1999	Walking Barbie & Baby Sister Krissy	22232	$18.00		Krissy

Year	Item	Number	Value	Specials	Doll
1999	Walking Barbie & Baby Sister Krissy (black)	22307	$18.00		Krissy
1999	Winter Coat Chelsie	18034	$5.00		Chelsie
1999	Wizard Melody	24599	$5.00		Melody
2000	Amusement Park Kelly	28391	$5.00		Kelly
2000	Amusement Park Marisa	29200	$5.00	Kelly Club	Marisa
2000	Amusement Park Ryan	28392	$5.00	Kelly Club	Ryan
2000	Cher	29049	$40.00	Timeless Treasures	Cher
2000	Cool Blading Christie	26230	$15.00		Christie
2000	Cool Blading Teresa	26231	Retail		Teresa
2000	Cool Clips Christie	26426	$14.00		Christie
2000	Cool Clips Teresa	26427	$17.00		Teresa
2000	Cool Skating Christie	26230	$15.00		Christie
2000	Cool Skating Teresa	26424	$15.00		Teresa
2000	Fashion Party Courtney	29104	$14.00		Courtney
2000	Fashion Party Nikki		$15.00		Nikki
2000	Flying Butterfly Teresa	50347	$13.00		Teresa
2000	Generation Girl Blaine	26111	$20.00	Generation Girls	Blaine
2000	Generation Girl Chelsie	26848	$20.00	Generation Girls	Chelsie
2000	Generation Girl Lara	25769	$20.00	Generation Girls	Lara
2000	Generation Girl Mari	26112	$20.00	Generation Girls	Mari
2000	Generation Girl Nichelle	25767	$20.00	Generation Girls	Nichelle
2000	Generation Girl Tori	25768	$20.00	Generation Girls	Tori
2000	Glam 'n Groom Teresa	26253	$15.00		Teresa
2000	Glam 'n Groom Christie	26252	$15.00		Christie
2000	Goldilocks and the Three Bears	29605	$19.00		Kelly
2000	Hansel & Gretel	28539	$19.00		Kelly & Tommy
2000	Hawaii Steven	24620	$5.00		Steven
2000	I Dream of Jeannie	29913	$50.00		Jeannie
2000	Kwanzaa Kayla	24606	$5.00		Kayla
2000	Love 'n Care Kelly	27039	$10.00		Kelly
2000	Movie Star Teresa		$15.00		Teresa
2000	Picture Pockets Kira	28704	$10.00	Toys "R" Us	Kira
2000	Nsync Christie w/CD	50535	$19.00		Christie
2000	Nsync Teresa w/CD	50536	$19.00		Teresa
2000	Picture Pockets Christie	28702	$9.00		Christie
2000	Picture Pockets Teresa	28703	$10.00	Toys "R" Us	Teresa
2000	Princess Kelly	25599	$5.00		Kelly
2000	Rain or Shine Christie		$15.00		Christie
2000	Rain or Shine	29181	$15.00		Teresa
2000	Scrub-a-dub-dub Krissy	26897	$9.00		Kira
2000	Scrub-a-dub-dub Krissy (black)	27244	$9.00		Krissy
2000	Surf City Christie	28418	$5.00		Christie
2000	Surf City Kira	28420	$5.00		Kira
2000	Surf City Midge	28421	$5.00		Midge
2000	Surf City Steven	28423	$5.00		Steven
2000	Surf City Teresa	28419	$5.00		Teresa
2001	Cowgirl Kelly	50733	$20.00	Toys "R" Us	Kelly

Barbie Doll Outfits

Listed Alphabetically

Item	Number	Year	Value	Specials
2 Different Prints in Yellow	2226	1978	$15.00	Best Buys
2-Piece Shocking Pink Evening Gown	2562	1978	$15.00	Best Buys
5th Avenue Fashions	1648	1992	$35.00	
6-Piece SuperStar Mix 'n Match	2580	1978	$140.00	Sears' Exclusive
64-Piece Accessory Set	1498	1970	$275.00	JCPenney
7-Piece Mix 'n Match	2579	1978	$40.00	Sears' Exclusive
8-Piece Coordinated Set	9670	1976	$45.00	Sears
9 to 5	2771	1986	$10.00	Finishing Touches
9-Piece Red/White/Blue Outfit	9078	1975	$60.00	Sears Fashion Originals
A Little Luxury	4810	1984	$10.00	Fashion Fantasy
Aboard in Blue	3346	1973	$40.00	Best Buys
Aboard Ship	1631	1965	$450.00	
Accessory Pack	923	1961	$250.00	
Accessory Pak (4 pairs shoes, pearl choker, etc.)	Pak	1962	$225.00	
Add-Ons	Pak	1968	$150.00	
After Five	934	1962	$175.00	
All About Plaid	3433	1971	$150.00	
All American Girl	3337	1972	$80.00	Best Buys
All Decked Out	17568	1997	$20.00	Barbie Millicent Roberts
All That Jazz	1848	1968	$300.00	
All the Trimmings (pak)	50	1970	$225.00	
All Turned Out	4822	1984	$20.00	Twice As Nice Fashions
American Airlines Stewardess	984	1961	$175.00	
Angel	12602	1995	$10.00	My First Fashions
Angel	68087	2000	$4.00	
Animal Lovin' Fashions	1601	1988	$30.00	
Anti-Freezers	1464	1970	$125.00	
Apple Print Sheath	917	1959	$200.00	
Apron and Utensils	Pak	1962	$55.00	
Aqua Locket Surprise Fashions	11560	1994	$5.00	Locket Surprise Fashions
Arabian Nights	874	1964	$375.00	Little Theatre Costumes
Baby Doll Pinks	3403	1971	$110.00	
Baby Sits	953	1962	$225.00	
Baby Sits (Layette)	953	1964	$400.00	
Backyard Barbecue	5719	1983	$20.00	Fashion Fun
Ballerina	12601	1995	$10.00	My First Fashions
Ballerina	7701	1973	$50.00	Get-Ups 'n Go
Ballerina	989	1961	$175.00	
Ballerina Costume	9650	1976	$45.00	Sears
Ballerina, One-Piece Hot Pink w/Shimmery Top	14666	1996	$4.00	My First Fashions
Bandana Skirt and Top, Red Cowboy Hat	12778	1995	$5.00	Western Fun Fashions
Barbie Disney Fun Fashions	68698	1999	$18.00	
Barbie in Hawaii	1605	1964	$175.00	Travel Outfits
Barbie in Holland	823	1964	$350.00	Travel Outfits
Barbie in Japan	821	1964	$375.00	Travel Outfits
Barbie in Mexico	820	1964	$225.00	Travel Outfits
Barbie in Switzerland	822	1964	$220.00	Travel Outfits
Barbie Learns to Cook	1634	1965	$525.00	

Item	Number	Year	Value	Specials
Barbie-Q	962	1959	$170.00	
Bashful Bunny Fashion	29156	2001	$5.00	Animation Styles
Bathrobe (yellow)	Pak	1963	$50.00	
Bathtime Chat Fashion	24294	1999	$5.00	Charm Styles
Beach	7788	1974	$60.00	Get-Ups 'n Go
Beach Dazzler	1939	1981	$10.00	Fashion Favorites
Beach Party	5541	1983	$20.00	Fashion Fantasy
Beau Time	1651	1966	$350.00	
Beautiful Bride	1698	1967	$2,000.00	
Bedtime Beauty	7081	1984	$10.00	Designer Collection
Belle Dress	Pak	1962	$100.00	
Belle Dress (orange)	Pak	1962	$90.00	
Benefit Performance	1667	1966	$1,250.00	
Bermuda Holiday	1810	1968	$300.00	
Best Bow	Pak	1967	$175.00	
Black & White Leopard Print Coat	22157	1999	$12.00	Fashion Avenue
Black Jeans, Shiny Pink Vest, Black Boots	68084	2000	$4.00	Jean Fashions
Black Magic Ensemble	1609	1964	$400.00	
Black Pants & White Top	12635	1995	$5.00	Paint The Dots Fashion
Black Pants and Oriental Tunic	2563	1978	$30.00	Best Buys
Black Shorts, Orange Jacket, White Top	12637	1995	$5.00	Paint The Dots Fashion
Black Tie Affair	1935	1981	$10.00	Fashion Favorites
Black, Blue & Yellow Bike Shorts & Shirt, Glasses	68085	1999	$2.00	Sun & Sea Fashions
Black/Rose Nightgown	9682	1976	$45.00	Sears' Exclusive Best Buys
Black/Silver Shimmer	9837	1977	$15.00	SuperStar Fashions
Black/White Bikers, Suspenders, Orange Top	2146	1990	$5.00	Cool Mix Fashions
Black/White Checked Bikers w/Suspenders, Halter	2144	1990	$5.00	Cool Mix Fashions
Black/White Checked Top, Multicolor Skirt	2132	1990	$5.00	Cool Mix Fashions
Black/White Dot Dress, Hat, Pants, Yellow Skirt	4795	1988	$10.00	Fashion Magic Fashions
Black/White Formal Long Gown with Gloves	1364	1980	$10.00	Fashion Collectibles
Black/White Long Halter Dress	3634	1982	$10.00	Best Buys
Black/White Polka Dot Culottes, Top, Jacket, Socks	3323	1989	$10.00	Cool Times Fashions
Black/White Two-Piece Pants and Top	2295	1986	$10.00	
Bloom Bursts	1778	1967	$450.00	Color Magic
Blue Bathing Suit	12645	1995	$5.00	Bath Paintin' Fashions
Blue Denim Dress and Hat	9907	1975	$40.00	Sears' Exclusive Best Buys
Blue Dress w/Silver Dots, Purse, Hose, Shoes	14368	1996	$5.00	Fashion Avenue
Blue Evening Gown	2769	1979	$15.00	Best Buys
Blue Evening Gown	8692	1973	$50.00	Best Buys
Blue Evening Gown, Lace Trim	9963	1977	$20.00	Best Buys
Blue Evening Gown, Sheer Coat	1021	1979	$15.00	Department Store
Blue Floral Print Halter Top and Shorts	3676	1982	$10.00	My First Barbie Fashions
Blue Gingham Boxers and Bustier w/Overshirt	14288	1996	$5.00	Fashion Avenue
Blue Gingham Top, Shorts, Blue Shoes	68014	2000	$2.00	Go in Style Fashions
Blue Glitter Trim Dress w/Long & Short Skirts	7392	1990	$5.00	Dance Magic Fashions
Blue Halter Dress	3637	1982	$10.00	Best Buys
Blue Halter Top, Blue/White Pants	1510	1989	$10.00	Feeling Pretty Fashions
Blue Halter, Blue Biker Pants, Yellow Ruffle Trim	2138	1990	$5.00	Cool Mix Fashions
Blue Halter, Pink Shorts w/Blue Trim, Flying Disc	2130	1990	$5.00	Cool Mix Fashions
Blue Jacket and White Short Outfit	12629	1995	$5.00	Sponge 'n Print Fashions
Blue Jumper, Orange Tube Top	2131	1990	$5.00	Cool Mix Fashions
Blue Jumper, White Print Top, White Purse	2131	1990	$5.00	Cool Mix Fashions
Blue Jumpsuit, Gold Belt and Collar	7910	1985	$10.00	B Active Fashions
Blue Long Halter Dress with Self-tie Belt	1358	1980	$10.00	Best Buys
Blue Long Skirt, Pink Top, Zebra Print Top	1597	1989	$10.00	Animal Lovin' Fashions

Item	Number	Year	Value	Specials
Blue Long Sleeve Long Sleeved Dress	3685	1982	$10.00	Fashion Collectibles
Blue Long Sleeve Outfit	2556	1978	$20.00	Best Buys
Blue Long Top and Leggings, Pink Scarf	4487	1988	$10.00	Sweatersoft Fashions
Blue Magic	7216	1984	$10.00	Spectacular Fashions
Blue Mist	1936	1981	$10.00	Fashion Favorites
Blue Outfit	12626	1995	$5.00	Bead Fun Fashions
Blue Outfit, Mask, Blue Ice Skates	4081	1990	$5.00	Ice Capades Fashions
Blue Pants and Tunic	2550	1978	$20.00	Best Buys
Blue Pants, Bandana Blouse	9161	1976	$35.00	Best Buys
Blue Pants, Checked Top	9579	1976	$35.00	Best Buys
Blue Pants, Silvery Blue Blouse	2564	1978	$20.00	Best Buys
Blue Pants, Striped Blouse	1006	1979	$15.00	Fashion Collectibles
Blue Pants, Yellow Top	9685	1976	$40.00	Sears' Exclusive Best Buys
Blue Party Dress	7840	1974	$100.00	Get-Ups 'n Go
Blue, Pink & White Print Dress, Shoes	68783	2000	$4.00	Glow-in-the-Dark Fashions
Blue Print and Red Dress	2219	1978	$20.00	Best Buys
Blue Print Baggy Pants	2217	1978	$20.00	Best Buys
Blue Print Dress w/White Collar and Cuffs	3679	1982	$10.00	Fashion Collectibles
Blue Print Long Dress	2227	1978	$20.00	Best Buys
Blue Print Short Halter Dress with Lace Trim	1895	1987	$10.00	My First Barbie Fashions
Blue Print Sundress, Black Sandals	68014	2000	$2.00	Go in Style Fashions
Blue Print Two-Piece Belted Dress	1424	1980	$10.00	Fashion Collectibles
Blue, Red & White Print Dress, Shawl, Shoes	68783	2000	$4.00	Glow-in-the-Dark Fashions
Blue Royalty	1469	1970	$250.00	Get-Ups 'n Go
Blue Sequin Trim Tutu w/Leggings	1862	1989	$10.00	My First Barbie Fashions
Blue Short Dress	1012	1989	$10.00	Fashion Finds Fashions
Blue Short Halter Dress w/Bow Trim, Pink Leggings	1466	1989	$10.00	Style Magic Fashions
Blue Short Ruffle Trim Dress, Long White Gloves	1308	1989	$10.00	Dinner Date Fashions
Blue Short Skirt, Top, Blue Dog	3656	1987	$10.00	Pet Show Fashions
Blue Short Sleeveless Dress	1019	1989	$10.00	Fashion Finds Fashions
Blue Shorts, White Top, and Yellow Jacket	13018	1995	$5.00	Yacht Club Fashions
Blue Skirt and Top, Red Pants	9143	1985	$6.00	Spectacular Fashions
Blue Skirt, Jacket, Pink Top	9170	1990	$5.00	Dinner Date Fashions
Blue Skirt, Yellow Jacket, Print Top	4529	1988	$10.00	Bright & Breezy Fashions
Blue Star Motif Top, Pink Print Pants	9271	1990	$5.00	My First Barbie Fashions
Blue Suit Jacket with Dark Blue Skirt	3682	1982	$10.00	Fashion Collectibles
Blue Top and Pants with Contrast Design on Top	1426	1980	$10.00	Fashion Collectibles
Blue Top with Lace Trim, White Pants	3791	1982	$10.00	Fashion Favorites
Blue Top, Blue/Pink Ruffle Short Skirt, Shawl	9249	1990	$5.00	My First Barbie Fashions
Blue Top, Print Ruffle Short Skirt, Red Belt	1527	1989	$10.00	Weekend Collection Fashions
Blue Top, White Skirt	3657	1987	$10.00	Pet Show Fashions
Blue/Flame Short Party Dress	9582	1976	$35.00	Best Buys
Blue/Fuchsia Lace Overlay Dress, Hat, Purse, Boa	1940	1989	$10.00	Private Collection Fashions
Blue/Gold Outfit, Hat, Blue Ice Skates	4082	1990	$5.00	Ice Capades Fashions
Blue/Green/Purple Jumpsuit, White Scarf	9618	1977	$15.00	Best Buys
Blue/Green/Purple Wrap Blouse and Cap	2052	1977	$25.00	Sears' Exclusive Best Buys
Blue/Hot Pink Two-Piece Jogging Suit	2180	1986	$10.00	B Active Fashions
Blue/Orange One-Piece Bathing Suit	12646	1995	$5.00	Bath Paintin' Fashions
Blue/Pink Short Ruffle Dress, Hat	1688	1989	$10.00	Jeans Fashions
Blue/Red Pants, Top, Jacket	2297	1986	$10.00	Twice As Nice Reversible
Blue/Silver Evening Gown	9626	1977	$15.00	Best Buys
Blue Sleeveless Dress, White Bow Trim	1453	1989	$10.00	Style Magic Fashions
Blue/White Checked Midi Suit	8621	1973	$50.00	Best Buys
Blue/White Print Long Sleeved Blouse, Skirt	1697	1989	$10.00	Jeans Fashions
Blue/White Print Nightgown	15873	1997	$5.00	Fashion Avenue Lingerie

Item	Number	Year	Value	Specials
Blue/White Striped Gown	2557	1978	$15.00	Best Buys
Blue/White Striped Top, Long Blue Skirt	7916	1985	$10.00	B Active Fashions
Boarding Outfit	None	1967	$500.00	Barbie Goes Braniff Fashions
Book Bag	4283	1984	$10.00	
Boudoir	Pak	1964	$125.00	
Bouncy Flouncy	1805	1967	$300.00	
Bridal Brocade	3417	1971	$275.00	
Bridal Gown	94196	1976	$40.00	Department Store
Bride	7176	1976	$40.00	Get-Ups 'n Go
Bride	7839	1974	$80.00	Get-Ups 'n Go
Bride In White	2300	1978	$20.00	Get-Ups 'n Go
Bride's Dream	947	1963	$300.00	
Bridesmaid's Dream	1417	1980	$15.00	Barbie & Ken Wedding Party
Bridesmaid's Dream	5745	1983	$10.00	Wedding of the Year
Bright 'n Brocade	1786	1970	$140.00	
Brocade Dream Steals the Scene	9740	1977	$15.00	Get-Ups 'n Go
Brocade Shine	9835	1977	$15.00	SuperStar Fashions
Brunch Time	1628	1965	$350.00	
Bubbles 'n Boots	3421	1971	$150.00	
Business Executive	9083	1985	$10.00	Day to Night Fashions
Busy Gal	981	1960	$415.00	
Busy Morning	956	1963	$230.00	
Butterfly	68087	2000	$4.00	Fantasy Costume Fashion
Butterfly Print Pants, Jacket, Top	3313	1988	$10.00	Beverly Hills Fashions
Camping	7702	1973	$55.00	Get-Ups 'n Go
Campus Belle	Pak	1964	$150.00	
Campus Sweetheart	1616	1964	$1,600.00	
Campus Sweetheart	5702	1983	$10.00	Fashion Classics
Can't Stop Dancin'	5538	1983	$10.00	Fashion Fantasy
Candlelight Nights	5898	1983	$10.00	Fashion Fun
Candy Striper Volunteer	889	1964	$300.00	
Capri Jeans, Pink Midi Top, Pink Sandals	68014	2000	$2.00	Go in Style Fashions
Cardigan	Pak	1962	$40.00	
Career Girl	954	1963	$350.00	
Caribbean Cruise	1687	1967	$230.00	
Casual Chic	1940	1981	$10.00	Fashion Favorites
Casuals	7242	1975	$40.00	Get-Ups 'n Go
Change-Abouts	Pak	1968	$150.00	
Check The Suit	1794	1970	$125.00	
Checked Pants, Solid Shirt	9576	1976	$40.00	
Cheerleader	876	1964	$200.00	
Cinderella	872	1964	$450.00	Little Theatre Costumes
City Fun	5717	1983	$10.00	Fashion Fun
City Nights	2770	1986	$10.00	Finishing Touches
City Shopping	5716	1983	$10.00	Fashion Fun
City Slicker Fashion	17570	1997	$20.00	Barbie Millicent Roberts
City Sophisticate	2671	1979	$20.00	Designer Originals
City Sparklers	1457	1970	$125.00	
City Suit in White	2342	1978	$10.00	
City Taylor	5542	1983	$10.00	Fashion Fantasy
Classic Cowgirl	1938	1981	$10.00	Fashion Favorites
Cling & Zing	2345	1978	$15.00	
Close-Ups	1864	1969	$125.00	
Cloud 9	1489	1969	$140.00	
Club Meeting	1672	1966	$400.00	

Item	Number	Year	Value	Specials
Coffee's On	1670	1966	$180.00	
Cold Snap	3429	1971	$75.00	
Collector Series IV	9258	1985	$40.00	Oscar De La Renta
Collector Series V	9259	1985	$40.00	Oscar De La Renta
Collector Series VI	9260	1985	$40.00	Oscar De La Renta
Collector Series VII	9261	1985	$40.00	Oscar De La Renta
Collector Series VIII	2762	1986	$40.00	Oscar De La Renta
Collector Series IX	2763	1986	$40.00	Oscar De La Renta
Collector Series X	2765	1986	$40.00	Oscar De La Renta
Collector Series XI	2766	1986	$40.00	Oscar De La Renta
Collector Series XII	2767	1986	$40.00	Oscar De La Renta
Color Coordinates	1832	1964	$100.00	
Color Floral Top and Bottoms	15874	1997	$6.00	Fashion Avenue Lingerie
Color Kick, The	3422	1971	$160.00	
Color Magic Set	4040	1966	$2,000.00	
Commuter Set	916	1959	$1,200.00	
Cook-Ups	Pak	1967	$250.00	
Cool Casual	Pak	1970	$140.00	
Coral Evening Gown	9595	1976	$35.00	Get-Ups 'n Go
Coral Evening Gown and Shoes	9972	1977	$20.00	Department Store
Costume Completers	Pak	1964	$150.00	
Cotton Casual	912	1959	$125.00	
Country Bride	15898	1997	$10.00	Fashion Avenue Bridal
Country Caper	1862	1969	$110.00	
Country Club Dance	1627	1965	$400.00	
Country Fair	1603	1964	$175.00	
Country Girl	5836	1983	$10.00	Designer Collection
Country Music	1055	1971	$300.00	Fashions 'n Sounds
Court Casuals	2787	1979	$15.00	Fashion Favorites
Court Favorite Fashion	17569	1997	$20.00	Barbie Millicent Roberts
Cream Pants, Leopard Print Top, Brown Fanny Pack	1594	1989	$15.00	Animal Lovin' Fashions
Crisp 'n Cool	1604	1964	$180.00	
Cruise Stripes	918	1959	$150.00	
Curtain's Up	4811	1984	$10.00	Fashion Fantasy
Daisy Duck Motif Dress, White Leggings, Socks	9207	1990	$5.00	Disney Character Fashions
Dance & Whirl, Golden Girl	2343	1978	$15.00	
Dance Sensation	7218	1984	$10.00	Spectacular Fashions
Dancer	9082	1985	$10.00	Day to Night Fashions
Dancing Doll	1626	1965	$475.00	
Dancing Lights	3437	1971	$325.00	
Dancing Stripes	1843	1968	$200.00	
Dandy Lines	3798	1982	$15.00	Barbie & Ken Designer Original
Dark Peasant Outfit	2561	1978	$15.00	Best Buys
Dark Peasant Print, Red Trim	2779	1979	$12.00	Fashion Collectibles
Dark Print	2768	1979	$12.00	Best Buys
Dark Print Jumpsuit	2778	1979	$12.00	Best Buys
Date Night	5654	1983	$10.00	Designer Collection
Day 'n Night	1723	1965	$75.00	Sew Free Fashion
Day in Town	1712	1965	$60.00	Sew Free Fashion
Dazzling Dancer	2743	1986	$30.00	Astro Fashions
Debutante Ball	1666	1966	$1,000.00	
Debutante Party	1711	1965	$75.00	Sew Free Fashion
Denim Dress, Pink Bandana Print Jacket	12779	1995	$5.00	Western Fun Fashions
Denim Jacket, Blue Dress, Pink Shorts, Overskirt	4593	1990	$5.00	Barbie and The Beat Fashion
Denim Jacket, Striped Short Skirt, Denim Top	4569	1990	$5.00	Barbie and The Beat Fashion

Item	Number	Year	Value	Specials
Denim Overalls w/Hip Pack, Lace Top, Beret	14670	1996	$5.00	Fashion Avenue
Denim Overalls with Red Top	3681	1982	$10.00	Fashion Collectibles
Denim Short Dress and Sparkly Golden Jacket	14673	1996	$5.00	Fashion Avenue
Denim Shorts and Bandana Print Halter	12776	1995	$5.00	Western Fun Fashions
Denim Skirt, Jacket w/Fur-like Trim, Purse	14671	1996	$5.00	Fashion Avenue
Denim Top & Skirt, Yellow Lace Trim	4573	1990	$5.00	Barbie and The Beat Fashion
Denim Top, Plaid Denim Trim Shorts, Purse	2496	1990	$5.00	All Stars Fashions
Denim Vest, Skirt w/Print Ruffle, Purple Halter	4596	1990	$5.00	Barbie and The Beat Fashion
Denim Vest, Skirt, Pink Top and Leggings	4595	1990	$5.00	Barbie and The Beat Fashion
Denim Vest, w/White Ruffled Blouse, Shorts	14672	1996	$5.00	Fashion Avenue
Dinner at Eight	946	1963	$250.00	
Dinner Date	5714	1983	$10.00	Fashion Fun
Disco Date	1633	1965	$275.00	
Disco Date	1807	1967	$280.00	
Disco Dazzle	1011	1979	$15.00	Fashion Favorites
Doctor	7700	1973	$75.00	Get-Ups 'n Go
Dog 'n Duds	1613	1964	$275.00	
Dolphin Print Top, Multicolored Jacket and Pants	4465	1988	$10.00	California Dream Fashions
Donald Duck Motif Top, Net Skirt, Biker Pants	9202	1990	$5.00	Disney Character Fashions
Dotted Skirt, Jacket, Yellow Top, White Shorts	4820	1988	$10.00	Fashion Magic Fashions
Double Date	4821	1984	$10.00	Twice As Nice Fashions
Double Dazzle	4824	1984	$10.00	Twice As Nice Fashions
Dream Team, The	3427	1971	$165.00	
Dream Time	5547	1983	$10.00	Fashion Fantasy
Dream Wraps	1476	1969	$80.00	
Dream-Ins	1867	1969	$115.00	
Dreamland	1669	1966	$160.00	
Dreamy Blues	1456	1970	$80.00	
Dreamy Delight for at Night	9743	1977	$15.00	Get-Ups 'n Go
Dreamy Designs for Dressy Dinners	7841	N/A	$80.00	
Dreamy Pair	2347	1978	$15.00	
Dreamy Pink	1857	1968	$100.00	
Dress and Jacket	11936	1994	$4.00	Fashion Forms Fashions
Dress and Shoulder Bag	11937	1994	$4.00	Fashion Forms Fashions
Dress Designer	9081	1985	$15.00	Day to Night Fashions
Dress w/Blue Top, Floral Skirt, Pink Jacket, Hat	4957	1990	$5.00	Private Collection Fashions
Dress w/Heart Print Top, Pink Bottom	9974	1990	$5.00	Fashion Finds
Dress w/Print Top, White Skirt, Red Jacket	1528	1989	$10.00	Weekend Collection Fashions
Dress w/Yellow Top, White Lace Skirt	1422	1980	$10.00	Fashion Collectibles
Dress, Bag	9573	1976	$30.00	Best Buys
Dress-Up Hats	Pak	1964	$125.00	
Dressed to a "T"	1403	1980	$10.00	Fashion Favorites
Dressed-Up	Pak	1968	$160.00	
Drizzle Dash	1808	1967	$200.00	
Drum Majorette	875	1964	$225.00	
Easter Parade	971	1959	$4,500.00	
Easy Slip On (pink short set)	1912	1981	$10.00	My First Barbie Fashions
Easy Slip On (plaid dress)	1913	1981	$10.00	My First Barbie Fashions
Elegant Evening Suit in Magenta with Bow	4622	1989	$10.00	Perfume Pretty Fashions
Enchanted Evening	983	1960	$325.00	
Evening Elegance	1414	1980	$15.00	Barbie & Ken Designer Original
Evening Enchantment	1695	1967	$550.00	
Evening Gala	1660	1966	$400.00	
Evening Gown	2062	1977	$50.00	Sears Exclusive
Evening Gown	2223	1978	$30.00	Best Buys

Item	Number	Year	Value	Specials
Evening Gown, Burnt Orange, Shawl	9422	1976	$40.00	Department Store
Evening Gown, Pink/Blue/Rose	9421	1976	$40.00	Department Store
Evening In	3406	1971	$150.00	
Evening Outfit	2221	1978	$30.00	Best Buys
Evening Rose	5548	1983	$10.00	Fashion Fantasy
Evening Splendour	961	1959	$275.00	
Evening Splendour (reissue)	961	1964	$150.00	
Everyday Outing	4804	1984	$10.00	Fashion Fun
Executive Lunch Fashion	22306	1999	$26.00	Barbie Millicent Roberts
Extra-Casuals	Pak	1968	$140.00	
Extravaganza	1844	1968	$350.00	
Eye Popper	1937	1981	$10.00	Fashion Favorites
Fab City	1874	1969	$350.00	
Fab Fur	1493	1969	$250.00	
Fabulous Fashion	1676	1966	$500.00	
Fabulous Gown for Night on the Town	2304	1978	$10.00	Get-Ups 'n Go
Faded Blue Skirt, Blue Sunburst Blouse	9621	1977	$10.00	Best Buys
Fairy, One-Piece Purple/Pink	14667	1996	$4.00	My First Fashions
Fall	15906	1997	$10.00	Fashion Avenue Internationale
Fancy Free	943	1963	$100.00	
Fancy Hair	2775	1986	$10.00	Finishing Touches
Fancy Pants	5703	1983	$10.00	Fashion Classics
Fancy That Purple	3362	1972	$125.00	Best Buys
Fancy Trimmin's	Pak	1967	$225.00	
Fancy-Dancy	1858	1968	$200.00	
Fashion Accents	1521	1970	$250.00	Sears
Fashion Accents (Pak)	1830	1964	$250.00	
Fashion Avenue Barbie Easter Fashion	21371	1999	$10.00	Fashion Avenue
Fashion Bouquet	1511	1970	$350.00	Sears
Fashion Editor	1635	1965	$800.00	
Fashion Extras	4918A	1984	$10.00	Department Store
Fashion Feet	Pak	1964	$75.00	
Fashion Firsts	Pak	1971	$90.00	
Fashion Hangers (10)	1065	1982	$5.00	
Fashion Luncheon	1656	1966	$1,100.00	
Fashion Original	7932	N/A	$75.00	
Fashion Shiner	1691	1967	$300.00	
Fashion Undergarment	919	1959	$75.00	
Festival Fashion	1056	1971	$370.00	Fashions 'n Sounds
Fiery Felt	1789	1970	$80.00	
Figured Gauchos and Jacket	9424	1976	$30.00	Department Store
Figured Skirt, Bolero, Cap, Beige Blouse	9629	1977	$30.00	Best Buys
Finishing Touches	Pak	1969	$175.00	
Firelights	1481	1969	$145.00	
Flamingo Print Top, Yellow Leggings	4464	1988	$10.00	California Dream Fashions
Flats 'n Heels	1837	1966	$275.00	
Flats 'n Heels	Pak	1968	$350.00	
Flats 'n Heels (10 pairs)	Pak	1969	$225.00	
Floating Gardens	1696	1967	$520.00	
Floral Petticoat	921	1959	$125.00	
Floral Print Halter Dress	3638	1982	$10.00	Best Buys
Floral Print Long Dress, Vest, Purse, Cowboy Hat	3578	1982	$10.00	Western Fashions
Floral Print Short Skirt, Blue Top	1025	1989	$10.00	Fashion Finds Fashions
Floral Print Sundress	4128	1988	$10.00	Pretty Choices
Floral Print Wrap Halter Dress	1362	1980	$10.00	Fashion Collectibles

Item	Number	Year	Value	Specials
Floral Print, Strapless Dress	1525	1989	$10.00	Feeling Pretty Fashions
Floral Printed Dress	9156	1976	$35.00	Best Buys
Flower Girl	5746	1984	$10.00	Wedding of the Year
Flower Print Dress	3343	1973	$60.00	Best Buys
Flower Wower	1453	1970	$70.00	
Flowery Delight is Party Right!	2302	1978	$15.00	Get-Ups 'n Go
Fluff Fashion	29154	2001	$5.00	Animation Styles
Flying Colors	3492	1972	$350.00	
Foot Lights (pak)	40	1970	$120.00	
For Barbie Dressmakers	1831	1964	$50.00	
For Rink and Court	Pak	1964	$75.00	
Formal Occasion	1697	1967	$500.00	
Four Pair Panties, One Glitter Hose, One Tan Hose	3181	1987	$10.00	Fancy Frills
Fraternity Dance	1638	1965	$600.00	
Fresh 'n Cool	1429	1980	$10.00	Fashion Favorites
Friday Nite Date	979	1960	$225.00	
Fringe Benefits	3401	1971	$100.00	
From Nine to Five	1701	1965	$60.00	Sew Free Fashion
Fuchsia Dress, White Fur Trim, Stole, Purse	14367	1996	$5.00	Fashion Avenue
Fuchsia Long Coat, Teal Cap, Bag, Pants	3309	1988	$10.00	Beverly Hills Fashions
Fuchsia Long Dress, Print Belt	4125	1988	$10.00	Pretty Choices
Fuchsia Long Dress, Purse, Hair Decoration	4958	1990	$5.00	Private Collection Fashions
Fuchsia Long Skirt, Top, and Shoes	7917	1985	$10.00	B Active Fashions
Fuchsia Robe, Pink Towels, and White Stand	9266	1985	$10.00	Bath Fun Play Set
Fuchsia Ruffle Trim Short Dress and Hat	4959	1990	$5.00	Private Collection Fashions
Fuchsia Short Dress and Print Belt	7915	1985	$10.00	B Active Fashions
Fuchsia Short, Strapless Party Dress, Scarf	9251	1990	$5.00	My First Barbie Fashions
Fuchsia Ski Jacket	16951	1997	$10.00	Fashion Avenue Boutique
Fuchsia/Blue Long Dress, Purse, Hat	1944	1989	$10.00	Private Collection Fashions
Fuchsia/Blue Print Long Dress, Purse, Hair Ribbon	1943	1989	$10.00	Private Collection Fashions
Fuchsia/Blue Reversible Short Dress	7953	1985	$10.00	Twice As Nice Reversible
Fun 'n Fancy	3800	1982	$10.00	Barbie & Ken Designer Original
Fun 'n Games	1619	1965	$320.00	
Fun at McDonald's	4274	1983	$20.00	Fashion Classics
Fun at the Fair	1624	1965	$300.00	
Fun Flakes	3412	1971	$120.00	
Fun Fur	3434	1971	$205.00	
Fun in the Sun	4801	1984	$10.00	Fashion Fun
Fun Shine	3480	1972	$175.00	Miss America
Funtime Slumbers Fashion	24297	1999	$5.00	Metro Styles
Fur Cape and Long Gown	2667	1978	$10.00	Department Store
Fur Coat, Hat, Brown Skirt, Boots, Bag	9470	1977	$15.00	Best Buys
Fur Hat/Bag	Pak	1963	$500.00	
Fur Sighted	1796	1970	$200.00	
Fur Stole with Bag	Pak	1962	$60.00	
Furry 'n Fun	3336	1972	$100.00	Best Buys
Galaxy A Go Go	2742	1986	$28.00	Astro Fashions
Gallery Opening		1998	$30.00	Barbie Collector's Club
Garden Party	5701	1983	$10.00	Fashion Classics
Garden Party	5835	1983	$10.00	Designer Collection
Garden Party	931	1962	$175.00	
Garden Tea Party	1606	1964	$210.00	
Garden Wedding	1658	1966	$525.00	
Gathered Skirt	Pak	1962	$45.00	
Gaucho Gear	3436	1971	$240.00	

Item	Number	Year	Value	Specials
Gaucho Pants, Boots, and Blouse	9572	1976	$35.00	Best Buys
Gay Parisienne	964	1959	$4,900.00	
Glamour Group	1510	1970	$350.00	Sears
Glamour Hats	Pak	1966	$400.00	
Glimmer Glamour	1547	1968	$4,800.00	Sears
Glittery Blue Pants, Long Blue Tunic	9969	1977	$15.00	Best Buys
Glittery Evening Outfit	2780	1979	$10.00	Fashion Collectibles
Glo-Go	1865	1969	$250.00	
Gloves, Ballerina Bag, Pink/White Cap	1879	1987	$10.00	My First Barbie Fashions
Glowin' Gold	3354	1972	$60.00	Best Buys
Glowin' Out	3404	1971	$110.00	
Going to the Ball	Pak	1964	$115.00	
Gold 'n Glamour	1647	1965	$1,500.00	
Gold Ballgown	13203	1995	$5.00	Fantasy Evening Fashions
Gold Halter Jumpsuit, Sequin Belt/Headband, Jacket	3304	1989	$10.00	Superstar Barbie Fashions
Gold Knit	620	N/A	$45.00	
Gold Long Coat w/White Fur Trim, Gold Hat	4961	1990	$5.00	Private Collection Fashions
Gold Long Skirt, Purple Print Jacket, Purple Pants	4511	1988	$10.00	Private Collection Fashions
Gold Parka w/Fur-like Trim, Leopard Leggings	14299	1996	$5.00	Fashion Avenue
Gold Spun	1957	1981	$15.00	Barbie & Ken Designer Original
Gold/Green Dress with Matching Shawl	1363	1980	$10.00	Fashion Collectibles
Gold/Purple Outfit, White Ice Skates	4083	1990	$5.00	Ice Capades Fashions
Gold/White Gown, Purse, Shoes	14303	1996	$10.00	Fashion Avenue
Gold/White Outfit, White Hat & Ice Skates	4078	1990	$5.00	Ice Capades Fashions
Golden Accent	1958	1981	$15.00	Barbie & Ken Designer Original
Golden Ball	1724	1965	$70.00	Sew Free Fashion
Golden Elegance	992	1963	$325.00	
Golden Evening	1610	1964	$275.00	
Golden Firelight	2670	1979	$15.00	Designer Originals
Golden Girl	911	1959	$175.00	
Golden Glamour	1412	1980	$15.00	Barbie & Ken Designer Original
Golden Glitter	3340	1972	$125.00	Best Buys
Golden Glory	1645	1965	$400.00	
Golden Mini	4802	1984	$10.00	Fashion Fun
Goldswinger	1494	1969	$250.00	
Golfing Greats	3413	1971	$200.00	
Good Sports	3351	1972	$70.00	Best Buys
Goodies Galore	1518	1970	$275.00	Sears
Goofy Motif Pink/White Shirt, Halter, Pants	9198	1990	$5.00	Disney Character Fashions
Graduation	945	1963	$60.00	
Great Coat	1459	1970	$90.00	
Green Dress and Black Top	12636	1995	$5.00	Paint The Dots Fashion
Green Jacket and Skirt, Stripped Top, Leggings	3391	1987	$10.00	Concert Tour Fashions
Green One Sleeved Shirt, White Pants & Pumps	2186	1986	$10.00	B Active Fashions
Green Outfit	12624	1995	$5.00	Bead Fun Fashions
Green Pants, Top, Jacket	9965	1977	$15.00	Best Buys
Green Pants, Yellow Top, and Silver Jacket	7955	1985	$10.00	Twice As Nice Reversible
Green Print Skirt, Bolero, Yellow Blouse	9627	1977	$15.00	Best Buys
Green Separates Set	7933	1975	$35.00	Fashion Originals
Green Short Halter Dress w/White Trim	3677	1982	$10.00	My First Barbie Fashions
Green Skirt, White/Green Blouse	12597	1995	$5.00	Picnic Pretty Fashions
Green Slip, Panties, and Camisole	2555	1978	$15.00	Best Buys
Green Thumb	19433	1998	$30.00	Barbie Millicent Roberts
Green Top and Yellow Pants	7911	1985	$10.00	B Active Fashions
Green/Yellow Beach Outfit	2976	1979	$15.00	

Item	Number	Year	Value	Specials
Groovin' Gauchos	1057	1971	$300.00	Fashions 'n Sounds
Guinevere	873	1964	$250.00	Little Theatre Costumes
Gypsy Spirit	1458	1970	$80.00	
Hair Originals	2457	1978	$40.00	Fashion Add-Ons
Hair Originals (bows and ribbons)	2457	1981	$30.00	Fashion Add-Ons
Halter Top, Denim Skirt, Pink Jacket, Denim Trim	4574	1990	$5.00	Barbie and The Beat Fashion
Halter, Pink/Black Shorts, Skateboard	2493	1990	$5.00	All Stars Fashions
Happy Go Pink	1868	1969	$200.00	
Harem-m-m's	1784	1970	$65.00	
Hats & Glasses	2460	1978	$15.00	Fashion Add-Ons
Hats & Glasses	2460	1980	$15.00	Fashion Add-Ons
Hats & Glasses (4 Hats)	2460	1981	$10.00	Fashion Add-Ons
Have Fun	Pak	1966	$325.00	
Heavenly Holiday	4277	1983	$10.00	Heavenly Holidays Fashions
Helenca Swimsuit	Pak	1962	$150.00	
Here Comes the Bride	1416	1980	$15.00	Barbie & Ken Wedding Party
Here Comes the Bride	1665	1966	$1,000.00	
Here Comes the Bride	5743	1984	$10.00	Wedding of the Year
Here Comes the Bride	5748	1983	$10.00	Wedding of the Year
Hip Hop	29073	2000	$8.00	Movin' to Music
Holiday Dance	1639	1965	$550.00	
Holiday Gown Collection I	697	1992	$55.00	Wholesale Club
Holiday Gown Collection II	697A	1993	$55.00	Wholesale Club
Holiday Hostess	4803	1984	$10.00	Fashion Fun
Hollywood Premier Fashion	N/A	1992	$35.00	
Hollywood T-Top, Pink Long Skirt, White Leggings	4468	1988	$10.00	California Dream Fashions
Homecoming	16076	1996	$30.00	
Hootenanny	1707	1965	$50.00	Sew Free Fashion
Horizontal Striped Halter Dress	3639	1982	$10.00	Best Buys
Horseback Ridin'	7080	1984	$10.00	Designer Collection
Hostess Pajamas	None	1967	$500.00	Barbie Goes Braniff Fashions
Hostess Set	1034	1965	$3,500.00	
Hot Pink Short Dress, Purple Bolero, Boots	1165	1986	$10.00	Barbie & the Rockers Fashions
Hot Pink Sleeveless Dress w/Blue Stripe	1466	1981	$10.00	Best Buys
Hot Pink Sparkle Gown w/Fur Trim, Purse	14305	1996	$10.00	Fashion Avenue
Hot Togs	1063	1972	$725.00	Put-Ons 'n Pets
Hurray for Leather	1477	1969	$75.00	
Ice Breaker	942	1962	$175.00	
Ice Dancing	29901	2000	$8.00	Movin' to Music
Ice Skater	12603	1995	$5.00	My First Fashions
Icy Mint Green Sheath w/Matching Jacket	4625	1989	$10.00	Perfume Pretty Fashions
Important In-vestment	1482	1969	$100.00	
In & Outfitted	4825	1984	$10.00	Twice As Nice Fashions
In Blooms	3424	1971	$90.00	
In Stitches	3432	1971	$175.00	
In The Limelight	2790	1979	$15.00	Designer Originals
In The Pink	7219	1984	$10.00	Spectacular Fashions
In The Spotlight	7082	1984	$10.00	Designer Collection
In The Swim	Pak	1964	$400.00	
Indian Print Separates	7241	1975	$35.00	Get-Ups 'n Go
International Fair	1653	1966	$500.00	
Intrigue	1470	1967	$425.00	
Invitation to Tea	1632	1965	$575.00	
It's Cold Outside (brown)	819	1964	$150.00	
It's Cold Outside (red)	819	1964	$225.00	

Item	Number	Year	Value	Specials
Ivory/Gold Dress, Purse, Hose, Shoes	14365	1997	$5.00	Fashion Avenue
Jazz Dancin'	4817	1984	$10.00	Fashion Fantasy
Jeans	Pak	1963	$55.00	
Jet Set Luggage Ensemble	17571	1997	$20.00	Barbie Millicent Roberts
Jewel & Glitter Fashions	12183	1994	$5.00	Jewel & Glitter
Jump into Lace	1823	1968	$150.00	
Jumpin' Jeans	Pak	1964	$85.00	
Jumpkey Fashion	29152	2001	$5.00	Animation Styles
Junior Designer	1620	1965	$350.00	
Junior Prom	1614	1965	$575.00	
Kiss Me in Miami Fashion	28132	2000	$5.00	Metro Styles
Kitchen Magic	Pak	1966	$200.00	
Kitty Kapers	1062	1972	$825.00	Put-Ons 'n Pets
Knit Accessories	Pak	1963	$125.00	
Knit Ensemble	9152	1976	$35.00	Get-Ups 'n Go
Knit Hit	1621	1965	$155.00	
Knit Hit	1804	1968	$150.00	
Knit Separates	1602	1964	$140.00	
Knit Sheath Dress with Fringed Collar	Pak	1963	$50.00	
Knit Sheath Skirt and Sash	Pak	1963	$50.00	
Knit Shorts and Top	Pak	1963	$50.00	
Knit Skirt (long blue with glitter)	Pak	1963	$60.00	
Knit Slacks	Pak	1963	$40.00	
Knit Top	Pak	1963	$55.00	
Knitted Sweater w/Chambray Pants, Mittens	14298	1996	$5.00	Fashion Avenue
Knitting Pretty (blue)	957	1963	$350.00	
Knitting Pretty (pink)	957	1963	$300.00	
Lace Bodice Wedding Gown, Veil, Bouquet	4507	1988	$10.00	Private Collection Fashions
Lace Caper, The	1791	1970	$125.00	
Lace Embellished White Wedding Gown, Veil	14398	1996	$10.00	Fashion Avenue
Lady in Blue	2303	1978	$15.00	Get-Ups 'n Go
Lamb 'n Leather	1467	1970	$245.00	
Lamé Sheath	Pak	1963	$200.00	
Lavender Jeans, Striped Turtleneck, Lavender Shoes	68084	2000	$4.00	Jean Fashions
Lavender Jumper	16952	1997	$10.00	Fashion Avenue Boutique
Lavender Short Robe, Matching Teddy	3180	1987	$15.00	Fancy Frills
Lavender Shorty Gown with Lace Trim	2122	1986	$10.00	My First Barbie Fashions
Lavender Top w/Skirt and Leggings	7393	1990	$5.00	Dance Magic Fashions
Lavender w/Silver Trim Short Dress, Pink Leggings	1465	1989	$10.00	Style Magic Fashions
Lavender/White Long Dress	1860	1987	$10.00	Jewel Secrets Fashions
Leisure Hours	Pak	1964	$175.00	
Leisure Leopard	1479	1969	$75.00	
Lemon Kick	1465	1970	$150.00	
Let's Dance	1428	1980	$10.00	Fashion Favorites
Let's Dance	5707	1983	$10.00	Fashion Classics
Let's Dance	978	1960	$190.00	
Let's Have a Ball	1879	1969	$300.00	
Letter Perfect	4815	1984	$10.00	Fashion Fantasy
Light 'n Lazy	3339	1972	$75.00	Best Buys
Light Blue Coat	22159	1999	$12.00	Fashion Avenue
Light Blue Fur Trimmed Ice Skating Outfit/Gown	3300	1989	$10.00	Superstar Barbie Fashions
Light Blue Long Halter Dress with Ruffle Bottom	3672	1982	$10.00	My First Barbie Fashions
Light Blue Long Pajamas with Pink Ruffle Trim	4575	1988	$10.00	My First Barbie Fashions
Light Blue Skirt, Blue Floral Print Top, Blue Sandals	68084	2000	$4.00	Jean Fashions
Light Blue Skirt Long and Short, Top, Jacket	9144	1985	$10.00	Spectacular Fashions

Item	Number	Year	Value	Specials
Light Green Top w/Pink Trim, Dark Green Pants	1902	1981	$10.00	Fashion Collectibles
Light Printed	2772	1979	$15.00	Best Buys
Lilac Chemise Embellished, Black Lace Trim	15875	1997	$5.00	Fashion Avenue Lingerie
Lilac Dress with Lace-up Top, Ruffle Skirt	4621	1989	$10.00	Perfume Pretty Fashions
Lime Green & Turquoise Soccer Outfit, Green Shoes	69312	2000	$3.00	Totally Sports Fashion
Lime Green and Purple Bowling Shirt and Pants	68312	2000	$3.00	Totally Sports Fashion
Lime Time (final touches)	17876	1997	$15.00	Barbie Millicent Roberts
Lingerie Pack	Pak	1962	$145.00	
Little Bow-Pink	1483	1969	$175.00	
Little Red Riding Hood and the Wolf	880	1964	$600.00	Little Theatre Costumes
London Tour	1661	1966	$405.00	
Long 'n Fringy	3341	1972	$100.00	Best Buys
Long Blue Halter Dress	1467	1981	$10.00	Best Buys
Long Blue/White Party Outfit	2784	1979	$15.00	Fashion Collectibles
Long Blue/White Printed Dress	9686	1976	$40.00	
Long Brown Striped Skirt w/Blue/White Top	9622	1977	$15.00	Best Buys
Long Coat, Private Collection	N/A	1988	$10.00	
Long Dark Printed Dress	2776	1979	$15.00	Best Buys
Long Dark Printed Dress	8620	1973	$40.00	Best Buys
Long Denim Dress, Pink Buttons/Belt, Denim Bag	1694	1989	$10.00	Jeans Fashions
Long Dress, Silver Lamé Top, Blue Skirt	1862	1987	$10.00	Jewel Secrets Fashion
Long Dress, White Halter Top, Lavender Skirt	1863	1987	$10.00	Jewel Secrets Fashion
Long Dress, White Ruffled Top, Blue Bottom	3788	1982	$10.00	Fashion Favorites
Long Evening Dress w/White Top	4623	1989	$10.00	Perfume Pretty Fashions
Long Floral Printed Sleeveless Dress w/Blue Trim	1360	1980	$10.00	Best Buys
Long Gold Skirt, White Blouse	8689	1973	$70.00	Best Buys
Long Green Skirt and White Bodice	9620	1977	$15.00	Best Buys
Long Off-White Dress	8684	1973	$60.00	Best Buys
Long Printed Dress	1027	1979	$15.00	Bargain Fashions
Long Printed Tricot Skirt and Hat, Green Top	3206	1973	$60.00	Best Buys
Long Printed Dress, Yellow Sleeves	9575	1976	$35.00	Best Buys
Long Printed Skirt, Yellow Blouse	8683	1973	$60.00	Best Buys
Long Purple Halter Dress w/White Belt	1470	1981	$10.00	Best Buys
Long Red Halter Dress	1357	1980	$10.00	Best Buys
Long Red Printed Dress	9571	1976	$35.00	
Long Red Skirt, Printed Blouse	2781	1979	$15.00	Fashion Collectibles
Long Red Sleeveless Dress w/Gold Belt	2087	1986	$10.00	Fashion Fun
Long Red Strapless Dress w/Silver Butterfly Pin	1859	1987	$10.00	Jewel Secrets Fashion
Long Red/White Dress	9687	1976	$35.00	
Long Red/White Outfit	2775	1979	$15.00	Best Buys
Long Rose Dress, Black Net Coat	8688	1973	$75.00	Best Buys
Long Skirt and Top	11935	1994	$4.00	Fashion Forms Fashions
Long Skirt, Blouse, Red/White/Black	3203	1973	$50.00	Best Buys
Long Skirt, White Blouse	9042	1975	$45.00	Sears' Fashion Originals
Long Tricot Print	8680	1973	$35.00	Best Buys
Long White Fur Coat, Gold Bowtie, Hat, Purse	4509	1988	$10.00	Private Collection Fashions
Long White Print Halter Dress w/Red Trim	3641	1982	$10.00	Best Buys
Long Yellow Dress w/Butterfly Bows	4620	1989	$10.00	Perfume Pretty Fashions
Long Yellow/Red Party Dress	9580	1976	$35.00	Best Buys
Loop Scoop	1454	1970	$80.00	
Lovely 'n Lace	5653	1982	$10.00	
Lovely 'n Lavender	3358	1972	$145.00	Best Buys
Lovely Lingerie	Pak	1964	$145.00	
Lovely Sleep-Ins	1463	1970	$100.00	
Lunch Date	1600	1964	$150.00	

Item	Number	Year	Value	Specials
Lunch Date	5713	1983	$10.00	Fashion Fun
Lunch Date	Pak	1966	$140.00	
Lunch on the Terrace	1649	1966	$350.00	
Lunchtime	1673	1966	$225.00	
Made for Each Other	1881	1969	$250.00	
Made for Malibu	1497	1971	$130.00	
Madras Mad	3485	1972	$120.00	
Magenta Dress w/Lace Detail, Purse, Hose	14369	1996	$5.00	Fashion Avenue
Magenta/Purple Blouse, Magenta Pants	2185	1986	$10.00	B Active Fashions
Magenta/Purple Long Sleeved Blouse, Pants	2184	1986	$10.00	B Active Fashions
Magenta/Silver Top with Denim Yoke, Skirt	15861	1997	$5.00	Western Fashions
Magnificence	1646	1965	$625.00	
Magnificent Midi	3418	1971	$325.00	
Mainly for Rain	3338	1972	$60.00	Best Buys
Majestic Blue	3216	1972	$530.00	Miss America
Make Mine Midi	1861	1969	$300.00	
Maroon Long, Velvet Gown w/Puffy Sleeves	14306	1996	$10.00	Fashion Avenue
Masquerade	944	1963	$200.00	
Match-Mates (pink formal)	Pak	1966	$240.00	
Matinee Fashions	1640	1965	$505.00	
Maxi 'n Mini	1799	1970	$350.00	
Mermaid Bride	15900	1997	$10.00	Fashion Avenue Bridal
Mermaid, Green Shimmery Two-Piece	14665	1996	$4.00	My First Fashions
Mickey Motif Top, Denim, Mickey Jacket, Skirt	9199	1990	$5.00	Disney Character Fashions
Midi Magic	1869	1969	$175.00	
Midi Mood	3407	1971	$80.00	
Midi Skirt, Yellow/White Blouse	3205	1973	$50.00	Best Buys
Midi-Marvelous	1870	1969	$160.00	
Midnight Blue	1617	1964	$775.00	
Mini and Jacket	11938	1994	$4.00	Fashion Forms Fashions
Mini Dress, Yellow Lace Skirt, Blue Top, Shawl	4988	1988	$10.00	Sensations Fashions
Mini Prints	1809	1967	$225.00	
Minnie Motif Long Top, Denim Short Skirt, Socks	9205	1990	$5.00	Disney Character Fashions
Minnie Mouse Motif Blue Dress, Lace Leggings	9197	1990	$5.00	Disney Character Fashions
Mint Green Nightgown w/Sheer Robe	14289	1996	$5.00	Fashion Avenue
Miss Astronaut	1641	1965	$625.00	
Mix 'n Match Set	9650	1976	$40.00	Sears
Mix 'n Match, Silver/Fuchsia Set	1023	1979	$15.00	Department Store
Mix 'n Matchers	1779	1967	$400.00	Color Magic
Modern Art	1625	1965	$525.00	
Mood for Music	940	1962	$200.00	
Mood Matchers	1792	1970	$140.00	
Moonlight 'n Roses	1721	1965	$80.00	Sew Free Fashion
Movie Date	5718	1983	$10.00	Fashion Fun
Movie Date	933	1962	$125.00	
Movie Groovie	1866	1969	$125.00	
Multicolored Bathing Suit w/Cover Up	2093	1986	$10.00	Fashion Fun
Multicolored Coat w/Fringe, Belt, Purse	14399	1996	$6.00	Fashion Avenue
Multicolored Coat, Scarf, Purple Dress, Hat, Boots	9950	1990	$5.00	Western Fun Fashions
Multicolored Dress, Jacket, Pink Leggings	3318	1989	$10.00	Cool Times Fashions
Multicolored Dress, Purple Jacket, Hat and Purse	4430	1988	$10.00	Citystyle Fashions
Multicolored Floral Print Top, White Shorts	4126	1988	$10.00	Pretty Choices
Multicolored Jacket, Black/White/Orange Pants Suit	3319	1989	$10.00	Cool Times Fashions
Multicolored Long Striped Halter Dress	1359	1980	$10.00	Best Buys
Multicolored One-Piece Ski Suit, Skis, Ski Boots	2553	1990	$5.00	All Stars Fashions

Item	Number	Year	Value	Specials
Multicolored Short Jacket, Black/White Skirt, Top	3320	1989	$10.00	Cool Times Fashions
Multicolored Striped Long Skirt	2229	1978	$30.00	Best Buys
Multicolored Striped Sweater, Gold Long Skirt	4479	1988	$10.00	Sweatersoft Fashions
Multicolored Striped Sun Dress	1354	1980	$10.00	Best Buys
Multicolored Striped Top & Socks, White Short Skirt	9253	1990	$5.00	My First Barbie Fashions
Multicolored Striped Top Dress w/White Skirt	2088	1986	$10.00	Fashion Fun
Multicolored Swimsuit, Blue Mesh Cover-up, Glasses	68085	1999	$2.00	Sun & Sea Fashions
Multicolored T-shirt, White Vest and Shorts	2187	1986	$10.00	B Active Fashions
Multicolored Top, Leggings, Yellow Boots	9953	1990	$5.00	Western Fun Fashions
Multicolored Vest, Purple Top, Print Skirt	9951	1990	$5.00	Western Fun Fashions
Music Center Matinee	1663	1966	$630.00	
Music Note & Record Print Shorts, Blue Halter	9967	1990	$5.00	Fashion Finds
My First Date	5614	1983	$10.00	My First Barbie Fashions
My First Day at the Park	4870	1984	$10.00	My First Barbie Fashions
My First Day of School	5609	1983	$10.00	My First Barbie Fashions
My First Frills	5613	1983	$10.00	My First Barbie Fashions
My First Party Dress	4868	1984	$10.00	My First Barbie Fashions
My First Picnic	4872	1984	$10.00	My First Barbie Fashions
My First Picnic	5611	1983	$10.00	My First Barbie Fashions
My First Ski Trip	5612	1983	$10.00	My First Barbie Fashions
My First Slumber Party	4869	1984	$10.00	My First Barbie Fashions
My First Slumber Party	5610	1983	$10.00	My First Barbie Fashions
Navy Blue Long Halter Dress w/White Trim	1472	1981	$10.00	Best Buys
Navy Dress Trimmed in Red	2092	1986	$10.00	Fashion Fun
Navy Short Dress, White Sailor Collar, Red Trim	2119	1986	$10.00	My First Barbie Fashions
Navy Wrap Dress w/White Trim and Belt	1905	1981	$10.00	Fashion Collectibles
Night & Day Extras	2462	1981	$10.00	Fashion Add-Ons
Night Clouds	1841	1968	$100.00	
Night Lighter	3423	1971	$175.00	
Nighty-Negligee	965	1959	$140.00	
Now Knit	1452	1970	$100.00	
Now Wow!	1853	1968	$125.00	
O-Boy Corduroy	3486	1972	$80.00	
Olympic Parade	7244	1975	$40.00	Get-Ups 'n Go
Olympic Warm-Ups	7243	1975	$40.00	Get-Ups 'n Go
On The Avenue	1644	1965	$495.00	
On The Go	Pak	1964	$80.00	
On-The-Go-Wardrobe	2070	1977	$40.00	Sears Exclusive
One-Piece Hot Pink Swimsuit, Wrap Skirt	14373	1996	$4.00	Barbie Floatin' Cool
One-Piece Nautical Swimsuit w/White Towel	14372	1996	$4.00	Barbie Floatin' Cool
Open Road	985	1961	$325.00	
Opening Night	5652	1983	$10.00	Designer Collection
Orange Blossom	987	1961	$225.00	
Orange Checked Shirt, Top	9153	1976	$40.00	Best Buys
Orange Slacks and Jacket	3208	1973	$70.00	Best Buys
Orangy Gauchos	2222	1978	$30.00	Best Buys
Outdoor Art Show	1650	1966	$500.00	
Outdoor Life	1637	1965	$325.00	
Overall Denim	3488	1972	$110.00	
Paint the Town Red	1955	1981	$15.00	Barbie & Ken Designer Original
Paint the Town Red	5700	1983	$10.00	Fashion Classics
Pajama Party	1601	1964	$80.00	
Pajama Pow!	1806	1968	$280.00	
Pan American Airways Stewardess	1678	1966	$4,800.00	
Pants for Town	2346	1978	$15.00	

Item	Number	Year	Value	Specials
Pants, Cape, Cap	9047	1975	$55.00	Sears' Fashion Originals
Pants, Jacket, Cap	9581	1976	$40.00	
Pants, Shirt, Socks	9574	1976	$30.00	Best Buys
Pants, Skirt, Hat, Blouse	8691	1973	$50.00	Best Buys
Pants-Perfect Purple	3359	1972	$90.00	Best Buys
Party Date	958	1963	$225.00	
Party in Pink Fashion	24289	1999	$5.00	Charm Styles
Party in Purple	5544	1983	$10.00	Fashion Fantasy
Party Lines	3490	1972	$175.00	
Party Nights	5848	1983	$10.00	Party Night Fashions
Party Pair	4828	1984	$10.00	Twice As Nice Fashions
Pastel Print Long Dress, Pink Rose Trim	1941	1989	$10.00	Private Collection Fashions
Patio Party	1692	1967	$350.00	
Patio Party	1708	1965	$50.00	Sew Free Fashion
Peach Locket Surprise Fashions	11559	1994	$5.00	Locket Surprise Fashions
Peach Strapless Slip & Bra, White Lace Bra	3184	1987	$15.00	Fancy Frills
Peach Tutu w/Rose Trim & Long Skirt	7394	1990	$5.00	Dance Magic Fashions
Peachy Fleecy Coat	915	1959	$160.00	
Peachy Fleecy Coat	Pak	1963	$65.00	
Peasant Dressy	3438	1971	$180.00	
Peasant Pleasant	3482	1972	$120.00	
Pedal Pushers	Pak	1968	$120.00	
Perfect Beginnings	60	1970	$90.00	
Perfectly Pink	4805	1984	$10.00	Fashion Fun
Pert Skirt	Pak	1966	$150.00	
Petti-Pinks	Pak	1969	$140.00	
Photo Fashion	1648	1965	$450.00	
Picnic in the Park	16077	1996	$30.00	Barbie Millicent Roberts
Picnic Party	5706	1983	$10.00	Fashion Classics
Picnic Set	967	1959	$325.00	
Picnic Set #2 (new hat, basket, fish)	967	1962	$300.00	
Picture in Plaid	7083	1984	$10.00	Designer Collection
Picture Me Pretty	3355	1972	$80.00	Best Buys
Pink Baby Dolls	9908	1975	$40.00	Sears' Exclusive Best Buys
Pink Ballgown	13024	1995	$5.00	Fantasy Evening Fashions
Pink Blouse and Silvery Skirt	1003	1979	$15.00	Fashion Collectibles
Pink Brushed Tricot Robe with B Monogram	12173	1997	$5.00	Fashion Avenue Lingerie
Pink Champagne	1427	1980	$10.00	Fashion Favorites
Pink Cowl Neck Halter Top, Leggings, Tutu	1870	1989	$10.00	My First Barbie Fashions
Pink Dress and Jacket, White Dog	3659	1987	$10.00	Pet Show Fashions
Pink Dress, Coat, Hat, and Scarf	4434	1988	$10.00	Citystyle Fashions
Pink Dress, White Dog	3658	1987	$10.00	Pet Show Fashions
Pink Dress, White Dog	3660	1987	$10.00	Pet Show Fashions
Pink Dress, White Lace Collar	1018	1989	$10.00	Fashion Finds Fashions
Pink Evening Gown	9594	1976	$40.00	Get-Ups 'n Go
Pink Formal	1681	1966	$2,200.00	Sears
Pink Full Skirt, Yellow Print Ruffle Top, Visor	1088	1990	$5.00	Wet 'N Wild Fashions
Pink Halter Dress w/White and Black Bottom	1908	1989	$15.00	Paris Pretty Fashions
Pink Halter Nightgown, Matching Short Robe	3182	1987	$10.00	Fancy Frills
Pink Halter Short Dress	9963	1990	$5.00	Fashion Finds
Pink Halter Top w/Long Floral Skirt	1906	1981	$10.00	Fashion Collectibles
Pink Halter Top, Floral Print Short Skirt	3675	1982	$10.00	My First Barbie Fashions
Pink Halter Top, Floral Print Skirt	9975	1990	$5.00	Fashion Finds
Pink Halter, Print Short Skirt, Stole, Leggings	1445	1989	$10.00	Style Magic Fashions
Pink Halter, Skirt, White Hat	2144	1990	$5.00	Cool Mix Fashions

Item	Number	Year	Value	Specials
Pink Jacket, Print Tank, Blue Skirt, Hose, Hat	1167	1986	$10.00	Barbie & the Rockers Fashions
Pink Jumpsuit, Figured Over Skirt	9966	1977	$35.00	Best Buys
Pink Knicker Jumpsuit, Zig Zag Hooded Jacket	9964	1977	$35.00	Best Buys
Pink Knit Top, Pink/White/Floral Print Short Skirt	1876	1987	$10.00	My First Barbie Fashions
Pink Lace Long Bridesmaid Dress, Hat, Bouquet	3105	1988	$10.00	Romantic Wedding
Pink Leotard, White Leggings, Warmers, Barbell	2610	1990	$5.00	All Stars Fashions
Pink Long Dress, White Trim and Long Gloves	1311	1989	$10.00	Dinner Date Fashions
Pink Long Sleeveless Dress	2089	1986	$10.00	Fashion Fun
Pink Mini Dress, Blue Leggings	1441	1989	$10.00	Style Magic Fashions
Pink Moonbeams	1694	1967	$300.00	
Pink Nightgown & Black Negligee	2558	1978	$15.00	Best Buys
Pink Outfit	12623	1995	$5.00	Bead Fun Fashions
Pink Palm Tree Top, Print Top, Short Skirt, Belt	4467	1988	$10.00	California Dream Fashions
Pink Pants Suit	8687	1973	$75.00	Best Buys
Pink Party Dress	9577	1976	$40.00	Best Buys
Pink Party Separates	7841	1974	$85.00	Get-Ups 'n Go
Pink Perfection	1402	1980	$10.00	Fashion Favorites
Pink Rain Slicker, Boots, Dotted Hat	14301	1996	$6.00	Fashion Avenue
Pink Ruffle Hem, Short Halter Dress	1039	1989	$10.00	Fashion Finds Fashions
Pink Ruffle Short Skirt, Yellow Halter, Leggings,	2689	1986	$10.00	Barbie & the Rockers Fashions
Pink Short Dress, Lace Leggings, Blue Jacket	2690	1986	$10.00	Barbie & the Rockers Fashions
Pink Shorts and Tank with Print Jacket	12438	1995	$5.00	Locket Surprise Fashions
Pink Shorts, White Top and Pants	12628	1995	$5.00	Sponge 'n Print Fashions
Pink Shorty Gown with Mirror	3635	1982	$10.00	Best Buys
Pink Skirt, Silver Top w/Ruffle Trim, Lace Leggings	9162	1990	$5.00	Dinner Date Fashions
Pink Sparkle	1440	1967	$250.00	
Pink Sparkler	1012	1979	$15.00	Fashion Favorites
Pink Sundress w/Blue Print Bottom, Teal Coat	1910	1989	$15.00	Paris Pretty Fashions
Pink Swimsuit and Long Gown w/Big Hat	3301	1989	$10.00	Superstar Barbie Fashions
Pink Swimsuit and Parasol	9263	1985	$10.00	Fashion Playsets
Pink Swimsuit/Gown with Star Print, Boa	3305	1989	$10.00	Superstar Barbie Fashions
Pink Tank Top, Blue Jean Jacket & Pants, Pink Boa	4335	1988	$12.00	The Jeans Look Fashions
Pink Tank, Leggings, Print Jacket, Yellow Belt	1166	1986	$10.00	Barbie & the Rockers Fashions
Pink Teddy with White Trim	1469	1981	$10.00	Best Buys
Pink Top w/Heart Motif, Pink, White Leggings	2121	1986	$10.00	My First Barbie Fashions
Pink Top w/Silver Trim, Jeans, Gray Boots	3393	1987	$10.00	Concert Tour Fashions
Pink Top, Blue Leggings, Striped Socks, Bag	2609	1990	$5.00	All Stars Fashions
Pink Top, Burgundy Pants, White Jacket	3790	1982	$10.00	Fashion Favorites
Pink Top, Hat, Socks, Shoes, White Shorts	1593	1989	$10.00	Animal Lovin' Fashions
Pink Top, Pink/White Striped Skirt, Tennis Racket	2588	1990	$5.00	All Stars Fashions
Pink Top, Ruffle Lace Skirt, Scarf	1292	1989	$10.00	Dinner Date Fashions
Pink Top, White Pants, Leggings, White Tank, Vest	4797	1988	$10.00	Fashion Magic Fashions
Pink Top, Yellow Skirt, Long Black/White Vest	4987	1988	$10.00	Sensations Fashions
Pink Tutu	1868	1989	$10.00	My First Barbie Fashions
Pink Vest, Yellow Halter, Blue Pants	1045	1990	$5.00	Wet 'N Wild Fashions
Pink/Black Polka Dot Dress & Jacket w/Ruffle Trim	9161	1990	$5.00	Dinner Date Fashions
Pink/Blue Halter with Shawl	4587	1988	$10.00	My First Barbie Fashions
Pink/Blue Print Skirt, Bolero, Pink Top, Belt	9245	1990	$5.00	My First Barbie Fashions
Pink/Blue Shorts, Halter, Playsuit	1506	1989	$10.00	Feeling Pretty Fashions
Pink/Blue/Striped Top, Pink Shorts	1882	1987	$10.00	My First Barbie Fashions
Pink/Blue/Yellow/White Top, Yellow Short Skirt	1028	1989	$10.00	Fashion Finds Fashions
Pink/Gold Evening Gown	2054	1977	$40.00	Sears' Exclusive Best Buys
Pink/Gold Long Sheer Wrap Dress	1421	1980	$10.00	Fashion Collectibles
Pink/Green Two-Piece Bathing Suit	12647	1995	$5.00	Bath Paintin' Fashions
Pink/Purple Long Strapless Dress with Print Belt	2299	1986	$10.00	Twice As Nice Reversible

Item	Number	Year	Value	Specials
Pink/Red Ruffle Trim Swimsuit, Long Skirt	7391	1990	$5.00	Dance Magic Fashions
Pink/Red Two-Tone Halter Short Dress	1519	1989	$10.00	Feeling Pretty Fashions
Pink/Silver Jumpsuit, Pink Jacket	9625	1977	$35.00	Best Buys
Pink/Silver Star Print Top, Blue Jeans	15859	1997	$5.00	Western Fashions
Pink/Silver/White, Long Halter Evening Dress	2298	1986	$10.00	Twice As Nice Reversible
Pink/White Ballet Tutu	2120	1986	$10.00	My First Barbie Fashions
Pink/White Ballgown	13025	1995	$5.00	Fantasy Evening Fashions
Pink/White Camisole, Slip, Panties, Bra	3687	1982	$10.00	Fashion Collectibles
Pink/White Gingham Corset with Pink Slip	15876	1997	$6.00	Fashion Avenue Lingerie
Pink/White Leggings, Blue Top, Yellow Headband	1170	1986	$10.00	Barbie & the Rockers Fashions
Pink/White Lights the Night	9738	1977	$15.00	Get-Ups 'n Go
Pink/White Long Halter Dress	1365	1980	$10.00	Fashion Collectibles
Pink/White Pants and Halter	12594	1995	$5.00	Picnic Pretty Fashions
Pink/White Short Skirt, Pink/White Striped Top	1508	1989	$10.00	Feeling Pretty Fashions
Pink/White Shorts, Short Skirt, Jacket, Top	4794	1988	$10.00	Fashion Magic Fashions
Pink/White Western Shirt, Cowboy Hat	3577	1982	$10.00	Western Fashions
Pink/White/Silver Dress w/White Biker Shorts	9163	1990	$5.00	Dinner Date Fashions
Pink/Yellow Dress w/Daisies, Beret, Hose	14363	1996	$5.00	Fashion Avenue
Plain Blouse and Purse	Pak	1962	$45.00	
Plantation Belle	966	1959	$550.00	
Pleasant Dreams	1400	1980	$10.00	Fashion Favorites
Pleasantly Peasanty	3360	1972	$70.00	Best Buys
Plush 'n Warm	Pak	1971	$75.00	
Plush Pony	1873	1969	$175.00	
Poncho Put-On	3411	1971	$150.00	
Poodle Doodles	1061	1972	$750.00	Put-Ons 'n Pets
Poodle Parade	1643	1965	$800.00	
Pool Party	5715	1983	$10.00	Fashion Fun
Pretty as a Picture	1652	1966	$475.00	
Pretty Beginnings	5897	1983	$10.00	Fashion Fun
Pretty Choices	2773	1986	$10.00	Finishing Touches
Pretty Pleasanty	2786	1979	$15.00	Fashion Favorites
Pretty Power	1863	1969	$125.00	
Pretty Traveler	1706	1965	$60.00	Sew Free Fashion
Pretty Wild	1777	1967	$450.00	Color Magic
Prima Ballerina	1787	1970	$75.00	
Princess	12600	1995	$5.00	My First Fashions
Princess Aurora	9329	1976	$40.00	Ballerina Costumes
Princess Bride	15899	1997	$10.00	Fashion Avenue Bridal
Princess, One-Piece Blue Outfit w/Poof Skirt	14668	1996	$4.00	My First Fashions
Print A Plenty	1686	1967	$275.00	
Print Culottes, Orange Tank and Sash	4527	1988	$10.00	Bright & Breezy Fashions
Print Dress, Pink Bolero	1008	1979	$15.00	Fashion Collectibles
Print Jacket, Black Mini, Pink Top, Orange Leggings	1176	1986	$10.00	Barbie & the Rockers Fashions
Print Long Full Skirt, Blue Top and Hat	4512	1988	$10.00	Private Collection Fashions
Print Long Skirt, Yellow Halter, Blue Hat	1530	1989	$10.00	Weekend Collection Fashions
Print Pants, White Blouse, Yellow Vest	8685	1973	$60.00	Best Buys
Print Skirt and Yellow Halter Top	12437	1995	$5.00	Make-Up Pretty Fashions
Print Skirt, Red Long Sleeved Top	4526	1988	$10.00	Bright & Breezy Fashions
Print Skirt, Red/Yellow Waist and Jacket	9968	1977	$15.00	Best Buys
Print Skirt, White Top	9046	1975	$35.00	Fashion Originals
Print Top, Blue Skirt	1529	1989	$10.00	Weekend Collection Fashions
Print Top, Denim Skirt with Lace Ruffle, Boots	4330	1988	$10.00	The Jeans Look Fashions
Print Top, Yellow Skirt	4523	1988	$10.00	Bright & Breezy Fashions
Pucino Serving Dress	None	1967	$500.00	Barbie Goes Braniff Fashions

Item	Number	Year	Value	Specials
Purple & White Print Dress, Shawl, Shoes	68783	2000	$4.00	Glow-in-the-Dark Fashions
Purple Dress with Floral Print Top	4127	1988	$10.00	Pretty Choices
Purple Flower Print Dress w/White Ruffle Trim	9964	1990	$5.00	Fashion Finds
Purple Halter, Blue Biker Pants, Ruffle Trim	2138	1990	$5.00	Cool Mix Fashions
Purple Leotard w/Pink Dots, White Leggings	1877	1987	$10.00	My First Barbie Fashions
Purple Locket Surprise Fashions	11558	1994	$5.00	Locket Surprise Fashions
Purple Long Sleeved Drop-Waist Dress	2181	1986	$10.00	B Active Fashions
Purple Paisley Print Jacket, Blue Long Skirt, Hat	4481	1988	$10.00	Sweatersoft Fashions
Purple Pleasers	3483	1972	$75.00	
Purple Shorts and Purple Jacket	12595	1995	$5.00	Picnic Pretty Fashions
Purple Sleeveless Dress	2091	1986	$10.00	Fashion Fun
Purple Trunks, Pink Blouse	2551	1978	$15.00	Best Buys
Purple Vest, Multicolored Shirt & Skirt, Gloves, Hat	9952	1990	$5.00	Western Fun Fashions
Purple, Coyote Motif Top, Leggings, Belt, Boots	9954	1990	$5.00	Western Fun Fashions
Purple/Blue/Red Shirred Top and Skirt	9971	1990	$5.00	Fashion Finds
Purple/Red Top, Tweed Slacks	4480	1988	$10.00	Sweatersoft Fashions
Purple/Red/Yellow Print Strapless Mini-dress	1909	1989	$15.00	Paris Pretty Fashions
Purple/Silver Outfit, Gloves, Hat, Purple Skates	4080	1990	$5.00	Ice Capades Fashions
Purple/White Long Dress, Hat	1304	1989	$10.00	Dinner Date Fashions
Purple/White Short Dress, White Belt, Ruffle Skirt	1526	1989	$10.00	Feeling Pretty Fashions
Purse Pack	Pak	1962	$60.00	
Rain or Shine	2788	1979	$15.00	Fashion Favorites
Rainbo Wraps	1798	1970	$350.00	
Raincoat	949	1963	$100.00	
Rare Pair	1462	1970	$125.00	
Raspberry Suit	None	1967	$500.00	Barbie Goes Braniff Fashions
Reception Line	1654	1966	$600.00	
Red Bandana-Print Top, Skirt, Bolo Tie	15858	1997	$5.00	Western Fashions
Red Blouse, Black/White Skirt	7950	1985	$10.00	Twice As Nice Reversible
Red Blouse, Red/White Check Print Skirt	2182	1986	$10.00	B Active Fashions
Red Brocade Ensemble	2670	1978	$35.00	Department Store
Red Coat with Hood	22160	1999	$12.00	Fashion Avenue
Red Delight	Pak	1966	$150.00	
Red Dress and Black Vest	12634	1995	$5.00	Paint The Dots Fashion
Red Dress and Head Scarf	1000	1979	$15.00	Fashion Collectibles
Red Dress with Gold Trim	1425	1980	$10.00	Fashion Collectibles
Red Dress, Red/Multistriped Jacket	2301	1986	$10.00	Twice As Nice Reversible
Red Evening Cape	7931	1975	$40.00	Fashion Originals
Red Evening Gown	1024	1979	$15.00	Bargain Fashions
Red Evening Gown	9962	1977	$15.00	Best Buys
Red Evening Gown and Cape	9650	1976	$45.00	Sears
Red Fantastic	1809	1967	$800.00	
Red Flair	939	1962	$175.00	
Red Floral Print Dress w/Black Belt, White Collar	3673	1982	$10.00	My First Barbie Fashions
Red Floral Print Sundress, Purple Leather Jacket	1907	1989	$15.00	Paris Pretty Fashions
Red Flowered Swimsuit, Red Beach Bag, Sunglasses	68085	1999	$2.00	Sun & Sea Fashions
Red for Rain	3409	1971	$70.00	
Red Fringe Trimmed Jacket and Pants, Cowboy	3579	1982	$10.00	Western Fashions
Red Front Tie Halter Top, Black Pants	1423	1980	$10.00	Fashion Collectibles
Red Hat, Red/White Coat	7951	1985	$10.00	Twice As Nice Reversible
Red Hot (final touches)	17878	1997	$15.00	Barbie Millicent Roberts
Red Jumper, Blue/White Striped Top	13017	1995	$5.00	Yacht Club Fashions
Red Jumpsuit	2553	1978	$15.00	Best Buys
Red Long Dress with Slit Skirt	3678	1982	$10.00	Fashion Collectibles
Red Long Jacket, Checked Skirt, Black Hat, Purse	4429	1988	$10.00	Citystyle Fashions

Item	Number	Year	Value	Specials
Red Palazzo Pants and Gold Halter	9650	1976	$45.00	Sears
Red Pants	2554	1978	$15.00	Best Buys
Red Pants and Jacket, Blue Blouse w/Bowtie	3786	1982	$10.00	Fashion Favorites
Red Pants and Over Dress	2559	1978	$15.00	Best Buys
Red Pants, Bull's Eye Blouse	9960	1977	$15.00	Best Buys
Red Pants, Sheer Over-Skirt, White Top	8622	1973	$70.00	Best Buys
Red Pants, Yellow Hat, Printed Scarf	2051	1977	$35.00	Sears' Exclusive Best Buys
Red Plaid Dress, Purse, Hose, Shoes	14366	1996	$5.00	Fashion Avenue
Red Plaid Pants and Jacket	9010	1975	$45.00	Sears' Exclusive Best Buys
Red Polka Dot Short Dress w/Ruffle Trim	1509	1989	$10.00	Feeling Pretty Fashions
Red Printed Dress	2767	1979	$15.00	Best Buys
Red Printed Dress	2771	1979	$15.00	Best Buys
Red Printed Dress w/Yellow Trim	1903	1981	$10.00	Fashion Collectibles
Red Printed Dress, Yellow Jacket	2783	1979	$15.00	Fashion Collectibles
Red Printed Long Skirt	2230	1978	$15.00	Best Buys
Red Printed Play Suit	2220	1978	$15.00	Best Buys
Red Printed Skirt & Kerchief, Blue/Yellow Blouse	2053	1977	$35.00	Sears' Exclusive Best Buys
Red Printed Skirt and Top	2224	1978	$15.00	Best Buys
Red Printed Strapless Dress	1468	1981	$10.00	Best Buys
Red Printed Tricot	9006	1975	$45.00	Sears' Exclusive Best Buys
Red Ruffled Neck Dress	2086	1986	$10.00	Fashion Fun
Red Sailor Top, White Tops, White Sailor Hat	3683	1982	$10.00	Fashion Collectibles
Red Satin Strapless Bustier	1911	1989	$20.00	Paris Pretty Fashions
Red Shine For Rain Time	9739	1977	$15.00	Get-Ups 'n Go
Red Short Dress w/Lace Trim	7920	1986	$10.00	My First Barbie Fashions
Red Short Overalls, Striped Bodysuit, Tights	14362	1996	$5.00	Fashion Avenue
Red Shorts and Top	3642	1982	$10.00	Best Buys
Red Shorts, Yellow Turtleneck, Socks	1532	1989	$10.00	Weekend Collection Fashions
Red Sizzle	7217	1984	$10.00	Spectacular Fashions
Red Skirt, Purse, Red/White/Blue Blouse	9628	1977	$15.00	Best Buys
Red Sleeveless Dress w/Printed Scarf	4119	1988	$10.00	Pretty Choices
Red Sleeveless Jumpsuit	3631	1982	$10.00	Best Buys
Red Striped Sheath Dress	1351	1980	$10.00	Best Buys
Red Suit	2560	1978	$15.00	Best Buys
Red Sweater, Plaid Jumper, Tights, Purse	14361	1996	$5.00	Fashion Avenue
Red Top w/Lace Trim, Ballerina Printed Skirt	4582	1988	$10.00	My First Barbie Fashions
Red Top, Striped Jacket, White Short Skirt	4581	1988	$10.00	My First Barbie Fashions
Red Top, Two-Tone Skirt	9146	1985	$10.00	Spectacular Fashions
Red Turtleneck and Black Pants	1367	1980	$10.00	Fashion Collectibles
Red Tweed Jumpsuit, Tam, Scarf	9625	1977	$15.00	Best Buys
Red Vest, Black Pants, White Shirt	7952	1985	$10.00	Twice As Nice Reversible
Red Wrap-Around Dress	1356	1980	$10.00	Best Buys
Red/Black Evening Gown, Turban	9967	1977	$15.00	Best Buys
Red/Black Lace Evening Gown	2552	1978	$15.00	Best Buys
Red/Blue Striped Long Sleeved Long Dress	1904	1981	$10.00	Fashion Collectibles
Red/Blue/Yellow Sun Dress	1353	1980	$10.00	Best Buys
Red/Gold Ruffled Dress, Bolero, Red Hat	4510	1988	$10.00	Private Collection Fashions
Red/White 'n Warm	1491	1969	$250.00	
Red/White Dress w/Red Yoke and Belt	1907	1981	$10.00	Fashion Collectibles
Red/White Floral Print Dress, White Hat, Scarf	3310	1988	$10.00	Beverly Hills Fashions
Red/White Halter Dress w/White Lace Leggings	9165	1990	$5.00	Dinner Date Fashions
Red/White Jogging Pants and Top, Sneakers	7913	1985	$10.00	B Active Fashions
Red/White Long Dress with White Belt	3680	1982	$10.00	Fashion Collectibles
Red/White Long Dress, Red Belt	1524	1989	$10.00	Feeling Pretty Fashions
Red/White Polka Dot Halter Dress	1465	1981	$10.00	Best Buys

Item	Number	Year	Value	Specials
Red/White Print Dress and Stole	9619	1977	$15.00	Best Buys
Red/White Shorts, Halter, Cap	1025	1979	$15.00	Bargain Fashions
Red/White Skirt, Red Sleeveless Top	4585	1988	$10.00	My First Barbie Fashions
Red/White Striped Cowl Neck Top, White Biker Shorts	9247	1990	$45.00	My First Barbie Fashions
Red/White Striped Dress	3636	1982	$10.00	Best Buys
Red/White Striped Jumpsuit	9958	1977	$15.00	Best Buys
Red/White Striped Long Halter Dress	1355	1980	$10.00	Best Buys
Red/White Swimsuit, Red/Blue Jacket	13020	1995	$5.00	Yacht Club Fashions
Red/White Wrap Dress	4821	1985	$10.00	Twice As Nice Reversible
Red/White/Blue Dress	9158	1976	$40.00	Best Buys
Red/White/Blue Print	9164	1976	$40.00	Best Buys
Regal Red	3217	1972	$550.00	Miss America
Registered Nurse	991	1961	$275.00	
Regular Olympic Outfit	9043	1975	$40.00	Sears' Fashion Originals
Resort Set	963	1959	$175.00	
Riding Gear	5834	1983	$10.00	Designer Collection
Riding in the Park	1668	1966	$600.00	
Right in Step	4808	1984	$10.00	Fashion Fun
Robe and Nightgown	8690	1973	$65.00	Best Buys
Roman Holiday	968	1959	$4,500.00	
Romantic Lady	1430	1980	$10.00	Fashion Favorites
Romantic Nights	5712	1983	$10.00	Fashion Fun
Romantic Ruffles	1871	1969	$225.00	
Romantic Valentine	4812	1984	$10.00	Fashion Fantasy
Romantic White	9836	1977	$15.00	SuperStar Fashions
Rose Dress, Stole, Hat	7934	1975	$35.00	Fashion Originals
Rose Evening Gown and Jacket	7934	1975	$40.00	Sears' Fashion Originals
Rose Nightgown	9157	1976	$30.00	Best Buys
Rose/White Printed Party Dress	9160	1976	$25.00	Best Buys
Royal Ball, The	2668	1979	$15.00	Designer Originals
Royal Velvet	3215	1972	$540.00	Miss America
Ruffles 'n Lace	Pak	1964	$130.00	
Ruffles 'n Swirls	1783	1970	$80.00	
Rust Short Giraffe Motif Top, Purple Skirt, Socks	1596	1989	$10.00	Animal Lovin' Fashions
Salmon Party Dress	7843	1974	$85.00	Get-Ups 'n Go
Salsa	29071	2000	$8.00	Movin' to Music
Salute to Silver	1885	1969	$110.00	Fan Club Offer
Satin 'n Rose	1611	1964	$375.00	
Satin 'n Shine	3493	1972	$325.00	
Satin Blouse	Pak	1963	$55.00	
Satin Bolero and Hat	Pak	1963	$100.00	
Satin Coat	Pak	1963	$100.00	
Satin Sheath Skirt	Pak	1963	$55.00	
Satin Slacks	Pak	1963	$100.00	
Satin Slumber	3414	1971	$160.00	
Satin Wrap Skirt	Pak	1963	$120.00	
Saturday Matinee	1615	1965	$875.00	
Scarfs and Such	2462	1978	$15.00	Fashion Add-Ons
Scarfs and Such	2462	1980	$10.00	Fashion Add-Ons
Scene-Stealers	1845	1968	$240.00	
Scoop Neck Playsuit	Pak	1962	$65.00	
Scuba Do's	1788	1970	$70.00	
Sea-Worthy	1872	1969	$225.00	
Sears' Natural Mink Jacket	1699	1964	$3,100.00	Sears
Seattle Latte Fashion	28137	2000	$5.00	Metro Styles

Item	Number	Year	Value	Specials
Senior Prom	951	1963	$200.00	
Set 'N Serve	Pak	1966	$350.00	
Sew-In, The	Pak	1971	$30.00	
Shape-Ups	1782	1970	$100.00	
Sharp Shift	20	1970	$110.00	
Sheath Sensation	986	1961	$150.00	
Sheath Skirt and Telephone	Pak	1962	$50.00	
Sheath with Gold Buttons	Pak	1962	$60.00	
Sheer Romance	1009	1979	$15.00	Fashion Favorites
Shift into Knit	1478	1969	$80.00	
Shimmering Magic	1664	1966	$1,400.00	
Shine at the Party	5546	1983	$10.00	Fashion Fantasy
Shiny Pants and Top	1001	1979	$15.00	Fashion Collectibles
Shirtdressy	1487	1969	$170.00	
Shoe Pack (12 pairs)	Pak	1963	$200.00	
Shoe Wardrobe	1833	1964	$225.00	
Shoes	3383	1977	$15.00	Best Buys
Shoes	8626	1973	$50.00	
Shoes	8626	1977	$15.00	Best Buys
Shoes & Bags (with white boots)	2458	1981	$10.00	Fashion Add-Ons
Shoes & Purses	2458	1982	$10.00	Fashion Add-Ons
Shoes and Bags	2458	1978	$15.00	Fashion Add-Ons
Shoes Scene	3382	1972	$70.00	Best Buys
Short 'n Sassy	5705	1983	$10.00	Fashion Classics
Short 'n Sassy Peach Ruffly Dress with Stole	4624	1989	$10.00	Perfume Pretty Fashions
Short Blue Dress, Gold Fishnet Leggings, Shawl	9166	1990	$5.00	Dinner Date Fashions
Short Blue/White Ruffled Halter Dress	2294	1986	$10.00	Twice As Nice Reversible
Short Denim Dress, Sailor Style Hat	1692	1989	$10.00	Jeans Fashions
Short Dress w/Blue Top, Print Ruffle on Hem	1067	1990	$5.00	Wet 'N Wild Fashions
Short Dress, Blue Top, Floral Skirt, Pink Belt	1523	1989	$10.00	Feeling Pretty Fashions
Short Dress, Denim Top, Striped Ruffle Skirt	1693	1989	$10.00	Jeans Fashions
Short Dress, Lace Ruffle Skirt, Yellow Top, Gloves	4986	1988	$10.00	Sensations Fashions
Short Dress, Orange Top, Fuchsia/Orange Skirt	5971	1988	$10.00	Sensations Fashions
Short Pink Tutu	1869	1989	$10.00	My First Barbie Fashions
Short Printed Dress	3347	1973	$30.00	Best Buys
Short Reddish Outfit	2774	1979	$15.00	Best Buys
Short Ruffle Skirt Dress, Pink Top and Gloves	4981	1988	$10.00	Sensations Fashions
Short Ruffle Skirt, Top, Leggings	4981	1989	$10.00	Cool Times Fashions
Short Set, The	3481	1972	$150.00	
Short Skirt, Fringe Jacket, Boots with Silver Studs	4329	1988	$10.00	The Jeans Look Fashions
Shoulder Gown	2344	1978	$15.00	
Showstopper	4806	1984	$45.00	Fashion Fun
Sightseeing	1713	1965	$60.00	Sew Free Fashion
Signature Series (final touches)	17875	1997	$15.00	Barbie Millicent Roberts
Silk Sheath (assorted colors)	Pak	1962	$75.00	
Silken Flame	977	1960	$175.00	
Silver Blues	3357	1972	$90.00	Best Buys
Silver Jacket w/Tails, Hat, Long Blue Gown, Boa	3303	1989	$10.00	Superstar Barbie Fashions
Silver Polish	1492	1969	$175.00	
Silver Sensation Fashion	7438	1984	$20.00	Collector's Series
Silver Serenade	3419	1971	$425.00	
Silver Sparkle	1885	1969	$110.00	Fan Club Offer
Silver Star Pattern Swimsuit & Gown, Pink/Blue Boa	3306	1989	$10.00	Superstar Barbie Fashions
Silver Sweater, Pink Poodle Skirt, White Lace Sock	4978	1988	$10.00	Sensations Fashions
Silver/Red Evening Gown	1975	1975	$35.00	Fashion Originals

Item	Number	Year	Value	Specials
Silvery Spark for After Dark	2301	1978	$15.00	Get-Ups 'n Go
Singing in the Shower	988	1961	$140.00	
Six to Midnight	7859	N/A	$30.00	Get-Ups 'n Go
Six to Mix, Match, and Pack	9742	1977	$15.00	Get-Ups 'n Go
Skate Mates	1793	1970	$130.00	
Skater's Waltz	1629	1965	$400.00	
Ski Party	7079	1984	$10.00	Designer Collection
Ski Party Pink	5708	1983	$10.00	Fashion Classics
Ski Queen	948	1963	$200.00	
Ski Scene, The	1797	1970	$180.00	
Skiing	7787	1974	$70.00	Get-Ups 'n Go
Skin Diver	1608	1964	$125.00	
Skirt Styles	Pak	1967	$115.00	
Slacks	Pak	1962	$30.00	
Sleek 'n Chic	2667	1979	$15.00	Designer Originals
Sleeping Pretty	1636	1965	$355.00	
Sleepy Set	3487	1972	$125.00	
Sleepy Time Gal	1674	1966	$275.00	
Sleeveless Dress, White Top, Blue/White Bottom	1062	1989	$10.00	Fashion Finds Fashions
Sleeveless Striped Dress with Turtleneck	1361	1980	$10.00	Best Buys
Slip On 'n Tie	1372	1980	$10.00	Beginner's Fashion
Slip On 'n Tie (gold dress)	1911	1981	$10.00	My First Barbie Fashions
Slip On 'n Tie (red pants and top)	1372	1981	$10.00	My First Barbie Fashions
Slip On, Snap, Tie	1371	1980	$10.00	Beginner's Fashion
Slip On, Wrap 'n Tie	1910	1981	$10.00	My First Barbie Fashions
Slip, Panty, and Bra	Pak	1962	$75.00	
Slumber Party	1642	1965	$275.00	
Smart Switch	1776	1967	$450.00	Color Magic
Smasheroo	1860	1968	$225.00	
Snap Dash	1824	1968	$140.00	
Snow Chic, So Chic	19772	1998	$30.00	Barbie Millicent Roberts
Snowflake Fairy	9327	1976	$40.00	Ballerina Costumes
Snug Fuzz	1813	1968	$250.00	
So Pretty Under it All	5549	1983	$10.00	Fashion Fantasy
Soft & Lacy	4807	1984	$10.00	Fashion Fun
Soft & Shimmering Silver & White	2252	1978	$15.00	SuperStar Fashions
Soft 'n Chic	4813	1984	$10.00	Fashion Fantasy
Soft 'n Snug	Pak	1971	$170.00	
Solid Red Dress	N/A	1974	$150.00	Sears
Solo In The Spotlight	982	1960	$350.00	
Sophisticated Lady	5720	1983	$10.00	Fashion Fun
Sophisticated Lady	993	1963	$400.00	
Sorority Meeting	937	1962	$275.00	
Sorority Tea	1703	1965	$50.00	Sew Free Fashion
Space Racer	2737	1986	$28.00	Astro Fashions
Sparkle Squares	1814	1968	$275.00	
Special Sparkle	1468	1970	$175.00	
Spectacular Spectators (final touches)	17877	1997	$15.00	Barbie Millicent Roberts
Spectator Sport	Pak	1964	$65.00	
Sport Star	3353	1972	$60.00	Best Buys
Sportin' Occasion	4816	1984	$10.00	Fashion Fantasy
Sporting Casuals	1671	1965	$275.00	
Spring	15904	1997	$10.00	Fashion Avenue Internationale
Springtime Magic Fashion	7092	1984	$20.00	Collector's Series
Square Neck Sweater	Pak	1962	$35.00	

Item	Number	Year	Value	Specials
Square Neck Sweater and Scarf	Pak	1963	$35.00	
Star of the Show in Golden Glow	9741	1977	$15.00	Get-Ups 'n Go
Star Struck	4814	1984	$10.00	Fashion Fantasy
Stardust	1722	1965	$70.00	Sew Free Fashion
Starlight Slumbers	2739	1986	$28.00	Astro Fashions
Stitch 'N Style	10	1970	$50.00	
Stormy Weather	949	1964	$100.00	
Striped Dress	9155	1976	$35.00	Best Buys
Striped Long Sleeved Dress	3689	1982	$10.00	Fashion Collectibles
Striped Long Top, Red Pants and Belt	4525	1988	$10.00	Bright & Breezy Fashions
Striped Pants and Purple Top	12439	1995	$5.00	Make-Up Pretty Fashions
Striped Shorts	2777	1979	$15.00	Best Buys
Striped Skirt and Green Top	12440	1995	$5.00	Make-Up Pretty Fashions
Striped Skirt, Blue Halter Top	4528	1988	$10.00	Bright & Breezy Fashions
Striped Top and Yellow/Blue Vest and Skirt	7954	1985	$10.00	Twice As Nice Reversible
Striped Top, Denim Yoke, Denim Long Skirt	4333	1988	$10.00	The Jeans Look Fashions
Striped Top, Red Shorts	1024	1989	$10.00	Fashion Finds Fashions
Stripes Away	1775	1967	$450.00	Color Magic
Stripes for Stretching	5539	1983	$10.00	Fashion Fantasy
Stripes Right for City Stripes	9152	N/A	$40.00	Get-Ups 'n Go
Student Teacher	1622	1965	$375.00	
Studio Tour	1690	1967	$275.00	
Style Setter Gets Rave Review	7843	N/A	$95.00	Get-Ups 'n Go
Suburban Shopper	969	1959	$225.00	
Suede 'n Fur	3491	1972	$225.00	
Sugar Plum Fairy	9326	1976	$40.00	Ballerina Costumes
Summer	15905	1997	$10.00	Fashion Avenue Internationale
Summer Dance	1401	1980	$10.00	Fashion Favorites
Summer Gown	9151	1976	$35.00	Get-Ups 'n Go
Summer Party	5711	1983	$10.00	Fashion Fun
Summer Picnic	5540	1983	$10.00	Fashion Fantasy
Summer Romance	2785	1979	$15.00	Fashion
Summer Sparkle	5545	1983	$10.00	Fashion Fantasy
Summertime Fun	5543	1983	$10.00	Fashion Fantasy
Sun Set Accessories	1497	1971	$550.00	J.C. Penney
Sun-Shiner	Pak	1969	$150.00	
Sunday Visit	1675	1966	$500.00	
Sunflower	1683	1967	$250.00	
Sunny Sleep Ins	3348	1973	$50.00	Best Buys
Super Scarf	3408	1971	$115.00	
Sweater Girl	976	1959	$180.00	
Sweet Dreams	3350	1972	$50.00	Best Buys
Sweet Dreams	Pak	1964	$155.00	
Sweet Dreams (pink)	973	1959	$400.00	
Sweet Dreams (yellow)	973	1959	$160.00	
Sweetheart Satin	3361	1972	$175.00	Best Buys
Swinging Easy	955	1963	$200.00	
Swirly-Que	1822	1968	$260.00	
Tailored Tops	Pak	1966	$100.00	
Tan Coat with Red Hat and Scarf	1908	1981	$10.00	Fashion Collectibles
Tan Coat, Fur Trim	8682	1973	$55.00	Best Buys
Tan Indian Dress w/White Fringe and Headdress	3633	1982	$10.00	Best Buys
Tan Shirt, Red Blouse	8681	1973	$55.00	Best Buys
Tangerine Scene	1451	1970	$75.00	
Tank w/Ballet Motif, Fuchsia Pants	4576	1988	$10.00	My First Barbie Fashions

Item	Number	Year	Value	Specials
Teacher, Firefighter, Veterinarian	10773	1995	$5.00	Caring Careers Fashion
Teachers	9085	1985	$5.00	Day to Night Fashions
Team Ups	1855	1968	$200.00	
Tennis	7842	1974	$50.00	Get-Ups 'n Go
Tennis Anyone	941	1962	$125.00	
Tennis Team	1781	1970	$75.00	
Terrific Twosomes	Pak	1969	$150.00	
Theatre Date	959	1963	$160.00	
Theatre Date (no hat)	1612	1964	$250.00	
Three-Piece White w/Fringed Vest and Skirt	14692	1996	$4.00	Western Fun
Togetherness	1842	1968	$175.00	
Top Twosome	Pak	1967	$100.00	
Topsy Twosider	4826	1984	$10.00	Twice As Nice Fashions
Tour-Ins	1515	1969	$50.00	
Tour-Ins	Pak	1969	$150.00	
Town 'n Travel	1011	1979	$15.00	Fashion Favorites
Trail Blazer	1846	1968	$250.00	
Travel Together	1688	1967	$250.00	
Tropicana	1460	1967	$170.00	
T-Shirt and Shorts	Pak	1962	$30.00	
Tunic 'n Tights	1859	1968	$300.00	
Turquoise Brushed Tricot and Denim Jacket	15860	1997	$5.00	Western Fashions
Turquoise Two-Piece Suit, Chain Belt, Purse	14360	1996	$5.00	Fashion Avenue
Turtle 'n Tights	3426	1971	$200.00	
TV News Reporter	9084	1985	$10.00	
Tweed Long Top, Black Skirt, Red Scarf	4478	1988	$10.00	Sweatersoft Fashions
Tweed Long Top, Red Long Skirt, Hat and Scarf	4484	1988	$10.00	Sweatersoft Fashions
Tweed Skirt, Blue Blouse	9048	1975	$35.00	Fashion Originals
Tweed Suit	9048	1976	$40.00	Best Buys
Twinkle Togs	1854	1968	$275.00	
Two for Fun	4823	1984	$10.00	Twice As Nice Fashions
Two for Tea	4827	1984	$10.00	Twice As Nice Fashions
Two-Piece Denim-Look Suit, Bag, Gold Trim	14374	1996	$4.00	Barbie Floatin' Cool
Two-Piece Pajamas	Pak	1962	$25.00	
Two-Piece Red/Beige Skirt, Top, Bolo Tie	14690	1996	$4.00	Western Fun
Two-Piece Turquoise/Silver/Magenta w/Jacket	14371	1996	$4.00	Barbie Floatin' Cool
Two-Piece w/Chambray Pants and Pink Jacket	14689	1996	$4.00	Western Fun
Two-Piece w/Purple Jacket, White Skirt	14691	1996	$4.00	Western Fun
Two-Tone Pink Dress, Bolero, Hair Bow	1295	1989	$10.00	Dinner Date Fashions
Two-Toned Green Wrap Dress w/Gold Belt	1464	1981	$10.00	Best Buys
Two-Way Tiger	3402	1971	$110.00	
Under Fashions	1655	1966	$500.00	
Under-Liners	1821	1968	$140.00	
Underprints	1685	1967	$250.00	
Underwear	9163	1976	$30.00	Best Buys
United Airlines Stewardess	7703	1973	$75.00	Get-Ups 'n Go
Vacation Time	1623	1965	$200.00	
Velvet Touch, The	2789	1979	$15.00	Designer Originals
Velvet Venture	1488	1969	$180.00	
Velveteens	1818	1967	$700.00	Sears
Vet Coat and Skirt with Dog	9267	1985	$10.00	Fashion Playsets
Victorian Velvet	3431	1971	$175.00	
Violet Panties and Negligee w/Floral Trim	14291	1996	$5.00	Fashion Avenue
Walking Pretty	Pak	1971	$130.00	
Wedding Belle	2965	1979	$15.00	Designer Originals

Item	Number	Year	Value	Specials
Wedding Day Set	972	1959	$400.00	
Wedding Gift	8623	1973	$110.00	Best Buys
Wedding Wonder	1849	1968	$360.00	
Weekenders	1815	1967	$900.00	Sears
Welcome to Venus	2738	1986	$28.00	Astro Fashions
What's Cooking	Pak	1964	$110.00	
White 'n With It	3352	1972	$60.00	Best Buys
White Blouse, Brown Pants, Brown Leopard Trim	4433	1988	$10.00	Citystyle Fashions
White Blouse, Reddish Plaid Skirt	2975	1979	$15.00	
White Coat with Fur Collar and Cuffs	22156	1999	$12.00	Fashion Avenue
White Delight	3799	1982	$15.00	Barbie & Ken Designer Original
White Dress with Navy Stripes	9683	1976	$45.00	Sears' Exclusive Best Buys
White Dress, Sheer Overlay, Wristbands, Veil	2688	1986	$10.00	Barbie & the Rockers Fashions
White Halter Dress, Floral Print, Pink Trim	1063	1989	$10.00	Fashion Finds Fashions
White Halter, Blue Scarf Skirt	1010	1989	$10.00	My First Barbie Fashions
White Halter, Red Short Skirt	1010	1989	$10.00	Fashion Finds Fashions
White Hat, Coat, Pink Scarf, Red Luggage	9264	1985	$10.00	Fashion Playsets
White Ice Cream Top, Yellow Shorts	4580	1988	$10.00	My First Barbie Fashions
White Jacket and Top, Purple Shorts	12631	1995	$5.00	Sponge 'n Print Fashions
White Jacket, Cap, Red Pants, Scarf	3302	1988	$10.00	Beverly Hills Fashions
White Jacket, Pants, Red Short Skirt, Striped Tops	4800	1988	$10.00	Fashion Magic Fashions
White Jacket, Skirt, Pants, Red Top	9145	1985	$10.00	Spectacular Fashions
White Jeans, Red Flowered Top, White Tennis Shoes	68084	2000	$4.00	Jean Fashions
White Lace Outfit, Hat, White Ice Skates	4079	1990	$5.00	Ice Capades Fashions
White Lace Wedding Dress, Veil, Pink Bouquet	3102	1988	$10.00	Romantic Wedding
White Long Dress with Silver Tie Belt	3789	1982	$10.00	Fashion Favorites
White Long Halter Dress, Lace Ruffle, Gloves	1300	1989	$10.00	Dinner Date Fashions
White Long Lace Trimmed Robe and Gown	3785	1982	$10.00	Fashion Favorites
White Long Shirt, Red Leggings, and Belt	7914	1985	$10.00	B Active Fashions
White Magic	1607	1964	$250.00	
White Outfit and Pink Vest	12630	1995	$5.00	Sponge 'n Print Fashions
White Pants and Red Shirt	9154	1976	$35.00	Best Buys
White Pants, Blue Print Tunic and Hat	2225	1978	$15.00	Best Buys
White Pants, Red Belt, Blue and White Halter	13019	1995	$5.00	Yacht Club Fashions
White Pants, Top, Multicolored Jacket, Leg Warmer	3322	1989	$10.00	Cool Times Fashions
White Print Pants and Top	3684	1982	$10.00	Fashion Collectibles
White Ruffle Shirt, Pink/Black Jumper	9265	1990	$5.00	My First Barbie Fashions
White Satin Baggy Pants, Blue Jacket, Red Shirt	2791	1986	$10.00	Barbie & the Rockers Fashions
White Satin Dress w/Lace Top, Veil, Pink Bouquet	3788	1990	$5.00	Wedding of the Year
White Slip and White Panties	1350	1980	$10.00	Best Buys
White Strapless Long Dress with Black Stripe	1901	1981	$10.00	Fashion Collectibles
White Sweater, Black Long Skirt, Black Hat, Purse	3298	1988	$10.00	Beverly Hills Fashions
White T, Silver/Yellow Jumper, Yellow Biker Pants	9272	1990	$5.00	My First Barbie Fashions
White Top, Blue Lace Trim, Blue Skirt	4583	1988	$10.00	My First Barbie Fashions
White Top, Blue Short Skirt, Red Leggings, Hat	4466	1988	$10.00	California Dream Fashions
White Top, Long Denim Skirt and Jacket	4334	1988	$10.00	The Jeans Look Fashions
White Top, Orange Shorts and Shoes	7912	1985	$10.00	B Active Fashions
White Top, Red Print Shawl	2228	1978	$15.00	Best Buys
White Turtleneck Sweater, White Leggings, Belt	3787	1982	$10.00	Fashion Favorites
White Two-Piece Suit, Gold Blouse, Black Boa	4417	1988	$10.00	Citystyle Fashions
White Vest, Skirt, Pink Ruffled Blouse, Pink Belt	2300	1986	$10.00	Twice As Nice Reversible
White/Black Dress, Black Hat	9961	1977	$15.00	Best Buys
White/Red Petal Point Hem	2773	1979	$15.00	Best Buys
Wild 'n Wintery	3416	1971	$300.00	
Wild 'n Wonderful	1856	1968	$250.00	

Item	Number	Year	Value	Specials
Wild Things	3439	1971	$250.00	
Winter	15903	1997	$10.00	Fashion Avenue Internationale
Winter Bride	15901	1997	$10.00	Fashion Avenue Bridal
Winter Holiday	975	1959	$280.00	
Winter Wedding	1880	1969	$200.00	
Winter Wow	1486	1969	$225.00	
Wrap 'n Snap	1373	1980	$10.00	Beginner's Fashion
Wrap 'n Tie (blue)	1368	1980	$10.00	Beginner's Fashion
Wrap 'n Tie (red)	1369	1980	$10.00	Beginner's Fashion
Wrap, Snap, Tie	1370	1980	$10.00	Beginner's Fashion
Yellow Bathing Suit, Matching Shorts, Headband	2183	1986	$10.00	B Active Fashions
Yellow Coat with Black Fur Collar and Cuffs	22158	1999	$12.00	Fashion Avenue
Yellow Evening Gown	1005	1979	$15.00	Fashion Collectibles
Yellow Evening Outfit	2565	1978	$10.00	Best Buys
Yellow Floral Print Dress with Blue Vest	1900	1981	$10.00	Fashion Collectibles
Yellow Flower Print Sun Dress	1352	1980	$10.00	Best Buys
Yellow Go, The	1816	1967	$800.00	Sears
Yellow Halter, Floral Print Pants	4122	1988	$10.00	Pretty Choices
Yellow Halter, Print Pants	1507	1989	$10.00	Feeling Pretty Fashions
Yellow Halter, Purple Skirt	9968	1990	$5.00	Fashion Finds
Yellow Hat, Denim Pants, Vest & Shirt	12777	1995	$5.00	Western Fun Fashions
Yellow Jumper, Blouse, and Scarf	9162	1976	$40.00	Best Buys
Yellow Jumpsuit with Red Belt	3674	1982	$10.00	My First Barbie Fashions
Yellow Jumpsuit with Striped Belt	3688	1982	$10.00	Fashion Collectibles
Yellow Long Coat and Skirt, Green Halter & Leggings	3390	1987	$10.00	Concert Tour Fashions
Yellow Long Dress w/Gold Glitter, Yellow Boa	1861	1987	$10.00	Jewel Secrets Fashion
Yellow Long Top, Blue Leg Warmers	1886	1987	$10.00	My First Barbie Fashions
Yellow Mellow	1484	1969	$125.00	
Yellow Music Note Top, Red Short Skirt, Socks	4579	1988	$10.00	My First Barbie Fashions
Yellow Outfit	12625	1995	$5.00	Bead Fun Fashions
Yellow Pants Outfit	2782	1979	$10.00	Fashion Collectibles
Yellow Pants, Multicolored Striped Top	1531	1989	$10.00	Weekend Collection Fashions
Yellow Playsuit, Red/Yellow Striped Socks	9959	1977	$15.00	Best Buys
Yellow Print Short Dress, Headband, Green Biker Pants	1054	1990	$5.00	Wet 'N Wild Fashions
Yellow Print Two-Piece Outfit	3686	1982	$10.00	Fashion Collectibles
Yellow Print, Orangy Halter Top	2770	1979	$15.00	Best Buys
Yellow Rain Slicker with Hat	2118	1986	$10.00	My First Barbie Fashions
Yellow Robe, Shower Cap	9623	1977	$15.00	Best Buys
Yellow Satiny Pants & Tunic, Glitter Coat	1022	1979	$15.00	Department Store
Yellow Short Dress w/Blue Flower Motif	1011	1989	$10.00	Fashion Finds Fashions
Yellow Short Dress, Blue Leggings, Stole	1464	1989	$10.00	Style Magic Fashions
Yellow Short Jumpsuit with Belt	2090	1986	$10.00	Fashion Fun
Yellow Skirt, Pants, Striped Top, Jacket	4819	1988	$10.00	Fashion Magic Fashions
Yellow Slicker Raincoat and Hat, Umbrella	3792	1982	$10.00	Fashion Favorites
Yellow Suit	9684	1976	$45.00	Sears' Exclusive Best Buys
Yellow Suit, Printed Halter	9909	1975	$45.00	Sears' Exclusive Best Buys
Yellow Sundress, Yellow Shoes	68014	2000	$2.00	Go in Style Fashions
Yellow Sweater with Giraffe, Orange Miniskirt	1595	1989	$15.00	Animal Lovin' Fashions
Yellow Top and Flare Leg Pants	12596	1995	$5.00	Picnic Pretty Fashions
Yellow Top, Pink Print Skirt	1069	1990	$5.00	Wet 'N Wild Fashions
Yellow Top, Pink Skirt and Jacket, Lace Leggings	1175	1986	$10.00	Barbie & the Rockers Fashions
Yellow Top, White Tutu, Yellow Leg Warmers	1874	1989	$10.00	My First Barbie Fashions
Yellow Two-Piece Gown	3183	1987	$10.00	Fancy Frills
Yellow Wrap Robe w/Red Trim	3640	1982	$10.00	Best Buys
Yellow/Black Dress, Black Boa and Hat	3314	1988	$10.00	Beverly Hills Fashions

Item	Number	Year	Value	Specials
Yellow/Black Jacket, Black Pants, Yellow Top	3394	1987	$10.00	Concert Tour Fashions
Yellow/Blue Long Dress, Ruffle Neckline	7956	1985	$10.00	Twice As Nice Reversible
Yellow/Burnt Orange Printed, Sunback Dress	2218	1978	$10.00	Best Buys
Yellow/Pink Two-Piece Bathing Suit	12648	1995	$5.00	Bath Paintin' Fashions
Yellow Printed Skirt, Printed Top	9011	1975	$45.00	Sears' Exclusive Best Buys
Yellow/Red Coat, Blue Scarf	2302	1986	$10.00	Twice As Nice Reversible
Yellow/White Top, White Pleated Short Skirt	1009	1989	$10.00	Fashion Finds Fashions
Zebra Printed Coat w/Pink Belt & Collar, Boots	68696	1998	$3.00	Coat Collection Fashions
Zig-Zag Bag, The	3428	1971	$175.00	
Zokko!	1820	1968	$200.00	

Barbie Doll Outfits

Listed by Stock Number

Number	Item	Year	Value	Specials
10	Stitch 'N Style	1970	$50.00	
20	Sharp Shift	1970	$110.00	
40	Foot Lights (pak)	1970	$120.00	
50	All the Trimmings (pak)	1970	$225.00	
60	Perfect Beginnings	1970	$90.00	
620	Gold Knit	N/A	$45.00	
697	Holiday Gown Collection I	1992	$55.00	Wholesale Club
819	It's Cold Outside (brown)	1964	$150.00	
819	It's Cold Outside (red)	1964	$225.00	
820	Barbie in Mexico	1964	$225.00	Travel Outfits
821	Barbie in Japan	1964	$375.00	Travel Outfits
822	Barbie in Switzerland	1964	$220.00	Travel Outfits
823	Barbie in Holland	1964	$350.00	Travel Outfits
872	Cinderella	1964	$450.00	Little Theatre Costumes
873	Guinevere	1964	$250.00	Little Theatre Costumes
874	Arabian Nights	1964	$375.00	Little Theatre Costumes
875	Drum Majorette	1964	$225.00	
876	Cheerleader	1964	$200.00	
880	Little Red Riding Hood and the Wolf	1964	$600.00	Little Theatre Costumes
889	Candy Striper Volunteer	1964	$300.00	
911	Golden Girl	1959	$175.00	
912	Cotton Casual	1959	$125.00	
915	Peachy Fleecy Coat	1959	$160.00	
916	Commuter Set	1959	$1,200.00	
917	Apple Print Sheath	1959	$200.00	
918	Cruise Stripes	1959	$150.00	
919	Fashion Undergarment	1959	$75.00	
921	Floral Petticoat	1959	$125.00	
923	Accessory Pack	1961	$250.00	
931	Garden Party	1962	$175.00	
933	Movie Date	1962	$125.00	
934	After Five	1962	$175.00	
937	Sorority Meeting	1962	$275.00	
939	Red Flair	1962	$175.00	
940	Mood for Music	1962	$200.00	
941	Tennis Anyone	1962	$125.00	
942	Ice Breaker	1962	$175.00	
943	Fancy Free	1963	$100.00	
944	Masquerade	1963	$200.00	
945	Graduation	1963	$60.00	
946	Dinner at Eight	1963	$250.00	
947	Bride's Dream	1963	$300.00	
948	Ski Queen	1963	$200.00	
949	Raincoat	1963	$100.00	
949	Stormy Weather	1964	$100.00	
951	Senior Prom	1963	$200.00	
953	Baby Sits	1962	$225.00	
953	Baby Sits (Layette)	1964	$400.00	

Number	Item	Year	Value	Specials
954	Career Girl	1963	$350.00	
955	Swinging Easy	1963	$200.00	
956	Busy Morning	1963	$230.00	
957	Knitting Pretty (blue)	1963	$350.00	
957	Knitting Pretty (pink)	1963	$300.00	
958	Party Date	1963	$225.00	
959	Theatre Date	1963	$160.00	
961	Evening Splendour	1959	$275.00	
961	Evening Splendour (reissue)	1964	$150.00	
962	Barbie-Q	1959	$170.00	
963	Resort Set	1959	$175.00	
964	Gay Parisienne	1959	$4,900.00	
965	Nighty-Negligee	1959	$140.00	
966	Plantation Belle	1959	$550.00	
967	Picnic Set	1959	$325.00	
967	Picnic Set #2 (new hat, basket, fish)	1962	$300.00	
968	Roman Holiday	1959	$4,500.00	
969	Suburban Shopper	1959	$225.00	
971	Easter Parade	1959	$4,500.00	
972	Wedding Day Set	1959	$400.00	
973	Sweet Dreams (pink)	1959	$400.00	
973	Sweet Dreams (yellow)	1959	$160.00	
975	Winter Holiday	1959	$280.00	
976	Sweater Girl	1959	$180.00	
977	Silken Flame	1960	$175.00	
978	Let's Dance	1960	$190.00	
979	Friday Nite Date	1960	$225.00	
981	Busy Gal	1960	$415.00	
982	Solo In The Spotlight	1960	$350.00	
983	Enchanted Evening	1960	$325.00	
984	American Airlines Stewardess	1961	$175.00	
985	Open Road	1961	$325.00	
986	Sheath Sensation	1961	$150.00	
987	Orange Blossom	1961	$225.00	
988	Singing in the Shower	1961	$140.00	
989	Ballerina	1961	$175.00	
991	Registered Nurse	1961	$275.00	
992	Golden Elegance	1963	$325.00	
993	Sophisticated Lady	1963	$400.00	
1000	Red Dress and Head Scarf	1979	$15.00	Fashion Collectibles
1001	Shiny Pants and Top	1979	$15.00	Fashion Collectibles
1003	Pink Blouse and Silvery Skirt	1979	$15.00	Fashion Collectibles
1005	Yellow Evening Gown	1979	$15.00	Fashion Collectibles
1006	Blue Pants, Striped Blouse	1979	$15.00	Fashion Collectibles
1008	Print Dress, Pink Bolero	1979	$15.00	Fashion Collectibles
1009	Sheer Romance	1979	$15.00	Fashion Favorites
1009	Yellow/White Top, White Pleated Short Skirt	1989	$10.00	Fashion Finds Fashions
1010	White Halter, Blue Scarf Skirt	1989	$10.00	My First Barbie Fashions
1010	White Halter, Red Short Skirt	1989	$10.00	Fashion Finds Fashions
1011	Disco Dazzle	1979	$15.00	Fashion Favorites
1011	Town 'n Travel	1979	$15.00	Fashion Favorites
1011	Yellow Short Dress w/Blue Flower Motif	1989	$10.00	Fashion Finds Fashions
1012	Blue Short Dress	1989	$10.00	Fashion Finds Fashions
1012	Pink Sparkler	1979	$15.00	Fashion Favorites
1018	Pink Dress, White Lace Collar	1989	$10.00	Fashion Finds Fashions

Number	Item	Year	Value	Specials
1019	Blue Short Sleeveless Dress	1989	$10.00	Fashion Finds Fashions
1021	Blue Evening Gown, Sheer Coat	1979	$15.00	Department Store
1022	Yellow Satiny Pants & Tunic, Glitter Coat	1979	$15.00	Department Store
1023	Mix 'n Match, Silver/Fuchsia Set	1979	$15.00	Department Store
1024	Red Evening Gown	1979	$15.00	Bargain Fashions
1024	Striped Top, Red Shorts	1989	$10.00	Fashion Finds Fashions
1025	Floral Print Short Skirt, Blue Top	1989	$10.00	Fashion Finds Fashions
1025	Red/White Shorts, Halter, Cap	1979	$15.00	Bargain Fashions
1027	Long Printed Dress	1979	$15.00	Bargain Fashions
1028	Pink/Blue/Yellow/White Top, Yellow Short Skirt	1989	$10.00	Fashion Finds Fashions
1034	Hostess Set	1965	$3,500.00	
1039	Pink Ruffle Hem, Short Halter Dress	1989	$10.00	Fashion Finds Fashions
1045	Pink Vest, Yellow Halter, Blue Pants	1990	$5.00	Wet 'N Wild Fashions
1054	Yellow Print Short Dress, Headband, Green Biker Pants	1990	$5.00	Wet 'N Wild Fashions
1055	Country Music	1971	$300.00	Fashions 'n Sounds
1056	Festival Fashion	1971	$370.00	Fashions 'n Sounds
1057	Groovin' Gauchos	1971	$300.00	Fashions 'n Sounds
1061	Poodle Doodles	1972	$750.00	Put-Ons 'n Pets
1062	Kitty Kapers	1972	$825.00	Put-Ons 'n Pets
1062	Sleeveless Dress, White Top, Blue/White Bottom	1989	$10.00	Fashion Finds Fashions
1063	Hot Togs	1972	$725.00	Put-Ons 'n Pets
1063	White Halter Dress, Floral Print, Pink Trim	1989	$10.00	Fashion Finds Fashions
1065	Fashion Hangers (10)	1982	$5.00	
1067	Short Dress w/Blue Top, Print Ruffle on Hem	1990	$5.00	Wet 'N Wild Fashions
1069	Yellow Top, Pink Print Skirt	1990	$5.00	Wet 'N Wild Fashions
1088	Pink Full Skirt, Yellow Print Ruffle Top, Visor	1990	$5.00	Wet 'N Wild Fashions
1165	Hot Pink Short Dress, Purple Bolero, Boots	1986	$10.00	Barbie & the Rockers Fashions
1166	Pink Tank, Leggings, Print Jacket, Yellow Belt	1986	$10.00	Barbie & the Rockers Fashions
1167	Pink Jacket, Print Tank, Blue Skirt, Hose, Hat	1986	$10.00	Barbie & the Rockers Fashions
1170	Pink/White Leggings, Blue Top, Yellow Headband	1986	$10.00	Barbie & the Rockers Fashions
1175	Yellow Top, Pink Skirt and Jacket, Lace Leggings	1986	$10.00	Barbie & the Rockers Fashions
1176	Print Jacket, Black Mini, Pink Top, Orange Leggings	1986	$10.00	Barbie & the Rockers Fashions
1292	Pink Top, Ruffle Lace Skirt, Scarf	1989	$10.00	Dinner Date Fashions
1295	Two-Tone Pink Dress, Bolero, Hair Bow	1989	$10.00	Dinner Date Fashions
1300	White Long Halter Dress, Lace Ruffle, Gloves	1989	$10.00	Dinner Date Fashions
1304	Purple/White Long Dress, Hat	1989	$10.00	Dinner Date Fashions
1308	Blue Short Ruffle Trim Dress, Long White Gloves	1989	$10.00	Dinner Date Fashions
1311	Pink Long Dress, White Trim and Long Gloves	1989	$10.00	Dinner Date Fashions
1350	White Slip and White Panties	1980	$10.00	Best Buys
1351	Red Striped Sheath Dress	1980	$10.00	Best Buys
1352	Yellow Flower Print Sun Dress	1980	$10.00	Best Buys
1353	Red/Blue/Yellow Sun Dress	1980	$10.00	Best Buys
1354	Multicolored Striped Sun Dress	1980	$10.00	Best Buys
1355	Red/White Striped Long Halter Dress	1980	$10.00	Best Buys
1356	Red Wrap-Around Dress	1980	$10.00	Best Buys
1357	Long Red Halter Dress	1980	$10.00	Best Buys
1358	Blue Long Halter Dress with Self-tie Belt	1980	$10.00	Best Buys
1359	Multicolored Long Striped Halter Dress	1980	$10.00	Best Buys
1360	Long Floral Printed Sleeveless Dress w/Blue Trim	1980	$10.00	Best Buys
1361	Sleeveless Striped Dress with Turtleneck	1980	$10.00	Best Buys
1362	Floral Print Wrap Halter Dress	1980	$10.00	Fashion Collectibles
1363	Gold/Green Dress with Matching Shawl	1980	$10.00	Fashion Collectibles
1364	Black/White Formal Long Gown with Gloves	1980	$10.00	Fashion Collectibles

Number	Item	Year	Value	Specials
1365	Pink/White Long Halter Dress	1980	$10.00	Fashion Collectibles
1367	Red Turtleneck and Black Pants	1980	$10.00	Fashion Collectibles
1368	Wrap 'n Tie (blue)	1980	$10.00	Beginner's Fashion
1369	Wrap 'n Tie (red)	1980	$10.00	Beginner's Fashion
1370	Wrap, Snap, Tie	1980	$10.00	Beginner's Fashion
1371	Slip On, Snap, Tie	1980	$10.00	Beginner's Fashion
1372	Slip On 'n Tie	1980	$10.00	Beginner's Fashion
1372	Slip On 'n Tie (red pants and top)	1981	$10.00	My First Barbie Fashions
1373	Wrap 'n Snap	1980	$10.00	Beginner's Fashion
1400	Pleasant Dreams	1980	$10.00	Fashion Favorites
1401	Summer Dance	1980	$10.00	Fashion Favorites
1402	Pink Perfection	1980	$10.00	Fashion Favorites
1403	Dressed to a "T"	1980	$10.00	Fashion Favorites
1412	Golden Glamour	1980	$15.00	Barbie & Ken Designer Original
1414	Evening Elegance	1980	$15.00	Barbie & Ken Designer Original
1416	Here Comes the Bride	1980	$15.00	Barbie & Ken Wedding Party
1417	Bridesmaid's Dream	1980	$15.00	Barbie & Ken Wedding Party
1421	Pink/Gold Long Sheer Wrap Dress	1980	$10.00	Fashion Collectibles
1422	Dress w/Yellow Top, White Lace Skirt	1980	$10.00	Fashion Collectibles
1423	Red Front Tie Halter Top, Black Pants	1980	$10.00	Fashion Collectibles
1424	Blue Print Two-Piece Belted Dress	1980	$10.00	Fashion Collectibles
1425	Red Dress with Gold Trim	1980	$10.00	Fashion Collectibles
1426	Blue Top and Pants with Contrast Design on Top	1980	$10.00	Fashion Collectibles
1427	Pink Champagne	1980	$10.00	Fashion Favorites
1428	Let's Dance	1980	$10.00	Fashion Favorites
1429	Fresh 'n Cool	1980	$10.00	Fashion Favorites
1430	Romantic Lady	1980	$10.00	Fashion Favorites
1440	Pink Sparkle	1967	$250.00	
1441	Pink Mini Dress, Blue Leggings	1989	$10.00	Style Magic Fashions
1445	Pink Halter, Print Short Skirt, Stole, Leggings	1989	$10.00	Style Magic Fashions
1451	Tangerine Scene	1970	$75.00	
1452	Now Knit	1970	$100.00	
1453	Blue Sleeveless Dress, White Bow Trim	1989	$10.00	Style Magic Fashions
1453	Flower Wower	1970	$70.00	
1454	Loop Scoop	1970	$80.00	
1456	Dreamy Blues	1970	$80.00	
1457	City Sparklers	1970	$125.00	
1458	Gypsy Spirit	1970	$80.00	
1459	Great Coat	1970	$90.00	
1460	Tropicana	1967	$170.00	
1462	Rare Pair	1970	$125.00	
1463	Lovely Sleep-Ins	1970	$100.00	
1464	Anti-Freezers	1970	$125.00	
1464	Two-Toned Green Wrap Dress w/Gold Belt	1981	$10.00	Best Buys
1464	Yellow Short Dress, Blue Leggings, Stole	1989	$10.00	Style Magic Fashions
1465	Lavender w/Silver Trim Short Dress, Pink Leggings	1989	$10.00	Style Magic Fashions
1465	Lemon Kick	1970	$150.00	
1465	Red/White Polka Dot Halter Dress	1981	$10.00	Best Buys
1466	Blue Short Halter Dress w/Bow Trim, Pink Leggings	1989	$10.00	Style Magic Fashions
1466	Hot Pink Sleeveless Dress w/Blue Stripe	1981	$10.00	Best Buys
1467	Lamb 'n Leather	1970	$245.00	
1467	Long Blue Halter Dress	1981	$10.00	Best Buys
1468	Red Print Strapless Dress	1981	$10.00	Best Buys
1468	Special Sparkle	1970	$175.00	
1469	Blue Royalty	1970	$250.00	Get-Ups 'n Go

Number	Item	Year	Value	Specials
1469	Pink Teddy w/White Trim	1981	$10.00	Best Buys
1470	Intrigue	1967	$425.00	
1470	Long Purple Halter Dress w/White Belt	1981	$10.00	Best Buys
1472	Navy Blue Long Halter Dress w/White Trim	1981	$10.00	Best Buys
1476	Dream Wraps	1969	$80.00	
1477	Hurray for Leather	1969	$75.00	
1478	Shift into Knit	1969	$80.00	
1479	Leisure Leopard	1969	$75.00	
1481	Firelights	1969	$145.00	
1482	Important In-vestment	1969	$100.00	
1483	Little Bow-Pink	1969	$175.00	
1484	Yellow Mellow	1969	$125.00	
1486	Winter Wow	1969	$225.00	
1487	Shirtdressy	1969	$170.00	
1488	Velvet Venture	1969	$180.00	
1489	Cloud 9	1969	$140.00	
1491	Red/White 'n Warm	1969	$250.00	
1492	Silver Polish	1969	$175.00	
1493	Fab Fur	1969	$250.00	
1494	Goldswinger	1969	$250.00	
1497	Made for Malibu	1971	$130.00	
1497	Sun Set Accessories	1971	$550.00	JCPenney
1498	64-Piece Accessory Set	1970	$275.00	JCPenney
1506	Pink/Blue Shorts, Halter, Playsuit	1989	$10.00	Feeling Pretty Fashions
1507	Yellow Halter, Printed Pants	1989	$10.00	Feeling Pretty Fashions
1508	Pink/White Short Skirt, Pink/White Striped Top	1989	$10.00	Feeling Pretty Fashions
1509	Red Polka Dot Short Dress w/Ruffle Trim	1989	$10.00	Feeling Pretty Fashions
1510	Blue Halter, Blue/White Pants	1989	$10.00	Feeling Pretty Fashions
1510	Glamour Group	1970	$350.00	Sears
1511	Fashion Bouquet	1970	$350.00	Sears
1515	Tour-Ins	1969	$50.00	
1518	Goodies Galore	1970	$275.00	Sears
1519	Pink/Red Two-Tone Halter Short Dress	1989	$10.00	Feeling Pretty Fashions
1521	Fashion Accents	1970	$250.00	Sears
1523	Short Dress, Blue Top, Floral Skirt, Pink Belt	1989	$10.00	Feeling Pretty Fashions
1524	Red/White Long Dress, Red Belt	1989	$10.00	Feeling Pretty Fashions
1525	Floral Print, Strapless Dress	1989	$10.00	Feeling Pretty Fashions
1526	Purple/White Short Dress, White Belt, Ruffle Skirt	1989	$10.00	Feeling Pretty Fashions
1527	Blue Top, Print Ruffle Short Skirt, Red Belt	1989	$10.00	Weekend Collection Fashions
1528	Dress w/Print Top, White Skirt, Red Jacket	1989	$10.00	Weekend Collection Fashions
1529	Print Top, Blue Skirt	1989	$10.00	Weekend Collection Fashions
1530	Print Long Skirt, Yellow Halter, Blue Hat	1989	$10.00	Weekend Collection Fashions
1531	Yellow Pants, Multicolored Striped Top	1989	$10.00	Weekend Collection Fashions
1532	Red Shorts, Yellow Turtleneck, Socks	1989	$10.00	Weekend Collection Fashions
1547	Glimmer Glamour	1968	$4,800.00	Sears
1593	Pink Top, Hat, Socks, Shoes, White Shorts	1989	$10.00	Animal Lovin' Fashions
1594	Cream Pants, Leopard Print Top Brown Fanny Pack	1989	$15.00	Animal Lovin' Fashions
1595	Yellow Sweater with Giraffe, Orange Miniskirt	1989	$15.00	Animal Lovin' Fashions
1596	Rust Short Giraffe Motif Top, Purple Skirt, Socks	1989	$10.00	Animal Lovin' Fashions
1597	Blue Long Skirt, Pink Top, Zebra Print Top	1989	$10.00	Animal Lovin' Fashions
1600	Lunch Date	1964	$150.00	
1601	Animal Lovin' Fashions	1988	$30.00	
1601	Pajama Party	1964	$80.00	
1602	Knit Separates	1964	$140.00	
1603	Country Fair	1964	$175.00	

Number	Item	Year	Value	Specials
1604	Crisp 'n Cool	1964	$180.00	
1605	Barbie in Hawaii	1964	$175.00	Travel Outfits
1606	Garden Tea Party	1964	$210.00	
1607	White Magic	1964	$250.00	
1608	Skin Diver	1964	$125.00	
1609	Black Magic Ensemble	1964	$400.00	
1610	Golden Evening	1964	$275.00	
1611	Satin 'n Rose	1964	$375.00	
1612	Theatre Date (no hat)	1964	$250.00	
1613	Dog 'n Duds	1964	$275.00	
1614	Junior Prom	1965	$575.00	
1615	Saturday Matinee	1965	$875.00	
1616	Campus Sweetheart	1964	$1,600.00	
1617	Midnight Blue	1964	$775.00	
1619	Fun 'n Games	1965	$320.00	
1620	Junior Designer	1965	$350.00	
1621	Knit Hit	1965	$155.00	
1622	Student Teacher	1965	$375.00	
1623	Vacation Time	1965	$200.00	
1624	Fun at the Fair	1965	$300.00	
1625	Modern Art	1965	$525.00	
1626	Dancing Doll	1965	$475.00	
1627	Country Club Dance	1965	$400.00	
1628	Brunch Time	1965	$350.00	
1629	Skater's Waltz	1965	$400.00	
1631	Aboard Ship	1965	$450.00	
1632	Invitation to Tea	1965	$575.00	
1633	Disco Date	1965	$275.00	
1634	Barbie Learns to Cook	1965	$525.00	
1635	Fashion Editor	1965	$800.00	
1636	Sleeping Pretty	1965	$355.00	
1637	Outdoor Life	1965	$325.00	
1638	Fraternity Dance	1965	$600.00	
1639	Holiday Dance	1965	$550.00	
1640	Matinee Fashions	1965	$505.00	
1641	Miss Astronaut	1965	$625.00	
1642	Slumber Party	1965	$275.00	
1643	Poodle Parade	1965	$800.00	
1644	On The Avenue	1965	$495.00	
1645	Golden Glory	1965	$400.00	
1646	Magnificence	1965	$625.00	
1647	Gold 'n Glamour	1965	$1,500.00	
1648	5th Avenue Fashions	1992	$35.00	
1648	Photo Fashion	1965	$450.00	
1649	Lunch on the Terrace	1966	$350.00	
1650	Outdoor Art Show	1966	$500.00	
1651	Beau Time	1966	$350.00	
1652	Pretty as a Picture	1966	$475.00	
1653	International Fair	1966	$500.00	
1654	Reception Line	1966	$600.00	
1655	Under Fashions	1966	$500.00	
1656	Fashion Luncheon	1966	$1,100.00	
1658	Garden Wedding	1966	$525.00	
1660	Evening Gala	1966	$400.00	
1661	London Tour	1966	$405.00	

Number	Item	Year	Value	Specials
1663	Music Center Matinee	1966	$630.00	
1664	Shimmering Magic	1966	$1,400.00	
1665	Here Comes the Bride	1966	$1,000.00	
1666	Debutante Ball	1966	$1,000.00	
1667	Benefit Performance	1966	$1,250.00	
1668	Riding in the Park	1966	$600.00	
1669	Dreamland	1966	$160.00	
1670	Coffee's On	1966	$180.00	
1671	Sporting Casuals	1965	$275.00	
1672	Club Meeting	1966	$400.00	
1673	Lunchtime	1966	$225.00	
1674	Sleepy Time Gal	1966	$275.00	
1675	Sunday Visit	1966	$500.00	
1676	Fabulous Fashion	1966	$500.00	
1678	Pan American Airways Stewardess	1966	$4,800.00	
1681	Pink Formal	1966	$2,200.00	Sears
1683	Sunflower	1967	$250.00	
1685	Underprints	1967	$250.00	
1686	Print A Plenty	1967	$275.00	
1687	Caribbean Cruise	1967	$230.00	
1688	Blue/Pink Short Ruffle Dress, Hat	1989	$10.00	Jeans Fashions
1688	Travel Together	1967	$250.00	
1690	Studio Tour	1967	$275.00	
1691	Fashion Shiner	1967	$300.00	
1692	Patio Party	1967	$350.00	
1692	Short Denim Dress, Sailor Style Hat	1989	$10.00	Jeans Fashions
1693	Short Dress, Denim Top, Striped Ruffle Skirt	1989	$10.00	Jeans Fashions
1694	Long Denim Dress, Pink Buttons/Belt, Denim Bag	1989	$10.00	Jeans Fashions
1694	Pink Moonbeams	1967	$300.00	
1695	Evening Enchantment	1967	$550.00	
1696	Floating Gardens	1967	$520.00	
1697	Blue/White Print Long Sleeved Blouse, Skirt	1989	$10.00	Jeans Fashions
1697	Formal Occasion	1967	$500.00	
1698	Beautiful Bride	1967	$2,000.00	
1699	Sears Natural Mink Jacket	1964	$3,100.00	Sears
1701	From Nine to Five	1965	$60.00	Sew Free Fashion
1703	Sorority Tea	1965	$50.00	Sew Free Fashion
1706	Pretty Traveler	1965	$60.00	Sew Free Fashion
1707	Hootenanny	1965	$50.00	Sew Free Fashion
1708	Patio Party	1965	$50.00	Sew Free Fashion
1711	Debutante Party	1965	$75.00	Sew Free Fashion
1712	Day in Town	1965	$60.00	Sew Free Fashion
1713	Sightseeing	1965	$60.00	Sew Free Fashion
1721	Moonlight 'n Roses	1965	$80.00	Sew Free Fashion
1722	Stardust	1965	$70.00	Sew Free Fashion
1723	Day 'n Night	1965	$75.00	Sew Free Fashion
1724	Golden Ball	1965	$70.00	Sew Free Fashion
1775	Stripes Away	1967	$450.00	Color Magic
1776	Smart Switch	1967	$450.00	Color Magic
1777	Pretty Wild	1967	$450.00	Color Magic
1778	Bloom Bursts	1967	$450.00	Color Magic
1779	Mix 'n Matchers	1967	$400.00	Color Magic
1781	Tennis Team	1970	$75.00	
1782	Shape-Ups	1970	$100.00	
1783	Ruffles 'n Swirls	1970	$80.00	

Number	Item	Year	Value	Specials
1784	Harem-m-m's	1970	$65.00	
1786	Bright 'n Brocade	1970	$140.00	
1787	Prima Ballerina	1970	$75.00	
1788	Scuba Do's	1970	$70.00	
1789	Fiery Felt	1970	$80.00	
1791	Lace Caper, The	1970	$125.00	
1792	Mood Matchers	1970	$140.00	
1793	Skate Mates	1970	$130.00	
1794	Check The Suit	1970	$125.00	
1796	Fur Sighted	1970	$200.00	
1797	Ski Scene, The	1970	$180.00	
1798	Rainbo Wraps	1970	$350.00	
1799	Maxi 'n Mini	1970	$350.00	
1804	Knit Hit	1968	$150.00	
1805	Bouncy Flouncy	1967	$300.00	
1806	Pajama Pow!	1968	$280.00	
1807	Disco Date	1967	$280.00	
1808	Drizzle Dash	1967	$200.00	
1809	Mini Prints	1967	$225.00	
1809	Red Fantastic	1967	$800.00	
1810	Bermuda Holiday	1968	$300.00	
1813	Snug Fuzz	1968	$250.00	
1814	Sparkle Squares	1968	$275.00	
1815	Weekenders	1967	$900.00	Sears
1816	Yellow Go, The	1967	$800.00	Sears
1818	Velveteens	1967	$700.00	Sears
1820	Zokko!	1968	$200.00	
1821	Under-Liners	1968	$140.00	
1822	Swirly-Que	1968	$260.00	
1823	Jump into Lace	1968	$150.00	
1824	Snap Dash	1968	$140.00	
1830	Fashion Accents (Pak)	1964	$250.00	
1831	For Barbie Dressmakers	1964	$50.00	
1832	Color Coordinates	1964	$100.00	
1833	Shoe Wardrobe	1964	$225.00	
1837	Flats 'n Heels	1966	$275.00	
1841	Night Clouds	1968	$100.00	
1842	Togetherness	1968	$175.00	
1843	Dancing Stripes	1968	$200.00	
1844	Extravaganza	1968	$350.00	
1845	Scene-Stealers	1968	$240.00	
1846	Trail Blazer	1968	$250.00	
1848	All That Jazz	1968	$300.00	
1849	Wedding Wonder	1968	$360.00	
1853	Now Wow!	1968	$125.00	
1854	Twinkle Togs	1968	$275.00	
1855	Team Ups	1968	$200.00	
1856	Wild 'n Wonderful	1968	$250.00	
1857	Dreamy Pink	1968	$100.00	
1858	Fancy-Dancy	1968	$200.00	
1859	Long Red Strapless Dress w/Silver Butterfly Pin	1987	$10.00	Jewel Secrets Fashion
1859	Tunic 'n Tights	1968	$300.00	
1860	Lavender/White Long Dress	1987	$10.00	Jewel Secrets Fashion
1860	Smasheroo	1968	$225.00	
1861	Make Mine Midi	1969	$300.00	

Number	Item	Year	Value	Specials
1861	Yellow Long Dress with Gold Glitter, Yellow Boa	1987	$10.00	Jewel Secrets Fashion
1862	Blue Sequin Trim Tutu w/Leggings	1989	$10.00	My First Barbie Fashions
1862	Country Caper	1969	$110.00	
1862	Long Dress, Silver Lamé Top, Blue Skirt	1987	$10.00	Jewel Secrets Fashion
1863	Long Dress, White Halter Top, Lavender Skirt	1987	$10.00	Jewel Secrets Fashion
1863	Pretty Power	1969	$125.00	
1864	Close-Ups	1969	$125.00	
1865	Glo-Go	1969	$250.00	
1866	Movie Groovie	1969	$125.00	
1867	Dream-Ins	1969	$115.00	
1868	Happy Go Pink	1969	$200.00	
1868	Pink Tutu	1989	$10.00	My First Barbie Fashions
1869	Midi Magic	1969	$175.00	
1869	Short Pink Tutu	1989	$10.00	My First Barbie Fashions
1870	Midi-Marvelous	1969	$160.00	
1870	Pink Cowl Neck Halter Top, Leggings, Tutu	1989	$10.00	My First Barbie Fashions
1871	Romantic Ruffles	1969	$225.00	
1872	Sea-Worthy	1969	$225.00	
1873	Plush Pony	1969	$175.00	
1874	Fab City	1969	$350.00	
1874	Yellow Top, White Tutu, Yellow Leg Warmers	1989	$10.00	My First Barbie Fashions
1876	Pink Knit Top, Pink/White/Floral Print Short Skirt	1987	$10.00	My First Barbie Fashions
1877	Purple Leotard w/Pink Dots, White Leggings	1987	$10.00	My First Barbie Fashions
1879	Gloves, Ballerina Bag, Pink/White Cap	1987	$10.00	My First Barbie Fashions
1879	Let's Have a Ball	1969	$300.00	
1880	Winter Wedding	1969	$200.00	
1881	Made for Each Other	1969	$250.00	
1882	Pink/Blue/Striped Top, Pink Shorts	1987	$10.00	My First Barbie Fashions
1885	Salute to Silver	1969	$110.00	Fan Club Offer
1885	Silver Sparkle	1969	$110.00	Fan Club Offer
1886	Yellow Long Top, Blue Leg Warmers	1987	$10.00	My First Barbie Fashions
1895	Blue Print Short Halter Dress w/Lace Trim	1987	$10.00	My First Barbie Fashions
1900	Yellow Floral Print Dress w/Blue Vest	1981	$10.00	Fashion Collectibles
1901	White Strapless Long Dress w/Black Stripe	1981	$10.00	Fashion Collectibles
1902	Light Green Top w/Pink Trim, Dark Green Pants	1981	$10.00	Fashion Collectibles
1903	Red Print Dress w/Yellow Trim	1981	$10.00	Fashion Collectibles
1904	Red/Blue Striped Long Sleeved Long Dress	1981	$10.00	Fashion Collectibles
1905	Navy Wrap Dress w/White Trim and Belt	1981	$10.00	Fashion Collectibles
1906	Pink Halter Top w/Long Floral Skirt	1981	$10.00	Fashion Collectibles
1907	Red Floral Print Sundress, Purple Leather Jacket	1989	$15.00	Paris Pretty Fashions
1907	Red/White Dress w/Red Yoke and Belt	1981	$10.00	Fashion Collectibles
1908	Pink Halter Dress w/White and Black Bottom	1989	$15.00	Paris Pretty Fashions
1908	Tan Coat w/Red Hat and Scarf	1981	$10.00	Fashion Collectibles
1909	Purple/Red/Yellow Print Strapless Mini-dress	1989	$15.00	Paris Pretty Fashions
1910	Pink Sundress w/Blue Print Bottom, Teal Coat	1989	$15.00	Paris Pretty Fashions
1910	Slip On, Wrap 'n Tie	1981	$10.00	My First Barbie Fashions
1911	Red Satin Strapless Bustier	1989	$20.00	Paris Pretty Fashions
1911	Slip On 'n Tie (gold dress)	1981	$10.00	My First Barbie Fashions
1912	Easy Slip On (pink short set)	1981	$10.00	My First Barbie Fashions
1913	Easy Slip On (plaid dress)	1981	$10.00	My First Barbie Fashions
1935	Black Tie Affair	1981	$10.00	Fashion Favorites
1936	Blue Mist	1981	$10.00	Fashion Favorites
1937	Eye Popper	1981	$10.00	Fashion Favorites
1938	Classic Cowgirl	1981	$10.00	Fashion Favorites
1939	Beach Dazzler	1981	$10.00	Fashion Favorites

Number	Item	Year	Value	Specials
1940	Blue/Fuchsia Lace Overlay Dress, Hat, Purse, Boa	1989	$10.00	Private Collection Fashions
1940	Casual Chic	1981	$10.00	Fashion Favorites
1941	Pastel Print Long Dress, Pink Rose Trim	1989	$10.00	Private Collection Fashions
1943	Fuchsia/Blue Print Long Dress, Purse, Hair Ribbon	1989	$10.00	Private Collection Fashions
1944	Fuchsia/Blue Long Dress, Purse, Hat	1989	$10.00	Private Collection Fashions
1955	Paint the Town Red	1981	$15.00	Barbie & Ken Designer Original
1957	Gold Spun	1981	$15.00	Barbie & Ken Designer Original
1958	Golden Accent	1981	$15.00	Barbie & Ken Designer Original
1975	Silver/Red Evening Gown	1975	$35.00	Fashion Originals
2051	Red Pants, Yellow Hat, Printed Scarf	1977	$35.00	Sears' Exclusive Best Buys
2052	Blue/Green/Purple Wrap Blouse and Cap	1977	$25.00	Sears' Exclusive Best Buys
2053	Red Print Skirt & Kerchief, Blue/Yellow Blouse	1977	$35.00	Sears' Exclusive Best Buys
2054	Pink/Gold Evening Gown	1977	$40.00	Sears' Exclusive Best Buys
2062	Evening Gown	1977	$50.00	Sears Exclusive
2070	On-The-Go-Wardrobe	1977	$40.00	Sears Exclusive
2086	Red Ruffle Neck Dress	1986	$10.00	Fashion Fun
2087	Long Red Sleeveless Dress w/Gold Belt	1986	$10.00	Fashion Fun
2088	Multicolored Striped Top Dress w/White Skirt	1986	$10.00	Fashion Fun
2089	Pink Long Sleeveless Dress	1986	$10.00	Fashion Fun
2090	Yellow Short Jumpsuit w/Belt	1986	$10.00	Fashion Fun
2091	Purple Sleeveless Dress	1986	$10.00	Fashion Fun
2092	Navy Dress Trimmed in Red	1986	$10.00	Fashion Fun
2093	Multicolored Bathing Suit w/Cover Up	1986	$10.00	Fashion Fun
2118	Yellow Rain Slicker with Hat	1986	$10.00	My First Barbie Fashions
2119	Navy Short Dress, White Sailor Collar, Red Trim	1986	$10.00	My First Barbie Fashions
2120	Pink/White Ballet Tutu	1986	$10.00	My First Barbie Fashions
2121	Pink Top w/Heart Motif, Pink, White Leggings	1986	$10.00	My First Barbie Fashions
2122	Lavender Shorty Gown w/Lace Trim	1986	$10.00	My First Barbie Fashions
2130	Blue Halter, Pink Shorts w/Blue Trim, Flying Disc	1990	$5.00	Cool Mix Fashions
2131	Blue Jumper, Orange Tube Top	1990	$5.00	Cool Mix Fashions
2131	Blue Jumper, White Print Top, White Purse	1990	$5.00	Cool Mix Fashions
2132	Black/White Checked Top, Multicolored Skirt	1990	$5.00	Cool Mix Fashions
2138	Blue Halter, Blue Biker Pants, Yellow Ruffle Trim	1990	$5.00	Cool Mix Fashions
2138	Purple Halter, Blue Biker Pants, Ruffle Trim	1990	$5.00	Cool Mix Fashions
2144	Black/White Checked Bikers w/Suspenders, Halter	1990	$5.00	Cool Mix Fashions
2144	Pink Halter, Skirt, White Hat	1990	$5.00	Cool Mix Fashions
2146	Black/White Bikers, Suspenders, Orange Top	1990	$5.00	Cool Mix Fashions
2180	Blue/Hot Pink Two-Piece Jogging Suit	1986	$10.00	B Active Fashions
2181	Purple Long Sleeved Drop-Waist Dress	1986	$10.00	B Active Fashions
2182	Red Blouse, Red/White Check Print Skirt	1986	$10.00	B Active Fashions
2183	Yellow Bathing Suit, Matching Shorts, Headband	1986	$10.00	B Active Fashions
2184	Magenta/Purple Long Sleeved Blouse, Pants	1986	$10.00	B Active Fashions
2185	Magenta/Purple Blouse, Magenta Pants	1986	$10.00	B Active Fashions
2186	Green One Sleeved Shirt, White Pants & Pumps	1986	$10.00	B Active Fashions
2187	Multicolored T-shirt, White Vest and Shorts	1986	$10.00	B Active Fashions
2217	Blue Print Baggy Pants	1978	$20.00	Best Buys
2218	Yellow/Burnt Orange Print, Sunback Dress	1978	$10.00	Best Buys
2219	Blue Print and Red Dress	1978	$20.00	Best Buys
2220	Red Print Play Suit	1978	$15.00	Best Buys
2221	Evening Outfit	1978	$30.00	Best Buys
2222	Orangy Gauchos	1978	$30.00	Best Buys
2223	Evening Gown	1978	$30.00	Best Buys
2224	Red Print Skirt and Top	1978	$15.00	Best Buys
2225	White Pants, Blue Print Tunic and Hat	1978	$15.00	Best Buys
2226	2 Different Prints in Yellow	1978	$15.00	Best Buys

Number	Item	Year	Value	Specials
2227	Blue Print Long Dress	1978	$20.00	Best Buys
2228	White Top, Red Print Shawl	1978	$15.00	Best Buys
2229	Multicolored Striped Long Skirt	1978	$30.00	Best Buys
2230	Red Print Long Skirt	1978	$15.00	Best Buys
2252	Soft & Shimmering Silver & White	1978	$15.00	SuperStar Fashions
2294	Short Blue/White Ruffled Halter Dress	1986	$10.00	Twice As Nice Reversible
2295	Black/White Two-Piece Pants and Top	1986	$10.00	
2297	Blue/Red Pants, Top, Jacket	1986	$10.00	Twice As Nice Reversible
2298	Pink/Silver/White, Long Halter Evening Dress	1986	$10.00	Twice As Nice Reversible
2299	Pink/Purple Long Strapless Dress with Print Belt	1986	$10.00	Twice As Nice Reversible
2300	Bride In White	1978	$20.00	Get-Ups 'n Go
2300	White Vest, Skirt, Pink Ruffled Blouse, Pink Belt	1986	$10.00	Twice As Nice Reversible
2301	Red Dress, Red/Multistriped Jacket	1986	$10.00	Twice As Nice Reversible
2301	Silvery Spark for After Dark	1978	$15.00	Get-Ups 'n Go
2302	Flowery Delight is Party Right!	1978	$15.00	Get-Ups 'n Go
2302	Yellow/Red Coat, Blue Scarf	1986	$10.00	Twice As Nice Reversible
2303	Lady in Blue	1978	$15.00	Get-Ups 'n Go
2304	Fabulous Gown for Night on the Town	1978	$10.00	Get-Ups 'n Go
2342	City Suit in White	1978	$10.00	
2343	Dance & Whirl, Golden Girl	1978	$15.00	
2344	Shoulder Gown	1978	$15.00	
2345	Cling & Zing	1978	$15.00	
2346	Pants for Town	1978	$15.00	
2347	Dreamy Pair	1978	$15.00	
2457	Hair Originals	1978	$40.00	Fashion Add-Ons
2457	Hair Originals (bows and ribbons)	1981	$30.00	Fashion Add-Ons
2458	Shoes & Bags (with white boots)	1981	$10.00	Fashion Add-Ons
2458	Shoes & Purses	1982	$10.00	Fashion Add-Ons
2458	Shoes and Bags	1978	$15.00	Fashion Add-Ons
2460	Hats & Glasses	1978	$15.00	Fashion Add-Ons
2460	Hats & Glasses	1980	$15.00	Fashion Add-Ons
2460	Hats & Glasses (4 Hats)	1981	$10.00	Fashion Add-Ons
2462	Night & Day Extras	1981	$10.00	Fashion Add-Ons
2462	Scarfs and Such	1978	$15.00	Fashion Add-Ons
2462	Scarfs and Such	1980	$10.00	Fashion Add-Ons
2493	Halter, Pink/Black Shorts, Skateboard	1990	$5.00	All Stars Fashions
2496	Denim Top, Plaid Denim Trim Shorts, Purse	1990	$5.00	All Stars Fashions
2550	Blue Pants and Tunic	1978	$20.00	Best Buys
2551	Purple Trunks, Pink Blouse	1978	$15.00	Best Buys
2552	Red/Black Lace Evening Gown	1978	$15.00	Best Buys
2553	Multicolored One-Piece Ski Suit, Skis, Ski Boots	1990	$5.00	All Stars Fashions
2553	Red Jumpsuit	1978	$15.00	Best Buys
2554	Red Pants	1978	$15.00	Best Buys
2555	Green Slip, Panties, and Camisole	1978	$15.00	Best Buys
2556	Blue Long Sleeved Outfit	1978	$20.00	Best Buys
2557	Blue/White Striped Gown	1978	$15.00	Best Buys
2558	Pink Nightgown & Black Negligee	1978	$15.00	Best Buys
2559	Red Pants and Over Dress	1978	$15.00	Best Buys
2560	Red Suit	1978	$15.00	Best Buys
2561	Dark Peasant Outfit	1978	$15.00	Best Buys
2562	2-Piece Shocking Pink Evening Gown	1978	$15.00	Best Buys
2563	Black Pants and Oriental Tunic	1978	$30.00	Best Buys
2564	Blue Pants, Silvery Blue Blouse	1978	$20.00	Best Buys
2565	Yellow Evening Outfit	1978	$10.00	Best Buys
2579	7-Piece Mix 'n Match	1978	$40.00	Sears' Exclusive

Number	Item	Year	Value	Specials
2580	6-Piece SuperStar Mix 'n Match	1978	$140.00	Sears' Exclusive
2588	Pink Top, Pink/White Striped Skirt, Tennis Racket	1990	$5.00	All Stars Fashions
2609	Pink Top, Blue Leggings, Striped Socks, Bag	1990	$5.00	All Stars Fashions
2610	Pink Leotard, White Leggings, Warmers, Barbell	1990	$5.00	All Stars Fashions
2667	Fur Cape and Long Gown	1978	$10.00	Department Store
2667	Sleek 'n Chic	1979	$15.00	Designer Originals
2668	Royal Ball, The	1979	$15.00	Designer Originals
2670	Golden Firelight	1979	$15.00	Designer Originals
2670	Red Brocade Ensemble	1978	$35.00	Department Store
2671	City Sophisticate	1979	$20.00	Designer Originals
2688	White Dress, Sheer Overlay, Wristbands, Veil	1986	$10.00	Barbie & the Rockers Fashions
2689	Pink Ruffle Short Skirt, Yellow Halter, Leggings	1986	$10.00	Barbie & the Rockers Fashions
2690	Pink Short Dress, Lace Leggings, Blue Jacket	1986	$10.00	Barbie & the Rockers Fashions
2737	Space Racer	1986	$28.00	Astro Fashions
2738	Welcome to Venus	1986	$28.00	Astro Fashions
2739	Starlight Slumbers	1986	$28.00	Astro Fashions
2742	Galaxy A Go Go	1986	$28.00	Astro Fashions
2743	Dazzling Dancer	1986	$30.00	Astro Fashions
2762	Collector Series VIII	1986	$40.00	Oscar De La Renta
2763	Collector Series IX	1986	$40.00	Oscar De La Renta
2765	Collector Series X	1986	$40.00	Oscar De La Renta
2766	Collector Series XI	1986	$40.00	Oscar De La Renta
2767	Collector Series XII	1986	$40.00	Oscar De La Renta
2767	Red Printed Dress	1979	$15.00	Best Buys
2768	Dark Printed Dress	1979	$12.00	Best Buys
2769	Blue Evening Gown	1979	$15.00	Best Buys
2770	City Nights	1986	$10.00	Finishing Touches
2770	Yellow Print, Orangy Halter Top	1979	$15.00	Best Buys
2771	9 to 5	1986	$10.00	Finishing Touches
2771	Red Printed Dress	1979	$15.00	Best Buys
2772	Light Printed Dress	1979	$15.00	Best Buys
2773	Pretty Choices	1986	$10.00	Finishing Touches
2773	White/Red Petal Point Hem	1979	$15.00	Best Buys
2774	Short Reddish Outfit	1979	$15.00	Best Buys
2775	Fancy Hair	1986	$10.00	Finishing Touches
2775	Long Red/White Outfit	1979	$15.00	Best Buys
2776	Long Dark Printed Dress	1979	$15.00	Best Buys
2777	Striped Shorts	1979	$15.00	Best Buys
2778	Dark Print Jumpsuit	1979	$12.00	Best Buys
2779	Dark Peasant Print, Red Trim	1979	$12.00	Fashion Collectibles
2780	Glittery Evening Outfit	1979	$10.00	Fashion Collectibles
2781	Long Red Skirt, Printed Blouse	1979	$15.00	Fashion Collectibles
2782	Yellow Pants Outfit	1979	$10.00	Fashion Collectibles
2783	Red Print Dress, Yellow Jacket	1979	$15.00	Fashion Collectibles
2784	Long Blue/White Party Outfit	1979	$15.00	Fashion Collectibles
2785	Summer Romance	1979	$15.00	Fashion
2786	Pretty Pleasanty	1979	$15.00	Fashion Favorites
2787	Court Casuals	1979	$15.00	Fashion Favorites
2788	Rain or Shine	1979	$15.00	Fashion Favorites
2789	Velvet Touch, The	1979	$15.00	Designer Originals
2790	In The Limelight	1979	$15.00	Designer Originals
2791	White Satin Baggy Pants, Blue Jacket, Red Shirt	1986	$10.00	Barbie & the Rockers Fashions
2965	Wedding Belle	1979	$15.00	Designer Originals
2975	White Blouse, Reddish Plaid Skirt	1979	$15.00	
2976	Green/Yellow Beach Outfit	1979	$15.00	

Number	Item	Year	Value	Specials
3102	White Lace Wedding Dress, Veil, Pink Bouquet	1988	$10.00	Romantic Wedding
3105	Pink Lace Long Bridesmaid Dress, Hat, Bouquet	1988	$10.00	Romantic Wedding
3180	Lavender Short Robe, Matching Teddy	1987	$15.00	Fancy Frills
3181	Four Pair Panties, One Glitter Hose, One Tan Hose	1987	$10.00	Fancy Frills
3182	Pink Halter Nightgown, Matching Short Robe	1987	$10.00	Fancy Frills
3183	Yellow Two-Piece Gown	1987	$10.00	Fancy Frills
3184	Peach Strapless Slip & Bra, White Lace Bra	1987	$15.00	Fancy Frills
3203	Long Skirt, Blouse, Red/White/Black	1973	$50.00	Best Buys
3205	Midi Skirt, Yellow/White Blouse	1973	$50.00	Best Buys
3206	Long Printed Tricot Skirt and Hat, Green Top	1973	$60.00	Best Buys
3208	Orange Slacks and Jacket	1973	$70.00	Best Buys
3215	Royal Velvet	1972	$540.00	Miss America
3216	Majestic Blue	1972	$530.00	Miss America
3217	Regal Red	1972	$550.00	Miss America
3298	White Sweater, Black Long Skirt, Black Hat, Purse	1988	$10.00	Beverly Hills Fashions
3300	Light Blue Fur Trimmed Ice Skating Outfit/Gown	1989	$10.00	Superstar Barbie Fashions
3301	Pink Swimsuit and Long Gown w/Big Hat	1989	$10.00	Superstar Barbie Fashions
3302	White Jacket, Cap, Red Pants, Scarf	1988	$10.00	Beverly Hills Fashions
3303	Silver Jacket w/Tails, Hat, Long Blue Gown, Boa	1989	$10.00	Superstar Barbie Fashions
3304	Gold Halter Jumpsuit, Sequin Belt/Headband, Jacket	1989	$10.00	Superstar Barbie Fashions
3305	Pink Swimsuit/Gown with Star Print, Boa	1989	$10.00	Superstar Barbie Fashions
3306	Silver Star Pattern Swimsuit & Gown, Pink/Blue Boa	1989	$10.00	Superstar Barbie Fashions
3309	Fuchsia Long Coat, Teal Cap, Bag, Pants	1988	$10.00	Beverly Hills Fashions
3310	Red/White Floral Print Dress, White Hat, Scarf	1988	$10.00	Beverly Hills Fashions
3313	Butterfly Print Pants, Jacket, Top	1988	$10.00	Beverly Hills Fashions
3314	Yellow/Black Dress, Black Boa and Hat	1988	$10.00	Beverly Hills Fashions
3318	Multicolored Dress, Jacket, Pink Leggings	1989	$10.00	Cool Times Fashions
3319	Multicolored Jacket, Black/White/Orange Pants Suits	1989	$10.00	Cool Times Fashions
3320	Multicolored Short Jacket, Black/White Skirt, Top	1989	$10.00	Cool Times Fashions
3322	White Pants, Top, Multicolored Jacket, Leg Warmer	1989	$10.00	Cool Times Fashions
3323	Black/White Polka Dot Culottes, Top, Jacket, Socks	1989	$10.00	Cool Times Fashions
3336	Furry 'n Fun	1972	$100.00	Best Buys
3337	All American Girl	1972	$80.00	Best Buys
3338	Mainly for Rain	1972	$60.00	Best Buys
3339	Light 'n Lazy	1972	$75.00	Best Buys
3340	Golden Glitter	1972	$125.00	Best Buys
3341	Long 'n Fringy	1972	$100.00	Best Buys
3343	Flower Print Dress	1973	$60.00	Best Buys
3346	Aboard in Blue	1973	$40.00	Best Buys
3347	Short Printed Dress	1973	$30.00	Best Buys
3348	Sunny Sleep Ins	1973	$50.00	Best Buys
3350	Sweet Dreams	1972	$50.00	Best Buys
3351	Good Sports	1972	$70.00	Best Buys
3352	White 'n With It	1972	$60.00	Best Buys
3353	Sport Star	1972	$60.00	Best Buys
3354	Glowin' Gold	1972	$60.00	Best Buys
3355	Picture Me Pretty	1972	$80.00	Best Buys
3357	Silver Blues	1972	$90.00	Best Buys
3358	Lovely 'n Lavender	1972	$145.00	Best Buys
3359	Pants-Perfect Purple	1972	$90.00	Best Buys
3360	Pleasantly Peasanty	1972	$70.00	Best Buys
3361	Sweetheart Satin	1972	$175.00	Best Buys
3362	Fancy That Purple	1972	$125.00	Best Buys

Number	Item	Year	Value	Specials
3382	Shoes Scene	1972	$70.00	Best Buys
3383	Shoes	1977	$15.00	Best Buys
3390	Yellow Long Coat and Skirt, Green Halter & Leggings	1987	$10.00	Concert Tour Fashions
3391	Green Jacket and Skirt, Stripped Top, Leggings	1987	$10.00	Concert Tour Fashions
3393	Pink Top w/Silver Trim, Jeans, Gray Boots	1987	$10.00	Concert Tour Fashions
3394	Yellow/Black Jacket, Black Pants, Yellow Top	1987	$10.00	Concert Tour Fashions
3401	Fringe Benefits	1971	$100.00	
3402	Two-Way Tiger	1971	$110.00	
3403	Baby Doll Pinks	1971	$110.00	
3404	Glowin' Out	1971	$110.00	
3406	Evening In	1971	$150.00	
3407	Midi Mood	1971	$80.00	
3408	Super Scarf	1971	$115.00	
3409	Red for Rain	1971	$70.00	
3411	Poncho Put-On	1971	$150.00	
3412	Fun Flakes	1971	$120.00	
3413	Golfing Greats	1971	$200.00	
3414	Satin Slumber	1971	$160.00	
3416	Wild 'n Wintery	1971	$300.00	
3417	Bridal Brocade	1971	$275.00	
3418	Magnificent Midi	1971	$325.00	
3419	Silver Serenade	1971	$425.00	
3421	Bubbles 'n Boots	1971	$150.00	
3422	Color Kick, The	1971	$160.00	
3423	Night Lighter	1971	$175.00	
3424	In Blooms	1971	$90.00	
3426	Turtle 'n Tights	1971	$200.00	
3427	Dream Team, The	1971	$165.00	
3428	Zig-Zag Bag, The	1971	$175.00	
3429	Cold Snap	1971	$75.00	
3431	Victorian Velvet	1971	$175.00	
3432	In Stitches	1971	$175.00	
3433	All About Plaid	1971	$150.00	
3434	Fun Fur	1971	$205.00	
3436	Gaucho Gear	1971	$240.00	
3437	Dancing Lights	1971	$325.00	
3438	Peasant Dressy	1971	$180.00	
3439	Wild Things	1971	$250.00	
3480	Fun Shine	1972	$175.00	Miss America
3481	Short Set, The	1972	$150.00	
3482	Peasant Pleasant	1972	$120.00	
3483	Purple Pleasers	1972	$75.00	
3485	Madras Mad	1972	$120.00	
3486	O-Boy Corduroy	1972	$80.00	
3487	Sleepy Set	1972	$125.00	
3488	Overall Denim	1972	$110.00	
3490	Party Lines	1972	$175.00	
3491	Suede 'n Fur	1972	$225.00	
3492	Flying Colors	1972	$350.00	
3493	Satin 'n Shine	1972	$325.00	
3577	Pink/White Western Shirt, Cowboy Hat	1982	$10.00	Western Fashions
3578	Floral Print Long Dress, Vest, Purse, Cowboy Hat	1982	$10.00	Western Fashions
3579	Red Fringe Trimmed Jacket and Pants, Cowboy	1982	$10.00	Western Fashions
3631	Red Sleeveless Jumpsuit	1982	$10.00	Best Buys

Number	Item	Year	Value	Specials
3633	Tan Indian Dress w/White Fringe and Headdress	1982	$10.00	Best Buys
3634	Black/White Long Halter Dress	1982	$10.00	Best Buys
3635	Pink Shorty Gown with Mirror	1982	$10.00	Best Buys
3636	Red/White Striped Dress	1982	$10.00	Best Buys
3637	Blue Halter Dress	1982	$10.00	Best Buys
3638	Floral Printed Halter Dress	1982	$10.00	Best Buys
3639	Horizontal Striped Halter Dress	1982	$10.00	Best Buys
3640	Yellow Wrap Robe w/Red Trim	1982	$10.00	Best Buys
3641	Long White Printed Halter Dress w/Red Trim	1982	$10.00	Best Buys
3642	Red Shorts and Top	1982	$10.00	Best Buys
3656	Blue Short Skirt, Top, Blue Dog	1987	$10.00	Pet Show Fashions
3657	Blue Top, White Skirt	1987	$10.00	Pet Show Fashions
3658	Pink Dress, White Dog	1987	$10.00	Pet Show Fashions
3659	Pink Dress and Jacket, White Dog	1987	$10.00	Pet Show Fashions
3660	Pink Dress, White Dog	1987	$10.00	Pet Show Fashions
3672	Light Blue Long Halter Dress w/Ruffled Bottom	1982	$10.00	My First Barbie Fashions
3673	Red Floral Print Dress w/Black Belt, White Collar	1982	$10.00	My First Barbie Fashions
3674	Yellow Jumpsuit with Red Belt	1982	$10.00	My First Barbie Fashions
3675	Pink Halter, Floral Print Short Skirt	1982	$10.00	My First Barbie Fashions
3676	Blue Floral Print Halter and Shorts	1982	$10.00	My First Barbie Fashions
3677	Green Short Halter Dress w/White Trim	1982	$10.00	My First Barbie Fashions
3678	Red Long Dress with Slit Skirt	1982	$10.00	Fashion Collectibles
3679	Blue Print Dress w/White Collar and Cuffs	1982	$10.00	Fashion Collectibles
3680	Red/White Long Dress w/White Belt	1982	$10.00	Fashion Collectibles
3681	Denim Overalls with Red Top	1982	$10.00	Fashion Collectibles
3682	Blue Suit Jacket with Dark Blue Skirt	1982	$10.00	Fashion Collectibles
3683	Red Sailor Top, White Tops, White Sailor Hat	1982	$10.00	Fashion Collectibles
3684	White Print Pants and Top	1982	$10.00	Fashion Collectibles
3685	Blue Long Sleeved Long Dress	1982	$10.00	Fashion Collectibles
3686	Yellow Print Two-Piece Outfit	1982	$10.00	Fashion Collectibles
3687	Pink/White Camisole, Slip, Panties, Bra	1982	$10.00	Fashion Collectibles
3688	Yellow Jumpsuit with Striped Belt	1982	$10.00	Fashion Collectibles
3689	Striped Long Sleeved Dress	1982	$10.00	Fashion Collectibles
3785	White Long Lace Trimmed Robe and Gown	1982	$10.00	Fashion Favorites
3786	Red Pants and Jacket, Blue Blouse w/Bowtie	1982	$10.00	Fashion Favorites
3787	White Turtleneck Sweater, White Leggings, Belt	1982	$10.00	Fashion Favorites
3788	Long Dress, White Ruffled Top, Blue Bottom	1982	$10.00	Fashion Favorites
3788	White Satin Dress w/Lace Top, Veil, Pink Bouquet	1990	$5.00	Wedding of the Year
3789	White Long Dress w/Silver Tie Belt	1982	$10.00	Fashion Favorites
3790	Pink Top, Burgundy Pants, White Jacket	1982	$10.00	Fashion Favorites
3791	Blue Top w/Lace Trim, White Pants	1982	$10.00	Fashion Favorites
3792	Yellow Slicker Raincoat and Hat, Umbrella	1982	$10.00	Fashion Favorites
3798	Dandy Lines	1982	$15.00	Barbie & Ken Designer Original
3799	White Delight	1982	$15.00	Barbie & Ken Designer Original
3800	Fun 'n Fancy	1982	$10.00	Barbie & Ken Designer Original
4040	Color Magic Set	1966	$2,000.00	
4078	Gold/White Outfit, White Hat & Ice Skates	1990	$5.00	Ice Capades Fashions
4079	White Lace Outfit, Hat, White Ice Skates	1990	$5.00	Ice Capades Fashions
4080	Purple/Silver Outfit, Gloves, Hat, Purple Skates	1990	$5.00	Ice Capades Fashions
4081	Blue Outfit, Mask, Blue Ice Skates	1990	$5.00	Ice Capades Fashions
4082	Blue/Gold Outfit, Hat, Blue Ice Skates	1990	$5.00	Ice Capades Fashions
4083	Gold/Purple Outfit, White Ice Skates	1990	$5.00	Ice Capades Fashions
4119	Red Sleeveless Dress with Printed Scarf	1988	$10.00	Pretty Choices
4122	Yellow Halter, Floral Printed Pants	1988	$10.00	Pretty Choices
4125	Fuchsia Long Dress, Printed Belt	1988	$10.00	Pretty Choices

Number	Item	Year	Value	Specials
4126	Multicolored Floral Print Top, White Shorts	1988	$10.00	Pretty Choices
4127	Purple Dress with Floral Print Top	1988	$10.00	Pretty Choices
4128	Floral Print Sundress	1988	$10.00	Pretty Choices
4274	Fun at McDonald's	1983	$20.00	Fashion Classics
4277	Heavenly Holiday	1983	$10.00	Heavenly Holidays Fashions
4283	Book Bag	1984	$10.00	
4329	Short Skirt, Fringe Jacket, Boots w/Silver Studs	1988	$10.00	The Jeans Look Fashions
4330	Print Top, Denim Skirt with Lace Ruffle, Boots	1988	$10.00	The Jeans Look Fashions
4333	Striped Top, Denim Yoke, Denim Long Skirt	1988	$10.00	The Jeans Look Fashions
4334	White Top, Long Denim Skirt and Jacket	1988	$10.00	The Jeans Look Fashions
4335	Pink Tank Top, Blue Jean Jacket & Pants, Pink Boa	1988	$12.00	The Jeans Look Fashions
4417	White Two-Piece Suit, Gold Blouse, Black Boa	1988	$10.00	Citystyle Fashions
4429	Red Long Jacket, Checked Skirt, Black Hat, Purse	1988	$10.00	Citystyle Fashions
4430	Multicolored Dress, Purple Jacket, Hat and Purse	1988	$10.00	Citystyle Fashions
4433	White Blouse, Brown Pants, Brown Leopard Trim	1988	$10.00	Citystyle Fashions
4434	Pink Dress, Coat, Hat, and Scarf	1988	$10.00	Citystyle Fashions
4464	Flamingo Print Top, Yellow Leggings	1988	$10.00	California Dream Fashions
4465	Dolphin Print Top, Multicolored Jacket and Pants	1988	$10.00	California Dream Fashions
4466	White Top, Blue Short Skirt, Red Leggings, Hat	1988	$10.00	California Dream Fashions
4467	Pink Palm Tree Top, Print Top, Short Skirt, Belt	1988	$10.00	California Dream Fashions
4468	Hollywood T-Top, Pink Long Skirt, White Leggings	1988	$10.00	California Dream Fashions
4478	Tweed Long Top, Black Skirt, Red Scarf	1988	$10.00	Sweatersoft Fashions
4479	Multicolored Striped Sweater, Gold Long Skirt	1988	$10.00	Sweatersoft Fashions
4480	Purple/Red Top, Tweed Slacks	1988	$10.00	Sweatersoft Fashions
4481	Purple Paisley Print Jacket, Blue Long Skirt, Hat	1988	$10.00	Sweatersoft Fashions
4484	Tweed Long Top, Red Long Skirt, Hat and Scarf	1988	$10.00	Sweatersoft Fashions
4487	Blue Long Top and Leggings, Pink Scarf	1988	$10.00	Sweatersoft Fashions
4507	Lace Bodice Wedding Gown, Veil, Bouquet	1988	$10.00	Private Collection Fashions
4509	Long White Fur Coat, Gold Bowtie, Hat, Purse	1988	$10.00	Private Collection Fashions
4510	Red/Gold Ruffled Dress, Bolero, Red Hat	1988	$10.00	Private Collection Fashions
4511	Gold Long Skirt, Purple Print Jacket, Purple Pants	1988	$10.00	Private Collection Fashions
4512	Print Long Full Skirt, Blue Top and Hat	1988	$10.00	Private Collection Fashions
4523	Print Top, Yellow Skirt	1988	$10.00	Bright & Breezy Fashions
4525	Striped Long Top, Red Pants and Belt	1988	$10.00	Bright & Breezy Fashions
4526	Print Skirt, Red Long Sleeved Top	1988	$10.00	Bright & Breezy Fashions
4527	Print Culottes, Orange Tank and Sash	1988	$10.00	Bright & Breezy Fashions
4528	Striped Skirt, Blue Halter Top	1988	$10.00	Bright & Breezy Fashions
4529	Blue Skirt, Yellow Jacket, Print Top	1988	$10.00	Bright & Breezy Fashions
4569	Denim Jacket, Striped Short Skirt, Denim Top	1990	$5.00	Barbie and The Beat Fashion
4573	Denim Top & Skirt, Yellow Lace Trim	1990	$5.00	Barbie and The Beat Fashion
4574	Halter Top, Denim Skirt, Pink Jacket, Denim Trim	1990	$5.00	Barbie and The Beat Fashion
4575	Light Blue Long Pajamas w/Pink Ruffle Trim	1988	$10.00	My First Barbie Fashions
4576	Tank w/Ballet Motif, Fuchsia Pants	1988	$10.00	My First Barbie Fashions
4579	Yellow Music Note Top, Red Short Skirt, Socks	1988	$10.00	My First Barbie Fashions
4580	White Ice Cream Top, Yellow Shorts	1988	$10.00	My First Barbie Fashions
4581	Red Top, Striped Jacket, White Short Skirt	1988	$10.00	My First Barbie Fashions
4582	Red Top w/Lace Trim, Ballerina Printed Skirt	1988	$10.00	My First Barbie Fashions
4583	White Top, Blue Lace Trim, Blue Skirt	1988	$10.00	My First Barbie Fashions
4585	Red/White Skirt, Red Sleeveless Top	1988	$10.00	My First Barbie Fashions
4587	Pink/Blue Halter w/Shawl	1988	$10.00	My First Barbie Fashions
4593	Denim Jacket, Blue Dress, Pink Shorts, Overskirt	1990	$5.00	Barbie and The Beat Fashion
4595	Denim Vest, Skirt, Pink Top and Leggings	1990	$5.00	Barbie and The Beat Fashion
4596	Denim Vest, Skirt w/Print Ruffle, Purple Halter	1990	$5.00	Barbie and The Beat Fashion
4620	Long Yellow Dress w/Butterfly Bows	1989	$10.00	Perfume Pretty Fashions
4621	Lilac Dress with Lace-up Top, Ruffle Skirt	1989	$10.00	Perfume Pretty Fashions

Number	Item	Year	Value	Specials
4623	Long Evening Dress w/White Top	1989	$10.00	Perfume Pretty Fashions
4625	Icy Mint Green Sheath w/Matching Jacket	1989	$10.00	Perfume Pretty Fashions
4800	White Jacket, Pants, Red Short Skirt, Striped Tops	1988	$10.00	Fashion Magic Fashions
4801	Fun in the Sun	1984	$10.00	Fashion Fun
4802	Golden Mini	1984	$10.00	Fashion Fun
4803	Holiday Hostess	1984	$10.00	Fashion Fun
4804	Everyday Outing	1984	$10.00	Fashion Fun
4805	Perfectly Pink	1984	$10.00	Fashion Fun
4806	Showstopper	1984	$45.00	Fashion Fun
4807	Soft & Lacy	1984	$10.00	Fashion Fun
4808	Right in Step	1984	$10.00	Fashion Fun
4810	A Little Luxury	1984	$10.00	Fashion Fantasy
4811	Curtain's Up	1984	$10.00	Fashion Fantasy
4812	Romantic Valentine	1984	$10.00	Fashion Fantasy
4813	Soft 'n Chic	1984	$10.00	Fashion Fantasy
4814	Star Struck	1984	$10.00	Fashion Fantasy
4815	Letter Perfect	1984	$10.00	Fashion Fantasy
4816	Sportin' Occasion	1984	$10.00	Fashion Fantasy
4817	Jazz Dancin'	1984	$10.00	Fashion Fantasy
4819	Yellow Skirt, Pants, Striped Top, Jacket	1988	$10.00	Fashion Magic Fashions
4820	Dotted Skirt, Jacket, Yellow Top, White Shorts	1988	$10.00	Fashion Magic Fashions
4821	Double Date	1984	$10.00	Twice As Nice Fashions
4821	Red/White Wrap Dress	1985	$10.00	Twice As Nice Reversible
4822	All Turned Out	1984	$20.00	Twice As Nice Fashions
4823	Two for Fun	1984	$10.00	Twice As Nice Fashions
4824	Double Dazzle	1984	$10.00	Twice As Nice Fashions
4825	In & Outfitted	1984	$10.00	Twice As Nice Fashions
4826	Topsy Twosider	1984	$10.00	Twice As Nice Fashions
4827	Two for Tea	1984	$10.00	Twice As Nice Fashions
4828	Party Pair	1984	$10.00	Twice As Nice Fashions
4868	My First Party Dress	1984	$10.00	My First Barbie Fashions
4869	My First Slumber Party	1984	$10.00	My First Barbie Fashions
4870	My First Day at the Park	1984	$10.00	My First Barbie Fashions
4872	My First Picnic	1984	$10.00	My First Barbie Fashions
4957	Dress w/Blue Top, Floral Skirt, Pink Jacket, Hat	1990	$5.00	Private Collection Fashions
4958	Fuchsia Long Dress, Purse, Hair Decoration	1990	$5.00	Private Collection Fashions
4959	Fuchsia Ruffle Trim Short Dress and Hat	1990	$5.00	Private Collection Fashions
4961	Gold Long Coat w/White Fur Trim, Gold Hat	1990	$5.00	Private Collection Fashions
4978	Silver Sweater, Pink Poodle Skirt, White Lace Sock	1988	$10.00	Sensations Fashions
4981	Short Ruffle Skirt Dress, Pink Top and Gloves	1988	$10.00	Sensations Fashions
4981	Short Ruffle Skirt, Top, Leggings	1989	$10.00	Cool Times Fashions
4986	Short Dress, Lace Ruffle Skirt, Yellow Top, Gloves	1988	$10.00	Sensations Fashions
4987	Pink Top, Yellow Skirt, Long Black/White Vest	1988	$10.00	Sensations Fashions
4988	Mini Dress, Yellow Lace Skirt, Blue Top, Shawl	1988	$10.00	Sensations Fashions
5538	Can't Stop Dancin'	1983	$10.00	Fashion Fantasy
5539	Stripes for Stretching	1983	$10.00	Fashion Fantasy
5540	Summer Picnic	1983	$10.00	Fashion Fantasy
5541	Beach Party	1983	$20.00	Fashion Fantasy
5542	City Taylor	1983	$10.00	Fashion Fantasy
5543	Summertime Fun	1983	$10.00	Fashion Fantasy
5544	Party in Purple	1983	$10.00	Fashion Fantasy
5545	Summer Sparkle	1983	$10.00	Fashion Fantasy
5546	Shine at the Party	1983	$10.00	Fashion Fantasy
5547	Dream Time	1983	$10.00	Fashion Fantasy
5548	Evening Rose	1983	$10.00	Fashion Fantasy

Number	Item	Year	Value	Specials
5549	So Pretty Under it All	1983	$10.00	Fashion Fantasy
5609	My First Day of School	1983	$10.00	My First Barbie Fashions
5610	My First Slumber Party	1983	$10.00	My First Barbie Fashions
5611	My First Picnic	1983	$10.00	My First Barbie Fashions
5612	My First Ski Trip	1983	$10.00	My First Barbie Fashions
5613	My First Frills	1983	$10.00	My First Barbie Fashions
5614	My First Date	1983	$10.00	My First Barbie Fashions
5652	Opening Night	1983	$10.00	Designer Collection
5653	Lovely 'n Lace	1982	$10.00	
5654	Date Night	1983	$10.00	Designer Collection
5700	Paint the Town Red	1983	$10.00	Fashion Classics
5701	Garden Party	1983	$10.00	Fashion Classics
5702	Campus Sweetheart	1983	$10.00	Fashion Classics
5703	Fancy Pants	1983	$10.00	Fashion Classics
5705	Short 'n Sassy	1983	$10.00	Fashion Classics
5706	Picnic Party	1983	$10.00	Fashion Classics
5707	Let's Dance	1983	$10.00	Fashion Classics
5708	Ski Party Pink	1983	$10.00	Fashion Classics
5711	Summer Party	1983	$10.00	Fashion Fun
5712	Romantic Nights	1983	$10.00	Fashion Fun
5713	Lunch Date	1983	$10.00	Fashion Fun
5714	Dinner Date	1983	$10.00	Fashion Fun
5715	Pool Party	1983	$10.00	Fashion Fun
5716	City Shopping	1983	$10.00	Fashion Fun
5717	City Fun	1983	$10.00	Fashion Fun
5718	Movie Date	1983	$10.00	Fashion Fun
5719	Backyard Barbecue	1983	$20.00	Fashion Fun
5720	Sophisticated Lady	1983	$10.00	Fashion Fun
5743	Here Comes the Bride	1984	$10.00	Wedding of the Year
5745	Bridesmaid's Dream	1983	$10.00	Wedding of the Year
5746	Flower Girl	1984	$10.00	Wedding of the Year
5748	Here Comes the Bride	1983	$10.00	Wedding of the Year
5834	Riding Gear	1983	$10.00	Designer Collection
5835	Garden Party	1983	$10.00	Designer Collection
5836	Country Girl	1983	$10.00	Designer Collection
5848	Party Nights	1983	$10.00	Party Night Fashions
5897	Pretty Beginnings	1983	$10.00	Fashion Fun
5898	Candlelight Nights	1983	$10.00	Fashion Fun
5971	Short Dress, Orange Top, Fuchsia/Orange Skirt	1988	$10.00	Sensations Fashions
7079	Ski Party	1984	$10.00	Designer Collection
7080	Horseback Ridin'	1984	$10.00	Designer Collection
7081	Bedtime Beauty	1984	$10.00	Designer Collection
7082	In The Spotlight	1984	$10.00	Designer Collection
7083	Picture in Plaid	1984	$10.00	Designer Collection
7092	Springtime Magic Fashion	1984	$20.00	Collector's Series
7176	Bride	1976	$40.00	Get-Ups 'n Go
7216	Blue Magic	1984	$10.00	Spectacular Fashions
7217	Red Sizzle	1984	$10.00	Spectacular Fashions
7218	Dance Sensation	1984	$10.00	Spectacular Fashions
7219	In The Pink	1984	$10.00	Spectacular Fashions
7241	Indian Print Separates	1975	$35.00	Get-Ups 'n Go
7242	Casuals	1975	$40.00	Get-Ups 'n Go
7243	Olympic Warm-Ups	1975	$40.00	Get-Ups 'n Go
7244	Olympic Parade	1975	$40.00	Get-Ups 'n Go
7391	Pink/Red Ruffle Trim Swimsuit, Long Skirt	1990	$5.00	Dance Magic Fashions

Number	Item	Year	Value	Specials
7392	Blue Glitter Trim Dress w/Long & Short Skirts	1990	$5.00	Dance Magic Fashions
7393	Lavender Top w/Skirt and Leggings	1990	$5.00	Dance Magic Fashions
7394	Peach Tutu w/Rose Trim & Long Skirt	1990	$5.00	Dance Magic Fashions
7438	Silver Sensation Fashion	1984	$20.00	Collector's Series
7700	Doctor	1973	$75.00	Get-Ups 'n Go
7701	Ballerina	1973	$50.00	Get-Ups 'n Go
7702	Camping	1973	$55.00	Get-Ups 'n Go
7703	United Airlines Stewardess	1973	$75.00	Get-Ups 'n Go
7787	Skiing	1974	$70.00	Get-Ups 'n Go
7788	Beach	1974	$60.00	Get-Ups 'n Go
7839	Bride	1974	$80.00	Get-Ups 'n Go
7840	Blue Party Dress	1974	$100.00	Get-Ups 'n Go
7841	Dreamy Designs for Dressy Dinners	N/A	$80.00	
7841	Pink Party Separates	1974	$85.00	Get-Ups 'n Go
7842	Tennis	1974	$50.00	Get-Ups 'n Go
7843	Salmon Party Dress	1974	$85.00	Get-Ups 'n Go
7843	Style Setter Gets Rave Review	N/A	$95.00	Get-Ups 'n Go
7859	Six to Midnight	N/A	$30.00	Get-Ups 'n Go
7910	Blue Jumpsuit, Gold Belt and Collar	1985	$10.00	B Active Fashions
7911	Green Top and Yellow Pants	1985	$10.00	B Active Fashions
7912	White Top, Orange Shorts and Shoes	1985	$10.00	B Active Fashions
7913	Red/White Jogging Pants and Top, Sneakers	1985	$10.00	B Active Fashions
7914	White Long Shirt, Red Leggings, and Belt	1985	$10.00	B Active Fashions
7915	Fuchsia Short Dress and Print Belt	1985	$10.00	B Active Fashions
7916	Blue/White Striped Top, Long Blue Skirt	1985	$10.00	B Active Fashions
7917	Fuchsia Long Skirt, Top, and Shoes	1985	$10.00	B Active Fashions
7920	Red Short Dress with Lace Trim	1986	$10.00	My First Barbie Fashions
7931	Red Evening Cape	1975	$40.00	Fashion Originals
7932	Fashion Original	N/A	$75.00	
7933	Green Separates Set	1975	$35.00	Fashion Originals
7934	Rose Dress, Stole, Hat	1975	$35.00	Fashion Originals
7934	Rose Evening Gown and Jacket	1975	$40.00	Sears' Fashion Originals
7950	Red Blouse, Black/White Skirt	1985	$10.00	Twice As Nice Reversible
7951	Red Hat, Red/White Coat	1985	$10.00	Twice As Nice Reversible
7952	Red Vest, Black Pants, White Shirt	1985	$10.00	Twice As Nice Reversible
7953	Fuchsia/Blue Reversible Short Dress	1985	$10.00	Twice As Nice Reversible
7954	Striped Top and Yellow/Blue Vest and Skirt	1985	$10.00	Twice As Nice Reversible
7955	Green Pants, Yellow Top, and Silver Jacket	1985	$10.00	Twice As Nice Reversible
7956	Yellow/Blue Long Dress, Ruffle Neckline	1985	$10.00	Twice As Nice Reversible
8620	Long Dark Printed Dress	1973	$40.00	Best Buys
8621	Blue/White Checked Midi Suit	1973	$50.00	Best Buys
8622	Red Pants, Sheer Over-Skirt, and White Top	1973	$70.00	Best Buys
8623	Wedding Gift	1973	$110.00	Best Buys
8626	Shoes	1973	$50.00	
8626	Shoes	1977	$15.00	Best Buys
8680	Long Tricot Print	1973	$35.00	Best Buys
8681	Tan Shirt, Red Blouse	1973	$55.00	Best Buys
8682	Tan Coat, Fur Trim	1973	$55.00	Best Buys
8683	Long Printed Skirt, Yellow Blouse	1973	$60.00	Best Buys
8684	Long Off-White Dress	1973	$60.00	Best Buys
8685	Print Pants, White Blouse, Yellow Vest	1973	$60.00	Best Buys
8687	Pink Pants Suit	1973	$75.00	Best Buys
8688	Long Rose Dress, Black Net Coat	1973	$75.00	Best Buys
8689	Long Gold Skirt, White Blouse	1973	$70.00	Best Buys
8690	Robe and Nightgown	1973	$65.00	Best Buys

Number	Item	Year	Value	Specials
8691	Pants, Skirt, Hat, Blouse	1973	$50.00	Best Buys
8692	Blue Evening Gown	1973	$50.00	Best Buys
9006	Red Printed Tricot	1975	$45.00	Sears' Exclusive Best Buys
9010	Red Plaid Pants and Jacket	1975	$45.00	Sears' Exclusive Best Buys
9011	Yellow Printed Skirt, Printed Top	1975	$45.00	Sears' Exclusive Best Buys
9042	Long Skirt, White Blouse	1975	$45.00	Sears' Fashion Originals
9043	Regular Olympic Outfit	1975	$40.00	Sears' Fashion Originals
9046	Print Skirt, White Top	1975	$35.00	Fashion Originals
9047	Pants, Cape, Cap	1975	$55.00	Sears' Fashion Originals
9048	Tweed Skirt, Blue Blouse	1975	$35.00	Fashion Originals
9048	Tweed Suit	1976	$40.00	Best Buys
9078	9-Piece Red/White/Blue Outfit	1975	$60.00	Sears' Fashion Originals
9081	Dress Designer	1985	$15.00	Day to Night Fashions
9082	Dancer	1985	$10.00	Day to Night Fashions
9083	Business Executive	1985	$10.00	Day to Night Fashions
9084	TV News Reporter	1985	$10.00	
9085	Teachers	1985	$5.00	Day to Night Fashions
9143	Blue Skirt and Top, Red Pants	1985	$6.00	Spectacular Fashions
9144	Light Blue Skirt Long and Short, Top, Jacket	1985	$10.00	Spectacular Fashions
9145	White Jacket, Skirt, Pants, Red Top	1985	$10.00	Spectacular Fashions
9146	Red Top, Two-Tone Skirt	1985	$10.00	Spectacular Fashions
9151	Summer Gown	1976	$35.00	Get-Ups 'n Go
9152	Knit Ensemble	1976	$35.00	Get-Ups 'n Go
9152	Stripes Right for City Stripes	N/A	$40.00	Get-Ups 'n Go
9153	Orange Checked Shirt, Top	1976	$40.00	Best Buys
9154	White Pants and Red Shirt	1976	$35.00	Best Buys
9155	Striped Dress	1976	$35.00	Best Buys
9156	Floral Printed Dress	1976	$35.00	Best Buys
9157	Rose Nightgown	1976	$30.00	Best Buys
9158	Red/White/Blue Dress	1976	$40.00	Best Buys
9160	Rose/White Printed Party Dress	1976	$25.00	Best Buys
9161	Blue Pants, Bandana Blouse	1976	$35.00	Best Buys
9161	Pink/Black Polka Dot Dress & Jacket w/Ruffle Trim	1990	$5.00	Dinner Date Fashions
9162	Pink Skirt, Silver Top w/Ruffle Trim, Lace Leggings	1990	$5.00	Dinner Date Fashions
9162	Yellow Jumper, Blouse, and Scarf	1976	$40.00	Best Buys
9163	Pink/White/Silver Dress w/White Biker Shorts	1990	$5.00	Dinner Date Fashions
9163	Underwear	1976	$30.00	Best Buys
9164	Red/White/Blue Print	1976	$40.00	Best Buys
9165	Red/White Halter Dress w/White Lace Leggings	1990	$5.00	Dinner Date Fashions
9166	Short Blue Dress, Gold Fishnet Leggings, Shawl	1990	$5.00	Dinner Date Fashions
9170	Blue Skirt, Jacket, Pink Top	1990	$5.00	Dinner Date Fashions
9197	Minnie Mouse Motif Blue Dress, Lace Leggings	1990	$5.00	Disney Character Fashions
9198	Goofy Motif Pink/White Shirt, Halter, Pants	1990	$5.00	Disney Character Fashions
9199	Mickey Motif Top, Denim, Mickey Jacket, Skirt	1990	$5.00	Disney Character Fashions
9202	Donald Duck Motif Top, Net Skirt, Biker Pants	1990	$5.00	Disney Character Fashions
9205	Minnie Motif Long Top, Denim Short Skirt, Socks	1990	$5.00	Disney Character Fashions
9207	Daisy Duck Motif Dress, White Leggings, Socks	1990	$5.00	Disney Character Fashions
9245	Pink/Blue Print Skirt, Bolero, Pink Top, Belt	1990	$5.00	My First Barbie Fashions
9247	Red/White Striped Cowl Neck Top, White Biker Shorts	1990	$45.00	My First Barbie Fashions
9249	Blue Top, Blue/Pink Ruffle Short Skirt, Shawl	1990	$5.00	My First Barbie Fashions
9251	Fuchsia Short, Strapless Party Dress, Scarf	1990	$5.00	My First Barbie Fashions
9253	Multicolored Striped Top & Socks, White Short Skirt	1990	$5.00	My First Barbie Fashions
9258	Collector Series IV	1985	$40.00	Oscar De La Renta
9259	Collector Series V	1985	$40.00	Oscar De La Renta

Barbie® Doll Outfits – Listed by Stock Number

Number	Item	Year	Value	Specials
9260	Collector Series VI	1985	$40.00	Oscar De La Renta
9261	Collector Series VII	1985	$40.00	Oscar De La Renta
9263	Pink Swimsuit and Parasol	1985	$10.00	Fashion Playsets
9264	White Hat, Coat, Pink Scarf, Red Luggage	1985	$10.00	Fashion Playsets
9265	White Ruffle Shirt, Pink/Black Jumper	1990	$5.00	My First Barbie Fashions
9266	Fuchsia Robe, Pink Towels, and White Stand	1985	$10.00	Bath Fun Play Set
9267	Vet Coat and Skirt with Dog	1985	$10.00	Fashion Playsets
9271	Blue Star Motif Top, Pink Print Pants	1990	$5.00	My First Barbie Fashions
9272	White T, Silver/Yellow Jumper, Yellow Biker Pants	1990	$5.00	My First Barbie Fashions
9326	Sugar Plum Fairy	1976	$40.00	Ballerina Costumes
9327	Snowflake Fairy	1976	$40.00	Ballerina Costumes
9329	Princess Aurora	1976	$40.00	Ballerina Costumes
9421	Evening Gown, Pink/Blue/Rose	1976	$40.00	Department Store
9422	Evening Gown, Burnt Orange, Shawl	1976	$40.00	Department Store
9424	Figured Gauchos and Jacket	1976	$30.00	Department Store
9470	Fur Coat, Hat, Brown Skirt, Boots, Bag	1977	$15.00	Best Buys
9571	Long Red Printed Dress	1976	$35.00	
9572	Gaucho Pants, Boots, and Blouse	1976	$35.00	Best Buys
9573	Dress, Bag	1976	$30.00	Best Buys
9574	Pants, Shirt, Socks	1976	$30.00	Best Buys
9575	Long Printed Dress, Yellow Sleeves	1976	$35.00	Best Buys
9576	Checked Pants, Solid Shirt	1976	$40.00	
9577	Pink Party Dress	1976	$40.00	Best Buys
9579	Blue Pants, Checked Top	1976	$35.00	Best Buys
9580	Long Yellow/Red Party Dress	1976	$35.00	Best Buys
9581	Pants, Jacket, Cap	1976	$40.00	
9582	Blue/Flame Short Party Dress	1976	$35.00	Best Buys
9594	Pink Evening Gown	1976	$40.00	Get-Ups 'n Go
9595	Coral Evening Gown	1976	$35.00	Get-Ups 'n Go
9618	Blue/Green/Purple Jumpsuit, White Scarf	1977	$15.00	Best Buys
9619	Red/White Print Dress and Stole	1977	$15.00	Best Buys
9620	Long Green Skirt and White Bodice	1977	$15.00	Best Buys
9621	Faded Blue Skirt, Blue Sunburst Blouse	1977	$10.00	Best Buys
9622	Long Brown Striped Skirt w/Blue/White Top	1977	$15.00	Best Buys
9623	Yellow Robe, Shower Cap	1977	$15.00	Best Buys
9625	Pink/Silver Jumpsuit, Pink Jacket	1977	$35.00	Best Buys
9625	Red Tweed Jumpsuit, Tam, Scarf	1977	$15.00	Best Buys
9626	Blue/Silver Evening Gown	1977	$15.00	Best Buys
9627	Green Print Skirt, Bolero, Yellow Blouse	1977	$15.00	Best Buys
9628	Red Skirt, Purse, Red/White/Blue Blouse	1977	$15.00	Best Buys
9629	Figured Skirt, Bolero, Cap, Beige Blouse	1977	$30.00	Best Buys
9650	Ballerina Costume	1976	$45.00	Sears
9650	Mix 'n Match Set	1976	$40.00	Sears
9650	Red Evening Gown and Cape	1976	$45.00	Sears
9650	Red Palazzo Pants and Gold Halter	1976	$45.00	Sears
9670	8-Piece Coordinated Set	1976	$45.00	Sears
9682	Black/Rose Nightgown	1976	$45.00	Sears' Exclusive Best Buys
9683	White Dress with Navy Stripes	1976	$45.00	Sears' Exclusive Best Buys
9684	Yellow Suit	1976	$45.00	Sears' Exclusive Best Buys
9685	Blue Pants, Yellow Top	1976	$40.00	Sears' Exclusive Best Buys
9686	Long Blue/White Printed Dress	1976	$40.00	
9687	Long Red/White Dress	1976	$35.00	
9738	Pink/White Lights the Night	1977	$15.00	Get-Ups 'n Go
9739	Red Shine For Rain Time	1977	$15.00	Get-Ups 'n Go
9740	Brocade Dream Steals the Scene	1977	$15.00	Get-Ups 'n Go

Number	Item	Year	Value	Specials
9741	Star of the Show in Golden Glow	1977	$15.00	Get-Ups 'n Go
9742	Six to Mix, Match, and Pack	1977	$15.00	Get-Ups 'n Go
9743	Dreamy Delight for at Night	1977	$15.00	Get-Ups 'n Go
9835	Brocade Shine	1977	$15.00	SuperStar Fashions
9836	Romantic White	1977	$15.00	SuperStar Fashions
9837	Black/Silver Shimmer	1977	$15.00	SuperStar Fashions
9907	Blue Denim Dress and Hat	1975	$40.00	Sears' Exclusive Best Buys
9908	Pink Baby Dolls	1975	$40.00	Sears' Exclusive Best Buys
9909	Yellow Suit, Printed Halter	1975	$45.00	Sears' Exclusive Best Buys
9950	Multicolored Coat, Scarf, Purple Dress, Hat, Boots	1990	$5.00	Western Fun Fashions
9951	Multicolored Vest, Purple Top, Print Skirt	1990	$5.00	Western Fun Fashions
9952	Purple Vest, Multicolored Shirt & Skirt, Gloves, Hat	1990	$5.00	Western Fun Fashions
9953	Multicolored Top, Leggings, Yellow Boots	1990	$5.00	Western Fun Fashions
9954	Purple, Coyote Motif Top, Leggings, Belt, Boots	1990	$5.00	Western Fun Fashions
9958	Red/White Striped Jumpsuit	1977	$15.00	Best Buys
9959	Yellow Playsuit, Red/Yellow Striped Socks	1977	$15.00	Best Buys
9960	Red Pants, Bull's Eye Blouse	1977	$15.00	Best Buys
9961	White/Black Dress, Black Hat	1977	$15.00	Best Buys
9962	Red Evening Gown	1977	$15.00	Best Buys
9963	Blue Evening Gown, Lace Trim	1977	$20.00	Best Buys
9963	Pink Halter Short Dress	1990	$5.00	Fashion Finds
9964	Pink Knicker Jumpsuit, Zig Zag Hooded Jacket	1977	$35.00	Best Buys
9964	Purple Flower Print Dress w/White Ruffle Trim	1990	$5.00	Fashion Finds
9965	Green Pants, Top, Jacket	1977	$15.00	Best Buys
9966	Pink Jumpsuit, Figured Over Skirt	1977	$35.00	Best Buys
9967	Music Note & Record Print Shorts, Blue Halter	1990	$5.00	Fashion Finds
9967	Red/Black Evening Gown, Turban	1977	$15.00	Best Buys
9968	Print Skirt, Red/Yellow Waist and Jacket	1977	$15.00	Best Buys
9968	Yellow Halter, Purple Skirt	1990	$5.00	Fashion Finds
9969	Glittery Blue Pants, Long Blue Tunic	1977	$15.00	Best Buys
9971	Purple/Blue/Red Shirred Top and Skirt	1990	$5.00	Fashion Finds
9972	Coral Evening Gown and Shoes	1977	$20.00	Department Store
9974	Dress w/Heart Print Top, Pink Bottom	1990	$5.00	Fashion Finds
9975	Pink Halter Top, Floral Print Skirt	1990	$5.00	Fashion Finds
10773	Teacher, Firefighter, Veterinarian	1995	$5.00	Caring Careers Fashion
11558	Purple Locket Surprise Fashions	1994	$5.00	Locket Surprise Fashions
11559	Peach Locket Surprise Fashions	1994	$5.00	Locket Surprise Fashions
11560	Aqua Locket Surprise Fashions	1994	$5.00	Locket Surprise Fashions
11935	Long Skirt and Top	1994	$4.00	Fashion Forms Fashions
11936	Dress and Jacket	1994	$4.00	Fashion Forms Fashions
11937	Dress and Shoulder Bag	1994	$4.00	Fashion Forms Fashions
11938	Mini and Jacket	1994	$4.00	Fashion Forms Fashions
12173	Pink Brushed Tricot Robe w/B Monogram	1997	$5.00	Fashion Avenue Lingerie
12183	Jewel & Glitter Fashions	1994	$5.00	Jewel & Glitter
12437	Printed Skirt and Yellow Halter	1995	$5.00	Make-Up Pretty Fashions
12438	Pink Shorts and Tank w/Printed Jacket	1995	$5.00	Locket Surprise Fashions
12439	Striped Pants and Purple Top	1995	$5.00	Make-Up Pretty Fashions
12440	Striped Skirt and Green Top	1995	$5.00	Make-Up Pretty Fashions
12594	Pink/White Pants and Halter	1995	$5.00	Picnic Pretty Fashions
12595	Purple Shorts and Purple Jacket	1995	$5.00	Picnic Pretty Fashions
12596	Yellow Top and Flare Leg Pants	1995	$5.00	Picnic Pretty Fashions
12597	Green Skirt, White/Green Blouse	1995	$5.00	Picnic Pretty Fashions
12600	Princess	1995	$5.00	My First Fashions
12601	Ballerina	1995	$10.00	My First Fashions
12602	Angel	1995	$10.00	My First Fashions

Number	Item	Year	Value	Specials
12603	Ice Skater	1995	$5.00	My First Fashions
12623	Pink Outfit	1995	$5.00	Bead Fun Fashions
12624	Green Outfit	1995	$5.00	Bead Fun Fashions
12625	Yellow Outfit	1995	$5.00	Bead Fun Fashions
12626	Blue Outfit	1995	$5.00	Bead Fun Fashions
12628	Pink Shorts, White Top and Pants	1995	$5.00	Sponge 'n Print Fashions
12629	Blue Jacket and White Short Outfit	1995	$5.00	Sponge 'n Print Fashions
12630	White Outfit and Pink Vest	1995	$5.00	Sponge 'n Print Fashions
12631	White Jacket and Top, Purple Shorts	1995	$5.00	Sponge 'n Print Fashions
12634	Red Dress and Black Vest	1995	$5.00	Paint The Dots Fashion
12635	Black Pants & White Top	1995	$5.00	Paint The Dots Fashion
12636	Green Dress and Black Top	1995	$5.00	Paint The Dots Fashion
12637	Black Shorts, Orange Jacket, White Top	1995	$5.00	Paint The Dots Fashion
12645	Blue Bathing Suit	1995	$5.00	Bath Paintin' Fashions
12646	Blue/Orange One-Piece Bathing Suit	1995	$5.00	Bath Paintin' Fashions
12647	Pink/Green Two-Piece Bathing Suit	1995	$5.00	Bath Paintin' Fashions
12648	Yellow/Pink Two-Piece Bathing Suit	1995	$5.00	Bath Paintin' Fashions
12776	Denim Shorts and Bandana Print Halter	1995	$5.00	Western Fun Fashions
12777	Yellow Hat, Denim Pants, Vest & Shirt	1995	$5.00	Western Fun Fashions
12778	Bandana Skirt and Top, Red Cowboy Hat	1995	$5.00	Western Fun Fashions
12779	Denim Dress, Pink Bandana Print Jacket	1995	$5.00	Western Fun Fashions
13017	Red Jumper, Blue/White Striped Top	1995	$5.00	Yacht Club Fashions
13018	Blue Shorts, White Top, and Yellow Jacket	1995	$5.00	Yacht Club Fashions
13019	White Pants, Red Belt, Blue and White Halter	1995	$5.00	Yacht Club Fashions
13020	Red/White Swimsuit, Red/Blue Jacket	1995	$5.00	Yacht Club Fashions
13024	Pink Ballgown	1995	$5.00	Fantasy Evening Fashions
13025	Pink/White Ballgown	1995	$5.00	Fantasy Evening Fashions
13203	Gold Ballgown	1995	$5.00	Fantasy Evening Fashions
14288	Blue Gingham Boxers and Bustier w/Overshirt	1996	$5.00	Fashion Avenue
14289	Mint Green Nightgown w/Sheer Robe	1996	$5.00	Fashion Avenue
14291	Violet Panties and Negligee w/Floral Trim	1996	$5.00	Fashion Avenue
14298	Knitted Sweater w/Chambray Pants, Mittens	1996	$5.00	Fashion Avenue
14299	Gold Parka w/Fur-like Trim, Leopard Leggings	1996	$5.00	Fashion Avenue
14301	Pink Rain Slicker, Boots, Dotted Hat	1996	$6.00	Fashion Avenue
14303	Gold/White Gown, Purse, Shoes	1996	$10.00	Fashion Avenue
14305	Hot Pink Sparkle Gown w/Fur Trim, Purse	1996	$10.00	Fashion Avenue
14306	Maroon Long, Velvet Gown w/Puffy Sleeves	1996	$10.00	Fashion Avenue
14360	Turquoise Two-Piece Suit, Chain Belt, Purse	1996	$5.00	Fashion Avenue
14361	Red Sweater, Plaid Jumper, Tights, Purse	1996	$5.00	Fashion Avenue
14362	Red Short Overalls, Striped Bodysuit, Tights	1996	$5.00	Fashion Avenue
14363	Pink/Yellow Dress w/Daisies, Beret, Hose	1996	$5.00	Fashion Avenue
14365	Ivory/Gold Dress, Purse, Hose, Shoes	1997	$5.00	Fashion Avenue
14366	Red Plaid Dress, Purse, Hose, Shoes	1996	$5.00	Fashion Avenue
14367	Fuchsia Dress, White Fur Trim, Stole, Purse	1996	$5.00	Fashion Avenue
14368	Blue Dress w/Silver Dots, Purse, Hose, Shoes	1996	$5.00	Fashion Avenue
14369	Magenta Dress w/Lace Detail, Purse, Hose	1996	$5.00	Fashion Avenue
14371	Two-Piece Turquoise/Silver/Magenta w/Jacket	1996	$4.00	Barbie Floatin' Cool
14372	One-Piece Nautical Swimsuit w/White Towel	1996	$4.00	Barbie Floatin' Cool
14373	One-Piece Hot Pink Swimsuit, Wrap Skirt	1996	$4.00	Barbie Floatin' Cool
14374	Two-Piece Denim-Look Suit, Bag, Gold Trim	1996	$4.00	Barbie Floatin' Cool
14398	Lace Embellished White Wedding Gown, Veil	1996	$10.00	Fashion Avenue
14399	Multicolored Coat w/Fringe, Belt, Purse	1996	$6.00	Fashion Avenue
14665	Mermaid, Green Shimmery Two-Piece	1996	$4.00	My First Fashions
14666	Ballerina, One-Piece Hot Pink w/Shimmery Top	1996	$4.00	My First Fashions
14667	Fairy, One-Piece Purple/Pink	1996	$4.00	My First Fashions

Number	Item	Year	Value	Specials
14668	Princess, One-Piece Blue Outfit w/Poof Skirt	1996	$4.00	My First Fashions
14670	Denim Overalls w/Hip Pack, Lace Top, Beret	1996	$5.00	Fashion Avenue
14671	Denim Skirt, Jacket w/Fur-like Trim, Purse	1996	$5.00	Fashion Avenue
14672	Denim Vest, w/White Ruffled Blouse, Shorts	1996	$5.00	Fashion Avenue
14673	Denim Short Dress and Sparkly Golden Jacket	1996	$5.00	Fashion Avenue
14689	Two-Piece w/Chambray Pants and Pink Jacket	1996	$4.00	Western Fun
14690	Two-Piece Red/Beige Skirt, Top, Bolo Tie	1996	$4.00	Western Fun
14691	Two-Piece w/Purple Jacket, White Skirt	1996	$4.00	Western Fun
14692	Three-Piece White w/Fringed Vest and Skirt	1996	$4.00	Western Fun
15858	Red Bandana-Print Top, Skirt, Bolo Tie	1997	$5.00	Western Fashions
15859	Pink/Silver Star Print Top, Blue Jeans	1997	$5.00	Western Fashions
15860	Turquoise Brushed Tricot and Denim Jacket	1997	$5.00	Western Fashions
15861	Magenta/Silver Top with Denim Yoke, Skirt	1997	$5.00	Western Fashions
15873	Blue/White Print Nightgown	1997	$5.00	Fashion Avenue Lingerie
15874	Color Floral Top and Bottoms	1997	$6.00	Fashion Avenue Lingerie
15875	Lilac Chemise Embellished Black Lace Trim	1997	$5.00	Fashion Avenue Lingerie
15876	Pink/White Gingham Corset with Pink Slip	1997	$6.00	Fashion Avenue Lingerie
15898	Country Bride	1997	$10.00	Fashion Avenue Bridal
15899	Princess Bride	1997	$10.00	Fashion Avenue Bridal
15900	Mermaid Bride	1997	$10.00	Fashion Avenue Bridal
15901	Winter Bride	1997	$10.00	Fashion Avenue Bridal
15903	Winter	1997	$10.00	Fashion Avenue Internationale
15904	Spring	1997	$10.00	Fashion Avenue Internationale
15905	Summer	1997	$10.00	Fashion Avenue Internationale
15906	Fall	1997	$10.00	Fashion Avenue Internationale
16076	Homecoming	1996	$30.00	Barbie Millicent Roberts
16077	Picnic in the Park	1996	$30.00	Barbie Millicent Roberts
16951	Fuchsia Ski Jacket	1997	$10.00	Fashion Avenue Boutique
16952	Lavender Jumper	1997	$10.00	Fashion Avenue Boutique
17568	All Decked Out	1997	$20.00	Barbie Millicent Roberts
17569	Court Favorite Fashion	1997	$20.00	Barbie Millicent Roberts
17570	City Slicker Fashion	1997	$20.00	Barbie Millicent Roberts
17571	Jet Set Luggage Ensemble	1997	$20.00	Barbie Millicent Roberts
17875	Signature Series (final touches)	1997	$15.00	Barbie Millicent Roberts
17876	Lime Time (final touches)	1997	$15.00	Barbie Millicent Roberts
17877	Spectacular Spectators (final touches)	1997	$15.00	Barbie Millicent Roberts
17878	Red Hot (final touches)	1997	$15.00	Barbie Millicent Roberts
19433	Green Thumb	1998	$30.00	Barbie Millicent Roberts
19772	Snow Chic, So Chic	1998	$30.00	Barbie Millicent Roberts
21371	Fashion Avenue Barbie Easter Fashion	1999	$10.00	Fashion Avenue
22156	White Coat with Fur Collar and Cuffs	1999	$12.00	Fashion Avenue
22157	Black & White Leopard Print Coat	1999	$12.00	Fashion Avenue
22158	Yellow Coat with Black Fur Collar and Cuffs	1999	$12.00	Fashion Avenue
22159	Light Blue Coat	1999	$12.00	Fashion Avenue
22160	Red Coat with Hood	1999	$12.00	Fashion Avenue
22306	Executive Lunch Fashion	1999	$26.00	Barbie Millicent Roberts
24289	Party in Pink Fashion	1999	$5.00	Charm Styles
24294	Bathtime Chat Fashion	1999	$5.00	Charm Styles
24297	Funtime Slumbers Fashion	1999	$5.00	Metro Styles
28132	Kiss Me in Miami Fashion	2000	$5.00	Metro Styles
28137	Seattle Latte Fashion	2000	$5.00	Metro Styles
29071	Salsa	2000	$8.00	Movin' to Music
29073	Hip Hop	2000	$8.00	Movin' to Music
29152	Jumpkey Fashion	2001	$5.00	Animation Styles
29154	Fluff Fashion	2001	$5.00	Animation Styles

Number	Item	Year	Value	Specials
29156	Bashful Bunny Fashion	2001	$5.00	Animation Styles
29901	Ice Dancing	2000	$8.00	Movin' to Music
68014	Blue Gingham Top, Shorts, Blue Shoes	2000	$2.00	Go in Style Fashions
68014	Blue Print Sundress, Black Sandals	2000	$2.00	Go in Style Fashions
68014	Capri Jeans, Pink Midi Top, Pink Sandals	2000	$2.00	Go in Style Fashions
68014	Yellow Sundress, Yellow Shoes	2000	$2.00	Go in Style Fashions
68084	Black Jeans, Shiny Pink Vest, Black Boots	2000	$4.00	Jean Fashions
68084	Lavender Jeans, Striped Turtleneck, Lavender Shoes	2000	$4.00	Jean Fashions
68084	Light Blue Skirt, Blue Floral Paint Top, Blue Sandals	2000	$4.00	Jean Fashions
68084	White Jeans, Red Flowered Top, White Tennis Shoes	2000	$4.00	Jean Fashions
68085	Black, Blue & Yellow Bike Shorts & Shirt, Glasses	1999	$2.00	Sun & Sea Fashions
68085	Multicolored Swimsuit, Blue Mesh Cover-up, Glasses	1999	$2.00	Sun & Sea Fashions
68085	Red Flowered Swimsuit, Red Beach Bag, Sunglasses	1999	$2.00	Sun & Sea Fashions
68087	Angel	2000	$4.00	Fantasy Costume Fashion
68087	Butterfly	2000	$4.00	Fantasy Costume Fashion
68312	Lime Green and Purple Bowling Shirt and Pants	2000	$3.00	Totally Sports Fashion
68696	Zebra Print Coat w/Pink Belt & Collar, Boots	1998	$3.00	Coat Collection Fashions
68698	Barbie Disney Fun Fashions	1999	$18.00	
68783	Blue, Pink & White Print Dress, Shoes	2000	$4.00	Glow-in-the-Dark Fashions
68783	Blue, Red & White Print Dress, Shawl, Shoes	2000	$4.00	Glow-in-the-Dark Fashions
68783	Purple & White Print Dress, Shawl, Shoes	2000	$4.00	Glow-in-the-Dark Fashions
69312	Lime Green & Turquoise Soccer Outfit, Green Shoes	2000	$3.00	Totally Sports Fashion
94196	Bridal Gown	1976	$40.00	Department Store
4918A	Fashion Extras	1984	$10.00	Department Store
697A	Holiday Gown Collection II	1993	$55.00	Wholesale Club
N/A	Hollywood Premier Fashion	1992	$35.00	
N/A	Long Coat Private Collection	1988	$10.00	
N/A	Solid Red Dress	1974	$150.00	Sears
None	Boarding Outfit	1967	$500.00	Barbie Goes Braniff Fashions
None	Hostess Pajamas	1967	$500.00	Barbie Goes Braniff Fashions
None	Pucino Serving Dress	1967	$500.00	Barbie Goes Braniff Fashions
None	Raspberry Suit	1967	$500.00	Barbie Goes Braniff Fashions
Pak	Accessory Pak (4 pairs shoes, pearl choker, etc.)	1962	$225.00	
Pak	Add-Ons	1968	$150.00	
Pak	Apron and Utensils	1962	$55.00	
Pak	Bathrobe (yellow)	1963	$50.00	
Pak	Belle Dress	1962	$100.00	
Pak	Belle Dress (orange)	1962	$90.00	
Pak	Best Bow	1967	$175.00	
Pak	Boudoir	1964	$125.00	
Pak	Campus Belle	1964	$150.00	
Pak	Cardigan	1962	$40.00	
Pak	Change-Abouts	1968	$150.00	
Pak	Cook-Ups	1967	$250.00	
Pak	Cool Casual	1970	$140.00	
Pak	Costume Completers	1964	$150.00	
Pak	Dress-Up Hats	1964	$125.00	
Pak	Dressed-Up	1968	$160.00	
Pak	Extra-Casuals	1968	$140.00	
Pak	Fancy Trimmin's	1967	$225.00	
Pak	Fashion Feet	1964	$75.00	
Pak	Fashion Firsts	1971	$90.00	

Number	Item	Year	Value	Specials
Pak	Finishing Touches	1969	$175.00	
Pak	Flats 'n Heels	1968	$350.00	
Pak	Flats 'n Heels (10 pairs)	1969	$225.00	
Pak	For Rink and Court	1964	$75.00	
Pak	Fur Hat/Bag	1963	$500.00	
Pak	Fur Stole with Bag	1962	$60.00	
Pak	Gathered Skirt	1962	$45.00	
Pak	Glamour Hats	1966	$400.00	
Pak	Going to the Ball	1964	$115.00	
Pak	Have Fun	1966	$325.00	
Pak	Helenca Swimsuit	1962	$150.00	
Pak	In The Swim	1964	$400.00	
Pak	Jeans	1963	$55.00	
Pak	Jumpin' Jeans	1964	$85.00	
Pak	Kitchen Magic	1966	$200.00	
Pak	Knit Accessories	1963	$125.00	
Pak	Knit Sheath Dress with Fringed Collar	1963	$50.00	
Pak	Knit Sheath Skirt and Sash	1963	$50.00	
Pak	Knit Shorts and Top	1963	$50.00	
Pak	Knit Skirt (long blue with glitter)	1963	$60.00	
Pak	Knit Slacks	1963	$40.00	
Pak	Knit Top	1963	$55.00	
Pak	Lamé Sheath	1963	$200.00	
Pak	Leisure Hours	1964	$175.00	
Pak	Lingerie Pack	1962	$145.00	
Pak	Lovely Lingerie	1964	$145.00	
Pak	Lunch Date	1966	$140.00	
Pak	Match-Mates (pink formal)	1966	$240.00	
Pak	On The Go	1964	$80.00	
Pak	Peachy Fleecy Coat	1963	$65.00	
Pak	Pedal Pushers	1968	$120.00	
Pak	Pert Skirt	1966	$150.00	
Pak	Petti-Pinks	1969	$140.00	
Pak	Plain Blouse and Purse	1962	$45.00	
Pak	Plush 'n Warm	1971	$75.00	
Pak	Purse Pack	1962	$60.00	
Pak	Red Delight	1966	$150.00	
Pak	Ruffles 'n Lace	1964	$130.00	
Pak	Satin Blouse	1963	$55.00	
Pak	Satin Bolero and Hat	1963	$100.00	
Pak	Satin Coat	1963	$100.00	
Pak	Satin Sheath Skirt	1963	$55.00	
Pak	Satin Slacks	1963	$100.00	
Pak	Satin Wrap Skirt	1963	$120.00	
Pak	Scoop Neck Playsuit	1962	$65.00	
Pak	Set 'N Serve	1966	$350.00	
Pak	Sew-In, The	1971	$30.00	
Pak	Sheath Skirt and Telephone	1962	$50.00	
Pak	Sheath with Gold Buttons	1962	$60.00	
Pak	Shoe Pack (12 pairs)	1963	$200.00	
Pak	Silk Sheath (assorted colors)	1962	$75.00	
Pak	Skirt Styles	1967	$115.00	
Pak	Slacks	1962	$30.00	
Pak	Slip, Panty, and Bra	1962	$75.00	
Pak	Soft 'n Snug	1971	$170.00	

Number	Item	Year	Value	Specials
Pak	Spectator Sport	1964	$65.00	
Pak	Square Neck Sweater	1962	$35.00	
Pak	Square Neck Sweater and Scarf	1963	$35.00	
Pak	Sun-Shiner	1969	$150.00	
Pak	Sweet Dreams	1964	$155.00	
Pak	Tailored Tops	1966	$100.00	
Pak	Terrific Twosomes	1969	$150.00	
Pak	Top Twosome	1967	$100.00	
Pak	Tour-Ins	1969	$150.00	
Pak	T-Shirt and Shorts	1962	$30.00	
Pak	Two-Piece Pajamas	1962	$25.00	
Pak	Walking Pretty	1971	$130.00	
Pak	What's Cooking	1964	$110.00	

Ken Doll Outfits

Listed Alphabetically

Item	Number	Year	Value	Specials
4-Piece Red/White Sports Outfit	2241	1978	$20.00	Best Buys
A Very Delux Tux	9745	1977	$20.00	Get-Ups 'n Go
Accessory Pack	Pak	1962	$100.00	
All Weather Favorite	2798	1979	$15.00	Fashion Favorites
American Airlines Captain	0779	1964	$300.00	
Arabian Nights	0774	1964	$200.00	
Army and Air Force	797	1963	$145.00	
At Ease	Pak	1964	$60.00	
Baseball	9168	1976	$70.00	Get-Ups 'n Go
Baseball, Two-Piece Striped, Bat, Ball	14376	1996	$8.00	Ken Career Fashions
Beach Beat	3384	1972	$80.00	
Beige Jumpsuit	2057	1977	$50.00	Sears' Exclusive Best Buys
Beige Pants, Yellow Scarf, Green Printed Shirt	9701	1977	$25.00	Best Buys
Belted Coat	7227	1975	$35.00	Best Buys
Best Foot Forward	Pak	1964	$30.00	
Best Man	1425	1966	$1,200.00	
Big Business	1434	1970	$75.00	
Black Pants	9116	1985	$15.00	Twice As Nice Reversible
Black Pants and Yellow/Black/Red Printed Shirt	2239	1978	$15.00	Best Buys
Black Pants, Polka Dotted Shirt	9002	1975	$20.00	
Black Tuxedo, Black/White Ruffled Shirt	3104	1988	$10.00	Romantic Wedding
Black/Red Turtleneck Sweater, Black Pants	4495	1988	$10.00	Sweatersoft Fashions
Black/Yellow T-shirt, Orange Pants	1375	1980	$10.00	Fashion Collectibles
Blazer	Pak	1962	$25.00	
Blue Animal Printed Top, Orange Shorts	1598	1989	$10.00	Animal Lovin' Fashions
Blue Coat, Checked Pants, White Shirt, Shoes	1912	1989	$10.00	Paris Pretty Fashions
Blue Gym Shorts, Hooded Jacket	2795	1979	$60.00	Fashion Collectibles
Blue Jacket and Clear Case	13570	1995	$10.00	On The Go Fashions
Blue Jacket, White Top, Brown Dog	3667	1987	$10.00	Pet Show Fashions
Blue Jeans, White Long Sleeved Top, Red Vest	9114	1985	$10.00	Twice As Nice Reversible
Blue Pants, Blue/White Jacket	9118	1985	$15.00	Twice As Nice Reversible
Blue Pants, Blue/White Striped Coat	2060	1977	$20.00	Sears' Exclusive Best Buys
Blue Pants, Blue/White Top w/Blue Pockets	1376	1980	$10.00	Fashion Collectibles
Blue Pants, Brown/Striped Shirt	2058	1977	$20.00	Sears' Exclusive Best Buys
Blue Pants, Printed Shirt	9696	1976	$20.00	
Blue Pants, Red/Blue Jacket	2240	1978	$20.00	Best Buys
Blue Pants, Vest, White Shirt	3793	1982	$10.00	Fashion Favorites
Blue Pants, White Shirt, Blue/Red Vest	9914	1985	$15.00	Twice As Nice Reversible
Blue Police Uniform w/Hat	12609	1995	$10.00	Cool Looks Fashions
Blue Shirt and Pouch	13569	1995	$10.00	On The Go Fashions
Blue Sweater, Pants, Red Scarf	4505	1988	$10.00	Sweatersoft Fashions
Blue Tuxedo, Vest, Tie, Shirt, Slacks	14678	1996	$10.00	Fashion Avenue
Blue/Red Sweater, Blue Pants	4504	1988	$10.00	Sweatersoft Fashions
Blue/White Baseball Uniform, Glove, Ball	3796	1982	$10.00	Fashion Favorites
Blue/White/Pink Jacket, Blue Pants, White Shoes	2410	1990	$5.00	Active Wear Fashions
Blue/Yellow Top, Blue Pants	2304	1986	$10.00	Twice as Nice Reversible
Bluechip Dressing	2800	1979	$20.00	Fashion Favorites
Blueprint for Success	1947	1981	$15.00	Ken Fashion Favorites

Item	Number	Year	Value	Specials
Bold Gold	1436	1970	$75.00	
Boxing Outfit	Pak	1963	$50.00	
Breakfast at 7	1428	1969	$70.00	
Bridegroom (blue and black)	7836	1974	$90.00	Get-Ups 'n Go
Bright Team for the Travel Scene	9744	1977	$20.00	Get-Ups 'n Go
Brown on Brown	1718	1972	$90.00	Fashion Originals
Brown or Gray Slacks	Pak	1962	$45.00	
Brown Pants, Argyle Shirt	7758	1974	$35.00	Best Buys
Brown Pants, Brown/Tan Striped Shirt	9703	1977	$20.00	Best Buys
Brown Pants, Sunrise Shirt	9702	1977	$22.00	Best Buys
Brown Suede Jacket, T-Shirt, Denim Pants	14677	1996	$5.00	Fashion Avenue
Brown Suit	7838	1974	$75.00	Get-Ups 'n Go
Brown/White Pants, Brown Jacket, Gold Shirt	3795	1982	$10.00	Fashion Favorites
Brown/White Striped Pajamas	3776	1982	$10.00	Fashion Collectibles
Business Appointment	1424	1966	$1200.00	
Business Suit	7246	1975	$60.00	Get-Ups 'n Go
Campus Corduroys	1410	1964	$75.00	
Campus Hero	0770	1961	$80.00	
Cardigan Sweater	Pak	1963	$30.00	
Casual All-Stars	1436	1970	$50.00	
Casual Cords	1717	1972	$75.00	Fashion Originals
Casual Scene	1472	1971	$70.00	
Casual Suit	9167	1976	$70.00	Get-Ups 'n Go
Casual Suit w/Shirt, Vest, and Slacks	13567	1996	$5.00	Fashion Avenue
Casuals (striped shirt)	0782	1964	$90.00	
Casuals (yellow shirt)	782	1961	$80.00	
Checked Pants, Denim Jacket	9904	1975	$15.00	Best Buys
Checked Pants, Red Sweater	7224	1975	$40.00	Best Buys
Cheerful Chef	Pak	1964	$100.00	
City Nights	2774	1986	$10.00	Finishing Touches
City Sophisticate	2801	1979	$15.00	Designer Fashion Originals
Classic Chambray Shirt and Khaki Pants	15182	1996	$5.00	Fashion Avenue
Classic Cowboy	1949	1981	$10.00	Ken Fashion Favorites
College Student	1416	1965	$550.00	
Construction Worker, T-Shirt, Jeans, Tools	14377	1996	$4.00	Ken Career Fashions
Cool Captain	5823	1983	$10.00	Fashion Classics
Cool 'n Casual	3379	1972	$70.00	
Cool 'n Casual	5822	1983	$10.00	Fashion Classics
Corduroy Jacket	Pak	1962	$60.00	
Corduroy Slacks	Pak	1962	$60.00	
Country Clubbin'	1400	1964	$140.00	
Country Flair	5820	1983	$10.00	Fashion Classics
Country Gentleman	5833	1983	$10.00	Designer Collection
Dandy Lines	3797	1982	$15.00	Barbie & Ken Designer Original
Dark Pants, Brightly Striped Top	2794	1979	$15.00	Fashion Collectibles
Dark Pants, Printed Shirt	9001	1975	$15.00	
Dashing Duo	4890	1984	$10.00	Twice As Nice Fashions
Date Night	5651	1983	$10.00	Designer Collection
Date with Barbie	5824	1983	$10.00	Fashion Classics
Denim Suit w/Red Plaid Trim	8618	1973	$30.00	Best Buys
Denim Top, Pants Trimmed in Yellow	1690	1989	$10.00	Jeans Fashions
Denims for Fun	3376	1972	$70.00	
Doctor	7705	1973	$80.00	Get-Ups 'n Go
Doctor, Green Scrubs, Mask, Bag, Chart	14378	1996	$4.00	Ken Career Fashions
Double Play	4886	1984	$10.00	Twice As Nice Fashions

Item	Number	Year	Value	Specials
Double Vested	4887	1984	$10.00	Twice As Nice Fashions
Dr. Ken	793	1963	$135.00	
Dr. Ken's Kit	Pak	1964	$90.00	
Dreamboat	785	1961	$135.00	
Drum Major	0775	1964	$200.00	
Evening Elegance	1415	1980	$15.00	Barbie & Ken Designer Original
Faded Pants, Green/Blue/Wine Sweater	9701	1977	$22.00	Best Buys
Fountain Boy	1407	1964	$165.00	
Fraternity Meeting	1408	1964	$100.00	
Fun at McDonald's	4276	1983	$15.00	Fashion Classics
Fun on Ice	791	1963	$125.00	
Fur-Trimmed Coat, Checked Pants, Sweater	4416	1988	$10.00	Citystyle Fashions
Go-Anywhere Gear	5819	1983	$10.00	Fashion Classics
Goin' Huntin'	1409	1964	$125.00	
Going Bowling	1403	1964	$85.00	
Golden Glamour	1413	1980	$15.00	Barbie & Ken Designer Original
Graduation	795	1963	$65.00	
Gray Tails, Vest, Trousers, Pink Striped Ascot	3789	1990	$5.00	Wedding of the Year
Green Pants and Hawaiian Shirt	7760	1974	$40.00	Best Buys
Green Printed Baggy Pants, Green Jacket, Tank	1177	1986	$10.00	Barbie & the Rockers Fashions
Green Striped Sweater, Brown Pants w/Pockets	2309	1986	$10.00	Twice as Nice Reversible
Groom	9596	1976	$15.00	
Guruvy Formal	1431	1969	$125.00	
Handsome Pair	4889	1984	$10.00	Twice As Nice Fashions
Here Comes the Groom	1426	1965	$1500.00	
Hiking Holiday	1412	1965	$260.00	
Holiday	1414	1965	$250.00	
Hunting Shirt	Pak	1963	$50.00	
In The Limelight	2802	1979	$20.00	Designer Fashion Originals
In Training	780	1961	$55.00	
Jazz Concert	1420	1966	$300.00	
Jean Jacket w/Studs, Top, Boots, Pants	4336	1988	$10.00	The Jeans Look Fashions
Jeans	Pak	1963	$50.00	
Jeans Suit, Red Printed Yoke	7225	1975	$40.00	Best Buys
Keeping in Shape	5821	1983	$10.00	Fashion Classics
Ken a Go Go	1423	1966	$700.00	
Ken in Hawaii	1404	1964	$180.00	
Ken in Holland	0777	1964	$170.00	
Ken in Mexico	0778	1964	$230.00	
Ken in Switzerland	0776	1964	$200.00	
King Arthur	0773	1964	$360.00	
Lifeguard, Jacket, Blue Shorts, T-Shirt	14379	1996	$4.00	Ken Career Fashions
Light Blue/White Shirt, Shorts, White T-Shirt	4469	1988	$10.00	California Dream Fashions
Light Brown Pants and Jacket, Gold Dickey	8617	1973	$30.00	Best Buys
Light Pants, Jacket w/Printed Yoke	9046	1975	$25.00	
Lounging Around	Pak	1964	$30.00	
Masquerade	794	1963	$125.00	
Midnight Blues	1719	1972	$115.00	Fashion Originals
Mod Madras	1828	1972	$115.00	Fashion Originals
Morning Workout	Pak	1964	$50.00	
Mountain Hike	1427	1966	$275.00	
Mr. Astronaut	1415	1965	$725.00	
Multi-Striped Top, Yellow Shorts, White Shoes	1332	1989	$10.00	Weekend Collection Fashions
Multicolored Striped Sweater, Red Pants	4496	1988	$10.00	Sweatersoft Fashions
Multicolored Striped Top, White Pants	9335	1990	$5.00	My First Ken Fashions

Item	Number	Year	Value	Specials
Multicolored Long Sleeve Shirt, White Pants	1380	1980	$10.00	Fashion Collectibles
Navy Pants, Plaid Jacket, Red Dickey	7229	1975	$30.00	Best Buys
Navy Slacks, Yellow and Navy #73 on Sweater	8616	1973	$30.00	Best Buys
Night Scene	1496	1971	$100.00	
Off to Bed	1413	1965	$200.00	
Off-White Jump Suit	2791	1979	$15.00	Fashion Collectibles
Olympic Hockey	7247	1975	$70.00	Get-Ups 'n Go
Olympic Outfit	7245	1975	$30.00	Best Buys
Orange Hooded Long Pullover	1932	1981	$10.00	Fashion Collectibles
Outdoor Man	1406	1980	$15.00	Ken Fashion Favorites
Paint the Town Red	1956	1981	$15.00	Barbie & Ken Designer Original
Pants, Jacket, Scarf	9128	1976	$22.00	Best Buys
Pants, Jacket, Shirt	9127	1976	$22.00	Best Buys
Pants, Shirt, Cap	9131	1976	$22.00	Best Buys
Pants, T-Shirt, Cap	9129	1976	$25.00	Best Buys
Pants, T-Shirt, Hat	9132	1976	$20.00	Best Buys
Party Fun	Pak	1964	$110.00	
Pattern Printed Shirt	Pak	1962	$15.00	
Pepsi Outfit	7761	1974	$40.00	Best Buys
Pilot Uniform (Braniff)	1427	1967	$550.00	Marx Company
Pink/Green/Black Top, Shorts, Surfboard	12607	1995	$6.00	Cool Looks Fashions
Plaid Jacket and Brown Case	13567	1995	$6.00	On The Go Fashions
Plaid Pants and Black Jacket	9047	1975	$25.00	
Plaid Pants Red Top	2792	1979	$20.00	Fashion Collectibles
Play Ball	792	1963	$120.00	
Play It Cool	1433	1970	$75.00	
Polo Shirt	Pak	1962	$25.00	
Prince, The	0772	1964	$400.00	
Purple Sleeveless Vest, White Pants & Shoes	1328	1989	$10.00	Weekend Collection Fashions
Purple Sweater, Tweed Pants	4502	1988	$10.00	Sweatersoft Fashions
Rain or Shine	4888	1984	$10.00	Twice As Nice Fashions
Rally Day	788	1962	$90.00	
Rally Gear	1429	1969	$90.00	
Red Pants and Beige Shirt	7226	1975	$30.00	Best Buys
Red Pants and Jacket	7762	1974	$30.00	Best Buys
Red Pants and Plaid Shirt	7759	1974	$15.00	
Red Pants and Printed Shirt	9698	1976	$40.00	Best Buys
Red Pants and Red/White/Blue Shirt	9704	1977	$15.00	Best Buys
Red Pants, Blue Vest, Shirt	9705	1977	$15.00	Best Buys
Red Pants, Blue w/Red Printed Top	2243	1978	$15.00	Best Buys
Red Printed Robe	3777	1982	$10.00	Fashion Collectibles
Red Shirt, Red/White Pants	9699	1976	$15.00	
Red Shirt, White Shorts	3773	1982	$10.00	Fashion Collectibles
Red Skirt w/White Fringe, White Pants, Cowboy Hat	3580	1982	$10.00	Western Fashions
Red Tank and Pants	1349	1989	$10.00	Weekend Collection Fashions
Red Top, Blue Jean Shorts	1930	1981	$10.00	Fashion Collectibles
Red Turtleneck, Blue Vest, Light Blue Pants	2308	1986	$10.00	Twice As Nice Reversible
Red V-Neck Sweater, Black Pants	1377	1980	$10.00	Fashion Collectibles
Red Vest	Pak	1962	$40.00	
Red/Black/White Top, Black & White Checkered Pants	9314	1990	$5.00	My First Ken Fashions
Red/Blue/Green V-Neck Sweater, Brown Pants	4503	1988	$10.00	Sweatersoft Fashions
Red/White Karate Top, White Pants	2304	1986	$10.00	Twice as Nice Reversible
Red/White Pajamas	9903	1975	$15.00	
Red/White Short Sleeved Top, Red Belted Pants	1933	1981	$10.00	Fashion Collectibles
Red/White Shorts, White Tank Red/White T-Shirt	2307	1986	$10.00	Twice As Nice Reversible

Item	Number	Year	Value	Specials
Red/White Striped Shirt and Pants	9115	1985	$10.00	Twice As Nice Reversible
Red/White Top, Denim Pants, White Shoes	2408	1990	$5.00	Active Wear Fashions
Red/White/Black Pants and Top	2059	1977	$30.00	Sears' Exclusive Best Buys
Red/White/Black Top, Black/White Striped Pants	2314	1990	$5.00	My First Ken Fashions
Red/White/Blue Short Sleeved Top, Blue Shorts	1379	1980	$10.00	Fashion Collectibles
Red/White/Blue Shorts and Shirt	12608	1995	$5.00	Cool Looks Fashions
Red/White/Blue Top, Blue Pants, White Shoes	2417	1990	$5.00	Active Wear Fashions
Red/White/Blue Top, Denim Shorts	9299	1990	$5.00	My First Ken Fashions
Red/White/Blue Top, Denim Shorts, White Shoes	9299	1990	$5.00	My First Ken Fashions
Red, White 'n Wild	1829	1972	$75.00	Fashion Originals
Reddish Pants, Yellow/Blue Printed Shirt	2242	1978	$15.00	Best Buys
Roller Skate Date	1405	1964	$130.00	
Roller Skate Date (cap omitted)	1405	1965	$70.00	
Rovin' Reporter	1417	1965	$325.00	
Running Start	1404	1981	$10.00	Ken Fashion Favorites
Safari	7706	1973	$70.00	Get-Ups 'n Go
Sailor	796	1963	$125.00	
Saturday Night Date	786	1961	$125.00	
Sea Scene	1449	1971	$60.00	
Seein' The Sights	1421	1966	$400.00	
Sewn Sweater	Pak	1962	$35.00	
Ship-Shape	4885	1984	$10.00	Twice As Nice Fashions
Shoe-Ins	Pak	1971	$25.00	
Shoes	8627	1973	$30.00	Best Buys
Shoes	8627	1977	$15.00	Best Buys
Shoes & Cases	2459	1978	$15.00	Fashion Add-Ons
Shoes & Cases	2459	1980	$10.00	Fashion Add-Ons
Shoes for Sport	Pak	1964	$25.00	
Shoes & Stuff	2459	1982	$10.00	Fashion Add-Ons
Shoes & Stuff (1 briefcase)	2459	1981	$10.00	Fashion Add-Ons
Shore Lines	1435	1970	$50.00	
Short Robe, Shorts & Sandals	2796	1979	$15.00	Fashion Collectibles
Silver Cape, Silver/White Tux, Silver Hat	1865	1987	$10.00	Jewel Secrets Fashion
Silver Pants, Blue Jacket, Red/Blue/White Top	2691	1986	$10.00	Barbie & the Rockers Fashions
Simply Dashing	7084	1984	$10.00	Designer Collection
Ski Champion	798	1963	$100.00	
Skiing Scene	1438	1971	$90.00	Get-Ups 'n Go
Skin Diver	1406	1963	$55.00	Sears
Slacks are Back	Pak	1970	$25.00	
Sleeper Set (blue)	0781	1964	$120.00	
Sleeper Set (long sleeves)	781	1961	$80.00	
Sleeper Set (short sleeves)	781	1961	$80.00	
Snorkel Gear	Pak	1963	$25.00	
Snow Bound	1948	1981	$10.00	Ken Fashion Favorites
Soccer Player, Black/Red Soccer Outfit	12608	1996	$4.00	Ken Career Fashions
Soda Date	Pak	1964	$120.00	
Solid Color Sport Shirt	Pak	1962	$20.00	
Special Date	1401	1964	$170.00	
Sport Shorts	783	1961	$60.00	
Sportman	Pak	1964	$90.00	
Striped Long Sleeved Shirt, Black Pants	3774	1982	$10.00	Fashion Collectibles
Striped Sweater and Knapsack	13568	1995	$5.00	On The Go Fashions
Striped Sweater, Blue Pants	3775	1982	$10.00	Fashion Collectibles
Striped Tank Top and Denims	9697	1976	$15.00	
Striped Top, White Pants & Shoes	9335	1990	$5.00	My First Ken Fashions

Item	Number	Year	Value	Specials
Suede Scene	1439	1971	$60.00	
Suit, Blue Pants, Red/Blue Jacket	7763	1974	$30.00	Best Buys
Suit with Vest for East or West	2306	1978	$15.00	Get-Ups 'n Go
Suited For The Groom	1418	1980	$15.00	Barbie & Ken Wedding Party
Suited For The Groom	5744	1983	$10.00	Wedding of the Year
Summer Job	1422	1966	$500.00	
Sun Fun	Pak	1970	$40.00	
Super Deluxe Silver/White Tux	2305	1978	$15.00	Get-Ups 'n Go
Surf's Up	1248	1971	$15.00	
Sweatshirt	Pak	1963	$50.00	
Tan Pants and Red/Tan Striped Shirt	9117	1985	$10.00	Twice As Nice Reversible
Tan Short Sleeved Sweater, Brown Pants	1378	1980	$10.00	Fashion Collectibles
Tan/White Long Coat, Brown Pants, White Scarf	2306	1986	$10.00	Twice As Nice Reversible
Tennis	7837	1974	$75.00	Get-Ups 'n Go
Tennis Everyone	1405	1980	$10.00	Ken Fashion Favorites
Terry Togs	784	1961	$80.00	
Time for Tennis	790	1962	$125.00	
Time to Turn In	1418	1966	$150.00	
Top It Off	Pak	1964	$75.00	
Touchdown	799	1963	$125.00	
Town Turtle	1430	1969	$75.00	
Turtleneck Sweater and Green Cuffed Slacks	14676	1996	$5.00	Fashion Avenue
Tuxedo	13026	1995	$5.00	Fantasy Evening Fashions
Tuxedo	787	1961	$175.00	
TV Sports Reporter	9086	1985	$10.00	Day to Night Fashions
TV's Good Tonight	1419	1966	$240.00	
Tweed Suit	9048	1975	$15.00	
United Airlines Pilot Outfit	7707	1973	$100.00	Get-Ups 'n Go
V.I.P. Scene	1473	1971	$75.00	
Vest Dressed	2799	1979	$15.00	Fashion Favorites
Victory Dance	1411	1964	$155.00	
Way-Out West	1720	1972	$65.00	Fashion Originals
Well Suited	1407	1980	$10.00	Ken Fashion Favorites
Western Shirt, Jeans, Hat, Vest, Bandana	12606	1995	$5.00	Cool Looks Fashions
Western Winner	3378	1972	$60.00	
White Clam Diggers, Red Top	2793	1979	$15.00	Fashion Collectibles
White Dress Shirt and Tie	Pak	1962	$25.00	
White Hanes Undershirt and Shorts	1931	1982	$10.00	Fashion Collectibles
White is Right	Pak	1964	$40.00	
White Jacket and Pants	2193	1986	$10.00	Fashion Collectibles
White Pants, Red/White Printed Shirt	8615	1973	$30.00	Best Buys
White Printed Pants, Blue Jacket, Yellow Tank	3395	1987	$10.00	Concert Tour Fashions
White Shorts and Tank, Blue Shirt	9113	1985	$10.00	Twice As Nice Reversible
White Sleeveless T-Top, White Undershorts	1931	1981	$10.00	Fashion Collectibles
White Sweatpants, Blue Printed Shirt	2238	1978	$15.00	Best Buys
White Tank, Brown Dog	3665	1987	$10.00	Pet Show Fashions
White Top, Blue/Red Shorts	2414	1990	$5.00	Active Wear Fashions
White Top, Gray Pants and Shoes	2409	1990	$5.00	Active Wear Fashions
White Tuxedo w/Tails, Black Pants, Shirt	4508	1988	$10.00	Private Collection Fashions
White/Blue Striped Top, Blue Jeans & Shoes	1327	1989	$10.00	Weekend Collection Fashions
White/Blue Sweater, Blue Dog	3663	1987	$10.00	Pet Show Fashions
Wide Awake Stripes	3378	1972	$60.00	
Windbreaker	Pak	1962	$50.00	
Yachtsman, The (no cap)	789	1962	$125.00	
Yachtsman, The (with cap)	0789	1964	$400.00	

Item	Number	Year	Value	Specials
Yellow and Blue Set	9130	1976	$15.00	
Yellow Hooded Rain Slicker, Blue Pants	3794	1982	$10.00	Fashion Favorites
Yellow Star Motif Tank, Pink/Blue Print Shorts	9334	1990	$5.00	My First Ken Fashions
Yellow Sweater Vest, Yellow Dog	3664	1987	$10.00	Pet Show Fashions
Yellow Top w/Stars, Red/Blue Star Printed Shorts	9334	1990	$5.00	My First Ken Fashions
Yellow/Blue/Red Sports Jacket, Blue Pants	2437	1990	$5.00	Active Wear Fashions
Yellow/Red/Blue Printed Shirt, Shorts, Shoes	68040	1998	$3.00	Stylin' Looks Fashions

Ken Doll Outfits

Listed by Stock Number

Number	Item	Year	Value	Specials
0770	Campus Hero	1961	$80.00	
0772	Prince, The	1964	$400.00	
0773	King Arthur	1964	$360.00	
0774	Arabian Nights	1964	$200.00	
0775	Drum Major	1964	$200.00	
0776	Ken in Switzerland	1964	$200.00	
0777	Ken in Holland	1964	$170.00	
0778	Ken in Mexico	1964	$230.00	
0779	American Airlines Captain	1964	$300.00	
780	In Training	1961	$55.00	
781	Sleeper Set (long sleeves)	1961	$80.00	
781	Sleeper Set (short sleeves)	1961	$80.00	
0781	Sleeper Set (blue)	1964	$120.00	
782	Casuals (yellow shirt)	1961	$80.00	
0782	Casuals (striped shirt)	1964	$90.00	
783	Sport Shorts	1961	$60.00	
784	Terry Togs	1961	$80.00	
785	Dreamboat	1961	$135.00	
786	Saturday Night Date	1961	$125.00	
787	Tuxedo	1961	$175.00	
788	Rally Day	1962	$90.00	
789	Yachtsman, The (no cap)	1962	$125.00	
0789	Yachtsman, The (with cap)	1964	$400.00	
790	Time for Tennis	1962	$125.00	
791	Fun on Ice	1963	$125.00	
792	Play Ball	1963	$120.00	
793	Dr. Ken	1963	$135.00	
794	Masquerade	1963	$125.00	
795	Graduation	1963	$65.00	
796	Sailor	1963	$125.00	
797	Army and Air Force	1963	$145.00	
798	Ski Champion	1963	$100.00	
799	Touchdown	1963	$125.00	
1177	Green Printed Baggy Pants, Green Jacket, Tank	1986	$10.00	Barbie & the Rockers Fashions
1248	Surf's Up	1971	$15.00	
1327	White/Blue Striped Top, Blue Jeans & Shoes	1989	$10.00	Weekend Collection Fashions
1328	Purple Sleeveless Vest, White Pants & Shoes	1989	$10.00	Weekend Collection Fashions
1332	Multi-Striped Top, Yellow Shorts, White Shoes	1989	$10.00	Weekend Collection Fashions
1349	Red Tank and Pants	1989	$10.00	Weekend Collection Fashions
1375	Black/Yellow T-shirt, Orange Pants	1980	$10.00	Fashion Collectibles
1376	Blue Pants, Blue/White Top w/Blue Pockets	1980	$10.00	Fashion Collectibles
1377	Red V-Neck Sweater, Black Pants	1980	$10.00	Fashion Collectibles
1378	Tan Short Sleeved Sweater, Brown Pants	1980	$10.00	Fashion Collectibles
1379	Red/White/Blue Short Sleeved Top, Blue Shorts	1980	$10.00	Fashion Collectibles
1380	Multicolored Long Sleeved Shirt, White Pants	1980	$10.00	Fashion Collectibles
1400	Country Clubbin'	1964	$140.00	
1401	Special Date	1964	$170.00	
1403	Going Bowling	1964	$85.00	

Number	Item	Year	Value	Specials
1404	Ken in Hawaii	1964	$180.00	
1404	Running Start	1981	$10.00	Ken Fashion Favorites
1405	Roller Skate Date	1964	$130.00	
1405	Roller Skate Date (cap omitted)	1965	$70.00	
1405	Tennis Everyone	1980	$10.00	Ken Fashion Favorites
1406	Outdoor Man	1980	$15.00	Ken Fashion Favorites
1406	Skin Diver	1963	$55.00	Sears
1407	Fountain Boy	1964	$165.00	
1407	Well Suited	1980	$10.00	Ken Fashion Favorites
1408	Fraternity Meeting	1964	$100.00	
1409	Goin' Huntin'	1964	$125.00	
1410	Campus Corduroys	1964	$75.00	
1411	Victory Dance	1964	$155.00	
1412	Hiking Holiday	1965	$260.00	
1413	Golden Glamour	1980	$15.00	Barbie & Ken Designer Original
1413	Off to Bed	1965	$200.00	
1414	Holiday	1965	$250.00	
1415	Evening Elegance	1980	$15.00	Barbie & Ken Designer Original
1415	Mr. Astronaut	1965	$725.00	
1416	College Student	1965	$550.00	
1417	Rovin' Reporter	1965	$325.00	
1418	Suited For The Groom	1980	$15.00	Barbie & Ken Wedding Party
1418	Time to Turn In	1966	$150.00	
1419	TV's Good Tonight	1966	$240.00	
1420	Jazz Concert	1966	$300.00	
1421	Seein' The Sights	1966	$400.00	
1422	Summer Job	1966	$500.00	
1423	Ken a Go Go	1966	$700.00	
1424	Business Appointment	1966	$1,200.00	
1425	Best Man	1966	$1,200.00	
1426	Here Comes the Groom	1965	$1,500.00	
1427	Mountain Hike	1966	$275.00	
1427	Pilot Uniform (Braniff)	1967	$550.00	Marx Company
1428	Breakfast at 7	1969	$70.00	
1429	Rally Gear	1969	$90.00	
1430	Town Turtle	1969	$75.00	
1431	Guruvy Formal	1969	$125.00	
1433	Play It Cool	1970	$75.00	
1434	Big Business	1970	$75.00	
1435	Shore Lines	1970	$50.00	
1436	Bold Gold	1970	$75.00	
1436	Casual All-Stars	1970	$50.00	
1438	Skiing Scene	1971	$90.00	Get-Ups 'n Go
1439	Suede Scene	1971	$60.00	
1449	Sea Scene	1971	$60.00	
1472	Casual Scene	1971	$70.00	
1473	V.I.P. Scene	1971	$75.00	
1496	Night Scene	1971	$100.00	
1598	Blue Animal Printed Top, Orange Shorts	1989	$10.00	Animal Lovin' Fashions
1690	Denim Top, Pants Trimmed in Yellow	1989	$10.00	Jeans Fashions
1717	Casual Cords	1972	$75.00	Fashion Originals
1718	Brown on Brown	1972	$90.00	Fashion Originals
1719	Midnight Blues	1972	$115.00	Fashion Originals
1720	Way-Out West	1972	$65.00	Fashion Originals
1828	Mod Madras	1972	$115.00	Fashion Originals

Number	Item	Year	Value	Specials
1829	Red, White 'n Wild	1972	$75.00	Fashion Originals
1865	Silver Cape, Silver/White Tux, Silver Hat	1987	$10.00	Jewel Secrets Fashion
1912	Blue Coat, Checked Pants, White Shirt, Shoes	1989	$10.00	Paris Pretty Fashions
1930	Red Top, Blue Jean Shorts	1981	$10.00	Fashion Collectibles
1931	White Hanes Undershirt and Shorts	1982	$10.00	Fashion Collectibles
1931	White Sleeveless T-Top, White Undershorts	1981	$10.00	Fashion Collectibles
1932	Orange Hooded Long Pullover	1981	$10.00	Fashion Collectibles
1933	Red/White Short Sleeved Top, Red Belted Pants	1981	$10.00	Fashion Collectibles
1947	Blueprint for Success	1981	$15.00	Ken Fashion Favorites
1948	Snow Bound	1981	$10.00	Ken Fashion Favorites
1949	Classic Cowboy	1981	$10.00	Ken Fashion Favorites
1956	Paint the Town Red	1981	$15.00	Barbie & Ken Designer Original
2057	Beige Jumpsuit	1977	$50.00	Sears' Exclusive Best Buys
2058	Blue Pants, Brown/Striped Shirt	1977	$20.00	Sears' Exclusive Best Buys
2059	Red/White/Black Pants and Top	1977	$30.00	Sears' Exclusive Best Buys
2060	Blue Pants, Blue/White Striped Coat	1977	$20.00	Sears' Exclusive Best Buys
2193	White Jacket and Pants	1986	$10.00	Fashion Collectibles
2238	White Sweatpants, Blue Printed Shirt	1978	$15.00	Best Buys
2239	Black Pants and Yellow/Black/Red Printed Shirt	1978	$15.00	Best Buys
2240	Blue Pants, Red/Blue Jacket	1978	$20.00	Best Buys
2241	4-Piece Red/White Sports Outfit	1978	$20.00	Best Buys
2242	Reddish Pants, Yellow/Blue Printed Shirt	1978	$15.00	Best Buys
2243	Red Pants, Blue w/Red Printed Top	1978	$15.00	Best Buys
2304	Blue/Yellow Top, Blue Pants	1986	$10.00	Twice As Nice Reversible
2304	Red/White Karate Top, White Pants	1986	$10.00	Twice As Nice Reversible
2305	Super Deluxe Silver/White Tux	1978	$15.00	Get-Ups 'n Go
2306	Suit with Vest for East or West	1978	$15.00	Get-Ups 'n Go
2306	Tan/White Long Coat, Brown Pants, White Scarf	1986	$10.00	Twice As Nice Reversible
2307	Red/White Shorts, White Tank Red/White T-Shirt	1986	$10.00	Twice As Nice Reversible
2308	Red Turtleneck, Blue Vest, Light Blue Pants	1986	$10.00	Twice As Nice Reversible
2309	Green Striped Sweater, Brown Pants w/Pockets	1986	$10.00	Twice As Nice Reversible
2314	Red/White/Black Top, Black/White Striped Pants	1990	$5.00	My First Ken Fashions
2408	Red/White Top, Denim Pants, White Shoes	1990	$5.00	Active Wear Fashions
2409	White Top, Gray Pants and Shoes	1990	$5.00	Active Wear Fashions
2410	Blue/White/Pink Jacket, Blue Pants, White Shoes	1990	$5.00	Active Wear Fashions
2414	White Top, Blue/Red Shorts	1990	$5.00	Active Wear Fashions
2417	Red/White/Blue Top, Blue Pants, White Shoes	1990	$5.00	Active Wear Fashions
2437	Yellow/Blue/Red Sports Jacket, Blue Pants	1990	$5.00	Active Wear Fashions
2459	Shoes & Cases	1978	$15.00	Fashion Add-Ons
2459	Shoes & Cases	1980	$10.00	Fashion Add-Ons
2459	Shoes & Stuff	1982	$10.00	Fashion Add-Ons
2459	Shoes & Stuff (1 briefcase)	1981	$10.00	Fashion Add-Ons
2691	Silver Pants, Blue Jacket, Red/Blue/White Top	1986	$10.00	Barbie & the Rockers Fashions
2774	City Nights	1986	$10.00	Finishing Touches
2791	Off-White Jump Suit	1979	$15.00	Fashion Collectibles
2792	Plaid Pants Red Top	1979	$20.00	Fashion Collectibles
2793	White Clam Diggers, Red Top	1979	$15.00	Fashion Collectibles
2794	Dark Pants, Brightly Striped Top	1979	$15.00	Fashion Collectibles
2795	Blue Gym Shorts, Hooded Jacket	1979	$60.00	Fashion Collectibles
2796	Short Robe, Shorts & Sandals	1979	$15.00	Fashion Collectibles
2798	All Weather Favorite	1979	$15.00	Fashion Favorites
2799	Vest Dressed	1979	$15.00	Fashion Favorites
2800	Bluechip Dressing	1979	$20.00	Fashion Favorites
2801	City Sophisticate	1979	$15.00	Designer Fashion Originals
2802	In The Limelight	1979	$20.00	Designer Fashion Originals

Number	Item	Year	Value	Specials
3104	Black Tuxedo, Black/White Ruffled Shirt	1988	$10.00	Romantic Wedding
3376	Denims for Fun	1972	$70.00	
3378	Western Winner	1972	$60.00	
3378	Wide Awake Stripes	1972	$60.00	
3379	Cool 'n Casual	1972	$70.00	
3384	Beach Beat	1972	$80.00	
3395	White Printed Pants, Blue Jacket, Yellow Tank	1987	$10.00	Concert Tour Fashions
3580	Red Skirt w/White Fringe, White Pants, Cowboy Hat	1982	$10.00	Western Fashions
3663	White/Blue Sweater, Blue Dog	1987	$10.00	Pet Show Fashions
3664	Yellow Sweater Vest, Yellow Dog	1987	$10.00	Pet Show Fashions
3665	White Tank, Brown Dog	1987	$10.00	Pet Show Fashions
3667	Blue Jacket, White Top, Brown Dog	1987	$10.00	Pet Show Fashions
3773	Red Shirt, White Shorts	1982	$10.00	Fashion Collectibles
3774	Striped Long Sleeved Shirt, Black Pants	1982	$10.00	Fashion Collectibles
3775	Striped Sweater, Blue Pants	1982	$10.00	Fashion Collectibles
3776	Brown/White Striped Pajamas	1982	$10.00	Fashion Collectibles
3777	Red Printed Robe	1982	$10.00	Fashion Collectibles
3789	Gray Tails, Vest, Trousers, Pink Striped Ascot	1990	$5.00	Wedding of the Year
3793	Blue Pants, Vest, White Shirt	1982	$10.00	Fashion Favorites
3794	Yellow Hooded Rain Slicker, Blue Pants	1982	$10.00	Fashion Favorites
3795	Brown/White Pants, Brown Jacket, Gold Shirt	1982	$10.00	Fashion Favorites
3796	Blue/White Baseball Uniform, Glove, Ball	1982	$10.00	Fashion Favorites
3797	Dandy Lines	1982	$15.00	Barbie & Ken Designer Original
4276	Fun at McDonald's	1983	$15.00	Fashion Classics
4336	Jean Jacket w/Studs, Top, Boots, Pants	1988	$10.00	The Jeans Look Fashions
4416	Fur-Trimmed Coat, Checked Pants, Sweater	1988	$10.00	Citystyle Fashions
4469	Light Blue/White Shirt, Shorts, White T-Shirt	1988	$10.00	California Dream Fashions
4495	Black/Red Turtleneck Sweater, Black Pants	1988	$10.00	Sweatersoft Fashions
4496	Multicolored Striped Sweater, Red Pants	1988	$10.00	Sweatersoft Fashions
4502	Purple Sweater, Tweed Pants	1988	$10.00	Sweatersoft Fashions
4503	Red/Blue/Green V-Neck Sweater, Brown Pants	1988	$10.00	Sweatersoft Fashions
4504	Blue/Red Sweater, Blue Pants	1988	$10.00	Sweatersoft Fashions
4505	Blue Sweater, Pants, Red Scarf	1988	$10.00	Sweatersoft Fashions
4508	White Tuxedo w/Tails, Black Pants, Shirt	1988	$10.00	Private Collection Fashions
4885	Ship-Shape	1984	$10.00	Twice As Nice Fashions
4886	Double Play	1984	$10.00	Twice As Nice Fashions
4887	Double Vested	1984	$10.00	Twice As Nice Fashions
4888	Rain or Shine	1984	$10.00	Twice As Nice Fashions
4889	Handsome Pair	1984	$10.00	Twice As Nice Fashions
4890	Dashing Duo	1984	$10.00	Twice As Nice Fashions
5651	Date Night	1983	$10.00	Designer Collection
5744	Suited For The Groom	1983	$10.00	Wedding of the Year
5819	Go-Anywhere Gear	1983	$10.00	Fashion Classics
5820	Country Flair	1983	$10.00	Fashion Classics
5821	Keeping in Shape	1983	$10.00	Fashion Classics
5822	Cool 'n Casual	1983	$10.00	Fashion Classics
5823	Cool Captain	1983	$10.00	Fashion Classics
5824	Date with Barbie	1983	$10.00	Fashion Classics
5833	Country Gentleman	1983	$10.00	Designer Collection
7084	Simply Dashing	1984	$10.00	Designer Collection
7224	Checked Pants, Red Sweater	1975	$40.00	Best Buys
7225	Jeans Suit, Red Printed Yoke	1975	$40.00	Best Buys
7226	Red Pants and Beige Shirt	1975	$30.00	Best Buys
7227	Belted Coat	1975	$35.00	Best Buys

Number	Item	Year	Value	Specials
7229	Navy Pants, Plaid Jacket, Red Dickey	1975	$30.00	Best Buys
7245	Olympic Outfit	1975	$30.00	Best Buys
7246	Business Suit	1975	$60.00	Get-Ups 'n Go
7247	Olympic Hockey	1975	$70.00	Get-Ups 'n Go
7705	Doctor	1973	$80.00	Get-Ups 'n Go
7706	Safari	1973	$70.00	Get-Ups 'n Go
7707	United Airlines Pilot Outfit	1973	$100.00	Get-Ups 'n Go
7758	Brown Pants, Argyle Shirt	1974	$35.00	Best Buys
7759	Red Pants and Plaid Shirt	1974	$15.00	
7760	Green Pants and Hawaiian Shirt	1974	$40.00	Best Buys
7761	Pepsi Outfit	1974	$40.00	Best Buys
7762	Red Pants and Jacket	1974	$30.00	Best Buys
7763	Suit, Blue Pants, Red/Blue Jacket	1974	$30.00	Best Buys
7836	Bridegroom (blue and black)	1974	$90.00	Get-Ups 'n Go
7837	Tennis	1974	$75.00	Get-Ups 'n Go
7838	Brown Suit	1974	$75.00	Get-Ups 'n Go
8615	White Pants, Red/White Printed Shirt	1973	$30.00	Best Buys
8616	Navy Slacks, Yellow and Navy #73 on Sweater	1973	$30.00	Best Buys
8617	Light Brown Pants and Jacket, Gold Dickey	1973	$30.00	Best Buys
8618	Denim Suit w/Red Plaid Trim	1973	$30.00	Best Buys
8627	Shoes	1973	$30.00	Best Buys
8627	Shoes	1977	$15.00	Best Buys
9001	Dark Pants, Printed Shirt	1975	$15.00	
9002	Black Pants, Polka Dotted Shirt	1975	$20.00	
9046	Light Pants, Jacket w/Printed Yoke	1975	$25.00	
9047	Plaid Pants and Black Jacket	1975	$25.00	
9048	Tweed Suit	1975	$15.00	
9086	TV Sports Reporter	1985	$10.00	Day to Night Fashions
9113	White Shorts and Tank, Blue Shirt	1985	$10.00	Twice As Nice Reversible
9114	Blue Jeans, White Long Sleeved Top, Red Vest	1985	$10.00	Twice As Nice Reversible
9115	Red/White Striped Shirt and Pants	1985	$10.00	Twice As Nice Reversible
9116	Black Pants	1985	$15.00	Twice As Nice Reversible
9117	Tan Pants and Red/Tan Striped Shirt	1985	$10.00	Twice As Nice Reversible
9118	Blue Pants, Blue/White Jacket	1985	$15.00	Twice As Nice Reversible
9127	Pants, Jacket, Shirt	1976	$22.00	Best Buys
9128	Pants, Jacket, Scarf	1976	$22.00	Best Buys
9129	Pants, T-Shirt, Cap	1976	$25.00	Best Buys
9130	Yellow and Blue Set	1976	$15.00	
9131	Pants, Shirt, Cap	1976	$22.00	Best Buys
9132	Pants, T-Shirt, Hat	1976	$20.00	Best Buys
9167	Casual Suit	1976	$70.00	Get-Ups 'n Go
9168	Baseball	1976	$70.00	Get-Ups 'n Go
9299	Red/White/Blue Top, Denim Shorts	1990	$5.00	My First Ken Fashions
9299	Red/White/Blue Top, Denim Shorts, White Shoes	1990	$5.00	My First Ken Fashions
9314	Red/Black/White Top, Black & White Checkered Pants	1990	$5.00	My First Ken Fashions
9334	Yellow Star Motif Tank, Pink/Blue Printed Shorts	1990	$5.00	My First Ken Fashions
9334	Yellow Top w/Stars, Red/Blue Star Printed Shorts	1990	$5.00	My First Ken Fashions
9335	Multicolored Striped Top, White Pants	1990	$5.00	My First Ken Fashions
9335	Striped Top, White Pants & Shoes	1990	$5.00	My First Ken Fashions
9596	Groom	1976	$15.00	
9696	Blue Pants, Printed Shirt	1976	$20.00	
9697	Striped Tank Top and Denims	1976	$15.00	
9698	Red Pants and Printed Shirt	1976	$40.00	Best Buys
9699	Red Shirt, Red/White Pants	1976	$15.00	

Number	Item	Year	Value	Specials
9701	Beige Pants, Yellow Scarf, Green Printed Shirt	1977	$25.00	Best Buys
9701	Faded Pants, Green/Blue/Wine Sweater	1977	$22.00	Best Buys
9702	Brown Pants, Sunrise Shirt	1977	$22.00	Best Buys
9703	Brown Pants, Brown/Tan Striped Shirt	1977	$20.00	Best Buys
9704	Red Pants and Red/White/Blue Shirt	1977	$15.00	Best Buys
9705	Red Pants, Blue Vest, Shirt	1977	$15.00	Best Buys
9744	Bright Team for the Travel Scene	1977	$20.00	Get-Ups 'n Go
9745	A Very Delux Tux	1977	$20.00	Get-Ups 'n Go
9903	Red/White Pajamas	1975	$15.00	
9904	Checked Pants, Denim Jacket	1975	$15.00	Best Buys
9914	Blue Pants, White Shirt, Blue/Red Vest	1985	$15.00	Twice As Nice Reversible
12606	Western Shirt, Jeans, Hat, Vest, Bandana	1995	$5.00	Cool Looks Fashions
12607	Pink/Green/Black Top, Shorts, Surfboard	1995	$6.00	Cool Looks Fashions
12608	Red/White/Blue Shorts and Shirt	1995	$5.00	Cool Looks Fashions
12608	Soccer Player, Black/Red Soccer Outfit	1996	$4.00	Ken Career Fashions
12609	Blue Police Uniform w/Hat	1995	$10.00	Cool Looks Fashions
13026	Tuxedo	1995	$5.00	Fantasy Evening Fashions
13567	Casual Suit w/Shirt, Vest, and Slacks	1996	$5.00	Fashion Avenue
13567	Plaid Jacket and Brown Case	1995	$6.00	On The Go Fashions
13568	Striped Sweater and Knapsack	1995	$5.00	On The Go Fashions
13569	Blue Shirt and Pouch	1995	$10.00	On The Go Fashions
13570	Blue Jacket and Clear Case	1995	$10.00	On The Go Fashions
14376	Baseball, Two-Piece Striped, Bat, Ball	1996	$8.00	Ken Career Fashions
14377	Construction Worker, T-Shirt, Jeans, Tools	1996	$4.00	Ken Career Fashions
14378	Doctor, Green Scrubs, Mask, Bag, Chart	1996	$4.00	Ken Career Fashions
14379	Lifeguard, Jacket, Blue Shorts, T-Shirt	1996	$4.00	Ken Career Fashions
14676	Turtleneck Sweater and Green Cuffed Slacks	1996	$5.00	Fashion Avenue
14677	Brown Suede Jacket, T-Shirt, Denim Pants	1996	$5.00	Fashion Avenue
14678	Blue Tuxedo, Vest, Tie, Shirt, Slacks	1996	$10.00	Fashion Avenue
15182	Classic Chambray Shirt and Khaki Pants	1996	$5.00	Fashion Avenue
68040	Yellow/Red/Blue Printed Shirt, Shorts, Shoes	1998	$3.00	Stylin' Looks Fashions

Francie Doll Outfits

Listed Alphabetically

Item	Year	Number	Value	Specials
Altogether Elegant	1970	1242	$200.00	
Altogether Elegant (reissue)	1974	1242	$200.00	
Beach Outfit	1973	7710	$60.00	Get-Ups 'n Go
Bells	1967	1275	$160.00	
Bloom Zoom	1970	1239	$100.00	
Bloom Zoom (reissue)	1974	1239	$100.00	
Border-Line	1967	1287	$180.00	
Bridal Beauty	1972	3288	$425.00	
Bridge Bit, The	1967	1279	$325.00	
Brown Coat and Hat	1973	8646	$45.00	Best Buys
Brown Skirt, Plaid Blouse	1973	8647	$35.00	Best Buys
Buckeroo Blues	1971	3449	$110.00	
Camping	1974	7846	$80.00	Get-Ups 'n Go
Candy Striper	1973	7709	$160.00	Get-Ups 'n Go
Change-Offs	1971	3460	$180.00	
Check This	1967	1291	$170.00	
Checker Chums	1972	3278	$150.00	
Checkmates	1966	1259	$160.00	
Cheerleading Outfit	1973	7711	$80.00	Get-Ups 'n Go
Clam Diggers	1966	1258	$215.00	
Clear Out!	1967	1281	$300.00	
Combination, The	1969	1234	$200.00	
Combo, The	1968	1215	$220.00	
Concert in the Park	1966	1256	$225.00	
Cool Coveralls	1972	3281	$110.00	
Cool White	1967	1280	$200.00	
Cool-It	1968	Pak	$90.00	
Corduroy Cape	1970	1764	$60.00	
Culotte-Wot?	1968	1214	$250.00	
Dance Party	1966	1257	$250.00	
Denims On!	1967	1290	$150.00	
Double Ups	1972	3286	$325.00	
Dreamy Duo	1971	3450	$100.00	
Dreamy Duo (reissue)	1974	3450	$45.00	
Dreamy Wedding	1968	1217	$370.00	
Entertainer, The	1970	1763	$85.00	
First Formal	1966	1260	$225.00	
First Things First	1966	1252	$125.00	
Floating-In	1968	1207	$215.00	Sears
Foot-Notes (hard-pointed heels)	1968	Pak	$130.00	
Foot-Notes (soft-pointed heels)	1967	Pak	$130.00	
For Francie Dressmaker	1967	Pak	$25.00	
Fresh as a Daisy	1966	1254	$155.00	
Frosty Fur	1971	3455	$80.00	
Frosty Fur (reissue)	1974	3455	$80.00	
Fur Out	1966	1262	$450.00	
Furry-Go-Round	1967	1296	$525.00	Sears
Gad-About	1966	1250	$200.00	

Francie® Doll Outfits – Listed Alphabetically

Item	Year	Number	Value	Specials
Get-Readies	1968	Pak	$80.00	
Go Gold	1967	1294	$480.00	
Go, Granny, Go	1966	1267	$160.00	
Gold Rush	1969	1222	$90.00	
Groovy Get-Ups	1967	1270	$425.00	Sears
Hair Dos	1967	Pak	$115.00	
Hair Dos	1968	Pak	$115.00	
Hi-Teen	1967	1272	$125.00	
Hill-Riders	1968	1210	$90.00	
Hip Knits	1966	1265	$225.00	
Ice Skating	1974	7845	$50.00	Get-Ups 'n Go
Iced Blue	1967	1274	$120.00	
In Step	1970	Pak	$85.00	
In-Print	1967	1288	$150.00	
It's a Date	1966	1251	$145.00	
Lace-Pace, The	1968	1216	$225.00	
Land Ho!	1969	1220	$90.00	
Lavender Dress	1974	7765	$35.00	Best Buys
Lavender Jumper	1974	7764	$35.00	Best Buys
Leather Limelight	1966	1269	$270.00	
Little Knits	1972	3275	$125.00	
Long Dark Printed Dress	1974	7769	$35.00	Best Buys
Long on Leather	1970	1769	$155.00	
Long on Looks	1969	1227	$180.00	
Long Red, White, Blue Halter Dress	1973	8644	$35.00	Best Buys
Long View, The	1972	3282	$85.00	
Long Black and White Pin Dot Dress	1974	7767	$35.00	Best Buys
Merry-Go-Rounders	1969	1230	$255.00	
Midi Bouquet	1971	3446	$125.00	
Midi Duet	1971	3451	$150.00	
Midi Duet (reissue)	1974	3451	$150.00	
Midi Plaid	1971	3444	$80.00	
Mini-Chex	1968	1209	$120.00	
Miss Teenage Beauty	1967	1284	$1,500.00	
Mod-Hatters	1967	Pak	$175.00	
Night Blooms	1968	1212	$95.00	
Nighty Brights	1970	Pak	$80.00	
Note the Coat	1967	1289	$85.00	
Olde Look	1971	3458	$200.00	
Olympic Outfit	1975	7273	$55.00	Best Buys
Orange Cozy	1966	1263	$250.00	
Orange Zip	1968	1548	$475.00	Sears
Pancho Bravo	1970	Pak	$45.00	
Partners in Print	1967	1293	$500.00	
Pazam!	1968	1213	$220.00	
Peach Plush	1971	3461	$250.00	
Peach Treats	1972	3285	$270.00	
Pepsi Outfit	1974	7766	$55.00	Best Buys
Pink Lightning	1969	1231	$220.00	
Pink 'n Pretty	1972	3369	$70.00	Best Buys
Pink Power!	1970	1762	$115.00	
Pink Printed Skirt and Vest, White Top	1975	7214	$35.00	Best Buys
Pink Sleep Suit	1975	7215	$35.00	Best Buys
Plaid Pants and Jacket	1975	7216	$36.00	Best Buys
Plaid Plans	1970	1767	$120.00	

Item	Year	Number	Value	Specials
Pleat-Neat	1967	Pak	$100.00	
Polka Dots 'n Raindrops	1966	1255	$130.00	
Pony Coat	1970	1240	$85.00	
Pony Coat (reissue)	1974	1240	$85.00	
Pretty Frilly	1972	3366	$75.00	Best Buys
Pretty Power	1970	1512	$265.00	
Prom Pinks	1967	1295	$1,400.00	Sears
Quick Shift	1966	1266	$200.00	
Ready! Set! Go!	1972	3365	$70.00	Best Buys
Red Baby Dolls	1973	8648	$34.00	Best Buys
Red Plaid Pants, Yellow/Blue Top	1973	8649	$37.00	Best Buys
Red Skirt, White Top	1975	7212	$35.00	Best Buys
Red, White 'n Bright	1972	3368	$60.00	Best Buys
Right for Stripes	1972	3367	$75.00	Best Buys
Satin Happenin'	1970	1237	$90.00	
Satin Happenin' (reissue)	1974	1237	$80.00	
Satin Supper	1971	3443	$75.00	
Shoes	1973	8625	$56.00	Best Buys
Shoppin' Spree	1966	1261	$150.00	
Short Red Printed Dress	1973	8645	$37.00	Best Buys
Short Red Printed Dress	1974	7768	$35.00	Best Buys
Side-Kick!	1967	1273	$90.00	
Silver Cage, The	1968	1208	$130.00	
Simply Super	1972	3277	$90.00	
Sissy Suits	1969	1228	$250.00	
Slacks 'n Caps	1970	Pak	$35.00	
Slacks Suit, The	1972	3276	$110.00	
Sleepy Time Gal	1972	3364	$55.00	Best Buys
Slightly Summery	1968	Pak	$95.00	
Slumber Number	1967	1271	$85.00	
Smashin' Satin	1972	3287	$375.00	
Snake Charmers	1970	1245	$180.00	
Snake Charmers (reissue)	1974	1245	$160.00	
Snappy Snoozers	1970	1238	$100.00	
Snappy Snoozers (reissue)	1974	1238	$100.00	
Snazz	1969	1225	$125.00	
Snooze News	1969	1226	$80.00	
Snooze News	1971	3453	$80.00	
Snooze News (reissue)	1974	3453	$80.00	
Solid Blue, Red, and White Printed Skirt	1975	7217	$35.00	Best Buys
Somethin' Else!	1969	1219	$65.00	
Striped Types	1970	1243	$75.00	
Striped Types (reissue)	1974	1243	$75.00	
Style Setters	1966	1268	$275.00	
Sugar Sheers	1969	1229	$230.00	
Suited for Shorts	1972	3283	$235.00	
Suits Me	1967	1293	$475.00	Sears
Summer Coolers	1967	1292	$460.00	
Summer Frost	1967	1276	$180.00	
Summer Number	1971	3454	$75.00	
Summer Number (reissue)	1974	3454	$75.00	
Sun Spots	1967	1277	$150.00	
Sunny Slacks	1970	1761	$70.00	
Super Shirt	1970	1736	$20.00	
Sweet 'n Swingin'	1967	1283	$500.00	

Item	Year	Number	Value	Specials
Swingin' Skimmy Time	1966	1264	$270.00	
Tennis Tunic	1969	1221	$75.00	
Tenterrific	1968	1211	$180.00	
Totally Terrific	1972	3280	$255.00	
Tuckered Out	1966	1253	$115.00	
Tweed-Somes	1967	1286	$325.00	
Twiggy Gear	1968	1728	$225.00	
Twiggy Turnouts	1968	1726	$225.00	
Twiggy-Dos	1968	1725	$200.00	
Twigster	1968	1727	$230.00	
Twilight Twinkle	1971	3459	$225.00	
Two for the Ball	1969	1232	$300.00	
Undies	1967	Pak	$100.00	
Vested Interest	1969	1224	$85.00	
Victorian Wedding	1969	1233	$240.00	
Waltz in Velvet	1970	1768	$225.00	
Wedding Whirl	1970	1244	$165.00	
Wedding Whirl (reissue)	1974	1244	$165.00	
Western Wild	1970	Pak	$25.00	
Wild Bunch	1970	1766	$475.00	
Wild Flowers	1971	3456	$70.00	
Wild Flowers (reissue)	1974	3456	$70.00	
Wild 'n Wooly	1968	1218	$140.00	
With-It Whites	1971	3448	$125.00	
Yellow Bit, The	1969	1223	$125.00	
Zig-Zag Zoom	1971	3445	$125.00	

Francie Doll Outfits

Listed by Stock Number

Number	Item	Year	Value	Specials
1207	Floating-In	1968	$215.00	Sears
1208	Silver Cage, The	1968	$130.00	
1209	Mini-Chex	1968	$120.00	
1210	Hill-Riders	1968	$90.00	
1211	Tenterrific	1968	$180.00	
1212	Night Blooms	1968	$95.00	
1213	Pazam!	1968	$220.00	
1214	Culotte-Wot?	1968	$250.00	
1215	Combo, The	1968	$220.00	
1216	Lace-Pace, The	1968	$225.00	
1217	Dreamy Wedding	1968	$370.00	
1218	Wild 'n Wooly	1968	$140.00	
1219	Somethin' Else!	1969	$65.00	
1220	Land Ho!	1969	$90.00	
1221	Tennis Tunic	1969	$75.00	
1222	Gold Rush	1969	$90.00	
1223	Yellow Bit, The	1969	$125.00	
1224	Vested Interest	1969	$85.00	
1225	Snazz	1969	$125.00	
1226	Snooze News	1969	$80.00	
1227	Long on Looks	1969	$180.00	
1228	Sissy Suits	1969	$250.00	
1229	Sugar Sheers	1969	$230.00	
1230	Merry-Go-Rounders	1969	$255.00	
1231	Pink Lightning	1969	$220.00	
1232	Two for the Ball	1969	$300.00	
1233	Victorian Wedding	1969	$240.00	
1234	Combination, The	1969	$200.00	
1237	Satin Happenin'	1970	$90.00	
1237	Satin Happenin' (reissue)	1974	$80.00	
1238	Snappy Snoozers	1970	$100.00	
1238	Snappy Snoozers (reissue)	1974	$100.00	
1239	Bloom Zoom	1970	$100.00	
1239	Bloom Zoom (reissue)	1974	$100.00	
1240	Pony Coat	1970	$85.00	
1240	Pony Coat (reissue)	1974	$85.00	
1242	Altogether Elegant	1970	$200.00	
1242	Altogether Elegant (reissue)	1974	$200.00	
1243	Striped Types	1970	$75.00	
1243	Striped Types (reissue)	1974	$75.00	
1244	Wedding Whirl	1970	$165.00	
1244	Wedding Whirl (reissue)	1974	$165.00	
1245	Snake Charmers	1970	$180.00	
1245	Snake Charmers (reissue)	1974	$160.00	
1250	Gad-About	1966	$200.00	
1251	It's a Date	1966	$145.00	
1252	First Things First	1966	$125.00	
1253	Tuckered Out	1966	$115.00	

Number	Item	Year	Value	Specials
1254	Fresh as a Daisy	1966	$155.00	
1255	Polka Dots 'n Raindrops	1966	$130.00	
1256	Concert in the Park	1966	$225.00	
1257	Dance Party	1966	$250.00	
1258	Clam Diggers	1966	$215.00	
1259	Checkmates	1966	$160.00	
1260	First Formal	1966	$225.00	
1261	Shoppin' Spree	1966	$150.00	
1262	Fur Out	1966	$450.00	
1263	Orange Cozy	1966	$250.00	
1264	Swingin' Skimmy Time	1966	$270.00	
1265	Hip Knits	1966	$225.00	
1266	Quick Shift	1966	$200.00	
1267	Go, Granny, Go	1966	$160.00	
1268	Style Setters	1966	$275.00	
1269	Leather Limelight	1966	$270.00	
1270	Groovy Get-Ups	1967	$425.00	Sears
1271	Slumber Number	1967	$85.00	
1272	Hi-Teen	1967	$125.00	
1273	Side-Kick!	1967	$90.00	
1274	Iced Blue	1967	$120.00	
1275	Bells	1967	$160.00	
1276	Summer Frost	1967	$180.00	
1277	Sun Spots	1967	$150.00	
1279	Bridge Bit, The	1967	$325.00	
1280	Cool White	1967	$200.00	
1281	Clear Out!	1967	$300.00	
1283	Sweet 'n Swingin'	1967	$500.00	
1284	Miss Teenage Beauty	1967	$1,500.00	
1286	Tweed-Somes	1967	$325.00	
1287	Border-Line	1967	$180.00	
1288	In-Print	1967	$170.00	
1289	Note the Coat	1967	$85.00	
1290	Denims On!	1967	$150.00	
1291	Check This	1967	$170.00	
1292	Summer Coolers	1967	$460.00	
1293	Partners in Print	1967	$500.00	
1293	Suits Me	1967	$475.00	Sears
1294	Go Gold	1967	$480.00	
1295	Prom Pinks	1967	$1,400.00	Sears
1296	Furry-Go-Round	1967	$525.00	Sears
1512	Pretty Power	1970	$265.00	
1548	Orange Zip	1968	$475.00	Sears
1725	Twiggy-Dos	1968	$200.00	
1726	Twiggy Turnouts	1968	$225.00	
1727	Twigster	1968	$230.00	
1728	Twiggy Gear	1968	$225.00	
1736	Super Shirt	1970	$20.00	
1761	Sunny Slacks	1970	$70.00	
1762	Pink Power!	1970	$115.00	
1763	Entertainer, The	1970	$85.00	
1764	Corduroy Cape	1970	$60.00	
1766	Wild Bunch	1970	$475.00	
1767	Plaid Plans	1970	$120.00	
1768	Waltz in Velvet	1970	$225.00	

Number	Item	Year	Value	Specials
1769	Long on Leather	1970	$155.00	
3275	Little Knits	1972	$125.00	
3276	Slacks Suit, The	1972	$110.00	
3277	Simply Super	1972	$90.00	
3278	Checker Chums	1972	$150.00	
3280	Totally Terrific	1972	$255.00	
3281	Cool Coveralls	1972	$110.00	
3282	Long View, The	1972	$85.00	
3283	Suited for Shorts	1972	$235.00	
3285	Peach Treats	1972	$270.00	
3286	Double Ups	1972	$325.00	
3287	Smashin' Satin	1972	$375.00	
3288	Bridal Beauty	1972	$425.00	
3364	Sleepy Time Gal	1972	$55.00	Best Buys
3365	Ready! Set! Go!	1972	$70.00	Best Buys
3366	Pretty Frilly	1972	$75.00	Best Buys
3367	Right for Stripes	1972	$75.00	Best Buys
3368	Red, White 'n Bright	1972	$60.00	Best Buys
3369	Pink 'n Pretty	1972	$70.00	Best Buys
3443	Satin Supper	1971	$75.00	
3444	Midi Plaid	1971	$80.00	
3445	Zig-Zag Zoom	1971	$125.00	
3446	Midi Bouquet	1971	$125.00	
3448	With-It Whites	1971	$125.00	
3449	Buckeroo Blues	1971	$110.00	
3450	Dreamy Duo	1971	$100.00	
3450	Dreamy Duo (reissue)	1974	$45.00	
3451	Midi Duet	1971	$150.00	
3451	Midi Duet (reissue)	1974	$150.00	
3453	Snooze News	1971	$80.00	
3453	Snooze News (reissue)	1974	$80.00	
3454	Summer Number	1971	$75.00	
3454	Summer Number (reissue)	1974	$75.00	
3455	Frosty Fur	1971	$80.00	
3455	Frosty Fur (reissue)	1974	$80.00	
3456	Wild Flowers	1971	$70.00	
3456	Wild Flowers (reissue)	1974	$70.00	
3458	Olde Look	1971	$200.00	
3459	Twilight Twinkle	1971	$225.00	
3460	Change-Offs	1971	$180.00	
3461	Peach Plush	1971	$250.00	
7212	Red Skirt, White Top	1975	$35.00	Best Buys
7214	Pink Printed Skirt and Vest, White Top	1975	$35.00	Best Buys
7215	Pink Sleep Suit	1975	$35.00	Best Buys
7216	Plaid Pants and Jacket	1975	$36.00	Best Buys
7217	Solid Blue, Red, and White Printed Skirt	1975	$35.00	Best Buys
7273	Olympic Outfit	1975	$55.00	Best Buys
7709	Candy Striper	1973	$160.00	Get-Ups 'n Go
7710	Beach Outfit	1973	$60.00	Get-Ups 'n Go
7711	Cheerleading Outfit	1973	$80.00	Get-Ups 'n Go
7764	Lavender Jumper	1974	$35.00	Best Buys
7765	Lavender Dress	1974	$35.00	Best Buys
7766	Pepsi Outfit	1974	$55.00	Best Buys
7767	Long Black and White Pin Dot Dress	1974	$35.00	Best Buys
7768	Short Red Printed Dress	1974	$35.00	Best Buys

Number	Item	Year	Value	Specials
7769	Long Dark Printed Dress	1974	$35.00	Best Buys
7845	Ice Skating	1974	$50.00	Get-Ups 'n Go
7846	Camping	1974	$80.00	Get-Ups 'n Go
8625	Shoes	1973	$56.00	Best Buys
8644	Long Red, White, Blue Halter Dress	1973	$35.00	Best Buys
8645	Short Red Printed Dress	1973	$37.00	Best Buys
8646	Brown Coat and Hat	1973	$45.00	Best Buys
8647	Brown Skirt, Plaid Blouse	1973	$35.00	Best Buys
8648	Red Baby Dolls	1973	$34.00	Best Buys
8649	Red Plaid Pants, Yellow/Blue Top	1973	$37.00	Best Buys

Skipper Doll Outfits

Listed Alphabetically

Item	Number	Year	Value	Specials
Aloha Lime	26987	2000	$5.00	Fashion Avenue
4-Piece Red/Blue Set	7221	1975	$45.00	Best Buys
Action Fashions	Pak	1971	$75.00	
All Over Felt	3476	1971	$125.00	
All Prettied Up	1949	1967	$165.00	
All Spruced Up!	1941	1967	$145.00	
Baby-Dolls	1957	1968	$100.00	
Ballerina	3471	1971	$75.00	
Ballerina	7714	1973	$45.00	Get-Ups 'n Go
Ballet Lessons (or Class)	1905	1964	$110.00	
Balloon Trim Top, Pink/White Skirt, Lace Hose	5857	1988	$10.00	Teen Fun Fashions
Bandana Printed Skirt & Dress, White Top	9023	1975	$36.00	Growing Up Skipper Fashions
Barbie Fan	5811	1983	$10.00	Fashion Fantasy
Beach	7848	1974	$50.00	Get-Ups 'n Go
Beach Party	1409	1980	$10.00	Skipper Fashion Favorites
Beachy-Peachy	1938	1967	$150.00	
Beauty Bath	Pak	1965	$100.00	
Beach Boardwalk	26990	2000	$5.00	Fashion Avenue
Bicentennial Fashions	9165	1976	$70.00	Get-Ups 'n Go
Black Floral Printed Dress	7773	1974	$45.00	Best Buys
Blue Dress, White Yolk, White Lace Hose	5870	1988	$10.00	Teen Fun Fashions
Blue Floral Dress w/White Lace Trim	3778	1982	$10.00	Fashion Collectibles
Blue Floral Printed Dress w/Dark Blue Jacket	1383	1980	$10.00	Fashion Collectibles
Blue Printed Skirt & Halter	2231	1978	$15.00	Best Buys
Blue Short Skirt, Blue Polka Dot Long Top w/Bead	2594	1989	$10.00	Lookin' Lively Fashion
Blue/Hot Pink Two-Piece Jogging Suit	2233	1986	$10.00	So Active Fashions
Blue/Pink Cheerleader Outfit/Pom Pons	12620	1995	$8.00	High School Fun Skipper
Blue/Pink Long Pajamas	2238	1986	$10.00	So Active Fashions
Blue/White Coat and Blue Belt and Yoke	1943	1981	$10.00	Fashion Collectibles
Blue/White Halter Dress w/Blue Purse	1942	1981	$10.00	Fashion Collectibles
Blue/White Striped Short Skirt, Cat Motif Top	2591	1989	$10.00	Lookin' Lively Fashion
Brown Skirt and Vest, White Lace Trimmed Blouse	1385	1980	$10.00	Fashion Collectibles
Brown Striped Skirt, Blue/White Top	9710	1977	$15.00	Best Buys
Budding Beauty	1731	1970	$70.00	
Camping	7715	1973	$50.00	Get-Ups 'n Go
Can You Play?	1923	1966	$155.00	
Change-Abouts	1411	1980	$10.00	Skipper Fashion Favorites
Check the Suit	Pak	1971	$45.00	
Chill Chasers	1926	1966	$75.00	
Chillin' at the Mall	28156	2000	$5.00	Fashion Avenue
Chilly Chums	1973	1969	$125.00	
City Shopping	2809	1979	$15.00	Super Fashion Favorites
Clan-Tastic	1953	1981	$10.00	Skipper Fashion Favorites
Confetti Cutie	1952	1968	$240.00	
Cookie Time	1912	1965	$125.00	
Country Picnic	1933	1966	$475.00	
Cut 'n Button Dress, Coat, Gown & Cap	Pak	1965	$100.00	
Daisy Crazy	1732	1970	$65.00	

Item	Number	Year	Value	Specials
Day at the Fair	1911	1965	$200.00	
Denim Jacket and Short Full Skirt	2579	1989	$10.00	Teen Time Fashion
Dog Show	1929	1966	$325.00	
Dotted Bliss	1410	1980	$10.00	Skipper Fashion Favorites
Double Dashers	3472	1971	$75.00	
Dream-Ins	3293	1972	$80.00	Fashion Originals
Dreamtime	1909	1964	$100.00	
Dress Coat	1906	1964	$130.00	
Dressed in Velvet	3477	1971	$125.00	
Drizzle Sizzle	1972	1969	$150.00	
Eeny Meeny Midi	1974	1969	$130.00	
Faded Skirt & Shorts, Sunburst Top	9706	1977	$15.00	Best Buys
Fancy Pants	1738	1970	$115.00	
First Dance	4882	1984	$10.00	Fashion Fantasy
Floral Printed Short Skirt, Yellow Tank	2592	1989	$10.00	Lookin' Lively Fashion
Flower Girl	1419	1980	$10.00	Barbie & Ken Wedding Party
Flower Girl	1904	1963	$160.00	
Flower Girl	5746	1983	$10.00	Wedding of the Year
Flower Girl	7847	1974	$70.00	Get-Ups 'n Go
Flower Girl Frills for Skipper	1419	1979	$25.00	
Flower Girl in a Party Whirl	2307	1978	$15.00	Get-Ups 'n Go
Flower Motif Top, Gold Skirt, White Leggings	9059	1990	$5.00	Cool Tops Fashions
Flower Power	3373	1972	$50.00	
Flower Showers	1939	1967	$140.00	
For Schooltime, Playtime, Anytime	9748	1977	$15.00	Get-Ups 'n Go
Fuchsia Dress, Blue Vest and Shoes	7982	1985	$10.00	B Active Fashions
Fun at McDonald's	4275	1983	$10.00	Fashion Fantasy
Fun Runners	3372	1972	$45.00	Best Buys
Funtime	1920	1965	$140.00	
Gauzeway to Fashion	2810	1979	$15.00	Super Fashion Favorites
Glad Plaids	1946	1967	$150.00	
Goin' Sleddin'	3475	1971	$75.00	
Green Long Halter Dress w/Bolero	3783	1982	$10.00	Fashion Collectibles
Green/Blue/Purple Dress, Blue Cap	9708	1977	$15.00	Best Buys
Happy Birthday	1919	1965	$525.00	
Happy Times	Pak	1970	$100.00	
Hats 'n Hats	Pak	1965	$45.00	
Hawaiian Printed Dress	7771	1974	$45.00	Best Buys
Hearts 'n Flowers	1945	1967	$300.00	
Hopscotching	1968	1969	$130.00	
Ice Cream 'n Cake	1970	1969	$165.00	
Ice Skatin'	3470	1971	$70.00	
'Jamas 'n Jaunties	1944	1967	$140.00	
Jazzy Jamys	1967	1969	$100.00	
Jeepers Creepers	1966	1969	$125.00	
Junior Bridesmaid	1934	1966	$480.00	
Just For Fun	Pak	1965	$110.00	
Knit Bit	1969	1969	$120.00	
Lacey Charmer & Partytimer	9746	1977	$15.00	Get-Ups 'n Go
Land and Sea	1917	1965	$140.00	
Lavender Top, Ice Cream Motif, Printed Shorts	2579	1989	$10.00	Lookin' Lively Fashion
Learning to Ride	1935	1966	$300.00	
Lemon Fluff	1749	1970	$90.00	
Let's Play House	1932	1966	$270.00	
Light Blue Lace Trim Dress, Pink Hose and Shoes	2616	1989	$10.00	Teen Time Fashion

Item	Number	Year	Value	Specials
Little Miss Midi	3468	1971	$80.00	
Lolapaloozas	1947	1967	$150.00	
Long Blue/White Dress	9123	1976	$38.00	Best Buys
Long Dark Printed Skirt, White Waist	7223	1975	$45.00	Best Buys
Long Dress, Blue/Yellow Print	2806	1979	$15.00	Fashion Collectibles
Long Dress, Solid Yellow & Print	2232	1978	$15.00	Best Buys
Long Green Bottom, White Overblouse	9709	1977	$35.00	Best Buys
Long Green/Pink Printed Dress	9125	1976	$36.00	Best Buys
Long Light Printed Dress	7775	1974	$45.00	Best Buys
Long 'n Short of It	3478	1971	$80.00	
Long Pink Dress	9711	1977	$25.00	Best Buys
Long Red Gown	2236	1978	$15.00	Best Buys
Long Red Printed Dress	7218	1975	$50.00	Best Buys
Long Red Printed Dress, White Trim	2234	1978	$15.00	Best Buys
Long Red Printed Head Scarf	9707	1977	$15.00	Best Buys
Long Red Printed Jumper	7774	1974	$45.00	Best Buys
Long Yellow Dress	8610	1973	$45.00	Best Buys
Lots of Lace	1730	1970	$75.00	
Loungin' Lovelies	1930	1966	$135.00	
Love to Ski	5815	1983	$10.00	Fashion Fantasy
Lullaby Time	3473	1971	$80.00	
Masquerade	1903	1964	$160.00	
Me 'n My Doll	1913	1965	$275.00	
Multicolored Pastel Top, Blue Short Skirt	7981	1985	$10.00	B Active Fashions
Multicolored Striped Long Ruffled Top, Pink Leggings	4535	1988	$10.00	Bright & Breezy Fashions
Multicolored Striped Top, Red Shorts & Shoes	7978	1985	$10.00	B Active Fashions
Multicolored Striped Jumper, Red Shirt	1386	1980	$10.00	Fashion Collectibles
Music Motif Top, Checked Skirt, Shawl, Socks	9052	1990	$5.00	Cool Tops Fashions
Nifty Knickers	3291	1972	$85.00	Fashion Originals
Nighty Night	Pak	1970	$50.00	
Olympic Outfit	7274	1975	$45.00	Best Buys
Olympic Skating	7251	1975	$70.00	Get-Ups 'n Go
Orange, Green, and Yellow Skirt, Pants, & Top	9513	1976	$36.00	Growing Up Skipper Fashion
Outdoor Casuals	1915	1965	$95.00	
Pants 'n Pinafore	1971	1969	$110.00	
Party Pair	3297	1972	$90.00	Fashion Originals
Party Perfect	5816	1983	$10.00	Fashion Fantasy
Party Pink	Pak	1965	$45.00	
Patent 'n Pants	1958	1968	$130.00	
Pepsi Outfit	7770	1974	$45.00	Best Buys
Perfectly Pretty Set	1962	1968	$125.00	
Pink, Blue, & Yellow Skirt and Blouse	9512	1976	$36.00	Growing Up Skipper Fashion
Pink Cat Motif Sweater, Denim Short Skirt	5860	1988	$10.00	Teen Fun Fashions
Pink Face Motif Top, Ruffled Skirt, Pink Socks	9080	1990	$5.00	Cool Tops Fashions
Pink Face Motif Top, Ruffled Skirt, Pink Socks	9088	1990	$5.00	Cool Tops Fashions
Pink, Lace Bodice Dress, w/Hair Decoration	3791	1990	$5.00	Wedding of the Year
Pink Lace Trimmed Long Sleeveless Dress	1944	1981	$10.00	Fashion Collectibles
Pink Party Dress	2803	1979	$15.00	Fashion Collectibles
Pink Princess	1747	1970	$90.00	
Pink Printed Drop Waist Dress w/White Yoke	2237	1986	$10.00	So Active Fashions
Pink Short Sleeved and Black/Pink Full Skirt	1381	1980	$10.00	Fashion Collectibles
Pink Sleep Set	8612	1973	$45.00	Best Buys
Pink Sleepers	7220	1975	$40.00	Best Buys
Pink Top, Blue Pants	3784	1982	$10.00	Fashion Collectibles
Pink Top, Printed Shirt & Hat, Pink Knickers	12619	1995	$8.00	High School Fun Skipper

Item	Number	Year	Value	Specials
Pink Waffle Dress, Floral Printed Leggings	14384	1996	$5.00	
Pink/Blue/White/Black Top, Heart Printed Pants	2598	1989	$10.00	Teen Time Fashion
Pink/Blue/Yellow Top, Blue Leggings	5849	1988	$10.00	Teen Fun Fashions
Pink/Silver Short Party Dress, Ribbon, Warmers	2608	1989	$10.00	Teen Time Fashion
Pink/White Short Dress	2640	1989	$10.00	Teen Time Fashion
Pink/White/Blue Top, Leggings, Pink Shorts	5874	1988	$10.00	Teen Fun Fashions
Plaid City	1977	1969	$135.00	
Plaid, Pleated Jumper, Lace Trimmed Shirt, Lace Hose	2633	1989	$10.00	Teen Time Fashion
Platter Party	1914	1965	$125.00	
Play Days	5814	1983	$10.00	Fashion Fantasy
Play Pants	3292	1972	$75.00	Fashion Originals
Pool Party	4876	1984	$10.00	Fashion Fantasy
Popover	1943	1967	$175.00	
Posey-Party	1955	1968	$170.00	
Printed Top, Blue Pants, Yellow Shoes	4534	1988	$10.00	Bright & Breezy Fashions
Printed Dress, White Lace Hose, Tea Set	12618	1995	$10.00	High School Fun Skipper
Purple Lace Long Dress, Hat, Bouquet	3106	1988	$10.00	Romantic Wedding
Purple Long Sleeved Top, White Printed Short Skirt	4538	1988	$10.00	Bright & Breezy Fashions
Purple Velvet Dress, Matching Purse	14382	1996	$5.00	
Purple Velvet Dress, Purse, Lace Shirt, Hose	14382	1996	$4.00	Skipper Fashions
Purple/Blue/Lavender Short Dress w/Bow Trim	2593	1989	$10.00	Lookin' Lively Fashion
Quick Changes	1962	1968	$135.00	
Rain or Shine	1916	1965	$95.00	
Rainy Day Checkers	1928	1966	$325.00	
Real Sporty	1961	1968	$145.00	
Red Blouse and Long Red Skirt	2807	1979	$15.00	Fashion Collectibles
Red/Blue Printed Jumpsuit	2233	1978	$15.00	Best Buys
Red Coat and White Trim	8613	1973	$35.00	Best Buys
Red Hat, Blue Jeans, Red/White Shirt	12617	1995	$8.00	High School Fun Skipper
Red Jacket, Black/White Skirt, Shirt, Hose	2629	1989	$10.00	Teen Time Fashion
Red Overalls, Yellow T-Shirt	1382	1980	$10.00	Fashion Collectibles
Red Plaid Coat and Cap	9121	1976	$38.00	Best Buys
Red Plaid Skirt, Blouse, Vest	9122	1976	$38.00	Best Buys
Red Plaid Skirt, White Top, Black Jacket	14383	1996	$5.00	
Red Printed Top and Blue Skirt	2237	1978	$15.00	Best Buys
Red Printed, Yellow Scarf	2804	1979	$15.00	Fashion Collectibles
Red Sensation	1901	1964	$140.00	
Red Set for When It's Wet	9747	1977	$15.00	Get-Ups 'n Go
Red Sweater and Blue Jeans	1384	1980	$10.00	Fashion Collectibles
Red Top, Red Plaid Skirt, White Belt	2234	1986	$10.00	So Active Fashions
Red, White, & Blue Skirt, Top, Pants, & Halter	9021	1975	$36.00	Growing Up Skipper Fashions
Red, White 'n Blues	3296	1972	$80.00	Fashion Originals
Red/White Dress, Red Hat and Shoes	7983	1985	$10.00	B Active Fashions
Red/White Long Skirt, White Top	9126	1976	$70.00	Best Buys
Red/White Striped Top w/White Shorts	3779	1982	$10.00	Fashion Collectibles
Riding Fun	5817	1983	$10.00	Fashion Fantasy
Right in Style	1942	1967	$180.00	
Rik Rak Rah	1733	1970	$70.00	
Rolla-Scoot	1940	1967	$180.00	
School Clothes	7250	1975	$52.00	Get-Ups 'n Go
School Days	1907	1964	$150.00	
School Days	4877	1984	$10.00	Fashion Fantasy
School Girl	1921	1965	$230.00	
School's Cool	1976	1969	$110.00	
Ship Ahoy	1918	1965	$175.00	

Item	Number	Year	Value	Specials
Shoe Parade	Pak	1965	$45.00	
Shoes	8624	1973	$40.00	Best Buys
Short Blue/White Skirt, Short Striped Top, Ruffle	2572	1989	$10.00	Lookin' Lively Fashion
Short Denim Jumper and Vest, Top, Backpack	14381	1996	$4.00	Skipper Fashions
Short 'n Sweet	4881	1984	$10.00	Fashion Fantasy
Short Red/Black/White Dress	8611	1973	$45.00	Best Buys
Shorts Subjects	2811	1979	$15.00	Super Fashion Favorites
Side Lights	Pak	1970	$60.00	
Sightseeing	4880	1984	$10.00	Fashion Fantasy
Silk 'n Fancy	1902	1963	$140.00	
Skate Motif Top, Blue Skirt, Jacket, White Socks	9060	1990	$5.00	Cool Tops Fashions
Skating Fun	1908	1964	$160.00	
Skimmer 'n Scarf	Pak	1971	$42.00	
Skimmy-Stripes	1956	1968	$200.00	
Sledding Fun	1936	1966	$315.00	
Sleep Set	7713	1973	$75.00	Get-Ups 'n Go
Sleeptime Stripes	5812	1983	$10.00	Fashion Fantasy
Slumber Party	1951	1981	$10.00	Skipper Fashion Favorites
Slumber Party, The	Pak	1971	$60.00	
Smooth Sailing	5810	1983	$10.00	Fashion Fantasy
Solid Red Top & Skirt, Floral Printed Halter and Pants	9022	1975	$36.00	Growing Up Skipper Fashions
Some Shoes	Pak	1971	$40.00	
Sporting Stripes	24300	1999	$5.00	Fashion Avenue
Sporty Shorty	Pak	1971	$40.00	
Striped Overalls and Red Blouse	7222	1975	$45.00	Best Buys
Striped Pants, White Top, Hot Pink Belt	2236	1986	$10.00	So Active Fashions
Striped Short Skirt, Yellow Top, Blue Jacket	4539	1988	$10.00	Bright & Breezy Fashions
Striped Top, Yellow Pants and Cap	2805	1979	$15.00	Fashion Collectibles
Summer Slacks	Pak	1970	$60.00	
Summer Sunshine	5813	1983	$10.00	Fashion Fantasy
Sunny Brights	1408	1980	$10.00	Skipper Fashion Favorites
Sunny Pastels	1910	1965	$165.00	
Sunny-Suity	1975	1969	$100.00	
Sunshine Special Set	1249	1971	$15.00	
Super Slacks	1736	1970	$60.00	
Super Snoozer	3371	1972	$55.00	Best Buys
Sweet Dreams	4878	1984	$10.00	Fashion Fantasy
Sweet Orange	3465	1971	$60.00	
Tan Fringed Top, Black Pants	3780	1982	$10.00	Fashion Collectibles
Tan, Yellow, & Orange Jumper & Skirt, Turtleneck	9024	1975	$36.00	Growing Up Skipper Fashions
Tea Party	1924	1966	$275.00	
Teeter Timers	3467	1971	$55.00	
Tennis Everyone	1952	1981	$10.00	Skipper Fashion Favorites
Tennis Time	3466	1971	$65.00	
Three-Piece School w/Red Plaid Skirt, Jacket	14382	1996	$4.00	
Three-Piece Short Jumper, Vest & Backpack	14381	1996	$5.00	
Toe Twinklers	Pak	1970	$60.00	
Town Togs	1922	1965	$140.00	
Trim Twosome	1960	1968	$90.00	
Triple Treat	1748	1970	$110.00	
Turn Abouts	3295	1972	$85.00	Fashion Originals
Turquoise Top and Pants w/White Trim	3781	1982	$10.00	Fashion Collectibles
Twice as Nice	1735	1970	$75.00	
Two-Piece Sleep Outfit, Pink w/Printed Leggings	14384	1996	$4.00	
Under-Pretties	1900	1964	$50.00	

Item	Number	Year	Value	Specials
Undertones	Pak	1970	$55.00	
Underwear	2808	1979	$15.00	Fashion Collectibles
Velvet Blush	1737	1970	$85.00	
Velvet 'n Lace	1948	1967	$215.00	
Warm 'n Wonderful	1959	1968	$160.00	
Weekend Wardrobe	9166	1976	$32.00	Get-Ups 'n Go
What's New at the Zoo?	1925	1966	$130.00	
White Blouse, Fuchsia Jumpsuit	7980	1985	$10.00	B Active Fashions
White, Bright 'n Sparkling	3374	1972	$55.00	Best Buys
White Lace Slip, Camisole, Lace Hose	5871	1988	$10.00	Teen Fun Fashions
White Pants and Blue Printed Blouse	7772	1974	$45.00	Best Buys
White Pants and Red T-Shirt	9124	1976	$36.00	Best Buys
White Top, Orange Shorts, White Shoes	7979	1985	$10.00	B Active Fashions
White Top w/Bow Trim, Printed Short Skirt, Leggings	2626	1989	$10.00	Teen Time Fashion
Winter Warmth	2812	1979	$15.00	Super Fashion Favorites
Wooly P.J.s	Pak	1965	$55.00	
Wooly Winner	1746	1970	$95.00	
Yellow Scarf, Yellow/Blue/Black Dress	2235	1978	$15.00	Best Buys
Yellow Short Sleeved Top w/Parrot Motif, Red Pants	1945	1981	$10.00	Fashion Collectibles
Yellow Short Sundress	2235	1986	$10.00	So Active Fashions
Young Ideas	Pak	1970	$150.00	Sears

Skipper Doll Outfits

Listed by Stock Number

Number	Item	Year	Value	Specials
1249	Sunshine Special Set	1971	$15.00	
1381	Pink Short Sleeved and Black/Pink Full Skirt	1980	$10.00	Fashion Collectibles
1382	Red Overalls, Yellow T-Shirt	1980	$10.00	Fashion Collectibles
1383	Blue Floral Printed Dress w/Dark Blue Jacket	1980	$10.00	Fashion Collectibles
1384	Red Sweater and Blue Jeans	1980	$10.00	Fashion Collectibles
1385	Brown Skirt and Vest, White Lace Trimmed Blouse	1980	$10.00	Fashion Collectibles
1386	Multicolored Striped Jumper, Red Shirt	1980	$10.00	Fashion Collectibles
1408	Sunny Brights	1980	$10.00	Skipper Fashion Favorites
1409	Beach Party	1980	$10.00	Skipper Fashion Favorites
1410	Dotted Bliss	1980	$10.00	Skipper Fashion Favorites
1411	Change-Abouts	1980	$10.00	Skipper Fashion Favorites
1419	Flower Girl	1980	$10.00	Barbie & Ken Wedding Party
1419	Flower Girl Frills for Skipper	1979	$25.00	
1730	Lots of Lace	1970	$75.00	
1731	Budding Beauty	1970	$70.00	
1732	Daisy Crazy	1970	$65.00	
1733	Rik Rak Rah	1970	$70.00	
1735	Twice as Nice	1970	$75.00	
1736	Super Slacks	1970	$60.00	
1737	Velvet Blush	1970	$85.00	
1738	Fancy Pants	1970	$115.00	
1746	Wooly Winner	1970	$95.00	
1747	Pink Princess	1970	$90.00	
1748	Triple Treat	1970	$110.00	
1749	Lemon Fluff	1970	$90.00	
1900	Under-Pretties	1964	$50.00	
1901	Red Sensation	1964	$140.00	
1902	Silk 'n Fancy	1963	$140.00	
1903	Masquerade	1964	$160.00	
1904	Flower Girl	1963	$160.00	
1905	Ballet Lessons (or Class)	1964	$110.00	
1906	Dress Coat	1964	$130.00	
1907	School Days	1964	$150.00	
1908	Skating Fun	1964	$160.00	
1909	Dreamtime	1964	$100.00	
1910	Sunny Pastels	1965	$125.00	
1911	Day at the Fair	1965	$200.00	
1912	Cookie Time	1965	$125.00	
1913	Me 'n My Doll	1965	$275.00	
1914	Platter Party	1965	$125.00	
1915	Outdoor Casuals	1965	$95.00	
1916	Rain or Shine	1965	$95.00	
1917	Land and Sea	1965	$140.00	
1918	Ship Ahoy	1965	$175.00	
1919	Happy Birthday	1965	$525.00	
1920	Funtime	1965	$140.00	
1921	School Girl	1965	$230.00	
1922	Town Togs	1965	$140.00	

Number	Item	Year	Value	Specials
1923	Can You Play?	1966	$155.00	
1924	Tea Party	1966	$275.00	
1925	What's New at the Zoo?	1966	$115.00	
1926	Chill Chasers	1966	$75.00	
1928	Rainy Day Checkers	1966	$325.00	
1929	Dog Show	1966	$325.00	
1930	Loungin' Lovelies	1966	$135.00	
1932	Let's Play House	1966	$270.00	
1933	Country Picnic	1966	$475.00	
1934	Junior Bridesmaid	1966	$480.00	
1935	Learning to Ride	1966	$300.00	
1936	Sledding Fun	1966	$315.00	
1938	Beachy-Peachy	1967	$150.00	
1939	Flower Showers	1967	$140.00	
1940	Rolla-Scoot	1967	$180.00	
1941	All Spruced Up!	1967	$145.00	
1942	Blue/White Halter Dress w/Blue Purse	1981	$10.00	Fashion Collectibles
1942	Right in Style	1967	$180.00	
1943	Blue/White Coat and Blue Belt and Yoke	1981	$10.00	Fashion Collectibles
1943	Popover	1967	$175.00	
1944	'Jamas 'N Jaunties	1967	$140.00	
1944	Pink Lace Trimmed Long Sleeveless Dress	1981	$10.00	Fashion Collectibles
1945	Hearts 'n Flowers	1967	$300.00	
1945	Yellow Short Sleeved Top w/Parrot Motif, Red Pants	1981	$10.00	Fashion Collectibles
1946	Glad Plaids	1967	$150.00	
1947	Lolapaloozas	1967	$150.00	
1948	Velvet 'n Lace	1967	$215.00	
1949	All Prettied Up	1967	$165.00	
1951	Slumber Party	1981	$10.00	Skipper Fashion Favorites
1952	Confetti Cutie	1968	$240.00	
1952	Tennis Everyone	1981	$10.00	Skipper Fashion Favorites
1953	Clan-Tastic	1981	$10.00	Skipper Fashion Favorites
1955	Posey-Party	1968	$170.00	
1956	Skimmy-Stripes	1968	$200.00	
1957	Baby-Dolls	1968	$100.00	
1958	Patent 'n Pants	1968	$130.00	
1959	Warm 'n Wonderful	1968	$160.00	
1960	Trim Twosome	1968	$90.00	
1961	Real Sporty	1968	$145.00	
1962	Perfectly Pretty Set	1968	$125.00	
1962	Quick Changes	1968	$135.00	
1966	Jeepers Creepers	1969	$125.00	
1967	Jazzy Jamys	1969	$100.00	
1968	Hopscotching	1969	$130.00	
1969	Knit Bit	1969	$120.00	
1970	Ice Cream 'n Cake	1969	$165.00	
1971	Pants 'n Pinafore	1969	$110.00	
1972	Drizzle Sizzle	1969	$150.00	
1973	Chilly Chums	1969	$125.00	
1974	Eeny Meeny Midi	1969	$130.00	
1975	Sunny-Suity	1969	$100.00	
1976	School's Cool	1969	$110.00	
1977	Plaid City	1969	$135.00	
2231	Blue Printed Skirt & Halter	1978	$15.00	Best Buys
2232	Long Dress, Solid Yellow & Printed	1978	$15.00	Best Buys

Number	Item	Year	Value	Specials
2233	Blue/Hot Pink Two-Piece Jogging Suit	1986	$10.00	So Active Fashions
2233	Red/Blue Printed Jumpsuit	1978	$15.00	Best Buys
2234	Long Red Printed Dress, White Trim	1978	$15.00	Best Buys
2234	Red Top, Red Plaid Skirt, White Belt	1986	$10.00	So Active Fashions
2235	Yellow Scarf, Yellow/Blue/Black Dress	1978	$15.00	Best Buys
2235	Yellow Short Sundress	1986	$10.00	So Active Fashions
2236	Long Red Gown	1978	$15.00	Best Buys
2236	Striped Pants, White Top, Hot Pink Belt	1986	$10.00	So Active Fashions
2237	Pink Printed Drop Waist Dress w/White Yoke	1986	$10.00	So Active Fashions
2237	Red Printed Top and Blue Skirt	1978	$15.00	Best Buys
2238	Blue/Pink Long Pajamas	1986	$10.00	So Active Fashions
2307	Flower Girl in a Party Whirl	1978	$15.00	Get-Ups 'n Go
2572	Short Blue/White Skirt, Short Striped Top, Ruffle	1989	$10.00	Lookin' Lively Fashion
2579	Denim Jacket and Short Full Skirt	1989	$10.00	Teen Time Fashion
2579	Lavender Top, Ice Cream Motif, Printed Shorts	1989	$10.00	Lookin' Lively Fashion
2591	Blue/White Striped Short Skirt, Cat Motif Top	1989	$10.00	Lookin' Lively Fashion
2592	Floral Printed Short Skirt, Yellow Tank	1989	$10.00	Lookin' Lively Fashion
2593	Purple/Blue/Lavender Short Dress w/Bow Trim	1989	$10.00	Lookin' Lively Fashion
2594	Blue Short Skirt, Blue Polka Dot Long Top w/Bead	1989	$10.00	Lookin' Lively Fashion
2598	Pink/Blue/White/Black Top, Heart Printed Pants	1989	$10.00	Teen Time Fashion
2608	Pink/Silver Short Party Dress, Ribbon, Warmers	1989	$10.00	Teen Time Fashion
2616	Light Blue Lace Trim Dress, Pink Hose and Shoes	1989	$10.00	Teen Time Fashion
2626	White Top w/Bow Trim, Printed Short Skirt, Leggings	1989	$10.00	Teen Time Fashion
2629	Red Jacket, Black/White Skirt, Shirt, Hose	1989	$10.00	Teen Time Fashion
2633	Plaid, Pleated Jumper, Lace Trimmed Shirt, Lace Hose	1989	$10.00	Teen Time Fashion
2640	Pink/White Short Dress	1989	$10.00	Teen Time Fashion
2803	Pink Party Dress	1979	$15.00	Fashion Collectibles
2804	Red Print, Yellow Scarf	1979	$15.00	Fashion Collectibles
2805	Striped Top, Yellow Pants and Cap	1979	$15.00	Fashion Collectibles
2806	Long Dress, Blue/Yellow Print	1979	$15.00	Fashion Collectibles
2807	Red Blouse and Long Red Skirt	1979	$15.00	Fashion Collectibles
2808	Underwear	1979	$15.00	Fashion Collectibles
2809	City Shopping	1979	$15.00	Super Fashion Favorites
2810	Gauzeway to Fashion	1979	$15.00	Super Fashion Favorites
2811	Shorts Subjects	1979	$15.00	Super Fashion Favorites
2812	Winter Warmth	1979	$15.00	Super Fashion Favorites
3106	Purple Lace Long Dress, Hat, Bouquet	1988	$10.00	Romantic Wedding
3291	Nifty Knickers	1972	$85.00	Fashion Originals
3292	Play Pants	1972	$75.00	Fashion Originals
3293	Dream-Ins	1972	$80.00	Fashion Originals
3295	Turn Abouts	1972	$85.00	Fashion Originals
3296	Red, White 'n Blues	1972	$80.00	Fashion Originals
3297	Party Pair	1972	$90.00	Fashion Originals
3371	Super Snoozer	1972	$55.00	Best Buys
3372	Fun Runners	1972	$45.00	Best Buys
3373	Flower Power	1972	$50.00	
3374	White, Bright 'n Sparkling	1972	$55.00	Best Buys
3465	Sweet Orange	1971	$60.00	
3466	Tennis Time	1971	$65.00	
3467	Teeter Timers	1971	$55.00	
3468	Little Miss Midi	1971	$80.00	
3470	Ice Skatin'	1971	$70.00	
3471	Ballerina	1971	$75.00	
3472	Double Dashers	1971	$75.00	
3473	Lullaby Time	1971	$80.00	

Number	Item	Year	Value	Specials
3475	Goin' Sleddin'	1971	$85.00	
3476	All Over Felt	1971	$125.00	
3477	Dressed in Velvet	1971	$125.00	
3478	Long 'n Short of It	1971	$80.00	
3778	Blue Floral Dress w/White Lace Trim	1982	$10.00	Fashion Collectibles
3779	Red/White Striped Top w/White Shorts	1982	$10.00	Fashion Collectibles
3780	Tan Fringed Top, Black Pants	1982	$10.00	Fashion Collectibles
3781	Turquoise Top and Pants w/White Trim	1982	$10.00	Fashion Collectibles
3783	Green Long Halter Dress w/Bolero	1982	$10.00	Fashion Collectibles
3784	Pink Top, Blue Pants	1982	$10.00	Fashion Collectibles
3791	Pink, Lace Bodice Dress, w/Hair Decoration	1990	$5.00	Wedding of the Year
4275	Fun at McDonald's	1983	$10.00	Fashion Fantasy
4534	Printed Top, Blue Pants, Yellow Shoes	1988	$10.00	Bright & Breezy Fashions
4535	Multicolored Striped Long Ruffled Top, Pink Leggings	1988	$10.00	Bright & Breezy Fashions
4538	Purple Long Sleeved Top, White Printed Short Skirt	1988	$10.00	Bright & Breezy Fashions
4539	Striped Short Skirt, Yellow Top, Blue Jacket	1988	$10.00	Bright & Breezy Fashions
4876	Pool Party	1984	$10.00	Fashion Fantasy
4877	School Days	1984	$10.00	Fashion Fantasy
4878	Sweet Dreams	1984	$10.00	Fashion Fantasy
4880	Sightseeing	1984	$10.00	Fashion Fantasy
4881	Short 'n Sweet	1984	$10.00	Fashion Fantasy
4882	First Dance	1984	$10.00	Fashion Fantasy
5746	Flower Girl	1983	$10.00	Wedding of the Year
5810	Smooth Sailing	1983	$10.00	Fashion Fantasy
5811	Barbie Fan	1983	$10.00	Fashion Fantasy
5812	Sleeptime Stripes	1983	$10.00	Fashion Fantasy
5813	Summer Sunshine	1983	$10.00	Fashion Fantasy
5814	Play Days	1983	$10.00	Fashion Fantasy
5815	Love to Ski	1983	$10.00	Fashion Fantasy
5816	Party Perfect	1983	$10.00	Fashion Fantasy
5817	Riding Fun	1983	$10.00	Fashion Fantasy
5849	Pink/Blue/Yellow Top, Blue Leggings	1988	$10.00	Teen Fun Fashions
5857	Balloon Trim Top, Pink/White Skirt, Lace Hose	1988	$10.00	Teen Fun Fashions
5860	Pink Cat Motif Sweater, Denim Short Skirt	1988	$10.00	Teen Fun Fashions
5870	Blue Dress, White Yolk, White Lace Hose	1988	$10.00	Teen Fun Fashions
5871	White Lace Slip, Camisole, Lace Hose	1988	$10.00	Teen Fun Fashions
5874	Pink/White/Blue Top, Leggings, Pink Shorts	1988	$10.00	Teen Fun Fashions
7218	Long Red Printed Dress	1975	$50.00	Best Buys
7220	Pink Sleepers	1975	$40.00	Best Buys
7221	4-Piece Red/Blue Set	1975	$45.00	Best Buys
7222	Striped Overalls and Red Blouse	1975	$45.00	Best Buys
7223	Long Dark Printed Skirt, White Waist	1975	$45.00	Best Buys
7250	School Clothes	1975	$52.00	Get-Ups 'n Go
7251	Olympic Skating	1975	$70.00	Get-Ups 'n Go
7274	Olympic Outfit	1975	$45.00	Best Buys
7713	Sleep Set	1973	$75.00	Get-Ups 'n Go
7714	Ballerina	1973	$45.00	Get-Ups 'n Go
7715	Camping	1973	$50.00	Get-Ups 'n Go
7770	Pepsi Outfit	1974	$45.00	Best Buys
7771	Hawaiian Printed Dress	1974	$45.00	Best Buys
7772	White Pants and Blue Printed Blouse	1974	$45.00	Best Buys
7773	Black Floral Printed Dress	1974	$45.00	Best Buys
7774	Long Red Printed Jumper	1974	$45.00	Best Buys
7775	Long Light Printed Dress	1974	$45.00	Best Buys
7847	Flower Girl	1974	$70.00	Get-Ups 'n Go

Number	Item	Year	Value	Specials
7848	Beach	1974	$50.00	Get-Ups 'n Go
7978	Multicolored Striped Top, Red Shorts & Shoes	1985	$10.00	B Active Fashions
7979	White Top, Orange Shorts, White Shoes	1985	$10.00	B Active Fashions
7980	White Blouse, Fuchsia Jumpsuit	1985	$10.00	B Active Fashions
7981	Multicolored Pastel Top, Blue Short Skirt	1985	$10.00	B Active Fashions
7982	Fuchsia Dress, Blue Vest and Shoes	1985	$10.00	B Active Fashions
7983	Red/White Dress, Red Hat and Shoes	1985	$10.00	B Active Fashions
8610	Long Yellow Dress	1973	$45.00	Best Buys
8611	Short Red/Black/White Dress	1973	$45.00	Best Buys
8612	Pink Sleep Set	1973	$45.00	Best Buys
8613	Red Coat and White Trim	1973	$35.00	Best Buys
8624	Shoes	1973	$40.00	Best Buys
9021	Red, White, & Blue Skirt, Top, Pants, & Halter	1975	$36.00	Growing Up Skipper Fashions
9022	Solid Red Top and Skirt, Floral Printed Halter & Pants	1975	$36.00	Growing Up Skipper Fashions
9023	Bandana Printed Skirt & Dress, White Top	1975	$36.00	Growing Up Skipper Fashions
9024	Tan, Yellow, & Orange Jumper & Skirt, Turtleneck	1975	$36.00	Growing Up Skipper Fashions
9052	Music Motif Top, Checked Skirt, Shawl, Socks	1990	$5.00	Cool Tops Fashions
9059	Flower Motif Top, Gold Skirt, White Leggings	1990	$5.00	Cool Tops Fashions
9060	Skate Motif Top, Blue Skirt, Jacket, White Socks	1990	$5.00	Cool Tops Fashions
9080	Pink Face Motif Top, Ruffled Skirt, Pink Socks	1990	$5.00	Cool Tops Fashions
9088	Pink Face Motif Top, Ruffled Skirt, Pink Socks	1990	$5.00	Cool Tops Fashions
9121	Red Plaid Coat and Cap	1976	$38.00	Best Buys
9122	Red Plaid Skirt, Blouse, Vest	1976	$38.00	Best Buys
9123	Long Blue/White Dress	1976	$38.00	Best Buys
9124	White Pants and Red T-Shirt	1976	$36.00	Best Buys
9125	Long Green/Pink Printed Dress	1976	$36.00	Best Buys
9126	Red/White Long Skirt, White Top	1976	$70.00	Best Buys
9165	Bicentennial Fashions	1976	$70.00	Get-Ups 'n Go
9166	Weekend Wardrobe	1976	$32.00	Get-Ups 'n Go
9512	Pink, Blue, & Yellow Skirt and Blouse	1976	$36.00	Growing Up Skipper Fashion
9513	Orange, Green, and Yellow Skirt, Pants, & Top	1976	$36.00	Growing Up Skipper Fashion
9706	Faded Skirt & Shorts, Sunburst Top	1977	$15.00	Best Buys
9707	Long Red Print, Head Scarf	1977	$15.00	Best Buys
9708	Green/Blue/Purple Dress, Blue Cap	1977	$15.00	Best Buys
9709	Long Green Bottom, White Overblouse	1977	$35.00	Best Buys
9710	Brown Striped Skirt, Blue/White Top	1977	$15.00	Best Buys
9711	Long Pink Dress	1977	$25.00	Best Buys
9746	Lacey Charmer & Partytimer	1977	$15.00	Get-Ups 'n Go
9747	Red Set for When It's Wet	1977	$15.00	Get-Ups 'n Go
9748	For Schooltime, Playtime, Anytime	1977	$15.00	Get-Ups 'n Go
12617	Red Hat, Blue Jeans, Red/White Shirt	1995	$8.00	High School Fun Skipper
12618	Printed Dress, White Lace Hose, Tea Set	1995	$10.00	High School Fun Skipper
12619	Pink Top, Printed Shirt & Hat, Pink Knickers	1995	$8.00	High School Fun Skipper
12620	Blue/Pink Cheerleader Outfit/Pom Pons	1995	$8.00	High School Fun Skipper
14381	Short Denim Jumper and Vest, Top, Backpack	1996	$4.00	Skipper Fashions
14381	Three-Piece Short Jumper, Vest & Backpack	1996	$5.00	
14382	Purple Velvet Dress, Matching Purse	1996	$5.00	
14382	Purple Velvet Dress, Purse, Lace Shirt, Hose	1996	$4.00	Skipper Fashions
14382	Three-Piece School w/Red Plaid Skirt, Jacket	1996	$4.00	
14383	Red Plaid Skirt, White Top, Black Jacket	1996	$5.00	
14384	Pink Waffle Dress, Floral Printed Leggings	1996	$5.00	
14384	Two-Piece Sleep Outfit, Pink w/Printed Leggings	1996	$4.00	
24300	Sporting Stripes	1999	$5.00	Fashion Avenue
26987	Aloha Lime	2000	$5.00	Fashion Avenue
26990	Beach Boardwalk	2000	$5.00	Fashion Avenue

Miscellaneous Doll Outfits

Listed Alphabetically

Item	Number	Year	Value	Doll	Specials
8-Piece Julia Set	1595	1969	$185.00	Julia	
Ballet, Black Leotard w/Pink Bow, Pink Tutu	14380	1996	$4.00	Stacie	Stacie Fashions
Beach	14394	1996	$3.00	Kelly	
Beach, One-Piece Yellow Swimsuit, Sundress	14389	1996	$4.00	Stacie	Stacie Fashions
Birthday Beauties	3617	1968	$160.00	Tutti	
Black/White Top, Pants, Skirt, Hat, Belt, Shoes	3775	1989	$10.00	Jazzie	Teen Scene Fashions
Black/White/Pink Top, Skirt, Belt, Pants, Shoes	3776	1989	$10.00	Jazzie	Teen Scene Fashions
Blue Hat, Blue/White Pants, Skirt & Shirt	12612	1995	$5.00	Stacie	Party Favorites Stacie
Blue Printed Sundress, Pink Sandals	68230	2000	$2.00	Kelly	Fashion Favorites
Blue Seashell Printed Shorts, Yellow Top, Sandals	68230	1999	$2.00	Kelly	Fashion Favorites
Blue/Green Skirt, Top, Pants, Belt, Tennis Shoes	3777	1989	$10.00	Jazzie	Teen Scene Fashions
Blue/White Striped Skirt, Red Printed Top, Sandals	68230	1999	$2.00	Kelly	Fashion Favorites
Brrr-Furrr	1752	1969	$175.00	Julia	
Candlelight Capers	1753	1969	$200.00	Julia	
Chris Set	3609	1967	$175.00	Chris	
Clowning Around	3606	1967	$190.00	Tutti	
Come to My Party	3607	1967	$100.00	Tutti	
Costume Contest	24310	1999	$5.00	Kelly	Fashion Avenue
Fashion 'n Motion	1508	1971	$15.00	P.J.	
Flower Girl	3615	1966	$290.00	Tutti	
Flower Maker	24307	2000	$5.00	Kelly	Fashion Avenue
Jewel & Glitter Fashions	12183	1994	$5.00	Christie	Jewel & Glitter
Jewel & Glitter Fashions	12183	1994	$5.00	Teresa	Jewel & Glitter
Leather Weather	1751	1969	$175.00	Julia	
Let's Explore	1506	1966	$130.00	Ricky	
Let's Play Barbie	3608	1967	$300.00	Tutti	
Lights Out	1501	1965	$95.00	Ricky	
Little League	1504	1965	$90.00	Ricky	
Mini Dress, Black/White Striped Top, Blue Skirt	3781	1989	$10.00	Jazzie	Totally Cool Fashions
Mini Dress, Yellow/Black Printed Top, Black Skirt	3783	1989	$10.00	Jazzie	Totally Cool Fashions
Nautical	14393	1996	$3.00	Kelly	
Nursery School	14392	1996	$3.00	Kelly	
Orange Blossom	987	1962	$75.00	Midge	
Party	14396	1996	$3.00	Kelly	
Party, One-Piece Glittery Floral Dress	14390	1996	$4.00	Stacie	Stacie Fashions
Pink Fantasy	1754	1969	$175.00	Julia	
Pink Lace Bodice Dress w/Hair Decoration	3970	1990	$10.00	Kira	Wedding of the Year
Pink P.J.'s	3616	1969	$125.00	Tutti	
Pink Top, Black/White Striped Shorts w/Suspenders	3784	1989	$10.00	Jazzie	Totally Cool Fashions
Pink/Black/White Top, Skirt, Pants, Hat, Belt	3774	1989	$10.00	Jazzie	Teen Scene Fashions
Pink/Blue Dress and Knickers	10749	1995	$5.00	Stacie	Party Favorites Stacie
Pink/Blue Jacket, Pants, Top, Belt, Tennis Shoes	3778	1989	$10.00	Jazzie	Teen Scene Fashions
Pink/Blue/Yellow Dress	12613	1995	$5.00	Stacie	Party Favorites Stacie
Pink/White Skirt and Blouse, Pink Sandals	68230	1999	$2.00	Kelly	Fashion Favorites
Pink/White Top and Pants w/Black Trim	3786	1989	$10.00	Jazzie	Totally Cool Fashions
Plantin' Posies	3609	1967	$125.00	Tutti	
Puddle Jumpers	3601	1966	$70.00	Tutti	
Purple/White Skirt, Lollipop Printed Top, Shoes	68230	1999	$2.00	Kelly	Fashion Favorites

Item	Number	Year	Value	Doll	Specials
Purple Short Jumper, Top	3785	1989	$10.00	Jazzie	Totally Cool Fashions
Red/White Striped Top, Blue Dot Pants	3780	1989	$10.00	Jazzie	Totally Cool Fashions
Sand Castles	3603	1966	$120.00	Tutti	
Saturday Show	1502	1965	$90.00	Ricky	
School, White Jacket and Satchel, Dress	14388	1996	$4.00	Stacie	Stacie Fashions
Sea-Shore Shorties	3614	1968	$140.00	Tutti	
Ship-Shape	3602	1966	$85.00	Tutti	
Skateboard Set	1505	1966	$110.00	Ricky	
Skippin' Rope	3604	1974	$80.00	Tutti	
Stripes Are Happening	1544	1968	$75.00	Stacey	
Sunday Suit	1503	1965	$95.00	Ricky	
Top, Skirt, Pants, Belt, Tennis Shoes, Green/Black	3773	1989	$10.00	Jazzie	Teen Scene Fashions
Twiggy Gear	1728	1968	$240.00	Twiggy	
Twiggy Turnouts	1726	1968	$250.00	Twiggy	
Twiggy-Dos	1725	1968	$250.00	Twiggy	
Twigster	1727	1968	$260.00	Twiggy	
Twist	1585	1970	$15.00	P.J.	
Yellow Jumper, Printed Jacket and Hat	12614	1995	$5.00	Stacie	Party Favorites Stacie

Miscellaneous Doll Outfits

Listed by Doll

Doll	Item	Number	Year	Value	Specials
Chris	Chris Set	3609	1967	$175.00	
Christie	Jewel & Glitter Fashions	12183	1994	$5.00	Jewel & Glitter
Jazzie	Black/White Top, Pants, Skirt, Hat, Belt, Shoes	3775	1989	$10.00	Teen Scene Fashions
Jazzie	Black/White/Pink Top, Skirt, Belt, Pants, Shoes	3776	1989	$10.00	Teen Scene Fashions
Jazzie	Blue/Green Skirt, Top, Pants, Belt, Tennis Shoes	3777	1989	$10.00	Teen Scene Fashions
Jazzie	Mini Dress, Black/White Striped Top, Blue Skirt	3781	1989	$10.00	Totally Cool Fashions
Jazzie	Mini Dress, Yellow/Black Printed Top, Black Skirt	3783	1989	$10.00	Totally Cool Fashions
Jazzie	Pink Top, Black/White Striped Shorts, Suspenders	3784	1989	$10.00	Totally Cool Fashions
Jazzie	Pink/Black/White Top, Skirt, Pants, Hat, Belt	3774	1989	$10.00	Teen Scene Fashions
Jazzie	Pink/Blue Jacket, Pants, Top, Belt, Tennis Shoes	3778	1989	$10.00	Teen Scene Fashions
Jazzie	Pink/White Top and Pants w/Black Trim	3786	1989	$10.00	Totally Cool Fashions
Jazzie	Purple Short Jumper, Top	3785	1989	$10.00	Totally Cool Fashions
Jazzie	Red/White Striped Top, Blue Dot Pants	3780	1989	$10.00	Totally Cool Fashions
Jazzie	Top, Skirt, Pants, Belt, Tennis Shoes, Green/Black	3773	1989	$10.00	Teen Scene Fashions
Julia	8-Piece Julia Set	1595	1969	$185.00	
Julia	Brrr-Furrr	1752	1969	$175.00	
Julia	Candlelight Capers	1753	1969	$200.00	
Julia	Leather Weather	1751	1969	$175.00	
Julia	Pink Fantasy	1754	1969	$175.00	
Kelly	Beach	14394	1996	$3.00	
Kelly	Nautical	14393	1996	$3.00	
Kelly	Nursery School	14392	1996	$3.00	
Kelly	Party	14396	1996	$3.00	
Kelly	Blue/White Striped Skirt, Red Printed Top, Sandals	68230	1999	$2.00	Fashion Favorites
Kelly	Blue Print Sundress, Pink Sandals	68230	2000	$2.00	Fashion Favorites
Kelly	Blue Seashell Print Shorts, Yellow Top, Sandals	68230	1999	$2.00	Fashion Favorites
Kelly	Costume Contest	24310	1999	$5.00	Fashion Avenue
Kelly	Flower Maker	24307	2000	$5.00	Fashion Avenue
Kelly	Pink/White Skirt and Blouse, Pink Sandals	68230	1999	$2.00	Fashion Favorites
Kelly	Purple/White Skirt, Lollipop Printed Top, Shoes	68230	1999	$2.00	Fashion Favorites
Kira	Pink Lace Bodice Dress w/Hair Decoration	3970	1990	$10.00	Wedding of the Year
Midge	Orange Blossom	987	1962	$75.00	
P.J.	Fashion 'n Motion	1508	1971	$15.00	
P.J.	Twist	1585	1970	$15.00	
Ricky	Let's Explore	1506	1966	$130.00	
Ricky	Lights Out	1501	1965	$95.00	
Ricky	Little League	1504	1965	$90.00	
Ricky	Saturday Show	1502	1965	$90.00	
Ricky	Skateboard Set	1505	1966	$110.00	
Ricky	Sunday Suit	1503	1965	$95.00	
Stacey	Stripes Are Happening	1544	1968	$75.00	
Stacie	Ballet, Black Leotard w/Pink Bow, Pink Tutu	14380	1996	$4.00	Stacie Fashions
Stacie	Beach, One-Piece Yellow Swimsuit, Sundress	14389	1996	$4.00	Stacie Fashions
Stacie	Blue Hat, Blue/White Pants, Skirt & Shirt	12612	1995	$5.00	Party Favorites Stacie
Stacie	Party, One-Piece Glittery Floral Dress	14390	1996	$4.00	Stacie Fashions
Stacie	Pink/Blue Dress and Knickers	10749	1995	$5.00	Party Favorites Stacie
Stacie	Pink/Blue/Yellow Dress	12613	1995	$5.00	Party Favorites Stacie
Stacie	School, White Jacket and Satchel, Dress	14388	1996	$4.00	Stacie Fashions

Doll	Item	Number	Year	Value	Specials
Stacie	Yellow Jumper, Printed Jacket and Hat	12614	1995	$5.00	Party Favorites Stacie
Teresa	Jewel & Glitter Fashions	12183	1994	$5.00	Jewel & Glitter
Tutti	Birthday Beauties	3617	1968	$160.00	
Tutti	Clowning Around	3606	1967	$190.00	
Tutti	Come to My Party	3607	1967	$100.00	
Tutti	Flower Girl	3615	1966	$290.00	
Tutti	Let's Play Barbie	3608	1967	$300.00	
Tutti	Pink P.J.'s	3616	1969	$125.00	
Tutti	Plantin' Posies	3609	1967	$125.00	
Tutti	Puddle Jumpers	3601	1966	$70.00	
Tutti	Sand Castles	3603	1966	$120.00	
Tutti	Sea-Shore Shorties	3614	1968	$140.00	
Tutti	Ship-Shape	3602	1966	$85.00	
Tutti	Skippin' Rope	3604	1974	$80.00	
Twiggy	Twiggy Gear	1728	1968	$240.00	
Twiggy	Twiggy Turnouts	1726	1968	$250.00	
Twiggy	Twiggy-Dos	1725	1968	$250.00	
Twiggy	Twigster	1727	1968	$260.00	

Accessories

Item	Year	Number	Value	Specials
10 oz. Water Bottle	1997	BD411B	$5.00	
At The Beach	1994	11730	$5.00	Paint 'n Dazzle
Baby-Sits	1974	7882	$25.00	
Baby-Sits	1976	7882	$25.00	
Barbie & Ken Hangers	1962	None	$80.00	
Barbie Bell	1995	BD540	$6.00	
Barbie Bicycle Accessory Kit	1995	BD935	$20.00	
Barbie Bicycle Basket	1995	BD519	$12.00	
Barbie Bicycle Handlebar Bag	1995	BD903	$10.00	
Barbie Chain Lock with Ring	1995	BD472	$10.00	
Barbie Cycling Gloves	1995	BD861	$10.00	
Barbie Glitter Pom Pon Streamers	1995	BD907	$10.00	
Barbie Key Clip	1995	BD438	$3.00	
Barbie Logo Plate	1995	BD487	$4.00	
Barbie Pad Set	1995	BD666	$10.00	
Barbie Seat Cover	1995	BD777	$10.00	
Barbie Spoke Covers	1995	BD902	$3.00	
Barbie Streamers	1995	BD437	$10.00	
Barbie Toddler Helmet (ages 1 – 4)	1995	BD956	$20.00	
Barbie Training Wheels	1995	BD224	$20.00	
Barbie Value Pack (includes BD777, BD666, and BD444)	1995	BD935	$20.00	
Barbie Water Bottle with Cage	1995	BD441	$8.00	
Beach Scene	1980	2319	$15.00	Play Paks
Blender	1987	1997	$5.00	Action Accents
Camp Barbie 20 oz. Water Bottle	1995	BD443	$5.00	
Camp Barbie Bicycle Canteen	1995	BD444	$12.00	
Camp Barbie Helmet (ages 4 – 14)	1995	BD958	$20.00	
Camp Barbie Value Pack	1995	BD937	$20.00	
Campin' Out	1980	2318	$40.00	Play Paks
Camping-Out Tent	1972	4288	$35.00	
Clip Hanger Pack	2000	68715	$2.00	Little Extras
Color 'n Curl Set	1965	4035	$150.00	
Color 'n Curl Set	1965	4038	$150.00	
Color 'n Curl Set	1966	4039	$150.00	
Color Magic Fashion Fun	1966	4041	$325.00	
Computer	1987	1981	$10.00	Action Accents
Dining Room	1996	67551-91	$18.00	
Dinner Party	1997	10819	$15.00	Tootsie Toy
Dough Dessert Maker	1994	11105	$40.00	
Fashion Decorator Pack	1994	10381	$18.00	
Fashion Decorator Refill Pack	1994	10970	$5.00	
Foam Refill for Seahorse	1995	13171	$2.00	
French-Style Telephone	1987	1980	$10.00	Action Accents
Fun Activities	2000	28870	$5.00	Fashion Avenue
Garden Patio with Real Growin' Plants	1972	4284	$30.00	
Get-Away	1980	2317	$15.00	Play Paks
Glamorous Shopping	1994	11731	$5.00	Paint 'n Dazzle
Glitter Barbie Helmet (ages 4 – 14)	1995	BD957	$20.00	

Item	Year	Number	Value	Specials
Glitter Gel Refill Pack	1994	11304	$5.00	
Golden Dream Barbie Fashion Face	1981	3274	$15.00	
Golden Dream Christie Fashion Face	1981	3306	$15.00	
Hair Blower	1995	12010	$15.00	
Hair Flair	1967	4042	$125.00	
Hair Flair	1969	4043	$125.00	
Hair Flair	1971	4044	$125.00	
Happy Face Boxers, T-Shirt, White Sandals	1999	68089	$2.00	Dreamy Touches Fashions
Horseback Ridin'	1983	4090	$15.00	Play Paks
Ice Cream Fun	1989	5323	$30.00	
Live Concert Instruments	1987	3611	$20.00	Barbie & the Rockers
Magic Moves CD Player	1994	67020	$2.00	
Magic Moves Dust Cleaner	1994	67020	$2.00	
Magic Moves Food Processor	1994	67020	$2.00	
Magic Moves Gumball Machine	1994	67020	$2.00	
Magic Moves Popcorn Maker	1994	67020	$2.00	
Magic Moves Toaster	1994	67020	$2.00	
Magic Plastic Molding Machine	1994	11813	$25.00	
Magic Plastic Molding Machine Repl. Pak	1994	12146	$5.00	
Outdoor Fun	1994	11732	$5.00	Paint 'n Dazzle
Paint 'n Dazzle Refill Kit	1994	11467	$26.00	
Patio	1980	2316	$15.00	Play Paks
Picnic Set	1984	5757	$15.00	Play Paks
Pink Flowered Lingerie	1999	68089	$2.00	Dreamy Touches Fashions
Pose Me Pretty Barbie Beauty Set	1984	7160	$4.00	
Radio/Tape Deck	1987	1996	$4.00	Action Accents
Romantic Glamour	1994	11729	$5.00	Paint 'n Dazzle
Sewing Machine	1987	1983	$5.00	Action Accents
Shoe Pack (Skipper, Kelly & Stacie)	2000	68715	$2.00	Little Extras
Shoe Packs	2000	68715	$2.00	Little Extras
Slumber Party Set	1985	9248	$10.00	Play Paks
Stereo & Speakers	1987	1993	$3.00	Action Accents
Straight Hanger Pack	2000	68715	$2.00	Little Extras
SuperStar Fashion Face (Barbie)	1980	9827	$15.00	
SuperStar Fashion Face (Christie)	1980	9952	$15.00	
Teen Time Skipper Sleep 'n Play Set	1989	1921	$10.00	
Treasure Fashion Accessories (basic)	1995	13762	$26.00	
Treasure Fashion Accessories (deluxe)	1995	13762	$26.00	
Water Sports	1981	3273	$10.00	Play Paks
Wedding	1984	4936	$15.00	Play Paks
Western Round Up	1981	5018	$9.00	Play Paks
White Felt Hat, White Fur Purse, Lace Tights	1999	68089	$2.00	Dreamy Touches Fashions

Adult Accessories

Item	Year	Number	Value	Specials
Backpack (large)	1994	none	$160.00	Nicole Miller
Checkbook Holder	1994	none	$40.00	Nicole Miller
Coin Purse with Keychain	1996	702191	$4.00	FAO Schwarz
Double-Mirrored Compact (Crystal Collection)	1996	738310	$200.00	FAO Schwarz
Drawstring Totes	1995	none	$125.00	Nicole Miller
Duffel Bag	1994	none	$120.00	Nicole Miller
Enchanted Evening Compact (decoupage)	1996	778852	$40.00	FAO Schwarz
Enchanted Evening Mini Purse (decoupage)	1996	778860	$200.00	FAO Schwarz
Evening Purse (Crystal Collection)	1996	790097	$1,875.00	FAO Schwarz
Eyeglass Case	1994	none	$30.00	Nicole Miller
Fanny Pack	1994	none	$60.00	Nicole Miller
Fanny Pack	1996	781526	$45.00	Nicole Miller
Hand Mirror (decoupage)	1993	164897	$90.00	Barbie at FAO
Handbag	1996	689760	$24.00	FAO Schwarz
Large Zippered Tote Bag	1994	none	$170.00	Nicole Miller
Lipstick Case (Crystal Collection)	1996	738336	$295.00	FAO Schwarz
Mega Scarf	1994	none	$70.00	Nicole Miller
Mini Purse (decoupage)	1993	164889	$200.00	Barbie at FAO
Necktie	1994	none	$50.00	Nicole Miller
Organizer/Eyeglasses Bag	1996	781518	$56.00	Nicole Miller
Overnight Duffel Bag	1996	781500	$85.00	Nicole Miller
Shoulder Strap Bag (large)	1994	none	$90.00	Nicole Miller
Shoulder Strap Bag (small)	1994	none	$80.00	Nicole Miller
Square Zippered Cosmetic Case	1994	none	$30.00	Nicole Miller
Tassel Purse	1995	none	$90.00	Nicole Miller
Travel Cosmetic Case	1996	781492	$38.00	Nicole Miller
Zippered Coin Purse	1994	none	$30.00	Nicole Miller
Zippered Cosmetic Pouch	1994	none	$35.00	Nicole Miller

Adult Clothing

Item	Year	Number	Value	Specials
Baseball Caps (denim)	1996	768036	$20.00	
Baseball Caps (pink)	1996	768044	$20.00	
Baseball Caps (white)	1996	781088	$20.00	
Blouse, Women's Short Sleeved	1994	none	$140.00	Nicole Miller
Bomber Jacket, Water Resistant	1994	none	$250.00	Nicole Miller
Boxer Shorts	1995	none	$50.00	Nicole Miller
Denim Jacket (with embroidered heart)	1996	788505	$75.00	
Embroidered Denim Shirt	1996	781450	$44.00	

Item	Year	Number	Value	Specials
Leather Biker Jacket (handmade)	1996	780841	$995.00	FAO Schwarz
Leather Jackets	1995	none	$1,100.00	JH Designs
Long Bathrobe	1994	none	$270.00	Nicole Miller
Long Pajamas	1994	none	$270.00	Nicole Miller
Nightshirt	1994	none	$130.00	Nicole Miller
P.J.'s (adult)	1995	none	$270.00	Nicole Miller
Shirt (men's short sleeved)	1995	none	$170.00	Nicole Miller
Silk Scarf (43" x 43")	1996	781476	$75.00	Nicole Miller
Silk Tie	1996	781468	$56.00	Nicole Miller
Sleep Shirt (adult)	1995	none	$130.00	Nicole Miller
Spaghetti Strap Chemise	1995	none	$100.00	Nicole Miller
Tank Top (adult)	1995	none	$50.00	Nicole Miller
Tony Alamo Coat (men's)	1995	none	$1,100.00	
Vest, Women's	1994	none	$100.00	Nicole Miller

Barbie® Bazaar Magazine

Year	Months	Value
1988	Premier Edition	$50.00
1988	September	$110.00
1988	October	$55.00
1988	November	$110.00
1988	December	$70.00
1989	January/February	$75.00
1989	March/April	$35.00
1989	May/June	$35.00
1989	July/August	$45.00
1989	September/October	$45.00
1989	November/December	$45.00
1990	January/February	$30.00
1990	March/April	$25.00
1990	May/June	$25.00
1990	July/August	$25.00
1990	September/October	$25.00
1990	November/December	$25.00
1991	January/February	$20.00
1991	March/April	$20.00
1991	May/June	$20.00
1991	July/August	$20.00
1991	September/October	$20.00
1991	November/December	$20.00
1992	January/February	$15.00
1992	March/April	$15.00
1992	May/June	$15.00
1992	July/August	$15.00
1992	September/October	$15.00
1992	November/December	$15.00

Year	Months	Value
1993	January/February	$15.00
1993	March/April	$15.00
1993	May/June	$15.00
1993	July/August	$20.00
1993	September/October	$20.00
1993	November/December	$20.00
1994	January/February	$20.00
1994	March/April	$20.00
1994	May/June	$20.00
1994	July/August	$20.00
1994	September/October	$20.00
1994	November/December	$20.00
1995	January/February	$20.00
1995	March/April	$20.00
1995	May/June	$10.00
1995	July/August	$10.00
1995	September/October	$10.00
1995	November/December	$10.00
1996	January/February	$8.00
1996	March/April	$8.00
1996	May/June	$8.00
1996	July/August	$8.00
1996	September/October	$8.00
1996	November/December	$8.00
1997	January/February	$8.00
1997	March/April	$8.00
1997	May/June	$8.00
1997	September/October	$8.00
1998	April	$5.00
1998	August	$5.00
1998	December	$5.00
1998	February	$5.00
1998	June	$5.00
1998	October	$5.00
1999	February	$5.00
1999	April	$5.00
1999	June	$5.00
1999	August	$5.00
1999	October	$5.00
1999	December	$5.00
2000	February	$5.00
2000	April	$5.00
2000	June	$5.00
2000	August	$5.00
2000	October	$5.00
2000	December	$5.00

Barbie® Doll Reading Books

Item	Year	Number	Value	Specials
A Fairy Princess Barbie Book	1977	N/A	$5.00	Golden Books
Animal Escapades	1993	N/A	$3.00	Price-Stern-Sloan
Ballet Debut	1993	N/A	$3.00	Price-Stern-Sloan
Ballerina Dance	1996	12822	$2.00	
Barbie	1974	N/A	$10.00	Little Golden Book
Barbie — A Picnic Surprise	1990	N/A	$10.00	Little Golden Book
Barbie — A Picnic Surprise (book and tape)	1990	N/A	$10.00	Golden Books
Barbie American Airlines	1974	N/A	$8.00	Golden Books
Barbie and Ken	1963	N/A	$12.00	
Barbie and Ken Pink Book	1961	N/A	$3.00	
Barbie and P.J. — A Camping Adventure	1973	N/A	$5.00	
Barbie and Skipper Go Camping	1973	N/A	$15.00	Whitman
Barbie and the Ghost Town Mystery	1965	N/A	$35.00	Random House
Barbie and The Rockers (Hottest Group in Town)	1987	N/A	$11.00	Golden Books
Barbie and The Rockers — The Fan	1987	N/A	$10.00	Golden Books
Barbie and the Scavenger Hunt	1996	98767	$2.00	
Barbie Goes to a Party	1964	N/A	$31.00	Wonder Books
Barbie in Dream Vacation	1984	N/A	$20.00	Hasbro
Barbie in Fashion	1995	N/A	$11.00	Tiny Folio
Barbie in Television	1964	N/A	$35.00	Random House
Barbie in the City	1983	N/A	$10.00	Kid Stuff
Barbie Magazine	1962	N/A	$45.00	
Barbie Magazine	1965	N/A	$25.00	
Barbie, Midge, and Ken	1964	534	$35.00	Random House
Barbie on Skates	1992	N/A	$8.00	Golden Books
Barbie Show Time	1992	N/A	$5.00	Golden Books
Barbie Soccer Coach	1995	N/A	$3.00	Little Golden Book
Barbie Solves a Mystery	1963	N/A	$35.00	Random House
Barbie — The Big Splash (2nd issue)	1992	N/A	$6.00	Little Golden Book
Barbie — The Island Resort Adventure	1992	N/A	$12.00	Golden Sound Story
Barbie (The Magazine for Girls) 1 – 47	N/A	02559	$3.00 each	
Barbie's Adventures at Camp	1964	N/A	$35.00	Random House
Barbie's Adventures to Read Aloud	1964	N/A	$25.00	Wonder Books
Barbie's Camping Adventure	1983	N/A	$10.00	Kid Stuff
Barbie's Christmas Party	1983	N/A	$10.00	Kid Stuff
Barbie's Fashion Success	1962	N/A	$35.00	Random House
Barbie's Neighborhood	1983	N/A	$5.00	Kid Stuff
Barbie's New York Summer	1963	N/A	$35.00	Random House
Barbie's Secret	1964	N/A	$35.00	Random House
Best Friends	1996	12939	$2.00	
Birthday Surprise for Skipper (sound)	1995	60908	$12.00	Golden Sound Story
Candy Striped Summer	1965	N/A	$35.00	Random House
Comic	1991	N/A	$10.00	Marvel
Comic Books 1 – 16	N/A	N/A	$3.00 each	
Dancing the Night Away	1993	N/A	$3.00	Price-Stern-Sloan
Dear Barbie Book Set	1997	296-508	$10.00	
Easy as Pie Cookbook	1964	N/A	$150.00	
Fashion Magazine 1 – 52	N/A	01580	$3.00 each	

Item	Year	Number	Value	Specials
Freckles	1997	10049	$3.00	
Glitter Fashion Fun	1993	2200-1	$3.00	Golden Books
Happy Go Lucky Skipper	1965	N/A	$35.00	Random House
Hawaiian Holiday	1963	N/A	$35.00	Random House
Here's Barbie	1962	534	$35.00	Random House
Hi, My Name Is Barbie	1994	10363	$5.00	Golden Books
Holiday Magic	1993	N/A	$3.00	Price-Stern-Sloan
International Collection (pamphlet)	N/A	N/A	$3.00	
Lace and Dress Dancing Doll	1975	930	$8.00	
Mermaid Island	1993	N/A	$3.00	Price-Stern-Sloan
My Very Own Diary by Barbie	1985	11752	$10.00	Golden Books
Portrait of Skipper	1964	N/A	$15.00	Wonder Books
Riding Champion	1996	12823	$2.00	
Skipper, Skooter, Ricky	1965	N/A	$10.00	
Smithsonian	Dec. 1989	N/A	$25.00	
Soda Shop Surprise	1993	N/A	$3.00	Price-Stern-Sloan
Star-Swept Adventure	1993	N/A	$3.00	Price-Stern-Sloan
Stories About the Fabulous Barbie	N/A	N/A	$35.00	
Story Diary	N/A	N/A	$5.00	
Target's 30th Anniversary Barbie Keepsake	1989	N/A	$20.00	Target
The Baby Sitter	1964	N/A	$5.00	Wonder Books
The Barbie Party Cookbook	1990	N/A	$15.00	Price-Stern-Sloan
The Big Splash (book and tape)	1992	107-94	$8.00	Golden Books
The Fairy Princess (SuperStar Barbie)	1977	111-38	$12.00	Little Golden Book
The Missing Wedding Dress	1986	107-63	$11.00	Little Golden Book
The Mysterious Dude of Ghost Ranch	1993	N/A	$3.00	Price-Stern-Sloan
The Phantom of Shrieking Pond	1993	N/A	$3.00	Price-Stern-Sloan
The World of Barbie	1962	533	$35.00	Random House
The World of Barbie Magazine	1964	9904	$30.00	
Very Busy Barbie	1993	N/A	$5.00	Little Golden Book
Who's the Boss	1997	12940	$3.00	
Wild Horse Run	1993	N/A	$3.00	Price-Stern-Sloan
Wildlife Rescue	1993	N/A	$3.00	Price-Stern-Sloan

Cases

Item	Year	Number	Value	Specials
Ballet Box	1969	5023	$20.00	
Barbie and Francie Case	N/A	3003	$15.00	
Barbie and Francie Dressing Room Case	1967	1024	$110.00	
Barbie and Francie Hat Box	N/A	5020	$20.00	
Barbie and Francie Overnighter	N/A	5022	$15.00	
Barbie and Francie Train Case	N/A	5021	$40.00	
Barbie and Ken Costume Trunk	N/A	5070	$175.00	
Barbie and Ken Trunk (orange blossom)	1964	N/A	$20.00	
Barbie Dnd Ken Trunk (tuxedo)	1964	N/A	N/A	
Barbie and Midge Case (blue)	1963	N/A	$25.00	

Item	Year	Number	Value	Specials
Barbie and Midge Case (lunch date)	1963	N/A	$20.00	
Barbie and Midge Trunk (red)	1964	9330	$35.00	Sears
Barbie and Skipper Case	1965	N/A	N/A	
Barbie and Skipper Closet Carrier Playcase	1988	7222	N/A	
Barbie at FAO Take Along	1996	781096	$35.00	FAO Schwarz
Barbie or Midge Carrying Case Black	1963	4418	$20.00	Montgomery Ward
Barbie and Midge Case (pink, 18"x4"x14")	1963	9330	$30.00	Sears
Beach Party Case	1979	N/A	$100.00	Department Store
Blue Trousseau Trunk	N/A	N/A	$150.00	
Carry-All	1972	4297	$12.00	
Case	N/A	390	N/A	
Case (beige)	N/A	N/A	$8.00	
Case, Blue, Barbie	1962	N/A	$20.00	
Double Fashion Doll Case	1986	2811	$20.00	
Easter Parade Case	1961	N/A	$15.00	
Enchanted Evening Case (red, blue, black)	1963	N/A	$20.00	
Fashion Doll Trunk	1980	1004	N/A	
Fashion Queen Barbie Carrying Case	N/A	N/A	$75.00	
Four-Doll Case, Black	1961	N/A	$20.00	
Four-Doll Trunk, Wedding Party	1965	N/A	$40.00	
Francie & Casey Case	N/A	1027	N/A	
Francie & Casey Double Case	N/A	1025	N/A	
Francie Case	N/A	1023	$25.00	
Francie Case	N/A	3002	$25.00	
Francie in Mod Clothes Case (white)	N/A	N/A	$95.00	
Goes Travelin' Blue Carrying Case	1965	N/A	$300.00	
Goes Travelin' Pink Carrying Case	1965	N/A	$300.00	
Goes Travelin' Yellow Carrying Case	1965	N/A	$300.00	
Green and White Diamond Case	1964	479	$1,800.00	
Hat Box	1962	4402	N/A	Montgomery Ward
House Mate Case	1965	N/A	$50.00	
Jamie Party Penthouse Case	1970	N/A	$65.00	Sears
Jamie's Room Case	1971	31121	$35.00	Sears
Ken Case (campus hero)	1964	N/A	$20.00	Ken
Ken Case (rally day)	1963	N/A	N/A	Ken
Ken Case Aqua (11"x4"x13")	1963	9328	$12.00	Sears
Large Barbie Doll Case	1962	N/A	$15.00	
Lavender Ken Case	1961	N/A	$15.00	Ken
Loving Care Play Case	1988	4927	$20.00	
Midge Case (movie date)	1964	N/A	$35.00	
Midge Case (red)	1964	9381	$35.00	Sears
Miss Barbie Black Patent Leather Case	1963	N/A	$165.00	
Miss Barbie Carrying Case	1963	Case	$75.00	
My First Barbie Dance and Dress Case	1989	2071	N/A	
One Doll Room Case	1971	N/A	N/A	Sears
Overnight Case	1972	4295	N/A	
Plane-Car Case	1965	N/A	N/A	
Ponytail Case	1962	N/A	$65.00	
Red Flair Case (blue, black, red, white)	1964	N/A	N/A	
Rockers Case	1987	1148	$15.00	Barbie & the Rockers
Silver Screen Barbie Case	1994	N/A	$45.00	FAO Schwarz
Single Doll Case	1981	1002	$50.00	Golden Dreams
Single Doll Case	1986	2810	$15.00	
Single Doll Case	1989	2069	$15.00	
Skipper & Skooter Case	1965	N/A	$200.00	

Item	Year	Number	Value	Specials
Skipper Case	1970	4966	$25.00	
Skipper Case	N/A	1045	N/A	
Skipper Case	N/A	360	N/A	
Skipper Case (School Days)	1964	N/A	$70.00	
Sleep 'n Keep Case (Barbie & Stacie)	1969	5023	$40.00	Sears
Stacey Case	N/A	1046	N/A	
Statue of Liberty Case	1996	748749	$25.00	FAO Schwarz
Tote Bag	1972	4296	$40.00	
Travel Case	1961	N/A	$20.00	
Travel Case #2	1961	N/A	$20.00	
Travel Trunk	N/A	4289	$175.00	
Travel Vanity Case Barbie & Skipper	1965	N/A	$25.00	
Trunk (Solo in the Spotlight)	1963	N/A	$30.00	
Trunk Carries All 3 (10"x7"x13")	1963	9331	$80.00	Sears
Tutti Case	N/A	3378	$35.00	
Tutti Case	N/A	3561	N/A	
Tutti Hat Box	N/A	5016	$29.00	
Tutti Overnighter	N/A	5018	$35.00	
Tutti Play Case	N/A	3001	$40.00	
Tutti Train Case	N/A	5017	$40.00	
Tutti Wears Swing a Ling Case (white)	N/A	N/A	$45.00	
Tutti and Chris Patio Picnic Case	N/A	N/A	$35.00	
Two Doll Trunk	1981	1004	$40.00	Golden Dreams
Two Doll Trunk	1984	1004	$40.00	
White 4 Doll Case	1961	N/A	$8.00	
World of Barbie 2-Doll Trunk	1969	1004	$30.00	
World of Barbie Doll Case	1969	1007	$75.00	
World of Barbie Single Doll Case	1969	1002	$25.00	

Catalogs

Item	Year	Number	Value	Specials
Barbie at FAO Schwarz Catalog	1995	N/A	$5.00	FAO Schwarz
Carnation Barbie Doll Catalog	1963	None	$30.00	
Collector Classic Catalog	1988	N/A	$16.00	
FAO Schwarz Fall Toy Catalog	1995	A1103	$5.00	FAO Schwarz
JCPenney Catalog	Fall 1997	None	$3.00	
JCPenney Doll and Collectible Catalog	1988	N/A	$5.00	JCPenney
JCPenney Doll and Collectible Catalog	1995	N/A	$3.00	JCPenney
Mattel 1980 Catalog	1980	7828	$40.00	Mattel Toy Company
Mattel 1981 Catalog	1981	N/A	$40.00	Mattel Toy Company
Mattel 1981 Department Store Catalog	1981	N/A	$30.00	Mattel Toy Company
Mattel 1982 Catalog	1982	N/A	$40.00	Mattel Toy Company
Mattel 1982 Spring White Space Sale Catalog	1982	N/A	$40.00	Mattel Toy Company
Mattel 1983 Catalog	1983	N/A	$40.00	Mattel Toy Company
Mattel 1983 Department Store Catalog	1983	N/A	$30.00	Mattel Toy Company
Mattel 1984 Catalog	1984	N/A	$40.00	Mattel Toy Company

Item	Year	Number	Value	Specials
Mattel 1985 Catalog	1985	N/A	$35.00	Mattel Toy Company
Mattel 1985 Department Store Catalog	1985	N/A	$30.00	Mattel Toy Company
Mattel 1986 Catalog	1986	N/A	$35.00	Mattel Toy Company
Mattel 1987 Catalog	1987	3692	$8.00	Mattel Toy Company
Mattel 1987 Department Store Catalog	1987	N/A	$15.00	Mattel Toy Company
Mattel 1989 Catalog	1989	0313	$30.00	Mattel Toy Company
Mattel 1990 Catalog	1990	0470	$20.00	Mattel Toy Company
Mattel 1991 Catalog	1991	N/A	$20.00	Mattel Toy Company
Mattel 1992 Catalog	1992	N/A	$15.00	Mattel Toy Company
Mattel 1993 Catalog	1993	N/A	$15.00	Mattel Toy Company
Mattel 1995 Catalog For Girls	1995	13951	$10.00	Mattel Toy Company
Permanent Counter Catalog	1964	1084	$40.00	
Sears Barbie Catalog	Fall 1995	N/A	$3.00	Sears
Sears Barbie Catalog	Spring 1995	N/A	$3.00	Sears
Sears Barbie Catalog	1994	N/A	$5.00	Sears
Sears Barbie Catalog	1995	N/A	$3.00	Sears
Spiegel Barbie Catalog	1995	N/A	$3.00	Spiegel
Timeless Creations Catalog	1990	N/A	$15.00	Timeless

Children's Accessories

Item	Year	Number	Value	Specials
Barbie Carry-All	1966	N/A	$30.00	Standard Plastic
Barbie Wallet	1966	N/A	$30.00	Standard Plastic
Book Bag	1984	7483	$20.00	On The Go Fashions
Caboodle Storage Kit	1993	092254	$20.00	
Canvas Tote Bag	N/A	N/A	$30.00	
In-Line Skates Knee and Elbow Pads	1993	161786	$20.00	
In-Line Skates for Girls	1993	161760	$60.00	
Shoulder Bag	1984	7481	$20.00	On The Go Fashions
Skipper Blue Coin Purse	1964	N/A	$35.00	
Skipper Blue Wallet	1964	N/A	$35.00	
Skipper Change Purse	1966	N/A	$15.00	Standard Plastic
Spring Green Canvas Wallet	N/A	N/A	$15.00	
Umbrella for Girls	1962	N/A	$65.00	
Wallet	1984	7478	$10.00	On The Go Fashions
Workout Bag	1984	7480	$20.00	On The Go Fashions

Children's Clothing

Item	Year	Number	Value	Specials
Barbie Costume	1963	203	$325.00	Ben Cooper
Blouse, Multicolored (sizes 7 – 12)	1964	4388F	N/A	Sears
Boxer shorts (kids)	1995	none	$40.00	Nicole Miller
Bra, Panty, and Pettipant	1963	5320	$75.00	
Chelsen Blouse (sizes 7 – 14)	1964	4386F	$40.00	Sears
Clear Jelly Clogs (girl sizes)	1993	N/A	$10.00	Payless Shoe Store
Denim Jacket (with embroidered heart)	1996	790089	$75.00	
Embroidered Denim Shirt	1996	781443	$42.00	
Evening Outfits for Girls	1963	1772	$40.00	
Girls' Tennis Shoes (sizes 10 – 2)	1995	N/A	$12.00	Payless Shoe Store
Hollywood Hair Rain Ensemble	1993	161125	$40.00	
Jacket (blue and white, sizes 7 – 14)	1964	4396F	$110.00	Sears
Jacket (bright rose and white, sizes 7 – 14)	1964	4397F	$110.00	Sears
Jumper (blue and white, sizes 7 – 14)	1964	4395F	N/A	Sears
Jumper (bright rose and white, sizes 7 – 14)	1964	4394F	$900.00	Sears
Nightshirt (Hollywood hair)	1993	129304	$20.00	
Peignoir and Sleeveless Pajama Set	1963	5319	$60.00	
Shirt #2 (blue and white, sizes 7 – 14)	1964	4392F	$60.00	Sears
Skirt #2 (bright rose and white, sizes 7 – 14)	1964	74393F	$60.00	Sears
Skirt (blue and white, sizes 7 – 14)	1964	4391F	$60.00	Sears
Skirt (bright rose and white, sizes 7 – 14)	1964	4390F	$60.00	Sears
Socks (sizes 5 – 10½)	1991	16CP	$5.00	
Vest (children's)	1995	none	$70.00	Nicole Miller

Children's Riding Toys

Item	Number	Year	Value	Specials
Camp Barbie Jeep	74780	1995	$150.00	Power Wheels
Barbie Lamborghini	78580	1995	$190.00	Power Wheels
10" Barbie Scooter	BD-7	1995	$35.00	Rand Int'l Leisure
10" Barbie Bicycle	BD1008	1995	$50.00	
10" Bicycle	BD1008	1997	$45.00	
10" Scooter	BD7	1997	$30.00	
10" Tricycle	BD411	1997	$35.00	
10" Barbie Tricycle	BD411	1995	$30.00	
12" Barbie Bike	BD1219T	1995	$70.00	Rand Int'l Leisure
12" Barbie Bicycle	BD1219	1995	$70.00	
12" Bicycle	BD129	1997	$60.00	
12" Cheerleader Scooter	BD15	1997	$30.00	
12" Glamour Bicycle	BD1239	1997	$60.00	

Item	Number	Year	Value	Specials
13" Barbie Low Rider	BD814	1995	$30.00	
16" Barbie Fashion Fun Bike	BD1629	1995	$80.00	Rand Int'l Leisure
16" Camp Barbie Bicycle	BD1639	1995	$80.00	
16" Cheerleader Bicycle	BD1639	1997	$80.00	
16" Deluxe Barbie Bicycle	BD1629	1995	$80.00	
16" Motorcycle Bike	BD1699	1995	$90.00	
20" Barbie Bicycle	BD2029	1995	$90.00	
34" Camp Barbie Wagon	BD34	1995	$45.00	
Barbie Beach Rider	BD-814	1995	$40.00	Rand Int'l Leisure
Barbie Beach Patrol	74560	1995	$240.00	Power Wheels
Barbie Wagon	BD34	1997	$45.00	
Butterfly Princess	78550	1995	$80.00	Power Wheels
Low Rider Tricycle	BD814	1997	$35.00	

Coloring & Activity Books

Item	Year	Number	Value	Specials
A Big Color Activity Book	1991	2963	$2.00	Golden Books
A Big Color Activity Book	1993	3999	$2.00	Golden Books
A Big Color Activity Book	1994	8585	$2.00	Golden Books
A Deluxe Color Activity Book	1994	5582	$3.00	Golden Books
A Giant Color Activity Book	1991	3105-16	$2.00	Golden Books
A Giant Color Activity Book	1992	3356-1	$2.00	Golden Books
Ballerina Barbie Coloring Book	1977	N/A	$8.00	
Barbie Fun Book	1993	3052	$10.00	Golden Books
Barbie Mark & See	1993	2887-2	$3.00	
Barbie and Ken Coloring Book	1963	N/A	$50.00	
Barbie and Rockers Activity Book	1987	1147-34	$3.00	Golden Books
Barbie and Skipper Coloring Book	1973	1015	$50.00	
Barbie's World: Bright Swinging Now	1968	None	$10.00	
Color by Number	1962	N/A	$30.00	
Colorforms Barbie Dress Up Set	1989	361	$3.00	
Crossword Puzzles	1976	1742-2	$10.00	
Francie Coloring Book	1967	1094	$85.00	
Giant Paint with Water	1993	2845-2	$3.00	Golden Books
Golden Dream Barbie Coloring Book	1982	N/A	$3.00	
Malibu Francie Coloring Book	1976	N/A	$10.00	
Mark & See	1993	2887-2	$3.00	Golden Books
Paint with Water	1993	1785-5	$2.00	Golden Books
Sand & Glitter Paint By Number Set	1997	296-656	$10.00	
The World of Barbie Fashions Book I	1967	None	$10.00	
The World of Barbie Fashions Book II	1967	None	$10.00	Trace and Color
Western Barbie Coloring Book	1982	1146-2	$6.00	Golden Books

Tea Sets & Dishes

Item	Year	Number	Value	Specials
17-Piece Tea Set (Chilton-Globe, Inc.)	1992		$15.00	
35th Anniversary (Chilton-Globe, Inc.)	1994		$40.00	JCPenney
35th Anniversary Miniature Nostalgic Tea Set (CG)	1994		$40.00	FAO Schwarz, LE
Barbie Doll Cake Pan	1992	N/A	$10.00	Wilton Enterprises
Color Change Party Set	N/A	N/A	$6.00	
Cutlery Set	1962	941	$50.00	Sears
Enchanted Tea Set (Chilton-Globe, Inc.)	1996		$20.00	
Frosty Mug	1996	651794	$12.00	FAO Schwarz
Heirloom Service Playset	1961	N/A	$150.00	
Holiday Tea Set, showing '88-'91 Holiday Barbies (CG)	1994		$27.00	
Holiday Tea Set, showing '92-'95 Holiday Barbies (CG)	1994		$27.00	
Large Ice Bucket with Tongs	1996	651786	$25.00	FAO Schwarz
Mattel Festival '94 (Chilton-Globe) (Mattel)	1994		$145.00	
Melamine Chip 'n Dip Platter	1996	651810	$20.00	FAO Schwarz
Musical Teapot Set (Plays "I'm a little Teapot")	1994		$9.00	Barbie for Girls
Party Set (31-piece cook 'n serve)	1983	N/A	$70.00	Chilton Globe
Pitcher	1996	651760	$14.00	FAO Schwarz
Plastic Dishes	1963	N/A	$60.00	
Playset	1994	N/A	$13.00	
Porcelain Barbie Tea Set (Chilton-Globe, Inc.)	1980	N/A	$85.00	
Serving Tray	1996	651778	$20.00	FAO Schwarz
Solo in the Spotlight Miniature Tea Set (CG)	1995	N/A	$45.00	J.C. Penney FAO Schwarz,
Tumblers (set of 4)	1996	651752	$16.00	FAO Schwarz

Electronics

Item	Year	Number	Value	Specials
Adventures with Barbie Ocean Discovery CD-Rom	1997	17764	$39.00	
AM Radio (Shape of Barbie)	1980	5203	$10.00	
AM-FM Radio	1984	20041	$15.00	Power Tronics
Barbie and Skipper Electric Drawing Set	N/A	N/A	$25.00	
Barbie Disco Record Player	1976		$145.00	
Barbie Electric Drawing Set	1970	15677	$75.00	
Barbie Electric Drawing Set	1983	8230	$75.00	
Barbie for Girls 35 mm Camera	1994	N/A	$30.00	
Barbie for Girls Cassette Player with Headset	1993	400	$40.00	Kiddesigns
Barbie Screen Styler	1997	18052	$20.00	
Barbie "Talk With Me" Phone	2000	BE-136	$20.00	
Cassette Player	1981	3742	$25.00	
Dance Club Doll and Tape Player	1989	N/A	$85.00	Children's Palace

Item	Year	Number	Value	Specials
Electronic Drawing Set	1963	N/A	$200.00	Sears
Electronic Keyboard (guitar shaped)	1993	131599	$40.00	Barbie at FAO
Fashion Designer CD-ROM, IBM Compatible	1997	16379	$34.00	
Fashion Designer Day 'N Play Wear CD-ROM	1998	17768	$34.00	
Fashion Designer Day 'N Play Wear Refill Kit	1998	17769	$24.00	
Fashion Designer, Macintosh Version	1997	18953	$39.00	
Fashion Designer Refill Kit	1997	16373	$19.00	
FM Microphone	1981	3456	$20.00	
Francie and Barbie Electric Drawing Set	1965	8278	$150.00	
Francie and Barbie Drawing Set	1966	8272	$150.00	
Glitter Star 110 Camera	1994	N/A	$25.00	
Magic Fairy Tales Barbie as Rapunzel CD-ROM	1997	16378	$29.00	
Magic Hair Styler CD-ROM	1997	16376	$29.00	
Mattel-a-Phone	1968	N/A	$100.00	
Party Print 'N Play	1997	17765	$24.00	
Phonograph (black)	1961	N/A	$1,200.00	Vanity Fair
Print & Play CD-ROM	1997	296-493	$25.00	
Radio	1981	3455	$30.00	
Record Player (red)	1961	N/A	$200.00	Montgomery Ward
Solo in the Spotlight Telephone	1995	N/A	$79.00	Kash 'n Gold
Storymaker CD-ROM	1997	16377	$32.00	
SuperStar Cameramatic Flash Camera	1978	8503	$20.00	
Super Talking Pager	1997	BD110	$14.00	
Talking "Play a Tune" Piano	2000	BE-127	$17.00	
Talking Voice Recorder	1997	BD265	$14.00	

Enesco

Listed Alphabetically

Item	Year	Number	Value	Specials
1850s Southern Belle Plate	1997	174785	$30.00	
1920s Flapper Plate	1996	174777	$30.00	The Great Eras Collection
After Five 1962 Mini Plate	1995	655058	$13.00	Fashion Barbie Series
After Five Figurine	1994	353647	$25.00	Fashion Barbie Series
Arabian Nights Figurine	1996	171026	$35.00	Barbie's Little Theatre
Arabian Nights Mini Plate	1996	171069	$13.00	Barbie's Little Theatre
Backer Card	1996	BAR013	$10.00	Barbie's Little Theatre
Ballerina 1961 Figurine	1994	113875	$15.00	Classic
Barbie as Dorothy Musical	1997	260185	$100.00	Wizard of Oz
Barbie as Dorothy Ornament	1997	260207	$14.00	Wizard of Oz
Barbie as Dorothy Plate	1997	260193	$35.00	Wizard of Oz
Barbie as Eliza Doolittle Musical	1997	270504	$150.00	My Fair Lady
Barbie as Eliza Doolittle Ornament	1997	270520	$14.00	My Fair Lady
Barbie as Eliza Doolittle Plate	1997	270512	$30.00	My Fair Lady
Barbie Cameo Collection Display Pack	1996	163503	$193.00	Cameo Collection
Barbie Classic Collection Display Pack	1994	141380	$120.00	Classic Collection
Barbie's Little Theatre Display Pack	1996	182753	$280.00	Barbie's Little Theatre
Barbie-Q 1959 Figurine	1997	259012	$30.00	
Bell with Heart Handle	1996	162272	$20.00	Cameo Collection
Bride Bell	1996	174734	$40.00	Glamour Collection
Bride Musical	1996	170976	$100.00	Glamour Collection
Bride's Dream 1963 Musical	1995	113905	$100.00	Glamour Collection
Brochures	1994	BAR005	$12.00	Fashion Barbie Series
Brunch Time 1965 Figurine	1997	259020	$30.00	
Bud Vase	1996	157570	$20.00	Cameo Collection
Button (Barbie Collectibles)	1997	Bar026A	$17.00	
Button (Enesco)	1995	BAR011	$10.00	
Buttons	1995	BAR001	$15.00	From Barbie with Love
Career Girl 1963 Ceramic Mug	1994	124435	$14.00	From Barbie with Love
Cinderella Figurine	1996	170992	$35.00	Barbie's Little Theatre
Cinderella Mini Plate	1996	171042	$13.00	Barbie's Little Theatre
Covered Box	1996	182036	$25.00	Nicole Miller
Dinner At Eight 1963 Figurine	1997	259039	$30.00	
Display Mini Figurines	1994	BAR010	$120.00	Classic
Display with 50 Brochures	1994	BAR004	$20.00	Fashion Barbie Series
Dream House Display	1997	Bar021	$15.00	
Easel Card	1997	Bar026D	$6.00	
Easter Parade 1959 Figurine	1995	353663	$25.00	Fashion Barbie Series
Easter Parade 1959 Mini Plate	1995	655074	$13.00	Fashion Barbie Series
Egyptian Queen Plate	1997	174793	$30.00	
Enchanted Evening 1960	1994	133396	$15.00	Classic
Enchanted Evening 1960 Ceramic Mug	1994	124443	$14.00	From Barbie with Love
Enchanted Evening 1960 Musical	1994	353620	$100.00	From Barbie with Love
Enchanted Evening 1960 Musical	1996	185787	$100.00	Glamour Collection
Enchanted Evening 1960 Plate	1996	175587	$30.00	Glamour Collection
Enchanted Evening 1960 Porcelain Bust	1995	115266	$70.00	From Barbie with Love
Enchanted Evening Oval Box	1996	157562	$25.00	Glamour Collection
Evening Splendor 1959 Figurine	1995	353728	$25.00	Fashion Barbie Series

Item	Year	Number	Value	Specials
Evening Splendor 1959 Miniature Bust	1995	125601	$25.00	From Barbie with Love
Evening Splendor 1959 Mug	1996	188905	$18.00	Glamour Collection
Evening Splendor 1959 Vase	1996	188913	$25.00	Glamour Collection
Gay Parisienne 1959 Miniature Bust	1995	125601	$25.00	From Barbie with Love
Gay Parisienne Figurine	1995	353655	$25.00	Fashion Barbie Series
Gibson Girl Plate	1996	174769	$30.00	The Great Eras Collection
Goddess of the Sun & Moon Goddess Set Plates	1997	270539	$125.00	
Gone with the Wind Music Box	1996	171107	$100.00	Hollywood Legends Collection
Gone with the Wind Musical	1996	171093	$100.00	Hollywood Legends Collection
Gone with the Wind Ornament	1996	182028	$13.00	Hollywood Legends Collection
Gone with the Wind Plate	1996	171085	$35.00	Hollywood Legends Collection
Graduation 1963 Vase	1994	124419	$25.00	From Barbie with Love
Graduation Mini Figurine	1994	113867	$15.00	Classic
Guinevere Figurine	1996	171018	$35.00	Barbie's Little Theatre
Guinevere Mini Plate	1996	171050	$13.00	Barbie's Little Theatre
Hand Mirror	1996	171204	$20.00	Nicole Miller
Happy Holidays 1988 Plate	1995	154180	$35.00	Happy Holidays Collection
Happy Holidays 1989 Musical	1996	188832	$100.00	Happy Holidays Collection
Happy Holidays 1989 Musical Box	1996	188840	$50.00	Happy Holidays Collection
Happy Holidays 1989 Plate	1996	188859	$30.00	Happy Holidays Collection
Happy Holidays 1994 Plate	1994	115088	$30.00	Happy Holidays Collection
Happy Holidays 1995 Plate	1995	143154	$30.00	Happy Holidays Collection
Happy Holidays 1996 Ornament	1996	188824	$13.00	Happy Holidays Collection
Happy Holidays 1996 Plate	1996	188816	$35.00	Happy Holidays Collection
Heart Covered Box	1996	157627	$15.00	Cameo Collection
Heart Shaped Plate	1996	157635	$18.00	Cameo Collection
Holiday Dance Hanging Ornament	1996	188808	$13.00	Glamour Collection
Holiday Dance Musical	1996	188786	$100.00	Glamour Collection
Holiday Dance Plate	1996	188794	$30.00	Glamour Collection
Let's Go To The Hop (music box)	1994	551538	$150.00	From Barbie with Love
Little Red Riding Hood Figurine	1996	171034	$35.00	Barbie's Little Theatre
Little Red Riding Hood Mini Plate	1996	171077	$13.00	Barbie's Little Theatre
Magnificence 1963 Musical	1995	143111	$100.00	Glamour Collection
Midnight Blue 1965 Musical	1995	113891	$100.00	Glamour Collection
Mobil Sign	1997	Bar026B	$7.00	
Music Box	1996	171220	$30.00	Nicole Miller
Musical Cake Topper	1997	260304	$50.00	From Barbie with Love
Original Swimsuit 1959 Figurine	1995	113700	$30.00	Fashion Collection Series
Ornament Holder	1997	260207	$10.00	Wizard of Oz
Oval Dresser Tray	1996	171212	$25.00	Nicole Miller
Perfume Bottle	1996	157589	$15.00	Cameo Collection
Photo Frame	1996	171166	$13.00	Nicole Miller
Picnic 1959 Figurine	1995	113727	$30.00	Fashion Collection Series
Plantation Belle 1959 Miniature Bust	1995	125601	$25.00	From Barbie with Love
Plate Stand (wood)	1997	274216	$13.00	Wizard of Oz
Poodle Parade 1965 Figurine	1995	113719	$30.00	Fashion Collection Series
Queen of Hearts Hinged Box	1995	157708	$50.00	Bob Mackie
Queen of Hearts Music Box	1995	157716	$50.00	Bob Mackie
Queen of Hearts Musical	1995	157651	$100.00	Bob Mackie
Queen of Hearts Ornament	1995	157724	$9.00	Bob Mackie
Queen of Hearts Plate	1995	157678	$35.00	Bob Mackie
Queen of Hearts Vase	1995	157694	$25.00	Bob Mackie
Record Action Mini Musical (Friday Night Date)	1997	271616	$35.00	From Barbie With Love
Red Flare 1962 Figurine	1994	353701	$25.00	Fashion Barbie Series
Red Flare 1962 Mini Plate	1995	655090	$13.00	Fashion Barbie Series

Item	Year	Number	Value	Specials
Registered Nurse 1961 Ceramic Mug	1994	124427	$14.00	From Barbie with Love
Registered Nurse 1961 Vase	1994	124397	$25.00	From Barbie with Love
Roman Holiday 1959 Figurine	1995	353671	$25.00	Fashion Barbie Series
Roman Holiday 1959 Mini Plate	1995	655082	$13.00	Fashion Barbie Series
Salt & Pepper Shakers (Ken & Barbie)	1995	113921	$30.00	From Barbie with Love
Senior Prom 1963 Musical	1995	124370	$100.00	From Barbie with Love
Senior Prom 1963 Musical	1995	125776	$100.00	Glamour Collection
Senior Prom 1963 Vase	1994	124400	$25.00	From Barbie with Love
Shopping Bag, 11¼"	1996	182044	$25.00	Nicole Miller
Shopping Bag, 6"	1996	926116	$15.00	Nicole Miller
Slumber Party 1965 Figurine	1997	259047	$30.00	
Small Powder Box	1996	157619	$13.00	Cameo Collection
Solo in the Spotlight 1960 Musical	1994	353752	$100.00	From Barbie with Love
Solo in the Spotlight 1960 Musical	1995	173533	$100.00	Glamour Collection
Solo in the Spotlight 1960 Oval Box	1996	157554	$25.00	Glamour Collection
Solo in the Spotlight 1960 Plate	1995	114383	$30.00	From Barbie with Love
Solo in the Spotlight 1960 Vase	1994	124389	$25.00	From Barbie with Love
Sophisticated Lady 1963 Musical	1995	113883	$100.00	Glamour Collection
Suburban Shopper 1959 Figurine	1995	113751	$30.00	Fashion Collection Series
Trio Display	1997	274224	$30.00	Wizard of Oz
Vanity Tray	1996	157643	$20.00	Cameo Collection
Vase	1996	171182	$40.00	Nicole Miller
Wedding Day 1959 Figurine	1994	113859	$15.00	Classic
Wedding Day 1959 Miniature Bust	1995	125601	$25.00	From Barbie with Love
Wedding Day 1959 Musical	1994	353639	$100.00	From Barbie with Love
Wedding Day 1959 Musical	1997	260274	$100.00	
Wedding Day 1959 Ornament	1997	260290	$14.00	
Wedding Day 1959 Plate	1997	260282	$30.00	
Wedding Day 1959 Oval Box	1996	157546	$25.00	Glamour Collection

Furniture

Item	Year	Number	Value	Specials
3-piece Dresser Set	1962	1383	$100.00	Sears
3-piece Wall Unit	1988	4772	$30.00	Living Pretty
Armoire	1988	4763	$30.00	
Armoire (light pink)	1980	2471	$35.00	Dream Furniture Collection
Armoire (pink & light pink doors)	1984	2471	$20.00	Dream Collection
Barbie and Midge Queen Size Chifforobe	1964	9384	$100.00	Sears
Barbie and Skipper Dining Room Furniture	1965	4010	$50.00	Go-Together Furniture
Barbie and Skipper Living Room Furniture	1965	N/A	$60.00	Go-Together Furniture
Bath and Beauty Center	1984	4345	$20.00	Dream Collection
Bath Chest and Commode (light pink)	1980	1045	$20.00	Dream Furniture Collection
Bathroom	1995	67151	$10.00	So Much To Do
Bathroom Accents	1986	2374	$6.00	
Bathroom Accents	1988	5988	$6.00	
Beauty Bath	1976	9223	$30.00	
Bed and Bath	1995	13204	$20.00	Double Fun Furniture
Bed and Nightstand (pink)	1984	2472	$25.00	Dream Collection
Bed, Nightstand, and Rug (light pink)	1980	2472	$20.00	Dream Furniture Collection
Bedding for 9248	1964	9358	$65.00	Sears
Bedroom	1970	4971	$45.00	
Bedroom	1995	67172	$17.00	So Much To Do
Bedroom Accents	1988	5986	$18.00	
Bedroom Set	1981	3768	$6.00	Dream House
Blanket Chest #1	1962	N/A	$30.00	
Blanket Chest #2 (round knobs)	1962	N/A	$30.00	
Bubble Bath	1968	5280	$25.00	
Bubbling Spa	1984	7145	$25.00	
Buffet/Server	1985	9479	$100.00	
Canopy Bed #1	1960	N/A	$150.00	Susy Goose
Canopy Bed #2	1962	N/A	$150.00	Susy Goose
Canopy Bed #3	1962	N/A	$150.00	Susy Goose
Chair	1964	0409	$20.00	Go-Together Furniture
Chair	1964	0410	$20.00	Go-Together Furniture
Chair and End Table	1978	2468	$30.00	Dream Furniture Collection
Chair and End Table (green)	1980	2468	$30.00	Dream Furniture Collection
Chair, Ottoman, and End Table	1964	N/A	$50.00	Go-Together Furniture
Chair, Ottoman, and End Table	1964	4440	$75.00	Sears Miss Barbie
Chair/Lounger, and End Table	1984	7403	$35.00	Wicker-Look Furniture
Chaise Lounge and Side Table	1964	4441	$60.00	Sears' Miss Barbie
Chaise Lounge	N/A	N/A	$50.00	
Chifforobe	1964	N/A	$275.00	Susy Goose
Commode and Towel Rack (pink)	1984	1045	$25.00	Dream Collection
Convertible Sofa-Bed and Coffee Table	1964	4439	$65.00	Sears' Miss Barbie
Cooking Center	1988	4777	$25.00	Living Pretty
Couch	1964	0408	$30.00	Go-Together Furniture
Desk and Seat	1978	2467	$12.00	Dream Furniture Collection
Desk and Seat (green)	1980	2476	$20.00	Dream Furniture Collection
Dinette	1970	4962	$25.00	
Dining Buffet/China Cabinet (blue)	1980	2470	$30.00	Dream Furniture Collection

Item	Year	Number	Value	Specials
Dining Buffet/China Cabinet (pink)	1984	2470	$30.00	Dream Collection
Dining Center Set (pink)	1984	4337	$25.00	Dream Collection
Dining Room Set	1985	9478	$25.00	
Dining Room Table and Chairs	1985	9480	$20.00	
Dining Table and Chair (blue)	1980	2475	$25.00	Dream Furniture Collection
Dining Table and Chair (pink)	1984	2475	$25.00	Dream Collection
Dining Table and Chairs	1988	4775	$20.00	
Dough Kitchen	1994	10949	$29.00	
Dream Bed	1983	5641	$25.00	
Dream Furniture Sofa & Coffee Table	1978	2474	$20.00	
Dream Glow Bed	1986	5461	$20.00	
Dream Glow Vanity	1986	2310	$20.00	
Dream Kitchen	1985	9119	$20.00	
Dream Kitchen and Dinette	1964	4095	$600.00	
Elegant Wardrobe	1962	9321	$50.00	Sears
Fashion Living Room Set	1984	7404	$30.00	Wicker-Look Furniture
Four Poster Bed Outfit	1962	N/A	$300.00	
Furniture Accents	1986	2376	$6.00	
Glamour Bath and Shower Set	1986	2552	$30.00	
Glitter & Glow Bed	1997	15327	$19.00	
Go-Together Dining Room Furniture	1964	4010	$175.00	Go-Together Furniture
Graceful Canopy Bed	1962	9248	N/A	Sears
Growing Up Skipper Bedroom	1976	9282	$45.00	
Home & Office	1985	7897	$40.00	
Ken Wardrobe	1963	N/A	$200.00	Susy Goose
Kitchen	1969	11498	$70.00	Montgomery Ward
Kitchen	1995	67158	$15.00	So Much To Do
Kitchen Accents	1986	2373	$8.00	
Kitchen Accents	1988	5987	$8.00	
Kitchen Set	1981	3770	$6.00	Dream House
Kitchen/Dining Room	1995	13205	$25.00	Double Fun Furniture
Lawn Swing and Planter	1964	0411	$100.00	Go-Together Furniture
Livin' Room	1971	4986	$85.00	Barbie's Place Setting
Living Room	1970	4993	$60.00	
Living Room	1981	3769	$6.00	Dream House
Living Room Accents	1986	2372	$12.00	
Living Room Accents	1988	5985	$12.00	
Living Room Furniture	1970	4963	$70.00	
Living Room Furniture Group	1965	4012	$60.00	Go-Together Furniture
Luxury Bathtub (light pink)	1980	1049	$25.00	Dream Furniture Collection
Luxury Bathtub (pink)	1984	1049	$20.00	Dream Collection
Miss Barbie Furniture Set	1964	4443	$70.00	Sears' Miss Barbie
Mod A Go-Go Bedroom	1966	N/A	$2,300.00	Susy Goose
My Very Own Vanity	1997	16964	$75.00	So Much To Do
Patio Barbecue	1981	1478	$50.00	Dream Pool Collection
Patio Table & Chairs	1969	1429	$52.00	
Patio Table & Chairs	1981	1479	$50.00	Dream Pool Collection
Picnic Set	1995	67032-91	$12.00	So Much To Do
Plastic Wardrobe (5" x 15" x 16")	1962	N/A	$175.00	
Plastic Wardrobe (7" x 4" x 14")	1963	N/A	$165.00	
Queen-sized Bed (Susy Goose)	1963	9357	$200.00	Sears/Susy Goose
Recliner & Serving Cart	1969	1480	$20.00	Dream Pool Collection
Refrigerator (white)	1984	2473	$18.00	Dream Collection
Refrigerator/Freezer	1988	4776	$30.00	Living Pretty
Refrigerator/Freezer (yellow)	1980	2473	$20.00	Dream Furniture Collection

Item	Year	Number	Value	Specials
Regal Bed (mint)	N/A	N/A	$1,700.00	Susy Goose
Ribbons & Roses Bed	1988	5620	$30.00	
Room-Fulls Country Kitchen	1974	7404	$40.00	
Room-Fulls Firelight Living Room	1974	7406	$45.00	
Room-Fulls Studio Bedroom	1974	7405	$45.00	
Skipper Jewel Vanity	1965	9350	$200.00	Sears/Susy Goose
Skipper Jeweled Bed	1965	9349	$225.00	Sears/Susy Goose
Skipper Jeweled Wardrobe	1965	9351	$200.00	Sears/Susy Goose
Skipper & Skooter Bunk Beds	1965	4011	$175.00	Go-Together Furniture
Sofa & Coffee Table (green)	1980	2474	$20.00	Dream Furniture Collection
Sofa/Bed & Chair Lounger	1988	4771	$30.00	Living Pretty
Sofa/Bed & Coffee Table	1984	7402	$35.00	Wicker-Look Furniture
Stove, Microwave Oven (pink, white)	1984	2417	$35.00	Dream Collection
Stove, Microwave Oven (yellow, orange)	1980	2417	$35.00	Dream Furniture Collection
Style Magic Barbie Vanity	1989	2761	$30.00	
Surf Set	1995	67032-91	$12.00	So Much To Do
Susy Goose Canopy Bed	1961	N/A	$140.00	
Susy Goose Hope Chest	1961	N/A	$25.00	
Susy Goose Piano	1964	None	$700.00	
Susy Goose Red Carpet	1961	N/A	$10.00	
Susy Goose Vanity	1961	N/A	$100.00	
Susy Goose Wardrobe	1961	N/A	$100.00	
Sweet Roses Accents	1988	7666	$30.00	
Sweet Roses Beauty Bath	1988	5156	$30.00	
Teen Dream Bedroom	N/A	N/A	$35.00	
Terrace Set	1994	67030	$13.00	
Tutti and Todd Dutch Bedroom Furniture	1965	N/A	$1,500.00	Susy Goose
Vanity & Bench	1963	9326	$125.00	Sears/Susy Goose
Vanity & Nightstand	1988	4764	$30.00	
Vanity & Seat (light pink)	1980	2469	$20.00	Dream Furniture Collection
Vanity & Seat (pink)	1984	2469	$20.00	Dream Furniture Collection
Vanity & Shower	1975	9056	$50.00	Sears

Games

Item	Year	Number	Value	Specials
A Glamorous Quest Full of Magic (video game)	1992	N/A	$35.00	Nintendo of America
Barbie and Her Magical Home (CD-Rom)	1994	N/A	$20.00	Hi Tech Expressions
Barbie Charms the World	1986	N/A	$35.00	Mattel
Barbie Game Board	1980	N/A	$20.00	Whitman
Barbie Game Girl (video game)	1992	N/A	$35.00	Nintendo of America
Barbie Super Model (video game)	1993	112026	$35.00	Sega
Barbie Travel Game — Cool Jobs	1992	N/A	$10.00	International Games
Barbie Travel Game — Pretty Party	1992	N/A	$10.00	International Games
Barbie Travel Game — Ultimate Vacation	1992	N/A	$10.00	International Games
Barbie's Little Sister Skipper Game	1965	5415	$55.00	Mattel
Butterfly Princess Game	1995	7200	$13.00	
Dream Date	1992	N/A	$12.00	Golden
Dress Up	1992	N/A	$12.00	Colorforms
Dress Up Game	1995	N/A	$15.00	International Games
Horse Back Riding LCD Game	1995	BRB111	$20.00	Micro Games
Hula Hoop	1991	N/A	$10.00	
In-Line Skating LCD Game	1995	BRB109	$20.00	Micro Games
Just Us Girls	1990	N/A	$20.00	Cardinal
Keys to Fame Game	1963	5410	$60.00	
Miss Lively Livin' Game	1970	5481	$35.00	
Mountain Bike Riding LCD Game	1995	BRB107	$20.00	Micro Games
Playing Cards (plastic coated)	1979	N/A	$16.00	Nasta
Queen of the Prom Game	1964	450	$175.00	Mattel
Queen of the Prom Game 1990s (reissue)	1991	N/A	$15.00	Golden
Shakin' Pinball	1995	BRB197	$20.00	
Shopping Spree (giant card game)	1991	N/A	$8.00	Golden
Shrinky Dinks	1979	N/A	$30.00	
Skipper Game	1964	5415	$25.00	
Sports Soccer LCD Game	1995	BRB105	$20.00	Micro Games
Sports Softball LCD Game	1995	BRB103	$20.00	Micro Games
Sports Volleyball LCD Game	1995	BRB101	$20.00	Micro Games
The Barbie Game	1980	4761	$18.00	Whitman
The Barbie Game 35th Anniversary Edition	1994	N/A	$60.00	Golden
The Barbie Game (Queen of the Prom)	1962	450	$80.00	Mattel
Vacation Adventure (video game)	1994	N/A	$35.00	Nintendo of America & Sega
We Girls Can Do Anything	1990	N/A	$15.00	Golden
We Girls Can Do Anything (reissue)	1992	N/A	$15.00	Golden
World of Fashion Game	1967	1746	$70.00	Mattel
Young Travelers Play Kit	1964	469	$50.00	Sears

Gift Sets

Listed Alphabetically

Item	Year	Number	Value	Specials
30th Anniversary Francie	1996	14608	$65.00	
35th Anniversary	1994	11591	$175.00	
Action Accents Set (Barbie)	1970	1585	$1,125.00	Sears
The Addams Family	2000	27276	$88.00	
Air Force Barbie & Ken (Thunderbirds)	1994	11581	$60.00	Stars 'n Stripes
Air Force Barbie & Ken (Thunderbirds, black)	1994	11582	$50.00	Stars 'n Stripes
All American Barbie & Star Stepper	1991	3712	$65.00	Wholesale Clubs
Army Desert Storm	1993	5626	$70.00	Stars 'n Stripes
Army Desert Storm (black)	1993	5627	$60.00	Stars 'n Stripes
Ballerina on Tour	1976	9093	$150.00	Department Store
Ballet Recital Barbie & Kelly	1998	18187	$15.00	
Ballet Recital Barbie & Kelly (black)	1998	21388	$15.00	
Barbie & Champion	1995	13831	$80.00	Wholesale Clubs
Barbie & Friends	1983	4431	$95.00	
Barbie & Friends (Disney)	1991	3177	$75.00	Toys "R" Us
Barbie & Her US Olympic Wardrobe	1975	9044	$105.00	Sears
Barbie & Keiko	1996	16214	$30.00	Ocean Friends
Barbie & Ken Mix 'n Match Set	1962	N/A	$1,500.00	Wards/Spiegel
Barbie & Ken Tennis Set	1962	892	$1,400.00	Wards/Spiegel
Barbie & Kenny Country Duet	1999	23498	$100.00	Grand Ole Opry
Barbie and Kelly Strolling Fun Set	1995	13742	$20.00	
Barbie and Kelly Strolling Fun Set (black)	1995	13743	$20.00	
Barbie Deluxe 100-piece(1st issue)	1992	7151	$40.00	Wholesale Clubs
Barbie for President	1991	3722	$65.00	Toys "R" Us
Barbie for President (black)	1991	3940	$45.00	Toys "R" Us
Barbie Loves Elvis	1997	17450	$90.00	
Barbie Loves Frankie Sinatra	1999	22953	$65.00	
Barbie Millicent Roberts	1996	16080	$75.00	Barbie Millicent Roberts
Bathtime	1991	9601	$25.00	Wholesale Clubs
Beach Fun	1994	11481	$35.00	Wholesale Clubs
Beautiful Blues Set (Barbie)	1967	3303	$3,000.00	Sears
Beauty Secrets Pretty Reflections	1980	1702	$95.00	
Bedtime Baby Barbie and Krissy	2000	28516	$16.00	
Bedtime Barbie	1994	12184	$45.00	Wholesale Clubs
Bendable Leg Ken	1970	1436	$800.00	
Birthday Fun At McDonald's	1994	11589	$45.00	
Birthday Fun Kelly	1996	15610	$40.00	Toys "R" Us
Birthday Surprise CD-ROM	1998	17765	$20.00	
Bright & Breezy (Skipper)	1969	1590	$975.00	Sears
Campin' Out	1983	4984	$100.00	
Caring Careers Fashion	1994	10773	$10.00	
Casey Goes Casual	1967	3304	$1,750.00	Sears
Color 'n Curl (Molded Barbie Head)	1965	4039	$600.00	
Color 'n Curl Set (Barbie & Midge)	1965	4035	$1,100.00	
Color Magic Barbie	1966	1043	$4,000.00	Sears
Color Magic Fashion Designer Set	1965	4038	$650.00	
Cookin' Goodies Playset (Tutti)	1967	3559	$300.00	
Cool City Blues (Barbie, Ken & Skipper)	1989	4893	$60.00	Toys "R" Us

Item	Year	Number	Value	Specials
Country Duet	1999	23498	$65.00	Grand Ole Opry
Cut 'n Button (Skooter)	1967	1036	$700.00	Sears
Dance Club (Barbie)	1989	4217	$50.00	Children's Palace
Dance Magic (Barbie & Ken)	1990	5409	$50.00	
Dance Sensation	1984	9058	$45.00	Toys "R" Us
Denim & Ruffles	1995	12371	$65.00	Wholesale Clubs
Denim Deluxe	1993	4893	$60.00	
Dinner Dazzle Set (Barbie)	1968	1551	$1,200.00	Sears
Disney Weekend Barbie	1993	10723	$50.00	
Disney Weekend Barbie & Ken	1993	10724	$75.00	
Dolls of the World I (Barbie)	1994	12043	$75.00	Dolls of the World Series
Dolls of the World II (Barbie)	1995	13939	$60.00	Dolls of the World Series
Dolls of the World III Barbie)	1996	15283	$65.00	Dolls of the World Series
Dr. Ken & Little Patient Tommy	1998	18898	$15.00	
Dr. Ken & Little Patient Tommy (black)	1998	18899	$15.00	
Dream Wardrobe	1992	3331	$40.00	
Dream Wedding	1993	10712	$55.00	Toys "R" Us
Dream Wedding (black)	1993	10713	$50.00	Toys "R" Us
Dressing Fun (pink dress)	1993	9518	$50.00	Wholesale Clubs
Dressing Fun (purple dress)	1993	9518	$50.00	Wholesale Clubs
Earring Magic Barbie Software Pak	1993	None	$45.00	Radio Shack
Easter Bunny Fun Barbie & Kelly	1999	21720	$25.00	
Easter Bunny Fun Barbie & Kelly (black)	1999	22187	$25.00	
Easter Egg Hunt Barbie & Kelly	1998	19014	$40.00	Target
Easter Egg Party Barbie & Kelly (black)	2000	25791	$25.00	
Fabulous Formal (Barbie & Ken)	1969	1595	$1,500.00	Sears
Fashion 'n Motion Set (P.J.)	1971	1508	$900.00	Sears
Fashion Fun Barbie	1999	24148	$25.00	
Fashion Queen & Her Friends	1963	863	$2,300.00	
Fashion Queen Barbie & Ken Trousseau	1963	864	$2,400.00	
Fluff Sunshine Special Set	1971	1249	$900.00	Sears
Foam 'n Color	1996	16567	$20.00	JCPenney
Francie & Her Swingin' Separates Set	1966	1042	$1,100.00	Sears
Francie Sportin'	1966	1044	$4,200.00	JCPenney
Fun to Dress	1993	3826	$25.00	
Fun-Timers Set (Chris)	1967	3301	$900.00	Sears
Furniture	1964	4005	$300.00	Go-Together Furniture
Gap Barbie & Kelly	1997	19014	$50.00	Gap Stores
Gap Barbie & Kelly (black)	1997	18548	$40.00	Gap Stores
Gardening Fun Barbie & Kelly	1997	17242	$30.00	Toys "R" Us
Generation Girl Barbie & Lara	1999	25502	$40.00	
Generation Girl Barbie & Nichelle	1999	25503	$40.00	
Giggles and Swing Barbie and Kelly	1999	20333	$15.00	
Giggles and Swing Barbie and Kelly (black)	1999	20534	$15.00	
Golden Dreams Glamorous Nights	1980	3533	$75.00	
Golden Greater Qi-Pao	1998	20649	$85.00	
Golden Groove Set (Barbie)	1969	1593	$1,600.00	Sears
Halloween Fun Barbie & Kelly	1999	23460	$25.00	
Halloween Fun Barbie & Kelly (black)	1999	23461	$25.00	
Halloween Fun Li'l Friends of Kelly	1999	23796	$25.00	
Halloween Party Barbie & Ken	1998	19874	$25.00	Target
Happy Birthday Barbie	1985	9678	$50.00	
Happy Birthday	1985	9514	$85.00	Department Store
Happy Halloween (Barbie & Kelly)	1997	17238	$30.00	Target
Harley-Davidson Barbie	2000	29208	$70.00	

Item	Year	Number	Value	Specials
Holiday Gown Collection I	1992	697	$75.00	
Holiday Gown Collection II	1993	697A	$60.00	
Holiday Party Set (Skipper)	1965	1021	$900.00	
Holiday Sisters Barbie, Kelly, and Stacie	1999	23617	$35.00	Holiday Sisters
Holiday Sisters Barbie, Stacie & Kelly	1998	19809	$25.00	Toys "R" Us
Hollywood Hair	1993	10928	$25.00	Wholesale Clubs
Horse Lovin' Barbie & Nibbles Gift Set	1996	15648	$25.00	Wholesale Clubs
Hostess Set (Barbie)	1965	1034	$4,600.00	
Hot Dancin' Set	1990	4841	$75.00	
Hot Skatin' Barbie & Mustang Deluxe	1995	13511	$45.00	Wholesale Clubs
I Love Lucy 50th Anniversary (episode 50)	2000	28553	$80.00	Timeless Treasures
Island Fun	1993	10379	$35.00	Wholesale Clubs
Julia Simply Wow Set	1969	1594	$1,100.00	Sears
Kelly & Baby Pony	1998	20346	$17.00	
Kelly & Ginger	1998	19810	$20.00	
Kelly & Tommy Power Wheels	1998	18717	$20.00	
Kelly & Tommy Power Wheels (black)	1998	18718	$20.00	
Ken & Barbie as King Arthur and Queen Guinevere	1999	23880	$100.00	Together Forever Collection
Ken Red, White & Wild Set	1970	1589	$525.00	Sears
Kissing Barbie Extra Value Set	1979	2977	$100.00	Department Store
Kissing	1980	2597	$45.00	
Let's Drive (Barbie and Skipper)	2000		$35.00	Toys "R" Us
Li'l Zoo Pals Sister	1998	19625	$30.00	
Little Theater Set	1964	1018	$5,000.00	
Living Room Furniture	1965	4012	$300.00	
Loves to Read	1993	10527	$50.00	Toys "R" Us
Loving You	1984	7563	$60.00	Department Store
Malibu Barbie and Her Ten Speeder Set	1978	N/A	$100.00	Montgomery Ward
Malibu Barbie Fashion Combo	1978	2753	$80.00	
Malibu Ken Surf's Up	1971	1248	$425.00	Sears
March of Dimes Walk America Barbie & Kelly	1999	20843	$18.00	
March of Dimes Walk America Barbie & Kelly (black)	1999	20844	$18.00	
Marine Corps	1992	4704	$45.00	Stars 'n Stripes
Marine Corps (black)	1992	2810	$45.00	Stars 'n Stripes
Matinee Today	1996	16079	$70.00	Barbie Millicent Roberts
McDonald's Fun Time Barbie & Kelly	2001	29395	$17.00	
Me & My Mustang	1995	11929	$35.00	Wholesale Clubs
Merlin & Morgan Le Fay	2000	27287	$100.00	Magic & Mystery Series
Midge Ensemble	1964	1012	$3,000.00	
Midge Mix 'n Match Set	1964	3807	$2,600.00	
Mix 'n Match Set (blonde)	1960	857	$1,800.00	
Mix 'n Match Set (brunette)	1960	857	$2,100.00	
Munsters, The	50544	2001	$235.00	Barbie Loves Pop Culture
My First Barbie	1991	2483	$35.00	
My First Barbie (Pink Tutu)	1986	1879	$25.00	
My Sister Stacie	1993	9365	$10.00	
Nite Lighting Set (Stacey)	1969	1591	$2,000.00	Sears
Ocean Friends	1996	N/A	$25.00	Department Store
Olympic	1996		$30.00	Wholesale Clubs
On Parade Set	1964	1014	$2,200.00	Sears
On The Go (Barbie)	1990	1007	$70.00	
Paint 'n Dazzle	1993	10926	$35.00	Wholesale Clubs
Party Set	1960	856	$2,100.00	
Party Time Set (Skipper)	1964	1021	$500.00	
Pep Rally Set	1964	4035	$1,500.00	

Item	Year	Number	Value	Specials
Perfectly Plaid (Barbie)	1971	1193	$1,200.00	Sears
Perfectly Pretty Set (Skipper)	1968	1546	$975.00	Sears
Perfectly Suited	1997	17567	$70.00	Barbie Millicent Roberts
Phantom of the Opera	1998	20377	$130.00	FAO Schwarz
Pink & Pretty Modeling Set	1982	5939	$65.00	Department Store
Pink Premier Set (Barbie)	1969	1596	$1,500.00	JCPenney
Polly Pocket	1995	14406	$20.00	J.Penney
Posable and Her Sew-Free Wardrobe	1965	8526	$1,500.00	Montgomery Ward
Pretty Pairs Angie 'n Tangie	1970	1135	$255.00	
Pretty Pairs Lori 'n Rori	1970	1133	$250.00	
Pretty Pairs Nan 'n Fran	1970	1134	$250.00	
Renaissance Rose	2000	28633	$40.00	
Rise & Shine (Francie)	1971	1194	$1,100.00	Sears
Rollerblade	1992	7142	$50.00	Wholesale Clubs
Romeo and Juliet	1998	19364	$70.00	Legendary Couples
Round the Clock	1964	1013	$4,500.00	
Secret Hearts	1993	10929	$50.00	Wholesale Clubs
Sharin' Sisters	1992	5716	$50.00	
Sharin' Sisters	1993	10143	$55.00	
Shoppin' Fun Barbie & Kelly Playset	1996	15756	$20.00	
Shoppin' Fun Barbie & Kelly Playset (black)	1996	15757	$20.00	
Show 'n Ride	1989	7799	$45.00	Toys "R" Us
Show Parade w/Star Stampin' Horse	1997	15059	$30.00	Toys "R" Us
Show Parade w/Star Stampin' Horse (black)	1997	15060	$30.00	Toys "R" Us
Silver 'n Satin Set (Barbie)	1968	1552	$1,500.00	JCPenney
Singing Holiday Sisters	2000	26260	$40.00	
Sisters Celebration Krissy and Barbie	2000		Retail	Sam's Club/Wholesale Clubs
Skipper & Her Swing-a-Round Gym	1972	1179	$350.00	Sears
Skipper On Wheels Set	1965	1032	$500.00	Sears
Snap 'n Play	1992	2262	$30.00	
Solo in the Spotlight	1995	14403	$50.00	JCPenney
Sparkle Eyes	1992	7131	$60.00	Wholesale Clubs
Sparkling Pink	1964	1011	$2,500.00	
Stacie & Butterfly Pony Gift Set	1993	10227	$25.00	
Star Trek Gift Set	1996	15006	$30.00	
Stripes Are Happening Set (Stacey)	1968	1545	$3,000.00	Sears
Sun Sensation	1992	7149	$75.00	Wholesale Clubs
Super Fashion Fireworks #1 (Barbie)	1976	9805	$75.00	Kresge Store
Super Fashion Fireworks #2 (Barbie)	1976	9805	$75.00	Kresge Store
Super Fashion Fireworks #3 (Barbie)	1976	9805	$75.00	Kresge Store
SuperStar Barbie & Ken Set	1978	2422	$125.00	Department Store
SuperStar Barbie Fashion Change-Abouts	1978	2586	$100.00	
SuperStar in the Spotlight Set	1977	2207	$80.00	Department Store
Swing-A-Ling (Tutti)	1967	3560	$300.00	
Swingin' in Silver Set (P.J.)	1970	1588	$1,200.00	Sears
Tennis Star (Barbie & Ken)	1988	7801	$65.00	Toys "R" Us
Travel in Style (Barbie)	1968	1544	$2,500.00	Sears
Travelin' Sisters	1995	14073	$50.00	
Tropical Malibu	1986	2996	$45.00	
Trousseau Set	1960	858	$1,900.00	
Tutti and Todd Sundae Treat Playset	1966	3556	$425.00	
Tutti Me and My Dog Playset	1966	3554	$375.00	
Tutti Melody in Pink Playset	1966	3555	$325.00	
Tutti Night-Night Sleep Tight Playset	1966	3553	$350.00	
Tutti Walkin' My Dolly Playset	1966	3552	$350.00	

Item	Year	Number	Value	Specials
Twinkle Town Set (Barbie)	1969	1866	$1,600.00	Sears
Twirly Curls	1983	4079	$95.00	Department Store
Vacation Sensation	1988	1675	$25.00	Toys "R" Us
Very Best Velvet Set (Skipper)	1970	1586	$600.00	Sears
Victorian Holiday Barbie and Kelly	2000	28395	Retail	Victorian Holiday
Walking Jamie Furry Friends Set	1970	1584	$1,000.00	Sears
Walking Jamie Strollin' in Style	1972	1247	$1,000.00	Sears
The Waltz Barbie and Ken	B2655	2003	$100.00	
Wedding Day Kelly & Todd	1991	9852	$35.00	
Wedding Fantasy	1997	17243	$40.00	Toys "R" Us
Wedding Fantasy (Barbie & Ken)	1993	10924	$75.00	Wholesale Clubs
Wedding Party Barbie Deluxe Set	1994	13557	$45.00	
Wedding Party Barbie Deluxe Set (black)	1994	13556	$45.00	Toys "R" Us
Wedding Party	1964	1017	$2,800.00	
Wedding Party Midge	1991	9852	$120.00	
Western Fun (with Horse Sun Runner)	1990	5408	$65.00	Toys "R" Us
Western (Barbie & High Stepper)	1995	12371	$95.00	B.J. Wholesale Club
Western Stampin' Deluxe Playset	1993	10927	$30.00	
Western Stampin'	1993	11020	$55.00	Wholesale Clubs
Western Stampin' Star Horse	1990	5408	$45.00	Wholesale Clubs
Western Stampin' Western Star Horse (black)	1993	13478	$45.00	Toys "R" Us
Winter Holiday	1996	15645	$40.00	
Winter Ride	1998	19850	$45.00	Toys " R" Us

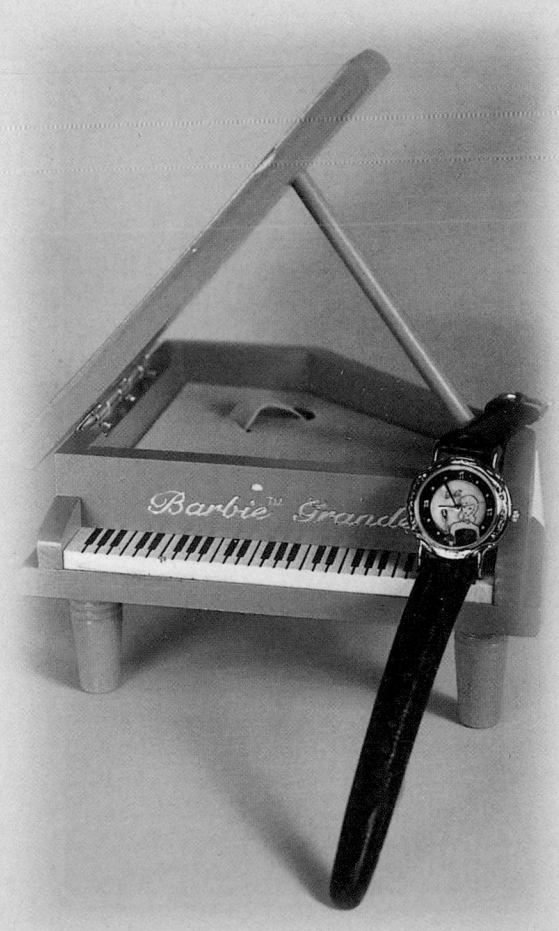

Gift Sets

Listed by Year

Year	Item	Number	Value	Specials
1960	Mix 'n Match Set (blonde)	857	$1,800.00	
1960	Mix 'n Match Set (brunette)	857	$2,100.00	
1960	Party Set	856	$2,100.00	
1960	Trousseau Set	858	$1,900.00	
1962	Barbie & Ken Mix 'n Match Set	N/A	$1,500.00	Wards/Spiegel
1962	Barbie & Ken Tennis Set	892	$1,400.00	Wards/Spiegel
1963	Fashion Queen & Her Friends	863	$2,300.00	
1963	Fashion Queen Barbie & Ken Trousseau	864	$2,400.00	
1964	Furniture	4005	$300.00	Go-Together Furniture
1964	Little Theater Set	1018	$5,000.00	
1964	Midge Ensemble	1012	$3,000.00	
1964	Midge Mix 'n Match Set	3807	$2,600.00	
1964	On Parade Set	1014	$2,200.00	Sears
1964	Party Time Set (Skipper)	1021	$500.00	
1964	Pep Rally Set	4035	$1,500.00	
1964	Round the Clock	1013	$4,500.00	
1964	Sparkling Pink	1011	$2,500.00	
1964	Wedding Party	1017	$2,800.00	
1965	Color 'n Curl (Molded Barbie Head)	4039	$600.00	
1965	Color 'n Curl Set (Barbie & Midge)	4035	$1,100.00	
1965	Color Magic Fashion Designer Set	4038	$650.00	
1965	Holiday Party Set (Skipper)	1021	$900.00	
1965	Hostess Set (Barbie)	1034	$4,600.00	
1965	Living Room Furniture Gift Set	4012	$300.00	
1965	Posable and Her Sew-Free Wardrobe	8526	$1,500.00	Montgomery Ward
1965	Skipper On Wheels Set	1032	$500.00	Sears
1966	Color Magic Barbie	1043	$4,000.00	Sears
1966	Francie & Her Swingin' Separates Set	1042	$1,100.00	Sears
1966	Francie Sportin'	1044	$4,200.00	JCPenney
1966	Tutti and Todd Sundae Treat Playset	3556	$425.00	
1966	Tutti Me and My Dog Playset	3554	$375.00	
1966	Tutti Melody in Pink Playset	3555	$325.00	
1966	Tutti Night-Night Sleep Tight Playset	3553	$350.00	
1966	Tutti Walkin' My Dolly Playset	3552	$350.00	
1967	Beautiful Blues Set (Barbie)	3303	$3,000.00	Sears
1967	Casey Goes Casual	3304	$1,750.00	Sears
1967	Cookin' Goodies Playset (Tutti)	3559	$300.00	
1967	Cut 'n Button (Skooter)	1036	$700.00	Sears
1967	Fun-Timers Set (Chris)	3301	$900.00	Sears
1967	Swing-A-Ling (Tutti)	3560	$300.00	
1968	Dinner Dazzle Set (Barbie)	1551	$1,200.00	Sears
1968	Perfectly Pretty Set (Skipper)	1546	$975.00	Sears
1968	Silver 'n Satin Set (Barbie)	1552	$1,500.00	JCPenney
1968	Stripes Are Happening Set (Stacey)	1545	$3,000.00	Sears
1968	Travel in Style (Barbie)	1544	$2,500.00	Sears
1969	Bright & Breezy (Skipper)	1590	$975.00	Sears
1969	Fabulous Formal (Barbie & Ken)	1595	$1,500.00	Sears
1969	Golden Groove Set (Barbie)	1593	$1,600.00	Sears

Year	Item	Number	Value	Specials
1969	Julia Simply Wow Set	1594	$1,100.00	Sears
1969	Nite Lighting Set (Stacey)	1591	$2,000.00	Sears
1969	Pink Premier Set (Barbie)	1596	$1,500.00	JCPenney
1969	Twinkle Town Set (Barbie)	1866	$1,600.00	Sears
1970	Action Accents Set (Barbie)	1585	$1,125.00	Sears
1970	Bendable Leg Ken	1436	$800.00	
1970	Ken Red, White & Wild Set	1589	$525.00	Sears
1970	Pretty Pairs Angie 'n Tangie	1135	$255.00	
1970	Pretty Pairs Lori 'n Rori	1133	$250.00	
1970	Pretty Pairs Nan 'n Fran	1134	$250.00	
1970	Swingin' in Silver Set (P.J.)	1588	$1,200.00	Sears
1970	Very Best Velvet Set (Skipper)	1586	$600.00	Sears
1970	Walking Jamie Furry Friends Set	1584	$1,000.00	Sears
1971	Fashion 'n Motion Set (P.J.)	1508	$900.00	Sears
1971	Fluff Sunshine Special Set	1249	$900.00	Sears
1971	Malibu Ken Surf's Up	1248	$425.00	Sears
1971	Perfectly Plaid (Barbie)	1193	$1,200.00	Sears
1971	Rise & Shine (Francie)	1194	$1,100.00	Sears
1972	Skipper & Her Swing-a-Round Gym	1179	$350.00	Sears
1972	Walking Jamie Strollin' in Style	1247	$1,000.00	Sears
1975	Barbie & Her US Olympic Wardrobe	9044	$105.00	Sears
1976	Ballerina on Tour	9093	$150.00	Department Store
1976	Super Fashion Fireworks #1 (Barbie)	9805	$75.00	Kresge Store
1976	Super Fashion Fireworks #2 (Barbie)	9805	$75.00	Kresge Store
1976	Super Fashion Fireworks #3 (Barbie)	9805	$75.00	Kresge Store
1977	SuperStar in the Spotlight Set	2207	$80.00	Department Store
1978	Malibu Barbie and Her Ten Speeder Set	N/A	$100.00	Montgomery Ward
1978	Malibu Barbie Fashion Combo	2753	$80.00	
1978	SuperStar Barbie & Ken Set	2422	$125.00	Department Store
1978	SuperStar Barbie Fashion Change-Abouts	2586	$100.00	
1979	Kissing Barbie Extra Value Set	2977	$100.00	Department Store
1980	Beauty Secrets Pretty Reflections	1702	$95.00	
1980	Golden Dreams Glamorous Nights	3533	$75.00	
1980	Kissing	2597	$45.00	
1982	Pink & Pretty Gift Set Modeling Set	5939	$65.00	Department Store
1983	Barbie & Friends	4431	$95.00	
1983	Campin' Out	4984	$100.00	
1983	Twirly Curls	4079	$95.00	Department Store
1984	Dance Sensation	9058	$45.00	Toys "R" Us
1984	Loving You	7563	$60.00	Department Store
1985	Happy Birthday Barbie	9678	$50.00	
1985	Happy Birthday	9514	$85.00	Department Store
1986	My First Barbie (Pink Tutu)	1879	$25.00	
1986	Tropical Malibu	2996	$45.00	
1988	Tennis Star (Barbie & Ken)	7801	$65.00	Toys "R" Us
1988	Vacation Sensation	1675	$25.00	Toys "R" Us
1989	Cool City Blues (Barbie, Ken & Skipper)	4893	$60.00	Toys "R" Us
1989	Dance Club (Barbie)	4217	$50.00	Children's Palace
1989	Show 'n Ride	7799	$45.00	Toys "R" Us
1990	Dance Magic (Barbie & Ken)	5409	$50.00	
1990	Hot Dancin' Set	4841	$75.00	
1990	On The Go (Barbie)	1007	$70.00	
1990	Western Fun (with Horse Sun Runner)	5408	$65.00	Toys "R" Us
1990	Western Stampin' Star Horse	5408	$45.00	Wholesale Clubs
1991	All American Barbie & Star Stepper	3712	$65.00	Wholesale Clubs

Year	Item	Number	Value	Specials
1991	Barbie & Friends (Disney)	3177	$75.00	Toys "R" Us
1991	Barbie for President	3722	$65.00	Toys "R" Us
1991	Barbie for President (black)	3940	$45.00	Toys "R" Us
1991	Bathtime	9601	$25.00	Wholesale Clubs
1991	My First Barbie	2483	$35.00	
1991	Wedding Day Kelly & Todd	9852	$35.00	
1991	Wedding Party Midge	9852	$120.00	
1992	Barbie Deluxe 100-piece (1st issue)	7151	$40.00	Wholesale Clubs
1992	Dream Wardrobe	3331	$40.00	
1992	Holiday Gown Collection I	697	$75.00	
1992	Marine Corps	4704	$45.00	Stars 'n Stripes
1992	Marine Corps (black)	2810	$45.00	Stars 'n Stripes
1992	Rollerblade	7142	$50.00	Wholesale Clubs
1992	Sharin' Sisters	5716	$50.00	
1992	Snap 'n Play	2262	$30.00	
1992	Sparkle Eyes	7131	$60.00	Wholesale Clubs
1992	Sun Sensation	7149	$75.00	Wholesale Clubs
1993	Army Desert Storm	5626	$70.00	Stars 'n Stripes
1993	Army Desert Storm (black)	5627	$60.00	Stars 'n Stripes
1993	Denim Deluxe	4893	$60.00	
1993	Disney Weekend Barbie	10723	$50.00	
1993	Disney Weekend Barbie & Ken	10724	$75.00	
1993	Dream Wedding	10712	$55.00	Toys "R" Us
1993	Dream Wedding (black)	10713	$50.00	Toys "R" Us
1993	Dressing Fun (pink dress)	9518	$50.00	Wholesale Clubs
1993	Dressing Fun (purple dress)	9518	$50.00	Wholesale Clubs
1993	Earring Magic Barbie Software Pak	None	$45.00	Radio Shack
1993	Fun to Dress	3826	$25.00	
1993	Holiday Gown Collection II	697A	$60.00	
1993	Hollywood Hair	10928	$25.00	Wholesale Clubs
1993	Island Fun	10379	$35.00	Wholesale Clubs
1993	Loves to Read	10527	$50.00	Toys "R" Us
1993	My Sister Stacie	9365	$10.00	
1993	Paint 'n Dazzle	10926	$35.00	Wholesale Clubs
1993	Secret Hearts	10929	$50.00	Wholesale Clubs
1993	Sharin' Sisters	10143	$55.00	
1993	Stacie & Butterfly Pony	10227	$25.00	
1993	Wedding Fantasy (Barbie & Ken)	10924	$75.00	Wholesale Clubs
1993	Western Stampin' Deluxe Playset	10927	$30.00	
1993	Western Stampin'	11020	$55.00	Wholesale Clubs
1993	Western Stampin' Western Star Horse (black)	13478	$45.00	Toys "R" Us
1994	35th Anniversary	11591	$175.00	
1994	Air Force Barbie & Ken (Thunderbirds)	11581	$60.00	Stars 'n Stripes
1994	Air Force Barbie & Ken (Thunderbirds, black)	11582	$50.00	Stars 'n Stripes
1994	Beach Fun	11481	$35.00	Wholesale Clubs
1994	Bedtime Barbie	12184	$45.00	Wholesale Clubs
1994	Birthday Fun At McDonald's	11589	$45.00	
1994	Caring Careers Fashion	10773	$10.00	
1994	Dolls of the World I (Barbie)	12043	$75.00	Dolls of the World Series
1994	Wedding Party Barbie Deluxe Set	13557	$45.00	
1994	Wedding Party Barbie Deluxe Set (black)	13556	$45.00	Toys "R" Us
1995	Barbie & Champion	13831	$80.00	Wholesale Clubs
1995	Barbie and Kelly Strolling Fun Set	13742	$20.00	
1995	Barbie and Kelly Strolling Fun Set (black)	13743	$20.00	
1995	Denim & Ruffles	12371	$65.00	Wholesale Clubs

Year	Item	Number	Value	Specials
1995	Dolls of the World II (Barbie)	13939	$60.00	Dolls of the World Series
1995	Hot Skatin' Barbie & Mustang Deluxe	13511	$45.00	Wholesale Clubs
1995	Me & My Mustang	11929	$35.00	Wholesale Clubs
1995	Polly Pocket	14406	$20.00	JCPenney
1995	Solo in the Spotlight	14403	$50.00	JCPenney
1995	Travelin' Sisters	14073	$50.00	
1995	Western (Barbie & High Stepper)	12371	$95.00	B.J. Wholesale Clubs
1996	30th Anniversary Francie	14608	$65.00	
1996	Barbie & Keiko	16214	$30.00	Ocean Friends
1996	Barbie Millicent Roberts	16080	$75.00	Barbie Millicent Roberts
1996	Birthday Fun Kelly	15610	$40.00	Toys "R" Us
1996	Dolls of the World III (Barbie)	15283	$65.00	Dolls of the World Series
1996	Horse Lovin' Barbie & Nibbles	15648	$25.00	Wholesale Clubs
1996	Foam 'n Color	16567	$20.00	JCPenney
1996	Matinee Today	16079	$70.00	Barbie Millicent Roberts
1996	Ocean Friends	N/A	$25.00	Department Store
1996	Olympic		$30.00	Wholesale Clubs
1996	Shoppin' Fun Barbie & Kelly Playset	15756	$20.00	
1996	Shoppin' Fun Barbie & Kelly Playset (black)	15757	$20.00	
1996	Star Trek	15006	$30.00	
1996	Winter Holida	15645	$40.00	
1997	Barbie Loves Elvis	17450	$90.00	
1997	Gap Barbie & Kelly	19014	$50.00	Gap Stores
1997	Gap Barbie & Kelly (black)	18548	$40.00	Gap Stores
1997	Gardening Fun Barbie & Kelly	17242	$30.00	Toys "R" Us
1997	Happy Halloween (Barbie & Kelly)	17238	$30.00	Target
1997	Perfectly Suited	17567	$70.00	Barbie Millicent Roberts
1997	Show Parade w/Star Stampin' Horse (black)	15060	$30.00	Toys "R" Us
1997	Show Parade w/Star Stampin' Horse	15059	$30.00	Toys "R" Us
1997	Wedding Fantasy	17243	$40.00	Toys "R" Us
1998	Ballet Recital Barbie & Kelly	18187	$15.00	
1998	Ballet Recital Barbie & Kelly (black)	21388	$15.00	
1998	Birthday Surprise CD-ROM	17765	$20.00	
1998	Dr. Ken & Little Patient Tommy	18898	$15.00	
1998	Dr. Ken & Little Patient Tommy (black)	18899	$15.00	
1998	Easter Egg Hunt Barbie & Kelly	19014	$40.00	Target
1998	Golden Greater Qi-Pao	20649	$85.00	
1998	Halloween Party Barbie & Ken	19874	$25.00	Target
1998	Holiday Sisters Barbie, Stacie & Kelly	19809	$25.00	Toys "R" Us
1998	Kelly & Baby Pony	20346	$17.00	
1998	Kelly & Ginger	19810	$20.00	
1998	Kelly & Tommy Power Wheels	18717	$20.00	
1998	Kelly & Tommy Power Wheels (black)	18718	$20.00	
1998	Li'l Zoo Pals Sister	19625	$30.00	
1998	Phantom of the Opera	20377	$130.00	FAO Schwarz
1998	Romeo and Juliet	19364	$70.00	Legendary Couples
1998	Winter Ride	19850	$45.00	Toys " R" Us
1999	Barbie & Kenny Country Duet	23498	$100.00	Grand Ole Opry
1999	Barbie Loves Frankie Sinatra	22953	$65.00	
1999	Country Duet	23498	$65.00	Grand Ole Opry
1999	Easter Bunny Fun Barbie & Kelly	21720	$25.00	
1999	Easter Bunny Fun Barbie & Kelly (black)	22187	$25.00	
1999	Fashion Fun Barbie	24148	$25.00	
1999	Generation Girl Barbie & Lara	25502	$40.00	
1999	Generation Girl Barbie & Nichelle	25503	$40.00	

Year	Item	Number	Value	Specials
1999	Giggles and Swing Barbie and Kelly	20333	$15.00	
1999	Giggles and Swing Barbie and Kelly (black)	20534	$15.00	
1999	Halloween Fun Barbie & Kelly	23460	$25.00	
1999	Halloween Fun Barbie & Kelly (black)	23461	$25.00	
1999	Halloween Fun Li'l Friends of Kelly	23796	$25.00	
1999	Holiday Sisters Barbie, Kelly, and Stacie	23617	$35.00	Holiday Sisters
1999	Ken & Barbie as King Arthur and Queen Guinevere	23880	$100.00	Together Forever Collection
1999	March of Dimes Walk America Barbie & Kelly	20843	$18.00	
1999	March of Dimes Walk America Barbie & Kelly (black)	20844	$18.00	
2000	The Addams Family	27276	$65.00	
2000	Bedtime Baby Barbie and Krissy	28516	$16.00	
2000	Easter Egg Party Barbie & Kelly (black)	25791	$25.00	
2000	Harley-Davidson Barbie	29208	$70.00	
2000	I Love Lucy 50th Anniversary (Episode 50)	28553	$80.00	Timeless Treasures
2000	Let's Drive (Barbie and Skipper)		$35.00	Toys "R" Us
2000	Merlin & Morgan Le Fay	27287	$100.00	Magic & Mystery Series
2000	Renaissance Rose	28633	$40.00	
2000	Singing Holiday Sisters	26260	$40.00	
2000	Sisters Celebration Krissy and Barbie		Retail	Sam's Club/Wholesale Clubs
2000	Victorian Holiday Barbie and Kelly	28395	Retail	Victorian Holiday
2001	McDonald's Fun Time Barbie & Kelly	29395	$17.00	

Greeting Cards

Item	Year	Number	Value	Specials
Ballerina Barbie Birthday Card	1989	N/A	$5.00	Gibson
Barbie Valentines (30 count)	1994	195TV57	$5.00	Hallmark
Children's Day Card (Feliz Dia del Nino)	1996	15310	$3.00	
Fashion Greeting Cards (all occasion)	1995	13041	$3.00	
Fashion Greeting Cards (birthday)	1995	13024	$3.00	
Fashion Greeting Cards (holiday)	1995	13062	$3.00	
Glamour Dream Collection	1994	N/A	$35.00	Hallmark
Happy Birthday	1996	13028	$3.00	
Happy Birthday	1996	13043	$3.00	
Happy Birthday	1996	13044	$3.00	
Happy Birthday	1996	13045	$3.00	
Happy Birthday	1996	13046	$3.00	
Happy Birthday	1996	13048	$3.00	
Happy Easter	1996	14680	$3.00	
Happy Easter	1996	14681	$3.00	
Happy Easter	1996	14683	$3.00	
Happy Holidays	1996	13056	$3.00	
Happy Holidays	1996	13059	$3.00	
Happy Holidays	1996	15443	$3.00	
Happy Holidays	1996	15444	$3.00	
Happy Holidays	1996	15445	$3.00	
Happy Valentine's Day	1994	5-7AA	$1.00	Hallmark
Happy Valentine's Day	1994	5-7AB	$1.00	Hallmark
Have Fun on Valentine's Day	1994	5-7AC	$1.00	Hallmark
Hope Your Valentine's Day is the Coolest	1994	5-7AD	$1.00	Hallmark
I Love You (Valentine card)	1996	14685	$3.00	
I Love You (Valentine card)	1996	14686	$3.00	
I Love You (Valentine card)	1996	14687	$3.00	
Let's Be Valentines	1994	5-7AE	$1.00	Hallmark
You're Special	1996	14881	$3.00	
You're Special	1996	14883	$3.00	
You're Special	1996	14884	$3.00	

Jewelry & Jewelry Boxes

Item	Year	Number	Value	Specials
16th Anniversary Child's Pendant	1974	N/A	$12.00	
Ballerina (music box)	1997	9603804	$30.00	
Ballerina (non-musical)	1997	9603798	$10.00	
Barbie and Me Jewels and Chest	1963	1771	$55.00	
Barbie at FAO Jewelry Collection	1996	782292	$25.00	FAO Schwarz
Bracelet for You	1988	4632	$10.00	Perfume Pretty Jewelry
Cameo Barrette, Blue	1982	5216	$5.00	Just For You
Cameo Barrette, Lilac	1982	5222	$5.00	Just For You
Cameo Barrette, Pink	1982	5090	$5.00	Just For You
Cameo Barrette, Yellow	1982	5219	$5.00	Just For You
Cameo Bracelet	1982	5114	$10.00	
Cameo Case	1982	3894	$10.00	Just For You
Cameo Locket	1982	5115	$10.00	
Cameo Ring	1982	5116	$10.00	
Costume Jewelry Set	1962	1311	$50.00	Sears
Diamond Collection	1987	1928	$10.00	
Emerald Collection	1987	1924	$10.00	
Enchanted Evening (music box)	1997	9603803	$30.00	
Enchanted Evening (non-musical)	1997	9603837	$10.00	
Fan Club Bracelet	N/A	N/A	$15.00	
Fashion Coordinated Jewelry	1962	1759	$10.00	Montgomery Ward
Fashion Fun	1997	9603796	$10.00	
Faux Pearl Bracelet 6½"	1997	296-417	$10.00	
Faux Pearl Earrings (pierced)	1997	296-402	$6.00	
Faux Pearl Necklace 15"	1997	017-040	$13.00	
Glamour Jewelry	1995	X-1052	$4.00	
Glitter and Stick Jewelry Kit	2000	29064	$17.00	Barbie Studio
Gold Collection	1987	1923	$5.00	
Gold Medal Jewelry	1975	8059	$75.00	
Jewel Secrets Collector Case	1987	3763	$15.00	
Jewelry and Purse For Barbie	1988	4637	$10.00	Perfume Pretty Jewelry
Jewelry, Belt, and Shoes For Barbie	1988	4635	$10.00	Perfume Pretty Jewelry
Jewelry Box with Jewelry	1963	N/A	$30.00	
Jewelry Gift Set	1982	5247	$10.00	
Jewelry, Hair Comb, and Belt	1988	4633	$10.00	Perfume Pretty Jewelry
Necklace Bronze Color	N/A	N/A	$15.00	
Nostalgic Charm Bracelet (collector's edition)	1990	none	$120.00	Peter Brams Designs
Nostalgic Pin	1989	N/A	$20.00	
Pendant for You	1988	4634	$10.00	Perfume Pretty Jewelry
Perfume Pretty Gifts for You	1988	5558	$20.00	Perfume Pretty Jewelry
Pin, 35th Anniversary Toy Club	1994	N/A	$11.00	
Pin, Barbie and the Bandstand Convention	1996	N/A	$25.00	
Play Jewelry	N/A	N/A	$152.00	
Play Ring	1960	N/A	$175.00	
Ponytail Charm, Silver and Gold	1995	N/A	$70.00	
Poodle Parade	1997	9603799	$10.00	
Red Flare	1997	9603801	$10.00	
Red Jewelry Box	1963	N/A	$25.00	

Item	Year	Number	Value	Specials
Ring For You	1988	4635	$10.00	Perfume Pretty Jewelry
Ruby Collection	1987	1929	$10.00	
Sapphire Collection	1987	1927	$10.00	
Silver Collection	1987	1926	$10.00	
Single Charm Bracelet	1963	N/A	$75.00	
Solo In The Spotlight (music box)	1997	9603802	$30.00	
Style Magic Hair Charm and Barrettes	1989	1649	$8.00	
Sweet 16 Promotional Necklace	1974	7796	$45.00	
Talking Jewelry Box	1995	12170	$8.00	
Tea Party	1997	9603797	$10.00	
Three-piece Jewelry Set	1963	N/A	$45.00	
40th Anniversary Barbie Pin	None	1999	$5.00	40th Anniversary Barbie

Keychains

Item	Year	Number	Value	Specials
Ballerina Barbie	1997	720-0	$5.00	
Barbie Bride	1997	712-0	$5.00	
Barbie & Ken Set	1996	710-0	$10.00	Basic Fun
Crystal Collection	1996	738286	$40.00	FAO Schwarz
Enchanted Evening (blonde)	1996	N/A	$5.00	Basic Fun
Enchanted Evening (brunette)	1996	N/A	$5.00	Basic Fun
Groom Ken	1997	714-0	$5.00	
Movin' Groovin' Barbie	1998	725-0	$5.00	
Ocean Friends Barbie	1997	721-0	$5.00	
Original Swimsuit (blonde)	1996	700-0	$5.00	Basic Fun
Original Swimsuit (brunette)	1995	700-0	$5.00	Basic Fun
Picnic Set	1996	704-0	$5.00	Basic Fun
Poodle Parade	1996	705-0	$5.00	Basic Fun
Solo in the Spotlight (blonde)	1996	701-0	$5.00	Basic Fun
Solo in the Spotlight (brunette)	1996	701-0	$5.00	Basic Fun
Twist & Turn Barbie	1997	713-0	$5.00	
University Barbie	1998	724-0	$5.00	

Kitchen

Item	Year	Number	Value	Specials
Baking Set	1997	67688	$10.00	Fun Fixin'
Barbeque Set	1997	67684	$5.00	Fun Fixin'

Item	Year	Number	Value	Specials
Dessert Set	1997	67682	$5.00	Fun Fixin'
Dishwasher Set	1997	67693	$15.00	Fun Fixin'
Makin' Breakfast	1997	67683	$5.00	Fun Fixin'
Makin' Breakfast (mini food set)	1997	67683	$10.00	Fun Fixin'
Picnic Set	1997	67686	$10.00	Fun Fixin'
Pizza Party	1997	67681	$5.00	Fun Fixin'
Refrigerator Set	1997	67691	$15.00	Fun Fixin'
Stove Set	1997	67692	$15.00	Fun Fixin'

Lunchboxes & Thermoses

Item	Year	Number	Value	Specials
Barbie and Midge Domed Lunchbox & black Thermos	1965	N/A	$350.00	
Barbie and Midge Lunchbox (black vinyl) & Thermos	1963	N/A	$100.00	
Barbie and Midge Thermos Bottle	1963	N/A	$110.00	
Black Ponytail Thermos	1962	2025	$60.00	
Campus Queen Lunchbox and Thermos	1967	N/A	$105.00	
Metal Lunchbox	1996	780858	$25.00	FAO Schwarz
Ponytail Lunchbox, 1960s Replica	1996	N/A	$50.00	FAO Schwarz

Barbie® Doll's Make-up

Item	Year	Number	Value	Specials
Bandages	1997	20150	$5.00	
Barbie Beauty Bundle	1997	215-761	$10.00	
Barbie Brush, Shampoo & Bow	1986	6085	$10.00	
Barbie Bubble Bath – Bain Mousse	1997	20100	$5.00	
Barbie Cologne	1986	6075	$3.00	
Barbie Cologne	1986	6085	$10.00	
Barbie Comb, Book & Lip Balm	1986	6085	$10.00	
Barbie Lip Balm	1986	6075	$3.00	
Barbie Lip Balm, Brush, & Nail Polish	1986	6085	$10.00	
Barbie Nail Polish	1986	6075	$3.00	
Barbie Pretty-Up Time	1964	4700	$130.00	Perfume Pretty Bath
Barbie Purse with Mirror	1997	20207	$15.00	

Item	Year	Number	Value	Specials
Barbie & the Rockers Bubble Bath	1987	6050	$5.00	Barbie & the Rockers
Barbie & the Rockers Color Foam Soap	1987	6060	$5.00	Barbie & the Rockers
Barbie & the Rockers Cosmetics Set	1987	622	$10.00	Barbie & the Rockers
Barbie & the Rockers Overnight Travel Case	1987	627	$10.00	Barbie & the Rockers
Barbie & the Rockers Vinyl Mini-Sets	1987	6025	$5.00	Barbie & the Rockers
Barbie & the Rockers Vinyl Purse (bows)	1987	6095	$15.00	Barbie & the Rockers
Barbie & the Rockers Vinyl Purse (brush)	1987	6095	$15.00	Barbie & the Rockers
Barbie & the Rockers Vinyl Purse (comb, cologne)	1987	6095	$15.00	Barbie & the Rockers
Basket with Toiletries	1994	20016	$15.00	Barbie For Girls
Bath Beauty Sponge	1997	20206	$5.00	
Bath Foam & Shampoo	1994	20046	$5.00	Barbie For Girls
Bath Foam & Shampoo	1995	20147	$5.00	
Bath Foam & Shampoo	1997	20147	$5.00	
Beautiful Hair Vanity Set	1994	20110	$10.00	Barbie For Girls
Beautiful Hair Vanity Set	1995	20145	$15.00	
Beauty Bath Set for Two	1988	5560	$10.00	Perfume Pretty Bath
Beauty Kit	1961	N/A	$100.00	
Beauty Parlor Set	1963	8643	$25.00	
Beauty Sets	1982	5119	$5.00	Just For You
Blush Peach	1982	5131	$5.00	Just For You
Blush Pink	1981	3591	$5.00	Just For You
Blush Plum	1982	5132	$5.00	Just For You
Blush Red	1981	3593	$5.00	Just For You
Body Lotion and Bow Barrette for Two	1988	5537	$5.00	Perfume Pretty Bath
Body Power	1997	294-414	$3.00	
Bubble Bath	1994	20100	$5.00	Barbie For Girls
Bubble Bath	1997	294-361	$5.00	Bath and Beauty Collection
Bubble Bath (Camp Barbie)	1995	20100	$5.00	
Cameo Comb, blue	1982	5217	$5.00	Just For You
Cameo Comb, lilac	1982	5223	$5.00	Just For You
Cameo Comb, pink	1982	5091	$5.00	Just For You
Cameo Comb, yellow	1982	5220	$5.00	Just For You
Cameo Ponytail Holder, blue	1982	5218	$5.00	Just For You
Cameo Ponytail Holder, lilac	1982	5224	$5.00	Just For You
Cameo Ponytail Holder, pink	1982	5089	$5.00	Just For You
Cameo Ponytail Holder, yellow	1982	5221	$5.00	Just For You
Cologne	1961	N/A	$125.00	
Cologne	1981	3603	$10.00	Just For You
Cologne Spray	1997	394-376	$7.00	Bath and Beauty Collection
Cosmetics Set	1994	20017	$10.00	Barbie For Girls
Cosmetics Case	1981	3548	$10.00	Just For You
Dream Cosmetics Set	1985	612	$15.00	
Dusting Powder and Powder Mitt for two	1988	5552	$10.00	Perfume Pretty Bath
Eye Shadow (lemon, orchid, pink)	1982	5133	$5.00	Just For You
Eye Shadow (lilac, sea blue, rose)	1981	3609	$5.00	Just For You
Eye Shadow (powder blue, aqua, warm brown)	1981	3596	$5.00	Just For You
Eye Shadow (sky blue, peach, plum)	1981	3595	$5.00	Just For You
Floating Soap Dish	1995	20133	$10.00	Baywatch
Fragrance and Perfume Purse for 2	1988	5536	$15.00	Perfume Pretty Bath
Fragrance Set	1994	20010	$10.00	Barbie For Girls
Glamour Cosmetics	1963	8643	$75.00	
Glamour Set	1994	20116	$10.00	Barbie For Girls
Glamour Set	1995	20135	$10.00	
Glamour Styling Set	1985	614	$15.00	
Hair Beauty Set (light blue)	1982	5214	$20.00	Just For You

Item	Year	Number	Value	Specials
Hair Beauty Set (pink)	1982	5215	$20.00	Just For You
Hand & Body Cream	1997	294-433	$3.00	Bath and Beauty Collection
I'm Into Barbie Hair Brush and Comb	1989	N/A	$10.00	Avon
Lip Balm	1997	294-380	$1.25	Bath and Beauty Collection
Lip Balm (passion fruit flavored) & Barbie Head Cap	1997	20131	$3.00	
Lip Balm (plain cap, passion fruit flavored)	1997	20149	$2.00	
Lip Balm Trio Set	1996	20165	$10.00	
Lip Gloss and Mirror for 2	1988	5554	$5.00	Perfume Pretty Bath
Lip Gloss, apple	1982	5175	$2.00	Just For You
Lip Gloss, cherry	1982	5172	$5.00	Just For You
Lip Gloss, plum	1982	5174	$5.00	Just For You
Lip Gloss, watermelon	1982	5173	$5.00	Just For You
Lipstick, coral (tropical fruit)	1981	3589	$5.00	Just For You
Lipstick, grape	1982	5135	$5.00	Just For You
Lipstick, hot pink (bubble gum)	1981	3590	$5.00	Just For You
Lipstick, pastel pink (peppermint)	1981	3587	$5.00	Just For You
Lipstick, red (strawberry)	1981	3588	$5.00	Just For You
Lipstick, tangerine	1982	5134	$5.00	Just For You
Liquid Soap and Sponge for 2	1988	5551	$5.00	Perfume Pretty Bath
Lotion	1961	N/A	$125.00	
Make-Up Case	1963	N/A	$25.00	
Mild Formula Bubble Bath	1997	20148	$3.00	
Nail Polish, coral	1981	3585	$5.00	Just For You
Nail Polish, deep violet	1982	5130	$5.00	Just For You
Nail Polish, hot pink	1981	3586	$5.00	Just For You
Nail Polish, pastel pink	1981	3583	$5.00	Just For You
Nail Polish, red	1981	3584	$5.00	Just For You
No-Tear Shampoo & Conditoner	1997	294-395	$4.00	
Overnight Travel Case	1997	20137	$15.00	
Perfume Maker Set	1980	2740	$20.00	
Perfumed Rollette	1997	294-400	$3.00	Bath and Beauty Collection
Pink and Pretty Deluxe Glamour Set	1997	20205	$15.00	
Pink Shades Beauty Set	1981	3598	$5.00	Just For You
Red Shades Beauty Set	1981	3599	$5.00	Just For You
Shampoo and Comb for 2	1988	5557	$10.00	Perfume Pretty Bath
Slumber Set	1985	610	$15.00	
Soap	1997	296-197	$3.00	Bath and Beauty Collection
Style 'N Go Set	1995	20136	$10.00	
Tote Bag with Toiletries	1994	20038	$10.00	Barbie For Girls
Travel Case	1994	20028	$10.00	Barbie For Girls
Travel Set	1995	20137	$10.00	
Vanity Set	1994	20044	$15.00	Barbie For Girls
Vinyl Drawstring Tote	1987	616	$10.00	
Vinyl Purse with Toiletries	1994	20036	$15.00	Barbie For Girls
Vinyl Purse with Toiletries	1995	20138	$10.00	
Workout Kit	1985	605	$15.00	

McDonald's Barbie Dolls

Item	Year	Number	Value
All American	1991	BA9140	$5.00
Bicyclin' Barbie	1994	BA9401	$3.00
Birthday Party	1993	BA9301	$4.00
Birthday Surprise	1992	BA9201	$4.00
Bridesmaid Skipper	1994	BA9408	$3.00
Bubble Angel	1995	N/A	$3.00
Butterfly Princess Teresa	1995	N/A	$3.00
Camp Barbie	1994	BA9403	$3.00
Camp Teresa #1	1994	BA9404	$3.00
Camp Teresa #2	1994	BA9419	$3.00
Cool Country	1995	N/A	$3.00
Costume Ball	1991	BA9141	$5.00
Dance Moves	1995	N/A	$3.00
Display/Premiums	1991	N/A	$175.00
Display/Premiums	1992	BA9226	$125.00
Display/Premiums	1993	BA9326	$100.00
Display/Premiums	1994	BA9426	$100.00
Display/Premiums	1995	N/A	$75.00
Display/Premiums	1996	N/A	$75.00
Display/Premiums	1997	N/A	$50.00
Dutch	1996	N/A	$2.00
Enchanted Evening (Tea Party Diorama)	1990	None	$8.00
Gymnast USA	1996	N/A	$5.00
Happy Birthday	1991	BA9143	$5.00
Happy Holidays	1990	None	$8.00
Happy Meal At Home	1991	BA9170	$3.00
Happy Meal Boxes (USA Banner)	1996	N/A	$2.00
Happy Meal On Stage	1991	BA9171	$3.00
Happy Meal Bag Barbie	1993	BA9330	$2.00
Happy Meal Beachfront Fun	1992	BA9220	$3.00
Happy Meal Magical World	1992	BA9221	$3.00
Hawaiian Fun	1991	BA9144	$5.00
Holiday Barbie	1995	N/A	$3.00
Hollywood Hair	1993	BA9302	$4.00
Hot Skatin'	1995	N/A	$3.00
Ice Capades	1991	BA9146	$5.00
Ice Skatin' Barbie	1995	N/A	$3.00
Japanese	1996	N/A	$2.00
Jewel & Glitter Bride	1994	BA9407	$3.00
Jewel & Glitter Shani	1994	BA9402	$3.00
Kenyan	1996	N/A	$2.00
Lights/Lace	1991	BA9142	$5.00
Lifeguard Barbie	1995	N/A	$4.00
Lifeguard Barbie (black)	1995	N/A	$4.00
Lifeguard Ken	1995	N/A	$4.00
Lifeguard Ken (black)	1995	N/A	$4.00
Locket Surprise Barbie #2 (Black)	1994	BA9420	$3.00
Locket Surprise Ken #2 (Black)	1994	BA9421	$3.00

Item	Year	Number	Value
Locket Surprise Barbie #1	1994	BA9405	$3.00
Locket Surprise Ken #1	1994	BA9406	$3.00
Mexican	1996	N/A	$2.00
Moonlight Ball (paper ballroom diorama)	1990	BA9004	$8.00
Movie Star (dressing room diorama)	1990	BA9001	$8.00
My First Ballerina	1992	BA9202	$4.00
My First Ballerina	1993	BA9303	$4.00
My First Barbie (Spanish)	1991	BA9147	$5.00
Paint 'n Dazzle	1993	BA9304	$4.00
Rappin' Rockin'	1992	BA9203	$4.00
Rollerblade	1992	BA9204	$4.00
Romantic Bride	1993	BA9305	$4.00
Rose Bride	1992	BA9205	$4.00
Secret Hearts	1993	BA9306	$4.00
Snap 'n Play	1992	BA9206	$4.00
Solo in the Spotlight (concert diorama)	1990	BA9020	$8.00
Sparkle Eyes	1992	BA9207	$4.00
Sun Sensation	1992	BA9208	$4.00
SuperStar	1990	None	$8.00
Train Car	1994	N/A	$3.00
Translite (large)	1991	BA9165	$30.00
Translite (small)	1991	BA9164	$20.00
Translite (small)	1992	BA9264	$10.00
Translite (small)	1993	BA9364	$10.00
Translite (small)	1994	BA9464	$8.00
Trayliner	1991	BA9183	$2.00
Twinkle Lights	1993	BA9307	$4.00
U-3 Ball, Lavender	1994	N/A	$3.00
U-3 Barbie Puzzle	1996	N/A	$3.00
U-3 Costume Ball	1991	BA9148	$5.00
U-3 Rose Bride	1993	N/A	$4.00
U-3 Sparkle Eyes	1992	BA9217	$5.00
U-3 Wedding Midge	1991	BA9149	$5.00
Wedding Day Midge	1991	BA9145	$5.00
Western Stampin'	1993	BA9308	$4.00

Miscellaneous

Item	Year	Number	Value	Specials
Accessory Case			N/A	Tara Toy Co.
Ballerina (large)	1997	9603821	$25.00	
Ballerina (medium)	1997	9604307	$15.00	
Ballerina (small)	1997	9604315	$10.00	
Ballerina Barbie Dress-Up Kit	1977	616	$10.00	
Balloon (mylar)	1995	1973	$3.00	
Barbie and Beauty Fashion Dress-Up Kit	1981	2363	$5.00	
Barbie and Me Dress-Up Set	N/A	N/A	$75.00	
Barbie and Me Vanity Set	1962	4719	$150.00	Montgomery Ward
Barbie and the Rockers — Out of This World	1987	N/A	$25.00	VHS Tapes
Barbie and the Sensations	1987	N/A	$25.00	VHS Tapes
Barbie as Florist (Suburban Shopper)	1997	9602193	$18.00	From Barbie With Love
Barbie Assorted Chocolate Eggs, 3¾ oz.	1997	302	$3.00 ea.	Russell Stover Candy
Barbie Assorted Chocolates, 8 oz.	1997	8804	$4.00	Russell Stover Candy
Barbie Bake w/Me Oven	2000	88888	$20.00	Tara Toy Co.
Barbie Bake w/Me Refill Set, brownie	2000	N/A	$5.00	Tara Toy Co.
Barbie Bake w/Me Refill Set, cake	2000	N/A	$5.00	Tara Toy Co.
Barbie Bake w/Me Refill Set, cookie	2000	N/A	$5.00	Tara Toy Co.
Barbie Birthday Ensemble	1989	N/A	$75.00	Unique Industries
Barbie Christmas Tin, 1¾ oz.	1997	8807	$2.00	Russell Stover Candy
Barbie Christmas Wreath Tin, 4 oz.	1997	8805	$5.00	Russell Stover Candy
Barbie Doll Display Boxes	1996	2923	$25.00	
Barbie Easter Basket, 6¾ oz.	1996	N/A	$35.00	Russell Stover Candy
Barbie Easter Basket, 7¼ oz.	1997	315	$30.00	Russell Stover Candy
Barbie Fashion Embroidery Set	1964	7520A	$100.00	
Barbie Fishing (Picnic Set)	1997	9602194	$18.00	From Barbie with Love
Barbie in Paris (Gay Parisienne)	1997	9602195	$18.00	From Barbie with Love
Barbie Nurse Kit	1962	1962	$300.00	
Barbie On a World Tour View-Master Set	1965	N/A	$35.00	
Barbie On Beach (original swimsuit)	1997	9602196	$18.00	From Barbie with Love
Barbie on Tour Poster	1986	N/A	$45.00	
Barbie Ornament, 3¾ oz. (hollow milk chocolate)	1997	8803	$3.00	Russell Stover Candy
Barbie Poodle Parade	1997	9602374	$18.00	From Barbie with Love
Barbie "Shop With Me" Cash Register	2000	BE-190	$45.00	
Barbie Surprise Egg, 3 oz.	1997		$3.00	Russell Stover Candy
Barbie Surprise Tin, ⅞ oz.	1997	8451	$2.00	Russell Stover Candy
Barbie Tin Egg, 3 oz.	1997	303	$3.00	Russell Stover Candy
Barbie Trunk with 3 Costumes	1993	164996	$98.00	FAO Schwarz
Barbie Wrap-an-Egg Decorating Kit	1983	N/A	$10.00	Easter Unlimited
Barbie's Around the World Trip	1965	N/A	$20.00	
Barbie's Birthday Party	1994	N/A	$15.00	VHS Tapes
Barbie, Ken, & Midge Embroidery Set	1963	7686	$100.00	
Bathroom Playset	2000	67555	$14.00	All Around Home
Beauty Secrets	N/A	N/A	$300.00	Store Display
Bedroom Playset (Barbie)	2000		$14.00	All Around Home
Bedroom Playset (Kelly)	2000	88703	$10.00	All Around House
Best Buys Fashion (shelf strip)	1982	5352	$20.00	Store Display
Black & White Bathing Suit (large)	1997	9603824	$25.00	

Item	Year	Number	Value	Specials
Black & White Bathing Suit (medium)	1997	9604301	$15.00	
Black & White Bathing Suit (small)	1997	9604309	$10.00	
Breakfast with Barbie Cereal	1989	16609	$10.00	
Christmas Stockings	N/A	N/A	$30.00	Joey Skilbred
Cleaning Set	1982	569	$10.00	
Collector's Club Kit	1999	23553	$40.00	
Compact Keychain	2000	729-0	$3.00	Basic Fun
Dance Workout with Barbie	1992	N/A	$15.00	VHS Tapes
Dining Room Playset (Barbie)	2000	67551	$10.00	All Around Home
Doll Stand (black)	1996	3246	$10.00	
Doll Stand (ivory)	1996	3247	$10.00	
Dr. Ken Kit	1963	1959	$50.00	
Dream House Playset	1979	N/A	$12.00	
Dress-Up Vanity Keychain	2000	729-0	$3.00	Basic Fun
Family Room Playset (Barbie)	2000	67553	$14.00	All Around Home
"Fan on Board" Window Suction	1990	N/A	$10.00	
Fashion Fun	1997	9603817	$3.00	Matrix
Free Cologne Sampler (shelf strip)	1982	N/A	$10.00	Store Display
Free Cosmetics Bag Offer (shelf strip)	1982	5351	$10.00	Store Display
Friendship Collection	1981	9001	$10.00	
Fun Fair Kelly Kiddie Rides	2000	88705	$9.00	
Fur and Jewels Safe	1978	2595	$10.00	
Ge-Tar	1964	524	$325.00	
Good Grooming Manicure Set	N/A	N/A	$75.00	
Hallmark Glamour Dream Collection	1994	N/A	$25.00	
Hat Box Keychain	1999	728-0	$3.00	Basic Fun
Have A Nice Trip — Nostalgic	1997	9602373	$3.00	Matrix
Heirloom Set	1962	4635	$100.00	Montgomery Ward
Hollywood Hair Styling Head	1993	N/A	$29.00	
Inflatable Pool, 54"	1993	1652	$15.00	
Julia Dress-Up Kit	1969	N/A	$10.00	
Kelly Playland	2000	88704	$14.00	
Kelly Surprise Birthday Party	1999	67346	$16.00	
Kitchen Playset (Barbie)	2000	67554	$14.00	All Around Home
Knitting For Barbie	1962	4767	$100.00	Montgomery Ward
Knitting Kit	1962	N/A	$30.00	
Let's Have a Party Case	1997	X1040	$10.00	
Lunch Kit Keychain	1999	728-0	$3.00	Basic Fun
Luncheon Embroidery Set	1962	4648D	$120.00	Montgomery Ward
Midge Fashion Embroidery Set	1964	7538A	$110.00	
Modern Miss Play Box	1963	593	$80.00	Sears
Nostalgic Barbie Shoes Replacement Pack	1996	10612	$10.00	
Nurse Kit	1962	1694	$70.00	Sears
Pillow, 18"x18"	N/A	N/A	$35.00	Joey Skilbred
Pillowcase (standard)	1991	DGB024	$5.00	J.P. Stevens & Co.
Pillowcases	1991	N/A	$5.00	
Poodle Parade (large)	1997	9603823	$25.00	
Poodle Parade (medium)	1997	9604303	$15.00	
Poodle Parade (small)	1997	9604303	$10.00	
Poof Valance	1991	356c	$6.00	J.P. Stevens & Co.
Purse, Shoe Set	1964	3295	$80.00	Sears
Queen of the Prom Keychain	1999	728-0	$3.00	Basic Fun
Record Tote	1961	N/A	$40.00	
Red Flare (large)	1997	9603826	$25.00	
Red Flare (medium)	1997	9604304	$15.00	

Item	Year	Number	Value	Specials
Red Flare (small)	1997	9604312	$10.00	
Red Shorts, Blue Printed Shirt, Shoes	2000	68230	$2.00	Fashion Favorites
Scoop 'N Swirl Ice Cream Shop Playset	2000	88706	$10.00	
Secret Bank	1993	BA00883	$7.00	
Sew Magic Add-Ons for Francie & Skipper	1973	N/A	$20.00	
Sewing Accessories	1964	3294	$60.00	Sears
Shoe Tube Keychain	2000	729-0	$3.00	Basic Fun
Song Bird	1997	9603818	$3.00	Matrix
Sports Fashion Set	1975	2352	$5.00	
Sweet 16 Promotional Set	1974	7796	$70.00	
Tablecloth	1978	N/A	$25.00	
Tea Party	1997	9603816	$3.00	Matrix
The Wonderful World of Barbie	N/A	N/A	$900.00	Store Display
The World of Barbie	1965	1093	$1,000.00	Store Display
Toothbrush	1981	3458	$10.00	
Towel & Washcloth	N/A	N/A	$15.00	
Ultimate Art Studio	1997	X1075	$13.00	
View Master Keychain	2000	730-0	$3.00	Basic Fun
Wedding — Nostalgic	1997	9602365	$3.00	Matrix
Western Barbie Dress-Up Set	1981	635	$15.00	
Western Barbie Dress-Up Set	1982	657	$5.00	
What's Cooking — Nostalgic	1997	9602375	$3.00	Matrix
Young Traveler's Play Kit	1964	469	$80.00	Sears
Zoo Babies Playset	2000	88716	$13.00	Zoo Babies

Ornaments

Item	Year	Number	Value	Specials
1962 Hat Box Doll Case	2000	N/A	$11.00	Hallmark
1989 Happy Holidays Barbie	1997	N/A	$25.00	Hallmark/Collector's Club Edition
1990 Happy Holidays Barbie	1998	N/A	$25.00	Hallmark/Collector's Club Edition
1991 Happy Holidays Barbie	1991	1999	$30.00	
1991 Happy Holidays Barbie	1999	N/A	$25.00	Hallmark/Collector's Club Edition
1993 Christmas Ornament (1988 Holiday)	1993		$100.00	Hallmark
1994 Christmas Ornament	1994	5216	$45.00	Hallmark
1995 Christmas Ornament	1995	N/A	$30.00	Hallmark
1995 JCPenney Christmas Ornament	1995	N/A	$20.00	JCPenney
1996 Christmas Ornament	1996	N/A	$15.00	Hallmark
1996 JCPenney Christmas Ornament (Winter Renaissance)	1996	N/A	$20.00	JCPenney
1997 Happy Holidays Barbie	1997	N/A	$10.00	Matrix
1997 Holidays Barbie	1997	N/A	$15.00	Hallmark/Holiday Barbie Series
1998 Happy Holidays Barbie	1998	N/A	$10.00	Matrix
1998 Holidays Barbie	1998	N/A	$15.00	Hallmark/Holiday Barbie Series
1999 Holidays Barbie	1999	N/A	$15.00	Hallmark/Holiday Barbie Series
24K Gold Finish	1996	N/A	$40.00	FAO Schwarz
35th Anniversary Ball	1994	N/A	$35.00	Mattel Festival

Item	Year	Number	Value	Specials
35th Anniversary Midge	1998	N/A	$15.00	Hallmark
40th Anniversary Barbie	1999	N/A	$17.00	Hallmark
40th Anniversary Barbie Lunchbox	1999	N/A	$15.00	Hallmark
African-American Holiday Barbie	1998	N/A	$15.00	Hallmark
Alpine Blush Barbie	1997	97Bar03	$45.00	Christopher Radko
Angel of Joy	2000	N/A	$15.00	
Ballerina	1996	9603031	$5.00	Matrix
Barbie & Ken	1997	N/A	$10.00	Matrix
Barbie Anniversary Edition Lunchbox	1999	47920	$14.00	Hallmark
Barbie as Cinderella	1999	47912	$16.00	Hallmark
Barbie as Dorothy	1997	260207	$10.00	Enesco
Barbie as Eliza Doolittle	1997	270520	$12.00	Enesco
Barbie as Eliza Doolittle (Embassy Ball)	1997	274305	$12.00	Enesco
Barbie as Eliza Doolittle (Ascot-disc)	1997	N/A	$12.00	Enesco
Barbie as Glinda the Good Witch	1997	274283	$14.00	Enesco
Barbie as Scarlett O'Hara	1996	182028	$14.00	Enesco
Barbie as Scarlett O'Hara	1997	260177	$13.00	Enesco
Barbie Black	1997	N/A	$35.00	Christopher Radko
Barbie 1996 Holiday	1996	64620	$19.00	Matrix
Barbie Stocking	1998	N/A	$35.00	Christopher Radko
Barbie Toy Block	1997	97Bar04	$38.00	Christopher Radko
Barbie Wedding Day	1997	N/A	$15.00	Hallmark
Barbie Wreath	1997	97Bar02	$36.00	Christopher Radko
Black/White Bathing Suit	1996	9603929	$5.00	Matrix
Campus Sweetheart	1998	295248	$10.00	Enesco
Career Girl	1996	N/A	$7.00	Ashton-Drake
Celebration	2000	N/A	$15.00	Hallmark
Chinese	1997	N/A	$15.00	Hallmark/Dolls of the World
Club Meeting	1996	N/A	$10.00	Ashton-Drake
Commuter Set	1996	N/A	$7.00	Ashton-Drake
Dorothy, Lion, Scarecrow, and Tin Man	1997	284335	$14.00	Enesco
Dorothy, Lion, Scarecrow, and Tin Man	1997	310832	$13.00	Enesco
Dreamhouse Playhouse	1999	N/A	$15.00	Hallmark
Easter Ornament	1995	8069	$25.00	Hallmark
Easter Parade	1996	N/A	$10.00	Ashton-Drake
Elegant Holiday	1998	N/A	$30.00	Christopher Radko
Enchanted Evening	1996	N/A	$10.00	Ashton-Drake
Enchanted Evening	1996	16541	$15.00	Hallmark
Enchanted Evening	1996	9603924	$5.00	Matrix
Evening Majesty	1997	N/A	$17.00	JCPenney
Evening Splendour	1996	N/A	$10.00	Ashton-Drake
Fashion Avenue	1997	N/A	$10.00	Matrix
Fashion Editor	1995	N/A	$10.00	Ashton-Drake
Fashion Fun	1996	9603933	$5.00	Matrix
Fraternity Dance	1996	N/A	$10.00	Ashton-Drake
Gay Parisienne	1996	N/A	$10.00	Ashton-Drake
Gay Parisienne	1997	N/A	$10.00	Matrix
Gay Parisienne Barbie	1999	38206	$16.00	Hallmark
Goddess of the Sun	1997	260223	$12.00	Enesco
Gone with the Wind (Barbie as Scarlett)	1996	182028	$13.00	Enesco
Hallmark Club 1996 Holiday Ornament	1996	N/A	$50.00	Hallmark
Happy Holidays 1989	1996	188867	$13.00	Enesco
Happy Holidays 1990	1997	N/A	$12.00	Enesco
Happy Holidays 1990	1997	274240	$10.00	Enesco
Happy Holidays 1996	1996	188824	$13.00	Enesco

Item	Year	Number	Value	Specials
Happy Holidays 1997	1997	274267	$10.00	Enesco
Harley-Davidson	2000	N/A	$15.00	Hallmark
Holiday Barbie	1997	97Bar01	$50.00	Christopher Radko
Holiday Barbie 3" (in acetate box)	1996	9604608	$5.00	Matrix
Holiday Barbie 4" (in acetate box)	1996	9604704	$15.00	Matrix
Holiday Barbie 4" (open window gift box)	1996	9604704	$15.00	Matrix
Holiday Dance	1997	188808	$10.00	Enesco
Holiday Dance 1965	1996	188808	$13.00	Enesco
Holiday Memories	1998	N/A	$15.00	Hallmark/Victorian Christmas
Holiday Traditions	1997	N/A	$15.00	Hallmark/Holiday Homecoming
Holiday Voyage	1998	N/A	$15.00	Hallmark/Holiday Homecoming
Little Bo Peep	1998	N/A	$15.00	Hallmark/Children's Collector Series
Mexican	1998	N/A	$15.00	Hallmark/Dolls of the World
Midnight	1997	N/A	$10.00	Matrix
Millennium Princess	1999	N/A	$26.00	Hallmark
Millennium Princess (black)	1999	N/A	$26.00	Hallmark
Moon Goddess	1997	260258	$10.00	Enesco
Native American	1996	5561	$20.00	Hallmark
Nostalgic Swimsuit	1994	N/A	$25.00	Hallmark
Original Swimsuit	1996	N/A	$10.00	Ashton-Drake
Ornament Holder, 6"	1997	274208	$10.00	Enesco
Picnic Set	1996	9603927	$5.00	Matrix
Poodle Parade	1996	9603925	$5.00	Matrix
Porcelain Barbie	2000	N/A	$30.00	Hallmark/Collector's Club Edition
Queen of Hearts (Bob Mackie)	1995	157724	$9.00	Enesco
Rapunzel	1997	N/A	$15.00	Hallmark/Children's Collector Series
Red Flare	1996	9603928	$5.00	Matrix
Roman Holiday	1996	N/A	$10.00	Ashton-Drake
Russian Barbie	1999	47874	$16.00	Dolls of the World
Saturday Matinee	1995	N/A	$10.00	Ashton-Drake
Scarlett O'Hara (green velvet-disc)	1996	N/A	$10.00	
Silken Flame	1996	N/A	$10.00	Ashton-Drake
Silken Flame	1997	N/A	$10.00	Matrix
Silken Flame	1998	N/A	$15.00	Hallmark
Solo in the Spotlight	1996	9603926	$5.00	Matrix
Solo in the Spotlight	1996	N/A	$10.00	Ashton-Drake
Solo in the Spotlight	1995	N/A	$25.00	Hallmark
Song Bird	1996	9603930	$5.00	Matrix
Spring Bouquet	1995	N/A	$20.00	Hallmark
Springtime #3	1997	N/A	$15.00	Hallmark/Springtime Barbie
Springtime #4	1998	N/A	$15.00	Hallmark/Springtime Barbie
Springtime Ornament	1996	N/A	$20.00	Hallmark
Sugar Plum Fairy	1997	N/A	$20.00	Avon
Summer Sophisticate	1996	N/A	Retail	Enesco
Summer Sophisticate	1996	N/A	$15.00	Spiegel
Tea Party	1996	9603932	$5.00	Matrix
Travel Case & Barbie Set	1999	N/A	$15.00	Hallmark/Miniatures
Travel Case & Silken Flame Barbie	2000	N/A	$15.00	Hallmark/Miniatures
Trio Display (plate & ornament)	1997	274224	$25.00	Enesco
Victorian Elegance Keepsake	1997	N/A	$15.00	Hallmark/Victorian Christmas
Wedding Day 1959	1959	260290	$10.00	Enesco
Winter Fun with Barbie & Kelly	2000	N/A	$15.00	Hallmark

Paper Dolls

Item	Year	Number	Value	Specials
Angel Face Barbie	1983	1982-45	$15.00	Golden
Angel Face Barbie (boxed)	1983	7407-E	$15.00	Golden
Ballerina Barbie	1977	1993-1	$30.00	Whitman
Ballerina Barbie (boxed)	1976	4391	$30.00	Whitman
Barbie	1962	1962	$90.00	Whitman
Barbie	1963	4601	$85.00	Whitman
Barbie	1963	11001	$85.00	Whitman
Barbie	1981	7408	$20.00	Whitman
Barbie	1990	1502	$12.00	Golden
Barbie	1990	1501-2	$12.00	Golden
Barbie	1990	1523-2	$10.00	Golden
Barbie	1991	1502-2	$12.00	Golden
Barbie	1992	1502-3	$12.00	Golden
Barbie	1992	1690	$12.00	Golden
Barbie	1993	1502-4	$12.00	Golden
Barbie	1993	1502-5	$12.00	Golden
Barbie	1994	2381	$7.00	
Barbie Fashion Originals	1976	1989	$15.00	
Barbie & Ken	1984	1527	$15.00	Golden
Barbie & Ken	1984	1985-51	$15.00	Golden
Barbie & Ken Coloring Book with Paper Dolls	1962	1883-B	$90.00	Western
Barbie & Skipper	1983	1944	$12.00	Whitman
Barbie & Skipper	1964	1944	$80.00	
Barbie & Skipper Campside at Lucky Lake Playbook	1980	1836	$25.00	Whitman
Barbie & the Rockers	1986	1528	$15.00	Golden
Barbie (boxed)	1962	4601	$25.00	Whitman
Barbie (boxed)	1967	4785	$50.00	Whitman
Barbie (boxed)	1971	4735	$30.00	Whitman
Barbie (boxed)	1981	74088-21	$29.00	Whitman
Barbie (boxed)	1991	5552	$10.00	Golden
Barbie 3-D Fashion Theater	1972	4350	$15.00	Colorforms
Barbie and Francie (boxed)	1976	4392-7411	$30.00	Whitman
Barbie and Francie, Barbie's Modern Cousin (boxed)	1966	4793	$75.00	Whitman
Barbie and Her 27-piece Wardrobe	1981	7408-B-1	$20.00	Whitman
Barbie and Her Friends All Sports Tournament	1975	1981	$18.00	Whitman
Barbie and Ken	1962	1963	$120.00	Whitman
Barbie and Ken	1962	1971	$120.00	Whitman
Barbie and Ken	1970	1976	$50.00	Whitman
Barbie and Ken	1970	1985	$40.00	Whitman
Barbie and Ken	1970	1986	$40.00	Whitman
Barbie and Ken (boxed)	1963	4797	$120.00	Whitman
Barbie and Ken (boxed)	1963	4797-100	$100.00	Whitman
Barbie and Ken All Sports Tournament (boxed)	1976	4389	$20.00	Whitman
Barbie and Ken Cut-Outs	1963	1976	$100.00	Whitman
Barbie and Ken Cut-Outs	1962	1971	$135.00	Whitman
Barbie and Ken Cut-Outs	1963	1976	$95.00	Whitman
Barbie and Ken Newport (boxed)	1974	4336	$30.00	Whitman
Barbie and Ken Suitcase Traveling Dolls	1962	4797	$100.00	Whitman

Item	Year	Number	Value	Specials
Barbie and Midge Travel Wardrobe (boxed)	1965	4785	$35.00	Whitman
Barbie and P.J. – A Camping Adventure	1973	1971-73	$26.00	Whitman
Barbie and Skipper	1983	1944	$15.00	Whitman
Barbie and Skipper	1964	1957	$85.00	Whitman
Barbie and Skipper Campsite at Lucky Lake	1980	1836-31	$20.00	Whitman
Barbie and Skipper Campsite at Lucky Lake	1980	1836-41	$20.00	Golden
Barbie and The Beat on Tour	1991	None	$10.00	Price-Stern-Sloan
Barbie and the Rockers	1986	1528-1	$15.00	Golden
Barbie Boutique	1973	1947	$15.00	
Barbie Boutique	1973	1996-1	$25.00	
Barbie Christmas Time	1984	1731	$20.00	Golden
Barbie Color 'n Play	1973	920A	$15.00	Colorforms
Barbie Costume Dolls with Skipper, Ken, Midge, and Alan	1964	1976	$100.00	Whitman
Barbie Country Camper	1973	1990	$30.00	Whitman
Barbie Country Camper and Paper Doll (boxed)	1973	4347	$30.00	Whitman
Barbie Country Camper Doll	1973	1983	$15.00	
Barbie Cut-Outs	1963	1962	$130.00	Whitman
Barbie Deluxe Edition	1994	2018	$3.00	Golden
Barbie Deluxe Edition	1994	2371	$3.00	Golden
Barbie Deluxe Edition	1994	2389	$3.00	Golden
Barbie Deluxe Edition	1994	2748	$3.00	Golden
Barbie Design-A-Fashion Paper Doll Kit	1982	4328-21	$15.00	Whitman
Barbie Doll Cut-Outs	1962	1963	$130.00	Whitman
Barbie Doll Cut-Outs	1962	1966	$110.00	
Barbie Doll Cut-Outs	1962	1957	$120.00	
Barbie Doll Cut-Outs	1963	1962	$85.00	
Barbie Dolls and Clothes	1969	1976	$70.00	Whitman
Barbie Dress-up Kit	1970	510	$15.00	Colorforms
Barbie Dress-up Kit	1977	510	$26.00	Colorforms
Barbie Fantasy	1984	1982-47	$15.00	Golden
Barbie Fashion Originals	1976	1989	$15.00	Whitman
Barbie Fashion Window Wardrobe (boxed)	1964	4605	$150.00	Whitman
Barbie Goin' Camping	1974	1961	$15.00	
Barbie Goin' Camping I	1974	1951	$25.00	Whitman
Barbie Goin' Camping II	1974	1951	$25.00	Whitman
Barbie Has a New Look	1967	1976	$90.00	Whitman
Barbie Lace and Dress Dancing Doll	1975	930A	$26.00	Colorforms
Barbie Magic (boxed)	1971	4331	$30.00	Whitman
Barbie Magic Dolls	1967	4785	$85.00	Whitman
Barbie Paper Doll	1983	7411D	$15.00	Whitman
Barbie Paper Doll	1990	1502	$10.00	
Barbie Paper Doll	1990	1502-1	$10.00	
Barbie Paper Doll	1990	1502-2	$10.00	
Barbie Paper Doll	1990	1523-2	$10.00	
Barbie Paper Doll	1990	1502-5	$10.00	
Barbie Paper Doll (boxed)	1967	4701	$235.00	Whitman
Barbie Paper Doll (boxed)	1993	5559	$8.00	Golden
Barbie Paper Doll (boxed)	1993	5570	$8.00	Golden
Barbie Paris Pretty Fashion	1990	1532-3	$10.00	
Barbie Sport Tournament Fashion Set	1975	2352	$23.00	Whitman
Barbie Sweet 16	1974	1981	$25.00	Whitman
Barbie's Beach Bus	1976	1996	$15.00	Whitman
Barbie's Beach Bus	1976	1996-1	$15.00	Whitman
Barbie's Boutique I	1973	1954	$32.00	Whitman

Item	Year	Number	Value	Specials
Barbie's Boutique II	1973	1954	$30.00	Whitman
Barbie's Boutique III	1973	1974-1	$30.00	Whitman
Barbie's Design-A-Fashion Paper Doll Kit	1979	4328-20	$20.00	Whitman
Barbie's Friendship	1973	1996	$24.00	Whitman
Barbie's Magic Paper Dolls (boxed)	1973	4322	$30.00	Whitman
Barbie's Travel Wardrobe (boxed)	1964	4616	$125.00	Whitman
Barbie's Wedding Dress 'n Fashion Clothes (boxed)	1964	4605	$130.00	Whitman
Barbie, 2 Magic Dolls with Stay-on Clothes (boxed)	1969	4763	$30.00	Whitman
Barbie, 2 Magic Dolls with Stay-on Clothes (yellow)	1969	4763	$30.00	Whitman
Barbie, Christie, and Stacey	1968	1978	$80.00	Whitman
Barbie, Christie, and Stacey, Barbie's New Friends	1968	1976	$75.00	Whitman
Barbie, Ken, and Midge	1963	1976	$75.00	Whitman
Barbie, Midge, and Skipper (boxed)	1964	4793	$80.00	Whitman
Barbie, Midge, and Skipper (boxed)	1965	4793	$70.00	Whitman
Barbie, Skipper, and Skooter	1966	1976	$60.00	Whitman
Crystal Barbie	1984	1983-46	$15.00	Golden
Crystal Barbie (boxed)	1984	7407-B	$10.00	Golden
Day-to-Night Barbie	1985	1521	$10.00	Golden
Day-to-Night Barbie	1985	1982-48	$12.00	Golden
Deluxe Paper Doll Barbie	1990	1699	$3.00	Golden
Deluxe Paper Doll Barbie	1990	1690	$12.00	Golden
Deluxe Paper Doll Barbie	1991	1695	$12.00	Golden
Deluxe Paper Doll Barbie	1991	1690-1	$12.00	Golden
Deluxe Paper Doll Barbie	1991	1690-2	$12.00	Golden
Deluxe Paper Doll Barbie (more fashions)	1991	1695-1	$12.00	Golden
Deluxe Paper Doll Barbie (more fashions)	1990	1690	$12.00	Golden
Fashion Photo Barbie	1979	1997	$25.00	Whitman
Fashion Photo Barbie (boxed)	1978	7408B	$30.00	Whitman
Fashion Photo Barbie and P.J.	1978	1982-32	$16.00	Whitman
Fashion Photo Barbie and P.J.	1978	1997-1	$16.00	Whitman
Fashion Photo Barbie and P.J.	1978	1997-21	$16.00	Whitman
Francie	1967	1094	$70.00	Whitman
Francie with Growin' Pretty Hair I	1973	1982	$35.00	Whitman
Francie with Growin' Pretty Hair II	1973	1982	$40.00	Whitman
Francie, Barbie's Modern Cousin & Casey, Francie's Fun Friend	1967	1986	$80.00	Whitman
Golden Dream Barbie	1982	1983-43	$15.00	Whitman
Golden Dream Barbie (boxed)	1982	7408C	$15.00	Whitman
Great Shape Barbie	1985	1522	$10.00	Golden
Great Shape Barbie	1984	1982-49	$10.00	Golden
Great Shape Paper Doll	1985	1525	$10.00	
Great Shape Paper Doll	1985	185-51	$10.00	
Groovy P.J. Fashions	1972	1974	$42.00	Whitman
Groovy World of Barbie & Her Friends	1971	1976	$55.00	Whitman
Growing Up Skipper	1976	1990	$25.00	Whitman
Growing Up Skipper Coloring Book with Paper Dolls	1978	1068	$20.00	Whitman
Hi, I'm Skipper Fashions	1973	1969	$32.00	Whitman
Jewel Secrets Barbie	1987	1537	$15.00	Golden
Jewel Secrets Barbie	1987	1537-1	$15.00	Golden
Malibu Barbie (boxed)	1972	1996	$30.00	Whitman
Malibu Barbie (boxed)	1982	7408E	$15.00	Whitman
Malibu Francie	1973	1955	$24.00	Whitman
Malibu Francie 21-piece Wardrobe (boxed)	1976	4393-7420	$28.00	Whitman
Malibu P.J. (boxed)	1972	4718	$30.00	Whitman
Malibu Skipper	1973	1945-2	$25.00	Whitman

Item	Year	Number	Value	Specials
Malibu Skipper I	1973	1952	$25.00	Whitman
Malibu Skipper II	1973	1952	$25.00	Whitman
Malibu Skipper III	1973	1952	$25.00	Whitman
Malibu Sunset Barbie I	1972	1994	$30.00	Whitman
Malibu Sunset Barbie II	1972	1994	$26.00	Whitman
Meet Francie, Barbie's Modern Cousin & Casey	1966	1980	$90.00	Whitman
Midge, Barbie's Best Friend Cut-Outs	1963	1962-29	$95.00	Whitman
Miss America	1973	1978	$15.00	
Miss America	1979	1976-3	$15.00	
New 'n Groovy P.J.	1970	1981	$50.00	Whitman
New 'n Groovy P.J.	1971	4332	$20.00	Whitman
Nostalgic Barbie (blonde)	1989	None	$20.00	Peck-Gandre
Nostalgic Barbie (brunette)	1989	None	$20.00	Peck-Gandre
Nostalgic Ken	1989	None	$20.00	Peck-Gandre
P.J. Cover Girl	1970	1981	$47.00	Whitman
Paper Doll Fashions P.J. and Barbie	1972	1975	$25.00	Whitman
Paris Pretty Fashion Barbie	1990	1532-2	$12.00	Golden
Peaches 'n Cream	1985	1525	$15.00	Golden
Peaches 'n Cream	1985	1983-48	$15.00	Golden
Perfume Pretty Barbie	1988	1500	$15.00	Golden
Pink & Pretty Barbie	1983	1836-43	$15.00	Golden
Pink & Pretty Barbie	1983	1838-45	$15.00	Golden
Pink & Pretty Barbie	1983	1983-44	$15.00	Golden
Pink & Pretty Barbie (boxed)	1983	7411-B	$15.00	Golden
Pos 'n Barbie Fashion	1972	1975	$39.00	Whitman
Pretty Changes Barbie (boxed)	1980	7410	$25.00	Whitman
Pretty Changes Barbie	1981	1982-34	$21.00	Whitman
Pretty Changes Barbie	1981	1982-42	$20.00	Whitman
Pretty Changes Barbie	1981	1982-42	$20.00	Golden
Quick Curl Barbie	1975	1644	$25.00	Whitman
Quick Curl Barbie (boxed)	1975	4399	$30.00	Whitman
Quick Curl Barbie and Her Friends I	1973	1984	$30.00	Whitman
Quick Curl Barbie and Her Friends II	1973	1984	$30.00	Whitman
Skipper & Skooter's Four Season Wardrobe (boxed)	1964	4778	$125.00	Whitman
Skipper (boxed)	1976	4395-7420	$28.00	Whitman
Skipper Design-A-Fashion Paper Doll Kit	1982	4329-21	$15.00	Whitman
Skipper Fashion Calendar Wardrobe (boxed)	1965	4607	$100.00	Whitman
Skipper's Day-By-Day Wardrobe	1964	4607	$100.00	
Skipper's Day-by-Day Wardrobe (boxed)	1964	4607	$100.00	Whitman
Skipper's Design-A-Fashion Paper Doll Kit	1979	4329-21	$20.00	Whitman
Skipper, Barbie's Little Sister	1962	1962	$35.00	Whitman
Skipper, Barbie's Little Sister	1965	1984	$25.00	Whitman
Skooter Fashion Go-Round (boxed)	1965	4639	$110.00	Whitman
Skooter, Skipper's Best Friend	1965	1985	$100.00	Whitman
Sun Valley Barbie and Ken (boxed)	1974	4338-7420M	$30.00	Whitman
Sunsational Malibu Barbie	1983	1982-44	$10.00	Golden
Super Teen Skipper	1980	1980-3	$15.00	Whitman
Super Teen Skipper	1980	1982-33	$15.00	Whitman
Super Teen Skipper & Scott	1981	7408C-1	$15.00	Whitman
Super-Teen Skipper	1980	1980-1	$14.00	
SuperStar Barbie	1977	1983	$21.00	Whitman
SuperStar Barbie	1977	1983-2	$20.00	Whitman
SuperStar Barbie	1989	1537-2	$20.00	Golden
SuperStar Barbie	1991	1537-3	$12.00	Golden
SuperStar Barbie (boxed)	1978	7413-D	$20.00	Whitman

Item	Year	Number	Value	Specials
Superstar Barbie Paper Doll	1989	1537-2	$10.00	
The 1959 Barbie (#1)	1994	None	$15.00	Peck Aubry
The 1961 Barbie (bubble cut)	1994	None	$15.00	Peck Aubry
The 1964 Barbie (Swirl Ponytail)	1994	None	$15.00	Peck Aubry
The 1965 Barbie (American Girl)	1995	None	$7.00	Peck Aubry
The 1966 Paper Doll (Color Magic)	1996	None	$7.00	Peck Aubry
The 1967 Paper Doll (twist 'n turn)	1996	None	$7.00	Peck Aubry
Tropical Barbie	1986	1523	$15.00	Golden
Tropical Barbie	1986	1523-1	$15.00	Golden
Tutti (boxed)	1967	4622	$60.00	Whitman
Tutti, Barbie & Skipper's Tiny Sister	1968	1991	$75.00	Whitman
Twiggy	1967	1999	$50.00	Whitman
Twirly Curls Barbie	1983	1982-46	$10.00	Golden
Western Barbie	1982	1982-43-G	$12.00	Golden
Western Barbie	1982	1982-43	$18.00	Whitman
Western Barbie (boxed)	1982	7408H	$21.00	Whitman
Western Fun Barbie	1990	1502	$12.00	Golden
Western Skipper	1983	7411-C	$12.00	Golden
World of Barbie	1971	1987	$50.00	Whitman
World of Barbie	1972	4367	$20.00	Whitman
World of Barbie (boxed)	1972	4376-B	$35.00	Whitman
World of Barbie Play Fun Box (boxed)	1972	4343	$35.00	Whitman
Yellowstone Kelly	1975	1956	$20.00	Whitman

Pets

Item	Year	Number	Value	Specials
Afghan	2000	25998	$9.00	Glam 'N Goom
Animal Lovin' Animal Assortment	1989	3499	$10.00	
Animal Lovin' Ginger Giraffe	1988	1395	$25.00	
Animal Lovin' Zizi Zebra	1988	1393	$25.00	
Baby Pony	1998	18498	$11.00	Walking Ponies
Beauty	1980	1018	$25.00	
Beauty and Puppies	1981	5019	$30.00	
Blinking Beauty Horse	1988	5087	$35.00	
Calico Cat	1996		$11.00	
Calico Cat	1995	14235	$10.00	Mattel
Candie (brown)	1997		$9.00	
Cat	2000	25998	$9.00	Glam 'N Groom
Cocker Spaniel	2000	25998	$9.00	Glam 'N Groom
Collie	1995	14234	$10.00	Mattel
Collie (barks)	1999		$7.00	Deluxe Pets
Dallas (horse)	1981	3312	$35.00	
Dalmatian	1999	20848	$9.00	Pet Lovin'
Dancer (horse)	1971	1157	$75.00	
Dream Horse Dixie	1984	7073	$20.00	

Item	Year	Number	Value	Specials
Dream Horse Prancer	1984	7263	$20.00	
English Pointer	1999	21726	$9.00	Pet Lovin'
Fluff (cat)	1983	5524	$30.00	
Flying Hero Horse	1996	14265	$20.00	
Ginger (Persian Kitty)	1996	67572	$5.00	
Ginger (white)	1997		$9.00	Pet Lovin'
Golden Retriever	1999	20848	$9.00	
High Stepper (horse)	1984	11766	$28.00	
High Stepper Walking Horse	1995	11766	$45.00	FAO Schwarz
Honey (gray)	1997		$9.00	
Honey (pony)	1983	5880	$25.00	
Honey (sheepdog)	1984	67572	$28.00	
Irish Setter	2000	25998	$9.00	Glam 'N Groom
Keiko (whale)	1996	15505	$16.00	Ocean Friends
Mandy (collie puppy)	1996	67572	$5.00	
Mandy (yellow)	1997		$9.00	
Midnight (horse)	1982	5337	$40.00	
Mitzi Meow (cat)	1994	11070	$10.00	
Mommy and Twin Poodles	1996	67573	$9.00	
Nibbles (horse)	1996	14879	$20.00	
Ocean Friends Keiko (whale)	1996		$15.00	
Poodle	2000	25998	$9.00	Glam 'N Groom
Prancing Horse	1994	11766	$30.00	FAO Schwarz
Prince (French poodle)	1985	7928	$25.00	
Puppy Ruff (dog)	1994	11069	$10.00	
Rainbow Horse	2000		$20.00	
Sachi (dog)	1991	N/A	$18.00	
Sassy Pony	1998	17970	$11.00	Walking Ponies
Sheep Dog (barks)	1999		$7.00	Deluxe Pets
Snow Dance (Horse)		9403	$25.00	
Snowball (dog)	1990	N/A	$18.00	Arco
Sparkle Beauties Amethyst (horse)	2000	67017-91	$12.00	
Sparkle Beauties Blue Diamond (horse)	2000	67019-91	$12.00	
Sparkle Beauties Emerald (horse)	2000	67022-91	$12.00	
Sparkle Beauties Pink Crystal (horse)	2000	67035-91	$12.00	
Sprint (horse)	1994	11550	$28.00	
St. Bernard	1999	20874	$9.00	Pet Lovin'
Stable Friends Families	1998		$11.00	
Starlight Unicorn & Serafina (horse)	2000	29041	$25.00	
Sun Runner (horse)	1990	9961	$35.00	
Sweetie Pony	1998	18498	$11.00	Walking Ponies
Tag A Long Tiffy	1992	3352	$15.00	
Tag A Long Wags	1992	N/A	$15.00	
Tropical Splash Seahorse	1995	12436	$12.00	
Tropical Tahiti (bird)	1965	2064	$40.00	
Walking Beauty Horse	1998	17718	$20.00	
Yorkie	1999	67572-91	$5.00	Barbie Pets
Zoo Babies Chika Chimp	2000	218936	$10.00	Zoo Babies
Zoo Babies Ping Ping Panda	2000	28938	$10.00	Zoo Babies
Zoo Babies Tika Tiger	2000	28935	$10.00	Zoo Babies

Plates

Item	Year	Number	Value	Collection	Company
1850s Southern Belle	1997	174785	$30.00		Enesco
1920s Flapper	1996	174777	$30.00	Great Eras Collection	Enesco
1995 Bride	1991	N/A	$25.00		Danbury Mint
After Five 1962 Mini Plate	1995	655058	$13.00	Fashion Collection	Enesco
Arabian Nights Mini Plate	1996	171069	$13.00	Fashion Collection	Enesco
Barbie as Scarlett O'Hara	1995	171085	$35.00	Hollywood Legends Collection	Enesco
Barbie at FAO Melamine Plate	1996	651844	$12.00	Barbie At FAO	
Barbie in England	1991	N/A	$20.00		Danbury Mint
Barbie in Russia	1991	N/A	$20.00		Danbury Mint
Barbie Paper Plates, 7"	1992	207	$2.00		C.A. Reed Inc.
Bride to Be	1990	N/A	$20.00		Danbury Mint
Cinderella Mini Plate	1996	171042	$13.00	Fashion Collection	Enesco
Circus Star Collector's Plate	1995	663914	$30.00		FAO Schwarz
Danbury Mini Collector Plates (set of 8)	N/A	N/A	$300.00		Danbury
Dessert Plates, 7"	1978	9148	$5.00		Ambassador
Debutante Ball	1990	N/A	$20.00		Danbury Mint
Easter Parade 1959 Mini Plate	1995	655074	$13.00	Fashion Collection	Enesco
Egyptian Queen	1997	174793	$30.00		Enesco
Enchanted Evening	1995	12711	$20.00		Bradford Exchange
Enchanted Evening	1994	N/A	$20.00		Bradford Exchange
Enchanted Evening 1960	1996	175587	$30.00	Glamour Collection	Enesco
Forever Glamorous	1994	N/A	$20.00		Bradford Exchange
Gibson Girl	1996	174769	$30.00	Great Eras Collection	Enesco
Goddess of the Sun & Moon Goddess Set Plates	1997	270539	$125.00		Enesco
Guinevere Mini Plate	1996	171050	$13.00	Fashion Collection	Enesco
Happy Birthday Paper Plates, 7"	1990	207	$2.00		C.A. Reed Inc.
Happy Birthday Paper Plates, 7"	1991	207	$2.00		C.A. Reed Inc.
Happy Holidays Barbie 1988	1994	154180	$40.00		Enesco
Happy Holidays Barbie 1989	1996	188859	$30.00		Enesco
Happy Holidays Barbie 1994	1995	115088	$40.00		Enesco
Happy Holidays Barbie 1995	1995	143154	$40.00		Enesco
Happy Holidays Barbie 1996	1996	188816	$30.00		Enesco
Here Comes The Bride 1966 (oval)	1966	170984	$30.00		Enesco
Holiday Dance	1990	N/A	$20.00		Danbury Mint
Holiday Dance 1965	1996	188794	$30.00	Glamour Collection	Enesco
Midnight Blue	1996	12714	$50.00		Bradford Exchange
Midnight Blue	1990	N/A	$20.00		Danbury Mint
Paper Plates, 6¾" Party Express	1995	207PL2033	$2.00		Hallmark
Paper Plates, 9"	1998	1275	$3.00	Unique Industries	
Queen of Hearts	1995	157678	$25.00	Bob Mackie	Enesco
Red Flare 1962 Mini Plate	1995	655090	$13.00	Fashion Collection	Enesco
Red Riding Hood Mini Plate	1996	171077	$13.00	Fashion Collection	Enesco
Roman Holiday 1959 Mini Plate	1995	655082	$13.00	Fashion Collection	Enesco
Senior Prom	1990	N/A	$20.00		Danbury Mint
Silver Screen	1993	N/A	$45.00		FAO Schwarz
Solo in the Spotlight	1995	12713	$20.00		Bradford Exchange
Solo in the Spotlight	1990	N/A	$20.00		Danbury Mint

Item	Year	Number	Value	Collection	Company
Sophisticated Lady	1995	12712	$50.00		Bradford Exchange
Sophisticated Lady	1990	N/A	$20.00		Danbury Mint
Statue of Liberty	1996	737239	$30.00		FAO Schwarz

Puzzles

Item	Pieces	Number	Year	Value	Company
Barbie & Ken Wishing Well			1963	$45.00	Whitman
Barbie and Ken Jigsaw Puzzle	100	N/A	1963	$40.00	Whitman
Barbie and Skipper on a Carousel Horse		N/A	1964	$45.00	Whitman
Barbie and the Rockers	200	4815	1987	$10.00	
Barbie in After Five at Fashion Shop		N/A	1963	$45.00	Whitman
Barbie in Guinevere at Little Theatre		N/A	1963	$45.00	Whitman
Barbie Puzzle Assortment (4 variations)		41659	1998	$3.00	
Barbie Sitting in Front of Mirror (Milton Bradley)			1976	$5.00	
Barbie Sticker/Glitter Puzzle Assortment (two styles)		41647	1998	$3.00	
Costume Ball Puzzle Card 2	8	1188-0362	1991	$1.00	Mattel
Costume Ball Puzzle Card 6	8	1188-0366	1991	$1.00	Mattel
Fashion Puzzle (Dream Date)		4565	1983	$5.00	
Fashion Puzzle (Horse Lovin')		4565	1983	$5.00	
Fashion Puzzle (Malibu)		4565	1983	$5.00	
Fashion Puzzle (Twirly Curls)		4565	1983	$5.00	
Floor Puzzle	63	4073A1	1993	$6.00	
Frame Tray Puzzle	12	4166A	1992	$1.00	Golden
Frame Tray Puzzle	12	4166B	1992	$1.00	Golden
Frame Tray Puzzle	20	8384	1992	$3.00	Golden
Jewel			1993	$14.00	
Jewel			1994	$14.00	
Jewel			1995	$14.00	
Jewel			1996	$14.00	
Jigsaw Puzzle in a Can (Malibu Barbie)		N/A	1975	$10.00	
Limited Edition 1988 Happy Holiday	120	5660A	1993	$10.00	
Limited Edition 1989 Happy Holiday	120	5660C	1993	$10.00	
Limited Edition 1990 Happy Holiday	120	5660D	1993	$10.00	
Limited Edition 1991 Happy Holiday	120	5660B	1993	$10.00	
Midge in Busy Morning by Bird Cage		N/A	1963	$60.00	Whitman
Nostalgic Barbie Jigsaw Puzzle	550	N/A	1989	$25.00	American Publishing
Nostalgic, 9 photos of Barbie (Western Publishing)			1994	$15.00	
Rapunzel Little Theater Puzzle		N/A	1984	$6.00	
Skipper & Skooter Puzzle (Picnic)	100	N/A	1965	$40.00	
Skipper & Skooter Under Umbrella with Sodas		N/A	1965	$45.00	Whitman
Skipper in Land & Sea Frame Tray Puzzle		N/A	1965	$40.00	Whitman
Twist 'n Turn Barbie		N/A	1972	$30.00	

Real Estate

Item	Year	Number	Value	Specials
Action Beauty Scene	1971	1016	$60.00	
Action Sewing Center	1972	4026	$50.00	
All Stars Sports Club	1990	4972	$40.00	
Apartment	1975	9188	$140.00	Department Store
Ballerina Barbie Stage	1976	9651	$75.00	
Barbie Beauty Boutique	1976	9795	$40.00	
Barbie Boutique Playset with Sound	1994	663765	$100.00	
Barbie Café Today	1971	4983	$400.00	
Barbie Goes to State College	1964	4093	$650.00	Sears
Barbie Loves McDonald's	1983	5559	$50.00	
Barbie and Francie's Campus	1966	9093	$330.00	Sears
Barbie and Ken Little Theater	1964	4090	$500.00	
Barbie and Skipper Deluxe Dream House	1965	N/A	$175.00	Sears
Barbie and Stacey Fashion Boutique	N/A	N/A	$1,000.00	Store Display
Barbie and the Beat Dance Café	1990	N/A	$35.00	
Barbie's Dream Kitchen	1965	4095	$500.00	
Beach Blast Patio and Pool	1989	3593	$45.00	
Beauty Salon	1983	4839	$30.00	
Bedroom Accents	1986	2375	$45.00	
Barbie Unique Boutique	1971	N/A	$180.00	Sears
Bubble Gum and Gift Shop	1995	12710	$35.00	
California Dream Surf 'n Shop	1988	4461	$30.00	
Cookin' Fun Kitchen	1971	4987	$95.00	Barbie's Place Setting
Cool Tops T-Shirt Shop	1990	4955	$45.00	
Country Living House	1973	8662	$75.00	Barbie's Place Setting
Dream Cottage (furnished)	1983	4718	$60.00	
Dream Cottage (unfurnished)	1983	4432	$50.00	
Dream House	1962	816	$225.00	
Dream House (furnished, pink)	1988	1667	$70.00	
Dream House (furnished, yellow)	1980	2587	$70.00	
Dream House (unfurnished, yellow)	1980	2588	$60.00	
Dream House Playset	1996	12709	$50.00	
Dream Pool (no furniture)	1981	1481	$40.00	
Dream Pool (with furniture)	1981	1496	$35.00	
Dream Store Deluxe Set	1983	4022	$65.00	
Dream Store Make-up Department	1983	4020	$40.00	
Family Deluxe House	1966	9342	$175.00	
Family House	1969	1106	$125.00	
Fashion Plaza	1976	9525	$80.00	
Fashion Salon	1964	9306L	$220.00	Sears
Fashion Shop	1962	817	$600.00	
Fashion Stage	1971	1148	$110.00	
Fashion Wraps Boutique	1989	4024	$35.00	
Feeding Fun Stable Playset	1996	15506	$25.00	
Folding Pretty House	1997	16961	$50.00	
Fold 'n Fun House	1994	1545	$50.00	
Fountain Pool	1994	0689	$25.00	
Francie & Casey Studio House	1967	1026	$150.00	

Item	Year	Number	Value	Specials
Francie House	1966	3302	$150.00	
Galleria	1989	4033	$75.00	
Glamour Home (furnished)	1985	9477	$125.00	
Glamour Home (unfurnished)	1985	9475	$100.00	
Hot Dog Stand	1988	4463	$35.00	
Hot Rockin' Stage	1986	1144	$40.00	
Hot Rockin' Stage	1987	1144	$40.00	Barbie & the Rockers
Ice Capades Skating Rink	1989	7547	$70.00	
Ice Cream Shoppe	1987	3653	$50.00	
Island Fun Hut	1987	4414	$50.00	
Jamie's Penthouse	1971	4990	$475.00	Sears
Juke Box Music Shop	1988	7361	$50.00	
K•B Toys Toy Shop	1999	67793-92	$16.00	
Lively Living House	1970	4282	$200.00	
Magic Sounds House	1992	N/A	$50.00	
Magical Mansion	1989	4438	$125.00	
Mall Food Court	1995	67273	$12.00	So Much To Do
McDonald's Playset	1994	11774	$50.00	
Mini Mart	1995	67029-92	$12.00	So Much To Do
Mountain Ski Cabin	1972	4283	$60.00	Sears
Movie Theatre	1996	14618	$24.00	
Movietime Prop Shop	1989	2768	$50.00	
New Dream House	1965	4092	$500.00	
New Restyled Dream House	N/A	4092	$250.00	
Olympic Ski Village	1975	7412	$55.00	
Party Garden Playhouse	1994	663625	$280.00	
Pop-Up Playhouse	1995	13198	$45.00	
Portable House	1962	1428	$225.00	Sears
Pretty Pet Parlor	1995	37154	$10.00	So Much To Do
Quick Curl Boutique	1973	8665	$70.00	Barbie's Place Setting
Record House	1989	4030	$40.00	
Rockers Dance Café	1987	3080	$50.00	Barbie & the Rockers
Skipper's Deluxe Dream House	1966	9343	$500.00	Sears
Skipper's Dream Room	1965	4094	$525.00	
Skipper's School	1965	N/A	$600.00	Sears
Soda Shoppe	1989	2707	$40.00	
Sports Shop	1989	4028	$40.00	
Step 'n Style Boutique	1989	2769	$40.00	
Surprise House	1972	4282	$100.00	
Sweet Shop	1995	67400	$12.00	So Much To Do
Teen Dream Bedroom	1971	4985	$80.00	Barbie's Place Setting
Three House Group	1967	N/A	$180.00	Sears
Three in One House	1995	11418	$70.00	FAO Schwarz
Town & Country Market	1971	4984	$130.00	
Townhouse (furnished)	1984	3764	$75.00	
Townhouse	1974	7825	$60.00	
Toys "R" Us Store	1999	67793-93	$17.00	
Travelin' Surprise House	1996	15427	$26.00	
Tropical Pool & Patio	1987	3041	$25.00	
Tutti & Chris Patio Picnic House	1968	5161	$140.00	Sears
Tutti & Chris Sleep & Play House	1967	5038	$150.00	
Tutti & Todd Playhouse	1966	3306	$175.00	
Tutti & Todd Playhouse without Dolls	1966	N/A	$60.00	Sears
Tutti Ice Cream Stand	1965	3563	$225.00	
Tutti Playhouse, no Doll	1967	3300	$90.00	

Item	Year	Number	Value	Specials
Tutti Playhouse with Doll	1966	3306	$175.00	
Tutti Summer House	1967	3317	$90.00	
Wet 'n Wild Lifeguard Stand	1990	3713	$25.00	
Wet 'n Wild Water Park	1990	7614	$35.00	
Workout Center	1985	7975	$30.00	
World of Barbie Family House, The	1969	1005	$160.00	
World of Barbie House, The	1968	1048	$170.00	

Records & Cassettes

Item	Year	Number	Value	Specials
"60s Style" CD	1996		$14.00	Barbie & the Bandstand
"Barbie Girl" (Aqua, MCA Records)	1997		$5.00	
"Barbie Girl" (Aqua, MCA Records)	1997		$9.00	
"Barbie Girl," 4 versions (Aqua, Universal Music)	1997		$11.00	
"Barbie Girl" Velva Blue Waxworks Collectables	1997	DS 5051-2	$15.00	
"I'm Still Here" (Steve Gideon) Collector's Anthem	1996		$25.00	
A Happy Barbie Birthday	1965	506	$100.00	Columbia
A Picnic for Skipper	1965	503	$100.00	Columbia
Barbie and Her Friends Record	1981	KD6003	$50.00	Kid Stuff
Barbie Christmas	1981	N/A	$10.00	Kid Stuff
Barbie Country Favorites	1981	N/A	$15.00	Kid Stuff
Barbie Country Favorites (record & cassette)	1981	N/A	$20.00	Kid Stuff
Barbie Looking Feeling Great Exercise Album	1982		$30.00	
Barbie Music "The Look" (Rincon Records)	1991		$14.00	
Barbie Sings (45 rpm record album)	1961	840	$75.00	
Barbie Sings (demo record)	1961	849	$125.00	
Barbie Sings Autograph and Beehive	1996		$20.00	Barbie & the Bandstand
Barbie Tune Tote (black vinyl case)	1993	N/A	$25.00	Barbie & the Bandstand
Barbie's Neighborhood	1981	KSR963	$10.00	Kid Stuff
Birthday Album	1981	N/A	$10.00	Kid Stuff
Busy Barbie	N/A	N/A	$12.00	
Camping Adventure	1981	KRS962	$10.00	Kid Stuff
Dance Club Cassette	1989	N/A	$15.00	Children's Palace
Dance Party (record & cassette)	1981	N/A	$10.00	Kid Stuff
Here in Nashville	1970	N/A	$10.00	
Living Doll (California Dream)	1988	N/A	$15.00	Beach Boys
Skipper, Skooter, and Ricky	1965	505	$100.00	Columbia
The Barbie Look	1965	504	$100.00	Columbia
The Big Game	1965	502	$100.00	Columbia
The World of Barbie	1965	501	$100.00	Columbia

Paper Products

Item	Year	Number	Value	Specials
12 Brilliant Colored Pencils	1994	9465	$3.00	
16 Crayons	1994	5593	$3.00	
24 Crayons	1994	5344	$6.00	
30th Anniversary Calendar	1989	N/A	$20.00	
8 Broad Line Markers	1994	8760	$6.00	
8 Fine Line Markers	1994	8757	$2.00	
Address Book (refillable)	1996	767921	$15.00	FAO Schwarz
Autograph Book (model AR-220)	1991	006-6	$10.00	Antioch Publishing Co.
Autograph Book (model AR-220)	1992	569-6	$10.00	Antioch Publishing Co.
Barbie Calendar	1989	N/A	$10.00	Design Look
Barbie Fun Stamper Set	1996	17420	$5.00	Tara
Barbie Memories Scrapbook	1991	N/A	$20.00	Antioch Publishing Co.
Barbie Name Tags	1990	0437-614	$2.00	C.A. Reed
Barbie Notes to Color & Send	1992	N/A	$12.00	Golden
Barbie World of Fashion Calendar	1976	N/A	$90.00	
Barbie and Skipper Notebook Ring Binder	1966	N/A	$30.00	Standard Plastic
Barbie at FAO Diary	1996	767905	$12.00	FAO Schwarz
Barbie at FAO Stamp & Sticker Set	1996	767897	$15.00	FAO Schwarz
Barbie at FAO Stationery	1996	767814	$8.00	FAO Schwarz
Bonus Pack (memo wipe-off board bookmark)	1991	0001	$15.00	Antioch Publishing Co.
Bonus Pak (7" x 11" wipe off board, bookmark)	1992	0016	$15.00	Antioch Publishing Co.
Calendar	1992	N/A	$10.00	Gibson
Calendar	1991	241	$10.00	
Calendar	1995	N/A	$10.00	Hallmark
Desk Calculator	1981	3457	$15.00	
Diary	1963	N/A	$30.00	
Dictionary Black	1963	N/A	$150.00	
Doorknob Hanger (Dreams Can Come True)	1991	D276	$3.00	Antioch Publishing Co.
Doorknob Hanger (Shhh – Barbie and Friends at Play)	1991	D189	$3.00	Antioch Publishing Co.
Dreams Can Come True Bookmark	N/A	N/A	$3.00	Antioch Publishing Co.
Fashion Maker Set	1981	3271	$15.00	
Figurine Stampers	1996	30289	$3.00	Tara
Fluorescent Watercolors	1994	9451	$3.00	
Gift Wrap (Nostalgic Papers)	1994	N/A	$15.00	
Gift Wrap by Gibson	1988	N/A	$10.00	
Gift Bag	1992	N/A	$5.00	Gibson
Gift Bag	1993	N/A	$5.00	Gibson
Goldtone Photo Album	1996	744938	$48.00	FAO Schwarz
Goldtone Picture Frame	1996	744920	$45.00	FAO Schwarz
Hallmark Barbie Calendar	1995	N/A	$15.00	
Journal	1996	767855	$10.00	FAO Schwarz
Key-Lock Diary (model AR-1106)	1991	005-8	$15.00	Antioch Publishing Co.
Key-Lock Diary (model AR-1106)	1992	570-X	$15.00	Antioch Publishing Co.
Large Barbie Photo Album	1963	N/A	$50.00	
Memo Wipe-Off Board (5" x 7")	1991	3023	$10.00	Antioch Publishing Co.
Memo Wipe-Off Board (5" x 7")	1992	3075	$10.00	Antioch Publishing Co.
Memo Wipe-Off Board (7" x 11")	1991	3028	$10.00	Antioch Publishing Co.
Memo Wipe-Off Board (7" x 11")	1992	3079	$10.00	Antioch Publishing Co.

Item	Year	Number	Value	Specials
Mini Posters	1974	N/A	$5.00	
Nostalgic Special 16-Month Edition Calendar	1990	N/A	$20.00	
Nice Goin' Bookmark	N/A	N/A	$3.00	
Nostalgic Barbie Calendar	1990	N/A	$10.00	Design Look
Notebook Memo Board	1991	3039	$10.00	Antioch Publishing Co.
Pencil Set	1984	7488	$10.00	On The Go Fashions
Party Party Party Bookmark	N/A	N/A	$3.00	Antioch Publishing Co.
Personal Size Address Book (model AR-430)	1991	007-4	$10.00	Antioch Publishing Co.
Personal Size Address Book (model AR-430)	1992	568-8	$5.00	Antioch Publishing Co.
Picture Frame (decoupage)	1993	164905	$120.00	Barbie at FAO
Poodle Parade Picture Frame	1996	790113	$12.00	
Poodle Parade Trinket Box	1996	790121	$20.00	
Postbound Scrapbook (model PB-421)	1991	009-0	$20.00	Antioch Publishing Co.
Postbound Scrapbook (model PB-421)	1992	562-9	$20.00	Antioch Publishing Co.
Really Cool	N/A	N/A	$3.00	
Ring-Bound Photo Album (model AR-204)	1991	388-X	$15.00	Antioch Publishing Co.
Ring-Bound Photo Album (model AR-204)	1992	561-0	$10.00	Antioch Publishing Co.
Ring-Bound Photo Album (model AR-46)	1991	008-2	$20.00	Antioch Publishing Co.
Scrapbook	1964	N/A	$50.00	
Snap Shot Album	1963	N/A	$40.00	
Sneak Preview Calendar	1991	N/A	$10.00	
Skipper and Skooter Pencil Case	1966	N/A	$15.00	Standard Plastic
Snaps and Scraps Scrapbook (red)	1961	N/A	$110.00	
Stationery Folio	1996	767871	$12.00	FAO Schwarz
Tasseled Bookmark (Dreams Can Come True)	1991	H-1221	$2.00	Antioch Publishing Co.
Tasseled Bookmark (I Think You're Special)	1992	H-1487	$2.00	Antioch Publishing Co.
Tasseled Bookmark (Really Cool)	1991	H-1219	$2.00	Antioch Publishing Co.

Vehicles

Item	Year	Number	Value	Specials
'57 Chevy (Chevrolet Bel-air) (pink)	1989	3561	$50.00	
Allan's Roadster (aqua)	1964	N/A	$500.00	
Around the Town Scooter (pink)	1992	N/A	$20.00	
ATC Cycle	1972	31229	$65.00	Sears
Barbie & Ken Hot Rod (red, turquoise)	1963	1460	$375.00	Sears
Barbie and Ken Dune Buggy	1970	5908	$300.00	
Barbie and Skipper's Speed Boat	1964	9314	$250.00	Sears
Barbie Country Ride Bike	1996	67560	$10.00	
Barbie's Sports Car (coral, lavender, red)	1962	N/A	$300.00	Austin Healey (Irwins)
Baywatch Rescue Boat	1995	N/A	$30.00	Baywatch
Baywatch Rescue Cruiser (remote control)	1995	7000-91	$40.00	Baywatch
Baywatch Rescue Wheels	1995	N/A	$20.00	Baywatch
Beach Bus	1974	7805	$45.00	
Beach Cruiser	2000	67389-91	$9.00	
California Dream Beach Taxi	1988	4520	$35.00	
Camp Barbie Sun Cruiser	1994	N/A	$25.00	Camp Barbie
Chevy Sidestep LE 7000	1994	13773	$50.00	Hot Wheels
City Nights Cycle (remote control)	1995	7005	$35.00	
Classy Corvette (yellow)	1976	9612	$40.00	Department Store
Country Camper	1971	4994	$40.00	
Cruise Ship	1994	10921	$70.00	
Cruisin' Car (red)	1997	16544	$25.00	
Dodge Caravan	1999	N/A	$30.00	Hot Wheels
Dream Boat	1975	7232	$70.00	
Drivin' Sports Car	1995	67532	$25.00	
Ferrari (red)	1991	3136	$50.00	
Ferrari 328 GTS (white)	1989	3564	$35.00	
Flight Time Airplane	1990	2081	$30.00	
Goin' Camping Set with Breeze Buggy	1973	8669	$75.00	
Going Boating Set	1973	7738	$70.00	Sears
Golden Dream Motorhome	1994	2555	$50.00	
Highway Hauler	1996	1174	$80.00	Hot Wheels
Hot Rockin' Van	1987	1810	$60.00	Barbie & the Rockers
Hot Rod (Ken)	1961	N/A	$325.00	Irwin
Hot Rod (red, Ken)	1964	1582	$900.00	Sears
Hot Wheels Racing K•B Toys Barbie Car	1999	23615	$10.00	NASCAR
Jaguar XJS	1994	N/A	$30.00	
Ken Dream 'Vette (dark blue)	1981	3299	$40.00	
Mini-Van	1995	13185	$50.00	
Motor Bike	1984	4856	$25.00	
Motor Bike (Skipper)	1989	N/A	$10.00	
Motorcycle	1994	419	$25.00	
Motorhome	1997	14614	$45.00	
Mustang (expands, 2" x 4")	1995	11929	$20.00	
Mustang (pink)	1993	65032	$20.00	
Mustang Convertible	2000	67391-91	$9.00	
Ocean Friends Speedboat	1996	67413	$14.00	
Paint 'n Dazzle Car	1994	10253	$25.00	

Item	Year	Number	Value	Specials
Pontiac Hot Wheels Toy Club LE 7000	1994	12873	$25.00	Hot Wheels
Pop Out Picnic SUV	2000	67384-91	$9.00	
Porsche 911 Cabriolet (white)	1994	10876	$30.00	
Ride 'N Shine Bike w/different baskets	2000	67560	$7.00	
Volkswagen Golf Cabriolet	1988	6803	$75.00	Hot Wheels
Volkswagen New Beetle (blue)	2000	28260	$23.00	
Volkswagen New Beetle (pink)	2000		$23.00	
Volkswagen New Beetle (red)	2000	28259	$23.00	
Volkswagen New Beetle (yellow)	2000		$23.00	
Western Fun Motorhome	1989	3366	$50.00	
Western Star Traveler Motorhome	1982	5345	$50.00	

Watches & Clocks

Item	Year	Number	Value	Specials
30th Anniversary Watch	1989	N/A	$80.00	
35th Anniversary Watch	1994	N/A	$150.00	Fossil Watches
Accessories	1996	737122	$34.00	Nostalgic Sportswatch
Asymmetrical Heart	1996	737080	$58.00	Nostalgic Barbie Watches
Barbie 3-in-1 Swap Watch	1996	26508	$29.00	
Barbie Action Digital Watch	1996	26251	$25.00	
Barbie and Ken Talking Alarm Clock	1983	8120	$15.00	
Barbie and Ken Watch	1963	N/A	$200.00	Bradley
Barbie Deck Alarm Clock	1995	26790	$25.00	
Barbie Deck Alarm Clock & Watch Set	1995	26791	$29.00	
Barbie Fashion Flip-Top Watch	1995	26451	$25.00	
Barbie for Girls Neon Orange Watch	1992	N/A	$10.00	
Barbie Interchangeable Bezel Quartz Watch	1995	2605	$29.00	
Barbie Jeweled Bracelet LCD Watch	1996	26112	$25.00	
Barbie Jeweled Necklace LCD Watch	1996	26111	$50.00	
Barbie Molded Watch	1996	26211	$25.00	
Barbie Multi-Lens Digital Watch	1996	26160	$25.00	
Barbie My First Clock	1996	26795	$25.00	
Barbie Silhouette TNT (link band)	1996	26501	$75.00	Nostalgic
Baywatch Barbie Digital Watch	1995	26442	$25.00	
Black Piano Watch	1996	26531	$125.00	Nostalgic
Black Stripe (black leather band)	1995	26532	$50.00	Nostalgic
Camp Barbie Digital Watch	1995	26431	$25.00	
Charm Bracelet Watch	1994	N/A	$90.00	Fossil Watches
Classic Pink	1996	737114	$45.00	
Clock Radio	1995	BE300	$20.00	
Clock Radio	1995	02362	$20.00	From Barbie with Love
Curly Bang Watch (light blue border)	1963	N/A	$350.00 Mint	Bradley
Curly Bang Watch (red border)	1963	N/A	$350.00 Mint	Bradley
Electric Wristwatch Wall Clock	1974	N/A	$350.00 Mint	
Fan Club Promotional Wristwatch	1981	N/A	$70.00	
Fashion Watch	1996	26451	$6.00	

Item	Year	Number	Value	Specials
Glamour	1996	737130	$34.00	Nostalgic Sportswatch
Official Wristwatch	1980	N/A	$30.00	
Golden Silhouette (black leather band)	1996	26536	$45.00	Nostalgic
My First Molded Watch	1995	26231	$25.00	
Oval with Lipstick Motif	1996	779033	$58.00	Nostalgic Barbie Watches
Petite Tank (brown leather band)	1996	26526	$75.00	Nostalgic
Picnic	1996	737148	$34.00	Nostalgic Sportswatch
Pink and Pretty Watch	1994	N/A	$80.00	Fossil Watches
Pink Profiles	1996	779041	$34.00	Nostalgic Sportswatch
Pink Watch		N/A	$50.00	
Plate Clock (Decoupage)	1993	164863	$120.00	Barbie at FAO
Ponytail Wristwatch #1	1963	N/A	$150.00	
Ponytail Wristwatch #2	1963	N/A	$150.00	
Ponytail Wristwatch #3	1963	N/A	$150.00	
Poodle Parade Watch (pink)	1996	776922	$80.00	Fossil Watches
Profiles of Barbie	1996	737098	$58.00	Nostalgic Barbie Watches
Silhouette Barrel (black grain band)	1996	26523	$35.00	Nostalgic
Silhouette Purple (leather band)	1996	26525	$45.00	Nostalgic
Silver Screen Watch	1994	N/A	$100.00	Fossil Watches
Solo in the Spotlight Collector Clock	1996	26794	$25.00	
Solo in the Spotlight Icons (resin band)	1996	26543	$35.00	Nostalgic
Starlight Boudoir Clock	1964	N/A	$1,000.00	Bradley
Swirl Ponytail Watch (necklace type)	1964	N/A	$400.00	
Swirl Watch (blue band)	1964	N/A	$400.00	
Swirl Watch (yellow band)	1964	N/A	$400.00	
Treasure Keeper Digital Watch	1996	26471	$5.00	
Twist 'n Turn Watch (blue rim)	1971	N/A	$125.00	
Watch with ¾ Face Looking Left	1963	N/A	$50.00	
Wristwatch (blue dial and band)	1964	N/A	$150.00	J.C. Penney
Wristwatch (red dial and band)	1964	N/A	$150.00	
Wristwatch with 3 Changeable Bands	1969	5211	$95.00	
Wristwatch with Large Dial	N/A	N/A	$50.00	
Wristwatch with Small Dial	N/A	N/A	$50.00	

Bibliography

Eames, Sara. *Barbie Fashions Vol. 1, 1959 – 1967.* Paducah, KY: Collector Books, 1990.

Augustyniak, J. Michael. *Barbie Doll Boom.* Paducah, KY: Collector Books, 1996.

Blitman, Joe. *Barbie and Her Mod, Mod, Mod World of Fashion.* 1996.

———. *Francie & Her Mod, Mod, Mod, World of Fashion.* 1996.

———. *Viva La Francie.*

Bryan, Sandra. *Ken Fashions, 1961 – 1976.* 1990.

———. *The Eyelash Era, 1967 – 1972.* 1990.

Deutsch, Stefanie. *Barbie, The First 30 Years.* Paducah, KY: Collector Books, 1996.

DeWein, Sibyl. *Collectible Barbie Dolls, 1977 – 1979.* 1980.

DeWein, Sibyl, and Joan Ashabraner. *Collector's Encyclopedia of Barbie Dolls.* Paducah, KY: Collector Books, 1980.

Fennick, Janine. *Collectible Barbie Dolls.* 1996.

———. *The Collectible Barbie Doll.* 1996.

Kimuro. *Barbie in Japan.* 1994.

Mandeville, A. Glenn. *5th Doll Fashion Anthology.* 1996.

Manos, Paris and Susan. *The Wonder of Barbie Dolls, 1976 – 1986.* Paducah, KY: Collector Books, 1987.

———. *The World of Barbie Dolls.* Paducah, KY: Collector Books, 1983.

Melillo, Marci. *Ultimate Barbie Doll Book.* 1996.

Olds, Patrick C. *The Barbie Doll Years.* Paducah, KY: Collector Books, 1995.

Pinkerton, Linda. *Skipper Fashion Guide, 1964 – 1976.*

Rana, Margo. *Barbie Exclusives I.* Paducah, KY: Collector Books, 1994.

———. *Barbie Exclusive II.* Paducah, KY: Collector Books, 1996.

Rupp, Rebecca Ann. *Treasury of Barbie Doll Accessories.* 1996.

———. *Treasury of Barbie Doll Accessories, 1961 – 1995.* 1996.

Sarasohn-Kahn, Jane. *Contemporary Barbie.* 1996.

Summers, Beth. *A Decade of Barbie Dolls, 1981 – 1991.* Paducah, KY: Collector Books, 1996.

Therault. I.D. Guide. 1993.

Therault's Barbie Rarities. 1992.

Therault Presents Barbie. 1985.

Westenhouser, Kitturah. *The Story of Barbie.* Paducah, KY: Collector Books, 1995.

DOLLS, FIGURES & TEDDY BEARS

6315	**American Character Dolls**, Izen	$24.95
6317	**Arranbee Dolls**, The Dolls that Sell on Sight, DeMillar/Brevik	$24.95
2079	**Barbie Doll** Fashion, Volume I, Eames	$24.95
4846	**Barbie Doll** Fashion, Volume II, Eames	$24.95
6823	The **Barbie Doll Years**, 6th Edition, Olds	$19.95
6546	Collector's Ency. of **Barbie** Doll Exclusives & More, 3rd Ed., Augustyniak	$29.95
6451	Collector's Encyclopedia of **Composition Dolls**, Volume II, Mertz	$29.95
6636	Collector's Encyclopedia of **Madame Alexander Dolls**, Crowsey	$24.95
5904	Collector's Guide to **Celebrity Dolls**, Spurgeon	$24.95
5599	Collector's Guide to **Dolls of the 1960s and 1970s**, Sabulis	$24.95
6030	Collector's Guide to **Horsman Dolls**, Jensen	$29.95
6455	**Doll Values**, Antique to Modern, 8th Edition, DeFeo/Stover	$14.95
5689	**Nippon Dolls** & Playthings, Van Patten/Lau	$29.95
6467	**Paper Dolls** of the 1960s, 1970s, and 1980s, Nichols	$24.95
5365	**Peanuts Collectibles**, Podley/Bang	$24.95
6336	Official **Precious Moments** Collector's Guide to Company **Dolls**, Bomm	$19.95
6026	**Small Dolls** of the 40s & 50s, Stover	$29.95
5253	Story of **Barbie**, 2nd Ed., Westenhouser	$24.95
5277	**Talking Toys** of the 20th Century, Lewis	$15.95
2084	**Teddy Bears, Annalee's & Steiff** Animals, 3rd Series, Mandel	$19.95
4880	World of **Raggedy Ann** Collectibles, Avery	$24.95

TOYS & MARBLES

2333	Antique & Collectible **Marbles**, 3rd Edition, Grist	$9.95
6649	Big Book of **Toy Airplanes**, Miller	$24.95
5150	**Cartoon Toys** & Collectibles, Longest	$19.95
6471	Collector's Guide to **Tootsietoys**, 3rd Edition, Richter	$24.95
6633	**Hot Wheels**, The Ultimate Redline Guide, 2nd Ed., Clark/Wicker	$29.95
6466	**Matchbox Toys**, 1947 to 2003, 4th Edition, Johnson	$24.95
5830	**McDonald's** Collectibles, 2nd Edition, Henriques/DuVall	$24.95
6840	**Schroeder's Collectible Toys**, Antique to Modern Price Guide, 10th Ed.	$17.95
6638	The Other **Matchbox Toys**, 1947 to 2004, Johnson	$19.95
6650	**Toy Car** Collector's Guide, 2nd Edition, Johnson	$24.95

FURNITURE

3716	American **Oak** Furniture, Book II, McNerney	$12.95
1118	Antique **Oak** Furniture, Hill	$7.95
6474	Collector's Guide to **Wallace Nutting** Furniture, Ivankovich	$19.95
3906	**Heywood-Wakefield** Modern Furniture, Rouland	$18.95
6338	**Roycroft** Furniture & Collectibles, Koon	$24.95
6343	**Stickley Brothers** Furniture, Koon	$24.95
1885	**Victorian** Furniture, Our American Heritage, McNerney	$9.95

JEWELRY, WATCHES & PURSES

4704	Antique & Collectible **Buttons**, Wisniewski	$19.95
6323	**Christmas Pins**, Past & Present, 2nd Edition, Gallina	$19.95
4850	Collectible **Costume Jewelry**, Simonds	$24.95
5675	Collectible **Silver Jewelry**, Rezazadeh	$24.95
6468	Collector's Ency. of Pocket & Pendant **Watches**, 1500 – 1950, Bell	$24.95
6554	**Coro Jewelry**, Brown	$29.95
6453	**Costume Jewelry** 101, Carroll	$24.95
4940	**Costume Jewelry**, A Practical Handbook & Value Guide, Rezazadeh	$24.95

5812	Fifty Years of Collectible **Fashion Jewelry**, 1925 – 1975, Baker	$24.95
6330	**Handkerchiefs**: A Collector's Guide, Guarnaccia/Guggenheim	$24.95
6464	Inside the **Jewelry** Box, Pitman	$24.95
5695	**Ladies' Vintage Accessories**, Johnson	$24.95
1181	100 Years of Collectible **Jewelry**, 1850 – 1950, Baker	$9.95
6645	100 Years of **Purses**, 1880s to 1980s, Aikins	$24.95
6337	**Purse Masterpieces**, Schwartz	$29.95
4729	**Sewing Tools** & Trinkets, Thompson	$24.95
6038	**Sewing Tools** & Trinkets, Volume 2, Thompson	$24.95
6039	Signed Beauties of **Costume Jewelry**, Brown	$24.95
6341	Signed Beauties of **Costume Jewelry**, Volume II, Brown	$24.95
6555	20th Century **Costume Jewelry**, Aikins	$24.95
5620	Unsigned Beauties of **Costume Jewelry**, Brown	$24.95
4878	Vintage & Contemporary **Purse Accessories**, Gerson	$24.95
5923	**Vintage Jewelry** for Investment & Casual Wear, Edeen	$24.95

ARTIFACTS, GUNS, KNIVES, TOOLS, PRIMITIVES

6021	**Arrowheads** of the Central Great Plains, Fox	$19.95
1868	Antique **Tools**, Our American Heritage, McNerney	$9.95
6469	Big Book of **Pocket Knives**, 2nd Edition, Stewart/Ritchie	$19.95
4943	Field Gde. to Flint **Arrowheads & Knives** of the N. American Indian, Tully	$9.95
3885	**Indian Artifacts** of the Midwest, Book II, Hothem	$16.95
4870	**Indian Artifacts** of the Midwest, Book III, Hothem	$18.95
5685	**Indian Artifacts** of the Midwest, Book IV, Hothem	$19.95
6565	**Modern Guns**, Identification & Values, 15th Ed., Quertermous	$16.95
2164	**Primitives**, Our American Heritage, McNerney	$9.95
6031	Standard **Knife** Collector's Guide, 4th Ed., Ritchie/Stewart	$14.95

PAPER COLLECTIBLES & BOOKS

5902	**Boys' & Girls' Book** Series, Jones	$19.95
6623	Collecting **American Paintings**, James	$29.95
5153	Collector's Guide to **Children's Books**, 1850 to 1950, Volume II, Jones	$19.95
6553	Collector's Guide to **Cookbooks**, Daniels	$24.95
1441	Collector's Guide to **Post Cards**, Wood	$9.95
6627	Early 20th Century **Hand-Painted Photography**, Ivankovich	$24.95
6936	**Leather Bound Books**, Boutiette	$24.95
3973	**Sheet Music** Reference & Price Guide, 2nd Ed., Pafik/Guiheen	$19.95

GLASSWARE

5602	Anchor Hocking's **Fire-King** & More, 2nd Ed., Florence	$24.95
6321	**Carnival Glass**, The Best of the Best, Edwards/Carwile	$29.95
5823	Collectible **Glass Shoes**, 2nd Edition, Wheatley	$24.95
6821	Coll. **Glassware** from the 40s, 50s & 60s, 8th Edition, Florence	$19.95
6626	Collector's Companion to **Carnival Glass**, 2nd Ed., Edwards/Carwile	$14.95
6830	Collector's Encyclopedia of **Depression Glass**, 17th Ed., Florence	$19.95
1664	Collector's Encyclopedia of **Heisey Glass**, 1925 – 1938, Bredehoft	$24.95
3905	Collector's Encyclopedia of **Milk Glass**, Newbound	$24.95
5820	Collector's Guide to **Glass Banks**, Reynolds	$24.95
6454	**Crackle Glass** From Around the World, Weitman	$24.95
6559	**Elegant Glassware** of the Depression Era, 11th Edition, Florence	$24.95
6334	Encyclopedia of **Paden City Glass**, Domitz	$24.95
3981	Evers' Standard **Cut Glass** Value Guide	$12.95
6126	**Fenton Art Glass**, 1907 – 1939, 2nd Ed., Whitmyer	$29.95

6628	Fenton Glass Made for Other Companies, Domitz	$29.95
6462	Florences' Glass Kitchen Shakers, 1930 – 1950s	$19.95
5042	Florences' Glassware Pattern Identification Guide, Vol. I	$18.95
5615	Florences' Glassware Pattern Identification Guide, Vol. II	$19.95
6142	Florences' Glassware Pattern Identification Guide, Vol. III	$19.95
6643	Florences' Glassware Pattern Identification Guide, Vol. IV	$19.95
6641	Florences' Ovenware from the 1920s to the Present	$24.95
6226	Fostoria Value Guide, Long/Seate	$19.95
5899	Glass & Ceramic Baskets, White	$19.95
6460	Glass Animals, 2nd Edition, Spencer	$24.95
6127	The Glass Candlestick Book, Volume 1, Akro Agate to Fenton, Felt/Stoer	$24.95
6228	The Glass Candlestick Book, Volume 2, Fostoria to Jefferson, Felt/Stoer	$24.95
6461	The Glass Candlestick Book, Volume 3, Kanawha to Wright, Felt/Stoer	$29.95
6648	Glass Toothpick Holders, 2nd Edition, Bredehoft/Sanford	$29.95
6329	Glass Tumblers, 1860s to 1920s, Bredehoft	$29.95
5827	Kitchen Glassware of the Depression Years, 6th Edition, Florence	$24.95
6133	Mt. Washington Art Glass, Sisk	$49.95
6556	Pocket Guide to Depression Glass & More, 14th Edition, Florence	$12.95
6925	Standard Encyclopedia of Carnival Glass, 10th Ed., Edwards/Carwile	$29.95
6926	Standard Carnival Glass Price Guide, 15th Ed., Edwards/Carwile	$9.95
6566	Standard Encyclopedia of Opalescent Glass, 5th Ed., Edwards/Carwile	$29.95
6644	Standard Encyclopedia of Pressed Glass, 4th Ed., Edwards/Carwile	$29.95
6241	Treasures of Very Rare Depression Glass, Florence	$39.95
6476	Westmoreland Glass, The Popular Years, 1940 – 1985, Kovar	$29.95

POTTERY

6922	American Art Pottery, 2nd Edition, Sigafoose	$24.95
4851	Collectible Cups & Saucers, Harran	$18.95
6326	Collectible Cups & Saucers, Book III, Harran	$24.95
6344	Collectible Vernon Kilns, 2nd Edition, Nelson	$29.95
6331	Collecting Head Vases, Barron	$24.95
6621	Collector's Encyclopedia of American Dinnerware, 2nd Ed., Cunningham	$29.95
5034	Collector's Encyclopedia of California Pottery, 2nd Ed., Chipman	$24.95
6629	Collector's Encyclopedia of Fiesta, 10th Ed., Huxford	$24.95
3431	Collector's Encyclopedia of Homer Laughlin China, Jasper	$24.95
1276	Collector's Encyclopedia of Hull Pottery, Roberts	$19.95
5609	Collector's Encyclopedia of Limoges Porcelain, 3rd Ed., Gaston	$29.95
6637	Collector's Encyclopedia of Made in Japan Ceramics, First Ed., White	$24.95
2334	Collector's Encyclopedia of Majolica Pottery, Katz-Marks	$19.95
5677	Collector's Encyclopedia of Niloak, 2nd Edition, Gifford	$29.95
5679	Collector's Encyclopedia of Red Wing Art Pottery, Dollen	$24.95
5841	Collector's Encyclopedia of Roseville Pottery, Vol. 1, Huxford/Nickel	$24.95
5842	Collector's Encyclopedia of Roseville Pottery, Vol. 2, Huxford/Nickel	$24.95
5917	Collector's Encyclopedia of Russel Wright, 3rd Edition, Kerr	$29.95
6646	Collector's Ency. of Stangl Artware, Lamps, and Birds, 2nd Ed., Runge	$29.95
3314	Collector's Encyclopedia of Van Briggle Art Pottery, Sasicki	$24.95
5680	Collector's Guide to Feather Edge Ware, McAllister	$19.95
6634	Collector's Ultimate Ency. of Hull Pottery, Volume 1, Roberts	$29.95
6829	The Complete Guide to Corning Ware & Visions Cookware, Coroneos	$19.95
1425	Cookie Jars, Westfall	$9.95
6316	Decorative American Pottery & Whiteware, Wilby	$29.95
5909	Dresden Porcelain Studios, Harran	$29.95
5918	Florences' Big Book of Salt & Pepper Shakers	$24.95

6320	Gaston's Blue Willow, 3rd Edition	$19.95
6630	Gaston's Flow Blue China, The Comprehensive Guide	$29.95
2379	Lehner's Ency. of U.S. Marks on Pottery, Porcelain & China	$24.95
4722	McCoy Pottery, Collector's Reference & Value Guide, Hanson/Nissen	$19.95
5913	McCoy Pottery, Volume III, Hanson & Nissen	$24.95
6333	McCoy Pottery Wall Pockets & Decorations, Nissen	$24.95
6135	North Carolina Art Pottery, 1900 – 1960, James/Leftwich	$24.95
5834	Occupied Japan Collectibles, Florence	$24.95
6335	Pictorial Guide to Pottery & Porcelain Marks, Lage	$29.95
5691	Post86 Fiesta, Identification & Value Guide, Racheter	$19.95
1440	Red Wing Stoneware, DePasquale/Peck/Peterson	$9.95
6037	Rookwood Pottery, Nicholson/Thomas	$24.95
3443	Salt & Pepper Shakers IV, Guarnaccia	$18.95
3738	Shawnee Pottery, Mangus	$24.95
6828	The Ultimate Collector's Encyclopedia of Cookie Jars, Roerig	$29.95
6640	Van Patten's ABC's of Collecting Nippon Porcelain	$29.95
5924	Zanesville Stoneware Company, Rans/Ralston/Russell	$24.95

OTHER COLLECTIBLES

5838	Advertising Thermometers, Merritt	$16.95
5898	Antique & Contemporary Advertising Memorabilia, Summers	$24.95
5814	Antique Brass & Copper, Gaston	$24.95
1880	Antique Iron, McNerney	$9.95
6622	The Art of American Game Calls, Lewis	$24.95
6472	The A-Z Guide to Collecting Trivets, Rosack	$24.95
1128	Bottle Pricing Guide, 3rd Ed., Cleveland	$7.95
6345	Business & Tax Guide for Antiques & Collectibles, Kelly	$14.95
3718	Collectible Aluminum, Grist	$16.95
6342	Collectible Soda Pop Memorabilia, Summers	$24.95
5060	Collectible Souvenir Spoons, Bednersh	$19.95
5676	Collectible Souvenir Spoons, Book II, Bednersh	$29.95
5666	Collector's Encyclopedia of Granite Ware, Book 2, Greguire	$29.95
5836	Collector's Guide to Antique Radios, 5th Edition, Bunis	$19.95
6558	The Encyclopedia of Early American Sewing Machines, 2nd Ed., Bays	$29.95
6561	Field Guide to Fishing Lures, Lewis	$16.95
5683	Fishing Lure Collectibles, Volume I, Murphy/Edmisten	$29.95
6328	Flea Market Trader, 14th Edition, Huxford	$12.95
6458	Fountain Pens, Past & Present, 2nd Edition, Erano	$24.95
6631	Garage Sale & Flea Market Annual, 13th Edition, Huxford	$19.95
4945	G-Men and FBI Toys and Collectibles, Whitworth	$18.95
2216	Kitchen Antiques, 1790–1940, McNerney	$14.95
6639	McDonald's Drinkware, Kelly	$24.95
6028	Modern Fishing Lure Collectibles, Volume 1, Lewis	$24.95
6131	Modern Fishing Lure Collectibles, Volume 2, Lewis	$24.95
6322	Pictorial Guide to Christmas Ornaments & Collectibles, Johnson	$29.95
6839	Schroeder's Antiques Price Guide, 24th Edition	$14.95
5007	Silverplated Flatware, Revised 4th Edition, Hagan	$18.95
6647	Star Wars Super Collector's Wish Book, 3rd Edition, Carlton	$29.95
6552	Summers' Guide to Coca-Cola, 5th Edition	$24.95
6827	Summers' Pocket Guide to Coca-Cola, 5th Edition	$12.95
4935	The W.F. Cody Buffalo Bill Collector's Guide, Wojtowicz	$24.95
6632	Value Guide to Gas Station Memorabilia, 2nd Ed., Summers & Priddy	$29.95
6841	Vintage Fabrics, Gridley/Kiplinger/McClure	$19.95
6036	Vintage Quilts, Aug/Newman/Roy	$24.95

This is only a partial listing of the books on antiques that are available from Collector Books. All books are well illustrated and contain current values. Most of these books are available from your local bookseller, antique dealer, or public library. If you are unable to locate certain titles in your area, you may order by mail from **COLLECTOR BOOKS**, P.O. Box 3009, Paducah, KY 42002-3009. Customers with Visa, MasterCard, or Discover may phone in orders from 7:00 a.m. to 5:00 p.m. CT, Monday – Friday, toll free **1-800-626-5420**, or online at **www.collectorbooks.com**. Add $4.00 for postage for the first book ordered and 50¢ for each additional book. Include item number, title, and price when ordering. Allow 14 to 21 days for delivery.

1-800-626-5420   Fax: 1-270-898-8890

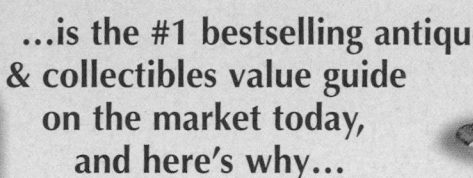
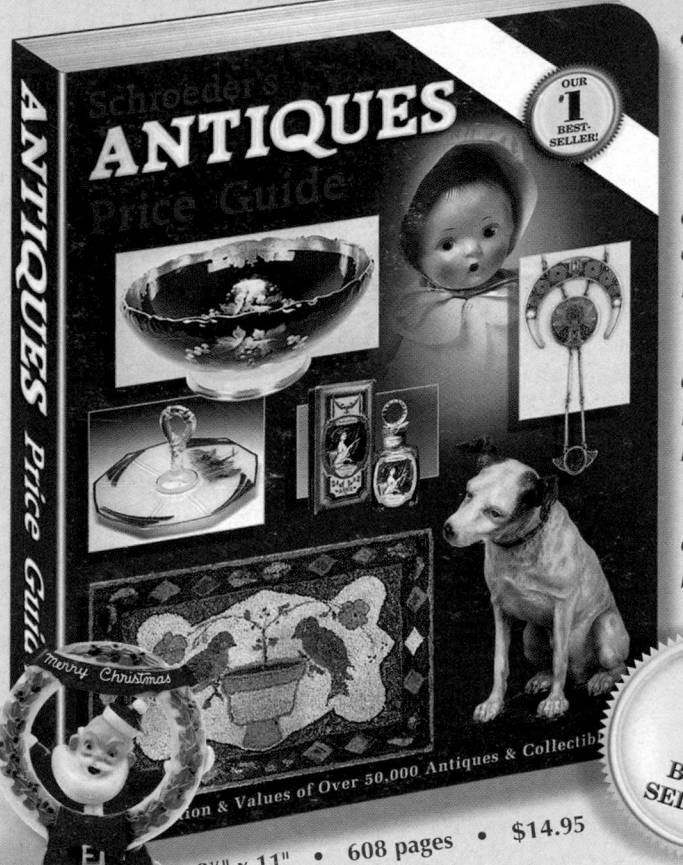